Montaigne

Montaigne

Hugo Friedrich

Edited and with an Introduction by
Philippe Desan

Translated by
Dawn Eng

UNIVERSITY OF CALIFORNIA PRESS
Berkeley · Los Angeles · Oxford

University of California Press
Berkeley and Los Angeles, California

University of California Press
Oxford, England

Originally published in German under the title
Montaigne by A. Francke AG Verlag, copyright 1949.
Second revised edition copyright 1967.

Library of Congress Cataloging-in-Publication Data

Friedrich, Hugo, 1904–1978
  [Montaigne, English]
  Montaigne / Hugo Friedrich ; edited and with an introduction by
Philippe Desan : translated [from the German] by Dawn Eng.
     p.   cm.
  Translation of: Montaigne.
  Includes bibliographical references and index.
  ISBN 0-520-06581-6
  ISBN 0-520-07253-7 (pbk)
  1. Montaigne, Michel de, 1533–1592. Essais.   2. French essays–
History and criticism.   I. Title.
PQ1643.F6913   1991
844'.3—dc20   90-47726
  CIP

Printed in the United States of America

1 2 3 4 5 6 7 8 9

The paper used in this publication meets the minimum requirements
of American National Standard for Information Sciences—Permanence
of Paper for Printed Library Materials, ANSI Z39.48-1984 ∞

Dedicated to the memory of
Leonardo Olschki (1885–1961)

Contents

Introduction

Philippe Desan

That reflecting on the human, all too human—or, as the
learned expression has it: psychological observation—is
among the expedients by means of which one can alleviate
the burden of living, that practice in this art lends presence
of mind in difficult situations and entertainment in tedious
circumstances, that one can, indeed, pluck useful maxims
from the thorniest and most disagreeable stretches of one's
own life and thereby feel a little better: that was believed,
that was known—in former centuries.

> —*Nietzsche*, Human, All Too Human, *section II,*
> *"On the History of Moral Sensations," trans. R.*
> *J. Hollingdale (Cambridge: Cambridge*
> *University Press, 1986).*

Many books have been written on Montaigne and his era, but few have
withstood the passage of time. The historical specificity of their preoccupations has rendered them generally out of date after a few years. However, Hugo Friedrich's *Montaigne* has resisted the course of time and is
still widely read in most graduate programs of French literature in this
country and in Europe. It is not, however, a work that addresses itself
solely to specialists of literature; historians and philosophers will also
find it provocative. In the grand German tradition of Curtius, Spitzer,
and Auerbach, Friedrich insists on a treatment of Montaigne that fully
takes into account the intertextual relationships that the Renaissance
authors entertained with Antiquity. His vast erudition enables him to
trace influences extending well beyond the field of French literature. For
intellectual boundaries were unknown to the Renaissance: Latin still
conveyed a humanistic ideology that, although on the decline, continued to call for a certain universality of thought. It is in the meanders of
this intertextuality that Friedrich is at his best.

Montaigne's *Essais* comprise a fine example of a "total" text, something that has always been troublesome to classify. The cause of this difficulty is apparent: the epistemology of the Renaissance is diametrically opposed to the critical categories that currently serve us as guidelines. Moreover, fields of knowledge had not yet been parceled out at the end of the sixteenth century; when one took up his pen it was to express himself on practically every subject. Friedrich understands that in the Renaissance literature was not separable from politics, philosophy, history, and even, in a certain way, science. Indeed, the *Essais* evoke an entire *Weltanschauung*. Therefore, the only approach that can truly do justice to the *Essais* is one that continually bears in mind the history of ideas or mentalities. Seen in this light, Montaigne is no longer an individual battling the currents of his time—an idiosyncrasy difficult to generalize, a writer who isolates himself in his ivory tower and blinds himself to the fray surrounding him—rather, he must be perceived as the epitome of an epoch. It is this epoch, distilled from accounts given by the best witness of the Renaissance, that is the true subject of Friedrich's book.

Writing at a time when psychological determinism still reigned (this book was written more than forty years ago), Friedrich postulates in the very first paragraph of his book that the events in Montaigne's life will be mentioned only if they are indispensable to an understanding of the *Essais*. The author's life is insufficient in explaining the text. In the second chapter ("Intellectual Inheritance and Education") Friedrich lays out for us the general setting of *his* Montaigne, where we discover the author of the *Essais* evolving within a milieu already structured by the ideology of the late Renaissance, and in fact propagating a certain continuity of thought. Far from being revolutionary, as has often been suggested, Montaigne's thought always situates itself in relation to the tradition and the culture that formed it. His "self" can be understood only through the relations that he entertained with the works of Antiquity. These relations, in turn, engender subjective reactions that he compares to his own lived experiences of the present.

If there is a tendency today among Montaignists to multiply the number of fragmentary studies and to indulge in analyses of single chapters—indeed often even the beginnings or the ends of chapters—thereby reinforcing the image of a Montaigne in "detached pieces" (II, 10, 300 A)* or in "patches" (*lopins*), to borrow Montaigne's expres-

---

*All quotations from Montaigne are from the translation of Donald M. Frame, *The Complete Essays of Montaigne* (Stanford: Stanford University Press, 1958).

sions, Friedrich already sensed the danger of this approach, which was just beginning to loom on the critical horizon. It is worthwhile to return to Friedrich's preface where, almost half a century ago, he warned against these mind games: "The more penetrating and sometimes brilliant interpretations of Montaigne we have are fragmentary—they treat one or several sides of his mind, but not its totality." Friedrich here echoes the methodological postulate of Georg Lukács, who also wanted to apprehend all artistic objects in their totality and incessantly reaffirmed the necessity of never losing sight of the work as a whole. For Friedrich, it is possible not only to generalize, to search for what forms the basis of thought, but one must also ground this generalization in what today we would call the mental climate of the epoch. Montaigne, in this view, would then be the propagator of what Friedrich calls a "popular philosophy." Friedrich emphasizes this point in chapter 1 as follows: "The *Essais* are an element in the philosophical anthropology of postclassical Europe." It is in this reifying and encompassing manner that Friedrich reads Montaigne.

What interests Friedrich above all are the great problems facing the late Renaissance, for which he offers a division privileging several of the larger themes found in the *Essais:* the self, death, literary consciousness. But since the *Essais* also constitute "a universal book," it is equally essential to relate the textual details to the overall project of the *Essais* so as not to lose sight of the work's unity of thought. For Friedrich strives to offer us more than just mere reflections on Montaigne; what emanates from his work is also a method of reading and analysis.

Friedrich displays a constant preoccupation that deeply marks his own reading of the *Essais*. Writing shortly after World War II—this book was published in 1949—Friedrich is primarily interested in morals and makes Montaigne into one of the first French moralists. Let us not be mistaken by this, for it is only in its broadest sense that we are to understand the notion of morality in the *Essais*. Nowhere does Friedrich find, for example, any prescriptive moral code or normative maxim in Montaigne's work. In chapter 1 the German critic himself explains to us precisely what he means by morals: "Something which has very little to do with morality, but a great deal to do with *mores,* that is, with man's living and being in their pure, even 'immoral' actuality." As he reaffirms later on (chapter 4), "This word must be understood in its broadest meaning. It encompasses traditions of every kind, lifestyles, characters, conditions of the time, inner make-up, essence—almost everything, apart from the purely physical, associated with man." Morals, such as

Friedrich understood them and such as we find them in the *Essais*, thus refer to a descriptive anthropology of the Renaissance man rather than to the defense of universal moral values.

The morals in which Friedrich is interested are visible in man's daily experiences. Yet it is important to point out that during the latter half of the sixteenth century these experiences increasingly run counter to Christian morals. Theory no longer corresponds to a practical reality in which political pragmatism reigns. It is precisely this contradiction between the theory and the practice of human actions that forms the basis for a moral crisis at the end of the Renaissance. This dichotomy between theory and practice—authority and experience—is reflected in the moral questions that Montaigne raises in most of the chapters of the *Essais*. It is in this sense that, for Friedrich, morals constitute the essential content of the *Essais*. Even if it is possible to reveal these morals in the text, we must remember that they are predicated on an anthropology and, consequently, never take shape in a vacuum. Friedrich makes it clearly understood that the historical context always forms the basis of any moral view. It is for this reason that the opposition between theory and practice in the moral domain is reflective of the very specific political and social reality of the late French Renaissance.

In the midst of the religious wars, the universal rules of Ciceronian ethics were suddenly overturned. A single example is sufficient to illustrate the profound upheaval making itself felt at the time. Let us take the famous literary *topos* of the lion and the fox. Cicero's moral axiom, according to which the fox's position is wholly incompatible with morality, is put into question by Machiavelli in the early sixteenth century. Machiavelli recommends that the prince be a lion at some moments and a fox at others, depending upon the necessities of power. Montaigne in turn takes up this literary *topos* in order to describe a reality that he establishes empirically every day: "The lion's skin will not suffice, we must sew on a bit of the fox's" (I, 5, 17 A). Montaigne most certainly condemns this moral *rapiéçage* (piecing together) on a theoretical level, but he is also bending to a practice that he must accept. It is no longer a matter of adopting a position but of merely describing things as they are.

Montaigne is not a moralist in the sense that we usually understand this term (and in this sense it is perhaps necessary to dissociate ourselves from Friedrich's statement), but rather is an anthropologist of moral man. The frequent confrontation of two contradictory concepts (two antinomical linguistic utterances) often leads to the emergence of a rift with the precepts of the Ancients and creates the moral questioning that one frequently finds as the theme of a chapter. Thus, the chapter entitled "Of the Useful and the Honorable," which begins the third book of the *Essais,* follows the same principle of comparison. The author here brings together two irreconcilable poles: on the one hand is a pragmatic and mercantile morality and on the other the remains of a nobiliary and courtly morality.

The late French Renaissance could be characterized as an era of contradictions and differences. One of the chief preoccupations of intellectuals at the time was to render an account of this perpetually changing world. This same preoccupation is also found in the *Essais:* "Finally, there is no existence that is constant, either of our being or of that of objects. And we, and our judgment, and all mortal things go on flowing and rolling unceasingly. Thus nothing certain can be established about one thing by another, both the judging and the judged being in continual change and motion" (II, 12, 455 A). It is from this perspective that in 1575 Loys Le Roy writes a treatise aimed precisely at gaining an understanding of the *Vicissitude ou variété des choses en l'univers.* One by one the systems collapse, and classical philosophy no longer occupies the position of an unimpeachable authority.

As a thinker on difference, on contradiction and the singular, Montaigne recommends an unpremeditated and fortuitous philosophy: "A new figure: an unpremeditated and accidental philosopher" (II, 12, 409 C). Distinction alone interests him: "*Distinguo* is the most universal member of my logic" (II, 1, 242 B). Henceforth, it is difference that allows an ordering of the world. In Michel Foucault's description of this epistemological break, which he situates in the seventeenth century, the author explains that order would no longer be organized according to a principle of similitude but instead would be based on a search for difference. "Resemblance does not make things so much alike as difference makes them unlike" (III, 13, 815 B) says Montaigne on this subject. The comparative method allows one to establish positively the difference between the particular and the universal, even if one considers the particular only to this universal. But for Montaigne the particular always remains particular, and this is the reason that the author of the *Essais* becomes for us a very unusual philosopher: he is a philosopher who resists any attempt at generalization. The *esprit de système* is conspicuous by its absence. Friedrich is correct in opposing the "philosophical" position of Montaigne to modern philosophy, whose center will soon be occupied by Kant, propagator of the systematizing mentality.

But, to stay closer to Montaigne's own era, one could also "read" Montaigne in relation to the first systematic philosopher of reason: Descartes. Such a comparison allows one to better situate the relative position of Montaignian thought in the history of ideas. Unlike Descartes, no definitive knowledge is possible for Montaigne; the only certainty is doubt. This is why the *Essais* will always be an almost irrecuperable text for philosophers. If one wants to profess philosophy, one must at a given time stop putting himself into question and consolidate his thoughts within a closed system. This will obviously be the task that Descartes will undertake. Montaigne is the eternal tailor, taking man's measurements without ever clothing him in a moral dress; he presents himself as a Sisyphus of thought who is constantly bringing his work back to the drawing board. For Montaigne, truth resides in the act of thinking and not in the product of the thought. The form that the thought takes reveals the content of the thought. Thus, if there is a crisis in the content of the thought, then the thought's discursive form should remain fluid and unstructured. For this reason, Montaigne promulgates a laissez-faire attitude toward thinking; the most flagrant digressions are systematically recouped through this process that will take the shape of a method. What counts is the judgment in action rather than the thing that is judged. In this way, the work of the essayist effaces any attempt to establish a normative morality.

From 1550 onward, an ideology of labor replaces an ideology based upon idleness and immediate pleasure. Henceforth, the authority of the Ancients is questioned and submitted to the destructive work of the interpreter. Truth soon comes to be viewed as nothing more than the product of mental labor, which in the end will lead back to the subject. People seem to realize that work, as Adam Smith will later say, best expresses the true wealth of nations (of thought, in Montaigne's case). This same mercantilist and exchangist ideology already strongly marks French thought of the second half of the sixteenth century. Consider, for example, the manner in which people speak of the French language at the time. It is through the slow and laborious accumulation of new words and expressions within a lexicon, all too impoverished up until this time, that they are able to enrich the language. The same logic of an accumulation of (linguistic) capital quickly finds its application in other spheres of knowledge. Personal labor rather than an inherited authority forms the basis of intellectual wealth.

Although the manner in which he writes his essays (by accumulation of successive layers of text—the famous *allongeails*) replicates the nascent ideology of labor, Montaigne nevertheless expresses his disapproval vis-à-vis this new way of perceiving man and the world. Hence, in a striking parallel, the author of the *Essais* opposes what we might call a "mercantilist conception of knowledge" (the absurd accumulation of a mass of knowledge such as that found, for example, in satirical form in Rabelais's *Gargantua*). But at the same time, Montaigne's disavowal of the accumulation of knowledge is testimony to this redealing of the cards in the moral domain. The only moral view possible is that which is continually put into question.

The mental displacement that moves from the object of thought back to the thinking subject brings about a weakening of the notion of the objectivity of history. For this reason one must consider Montaigne not only as one of the first modern thinkers but also as one of the first bourgeois thinkers: he provides a glimpse of an ideology aimed at the end of history, a type of thinking that draws everything into its own subjectivity. History performs quite an unusual function in the *Essais*, serving primarily to define an object of discourse and setting as its goal the inscription of the self "in words."

Two ways of approaching the objectivity of history emerge in the *Essais:* first, there is a certain detachment in relation to the verification and the veracity of the stories that Montaigne employs. As our essayist notes, the objective of his discourse does not lie in those stories: "I refer the stories that I borrow to the conscience of those from whom I take them" (I, 21, 75 A). Second, there is "fortuitous" reading, an approach that might appear disorderly in an era when people were very concerned with historical method. In "Of Books" (II, 10), Montaigne explains to us in detail his literary relation to history: "In this kind of study of history we must leaf without distinction through all sorts of authors, both old and new, both gibberish and French, in order to learn in them the things of which they variously treat" (II, 10, 303 A). Montaigne therefore uses history in order to find in it the *topoi* that will allow him to speak.

The histories of great army captains drawn from various writings offer Montaigne the opportunity to initiate dialogue. But this dialogue quickly transcends the territory defined by the historian. At each turn, Montaigne surpasses the history he has before him to create a new object that he brings back to himself in the end: "This is the material of history, naked and unformed; each man makes his profit of it according to his understanding. The really outstanding ones have the capacity to choose what is worth knowing; they can pick out of two reports the one that is more likely" (II, 10, 304 A).

Montaigne understood that history does not exist as an immutable object; only by submitting history to the rigors of the essay does it acquire an existence. The degree of malleability of the historical object depends upon the epoch in which it is being written. In the *Essais,* the intention of the historian always prevails over notions of objectivity and truth, which no longer belong to the historical object itself but reside thereafter in the interaction between that object and the interpreting subject. For Montaigne truth springs from the realm of persuasion: "Our truth of nowadays is not what is, but what others can be convinced of" (II, 18, 505 A). The other and his history exist only as a function of the self in an interactional relation: "My history needs to be adapted to the moment. I may presently change, not only by chance, but also by intention. This is a record of various and changeable occurrences, and of irresolute and, when it so befalls, contradictory ideas: whether I am different myself, or whether I take hold of my subjects in different circumstances and aspects. So, all in all, I may indeed contradict myself now and then; but truth, as Demades said, I do not contradict" (III, 2, 611 B). Truth abandons the historical object in order to side with the subject *writing* history.

The whole question of knowledge can be summed up under the notion of truth in Montaigne. Before the cosmogonic chaos, the parceling out of Aristotelian morals, the splintering of politics, the discovery of the new world and the individual (to employ the expression of Jacob Burckhardt), Montaigne discovers that, in a way, language alone is the basis of all truth. Let us listen to him when, speaking on this subject, he declares that "this capacity for sifting truth, whatever it may amount to in me, and this free will not to enslave my belief easily, I owe principally to myself" (II, 17 499 A). The theoretically possible would then enter into the struggle on the side of the notion of truth, the two soon converging to form one and the same thing. Here, clearly, is a discourse sufficient unto itself. So seen, the essayist would first choose the object of his analysis, proceeding next to the task of interpretation, and the totalizing truth of his remarks would be validated in the end only by his own act of taking the floor and writing. Every possibility becomes truth.

As it is conceived by Montaigne, the essay universalizes the self by denying the history of the other; it proposes a new and truer history that diminishes the other's experience in relation to that of the self. As a critical act, the essay also supposes a method and therefore provides a form for analyzing historical material. Friedrich stresses the importance of the essay as a form and tells us that, far from expressing a necessary content, Montaigne "does not associate any literary concept with this, but only a methodical one." Having already denied the objective content of history, Montaigne ends by proposing to us a new form: "By long usage this form of mine has turned into substance" (III, 10, 773 B). The self has become history and his writing is thus authorized. The particular has just been transformed into a universal. Montaigne speaks to us then of his "nature as a whole" (*forme universelle*) (III, 2, 617 B) and puts forward his own body as the only witness of his historical existence.

The *Essais,* a horn of plenty for the future reader, are self-regenerating. As a single document, they will engender all the documents necessary for the reader's rewriting of history. Montaigne rests assured that the "able reader" will see in his book the sum total of all preceding histories, and it will thereafter be possible for that reader to find *all* of history inscribed in the *Essais* without having to look elsewhere. In this way Montaigne attempts to replicate for the reader the same relationships that he maintained with the various documents that passed before his own eyes. By removing the element of choice that Montaigne himself had, the *Essais* symbolize the only possible historical solution for the reader who desires to reconstruct history by taking the self as the point of departure.

The same notion of a subjective truth serving as a point of departure for thought will be taken up once again by Descartes, who will oppose the concept of truth to the idea of an empirically identifiable reality, an objective reality defended by Francis Bacon only a half century later. In this view, there will be as many truths as interpretations of the world. The subject who aspires to reconstruct this world could found his own morality based upon personal experience, which would then be just as valuable as all the authority of the thinkers of Antiquity. Friedrich astutely analyzes this epistemological break that inevitably draws Montaigne toward moral relativism. It is this break that gives birth to the notion of the savage (the famous cannibal, so dear to Montaigne), possessor of a system of morals equal, if not superior, to the Christian morals behind which the conquerors of the New World take refuge.

All the critics agree on one point: moral relativism emerges forcefully from the *Essais.* The cause of this relativism is not very difficult to pinpoint. The late Renaissance experienced a series of serious crises in almost every domain (moral, political, scientific, philosophical, cosmo-logical). These crises brought about a questioning of the authority of the Ancients and sapped the foundations of humanism. It is no longer possi-ble to believe in universal truth. There will be only particular truths that take form through the intervention of individual thought. Friedrich sums up better than anyone else this very distinctive approach to the world: "His [Montaigne's] concept of truth separates itself from the goal of a knowledge of things and existence and is transformed into the concept of personal truthfulness. Its rigorousness consists in the preci-sion of listening in on one's self. It only states what is valid for the author in the instant in which he is writing, but in allowing contradic-tion he becomes genuine." With such an understanding of the world, the concept of time, too, undergoes redefinition. The present moment and everyday experience acquire as much value as ideas that have rip-ened slowly and been transmitted through the centuries. Personal labor aiming at the enrichment of knowledge gains precedence over the no-tion of the legacy of a linguistic, scientific, or moral capital.

Yet no system of thought in the process of formation could so readily replace the previous system. The late French Renaissance represents a key moment when several ideologies superimpose themselves upon one another and yield contradictory images of man. The effect of linguistic and ideological—and therefore moral—polyphony has inevitable reper-cussions in writing. One of the strengths of the *Essais* is to account effectively for what Friedrich calls a "polyphonic juxtaposition of hu-man spheres." We encounter the same criticism of ideological polyph-ony in Bakhtin. Throughout the *Essais* we can see, for example, how nobiliary and bourgeois ideals are superimposed in the same text, the language reflecting the tensions between these two value systems—a phenomenon that once again is the product of an entire epoch, of which Montaigne tries to record the visible signs.

As Friedrich points out, "Authors were trying to express the totality of man through mass, quantity, even chaos." During the Renaissance, one could express the totality of man only in a quantitative fashion and according to a geometric model. One might say that in this era the quantitative replaces the qualitative. Montaigne attempts to take man's measurements, placing him on the scales of his balance which are the *Essais*. It is no coincidence that the etymology of the word *essai* refers directly to *exagium*, that is to say, to the balance and to weighing. For Montaigne is engaged in a veritable weighing of the most diverse events. Writing, then, is a documentation of this weighing process and the means by which Montaigne tries to calculate the chaos described by Etienne Pasquier in his *Recherches de la France*. Incertitude reigns in every domain and chaos becomes the referential norm. Montaigne often reaffirms this state of incertitude: "Everything is crumbling about us; in all the great states that we know, whether in Christendom or elsewhere, take a look: you will find an evident threat of change and ruin" (III, 9, 734 B). Let us recite the famous phrase of Montaigne according to which: "The world is but a perennial movement" (III, 2, 610 B).

One thing is certain: the authority of the Ancients is no longer sufficient. In one of the numerous profound and lapidary statements strewn throughout his work, Friedrich summarizes the spirit of this declining humanism: "That is a late humanistic way of thinking: reverent yet critical." The Aristotelian world view no longer suffices to explain contemporary life. If, as Friedrich observes, it is true that "Montaigne did not devote himself fully to any of the classical eudemonological schools. One cannot really call him a stoic; an Epicurean, or even a pure skeptic," it is also quite certain that Montaigne's inclinations lean toward readings of Plato. This is in no way happenstance. Traces of a reading of Aristotle are not, in fact, very numerous in the *Essais*, and it is apparent that Montaigne shows a strong preference for Plato over the founder of the Peripatetic school. Socrates will ultimately be Montaigne's true model, and it is he who Montaigne will seek in Plato. Montaigne was participating in a movement slowly beginning to take shape in 1550 that aims to replace Aristotle with Plato. Pierre de La Ramée is just one philosopher who took such an approach. Montaigne's interest in neoplatonism results largely from his emphasis on the dialogic form. This period clearly no longer valorizes the authoritarian and monologic discourse used in treatises of the early part of the century.

In works of this period, we discover a horizontal richness that can only be expressed in a contradictory and piecemeal fashion, rather than a vertical hierarchy. Polyphony reigns, with the resulting effect that all is brought to the same level in the course of analysis. The originality of the *Essais* resides in what Friedrich calls the force of "leveling": "The secret of man should now be revealed precisely in the confused comings and goings of the random contents of his life. To understand him here means: to know that he is a polymorphous being moving along ungraded planes, a being that can only be deciphered by observation of his surprising inconsistencies and disorder." But how does one account for this human rhapsody of which Montaigne is speaking? What form and what style must one adopt in order to write man's chaos?

Although Plato and Socrates interest Montaigne from the perspective of dialogue and the maieutic method, Montaigne's two great literary models were Seneca, chosen for his open and easy style, and Plutarch, chosen for his taste for psychological portraits. According to Friedrich, "The *Essais* constitute the mediating element that establishes the connection between the newer more modern study of morality, that is, the descriptive, nonnormative comprehension of intimate individualities, and Plutarch." Plutarch knew how to reduce all men to a common denominator. The great army captains are transformed to mere individuals whose psychology differs only slightly from that of a man of average rank and status. From then onward, one must no longer concern oneself with the education of the prince but with man in general, whom Friedrich calls "the abased man." The peasant as well as the prince possesses within himself the imprint of the human mold, or, as Montaigne so aptly puts it, "Each man bears the entire form of man's estate [*l'humaine condition*]" (III, 2, 611 B).

Friedrich does not see a linear progression or evolution in Montaigne's reconstruction/discovery of the self; rather, he shows how mental states blend together and are simultaneously present from the beginning of the writing of the *Essais:* "a certain structuring which we must keep in mind is apparent in the viewpoint under which Montaigne observes man. The first consists in abasement; he stresses every conceivable thing that forces man down into an animal helplessness. The next renounces the negative value judgments though leaving the humbled creature in his abasement, discovers this creature's life circumstances there, and describes and affirms them. Finally, the third turns his back on Montaigne; this observer of man, in describing himself, seizes the closest and least falsified material to answer the question of what we really are." Friedrich distances himself then from the thesis of Pierre Villey, who considered these "stages" as being independent of one another—stages corresponding to reader reactions that one could situate in different time periods. For Friedrich, on the contrary, "these three viewpoints cannot be considered as an historical development, as if Montaigne had first abased, then affirmed, and finally chosen himself as subject matter. All three points of view are present from the beginning."

The superimposition of these three attitudes, or "structurings" as Friedrich prefers to call them, explains in part many of the contradictions inherent in the text. Montaigne often wields a double-edged sword in the logic of his argumentation, almost always returning immediately to the drawing board with what he just announced. The causes that he believes he is defending often have the unfortunate habit of turning against him. The best example of this phenomenon of "sabotage" is without a doubt the "Apology for Raymond Sebond" (II, 12). Let us briefly recall the history of this apology. Pierre Brunel recommended to Montaigne's father one day that he read the work of Raymond Sebond, *Theologia naturalis sive liber creaturarum,* written in 1434–36 and published in 1484. Montaigne translated this work for his father in 1569. The "Apology," composed in several stages between 1573 and 1580, set for itself the task of proving that a natural theology based on rational knowledge is impossible. The opening of this essay clearly poses the problem: "In truth, knowledge is a great and very useful quality; those who despise it give evidence enough of their stupidity. But yet I do not set its value at that extreme measure that some attribute to it, like Herillus the philosopher, who placed in it the sovereign good, and held that it was in its power to make us wise and content. That I do not believe, nor what others have said, that knowledge is the mother of all virtue, and that all vice is produced by ignorance. If that is true, it is subject to a long interpretation" (III, 12, 319 A). Montaigne does undertake this hardy interpretation, but he quickly loses the thread of his argument, and, in what will become the longest chapter of the *Essais,* he concludes by saying the opposite of what he had stated at the start.

The beginning of the essay is symptomatic of Montaigne's thought and of his desire to avoid all polemics on the origin and transmission of knowledge. But the author of the *Essais* does not respect the framework that he laid down in his initial plan, precisely because he cannot keep his argument on the theoretical level. Practice shows up the weakness of theory, and soon he is turning in a circle, attempting to recover what is irrecoverable. Clearly, Montaigne knows that one cannot uphold truths on the purely logical and discursive level (precisely what he pokes fun at in the philosophers), for if one attempts to do this, one ends up arguing in syllogisms and proving the most enormous absurdities. According to Montaigne, reason cannot demand its autonomy; sense and experience remain the only true guarantors of truth. But even an argument of this type is the result of a process of reasoning, and it is here that Montaigne sabotages his own argument. As Friedrich himself notes in this regard, "where man is involved, there is no ideality—and we do not have access to any areas, in which man would not be involved." Anecdotes very quickly invade Montaigne's argument and finally "the possible unconditional quality of faith fades before the daily evidence of man's limitedness."

Reasoned discourse marks the limits of experience and can never render a total account of it, but experience itself can be expressed only through the understanding. The contradiction that emerges from this essay is once again perfectly summarized by Friedrich: "As representative of natural theology, he [Montaigne] has in mind the rationalistic critics of Sebond. But since methodologically they are related to him (namely in their rationalistic handling of theological questions), in the end he still encounters Sebond; without expressly intending this or stating it, he becomes Sebond's opponent." According to Friedrich, it is in the "Apology for Raymond Sebond" that one comes across the clearest trace of abased man. It is also perhaps the chapter that best corresponds to Friedrich's thesis concerning the superimposition of the three structurings present in Montaignian discourse on man.

If Montaigne finds reasoning and rhetoric somewhat displeasing, conversation remains his favorite activity. Thus, in "Of the Art of Discussion" (III, 8) the author of the *Essais* declares that "the most fruitful and natural exercise of our mind, in my opinion, is discussion. I find it sweeter than any other action of our life; and that is the reason why, if I were right now forced to choose, I believe I would rather consent to lose my sight than my hearing or speech" (III, 8, 704 B). But conversation, as Montaigne understands it, is quite different from that "science of guzzling" (I, 51, 222 A) that was being taught in the schools at the time. Theoretical battles do not interest Montaigne; practice alone counts. These rhetorical jousting matches are not dangerous in the least if they are never introduced into practice. As Friedrich notes, one could even go so far as to suppose that Protestantism might have been tolerable to Montaigne had it not gone beyond the level of a mere theory.

Likewise, the author of the *Essais* is more interested in things than in causes. He finds the observable more essential than its logical explanation: "I see ordinarily that men, when facts are put before them, are more ready to amuse themselves by inquiring into their reasons than by inquiring into their truth. They leave aside the cases and amuse themselves treating the causes" (III, 11, 785 B). The study of cases allows Montaigne to erect a comparative table of types of moral behavior. The causes of these types of behavior, however, are ungraspable, which is why the moral anthropologist contents himself with recording the cases. But we are not to mistake this, as Montaigne does not possess the scientific basis that some have wanted to grant him. It is by no means in order to obtain a greater degree of certitude that he refuses to search for causes.

In truth, man never exists in an abstract manner. He lives in society, and it is for this reason that we can speak only of *men,* that is to say, individuals grounded in an anthropology and sociology but never in a philosophy. From 1580 onward Montaigne recognizes this inescapable truth: "We do not care so much what we are in ourselves and in reality as what we are in the public mind" (III, 9, 729 B). One must, therefore, be wary of any interpretation that would attempt to depict Montaigne as the sage who sequesters himself in his ivory tower. Let us not forget that Montaigne was the mayor of Bordeaux and that he led a very active social life. With this we are taking on one of the thorniest problems of the *Essais:* the goal and the finality of writing for Montaigne.

In the last chapter of his book, Friedrich tackles the problem of the writing of the *Essais* and of Montaigne's literary consciousness. For Friedrich Montaigne is without doubt the first writer desirous of distinguishing his writing from those of the theologians, jurists, and philologists of his time. For this reason Montaigne could be called the first *honnête homme.* The "honnête homme" is always conscious of his listeners and concerned with the public and the reader. The preface "To the Reader" reflects all the ambiguity of this question of the reader. There we encounter a profound hesitation when faced with a choice between two opposing poles: the particular or the universal. Montaigne first makes the declaration that his book, unique in all the world, addresses itself to a very restricted public, namely his parents and friends: "I have dedicated it to the private convenience of my relatives and friends" (To the Reader). He goes so far as to discourage the reader from spending too much time on his work: "You would be unreasonable to spend your leisure on so frivolous and vain a subject." Yet, this advice is addressed to a generic "Reader," and on several occasions, Montaigne clearly leads us to understand that the "able reader" (*le suffisant lecteur*) (I, 24, 93 A) will find a model in his book.

At first, this hesitation toward the public might appear baffling. It gives evidence, however, of a refusal to teach: "I do not teach, I tell" (III, 2, 612 B). If Montaigne constantly wavers back and forth between the particular and the universal, it is because he refuses to fix his own judgment in a moral. Whereas the moralist teaches, the moral anthropologist merely reports what he observes. Nevertheless, as we know, any moral must pass sooner or later from the particular to the universal, a phenomenon that we will encounter again in La Bruyère and La Rochefoucauld in the following century. Montaigne refuses this progressive movement, demonstrating the incessant desire to return to the individual and to the particular, nongeneralizable body. Subjectivity affirms itself both as a method and as a principle of living. Montaigne "knows that thinking, to the extent that it cannot avoid becoming language, becomes subject to the communicative function of language. With the transition from silent to written meditation, one necessarily enters the public realm. The fact that Montaigne recognizes this is what really prompts his question about audience." For this reason the public is always present, even if Montaigne wants to deny its existence.

To accept an audience would also be to play the game of exchange and to entertain literary relationships in order to please others. This would present an impossible situation for Montaigne who, on the contrary, endeavors to preserve the greatest amount of his self and to avoid dividing up the subject. It is a question of giving everything while skimming nothing off for oneself. This is the essence of public life for Montaigne: "[B] I have been able to take part in public office without departing one nail's breadth from myself, [C] and to give myself to others without taking myself from myself" (III, 10, 770), Montaigne confesses to us with a certain pleasure. The problem with public life is that one must give oneself to others, lose one's own subjective existence. Even the king, a public figure *par excellence,* "has nothing that is properly his own; he owes his very self to others" (III, 6, 689 B). The public figure is completely indebted to those whom he governs or administers, for this type of authority is based on a vertical, hierarchical scheme: "The authority to judge is not given for the sake of the judge, but for the sake of the person judged. A superior is never appointed for his own benefit, but for the benefit of the inferior" (III, 6, 689 C). Such a hierarchical model would challenge the leveling principle that Montaigne is striving to develop. All things considered, Montaigne's practice of weighing may simply be a search for stability within human relationships. Were this true, it would merely be a matter of finding equivalences between men, this human condition that each one possesses to the same degree, regardless of rank or class. But a paradox soon arises: when all is said and done, man's common denominator is nowhere more readily visible than in death.

Death, for this reason, is one of the great themes that runs through practically every chapter of the *Essais.* Yet it is difficult to form a clear idea of Montaigne's exact position on death. As Friedrich points out in his chapter on Montaigne and death, the author of the *Essais* broaches this topic from different angles (loss of the friend, suicide, accident, etc.) in order to view its full dimensions. In fact, Montaigne combines several conceptions of death, conceptions that counterbalance one another. Thus, as Friedrich puts it, Montaigne is neither stoic, nor Christian; he "intends to interpret and withstand death from a pre-Christian, that is, classical, understanding of death as an order—but at the same time from the Christian definition of man as a temperamental being—but without the devices of grace and faith which are part of the Christian religion. He takes death as seriously as a Christian, though for different reasons, but he denies himself Christian comfort." Montaigne actually means to assume death in a serene manner and therefore one that is independent of any moral concerns. The subject divests himself of all consolation and restores death as a personal experience, open to variation depending upon the context.

The moral anthropology that Montaigne strives to elaborate corresponds to a very specific period in history where it is difficult to judge the tyranny invading everyday life. It is more difficult yet to give a definition of tyranny and the inhuman. Perhaps in this regard Friedrich felt a certain affinity between himself and the author of the *Essais*. It seems that Friedrich, writing his book on Montaigne shortly after World War II, finds himself following in Montaigne's path. The morals that so interest Friedrich certainly must condemn but in no way try to change; they are purely descriptive. Like Montaigne, Friedrich does not think in terms of natural law. In this perennial movement where synthesis becomes problematic, one must return to the individual and the particular. It is impossible to lay the foundations of morality without this return to man. History has just annulled the moral code that was believed to be well established. After this, one can only judge in relative terms hinged upon the ideological position of the subject who interprets the events of history. As Friedrich states, "The *Essais* do not contain a constructive concept of history. Here it is really not much more than the whirling fair of what is human. Broader contexts, subjects of a higher unity (nations, peoples, institutions) do not appear." Friedrich's project, carried out soon after the outburst of inhumanity that characterized World War II, seems to resemble closely that of Montaigne.

When history is obliterated, all that remains are stories and anecdotes, each one every bit as proper and terrible as the next. Montaigne was able to counter the current of his times by bringing himself down to the human level. Well before Nietzsche, he made the "all too human" the only philosophical category possible. He, too, could very well have exclaimed: "Here is Man stripped bare, and he is only that." In the end Montaigne "becomes entangled in his all-too-human qualities neither with misery nor with vanity. He has at his disposal that compelling power that flows from people who have the courage to be themselves completely." It is thus understandable why Friedrich ends by finding in Montaigne the traces of a wisdom, the logical result of this stepping back before the events of history. This wisdom sets itself up as a model, no longer solely for the Renaissance, but also for the postwar West. A harmony between the world and the self: therein lies genuine wisdom according to Friedrich. From this moment onward "the inner form of the *Essais* resembles a journey on which one leaves the wide through-way that ignores the surrounding landscape for the sake of leading directly to the destination in order to move into the forest. The traveler walks on, discovers unknown or forgotten trees, plants, animals, and suddenly finds himself at the throughway again, but richer and more knowledgeable than before." The traveler has arrived at the end of history; nothing can amaze him anymore; he has just encountered within himself the entire form of the human condition—as of that moment, the end of morality opens onto a new morality.

Preface to the First Edition

This book is an attempt at as encompassing a presentation and interpretation of Montaigne as possible. Events of his life are only included to the extent that they are indispensable for an understanding of the *Essais*.

The most reliable and exhaustive material available in the secondary literature on Montaigne concerns biographical questions and those of text criticism and source history. But when these studies move into an interpretation of the *Essais*, they are no longer satisfying. On the other hand, the more penetrating and sometimes brilliant interpretations of Montaigne we have are fragmentary—they treat one or several sides of his mind, but not its totality. But what sort of mind is he, and what is his place in the history of thought? This question has been answered in various ways, and often quite inadequately. He has been categorized with the theorists of cognition and even with pedagogues, he has been explained as a trailblazer for the Enlightenment or even for Rousseau's nature ideology, and then again as a sort of pre-Bergsonian Bergson. Whatever could not be fit into these oblique categories was called pleasant conversation or popular philosophy. But where is that popular man who would really have understood him? Strangely, the society of readers which has found Montaigne over the three and a half centuries since his death is an intellectual aristocracy of all possible strata, activities, and occupations. It will be valuable to look in greater depth at this "popular philosophy" content of Montaigne's, that content which has been shifted back and forth among academic disciplines with an embarrassed denial of competence, but which has deeply affected an elite of experts beyond the boundaries of particular disciplines. And it will be worthwhile to treat him in such a manner that the parts that have been inappropriately delimited by many critics (skepticism, Epicurianism, etc.) can be understood as elements of a very organic mind whose coherence will clearly not emerge if one breaks it down into latecomer and forerunner categories.

Moreover, since the end of the great philosophical systems, our eyes have again been opened to the values of concrete thinking and wisdom. We know that essaistic meditation and writing do not represent a lower form of thinking which is nourished with crumbs from the table of the Greats, but rather that it is an irreplaceable alternate way of thinking which has its own history and use of verbal form. We can no longer dismiss an author as a popular philosopher simply because for him truth is his personal truth, because to him, the only thought that seems worth thinking is one that plays upon the strings of his heart, only because he says again something that has already been said many times before, only because he drifts into narrative and semifiction and is an author who is easy to read—as if something that is created easily due to great talent and intellectual superiority is also necessarily lightweight in content!

I have taken Montaigne more seriously than has generally been the case precisely in those passages in which he seems to be merely playing with intellectual matters. But I am also aware how much of his direct and indirect appeal could be lost in doing so. So I hope to assure the reader frequently of the charm that awaits him when he reads the *Essais*. Montaigne's fellow countryman Malebranche, who is a stern critic, chastised the *Essais* for being nothing more than charm and tone. Nothing more? Could a tone have such power if the string were not noble and strong?

In the narrower historical sense, I hope with my book to define Montaigne's place in modern studies of morality. My understanding of this concept, which must be clearly defined, in contrast to its customary, vacillating usage, is presented in several passages, particularly in the fourth chapter. In this respect, this book is a starting point for the analysis of moralistic thinking based upon a monographically limited individual case.

The emphasis of the book can be found in chapters 3 through 7. Here is where the reader will find the greatest departures from previous Montaigne research which I considered necessary. However, I am not forget-

ting the great debt I owe to previous researchers—particularly Villey.
The first chapter anticipates most of what follows in broad outline. It
stakes out the field, makes apparent those contours and accents that I
consider correct and that must be kept in mind from the beginning so
that subsequent individual studies can be understood in proper perspective, without a view of the totality of Montaigne's intellect being lost.
The last pages of the concluding chapter deal with stylistic matters, and
they end in intimations. I intended to bring it only far enough along that
one could see how the older form of rhetorical artistic prose has given
way in the *Essais* to an individual style of expression.

As a rule, I have only spoken of Montaigne's numerous sources and
parallels from antiquity when Villey overlooked them in his admirable
commentary, or, in his most sensitive omission, when he disregarded the
fact that they had become something quite different when Montaigne
adopted them. Only the second chapter, in accordance with its theme,
deals extensively with the sources, but even in this case they are considered primarily from the perspective of how they have been transformed.
In many instances I have deliberately avoided naming Montaigne's
sources, as I did not want to weaken the force of his thought, which
transformed these in any case. Unfortunately, with our historicist education, when we discover an author's source we all too easily combine this
with the opinion that since the author is making use of something that
was thought once before, he has not done any thinking himself. The
motto from Montesquieu which precedes the second chapter can be
taken as a methodological confession.

It is the exception for me to deal with an individual Essay as an
entity, for very few Essays are entities. I have structured my consideration of Montaigne thematically and according to the sequence of his
perspectives—according to his "dialectic," so to speak. Since he himself never quite surveys what he has already said about a matter, and
since no single passage expresses the totality of his thought concerning
it, one can collect the scattered passages and compare them to one
another. In so doing, I hope I have adequately avoided trying to system-
atize him. For the best way to get a sense of Montaigne without
stifling him is with an accompanying description. I have admittedly
not gone into all of his fluctuations and contradictions. Critics will
have an easy time coming up with evidence that opposes many of my
interpretations. For what didn't Montaigne say! But the definitive factor is not what he said in one passage, but rather when and how often
and in what context he said it. I have essentially only brought out the

dominant thoughts of the middle and later periods, particularly those
for which it is established through several repetitions that they have
remained an integral part of his intellectual organism. Despite this, it
was impossible to avoid some tediousness and repetition in this description. That is due to the character of the author portrayed and his
nimble, orbital style of thinking, which the accompanying description
should not suppress completely. I would not consider it a reproach if at
some point it were said of me what Ranke once stated: "One notices
many who are gripped by his style when they so much as speak of
him!"

Let me mention the following regarding the quotes used in the book:

1. [In the original edition, Hugo Friedrich quoted Montaigne from
Thibaudet's one-volume edition of the *Essais*. Donald M. Frame's English translation of the *Essais* (*The Complete Essays of Montaigne*,
Stanford: Stanford University Press, 1958) is used here instead. When
quoting Montaigne, the layers of the text are identified: A = 1580; B =
1588; C = additions since 1589 and until Montaigne's death in 1592.]
This distinction is essential so one can see with which phase the particular thought is associated. [For consistency all titles of works cited are
given in the original language.]

2. Reading in Middle French presumes schooling in linguistic history. Thus I have translated any quotes that might cause problems for
readers only familiar with modern French, except for those in chapter 8
which serve to illustrate Montaigne's stylistic devices. In translating
them, I have placed greater emphasis on clarity than on absolute literal-
ness. The reader will be able to find his way alone in the older orthography of the easier quotes that I did not translate.

3. Greater significance is attributed to some quotes than their context justifies. But it is permissible to do this with Montaigne if the quote
in the passage in question expresses particularly well a thought that
appears elsewhere in the *Essais*, even though to a limited degree. Montaigne, who disliked the abstract, tended to prefer limiting even his basic
ideas to concrete situations and things. Thus a thought may frequently
be understood in the broader sense that is perhaps not found in the
passage, but is certainly behind it, assuming that it has been established
in other passages that it really is one of his basic ideas.

Let me also add that I write *Essais* when referring to the title of
Montaigne's book as a whole, but "Essay" or "Essays" when individual
items are discussed, herein conforming to the English spelling that has
also been adopted in German.

Other than that, I can only hope that this description, written by a scholar of Romance languages and literatures, will also once again open the hearts of philosophers to our author and invite them to provide a philosophical interpretation of his statement about himself: "I am not a philosopher."

Freiburg im Breisgau   H. F.
March 20, 1949

CHAPTER I

Introductory Description of the *Essais*

1. SUBJECTS AND THEMES

Michel de Montaigne's *Essais* are the free observations of a French nobleman of the late humanistic period of the sixteenth century, written between his fortieth and sixtieth years of life. He published them himself as a means of filling his time in the idleness of his secluded old age. They were frequently revised, never completed, and in fact are inconceivable as a finished work. They deal with all imaginable subjects of varying significance: the powerlessness of reason to attain knowledge, for example, or disputed confessional questions, the healing arts, calendar reform, witch trials, books, horses, household matters, exotic peoples . . . Intertwined with all these are the author's reflections on the living of his own life, from the simple day-to-day to the great concerns of mankind, such as friendship, social intercourse, loneliness, freedom, dying.

At first glance, a confused randomness seems to prevail in this book. The significant and the mundane, quickly outdated themes and universal ones are interspersed seemingly at random. Only after reading one's way well into it can one uncover several central ideas that form the calm yet meandering basic stream of thought of the work. But countless rapid little waves of anecdotes and apercus play along its surface. The *Essais* do not fit neatly into the familiar treatise style. Montaigne does not reach for his themes with methodical deliberation. Rather, he listens, lets everything, even the lowliest, come to him, and yet he is absolutely certain that things will unfold and organize themselves eventually, if one can only wait for them. His much-discussed skepticism must be understood in the older sense of the word: it is a *peering in* that leaves the world and men richer, not poorer, an inferential skepticism with a reverence for the superiority of the pure appearance of a matter to its interpretation, which cannot be other than imperfect.

The *Essais* have become a universal book. They radiate a particular appeal to which a great variety of readers responds, even some whom one would not expect to find among the readership of a philosopher. It is an appeal that is due not so much to the content of the thought as to the flux of the thinking. Its ripples continue beyond the individual thought that springs from the moment and is then let go. And the manner in which Montaigne speaks also contributes to that appeal. The language is vivid, filled with irony, never histrionic, each phrase pure, usually familiar and relaxed, sometimes with considerable depth, but never with an effort to drive the point home. Montaigne shows an amazing readiness for the contradictory in himself and in things, as if he really felt completely in harmony only in the enjoyment of this all-encompassing contradiction. Yet there is no desire to impose his opinion on others or to be seen as knowing it all. There is no lecturing. The *Essais* are essentially an inner dialogue. From no one do they expect more than the inclination to listen to what they say. In fact, they do not even presume this inclination with certainty. Their only real aim is to come to a clear understanding of themselves and to invite others to do the same in their own manner. They grant every person the same right to the freedom of being himself that the author claims for himself. Nietzsche said it well: "The fact that such a person has written has truly enhanced the joy of living in this world. At least for me, since my acquaintance with this free and powerful soul, I find that I must say what he said of Plutarch: 'The moment I laid eyes upon him I grew a drumstick or a wing.' I would stay with him if the task were assigned to me to be at home in this world."[1]

Of course Montaigne is not one of the Greats. He ranks more to the middle—an intelligent, educated intellect can reach him. But he is a very comprehensive man in whom the most varied possibilities of the Western world up to this time have been preserved and encounter or pervade one another, and in whom the ground is prepared for varied future possibilities. The richness of the man and the themes, the manners and inflections of which he is capable can be seen, for example, in the fact that one can mention names such as Socrates, Horace, Seneca, Plutarch, Marcus Aurelius, and Erasmus, Rabelais, Ariosto, Cervantes, La Fon-

taine, Sterne, Lichtenberg, Diderot, Sainte-Beuve—even Goethe, and
also Jacob Burckhardt and Fontane in the presence of his work—and
each time something vibrates from his work in response. Admittedly, the
idealists and tragedians, the visionaries, dreamers, and believers, and
the teachers of rigorous thinking are not a part of his world.

Everything that interests Montaigne can be related to the single basic
question: What is man? Or more precisely, to express this using modern
terms, one could say that the *Essais* are an element in the philosophical
anthropology of postclassical Europe—and the most content-rich the
spirit of the French late Renaissance could add. Almost all of the study
of the basic nature of mankind pursued in France since that time has its
origin in the *Essais*. Or, to use another key term, one can define the
Essais as a major work of the modern study of morality—this major
current, separate from the exact sciences and running parallel to them
only in time, which came from Italy and extended over France, Spain,
England, and later over Germany as well. Morality, though, is something that has very little to do with morals, but a great deal to do with
mores, that is, with man's living and being in their pure, even "immoral" actuality. Moralists are neither educators nor moral philosophers. They are observers, analysts, and describers of mankind. They
find themselves facing an endless task. Their studies concern the contradictory nature and commonplace elements of mankind which only come
to the fore when ethics recede and leave the field open for objective
observation of what is real.

Montaigne is this type of moralist. When he says: "Others form man,
I tell of him" (III, 2, 610 B), he concisely expresses what is essential:
namely, that his *Essais* do not reason normatively from how matters
should be, but rather from the actuality of how they are. No wise man
in the stoic mode, no holy one, in fact no ideal character of any kind
moves through this book as an educational, absolute paragon. The
cosmopolitan societal education that Montaigne imagines to be the
most beautiful flowering of humanity at that time is intended as a
recommendation to be freely chosen, not as a lesson. Instead of concerning himself with what man can become, Montaigne concerns himself
with the discovery of what man in general is: an essence of ordinariness,
humanitas in the sense of what is only too human and temperamental, a
creature of surprising variety who is more likely to hide than come to
light through his ethical, social, even religious culture. The basic idea of
the *Essais* states again and again that actual man is richer than all
paragons upon which he strives to model himself: "We are each richer

than we think, but we are trained to borrow and beg; we are taught to use the resources of others more than our own" (III, 12, 794 B). The generic concept of man is replaced with the concept of the multiplicity, the individuality, and the variability of what is human. Words such as *diversité, variété, dissemblance* are the catchwords of Montaigne's anthropology. The wealth of what is human is described in the temporal and spatial diversity, in the individual phases of life, opinions, attitudes, moods. The description delves with a special passion precisely into what is paradoxical and inconsistent. It avoids any grouping and premature interpretation that would subordinate fact to a general coherence. Montaigne is pervaded by the insight that no individual thing disappears into what is general, such as the lower into the higher. He does not look for the law, but rather for the single image. Thus he, like the study of morality as a whole, stands well apart from the methodology of the natural sciences, which does not seek the individual element and the particular image, but rather the governing law. His book contains a moralistic phenomenology. It arrives at a previously unattained refinement of the study of man by exposing the crude and much too broad categories with which psychology and moral philosophy had up till then busied themselves and schematized things. Finally, the power of visualization with which Montaigne succeeds in portraying what is unique determines his place in the realm between philosophy and literary work—a place in which so many other skeptics are also at home.

Admittedly, he hardly concerns himself at all any more with one question, namely, the metaphysical question of what role man plays in the totality of the order of existence. But he does deal, in fact quite extensively, with the fragility of human existence, the *condition humaine*. This resembles the Christian ranking that declares man, to the extent that he is part of nature, to be a creature of misery and thus speaks of the *miseria hominis*. These types of Christian motifs linger on often enough in the language used in the *Essais*. But they also fade away. Their task consists only in pointing the way leading to the view of the natural qualities of man. Once this has become visible, Montaigne leaves it as it is. Christianity also has another concept of man: the *dignitas hominis,* man created by God, in the image of God, and the possibility of his being redeemed. And between Miseria and Dignitas Christianity lays the ascending path to saving grace which man can embark upon by means of a moral transformation of self. Montaigne has no interest in this path to saving grace or that supernatural dignity of existence. Since their intensity is lacking, so is the remorse and longing for redemption. The staircase Montaigne travels to human reality leads from top to bottom, from hubris to modesty. But having arrived at the end of this descent, he does not bring man despair or the hope of grace. The *Essais* were not written to make man weary of himself. They do expose him, but without anger, misery, or cynicism. The same hand that strikes down human hubris soothes him and shows him what is bearable about his stay in the common realm of all creatures of nature. This is the serenity and wisdom that threads through the *Essais:* a profound trust that the mortality under which we suffer is at the same time the condition of our existence. Man who has been devalued through the helping motifs of Christianity (and antiquity) becomes the affirmed man. Goethe spoke with good reason in the Cardano section of his *Geschichte der Farbenlehre* of Montaigne's "incalculably serene phrasing."

However, he himself, Michel de Montaigne, is the dominant figure in the *Essais.* His question of what man is can be stated more precisely as: What am I? One can only bring his book into a very loose historical connection with Christian confessional literature and with autobiographies, for it has decisively altered their conception and purpose. But it does share this one aspect with them: it bases its knowledge of man upon the old principle of "Know thyself." This is accomplished in a quite literal way, as self-observation of the individual named Montaigne. What results from this is not a uniform self-portrait but rather a portfolio of sketches and figure studies such as a painter might make at various times during the day, sometimes in this, sometimes in that pose and lighting, captured quickly in the chance moment. And yet a strict method prevails in them. It is the method of an attentive honesty that only says about itself what it can be sure of as the content of the self in that moment. Montaigne knows how difficult it is to perceive the center and the hairline boundaries of the self, and how dangerously quickly man can stray into self-falsification, how agilely he attributes motives to his behavior which are not the true motives, and how comfortable he can make things for himself by imitating clichés rather than heeding the uncovered source of his being. Montaigne summons up all his energy to find rather than to invent himself. Precisely the fact that man can only approach knowing where and what his self is compels the self-analyst in him to constantly retest his individuality. Thus we find the unending, contradictory line of his descriptions of himself and this tenacious consent to the most fleeting moments of his existence, which is probably a synthesis, but one that remains open and tends toward erratic transformation.

The countless personal and often trivial details that are scattered through the *Essais,* such as physical and moral habits, favorite foods, clothing, manner of travel, and so forth—things that make his work the most intimate book written up to that time—serve his aim of self-discovery. They permit us a view of the author in personified precision before us, so close as to belie the nearly four centuries between him and us. Montaigne is the first great postclassical author of concrete individuality who is not diverted from himself by a need for moral exemplariness or by the observation of the human condition of sin, as was still true of Petrarch.

And to this is added a style of thinking that intentionally remains within the sphere of mere private opinions and personal taste. By listening in on his own spontaneous reactions, the observer of self hopes to find the traces of his individual makeup: ". . . the opinion I give of them is to declare the measure of my sight, not the measure of things" (II, 10, 298 A). It seems as if to him all things, all things that are done or thought by man, are only windows allowing him to look inside himself, as if they were only means to the reproduction of himself. The intellect has become more interesting to itself than all the materials that start it in motion. Montaigne has the consistency of resolute subjectivity. In his position in history, this means that he has found a basis upon which to bear the force of the educational weights encumbering his century, and to balance these with the opposing force of free individuality. The weight of instructional content had become overwhelming in the sixteenth century as a result of the growth of humanistic knowledge, and it had finally suppressed the ordering principle, still possible in older humanism, of relating what was classical and what was Christian to one another concordistically, and thus keeping them distinct. The result was a chaotic quantitative approach to knowledge, a formless accumulation of material. These masses of material could only be managed in that individuality risked either relating all theorems to itself and injecting them into the content of its own life and soul or boldly holding them at arm's length, disregarding authoritarian demands. The established elements of general education included in the *Essais*—still considerable in scope—form an open space in which the individual may wander around at will, discover his own nature, remain true to it, and speak his own honest words without feeling annihilated by the multiplicity available.

With his return to the self, Montaigne attains access to the knowledge—for him the only possible access—of what it is to be human using the particular case of his own individuality. If indeed individuality is the actual reality of being human, then self-observation provides the closest proximity to this reality. It does this along the path leading through inner experience, which has the advantage of directness over objective knowledge of mankind—and also the directness that offers the self-analyst the assurance that he is close to the core of the matter. Thus the search for self of the *Essais* is the main method used in this unconventional, descriptive study of mankind.

And at the same time it is Montaigne's decision to conduct his life in undisturbed, self-defined legitimacy as the way shown him for being human, without regret or correction, without gazing up at a superior thought content, and fearing only one thing—alienation from himself. In contrast to Augustine's *Confessiones,* for example, or to any ordering type of self-understanding, he recognizes no hidden basic nature of his being that is imposed upon it from the outside, no central event in his life history in which such a nature would have broken through and fulfilled itself. Nor does he therefore recognize any crises or high points; rather he sees his life as a continuous flow into which he can dip, living and reflecting—in the full awareness that he is risking something new when he makes this the subject matter of a book. "It is the only book in the world of its kind" (II, 8, 278 C) is what he himself said of the *Essais* at the end of his life, and one must admit that he is right.

2.   ON MONTAIGNE THE MAN

Montaigne's ancestors, with the name Eyquem, were wealthy large-scale merchants of the bourgeois class. His great-grandfather acquired the Castle Montaigne in the fifteenth century, which had belonged to the archbishops of Bordeaux as a fief. Thus our author's nobility was rather recent and was based upon the purchase of goods. Michel Eyquem, as he was still known at first, as the son of a family that had become castle lords, received after his initial Latin humanistic education an ongoing education appropriate to his station as a nobleman at one of the so-called noblemen's academies. His father planned a civil service career of the *noblesse de robe* for him. Thus he studied law and at twenty-four years old entered the parliament of Bordeaux as judge and councilor. In this capacity, he came into contact with the religious battles then flaring up, and which continued to constitute the major contemporary historical background of his life. As a civil servant, as in his conducting of his life as a whole, he always remained Catholic-conservative. This is all the more remarkable because in the circle of his immediate family, there were considerable denominational differences. A brother and two sisters embraced the Reformation. A niece who had grown up a Calvinist later converted—purportedly under his influence—to Catholicism (and in the following century was even beatified). One of his cousins was a Jesuit. His wife's family consisted of notorious opponents of the Huguenots. The religious divisions of the epoch were thus also mirrored in Montaigne's immediate environment. He gained a direct perspective of denominational disunity. This is significant for his stance with respect to religious questions, which will be described later.

Performance of his official duties in Bordeaux was correct and loyal to the king, neither distinguished by unusual ambition nor tarnished by any negligence worthy of mention. He did what was expected of a civil servant in fulfilling the judicial and administrative responsibilities of his office. As a member of Parliament, he went to the king's court several times. In 1570, he gave up his office and shortly thereafter withdrew to the Castle Montaigne, which had been left him after his father's death; he had been known since 1568 as messire Michel, Seigneur de Montaigne. He began work on the *Essais* around the year 1572. After the first two books appeared, he made a trip to the therapeutic baths in Italy. We know about these through the *Journal de Voyage,* which was published posthumously. During this journey (1581), he received news that the city of Bordeaux had offered him the office of mayor. He accepted, and was selected again after his term expired. This worthy and responsible position—which had even been held by princes on occasion—combined judicial and city administration duties with the delicate political task of maintaining the connection between the city and the king. Montaigne took care of his office with the conviction of a man who loves order and balance, avoids adventure, and holds to the preservation of the existing order despite its faults. In so doing, he knew how to preserve his inner freedom. One of his most content-rich Essays (III, 10) resulted from his reflections on the conducting of his office and freedom. He was able to continue in mediation activity, which he had already performed in the earlier period in conflicts between league and crown, even beyond the scope of his mayoral office, which brought him the favor of Henry of Navarre. He appears later to have exercised direct or indirect influence over King Henry IV and to have played a preparatory role in his conversion. One must bear these facts in mind to understand that under the private appearance of the *Essais* there is a layer of experiences that reach in to the great affairs of crown and church in France of that time. Montaigne tested out the problems running through the *Essais* concerning philosophical freedom and balancing these against societal and political existence, as he did the central concept of a skeptical conservatism, against a reality in which he himself had taken active part.

3. PRETENSION TO NOBILITY

What all contemporary readers of the *Essais* observed was the author's pretense of nobility when he liked to reach a bit higher than the offspring of the mercantile bourgeoisie was entitled. Montaigne spoke of himself as if he belonged to long-established nobility. This man who was otherwise so willing to deprecate himself here appeared unable to master his vanity. The fact that after giving up his office he performed occasional military service as officer among the ranks of the Perigord nobility enticed him into counting himself as a member of the military nobility. This was soon ridiculed or dismissed with scorn, and it constitutes one of the few points in which his contemporaries and people of the next generation did not take him completely seriously. Scaliger, Brantôme, and later Guez de Balzac sneered about this. Even in the extensive critique of Montaigne in the *Logique de Port-Royal* this plays a role as evidence of human foolishness, vanity, and egoism, for which in Jansen's circles Montaigne was seen as a prime example.

But today we can see these things in a somewhat different light. Montaigne had several reasons for his need for class validity. They are connected with his task as an author and with his concept of education. European and particularly French literature of the sixteenth century was in the process of moving the author out of the specializations of theologians and jurists into the "larger" world, that is, the world of society and class, and conversely of exposing this world to the realm of intellectual property. This had been begun at the Upper Italian courts of the fifteenth century and the beginning of the sixteenth century. Measured against their culture, the French nobility was quite backward. Its lack of education was proverbial, as one can read in Castiglione, in Italian novellas, in embassy reports, and even in Tasso. Nevertheless, the French nobility was supposed to be lifted from the coarseness of its military virtues to a higher level of culture, indeed to the privileged foundation of world culture. Montaigne participated in this process. Even when functioning as an author, he spoke—at least at first—to members of the nobility. This required that he make a number of accommodations before he could be heard at all. The first consists in the protestation that he himself is a man of the upper classes. The other consists in consideration of the tastes of the nobility, which had an aversion to any pedantic specialization. Montaigne had to push his consciousness as an author through the reservation that noblemen did not write books, or at the very least could not display any scholarly and rhetorical schooling. The nobleman who wrote would stress that he owed his rank to his position in society, not to his writing activities. Writing books was only valued when it upheld the allure of freely occupying one's spare time. And even this still seemed strange to the backward nobility in the provinces. Montaigne complains late in his life that in his home, the Gascogne, people thought it a kind of joke to see him, their lord of a neighboring castle, in print (III, 2, 614 C).[2] He finds that he is resisting the nobility's lack of education of the older and provincial mode. But he has the more open-minded of them on his side, or he brings them to his side with the express assurance that he is one of their own. He did everything possible to assure for his writing occupation the high regard that could be granted him only by the aristocracy that was elevating itself to a cosmopolitan education. Thus the often strange character of his claims to social standing. It is important to him to appear with a good name, and he helps the somewhat faint luster of his name along a bit. He writes such that the aristocrats will not suspect him of being a scholar and disregard him. He writes in the only way open to him among men of the world, in an enthusiastic, conversational informality. By using this accommodation to class standing, Montaigne initiated a then new dignity for the independent writer, and he facilitated the movement of the French aristocracy, to the extent that they detached themselves from their military or landed gentry isolation, along the path toward the great flowering of culture of the seventeenth century. And this also brought success. The *Essais*, after they had broken through the initial resistance, even became fashionable reading for the French nobility, and soon it was considered good taste to have the book lying on the hearth in castles and salons.[3]

Of course neither the oft-repeated self-interpretation of the *Essais* as the pastime of a nobleman nor the corresponding assessment by its first readers does justice to its scope. It is a book that reaches not only beyond specific professions but also beyond any single class of society. One no longer needs to restrict its author to a single caste in order to understand him. And he himself was not without a feeling of disquiet regarding the limitedness of those of his class. He had different points of view. He once somewhat contemptuously separated the exclusively militaristic and inordinately ambitious occupation of the nobility from "philosophical valor," that is, the great soul that is capable from the strength of its own powers, and he knows that this is not bound to presumptions of class (II, 7, 277 A). Another passage is even clearer: "I know of nothing worthy of great admiration . . . and those I come in contact with most commonly through my situation are for the most part men who have little care for the culture of the soul" (II, 17, 500 A); indeed they are people who know no happiness other than honor, and no perfection other than soldierly competence. This is informative, for it shows how little the bases of the noble class of which he considers himself a part really satisfy him, and how greatly he feels urged forward toward—here expressed with the Ciceronian formula of the *cultura animi*—humanity.[4] And still later he writes that nobility by birth is indeed a pleasant, but also a questionable matter; it can just as easily be the lot of a competent man as of a depraved one. Here one hears the concept, never-ending since antiquity, of the distinction between nobility of birth and nobility of essence.

Thus Montaigne finds himself in the middle between the ambition of his class, which he still needs in order to secure his reputation as a writer, and an ever-developing ideal of the culture of personality which is free of class ties.

4. WRITING AS AN OCCUPATION

Montaigne was thirty-eight years old when he retired to the room in the tower of his castle and began to write the *Essais*. His early age at the time of his retreat from professional life was rather unusual for a member of the nobility by office. The reasons are merely a matter of conjecture, for he expressed himself only very generally on this subject. But they would have been related to his obligation as heir to the castle after his father's death of assuming responsibility for management of the household. Also, political disappointments, weariness of civil activity, and mourning for his deceased friend La Boétie may have played a role. We know in any case that he settled into his room in the tower surrounded by books, the majority of them from the bequest of La Boétie. We also know that there was engraved in this room a Latin inscription, adapted to classical script, and also dressed up somewhat coquettishly with archaic forms of words. This inscription said that "Mich. Montanus" had been weary of the burden of public service for some time, and thus *quietus et omnium securus* had dedicated the remainder of his life to peace and freedom in the lap of the muses (*in doctarum virginum sinus*). He also had fifty-four key phrases by classical authors and from the Bible burned into the crossbeams on the ceiling; they outline, in the manner of mnemonics, the skeptical main themes of the first two books of the *Essais*, in which a part of them is repeated.[5]

There is an unmistakable imitation of classical style in this decision to retreat to solitude. To conclude a period of official and political duties by turning inward to a state of meditative idleness was considered the appropriate behavior of one of advanced years among those with an Augustinian education. Cicero in *De senectute*, Seneca, and Pliny the Younger addressed this in their letters. The *otium cum litteris* (Seneca, *epistolae* 82) is a common lifestyle of Renaissance humanists. Petrarch demonstrates this for them: he is the original model for book-reading solitude, which has been transplanted from the monk's cell into the scholar's room, and which henceforth should move alongside the various forms of religious separation from the world as a secular variant. Later on, and modeled on the Platonic *Symposium* motif, some attempted seclusion from the world in groups: an example is the esoteric circles of the Medician Academy. This then spread to France: Rabelais' utopia of the Abbey of Thelem is the best known literary reflection. Montaigne's retreat is also along the lines of this form of education. He decided upon personal solitude in the sphere of his private residence. An air, though a dilute one, of humanistic, muse-inspired turning away from the world and the mood of soliloquy-like meditation hovers over the *Essais* to the end and more closely reflects its inclination than class-related, political and conversational traffic with the world. Still, without revealing a strict desire to escape the world or any sort of esoteric arrogance, Montaigne's book belongs in a quiet space into which the rest of the author's life, which is still not without activity, can penetrate only in muted form, quieted by the distance of observation. Shortly after moving into the room in the tower, he declares in words in which his consciousness speaks that he has entered into a clearly delineated last phase of his life in which self-occupation of the spirit is more important than outwardly directed involvement: "Lately when I retired to my home, determined so far as possible to bother about nothing except spending the little life I have left in rest and seclusion, it seemed to me I could do my mind no greater favor than to let it entertain itself in full idleness and stay and settle in itself . . ." (I, 8, 21 A). The Essay is believed to be from the year 1572.

5. WRITINGS BEFORE THE *ESSAIS*

Montaigne was not a newcomer to the wielding of a pen when he began to write the *Essais*. He had already accomplished the translation of the extensive *Theologia naturalis* by Sebond (1569). We will have the opportunity to discuss this later (chapter 3). And the letters must be mentioned. Of the thirty-six in publication today—all of these in French—several belong to the period of his participation in the parliament in Bordeaux and to the first period of his seclusion in the Castle Montaigne.[6] There is no need to discuss the official letters here. However, of significance is a series of letters which are written with literary intent and which adhere undeniably to the rules of style of the art epistles. Montaigne published them himself (1571) as accompaniment to his publication of the verse and the Plutarch and Xenophon translations of his friend La Boétie, who died in 1563.

The most valuable and extensive letter is the one from the end of August 1563, in which he reports to his father on La Boétie's death. It is a well-proportioned work of art, consisting of a description of the illness, six speeches by the dying man to his relatives and to his friend Michel, and of the large concluding piece that provides the details of the act of dying itself. This portrait of the Christian death of La Boétie has classical elements of the hero's courage in death and the customary *consolatio* themes woven through it, though without these gaining the upper hand. This is Montaigne's most significant prose before the *Essais*, and it also involves an art of composition which he consciously gives up in the *Essais*. However, evidence of the Montaigne of the future is perceptible in the obvious thoroughness with which he involves himself in the tortured details of a death. Here we already see something of his drive for knowledge, which ever more intensely revolves around all appearances and ways of experiencing death. Even the tendency to pay greater attention to the human-natural process than to the Christian or classical classifications, then the perceptible dropping of the initial intention to show the dying man as a stoic who is superior to the body and to pain, in fact, his declining to make something violently pathetic of his friend's dying in itself: all this betrays the fact that even here he is secretly involved in the study of actual dying, and not in interpreting death, taken from whatever source, or in consolation. He wants to *see* the process, not deflect it from himself by explanation and acquisition of knowledge.

Other than this, Montaigne's spiritual personality was either not expressed at all or was expressed only in a faint reflection in his letters. This is true of the later letters as well. They shed no light on the *Essais*, to which they refer only in an insignificant way. They are only significant for biographical reasons. Only the last (or the last found) letter of 1590 is noteworthy. It was written to Henry IV. With proud free-spiritedness Montaigne rejects the king's intention to compensate him, the *gentilhomme,* for his services with money. Around the same time he notes in his *Essais:* "[C] I look upon our kings simply with a loyal and civic affection, which is neither moved nor removed by private interest. For this I congratulate myself . . . [B] This is what makes we walk everywhere head high, face and heart open" (III, 1, 601). The letter confirms that Montaigne acted in the same manner as he thought in the *Essais*. He shows in both cases an independence born of strong character, the equal of the best of the feudal noblemen. Here we perceive the noble tone of France before absolutism.

6. SELF-DEPRECATION

Questions of the literary stimulus connected with the genesis of the *Essais* will be discussed later (chapter 8). However, we must point out a characteristic that is one of the central features of the *Essais:* the persistent self-deprecation of the author. It takes the form of the author's assurance that he is an old man to whom no one need listen and of his devaluation of his writing, which he is offering as an artless game, free of expectations.

Montaigne exercises the particularization he requires for his view of man upon his own person to such a great extent that he does not see it as a whole, but rather understands it in its movement from phase to phase. "I do not portray being: I portray passing. Not the passing from one age to another, or, as the people say, from seven years to seven years, but from day to day, from minute to minute," so reads one of his most significant statements (III, 2, 611 B). At least in Montaigne's intent, these parts of this continuous, transitional movement are small— extremely small units, for which a differentiation based upon chronological age should seem too rough and too broad. Yet the analysis of the whole of his life in the *Essais* does contain a classification into periods based upon age. Montaigne expressly wishes to limit his statements to the part of his life during which they were made. That is the period between his fortieth and sixtieth years of life. By means of this limitation, his *Essais* were to be characterized as something that could only be evaluated to diagnose his own individuality, as determined by age. They were to make no claim of having any normative value for his own life as a whole or for mankind in general.

This is why the *Essais* are so liberally permeated with comments that their author is an aging, in fact old, man. We find such comments even in the sections that are part of the oldest level of the text. Of course they increase in frequency in the third book and in the handwritten additions of the Bordeaux edition. Montaigne feels that he is in the twilight of his life and is accustoming himself to seeing everything with the eyes of one in a final encounter. An air of autumn surrounds the *Essais,* as was true of the authors he liked to quote, Seneca and Plutarch. And he considered old age the most appropriate time for writing what was to be self-description. It was the age in which the external movements of life no longer held surprises, when only the horizon of death was visible before him, and when it is assumed that one's own nature will no longer exceed the development measured out for it. When he was approximately fifty-four years old he wrote: "I have chosen the time when my life, which I have to portray, lies all before my eyes; what is left is more related to death" (III, 12, 809 B).

But even with the degree of coquetry and mischievousness apparent in these protestations of old age, they do have a seriousness as well. Montaigne does not see advanced age or even very old age as a stage of serenity in which the physical powers that have come to rest now free the spirit to indulge in pure observation. He sees it as decline and weariness. He does not separate spirit and body; for him, when the one declines, so does the other. The fact that he confesses to being old means, without glossing it over, that the best is behind him and that he could easily seem laughable, unworthy of being heard, to the young. But it must also be understood to mean that he is obediently grasping the natural urge of one his age to be whatever is left for him to be. Montaigne felt deeply how each period of a life had its own inalienable value that needed to be lived regardless of whether it came before or after another period, indeed, how full authenticity of a man could only succeed where the law and also the questionable character of the moment were fulfilled. This brought him the fortunate feeling of being part of some order—it did not matter whether it pointed upward or downward. He consents to live in the last phase of the great rhythm consisting of turning green, blossoming, harvesting, and wilting. What makes his resonating contact with the tides more intimate is that he does not evade the difficulties of this last phase. Since he does not connect human acts of recognition, assessment, and forming opinions to encroaching objective interconnections, but rather to the particular individuality that is expressed in it, he must also qualify his own thinking and writing in every way as a symptom of the brief final period of life in which he finds himself: "My history needs to be adapted to the moment" (III, 2, 611 B). The more he follows the law of this period, the closer he feels to the honesty for which he strives. It is not a matter of *the* wise man speaking to *men*. Rather, an aging man is speaking to a public that he cannot determine and which he leaves to chance.

Later we will again discuss the aging theme at length (chapter 5). But here it was important to stress, because it is significant for an understanding of the *Essais* from the beginning, that in confessing to old age Montaigne is deliberately placing his book under a negative sign. And this is the case because an honest establishing of the natural difficulties of age should bring forth what is special at that time, and for him that is the full reality of his being human. As he does everywhere else, here too he uses that which is imperfect as the unsuspicious contour of what is concrete.

The self-effacements of his writing are also part of this. He loves to speak contemptuously of his *Essais*. In fact, he presses an undervaluing of the book upon the reader—admittedly, upon the reader who has been made wiser, the one he is counting on to make his own judgment. A case in point: ". . . I place the *Essais* now low, now high, very inconsistently and uncertainly" (III, 8, 718 B). Even this is a fluctuating judgment. As a rule, he expresses himself less ambivalently. For example: "My works are so far from delighting me that as many times as I sample them again, so many times I am vexed with them" (II, 17, 482 A). Or: ". . . these are nothing but reveries of a man who has tasted only the outer crust of sciences . . ." (I, 26, 106 A), and: ". . . in these ramblings of mine . . ." (III, 9, 734 B). Calling his thinking and writing *rêveries* in the usage of that time has a frankly disparaging meaning; the word in no sense means emotional, beautiful fantasies, as it has since about the middle of the eighteenth century, but rather (and not only in its pejorative form *ravasseries*) has the sense of insanities, hallucinations, delirium of a semicomatose mind.[7] ". . . these fancies of mine that you see here" can be found in another passage (III, 3, 629 B). Or he speaks of his flow of babble, *flux de caquet* (III, 5, 684 B), or even calls the *Essais* "some excrements of an aged mind," this following a quite unappetizing anecdote that one can read in the text (III, 9, 721 B).

There are countless such comments. Should one take them seriously? Certainly not more but also not less than one should take the hidden intention in irony seriously. They are amusing and belong to the animating appeal of the *Essais*. It is certainly not true remorse when Montaigne speaks so dismissingly of himself. Sometimes it can seem that the reason he performs this comedy of professing unworthiness is quite transparent. It is reminiscent of the formula of "feigned modesty" (called this by Eduard Norden), which has long been an author's device: the author hides his self-esteem behind alleged inferiority. It is possible that Montaigne here and there made use of this type of convention, with which the reader would have been familiar, and would not have taken literally. But he, ever ironic toward himself, is smart enough to know that too clever modesty becomes suspicious: "There is a certain type of subtle humility that is born of presumption . . ." (II, 37, 578 A). Then there is a sort of trick in his self-deprecation which takes the dangerous edge from what he says—and he says some bold things—when he passes his remarks off as only opinions, hallucinations. He can in this way avoid efforts to nail him down: I am nothing, I am not competing with the recognized authorities. This is an element of the "double truth" tactic, or of all those works that appeared purportedly as mere exercises in style, such as Erasmus' *Laus stultitiae*, More's *Utopia*, Agrippa von Nettesheim's *De vanitate*. Or it resembles the *locura*-motif beloved by Spanish writers which involved making a character in a novella or novel insane, then being able to put extremely dangerous material into his mouth, since what he says cannot be attacked: the speaker is, after all, only a fool. Furthermore, the literary self-deprecation Montaigne uses also serves his pretension of having a cosmopolitan nobleman's education. There must be no hint of pedantry or rhetorical display, for scholarly literateness would be inappropriate and ineffective. It should all remain a private chat: this is how the taste of the larger world wants it, and this world pervades the *Essais*—at least their surface—to a much greater degree than we might perceive at first glance today.

Precautions and capricious game pieces are thus entwined in the self-deprecation displayed in the *Essais*. But it is more. It is an element of the method Montaigne uses to tone man down in order to get a real look at him. If that man who is observing himself like a lab specimen claims to be *so* insignificant that he even treats his book with contempt—then, as is true of moral and biological self-deprecation, that implies that he wants to be on solid ground that no one can dispute: the solid ground of ordinariness. He would rather diminish himself by several degrees more than he himself believes in order to feel protected against the distortions of posing and dignity. He wants to be at home where man is only a beginning, a simple possibility, a creature that receives itself from the hands of nature, unprocessed, undistorted, unshaped. His desire is to bring this naked humanity to light, for the tedious monotony of being significant flees before it. I am such a nothing—therefore I am: this is the amazing conclusion of Montaigne's self-knowledge. This is why in the *Essais* he reaches so obstinately for every opportunity that presents itself, even the conventional ones, to diminish himself. He compares his *Essais* with great artistic prose, and with authoritarian books, to say: these cannot compare with those—they are incomparable. They present themselves modestly in order to declare that they are unique. That which is imperfect is to them a genuine trace of individuality. Here a remarkably arabesque interplay of true modesty and philosophical awareness of individuality comes into being. There, as is often the case with Montaigne, it is difficult to cite the passage where irony ends and seriousness begins. The irony lies in the execution, not in the core of the matter. The irony shields the desire to remain insignificant from being misinterpreted as a sense of guilt and sin. It is the outward shimmer of an inner freedom, joyousness, and complete lack of vulgarity. For someone who intends so strongly to be himself, even under the condition of being insignificant, and who gives others room to do the same is not common but rather elite. A breath of Socratic spirit rests upon him.

7. BANALITY

When Montaigne seeks the reality of what it is to be human he seeks it in the observation of the most ordinary, the most banal things—in himself as in others. Every reader of the *Essais* will have made the discovery that one can become impatient or bored when very unprepossessing things are discussed, often for page after page, such as meals and favorite foods, trivialities occurring at the table, when riding, when greeting someone, in the performance of household duties. The author's joy in details is boundless, and also often undisciplined. The "tedium" of certain passages in the *Essais* always arises when Montaigne dwells in the random abundance of ordinary things; and he loves to do this. To him everything is worthy of being observed: "There is no subject so vain that it does not deserve a place in this rhapsody" (I, 13, 32 A). Here he must be read as one pages through a picture book. It can happen that he leaves the banal material unprocessed. But it can also happen, and much more frequently, that he turns it over in his hands reflectively until suddenly a thought flares up in the light of which it becomes transparent. A curious disparity between substance and idea prevails, and in the midst of his most casual "flow of babble" (*flux de caquet*) he can unintentionally encounter a point that ignites his interest. He starts anywhere; he can begin his contemplation at any point, discontinue it at any point. "Judgment is a tool to use on all subjects, and comes in everywhere. Therefore in the tests that I make of it here, I use every sort of occasion," he says himself (I, 50, 219 A). Another time he interrupts his digressions (but are they?) with the confession: "Any topic is equally fertile for me. A fly will serve my purpose . . ." (III, 5, 668 B). He draws upon so much raw material because he is always awaiting a new perspective that he takes into himself from the particular thing: "A new figure: an unpremeditated and accidental philosopher" (II, 12, 409 C). He knew that this process of awaiting was a method. He sees man as woven into the weave of the coincidences of his daily life. Thus he secretly watches as many of those sorts of coincidences as possible for what they may have to say about the nature of an individual—and from this for the variable structure of what it is to be human. The most banal, intimate, inapparent thing can open up the most fertile insight into being. Thus Montaigne's most content-rich observations appear bound to the images of what is lowliest. Everywhere we find solid tangibility, visibility, a confidential, comfortable aura circulating in a peaceful contemplativeness. This empirical method is far more than the usual collections of curiosities and facts of contemporary popular literature. Montaigne's method has the incomparable art of portraying the ordinary such that its mysteriousness begins to shine through. And this happens in that he prefers to let a matter emerge with its appearance rather than to wear it out prematurely with theorems, thus robbing it of its ambiguity: "I uncover things more than I discover them" (II, 12, 370 C).[8] Even his most thorough insights into being do not lose the freshness of their origin in perception. Even when he formulates something abstractly, there is always an anecdote, a little story from his own experience along with it. The individual thing should remain individual, rather than to disappear in a whole that is inaccessible or only artificially conceivable. This is skeptical fragmentarism: "For I do not see the whole of anything; nor do those who promise to show it to us" (I, 50, 219 C). He appears to consider not teaching but rather simply narrating to be the right method of finding a clue to the secrets: "I do not teach, I tell" (III, 2, 612 B). He has succeeded completely in stating his insights without imposing them. He does not even impose them upon himself. He could think differently another time—or (with the major basic ideas) could stumble upon something he himself had thought before as ingenuously as if he had forgotten it, and as if he were obtaining it only now for the first time from the directness of the thing he is looking at: the perpetual condition of the pupil who always begins from the beginning. "He left his disciples in order to become a disciple himself"—this was how his adopted daughter, helper, and pupil, Marie de Gournay, so eloquently put it in speaking of him.[9]

8.   CONTRAST TO THINKING IN SYSTEMS

One can get a picture of the *Essais* by comparing the book with its extreme contrast, the "system." Proof of this could be found in the known definition of the system in Kant's *Critique of Pure Reason* (third main section in the "Transcendental Doctrine of Method"). Kant writes: "In accordance with reason's legislative prescriptions, our diverse modes of knowledge must not be permitted to be a mere rhapsody, but must form a system . . . By a system I understand the unity of the manifold modes of knowledge under one idea. This idea is the concept provided by reason—of the form of a whole—insofar as the concept determines *a priori* not only the scope of its manifold content, but also the positions which the posts occupy relatively to one another . . . The whole is thus an organized unity (*articulatio*), and not an aggregate (*coacervatio*). It may grow from within (*per intussusceptionem*), but not by external addition (*per appositionem*)." Let us simply turn this around. Montaigne, skeptical of the efficiency of reason, does not subject himself to its "rule," rather, he keeps himself free in the hovering realm of conjecture. This moves through the interplay of diverse perspectives and avoids stopping in definitive insights. He knows of no idea that radiates out into diversity with a unifying effect. If one wanted to summarize the *Essais* into a core idea (as in *que sais-je?*) and its parts, too much of what they are in their full breadth would be lost; but their breadth, which runs toward open horizons, belongs no less to their essence than the depth of their momentary thoughts. They have no predetermined scope of diversity which it occurs to them to express. They are neither internally nor externally complete, rather they could have continued to grow in an unforeseen direction. Their thoughtfulness and concreteness, their wit and their changeability do not permit an abbreviated rendering any more than would a meditation or a story. They do not evade contradiction, instead, they drive it forward as a fresh symptom of the intellect in perpetual motion; its nature—constantly an initial trying things out—not its result is what interests the author. Thus its presentation, too, is not a structuring but rather an accumulating one, an aggregate with an intentionally random character. Montaigne designates his *Essais* as *rapsodie* (I, 13, 32 A) with good reason, that is (according to French usage of his time and the present), as a disjointed fragmentary work. Thus he himself provides the catchword that has been used for some time by strictly system-oriented philosophers—and was still used by Kant—to designate prescientific thinking.

We will be concerned later with the fact that the open manner of thinking and presentation in the *Essais* continues a process that since the late Middle Ages had begun to dissolve the formalism of the scholastic method and its system concept and thus the idea of an integral science of knowledge (chapter 8). At the moment, we only hope to show a first characteristic. If one applies as strict a standard as Kant's specification of the system (though it could also have been Aristotelian and Thomistic specifications), then the *Essais* appear to be the classical example of vagueness, of an unscientific character, and of a comfortable dwelling in a state in which one knows and sees many things yet does not want to be pinned down to anything. Montaigne supports this type of impression with his numerous programmatic statements in which, in his usual self-deprecating manner, he gives the impression that he is making quite light of his subject. But his self-abandonment to the boundless, his relinquishment of relationship, order, and a unified whole is not as easy as one might think. There is also a courage and rigorousness in it, particularly in those historical instants in which a rigid, formalistic tradition does not give subjectivity room to breathe and denies access to knowledge of concrete humanity. In resisting this rigidity Montaigne strives for unconditional subjectivity. His concept of truth separates itself from the goal of a knowledge of things and existence and is transformed into the concept of personal truthfulness. Its rigorousness consists in the precision of listening in on one's self. It only states what is valid for the author in the instant in which he is writing, but it says this without restriction. Thus Montaigne continuously contradicts himself, but in allowing contradiction he becomes genuine. Thus we find in the meaningful introduction of Essay III, 2: "This [my book] is a record of various and changeable occurrences, and of irresolute and, when it so befalls, contradictory ideas: whether I am different myself, or whether I take hold of my subjects in different circumstances and aspects. So, all in all, I may indeed contradict myself now and then; but truth . . . I do not contradict (611 B). By breaking down an objective compulsoriness and consistency, Montaigne enhances the freedom of individual subjectivity and the capacity to perceive each new moment arising in it. He masters the art of expressing the diversity that runs through the mind when one is in a reflective mood and the condition of being "lost in thought" without being engaged in the process of rigorous thinking. His writing, which from the point of view of one requiring a system is an unfocused drifting, reveals itself to be the organic radiation of a self that is capable of being entirely with itself. Behind the disorder of thought and form of the *Essais* the spiritual and human gestures of Michel de Montaigne thrive, or as Ranke once expressed it, "which, as he was, henceforth applied to himself."[10] The other difficulty of the drifting style of writing and thinking is that it has to fill his statements from the force of autonomy of the particular object and moment. It has to fend for itself completely. It cannot rely on the automatism of a system schema that steers everything along marked out lines and which for the sake of completeness, transitions, and logical linkage compels the author to make statements that would not otherwise be made for their own sake. It draws its light from sudden inspiration and knows that inspiration can be more beneficial than the systematic approach: in its glow banal and oft-repeated things again become a wonder.

This style of thinking and writing, which moves elastically in chance ideas, makes it possible to open up the *Essais*—other than the earliest ones—to any random passage. A few pages suffice in drawing the reader into the author's suggestive proximity and in stimulating his own reflectiveness. And this is how Montaigne has been read all along. Alfieri, who loved him and carried the book along with him on his travels, commented how he read here and there in the *Essais,* put them away, ". . . and in my way meditating for several hours over two of his pages" (*Vita,* III, 8). Sainte-Beuve recommends the same approach. In his journal, Gide notes: "Morning at the Louvre; delightful morning. I had a little Montaigne with me, but only read from it periodically as I walked, and only what was necessary to sustain the joyful elation of my thoughts."[11] Montaigne is one of the classical authors who are re-read because he fills the background of what is said with unspoken or only half-spoken possibilities that the reader can spin out in a different manner each time. He is open to any reading mood, always offers a word that one needs at that moment. Even overinterpretation, otherwise so risky, cannot go too far wrong with his work. And the more often one reads him, the better he becomes. "It is a wine that improves with age" was the clever Marie de Gournay's comment on the *Essais*.[12]

9. POSITION IN CONTEMPORARY HISTORY

In the course of our presentation we will be able to go into greater detail on Montaigne's position in his epoch—the "Renaissance" centuries. For the sake of an overview, only the most general elements will be mentioned here.

First let it be said that the *Essais* represent an event in the history of language. Theoretical prose written in the language of ordinary people had appeared before Montaigne in France, Italy, and Spain. Yet among the Romanic peoples within the category of philosophical writings in the narrower sense—and despite the difficulties of specifying their exact place, the *Essais* belong here—Montaigne is the first to express a significant and original body of thought *exclusively* in the language spoken by ordinary people. The philosophical literature written in French which had come to light in France up till then—Pierre de La Ramée, for example—cannot be compared with Montaigne, and it did not become a national treasure that still lives today, as did the *Essais*. The greatest works in philosophy but also in theology, moral theory, and science of the post-Middle Ages Romanic regions were predominantly written in Latin up to the time of Montaigne. The awakening of national language consciousness during the late Middle Ages and shortly thereafter was being felt in theoretical literature as well, with the result that some authors— since Dante and Ramón Lull—wrote alternately in Latin and in their ordinary language. This use of two languages, which reflected the rivalry of national and humanistic considerations, persisted into Montaigne's century (Calvin, Bodin) and continued (though the reasons had changed) to Descartes and beyond. Montaigne, however, although he had known Latin from his youth on, did not vacillate in his choice of French. For him this is a further sign of his intended departure from specialized knowledge and traditional philosophy: philosophizing would be done by the man and cosmopolitan layman, not the "philosopher." Only the passages he quotes are still in Latin. But he converts the enormous humanistic educational store he is processing into the expressions of his native tongue. In that time period, really only the Italian dialogues written by Giordano Bruno (1584/1585) can compare with the intellectual force of the *Essais*. Thus the two most original philosophical products of the sixteenth century arose at close to the same time. Apart from the ideational differences of the two—the Italian expressing an ecstatic cosmology, the Frenchman a calm, empirical analysis of man—Montaigne differs from Bruno in that he used his national language alone, whereas Bruno also left works in Latin. Montaigne's resoluteness concerning his national language is more unwavering than that of any of his ranking philosophical contemporaries. (The parts of the *Journal de Voyage* which were written in Italian can be ignored here, since they were supposed to be a casual exercise.) He uses French in the *Essais* with the full awareness that he is entrusting himself to a shifting foundation. As a humanist, he indeed theoretically gives Latin its full due as the most enduring and authoritative language (III, 9, 751 B). For his way of thinking, however, this is just a further incentive to express himself in French: his fluid thinking requires a living and thus changeable language, for this thinking consents all the more readily to changeability, the more concrete it feels in the language. Independent of this particular motivation, one can in any case say that Montaigne till then had decided for himself upon a more tentative than purposeful striving of the Romance spirit to carry over even his liberated thinking into the ordinary languages (which had been considered suitable for literary work for some time). The historical form of a Romance language of the late sixteenth century has become for Montaigne a fully transparent medium of individual thinking. One can no longer conceive of the *Essais* in any other medium. They are untranslatable to the same degree as literature, and they are bound just as tightly as literature to the means of expression of their time and nation.

Certain essential features of the thinking of the Renaissance centuries are repeated in numerous themes of the *Essais*, that is almost self-evident. But less self-evident is the answer to the question of whether and how Montaigne encountered the great Renaissance texts from Petrarch to Pomponazzi. Almost the only thing for which there is evidence is his reading of popular literature of the sixteenth century which was written in or translated into French. Thanks to Villey's research we can claim with certainty that these "influenced" him. But this popular literature of the kind produced by Boaistuau, Guy de Brues, and Antonio Guevara is a low-level sort of literature. It involves compilations of adopted ideas with their origin in a long series of authors of the fourteenth, fifteenth, and sixteenth centuries in Italy. It is possible that this is how Montaigne became acquainted with a body of thought which, though it did not constitute a unified whole, left its mark on the intellectual life of these three centuries. However, what remains astounding is that the *Essais* belong at a level well above the derivative popular literature and are equal or even superior to the best of that series of authors, Petrarch, Alberti, Valla, and others, and that in certain passages the *Essais* approximate their themes so closely that it is as if Montaigne had read them. But we have no evidence that this is the case. Thus we cannot clarify the fact that so much of the body of thought of the three Renaissance centuries is repeated in the *Essais* by pointing to definitive influences. The only solution is to speak of the effect of a "spirit of the times"—an awkward solution which leads nowhere, because it begins with nothing, namely with the "spirit of the times," that most confused and speculative of all historical categories. The correspondences that do exist between the *Essais* and the major themes of the Renaissance centuries and what makes this author with all his autonomy a member of a family of spirits moving in the same direction can only be determined and described in the particular degrees of similarity of each instance. The trail of sources leading to them is no longer evident.

The thinking of the Renaissance centuries was directed in two traditional classifications, but with the increasing use of classical texts, and thus in an altered response to problems. It looked outward with God, cosmos, and nature, and inward with human society, history, and soul.[13] Both sides are represented in the wealth of themes found in the *Essais*. But the latter prevails. Montaigne signifies the fulfillment of Renaissance anthropology in the French manner. When God and cosmos appear in his work at all, they appear as trigger points of a skeptical and fideistic critique of cognition. To him, nature is the felt content of inner experience. He dissolves society and history in the realm of the empirical-coincidental. But the soul is the focal point of his observation as the goal of earthly self-analysis of the individual. Nothing connects him to the metaphysical productivity of the Italians (from Ficino to Bruno). The dying out of Platonism, so characteristic for the French spirit of the sixteenth century, in the midst of Ronsard's literary work shows traces of the air of the *Essais:* an air of the earth and of humanity. Montaigne's human and self-interest exists in a particular anthropological context that reaches back to Petrarch. What he set down in his Latin tracts and letters affected, whether to a hidden or open degree, the moral theory and autobiographical literature of about three centuries. Even Montaigne is still affected by this, thus later we will be able to specify his position by using a comparison with Petrarch, among other things. This context that illuminates the *Essais* as a final release of Petrarchian striving is not lessened by the fact that Montaigne probably only knew Petrarch's Italian literary works, thus one cannot speak of a direct influence of his main autobiographical and anthropological works (*Secretum* or the dialogue-form tract *De remediis utriusque fortunae*).

Among the assumptions most significant for the *Essais* is the tendency to see the creation as more important than the creator. In the development from Cusanus to Bovillus, it is embedded in the idea of the microcosm: Man should and can attain the boundless richness of his own essence by developing all of the forces inherent in him, and this richness corresponds to the richness and the framework of the macrocosm. He will be relieved of the position of animal submissiveness. Just as he honors all creations as manifestations of the divine in the immanent, he honors himself. And if the speculative microcosm idea fades, he emerges all the more concretely as a creation of nature, which reigns over all. And nature itself—despite all of the theological means of expression that continue along the surface—is granted an autonomy that can no longer be maintained from a theological-orthodox standpoint, be it that God is moved away to nature's remote principle of creation, or be it that He is identified with it in the concepts of infinity and omnipotence. The strong Pliny reception in the fifteenth and sixteenth centuries favors the latter solution. Theologically, the elevation of nature and man is expressed through the blurring of the difference in essence between nature and grace. This was initiated in Telesio, Varchi, Rhodiginus, and others, and was expressed emphatically in Campanella, shortly after Montaigne. It was a common ground of sixteenth-century free-thinking in Italy and France to conceive of nature as the autonomous representative of God and as the free molder of all human individuals with their powers and defects. Montaigne also thinks along these lines. To him man is a creature indeed obedient to and in the care of God, but which no longer requires God; man is a creature of a nature that has its own power, that forms the single instance of the living of a life, and that carries within it an order that no longer relies upon grace. Montaigne could confirm all of this based on classical texts, and did so, as others had; but the fact that his eye was drawn precisely to these types of passages in the classical interpretations of nature is already the result of a modern free-thinking intellect that was the result of long preparation. Something that is also important is Montaigne's abandonment of the idea of gradation. This concept had served to classify the cosmos as a giant gradient, limited as a whole and separating the individual steps, from the intelligence closest to God down to men, animals, and the elements. Continuing beyond the Dominican and Franciscan metaphysics of the high Middle Ages, this was one of the most durable elements of Neoplatonic-Plotinic speculation. But even in Cusanus, besides this the conception of a homogeneous cosmos begins to appear. The leveling of the hierarchical ladder characteristic of nature philosophy is repeated in anthropology as moderation, and finally as the relinquishment of the superiority of the soul over the body, and in reference to the soul, as abandonment of a graduation upward and downward according to intellectual and affective ability. It is true that large spheres of the interpretation of man in the fifteenth and sixteenth centuries did not participate in this process and were satisfied with the secular release of man; otherwise, the renewal of the stoic ethic that was based upon the duality of body and soul would not have been possible. But Montaigne, who was never a true stoic and who did not base his wisdom on the authority of ethical reason but rather on the harmonious breadth of the equivalent capacities of body and soul, belongs to those theorists, like Pomponazzi, for example, who no longer divided man dualistically into higher and lower functions. Other than this, these levelings were to a large extent not expressed theoretically at all, though they had been used for some time and with confidence, almost like something self-evident, in descriptions of man. Since the fourteenth century there had been the beginnings of a decentralization of the content and interests of life, a horizontally directed expansion, whereby what were at one time the contents of various levels were isolated in individual spheres whose mutual incompatibility was ignored or no longer felt. One sees this in the novella-like and moralistic literature of Italy and France. Petrarch can be mentioned as an early example. In his short tract *De vita solitaria* he describes the secluded life of philosophical and religious contemplation in contrast to the noisy, unfocused life of a courtier. But the description of the latter is such that one notices the following: the author's interest is an aesthetic one and it belongs to both spheres. The judgmental ranking of quiet idleness above the public nature of court life disappears behind his literary involvement in both scenes. Even the division of Eros into a "heavenly" and an "earthly" love as it was found in the novellas and love treatises of the fifteenth and sixteenth centuries is connected with the waning of a sense of gradation in that the portrayal of the two forms of love increasingly amounts to a difference in kind rather than a hierarchy. One sees this most clearly where the two kinds of love are described by one and the same author with equal virtuosity, such as Bandello.

France of the late Middle Ages and the Renaissance displays this polyphonic juxtaposition of human spheres to a significantly higher degree than Italy, which is still restrained by its sense of proportion and honesty. The curiosity, almost inconceivable today, in *Heptameron* by Marguerite de Navarre, of portraying ideal Eros and obscene crudeness side by side is just as much a symptom of this as is the day of the young Gargantua by Rabelais, wherein reading the Bible and digestive functions are reported with equal emphasis. It could serve as a motto for this desire for ungraded multiplicity when at one point we read in Marguerite de Navarre: "The more diversified our bouquet, the handsomer it will be" (Novella 48). The sentence means far more than a variation in rhetorical style and subject. It could be written identically in Montaigne in its fundamental meaning (mixing and leveling of what is human). Under the pressure of the wealth of material, characters, and situations in French Renaissance literature the gradation breaks down completely. Authors were trying to express the totality of man through mass, quantity, even chaos. And despite how much more serene that all is in Montaigne, his portrayal of man in a horizontally expanded empirical richness lacks a ranking by value just as theirs do. The characteristic of the *Essais* described above of declining to give any sphere of life priority over another, of refusing to consider any theme more worthy of contemplation than another, and then the book's indulgence in banal commonplace subjects and its sudden jump from these to the greater questions, as well as the parity granted to body and soul, receive their impetus from the processes just mentioned. The *Essais* continue a leveling of everything with everything else begun in the preceding centuries, though admittedly in a newly thought-out manner. The secret of man should now be revealed precisely in the confused comings and goings of the random contents of his life. To understand him here means: to know that he is a polymorphous being moving along ungraded planes, a being that can only be deciphered by observation of his surprising inconsistencies and disorder.

As a result of this definition of man, however, numerous traces of the Renaissance anthropology that was active up to a time quite close to Montaigne's are not included in the *Essais*. Thus, for example, one could characterize the *Essais* by saying that they completely lack the enthusiastic "Faustian" picture of man in which, possessed of his finiteness by a never-ending, joyful restlessness for knowledge, he rises into the vision of truth and fans the spark of the divine which sleeps within him into an ardent flame. This picture, last conceived in Florentine Neoplatonism and then by Bruno, does appear here and there in the *Essais*. Even Montaigne can speak of the "hunt for knowledge" (which is reminiscent of the *venatio sapientiae* by Cusanus), and he can say: "It is a sign of contraction of the mind when it is content . . . A spirited mind never stops within itself; it is always aspiring and going beyond its strength . . ." (III, 13, 817/818 C). But this is meant critically, as the continuation of this passage and numerous others shows: The upswing of endless research that is never satisfied with what it has attained is noted as a special case of spiritual danger which, not unlike other cases of the striving for knowledge, ends in confusion and self-deception. Montaigne neither took up Neoplatonism nor let Plato affect him at a deep level. He no longer sees man as executor of super-individual functions of reason which proceed from the order of being itself, nor as the creature who rises from the prison of his body into the light of ideas.

But he withdraws not only from the Platonic-speculative approach, but also from the thirst for knowledge of the natural sciences, which were so tightly intertwined with that in the sixteenth century. He does not distinguish between them. To him, both are only suitable as symptoms of error, or, as seen from a more elevated standpoint, as symptoms of the spirit's passion to create, independent of knowledge and as an end in itself: ". . . philosophy is but sophisticated poetry" (II, 12, 401 C). But man should not break the bonds of his wandering, delusion-evoking finite nature, but rather should seek a serene consent in it. One could look at it as Montaigne's greatest poverty that he is not interested in the divine in man. But this poverty has revealed another treasure: the wisdom of contentment in earthly reality, and the joy that our finiteness is exhaustive enough to create the good fortune of an eventful richness.

Finally, Montaigne was quite reserved concerning the metaphysical instructional pieces that had come into France from the school of Padua through Dolet's efforts and there permeated all of free-thinking literature of the sixteenth century. He, the free thinker, treats them just as he does the instructional content of classical philosophy, that is, doxographically and eclectically. He does not commit himself to any one. Any conceivable affinity to the Paduans dissolves upon closer scrutiny into a vague semi-similarity. It is conspicuous that Montaigne never seriously takes up the most acute questions that came to his century with Pomponazzi and his followers as well as from theological controversies, namely the questions of free will, divine providence, fate, and the eternal nature of the world. If he touches upon these and the solutions offered to them, he simply becomes aware of them and classifies them as part of the panorama of human attempts at knowledge, sometimes turning out one way, sometimes another, thus interesting at best as a symbol of the undefinable play of the intellect. Otherwise, his caution avoided making a categorical decision, even one of a free-thinking nature. What results is the strange situation in which Montaigne—with the exception of his concept of death—as a result of his deductive, nonsubversive skepticism remained well behind in the risks taken by some in his epoch. Dolet, Rabelais, Des Periers, Bodin: all of them were bolder than he in taking on faith and the Church. Montaigne shies away from a radical free-thinking movement just as he does from authoritative dogmatism. Both of these contain too much hubris of knowledge for him. He holds everything in balance, but without suppressing it. He attacks neither faith nor lack of faith expressly. For to do so, he would have to know better than the one he attacks. But he does not know better, he only knows socratically that he knows nothing. He did despecialize and humanize the great theological questions. But the religious substance itself he simply transfers into a wisdom of obedience for which a precise theological or metaphysical justification would have only meant getting left behind when only halfway there.

CHAPTER II

Intellectual Inheritance and Education

... in order to judge [in a man] the qualities that are most his own and most worthy, the strength and beauty of his mind, we must know what is his and what is not; and in what is not his, how much is due him in consideration of the choice, arrangement, embellishment, and style that he has supplied.

—*Montaigne* [III, 8, 718 B]

We must render this justice to authors who have appeared original to us in various places in their works, that they did not lower themselves to the quality of copyists.

—*Montesquieu* [Pensées et Fragments, *No. 793*]

1. CLASSICAL EDUCATION

A massive store of learning has been collected in the *Essais*. This is the first thing that strikes one who gives the work a casual glance. The research done on sources has methodically expanded this first impression. Villey's major commentary shows how almost every page of the book is connected by many threads to earlier writings, particularly works of antiquity. But even this commentary, which is the most comprehensive to date and has a remarkable feel for tracking down sources, did not uncover all of the sources and outside stimuli which can be detected or at least suspected in the work.

Montaigne himself is fond of giving the impression that he has a poor memory. He presents himself as a dilettante who pages through his library at random and either writes down or forgets his chance findings, depending on his mood. But this—a sophisticated self-protection against the suspicion of pedantry—as well as the disorderly manner in which he spills out his accumulated education cannot conceal the fact that he is

well versed in the literary works of the past. He reaches for the appropriate quotation, the apt example, with a sureness that only a well-read
scholar has at his command. When he has the broad contents of his
education so easily at his fingertips and yet tries to give the impression
that he is only playing with them, this characterizes him as belonging to a
historical situation in which one is still conscious of tradition and yet,
though showing traditional forbearance, strives for one's own freedom.
The humanistic orientation toward authority and the modern urge toward self-assertion are attempting to come into balance.

Montaigne's literary education is predominantly humanistic, that is,
of classical origin. He, too, experiences the contents of life of any kind
as shaped to such a great extent by what was handed down from antiquity that his own thinking and the living of his own life is accommodated to or measured against this pre-shaping. For him it is self-evident
that he will consult the ancients in all that occupies him. They provide
him with his daily reference books and they are his authorities—though
no longer in the sense of their having absolute validity. He does not read
them in order to obey them, but rather to let them stimulate his thinking. He knows enough of their weaknesses and errors and sees them as
human. But he tends them, treating them as still the noblest treasure
chamber of the spirit, the only one worthy of being looked to for answers or quoted. That is a late-humanistic way of thinking: reverent yet
critical.

Montaigne's quotations, anecdotes, and examples speak for the fact
that the works of antiquity have priority in his education. They create a
constant presence of classical life and history in the *Essais*. But they are
only the outermost signs. Even more is revealed by the unidentified
derivations, even the themes and couplings of themes in the *Essais*. One
could say that the entire stock of ideas in Montaigne, that is, not merely
his material, but also the shape of his thinking, is determined by antiquity. There is not a single theme in the *Essais* which could not be
identified as a repetition or further development of one or usually several classical writers, or which could not be justified because it was dealt
with before by some classical author, or for which at least a classical
confirmation could not be sought, and this confirmation would then be
inserted in his work, though often in a quite contrived manner. Montaigne sees problems in areas pointed out to him by the ancients. Admittedly, he does not always make this obvious, even when in his solution
he sticks quite closely to the classical text or even writes it out in full. So
it can happen that in admiring him one is actually admiring one of the

classical authors. However, in most cases Montaigne goes beyond his sources—though again, never far enough that he loses sight of the classical world. As is also true of Machiavelli and Bodin, Montaigne is able to express all essential and new things that he has to say at any point with a classical quotation—even if at times he has to bend it to fit.

His need to remain in the glow of antiquity is so strong that even when Montaigne takes up a subject arising from entirely personal matters, one can ask whether he does not do so with the feeling that it is proper to speak of this because the ancients spoke of it. An example: he frequently discusses matters of his household affairs, the most detailed case found in Essay III, 9. This seems so reasonable because of his function as castle lord that one would not tend to look for outside stimuli. Yet the treatment of household and family life is a convention of moral philosophy. Specifically, it belongs to the "economics" group, which usually follows the groups of ethics and politics according to the Aristotelian divisions. (Even Amyot, for example, reproduces this division in the preface to his translation of Plutarch's *Moralia.*) The classical model for treating those questions was Xenophon's *Oeconomicus.* This document, which even had an effect on Alberti's *Della famiglia,* was translated by La Boétie under the title *De la mesnagerie.* Montaigne published the translation in 1571. He could have experienced the simple fact that this document existed as a justification for treating this subject himself. In fact, what he writes is far removed from the ideal type of life as household manager prescribed as a standard by Xenophon and others. Montaigne speaks in *his* way about *his* household affairs, narratively, without pedagogical intent, with the sole aim of self-portrayal, and there, as everywhere, he achieves his individual expression. But he still moves within a preestablished set of topics, and he has beneath his feet the ground already tread in antiquity. Thus it is very probable that those household affairs described in detail in Essay III, 9 within their framework are of literary origin, although individually they may indeed bear the mark of his personal affairs. This cannot be proven definitively. But one cannot help thinking this, since Montaigne, when handling the major themes of the *Essais,* has been proven to proceed in seeking his freedom not by leaving the larger realm of classical tradition but rather by indulging in it in his own individual manner. He allows himself the full right to his own opinion in a matter. But he reflects upon a subject because the ancients pointed it out as something worthy of reflection.

Admittedly, his involvement with the ancients shows nothing of the typical humanistic philological faithfulness to the source. He does not

concern himself with doing historical justice to a text. There is no room in
the *Essais* for the hermeneutical care taken by Budé, Henri Estienne, and
others. There is a world of distance between Montaigne's method of
quoting from Seneca and the spirit that guided, for example, Erasmus'
edition of Seneca. Precisely because of his respectful yet also baronial and
thoroughly eclectic treatment of the texts, the task of researching his
sources can bring one to wit's end. Only in relatively few passages can one
be absolutely certain where he got a quotation, a paraphrase, or a theme.
Research into the sources used in the *Essais* must make complicated
differentiations between first-level classical sources, second-level classical sources (for example, Seneca with his Epicurus quotations or Cicero
with his presentations of Plato), and later sources imparting these from
the church fathers of the Renaissance period. The material found in
Montaigne's quotations and themes has for the most part been repeated
so often by eclectic writers along its path from the original source to the
sixteenth century that one can rarely be certain from whom Montaigne
took it. For he does not only read the classical writers of antiquity, he also
reads the demographic literature of late antiquity and he is acquainted
with the massive market in examples and motifs of humanism, which
trades with this classical material as if with merchandise that has no
owner. So it is quite possible that he will quote Lucretius or Virgil, whom
he reads often and carefully in the original, not from the original source
but from an anthology. One finds Cicero or Tacitus quotations in his
work which can be identified as coming from Gentillet and Bodin by
specific errors present in them, even though Montaigne was familiar with
the original text. Since one can prove this sort of thing in various instances, there is also uncertainty in assigning the sources for the other
quotations. Montaigne does this as many others do, and he admits:
"Some people quote Plato and Homer who have never looked at them.
And I myself have taken enough passages elsewhere than at their source"
(III, 12, 808 B).

Where Montaigne takes material from first- and second-level classical sources, he does so eclectically. He does not reproduce a single
author in that author's systematic entirety, rather, he takes individual
items and contaminates them with items from other authors. When, for
example in the early Essays, he sticks relatively closely to his sources,
this is a sign that he does not yet dare to venture forth with his own
thinking. The eclectic contaminations expand in proportion to the freedom he allows his thinking. Thus identification of the sources corre-

spondingly becomes increasingly difficult. It remains a matter of speculation whether his doctrine on modifications of judgment go back to
Lucretius or to Sextus Empiricus, or whether his favorite psychological
theme, the incongruence of action and motive, was inspired by Plutarch
or Seneca. The quotations in the pertaining passages do not provide
certainty regarding the actual origin of the thought. For a long period of
processing lies between its adoption and its production, and during this
period the material so eclectically collected has been mixed and combined several times. But the decisive factor is that Montaigne always
strives to again establish a relationship between his own result and
antiquity. He makes this relationship clear by his use of quotations.
They are questionable as a statement of the sources of his thinking, but
they are all the more important as a symptom of his attitude of wanting
to remain within the glow of antiquity.[14]

2. FREE RELATIONSHIP TO HIS INTELLECTUAL INHERITANCE

But what relationship does Montaigne want with what was handed
down from antiquity? Despite his acknowledgment of the literary authority of the ancients, it is important to him to be more than a mere
compiler. In the midst of his humanistic attitude toward tradition he
tries to create space for his need of his own originality. He assures the
reader several times that he first did his thinking from his personal
situation and only subsequently drew upon classical authority. Thus he
writes in a late passage: "My behavior is natural; I have not called in the
help of any teaching to build it. But feeble as it is, when the desire to tell
it seized me, and when, to make it appear in public a little more decently, I set myself to support it with reasons and examples, it was a
marvel to myself to find it, simply by chance, in conformity with so
many philosophical examples and reasons" (II, 12, 409 C). Even earlier
he wrote: ". . . the firmest and most general ideas I have are those
which, in a manner of speaking, were born with me. They are natural
and all mine. I produced them crude and simple, with a conception bold
and strong, but a little confused and imperfect. Since then I have established and fortified them by the authority of others and the sound
arguments of the ancients, with whom I found my judgment in agreement. These men have given me a firmer grip on my ideas and a more
complete enjoyment and possession of them" (II, 17, 499 A). And then

he again assures the reader that he has read the authors "not at all to form my opinions, but certainly to assist, second, and serve those which I formed long ago" (II, 18, 505 C).

All these statements taken from different time periods agree that Montaigne explains his involvement with classical texts as a subsequent enrichment of his own discovery of truth. This is an exaggeration, one of many examples of his play-acting. We know that at least the oldest level of the *Essais* is a product of the stimuli in his reading. Later he did become more independent. But one cannot take his assurance that he only consulted other authors after he had completely formed his own opinion as the literal truth for any phase of the *Essais*, at least to the extent that it hardly applies to the actual process. But it is important in another respect. It is an expression of the need for freedom. It is sufficient to know that this need is at least present as an intention and that it strives to conceal the actual adoptive connections of the *Essais*. The path should not proceed from the book to the self, but in the other direction. Montaigne as late humanist does not want to be an emulator, rather he wants to be an individual whose intellectual life consists in the unfolding of his own essence. He wants his reader to understand the classical quotations, examples, and hypotheses as accessories, as fortunate yet not indispensable agreement existing between him and some authorities. The classical material that is included eclectically here and there is only intended as a fitting means to aid understanding ("to make it [my behavior] appear in public a little more decently" (II, 12, 409 C)), an aid in organizing his own thoughts, to master them and allow him to portray them. A very free independence creates for itself an at least programmatic consciousness vis-à-vis tradition. The contact with the ancients is supposedly more or less terminable at any time. Even under the weight of his inheritance, it is always Montaigne's intention to remain himself. As much as the development of the *Essais* conceals this, one thing is true: Montaigne does not repeat anything, at least at his mature stage, from the store of thought which has been handed down without first having transformed it into his own conviction. Only from this perspective does what was handed down become valid for him. He only writes the sentences drawn upon above to express the productive moment, the integration forming a new originality. From time to time he protests against the assumption that because his thinking agrees with that of one of the ancients, it is merely parroting what the earlier author thought. "Not because Socrates said it, but because it is really my feeling, . . . I consider all men my compatriots . . ." he says at one point

(III, 9, 743 B): due to his classical education, he cannot express cosmopolitan thoughts at all without being reminded of the common ground,
"Socrates taught cosmopolitanism"; the motif from his education is so
consistent that he is compelled to both quote it and fend it off. As a
result of his intention, and in a deeper sense, in actuality also, Montaigne does not simply parrot tradition, rather, he speaks as himself
from the mouth of tradition.

Thus the *Essais* become one of the finest blossoms at the vertex of
occidental culture, where an educated person was still able to possess
the full wealth of his classical inheritance and at the same time had the
power to dispose over it from his own, now autonomous, essence.
Montaigne feels secure within a vast, ancient company of spirits. This
gives him the assurance that he is not standing in an empty space, and
yet it also feeds his courage in himself. He knows that to speak his own
mind will not damage the standing of the authorities—and also that
thinking what has been thought before, restating what has been said
before does not diminish one's own validity. Such a consciousness,
which was also shared by other late humanists, is not yet associated
with the melancholy tone expressed a century later in the following
sentence from La Bruyère: "All has been said, and we have been arriving
too late for more than seven thousand years, since there have been
thinking men." Montaigne lives in the joy of participating in the eternal
and varied discussion of wisdom in his own way.

He does not simply reproduce what was handed down by the ancients, he reincarnates it by recasting it. Using an allegory that was used
frequently from Petrarch on, and which can be traced back to Lucretius,
Horace, and Seneca, at one point he writes with regard to the pupil of
his Essay on education, and with regard to himself: "The bees plunder
the flowers here and there, but afterward they make of them honey,
which is all theirs; . . . Even so with the pieces borrowed from others; he
will transform and blend them to make a work that is all his own, to
wit, his judgment" (I, 26, 111 A). This is certainly all the way down to
the wording a repetition of a passage from Seneca's eighty-fourth letter,
and it stresses, as Seneca already had, not the adoptive but rather the
productive act, whereby the spirit impresses its own form upon what is
acquired (*formam suam impressit* in Seneca's words), so that a unit may
arise from many foreign elements (*ut unum fiat ex multis*). But in Montaigne this has an unequally strong breath of freedom to that in Seneca
or even Petrarch and the Ciceronians of the fifteenth and sixteenth
centuries.[15] And the following thought is clearer in Montaigne than in

those who came earlier: only when the individual makes that which is foreign, that which no one is able to dispense with, his own and it has become the sound of *his* voice does education rise above imitation and into originality. The personal truth at which everything is aimed here only comes into being by testing what is inherited against its beneficial effect on the heirs. This is why his defense against a constrained following of authority has such a sharp tone: "He who follows another follows nothing" (I, 26, 111 C).

Montaigne defended himself against the possible reproach that he was decorating himself with someone else's feathers: "Even so someone might say of me that I have here only made a bunch of other people's flowers, having furnished nothing of my own but the thread to tie them. Indeed I have yielded to public opinion in carrying these borrowed ornaments about on me. But I do not intend that they should cover and hide me; that is the opposite of my design, I who wish to make a show only of what is my own, and of what is naturally my own" (III, 12, 808 B). He is not exaggerating when he says this. He only appropriates that which is in harmony with his own essence. His contaminating acts of selection which bring in this and that from the material that has been handed down and ignore or restructure or distort other parts of it are determined by a will that is working on his own character. What he leaves out characterizes him no less than what he includes. This involvement with his intellectual inheritance consists of the instinctive actions of a strong spirit which senses precisely where and where not to find confirmation or nourishment for its predisposition. Its actions transform the truths of others into his own and give them a new, organic coherence that will certainly not be recognized if one tries to examine the *Essais* only from the standpoint of their sources. "Paragons are not objects of imitation and blind subjection, they only pave the way to hearing the call of our own person," as Max Scheler once wrote,[16] and this is precisely Montaigne's thinking. A principle he not only knew, as did so many humanists, but also practiced as few others, was this: that only in the incorporation of what is foreign into what is one's own (*transformer, digérer, confondre* are common terms for this) does knowledge by memory, mere knowledge of literature, ripen into education. Thus one can apply to Montaigne Lichtenberg's comment: "It would certainly be useful to show to the world those writers who have reached into themselves with a knowledge of those who came before them." He is such a writer, and he is, to again speak with Lichtenberg, not one of those who "mint coins from an earlier mold yet in their own intellect are counterfeiters."[17]

One cannot stress these things enough. For the conclusion to be drawn from them is that the research into the sources must watch its limits despite the enticement of the massive quantity of knowledge to be found in the *Essais*. This leads only up to the point at which the vegetative-like growth of Montaigne's intellectual personality begins. The scholarly pleasure of checking an author's work to say "many others have already said that" is insidious. Its basis is the simple delusion that when two persons say the same thing, it really is the same. A community of intellects does not consist only of the business of mutual reproduction. This is only the case in the depths of the impersonal. But among the higher level intellects, what is borrowed comes together into an entirely new creation. By virtue of the instinctive confidence of their own organism they themselves become historical in that they recast historical material, thereby reincarnating it. This new historicism cannot be understood from research into sources alone when it does not take the recasting process into account. Only the educational realm in which Montaigne found himself can show it, as well as the authorities in whose proximity he discovered himself, always aware of his connection with them and speaking through their medium.

I cannot and do not intend to be what the ancients were, but I would be poor without involvement with them: this approximates Montaigne's attitude toward antiquity. Thus one might well hesitate to call him a full humanist. Nevertheless, one must concede that he is "one of the most perfect products of classical education," as Ivo Bruns said.[18]

Otherwise, he sees antiquity as apart from temporal proximity or remoteness. It seems as if it never occurred to him that a period of twelve to twenty centuries lay between the sources of his quotations and his own writing. He himself makes the comment upon the occasion of an observation concerning the Romans that: it does not matter whether someone one loves has been dead for eighteen years or sixteen hundred (III, 9, 762 B). If only the past is known, then it is present like any other memorable humanity in an intimate, familiar, naive presence for which the time interval is inconsequential. Montaigne neither has a historicizing consciousness of the historical conditions of antiquity, as Budé does, for example, nor even—or at best only in momentary impulses—a transfiguring longing for it, as do the Italian humanists. While the latter attempt to transfer ancient customs to the present and to stylize them in the classical mode, for him both spheres blend into each other in an informal sociability without a difference in tone and level. He does not mask himself with classical gestures and garments, rather, he stands beside the ancients, in his own way sometimes comparing himself with them, sometimes differentiating himself from them. The life of people from classical times is like a diagram in outline within which he draws his own life. But it is not expected to acquire dignity or a festive point of reference in the process, as once was true for Petrarch when he entered his own opinions and events into the Virgil manuscript. Montaigne is more likely to seek out the all-too-human than the super-human in the ancients. This is the common ground upon which he fraternizes with them. The few examples in which he honors one of the Greeks or Romans unreservedly contrast sharply with the many other examples in which he mixes criticism or irony with his admiration. His eye for the polarity of man is incorruptible when it comes to the ancients. Even in them, as everywhere, he sees the "feet of the peacock," as he puts it, using his metaphorical expression from medieval animal symbolism, alluding to the imperfection of even the most beautiful of creatures (III, 5, 669 B). He can say frankly that in even the most beautiful Greek and Latin we risk being inoculated with "the most inane humors of antiquity" (II, 17, 501 A). There is no hint of the rebirth idea and that accusatory flight from the present into the past. Indeed, on one occasion he does state: "Finding myself useless for this age, I throw myself back upon that other" (III, 9, 763 B). But this is only intended as a diminishment of himself, along the lines of his other instances of self-deprecation; it does not signify a gilding of antiquity. There is a world of difference between this type of occasional utterance and Petrarch's effusive confession that he would like to forget the bustle about him and the commonness of men in order to live in the contemplation of even the tiniest fragments of the classical works handed down (to Livius, *Familiares*, XXIV, 8).

Montaigne no more acknowledged a theoretical tension between antiquity and Christianity than his personality entered into a romantic tension with antiquity. And to even less an extent did he acknowledge the early and high medieval release of the former tension, practiced long thereafter in humanism, using the idea of concordance, which attributes to antiquity a natural knowledge of truth built into mankind before the revelation of God and which allows Christian theology to make use of the products of classical knowledge as a preliminary stage of and support to human reason for the revealed truth. He required no particular speculation to bring classical and Christian content together into a salvation context. Just as naively and self-confidently as he prayed the Our

Father and followed it with a classical quotation before going to sleep (III, 9, 741 B), he was able to cope with texts handed down to him which for others contained the stuff of enormous conflict. He never reflected upon the fact that a theological justification really was needed when he wove classical quotations into his explanations of his faith in the way that Erasmus was prone to reflect upon this. He never constructed a connection between stoic and Christian moral philosophy, as Lipsius did later. The remainder of Christian elements alive in him, after any differences were dealt with theoretically, peacefully, and undemandingly accepted the intellectual inheritance of hellenism which he was processing, just as the contents of his personal life became peacefully interwoven with classical images of life.

3.   OCCUPATION WITH BOOKS

Montaigne's double-edged position regarding the material handed down, described above—respect and distance, love and independence— is reflected manifestly in his relationship with books. Anecdotes in the *Essais* about his occupation with books form a part of Montaigne's graphically intimate portrayals of himself. He valued this occupation very highly. In Essay III, 3 he writes that reading materials create the most constant and reliable companionship, following his discussion of the company of noble persons and women. Books are always right there at hand, a never-failing occupation if one is disappointed by human interaction, or when one is bored. They are a comfort in old age and in solitude, soothing in times of pain, and a healing diversion from bad moods; and books are patient, not taking offense when one reaches for them due to a lack of human companionship. They always welcome the one who seeks them with the same friendly face. He then relates how he takes them along on his journeys, an always available reserve of the spirit for one's journey of life: "I cannot tell you what ease and repose I find when I reflect that they are at my side to give me pleasure at my own time, and when I recognize how much assistance they bring to my life. It is the best provision I have found for this human journey, and I am extremely sorry for men of understanding who do not have it" (III, 3, 628 B). He describes with satisfaction his library on the fourth floor of the castle tower where the books surrounded him five shelves high with three windows in between them, looking out upon the garden, the courtyard, and into the distance. Here is where he spends most of his time, and he considers whether he should have galleries built on where he might walk up and back, for he is fond of walking and believes that one's thoughts sleep when one's legs are not in motion.

One can often read similar things in Petrarch: the library he has collected himself as the place of seclusion from the world, the books as comforting, reminding, reprimanding friends, and the corresponding passages in his writings bear appropriate quotations from Cicero's Atticus letters, from which humanism was long accustomed to borrowing formulations for its love of books. But this similarity with the humanists is only a superficial one. Montaigne's occupation with books lacks the passionate, cultish, reverent elements. He does not let them dominate him. His respect for them survives, as does his respect for tradition as a whole, under the presumption of his independence. On the page cited above he relates how he actually prefers to keep them in the background, like the miserly man who does not spend his treasure, being completely content in the knowledge that he has it. As often as he speaks of his favorite authors, Seneca and Plutarch, we never find that he handles his editions of them with the passion of a Plutarch, who confessed that he kissed his Virgil manuscript, or Erasmus, who later said the same of some of his copies of Cicero. There is no more of enraptured vigils over a timidly sanctified text. Is it a side-swipe at the humanists' reports, repeated often from Petrarch on, of their nightly studying in their libraries, when Montaigne in describing his book tower drops the sentence: "I am never there at night" (III, 3, 629 C)? One never finds him in a situation like that of Machiavelli, who, as he reports in his letter of December 10, 1513, puts on festive garments after the day of effort and impurity before he opens books by the ancients in his office. For all his interest in it, Montaigne's style of reading remains down-to-earth. His baronial distance from what has been handed down tempers even his occasional occupation with the book into a satisfying game with an attractive possession, but one that can be pushed aside at any time. He has more the nature of an outdoorsman than a bookworm. The scenes of his daily life are far more likely to show him on horseback, on journeys, conducting household affairs and those of his office, or in society than in his library. The quotation from III, 3 above does not however conceal the fact that he never permits his books to contest his right to unbound meditation and actual living. His fear of being perceived as pedantic causes him to emphasize this more strongly than the facts really justify. He goes so far as to say: "We who have little contact with books are in this strait" (III, 8, 718 B). He assures his reader that he only really learned to read properly in old age:

not to impress others, not to become more clever, but only for amusement, and "never for gain" (III, 3, 629 B). To him books serve more as impetus than instruction. He pages through them, first here, then there, without a plan and without organization ("by disconnected fragments," 629 B). He reads in contemplative comfort in such a manner that he might dwell for several moments over a passage to which he has just opened, then glance away and lose himself in the reverberation of his own intellect. He assures the reader that he cannot even read a book for a full hour; only Tacitus can seize his interest so strongly that he can read through it all at one sitting, which he notes is a great exception. His lively temperament would lose all its joy if it had to rein itself in to perseverance: "I do nothing without gaiety; continuation and too strong contention dazes, depresses, and wearies my judgment" (II, 10, 297 B/C).

This enthusiast's orientation toward books allows him to avoid all difficulties of comprehension: "If I encounter difficulties in reading, I do not gnaw my nails over them; I leave them there, after making one or two attacks on them" (II, 10, 297 A).[19] Even when he does not understand difficult passages, he can still use these to discover the measure of his own judgment, thus, again, himself, which is the aim of all his reflection. He takes a certain pleasure in letting difficult material go and being thrown back upon his own averageness (II, 10, 298 A). He states this quite uninhibitedly and cheerfully, and dares to be as he is. He does not want to wrestle with the great authors: "I do not wrestle with those old champions wholesale and body against body; I do so by snatches, by little light attacks. I don't go at them stubbornly; I only feel them out; and I don't go nearly as much as I think about going" (I, 26, 108 C). His involvement with books—objectively as well as ideally—is carefully restricted to the degree to which it does not interfere with the reader Montaigne's self-development and formation of opinions. For the intellect that seeks itself runs the risk of being diverted from its goals in the presence of others. Thus he writes a sentence like this: "When I write, I prefer to do without the company and remembrance of books, for fear they may interfere with my style" (III, 5, 666 B). For him, who with each reading is brought productively and further along the path to himself, it suffices to be affected briefly and powerfully by books. Then he pushes them aside, and this gesture appears no less frequently in the *Essais* than the other, namely that of opening the books. Authors he has read lie behind him as traces along the path of his own intellectual motion; if they are called for again, then it is from a new point in his own movement. What is in them is much less important than what he becomes through them. Thus the beautiful Essay in which he speaks of his favorite authors, "Of Books" (II, 10), consists entirely of the subjectivity of commentary-like insights arising from his readings. The Essay is really nothing other than a reworked reproduction of margin notes that Montaigne had made in his texts, enriched by methodical comments. What he seeks in books is above all the author who wrote them. He who makes such a great effort on behalf of his own individuality wants also to perceive the individuality in others: "And every day I amuse myself reading authors without any care for their learning, looking for their style, not their subject. Just as I seek the company of some famous mind, not to have him teach me, but to come to know him" (III, 8, 708 C). His occupation with books becomes occupation with men and a curiosity for the variety in their personal ingenuity. This turning of one's eye from the work to the individual radiating forth from the work can be found even in Erasmus. It is conceivable that this recurs to an intensified degree in Montaigne.

Just as the material handed down had ceased to be a compulsory authority in the *Essais,* the book had ceased to be a sacred object or even only an honored monument in its entirety. To the reader Montaigne the book became his equal, indeed a witness to the wealth of what is human, but still standing on the same level ground, so to speak, upon which the reader stood. And most important, the book did not replace one's own experience. For the earlier humanists it did. They often compared reading with traveling; Petrarch praised these types of intellectual journeys as not tiring one out, not wearing out the shoes, and free of dust, thorns, and stones (*Seniles* IX, 2). But Montaigne welcomes the dirt, stones, and thorns of physical travel and the journey of life: only here does he gain the experience that brings him to the full reality of himself as well as of men. No book makes this superfluous. It can only offer assistance, half friend, half servant. It has no power over the innermost space of the self. It deserves thanks and love, but not submission.

4.   THE KNOWLEDGE OF ANTIQUITY

The period of classical writing for which Montaigne was familiar with the major figures from his own reading (whether in the original or in translations) extends from Herodotus and Plato up to the historians of the fourth century A.D.

Notable but difficult to explain is the absence of Thucydides, Lucian, Marcus Aurelius, and Boethius. Multiple similarities in kind could have led him to these sources. Since he valued Livius and Tacitus, why not Thucydides as well? Marcus Aurelius is so close to his own pearls of wisdom that these could be expressed to not a small extent with sentences from this philosopher of obedience. The dash of Erasmian and Rabelaisian spirit alive in Montaigne would have also made Lucian appeal to him. The texts by those named were within his reach; the Greeks among them were available in Latin, and in part also in French, translations. Boethius' name can be found in most of the library lists that we have from the sixteenth century. Their absence can probably be explained simply from the chance contents of his library, the basis of which came from the bequest of his friend La Boétie and which he supplemented continuously afterward, but without the well-organized passion of a collector.

In another respect as well he did not know classical works to as great an extent as they were available to his contemporaries. His classical horizon was Latin. He could only read the Romans in the original. The Greeks were only accessible to him in Latin and French translations. He had very little command of Greek, at least not beyond spelling out some of the aphorisms that he took from anthologies and from Erasmus. Nevertheless, his instinct for intellectual ranking, surprising elsewhere as well, which intuits the proper proportions of even that which he only knows in fragmentary form or indirectly, sometimes permits him to express astoundingly appropriate assessments of the Greeks, for example of Homer or Plato. But he did not feel compelled to study them in the original language. In contrast to some of his contemporaries and predecessors, he appears to be unaware of the difference in essence between Greek and Roman nature. The Socrates called upon so often in the *Essais* has not a Greek but a human, or more precisely, a Montaignian face.

Montaigne represents an important stage in the renewed Latinization of the French spirit. Knowledge of Greek as it came to the French via Italian and Byzantine humanists, in the end prevailing in the circles around Dorat and the Pléiade, here, too, leading to several translations, really finally remained only a scholarly, philological matter. Whereas Rabelais was able to correspond in Greek with Budé in the first half of the century, at the end of the century Montaigne remained cool to this sort of educational ambition. One can conclude from various comments in the *Essais* that he sensed pedantry in this. With Ronsard's relinquishment of the Graecized odes of his early period and with Montaigne's

Essais, leading French writing was again freed from the transitorily narrowed bond to hellenism. Later on Racine, Chénier, and Renan will represent isolated exceptions. Even in their humanistic sense of inheritance the French remained a Latin people that saw its intellectual ancestors in Virgil and Horace, not in Homer or Sophocles, and which essentially knew the Greek world in Latin excerpts.

When Montaigne assesses classical literary work—Roman literary work—he shows an unerring feeling for rank. He sharply separates classical Latin works from the later Caesar period. This is not self-evident. The group of poets of the Pléiade, for example, as with earlier epochs, had seen the Augustinian, late Roman, and new Latin literary work as a unit. But Montaigne declares with full confidence in his taste that the highest rank includes the poetry of Lucretius, Virgil, Horace, and Catullus (II, 10, 298 A). He praised precisely those Roman poets who displayed the relatively greatest originality vis-à-vis the Greeks. Besides those just mentioned in another passage he mentions Terence, Plautus, and Ovid.[20] He never in his value judgments erred to the extent that we would seriously have to contradict him. He only treated the classical philosophers without a careful differentiation of rank; in part it sufficed to him to become acquainted with these from the later doxographic literature, that is, in derivative form. But that belongs on another page. Here, where aesthetic qualifications were not a consideration (at least not for him) he could give himself over to his eclecticism, which took something wherever it found it. But where literary work was concerned he held to his standards. As much as the way was paved for individual ones of his judgments by humanistic establishment of value, which for its part went all the way back to Quintilian, his statements still had to pass monitoring by his personal taste and were not parroted, but were rather experienced. He disliked any refinement of form. Perhaps his ignoring of Statius can be explained by this discontent. In any event, he did not attribute a particularly high stylistic value to Lucian.

Virgil was at the top of his list of favorite poets: "The master of the choir," as he called him (I, 37, 172 A). What Montaigne says about him is among the most beautiful Virgil confessions of his countrymen, in fact of the Romantic peoples as a whole, who experience this founder of Latin pastoral poetry, the perfecter of Latin didactic and epic poetry, as the forefather of their own poetry and the archetype for their view of art, which ranks mature mastery above early originality. Montaigne was familiar with him from childhood on. He once wrote that he treasured the *Georgics* as the most perfect of all poems (II, 10, 298 A). He thereby repeats an assessment that was last common in the Pléiade circle and can be found somewhat frequently later on as well. But he saved his most lavish praise for the *Aeneid*. His favorite part was the fifth book (II, 10, 298 B), though this was just a personal preference for which he gives no reason. The fifth book is the book of festivals and games, a cheerful pause in his artfully composed middle work between the Dido tragedy and the descent of Aeneas into Hades; perhaps it was this brightening and balance which pleased him? He reads the *Aeneid* without using the customary approach of reading things into it. Although he does consult the Servius commentary (*Journal de Voyage*), he remains uninfluenced by its research of real facts which had molded the understanding of Virgil from the early Middle Ages into the nineteenth century. Nor is there any trace of the Christianizing viewpoint that was also encountered in his epoch; to him, Virgil is no longer the *anima naturaliter christiana* (Tertullian). Unlike Ronsard and Pasquier, he does not seek the mythology of the Trojan origin of the Franco-Gauls in the *Aeneid*. He reads it with a pure sense of art which cannot be spoiled by an interest in the subject matter, which he also had, though to an inhibited degree. At one point he compares it with Ariosto's *Orlando Furioso*. This leads to the following memorable image: the *Aeneid* strives on powerful wings directly toward its destination in a high, steady flight— while Ariosto hops from episode to episode like a feeble bird from branch to branch, in each instant settling on the ground from fear that it could run out of breath (II, 10, 300 A). In Essay III, 5, "On Some Verses of Virgil," Montaigne gives his assessment of the stylistic value of the *Aeneid*, in a passage that also refers to Lucretius (664 B). He sees in both poets' art a powerful fullness of fantasy, solid substance, balanced distribution of a sinewy, thrilling force of language in which what is well said has also been well thought-out, and an avoidance of any empty subtlety of form. This recognition is evidence of his highly developed sense of art and language. These few sentences in their personal freshness stretch way beyond the formulaic praise of Virgil and Lucretius which one could read at that time, for example in Ronsard's prefaces to the *Franciade* or in Denis Lambin's Lucretius edition of 1563. We will come back to this passage later (in chapter 8) since it also has programmatic significance for Montaigne's own art as a writer.

The fact that Montaigne's praise of art lumps Virgil and Lucretius together results in the high aesthetic rank he grants the didactic poem *De rerum natura*. In the *Essais* only Horace is quoted almost as frequently as Lucretius. The reason for this lies in the nature and moral philosophy content of the poem, from which Montaigne borrows freely. His use of this need not be explained at the moment. Comparing Lucretius and Virgil was traditional in the Renaissance epochs, particularly in sixteenth-century France. It was also traditional to appreciate Lucretius aesthetically: this was an attempt to free him from the stigma of the unpopular Epicureanism.[21] Noteworthy here is, however, the fact that Montaigne does not conduct the comparison in favor of one or the other. Both are to him nearly equally great poets. He had no need of de-stigmatizing Lucretius, since he understood the doctrines of happiness and wisdom taken from him to be at such a spiritual height that their differences from those of the theological authorities no longer contained anything provocative, any more than was the case with Erasmus' epicurean motifs. He ignores Lucretius' atheism as he does the cosmological speculations. Montaigne probably read him as a source of ideas, but he loved him for the sake of the poetic sensuousness that recast the abstraction of the doctrines into the glow of the images. Presumably, the personal passion with which Lucretius fired the doctrines also appealed to him. Furthermore, the verses that were the occasion of his praise of art in Essay III, 5—namely from Book I, 33 ff: Venus beds Mars—are among the most famous, most often discussed verses in Lucretius; Botticelli took the subject matter of his painting of Venus and Mars from them. Here, too, Montaigne put in his word on a conventional topic, but it is a more striking and memorable word than the worn-out praise of Lucretius uttered by his predecessors.

Of the Roman lyric poets, Horace was closest to his heart. Montaigne does not say much about him, but uses much from him, namely in the form of quotations. But this was before 1588; he does not appear to have picked him up anymore in his last years. It is possible that Horace, who described his own intimacies, encouraged Montaigne's self-portrayal. Some of the most beautiful odes (II, 16; II, 17; II, 18; III, 29) are reproduced several times. The last quotation in the *Essais*, and at the same time its last word, consists of the famous Horace verses starting with *Frui paratis et valido mihi . . . (Carm.* I, 31, v. 17 ff). The Epistles are mentioned almost as frequently. He borrows from both sources those verses that express the wisdom that speaks to him: seclusion and security, self-confidence, relinquishment of the great positions, openness to illusion, and carefreeness about the fact that the person in this world who enjoys himself and his own modest, comfortable possessions is considered a fool, and the awareness of how much everything in existence is merely fluctuation and contradiction. There is a fairly strong affinity between

Montaigne and this Roman spirit of mature, cheerful, cool-headed manliness which has been initiated into what is questionable in our life. The *Essais* are also ruled by the relaxed serenity of Horace's advice *et amara lento temperet risu* ("and the gentle bitter with a calm smile," *Carm.* II, 16). "Montaigne is our Horace," as Sainte-Beuve once put it (*Lundis* IV), and others have reiterated this. And Montaigne also praised the Roman as the artistic master who carefully worked through the stores of words and figures to state what he saw so deeply and clearly, what he thought so boldly, with bold and carefully chosen means (III, 5, 665 B). Do we perhaps hear the echo of Quintilian? In the *Institutio oratoria* we find: *Nam et insurgit aliquando et . . . variis figuris et verbis felicissime audax* ("For from time to time he elevates himself to the heights and expresses a felicitous boldness in his varied figures and words," X, I, 96) about Horace.[22]

We need not discuss those Roman writers who were more in the background of Montaigne's education—Ovid, Catullus, Persius, Juvenal, and so forth. Yet a brief digression on his overall relationship to poetry must be permitted for the sake of understanding his aesthetic judgments.

It is astounding how fond this skeptic is of poetry. Even late he writes "from my earliest childhood poetry has had that power to transpierce and transport me" (I, 37, 171 C). He has a receptivity to the magic of verses which is direct, not derived from some theory. Among his many comments on poetry, the following is perhaps the most beautiful: "It is easier to create it than to understand it. On a certain low level it can be judged by precepts and by art. But the good, supreme, divine poetry is above the rules and reason. Whoever discerns its beauty with a firm, sedate gaze does not see it, any more than he sees the splendor of a lightning flash. It does not persuade our judgment, it ravishes and overwhelms it. The frenzy that goads the man who can penetrate it also strikes a third person on hearing him discuss it and recite it, as a magnet not only attracts a needle but infuses into it its own faculty of attracting others" (I, 37, 171 C). Since expressions from Plato's *Ion* and Ficino's *Ion* commentary are apparent here, it seems as if Montaigne is only repeating the Platonic-Neoplatonic theory of *furor poeticus*. The Neoplatonic fashion of his century may also have led him here. But knowledge of this sort only became true for him from the enthusiastic disposition of his own nature, which he never denies. Other than in his confessions of friendship, he nowhere more than in consideration of poetry so freely, almost sentimentally, reveals his capacity to give himself over to enchantment, nor sets aside his usual understatement and irony. To him, poetry is a primeval force, a bolt of lightning, a fervently experienced ecstasy and overwhelming of reason. He takes this nonrational enchantment seriously as a fundamental event of spiritual life in others and in himself. Thus he once describes how easily man is conquered by the effect of music, from dim, wide church chambers, the tones of the organ and cult ceremonies; he thereby uses the expression *frisson de cœur,* which will not be used again in the French language until the eighteenth and nineteenth centuries to express the force of emotional shocks; and he adds the following: "As for me, I do not consider myself strong enough to listen sedately to verses of Horace or Catullus sung by an adequate voice from a young and beautiful mouth" (II, 12, 448 B).

But all this is just one side of the coin. The admitted susceptibility becomes the material of observation for an analysis of spiritual findings, of human subjection to "irrational" powers in general. For Montaigne, poetic rapture does not have the sense of a spectacle of being or of ideas, as it does for the Neoplatonists. It does not signify an elevation of man. It is rather the complete escape of our staggering being, permitted and lauded because it makes us blissfully happy—but also distanced again to be made the object of a curious anthropology that hopes to learn how things are with us. Those sentences on the effect of church chambers, organ playing, and verses sung by a lovely mouth are found in the midst of an explanation of the clouding of judgment by the emotions. One must always keep in mind the fact that Montaigne is exercising two capacities: he is the expressor of his inner experience and also the critical analyst who evaluates that experience for a knowledge of human fragility. His words on being overwhelmed by the lightning bolt of poetry seem like something that contains its own purpose, poetry about poetry. And yet they come from the need of a tester of mankind to collect examples of the susceptibility of the human spirit to seduction. Man is permitted to be what he is. He is permitted to immerse himself in this susceptibility. The only requirement is that he be cognizant that this is so, that he has an essence that is not capable of knowledge and that his happiness remains connected to the condition of this delusion. Thus, according to Montaigne, this susceptibility to the seductive power of poetry is both a defect and a benefit: a defect because it arises from our dependence on delusion—a benefit because it brings with it one of the highest fulfillments available to our kind, one to which it is wise to consent. This is quite far removed from the fashionable Neoplatonism of the sixteenth century.

We will return to discuss these matters several times. But here the point is only to be aware that Montaigne's love of poetry is not only of an aesthetic nature, rather, it is part of his highly reflected adaptability vis-à-vis mankind, moving between the poles of yes and no. And that love is also connected with his skepticism. Its rejection of abstraction exposes the desire to see and portray the unexplainable clearly in a form perceptible to the senses in which it remains superior to all questionable theories due to its vivid actuality. This desire is satisfied by poetry. And finally, the language of the *Essais,* blooming in images, already betrays the close affinity between the author's sense-oriented manner of observation and that of poetry.

The philosophical writings of antiquity stimulate Montaigne's store of ideas or challenge them to contradiction. But the classical-hellenistic authors Plato and Aristotle, whom he knew only in Latin translation, exercised relatively little influence. Montaigne never studied them coherently.

One can find an extensive occupation with Plato in the last years of his life. But it is not systematic, nor does it weaken his distance from Plato. He did not internalize any of Plato's major idealistic teachings. He uses him to obtain information on this or that. One sees from the manner in which and from where he calls upon Plato that as a rule he just paged through individual passages—usually the *Politicus* or the *Laws*—without concerning himself with the further context of the text, resulting in a quotation that often distorts the intention of the original. But it is obvious that he enjoys Plato the writer who unfolds his presentation of a matter in its changing perspectives, using a multiplicity of speakers. Montaigne interprets Platonic dialogue, and to a certain extent he is right, as the appropriate form for an open-ended, fluctuating way of thinking (II, 12, 377 C). The modern artist of the Essay discovers Plato's artistic elegance and sympathizes with his "prose poetry in several styles"[23] because he himself has the capacity for expression that is not constricted by rigid divisions of style, and because he only sees poetic conceptions in the philosophies. (More about this in chapter 8.) However, he also expressed himself more critically when he spoke of Plato's "dragging dialogues" and regretted the time spent by this man, who could have had so many better things to say, on involved, merely preparatory dialogues (II, 10, 301 C). This would not have been presented here if it did not confirm the low energy level of his readings in Plato. He did not notice that even the breadth of Plato's dialogues is narrow compared to the internal extent of their content.

But what interested Montaigne above all in Plato's texts was Socrates. Thus we will discuss Montaigne's conception of Socrates here. It should be noted that this was not obtained from Plato alone, but was also drawn liberally from Xenophon (*Memorabilia* and *Symposium*) and from Plutarch's *Moralia;* additionally, individual excerpts were also found in the Roman literature available to him.

What drew him to Socrates appeared at first to be the fortunate occasion of seeing before him the one among the Greats of antiquity who was best preserved as a personality over the course of time, a great man about whom many intimate details were handed down (III, 12, 793 B). Such an occasion must have moved Montaigne's impassioned feeling for the most intimate human detail with joy. But this is not the only thing. He has a deeper affinity with the Athenian. "Montaigne is our Socrates" said Albert Thibaudet in 1933.[24] Socrates is the sage of Montaigne's taste. It is precisely in the last Essays and in the late insertions that this confession emerges: he is *le maistre des maistres* in the knowledge of his sole conscience, namely of lack of knowledge (III, 13, 823 B/ C)—the "first love" that relinquishes all violence to glide easily and joyfully into what is natural (I, 26, 120). In the classical horizon of the mature Montaigne, Socrates is the only one who endures, despite some protests against certain rigors. One in fact often has the impression when Montaigne describes him that he is describing himself.

His image of Socrates is not Platonic. Montaigne noted that Socrates and Plato are not identical and that in the latter's dialogues, the historical Socrates was transcended by a mythical one. He does not, it is true, say this expressly, but rather in what is left out. To the extent that his knowledge of Socrates comes from Plato at all, it is predominantly limited to the *Apology,* and more precisely to the last speech before death (*Apology* 36 ff.), and to the great speech of praise by the intoxicated Alcibiades in the *Symposium,* which describes the mysterious, two-sided magic of Socrates' personality (*Symposium* 215 ff.). However, Socrates is nowhere in the *Essais* mentioned as the herald of the doctrine of ideas, of proof of immortality, of cosmology. Montaigne goes even further and also reaches for the original core of Socrates. He strikes out the consciousness of demon and mission; when he does take up the subject, he only does so polemically (III, 13, 856 C). This eliminates the mysterious-numinous element for which Montaigne has no feel even in other cases. He completely leaves out the actual—and transcendent, symbolic—Socrates tragedy, namely that the sage is sentenced to death by precisely those whom he intended to make "better and more reasonable" (*Apology* 36b/c). His Socrates dies of human mortality. Montaigne is unable to see spirit as destiny. He also leaves out the Socratic epistemological elements, the sharp, dialectical art of definition which, while it claimed to know nothing else, did base ethical principles upon an insight into the objective continued existence of the Good, and thus replaced a validity based upon raw authority and convention with an absolute, moral awareness, at the same time determining the bearing of critical science for the entire future.

These passages left out are characteristic. They come precisely at the points in which Montaigne's own thinking stops. There is still enough consideration given the material handed down that one could not say that he misrepresented Socrates. He simply drew the boundaries closer in. But within these boundaries he understood and loved Socrates— understood him better at least than his contemporaries. Nothing can be found in European writing of the sixteenth century and before which compares with the rebirth of Socrates in the *Essais*.

Initially Montaigne stuck with the skeptics and agnostics who dissolved long-held beliefs without replacing them with something new, instead striving for *one* outcome, the awareness of ignorance. This line of thinking, handed down equally by Plato, Xenophon, and Cicero, confirms Montaigne's own manner of thinking. Thus one finds corresponding references to Socrates in the handwritten additions to Essay II, 12, which represents the major text of his skepticism.[25] Socrates is to him the liberator of original, relentless, curatively bewildering thinking from the rigidities and ceremonial dignities of school philosophy—the deliverer of mankind from the specialized competencies of a profession—the liberator of genuine wisdom from the factual knowledge that burdens the memory. Like Socrates, Montaigne himself waives the claim to being a teacher and authority, and like him he also wants only to be a "layman," a tester of human ignorance who deliberates carefully and seeks the counsel of others. His own mature skepticism expects no more from thinking than the stimulus for intellectual movement and critical conscience, for it knows no certainty and is indifferent to where we go, as long as we go at all, guarding us and others against sleep. Thus in one passage that explains this, he happily repeats the famous *Theaetetus* sentences (150c–151c) in which Socrates develops his maieutic method (II, 12, 377 C).

But he then also praises Socrates because he deflects one's view from the unknowable things—the external things, the stars, the cosmos— back to the only relevance, to man's knowledge of self. Using a formulation of Cicero's he writes: "It is he who brought human wisdom back

down from heaven, where she was wasting her time, and restored her to
man, with whom lies her most proper and laborious and useful business" (III, 12, 793 C).[26] He comes back to the topic of this return of
focus repeatedly. Thanks to it, Socrates becomes for him a companion in
his own concerns, a companion found late, for he only occupied himself
extensively with him in the last years of his life after he had followed his
own path almost to the end. He describes the Socratic knowledge of self
in the manner of his own. He accentuates the connection between self-
knowledge and self-abasement: "Because Socrates alone had seriously
digested the precept of his god—to know himself—and because by that
study he had come to despise himself, he alone was deemed worthy of
the name wise. Whoever knows himself thus, let him boldly make himself known by his own mouth" (II, 6, 275 C). Since Montaigne had
freed himself from the Christian striving for God's saving grace, he sees
the special, entirely unremorseful character of this self-abasement,
which is more likely to serve to further the knowledge of man's proper
place from an analytical-descriptive standpoint than an ethical-active
one. He recognizes its right to irony concerning others and with respect
to itself. Because he practices it himself, he sees through this irony's
double edge, that it is mere play and yet serious, as well as the methodical direction of the ironic modesty of leading into the freedom of being
oneself.

To Montaigne Socrates is the man who, because of his awareness of
his own insignificance, discovered the chance of being able to live in this
insignificance and with trust in the blessing of what is natural and
simple. He once stated the following as a summary of Socratic wisdom:
"Lead the life of man in conformity with its natural condition" (III, 2,
614 B). The Socrates passages in the *Essais* point again and again to this
characteristic of an intellect that rose to the highest awareness of the
boundaries and of the wealth of being human contained within such
boundaries. They love the sage who is the greatest one in that he remains the simplest, and in that he does less theorizing than actually
fulfilling nature's allocation to mankind in the way that he lives. Montaigne calls him a saintly model of human nature (III, 12, 807 C). He has
given mankind trust in itself, even when it has been divested of hubris:
"He did a great favor to human nature by showing how much it can do
by itself" (III, 12, 794 B). This is stated in view of Socrates' behavior
before his death, and Montaigne paraphrases the last speech in the
Apology in the same Essay. There Socrates appears as the admirable
spirit who overcomes the most difficult thing possible, namely dying,

from a simple obedience to nature—the same thing Montaigne hopes also to practice in the face of death.

But it is not only in the great moments but also in the relaxed joys of body and soul that Socrates appears as the appropriate model, in fact the wonder of his personality consists in its overall capability in any situation. To show this, Montaigne refers several times to the Alcibiades speech in the *Symposium*. The last Essay contains a rather long paraphrase from it. Here we find praise of his gift for pondering in the most enraptured thoughts, then his courage in battle, but also his perseverance in the adversities of daily life and his talent for recovering in drink, dance, or play with the children (III, 13, 851 B/C). The latter trait— found in Xenophon and handed down in Roman literature—was particularly emphasized by Montaigne, as well as by his epoch.[27] On another occasion he states (from Xenophon's *Symposium* IV, 27/28) that even when an old man Socrates fell in love and joked about this: "Indeed, why not? Socrates was a man, and wanted neither to be nor to seem anything else" (III, 5, 680–681 C).

Montaigne certainly did not grasp the full scope of Socratic thinking, at best he only suspected it. But what he did see was the full, capable, joyful, informal man who knew to reconcile his wisdom with the limitations of our nature and to keep it fluid in the play of irony, and who endured through all the comings and goings of various dogmas, an aid to humanity, needed again and again. Thus in the *Essais* Socrates becomes the antitype to the drawn up, ascetic, solemn ethicists of will and to any form of intellectual arrogance. And Montaigne knows it is difficult to be as Socrates was, so human, so charming, so able to resolve what is laborious into something easy, so capable of expressing the divine completely without pathos or artistic manipulation in the language of the farmers, carpenters, coachmen, and women: "If anything of the kind were brought forth at this time, there are few men who would prize it." And he continues that the magic of Socrates is a tender, concealed beauty: ". . . we need a clear and well-purged sight to discover their secret light" (III, 12, 792–793 B). Montaigne did have this "clear and well-purged sight," even if much else about the greatness of the Athenian escaped him. He knew more about him than the anecdote collectors Erasmus and Henri Estienne, or than Rabelais, who threatened to distort Socrates into a burlesque fool and boozer.

Traces of readings in Aristotle are weak in the *Essais*. That is no longer something out of the ordinary for a sixteenth-century author. In this period Aristotle had one last major effect as a source of the humanists' poetics, which would soon lead to classicism. But this lay outside of Montaigne's sphere. The Aristotelian doctrine of categories and being which was once closely integrated into Christian metaphysics increasingly fell victim along with the latter to secular-philosophical disapproval from the fourteenth century on. The Neoplatonic and Neo-Averroistic movements and the reception of Roman moral philosophy forced Aristotle back into the field of specialized theology, where he persisted for a long time as a source, and was precisely for this reason condemned in nontheological circles that took over the conducting of modern education as a symptom of orthodox scholasticism. And this is precisely how he appears in Montaigne as well. Montaigne sees him as the embodiment of the school authority that stands in the way of his free relationship to his intellectual inheritance: "His doctrine serves us as magisterial law, when it is peradventure as false as another" (II, 12, 403 A). This dry sentence, which at that time no longer required any particular courage, shows Montaigne's affiliation with humanistic education and its altered constellation of authorities. His aversion to Aristotle stems from the same reason that makes his attraction to the writer and "skeptic" Plato possible: dissatisfaction with apodictic and systematic thinking. It cannot be established to what extent he had actually read Aristotle; certainly it was not a thorough study. The thoughts presented in Aristotle's name in the *Essais* could have been taken from middlemen. Not even the *Nicomachean Ethics* appear to have moved him more deeply, although the work is used relatively frequently. Perhaps the following sentence is aimed at this work or its commentators: "I do not recognize in Aristotle most of my ordinary actions: they have been covered and dressed up in another robe for the use of the school" (III, 5, 666 B). This is significant for Montaigne's disapproval of a merely categorically general and ethically normative concept of man in which the relationship to concrete, individual, average humanity is lacking—a disapproval that can, by the way, also be found many years earlier in Lefèvre d'Etaples.[28]

Montaigne's involvement with the philosophical writings of later hellenism are of a different scope entirely. It is true that he processes this, too, only eclectically, but here he feels himself to be in the area of classical thinking which comes closest to his interests. The Stoic school, the Epicurean school, and Pyrrhonism are his intellectual home. It can be shown of Montaigne, as of so many authors continuing into the eighteenth century, what a major influence that hellenistic wisdom ethic really was, though it was so often reduced with the best of intentions to the rank of the latecomers of popular philosophy in later writings on the history of philosophy. Although one can detect a canon of what is classical in Montaigne's assessment of ancient poetry and though he reacts sensitively against the mannerisms of later Latinism, nothing in the *Essais* indicates that he saw in hellenism a decline from the heights of the philosophy of the fifth century before Christ.

One ought not to be surprised at this broad contact with hellenistic wisdom, particularly with its Roman representatives. It is a part of the direction of moral theory as a whole from Petrarch on, in fact it extends back before Petrarch into early Christian theology and its adoption of Cicero, Seneca, and Epictetus. The full bloom of the lay culture in late humanism was sympathetic, even without a Christian reinterpretation, to a philosophical inheritance that taught men how to handle themselves without burdening them with metaphysical speculations. The same is true of Montaigne. As did every movement in moral theory, he had only a doxographical interest in such speculations. This in itself is a fundamental characteristic of the sixteenth century. Itself a mixture of disintegration and reestablishment, it moves in a whirlpool-like multiplicity of directions of thinking which skeptically takes delight in the panorama of metaphysical theories and feels liberated to follow its own subjective independence. "That infinite confusion of theories and views"—so reads the judgment with which Montaigne, no differently than Agrippa von Nettesheim, levels the countless number of works of nature philosophy and cosmology which have been handed down to him into equivalent meaninglessness or into the characteristic of reason's impotence where knowledge is concerned (II, 12, 403 A). However, he turns his full attention to themes of moral philosophy.

Montaigne did not devote himself fully to any of the classical eudemonological schools. One cannot really call him a Stoic, an Epicurean, or even a pure skeptic. It is all the more remarkable how the general basic characteristics of the hellenistic spirit are reflected in him.

Hellenism developed from the fourth century before Christ on as a world culture that expanded from its origins in the polis and the national self-awareness of the Greeks to include Europe and the Near East.[29] The idea of a cosmopolitan humanity developed in its womb. Roman writers from Cicero to Marcus Aurelius passed on this idea, which had been justified by the stoics as based in natural law, to later centuries as one of the noblest possessions of the Occident. Along with the process of becoming aware of a wide horizon of countries, people, and religions came the interest (the ground for it prepared by the sophists) in a culture of personality which connected the feeling for the individuality of others—which arose along with the broadening of horizons—with the feeling of the worth of one's own. The individual man became significant in his empirical peculiarities, and he was portrayed biographically or autobiographically in the most improbable degree of intimacy. But he was even more significant as a being who was able from his own reason to integrate himself into the world's reason in order in this way to find his own moral self-assertion and happiness independently of any authority. The highest strivings of hellenistic philosophy were collected in this conception: it became ethics. The history of the Stoic and Epicurean schools attests to the exhausting of the speculative forces and the growth in ethical nurturing of the personality. The ideal model of a wise man develops in the sphere of an art of living which strives to protect men from external and internal life deprivation. Anyone can become wise; the conditions for this lie within his powers, not within a socially, politically, or clerically privileged position. Wisdom elevates itself above factual knowledge and above the speculations of theology or the philosophy of nature. To the extent that the latter is heeded, it is to serve the manner in which one conducts one's life and is satisfied by eclectic adoption as something coordinate or even subordinate. Philosophical spiritual work arises which has something other than the glory of the heroic deed in mind. Man, who wants to know as an individual what he is and how by means of the moral intensification of the capacity he has within him he can attain harmony with himself and with world reason, has built his doctrine of happiness and wisdom upon a consideration of personal variety for which the earlier hellenistic generic concept of man is no longer adequate.

However the aims of the different doctrines of wisdom may appear, they all have in common the fact that they advocate an independence of the personality from the outside world, but also from strata foreign to the will which threaten the personality itself. It is even more significant and of greater consequence for later after-effects that this ethical philosophy that speaks of affects and invents maxims to guide or eliminate them enters at all into a sphere that is superior to factual knowledge by virtue of its direct content, which concerns every man in the deprivations of his life: being oneself. All of the mental events that are awakened in the course of daily living or accompany the view of one's life as a whole, or which really transform this life as a whole and man's concern for his position in it into an intense experience: anxiety, pain, sympathy, melancholy, the feeling one has had enough, fear of death—all these

appear here in their full gravity, worthy of reflection. The great influence exercised by the post-Aristotelian doctrine of wisdom over the
centuries is due not so much to its intention of overcoming emotions as
to the fact that here man feels himself addressed in his intimate inner
space in which the experience of discontent, of disturbed balance, of a
discrepancy in his desired life plan is at home and in which the freedom
of being himself is endangered by submerged reasons that he carries
within himself and which are nevertheless as foreign as external fate.
What is added to this development of human inner space as stoic or
epicurean ethics is an addition that carries less weight than the development itself. The pathology of the ethicist has always had greater effect
than its therapy.

Joining these features of hellenistic thinking is a more relaxed form of
literary presentation which is more open to the attractive initial contact
the ethical philosopher seeks to establish with the reader than the major
treatise form used for strict systems. Insofar as the culture of wisdom
does not remain completely restricted to oral communication within an
initiated circle of teachers and pupils, it creates a form of communication which cleaves to free, ever-renewing meditation and is well suited
to work its way into the daily living of a broader public. Structures of
open and brief form which flowed into one another without sharply
defined boundaries were cultivated: letters, polemics, dialogues, table
talk, collections of maxims, curiosities, and apothegms. Vividness, essayistic treatments, avoidance of prerequisite special knowledge, aesthetic
stylistic stimuli that allow the restatement with variation of what has
often been said before, as well as the colorfulness of the liberal quoting
and relating of anecdotes are characteristic of these. After the individual
schools in the Roman expansion of hellenism had become similar to one
another in their essential features and forms of representation, the Stoic-
Epicurean wisdom of the Romans finally also expanded to other genres
and became scarcely less expressive in lyric and epic poetry and in
history writing than in theoretical works. Thus Horace, Virgil, and even
Tacitus come under consideration to just as great an extent as Seneca
and Epictetus for the after-effect of late-hellenistic stores of wisdom—
quite apart from an author such as Lucretius who belongs somewhere
between poetry and didactic writing.

All these features preserve their solid, organic coherence and return
reconciled where in the future the wisdom of the further receding antiquity is taken up. We also find them in Montaigne. Cosmopolitan breadth;
turning to the culture of personality; preeminence of wisdom as occupa-

tion with the need of the self for happiness; eclectic balance among the various schools; open form of meditating and writing: these are Montaigne's most general features that cloak themselves in hellenism and its Roman heirs. But in his work, ethical ideality, the therapeutic aim, recedes considerably and makes way for a descriptive observation of the individual.

Within this typological framework the *Essais* perform their transformative process of Stoic, Epicurean, and Pyrrhonistic instructional material.

First the Stoic school. Montaigne was familiar with it through Seneca, through its remnants and reports of it in Cicero, and through the anti-stoic passages of Plutarch's *Moralia;* his study of Diogenes Laërtius supplemented this.

However, his readings of Seneca were the most comprehensive. This requires that we linger over this subject.

Montaigne began reading the Roman ethicist at about the same time he began writing out the first Essay. Books I and II are filled with borrowings from him. His influence has receded somewhat in the third book, only to increase again after 1588. The passages he values most highly are the Lucilius letters, which together with Plutarch's *Moralia* accommodate his taste for reading by randomly paging through works. It is Seneca's open style of thinking and use of form which appeal to him as familiar and pleasant. He takes the Roman's philosophical energy very seriously, namely as the product of a personal manner of living which adheres to what the theory promises (II, 31, 541 A). Thus he shields him from the conventional judgment that suspects he is a posturer,[30] and it is significant when Montaigne, to whom any deceptive affectation is repugnant, believes in an intellect's honesty. He notes in his traveler's journal the good fortune granted him when he was permitted to see a Seneca copy in the Vatican. Often he groups Seneca with Plutarch; these two are the authors he consults most frequently. "I have not had regular dealings with any solid book, except Plutarch and Seneca, from whom I draw like the Danaïds, incessantly filling up and pouring out," he comments even late in life (I, 26, 107 C). The grouping and comparison of the two—carried out in one particular Essay (II, 32)—is customary. But less conventional is the fact that Montaigne's comparison is always resolved in favor of the Greek. He considers Plutarch the richer, more accessible, more human, warmer spirit who is superior to the tension of will and intellectual acuity of the Roman (II, 10, 300–301 A/B and III, 12, 795 B/C). This is the first indication of the

point of view from which Montaigne carries out his selection or rejection of Seneca's ideas. The frequent reference to Seneca in the *Essais*
must not be interpreted as proof of a stoic phase or level in Montaigne.
He only borrows fragments from the Roman, specifically those that lie
at the periphery, not the core, of stoic ethics.

When Seneca was writing, the Stoic school had long since stripped
away the ascetic rigidity of its beginnings. Since its penetration into
Roman educational circles (in the second century before Christ), a moderation and urbanization had taken place which no longer elevated
sages to a superhuman or nonhuman level, but rather considered wisdom possible even within the societal culture and day-to-day activities
guided by reason. Interest had turned to those who were striving, who
were on the way, those "who were progressing" (*procedentes*). These
were the ones to whom philosophy wanted to offer pastoral help, by
cautious attention to the natural dimensions of life. Seneca's writings
are also permeated by this more liberal attitude, particularly his Lucilius
letters. With their frequent quotations from Epicurus, they express the
fact that they do not intend to teach orthodox stoicism, but rather the
wisdom of mastering self and world, from whatever source it might be
taken.

Nevertheless, the basic idea of Seneca's ethics is strict and rigid
enough. It differentiates between man as he is and man as he should be
and bases this on the opposition of two value categories, of which the
first has the character of illness, the other the character of good health.
Man has in him a restless disharmony, in Seneca's view, a struggle
between the high and the low. This can only be mastered by a force of
will which achieves the triumph of the higher over the resistance of the
lower. The spiritual strength (*firmitas animi, ep.* 20) aspired to bring the
flow and vacillation (*fluctuare, vacillare, ep.* 20) of the underlayer
which is determined by one's drives to a stop and covers it with a peace
that is independent of all conditions foreign to the will: *Nulla placida
quies est nisi quam ration composuit (ep.* 56; "There is no joyfulness
and peace other than that created by reason"). Man even as individual
personality gains the imperial power and rank over destiny and over
himself. He becomes *sui possessor (ep.* 12) and is capable of *supra
fortunam surgere (ep.* 44). With his reason he joins himself to the reason
of the world order. Indeed he does have consciousness of the unceasing
ebb and flow of circumstances in which nothing can be predicted. But
he can free himself from the danger of evaluating circumstances in an
illusionary manner, whereas the one lacking wisdom will see circum-

stances sometimes as too great, sometimes as too small. He learns to distinguish between reality and appearance: *Non hominibus tantum, sed et rebus persona demenda est, et reddenda facies sua* (*ep.* 24; "not only man, but also things, must have their mask stripped away and their true face shown"). He understands reality when it has been restored to its objective dimensions, no longer concealed by the horrors of appearance, as an imposed necessity; he becomes one with it and becomes free because he incorporates it into his own will: *Nihil invitus facit sapiens. Necessitatem fugit, quia vult quod ipsa coactura est* (*ep.* 54; "The wise man does nothing against his will. He eludes necessity because he wills that to which it wishes to compel him"). Man who is becoming wise, practiced in borderline and crisis situations, endures all. Poverty, loss of honor, threat of death, but also the small, trying disturbances of everyday life flow past him without causing injury. He serenely withstands even the agonizing emptiness of existence which opens up in the form of loathing of life—and Seneca expressed this emptiness in an unforgettable formulation: we are ignited like the light and extinguished like the light, but in the brief period in between we are destined for suffering (*ep.* 54). Man does not know what the necessary is beyond its mere necessity; he can only know how he should behave with respect to it. In the midst of metaphysical uncertainties he is a being who has done enough for his dignity if he has succeeded in transforming what is necessary into an act of his own will. But this will is imperious, not obedient. Within it lives an unmistakable desire to find resistance and to grow as a result of it: *Crescit animus ipsa rerum difficultate* (*ep.* 22; "The spirit grows precisely because of difficulty"). There is something militant about these ethics; it is not for nothing that its language so frequently reaches for military terms and images. It is true that Seneca likes to speak of the joyfulness of being wise. But this is an acquired, dark joyfulness, not a liberated one. It still bears the scent of the old stoic asceticism.

Yet the picture of Seneca would be incomplete if we tried to limit it to the stoic-voluntary core. This core is surrounded by a wreath of moderating features. Seneca wants to heal himself and others, not with strong medicine, but in small, easily tolerated doses. As relentlessly as he separates man into an inimically tense higher and lower direction, his ascetic idealism still has no rumbling pathos. His style alone betrays this fact. The sentences containing the results of his reflections fall like heavy, hesitant droplets into the depths and coagulate into unbreakable yet never challenging or hurtful formulations. His knowledge of human susceptibilities is not only polemical, it is also understanding. He knows that we need kindness. He comes close to humanity in the later sense of the word, admittedly without being able to take the final step into it. For in the end he is always bound by the isolated dignity of the personality, which always stands still through all of the surging and developing. But he always sees the ethical task in reference to the internally transforming individual and shows consideration for his aptitude and life circumstances. In his most accommodating letters he offers wisdom like an easily picked, lovely fruit. He courts him and practices with him using daily trivialities with which he shows him how freedom must remain on guard against even the lowliest things and how it has its weapons within reach, namely in his own reason. Just as the doctor can only give orders for recovery with the assurance of success if he has first felt the patient's pulse, the philosopher cannot simply issue general maxims, but rather must thoroughly look into the particular case, as we find in one passage, and: *ex longinquo nemo suadebit, cum rebus ipsis deliberandum est* (*ep.* 27; "no one can be convincing from afar; the matters themselves must be weighed"). Thus the heartwarming involvement in the details of life which make the letters so rich. Seneca presents himself in a series of concrete situations in which he shows the development and actions of reason with which he masters them: a walk in his garden of autumn with its warnings of aging and dying, participation in a banquet, official duties, residence in the vicinity of a noisy bath house, the frightening grotto of Naples, and so forth. Even when all this resounds with the cadence of exemplary behavior and when individuality only speaks of itself because it wishes to provide a didactic example, these easily perceived passages suffice to brighten up the monotonous fundamental theory of the ethics.

A further softening takes place through the psychological sensitivity that can detect the most secret seductions of the will which threaten one from the soul's need for enjoyment and illusion. The intention of this is to drive the ethical will for mastery into the last depths of one's being. But analyses such as these (for example, of melancholy, of a dream, of vanity, etc.) produce some of the most intelligent insights attained by classical psychology, and they have a validity for man which extends beyond their ethical intent. The rich experience of himself and of man which Seneca has at his disposal is not without influence upon his actual practice of wisdom. Even the earlier Roman stoics, as we already mentioned, had moderated the unconditional, unworldly asceticism of the Greek school. He moderates it still further (particularly compare *De vita beata*, chaps. 23–25). He shifts the tension between world and personality into the interior of the personality itself, where it is mastered to become an unpathetic form of overcoming which need no longer appear as physical escape from the world. He does not want to wrench man violently out of his life's circumstances. The direction of his internalized wisdom is to be independent of the world while in the midst of it. This urbane Roman with his knowledge of life no longer cuts through one's bond to the world, instead, he depletes its power with a concealed distance. He moves unaffected through the midst of given circumstances and practices the *secum morari* (*ep.* 2) in the showplaces of public life in which the weaker ones tend to fall prey to self-alienation. Seneca resolves the classical problem of the ethics of antiquity, the relationship of the wise to the unwise, to the *vulgus,* in that he closes off the internal lack of vulgarity of being wise behind a visage adapted to the world: *Intus omnia dissimilia sint: frons populo nostra conveniat* (*ep.* 5; "All may be different inside; but our exterior is adapted to the world"). One is advised to seek a middle ground between internal distance and external affability which offers the wise man protection from the scorn of those who lack understanding. Thus in Seneca a high, world-wise culture is achieved. It is able simultaneously to encompass the particularities of the individual and his situation in life as well as the universally relevant freedom of a personal being oneself, and shows everyone, the knight as well as the slave (cf. *ep.* 31), the chance for ethical dignity.

Because Seneca's moral philosophy does not consist merely of a stoic core idea, but rather also includes numerous sophisticated concomitants, he can also be valued by nonstoic readers. This is the case with Montaigne. If one looks through his quotations and borrowings from Seneca, one finds only a small number of the strict kind of will and resistance maxims. These are found in the Essays drafted before 1580, but even here, they are without exception in passages in which Montaigne has not yet completely written his way to his own free self. They serve the role of stimuli. He distances himself from the sense they had in the original in that he moves from them into hedonistic or descriptive, psychological explanations. Thus the concept of solitude of Essay I, 39 which presumably arose soon after 1572, although stimulated by Seneca's recommendation of ethical contemplation of self, turns into the description of an aesthetic-contemplative enjoyment of self with express rejection of any excessive virtue (*vertu excessive,* 179 A). Essay II, 11, which probably stems from the same period, begins with praise of active virtue and extols how this rises all the more triumphantly, the more resistance it must overcome. This is completely in the style of Seneca.

But a few pages later (though supported by later additions), the text pushes this ethic of resistance aside, and another form of completion arises in its place: composure. In the death Essay I, 20, the stoic doctrine, paraphrased from Seneca, of strength of soul against the fear of death occupies a fair amount of space. But it is just a beginning, surrendered even in this Essay, but still more in the later ones, in favor of a relaxed willingness for death. Also, in this Essay on death the stoic maxims decrease in number and importance in favor of borrowings from Seneca which linger even in the description of the inherency of death in life. One can see that Montaigne extrapolates his Seneca in a direction that in the original was always only a digression leading back to the core stoic idea, whereas in the *Essais* it becomes a movement leading away from the stoic idea.

There will be frequent opportunities in the course of our description to show in detail that Montaigne did not read the Roman as a normative ethicist, but rather as a psychologist. He takes up and develops further material that Seneca only designed as a facilitating preparatory lesson: the anthropological sensitivity and the agent for all the individual cases of daily life in which man is confronted with himself and his own inadequacies. Yet he ignores or dispels or disapproves of the moral purpose with which the fullness of the knowledge of man is encircled there. What Seneca intended as a diagnosis of moral "illnesses" serves here to make human nature, as such, visible. In the Plutarch-Seneca comparisons, the extravagance faulted in the latter marks the critical point in which Montaigne's appropriation of the hellenistic and Roman Stoic school ceases. Only now, in the sixteenth century, are those possibilities of a descriptive understanding of individuality completely set free which in that tradition were only touched upon and then suppressed again. Despite Seneca's willingness to respond to the particularities of philosophizing men of the world, his ethical aim only took people's individuality into account; when wisdom was complete, these individual particularities were to disappear. But Montaigne's concept of wisdom brings individual particularities, especially his own, to the forefront in all their phases. It is a wisdom that has incorporated fluctuation, not brought it to a standstill. Its freedom is not that of imperial will over self and destiny, not *supergradi se ipsum* (Seneca *ep.* 34), but rather obedience. Its calmness comes from this, not from the efforts of moral reason. His keen observation of differentiated spiritual processes and their interplay with physical conditions, as much as it might have been learned from Seneca, sees no application for a reduction of man into a higher force of reason and a lower level of affect. His belief in healing forces inherent in natural life is not capable of understanding this life as an unworthy delay of a spirit of reason which belongs to other orders of being. It is instructive that even in Seneca he pays no heed to the two Platonic motifs of the duality of body and soul and the concept of life as imprisonment, though in Seneca as in stoicism as a whole there are still strong traces of these. Thus his lack of responsiveness to Platonic thinking is also revealed in his adoption of Seneca. The *Essais* do not provide an elaborately devised medicine. They are content in what is given. Even the urbane Seneca, who is so moderate compared to the earlier stoics, is still too harsh for Montaigne and appears to spoil for him the mystery of what is given with his rationalized discipline of will. Thus Montaigne's does not write to admonish, to direct, or to educate, as does the Roman; his writing is not *clamore juvare* (*De tranquil. animi*, III), rather, it is a broadening of his own perspectives, a form of talking with himself, to which any form of instructive brow-beating is undesirable.

There is no such thing as Montaigne's much discussed "stoic phase." In the early Essays there are several inclusions of stoic maxims, and it can happen in the late period that when rereading them Montaigne comes across some of these earlier examples of heroic greatness of soul and is again moved by them fleetingly, as the insertions prove. But that must not blind one to the fact that these reproductions are always qualified by completely different material immediately before or after them in the text. Montaigne's "stoicism" is more of a literary than a personal nature. It was a misunderstanding when some contemporaries—the foremost being Lipsius—saw him as a stoic. Montaigne is fundamentally differentiated from the so-called neo-Stoics of the sixteenth and seventeenth centuries in that he makes a descriptive study of morality out of Seneca's normative moral philosophy. The line of neo-stoicism proceeds, without touching Montaigne, from the humanistic philologists to Du Vair, Lipsius, Quevedo, Descartes, and Corneille. Montaigne's originality is apparently precisely from this line in that he avoided a fashion that was in the air. He seeks his closer allies in Socrates, Horace, and Plutarch and is indebted to the psychologist, not the ethicist, Seneca—he, the perfecter of that relaxed way of thinking which had lived within the more finely organized intellects of the sixteenth century from Erasmus on.[31]

It is far more difficult to specify the role Epicurus and Epicureanism play in the *Essais*. It can be proven that Montaigne dipped into the most important first and second level Epicurean sources that were accessible at that time. He was acquainted with the life and teachings of Epicurus from the tenth book of Diogenes Laërtius, particularly the Epicurus letters woven into it, and on several occasions consulted the most content-rich letter—to Menoikeus. Also, Lucretius and the Epicurus quotations and reports in Cicero, Seneca, and Plutarch come under consideration. But one seldom finds an overall assessment of Epicurus in the *Essais*. On occasion Montaigne calls his teachings "closer to my style" (III, 4, 631 C), or he speaks sympathetically of the "sweet fruits of the enervating gardens of Epicurus" (II, 12, 399 B). But he only touches upon epicurean teachings in their insignificant details. And Montaigne's hedonistic tendencies, particularly in the third book, are so unmistakable that even in the seventeenth century it seemed obvious to label him an epicurean. But he himself never called upon Epicurus for these particular tendencies. Was this because the name was still so stigmatized? We do not know. We can only establish that his wisdom regarding life with its moderate and highly reflected willingness for enjoyment represents a high point of Renaissance epicureanism—and we can also suspect that he owes much more to epicurean writings of antiquity than he admits.

Epicurus and his school restricted themselves to a much greater extent than the stoics to the nurture of the unspoiled personality. All bonds to extra-individual connections drop away. State and society are seen only as a union formed to serve particular ends, constructed in a realm beyond right and wrong, and the wise man removes himself from it insofar as possible. The world and life as a whole lie under a fog of worthlessness and senselessness. One's only security consists in perceiving the remaining moments of pleasure and in a readiness to do without desires that cannot be realized. No dualistic division of man, as that of Stoicism, forces one to cut away one's natural joys, physical or spiritual. What is given is grasped, not overpowered by the rationalized ideal configuration of a concept of moral virtue. It is grasped all the more willingly, but also all the more free of illusion, when man knows he is a questionable interplay between the nothingness of his current condition of not yet being and the nothingness of his future no-longer-being. This type of nihilism is also present in Stoicism—but in contrast to this, the Epicurean does not propose to climb to imperial dignity in his brief life, suspended between the two poles of nothingness. His enjoyment principle sometimes takes on a provocative sharpness, as if the only aim were the craving for lower pleasures. But these are isolated moments, usually with a polemical cause. Overall we find that this quiet state of readiness for life's lack of value, for one's desires to fail, for poverty and deprivation, has the power to elevate the enjoyment principle to the level of a transfigured renunciation. It finds appropriate expression in a form of life which embraces seclusion, the esoteric cult of friendship with its selection of the best, and the practice of kindness and a willingness to be understanding. In this manner the noblest spirituality possible within the limits of a nihilistic consciousness arises. It is a "disposition as calm as the sea," an undoctrinaire circulating of the personality within itself, an autumn-like clarity but also inclination of one's feeling for life, a modesty of needs conscious of moderation which knows what is worth doing and what is not—in any case, it is something quite different from the vulgar misunderstanding that Prasser and Schlemmer had of the epicureans. Jacob Burckhardt put it this way: "One fears that but few men would be content with epicurean pleasure properly understood."[32]

There is much in this that must have appealed to Montaigne. Both the ἡδονή of the Greeks and the *volupté* of the French proceed from a long reflection that from all the paths leading to happiness selected the one that does not lead beyond man, but rather leads back and into his own natural content to thankfully receive it without passionately seeking it. Montaigne's spiritual sensuality of life rises up as a more genuine understanding of Epicurean wisdom above the vituperation, still freely repeated in the sixteenth century, which called the Epicureans "swine" (this goes back to the misunderstood concluding verses in Horace's *epistola* I, 4, among other things). Thus he places himself—perhaps without knowing it—in the company of Erasmus, who in his "Epicurus" conversation in the *Colloquia* as well as in *Paraclesis* reconciles the Epicurean pleasure concept with the concept of spiritual bliss, and in the company of Lorenzo Valla's *De voluptate*, wherein the Christian's eternal salvation is interpreted as the most highly sublimated form of that which even in common life is desire. Admittedly, Montaigne does not include such a Christian deliverance of Epicurus. As he once put it, Epicurus lived piously without having thought piously—and then a question follows in which Montaigne's own way is expressed, to live piously, that is, with trust in the forces of nature which are unknowable, and thus cannot be presaged dogmatically: "Could it be true that to be wholly good we must be so by some occult, natural, and universal property, without law, without reason, without example?" (II, 11, 312 C). He understood that even with Epicurus all depended upon the personality being itself.

But much in the original teachings of Epicurus is missing from the *Essais*. The total devaluation of the purpose of life is missing. The nature philosophy is missing, or rather Montaigne only considers it doxographically in order to dismiss it as the playfulness of the imagination, as he does with all speculative ideas. He is far more agnostic than was Epicurus, who permitted theoretical knowledge to the extent that it was able to free men of fear and delusion. These differences are revealed in the manner in which Montaigne receives Lucretius, the Roman source of Epicureanism.

Thus we return again to this poet, but this time with a view toward his teaching system. Montaigne became acquainted with a considerable portion of Epicurus' work from Lucretius, and this was true before he got his hands on Diogenes Laërtius. He read him without prejudice, that is, neither with the critique of his aesthetic principles which was customary earlier, nor with the attempt to reinterpret him in Christian terms[33]—an example is Lambin's foreword to his edition of 1563. As we saw earlier, he first evaluated him aesthetically. To the extent that he read him as a philosopher at all, he did not concern himself with the system as a whole. He borrowed individual passages from the didactic poem *De rerum natura* in a random manner, which often distorted the original meaning. The passages are so numerous that Montaigne proves to be the heaviest borrower from Lucretius in the sixteenth century. More than a sixth of the didactic poem is quoted or paraphrased in the *Essais*.[34]

Nevertheless, the question of to what extent his hedonistic wisdom was stimulated by the Epicureanism of Lucretius must remain open, as must the other question concerning the role of the (later) borrowing from Epicurean sources in Diogenes Laërtius. One can only speak of general and fragmentary correspondence with respect to Lucretius, without this establishing comprehensible influences. On one occasion (III, 1, 600 B) he quotes the famous beginning of the second book (*Suave, mari magno* . . .), wherein the wise one's dwelling in the pure, joyful heights of the temple, his serene glance falling upon the ambitious, empty tumult of men below, his keeping spiritual unrest and physical pain at a distance are expressed so splendidly. But Montaigne quotes this only in passing—the only reason being perhaps that all educated men were accustomed to quoting these verses. For this claim of wisdom reaches higher than that of Montaigne. All they have in common is the joyful tone. Montaigne does not want the heights far removed from the throng; his concept of wisdom takes part in the surge of his own humanity and that of others. He completely excluded the Epicurean doctrines of the gods, the atom and the soul, everything which at the beginning of the century in Pomponazzi and others supported a turning away from the Christian doctrine of the creation of the world and Christian anthropology. The panvitalistic eros concept from the first and second books of the poem is repeated in only a muted form in the *Essais,* in contrast to Ronsard, for example. On the other hand, Montaigne had several features of his interpretation of man expressly confirmed by Lucretius, perhaps even took them from him. For example, when again and again he loves to look into the broad expanse of the universe, measured against which the Earth and man are only tiny specks, in fact whenever he lets go of any anthropocentric thinking, it is not difficult to recognize in this one of Lucretius' leitmotifs. He had two verses from a passage of the sixth book which is particularly important for this (v. 678–679) inscribed on the ceiling in his library, and he quoted them in II, 12 (389 A):

> *Omnia cum caelo terraque marique*
> *Nil sunt ad summam summai totius omnem.*

> "The sky, the land, the sea, and all
> Are nothing to the universal whole."

Also reminiscent of Lucretius is the personification of nature in the Essay on death (I, 20), in fact his entire conception of nature as a helping, motherly power. And he also uses Lucretius to prove his teachings on the clouding of judgment by the emotions and on the body-soul totality of man. But as mentioned before, all this remains fragmentary. Within Montaigne's eclecticism, Lucretius has a considerable effect from a literary standpoint, but ideationally only a coordinate, supporting effect that is comparable to the similar effect Cicero has.

Montaigne is also familiar with the third (and oldest) of the hellenistic types of wisdom, Pyrrhonic skepticism. He became acquainted with it from Sextus Empiricus and Diogenes Laërtius, but coupled it with the moderated skepticism of the newer Academy to which he had access in Cicero. We will save the greater details of this till the next chapter where Montaigne's skepticism is discussed.

But one author of antiquity predominates all others in his effect on Montaigne, and that is Plutarch. He speaks of no other with such constant gratefulness and warmth. He mentioned before that he liked to refer to Plutarch together with Seneca, and always to the latter's disfavor. Plutarch is so universal and content-rich, he writes on one occasion, that in all things with which man is occupied, even the oddest, he is available to help with a hand that holds an inexhaustible supply of riches and decorations—and this is followed by a comment referred to earlier: "I cannot be with him even a little without taking out a drumstick or a wing" (III, 5, 666 B/C).[35] Montaigne loves his more suggestive than explanatory writing which maintains suspense, leaves questions open, makes one productive, sows seeds from which entire intellectual worlds could be developed (I, 26, 115 A). For him, the *Moralia*, like Seneca's letters, are valuable as "detached pieces" that one can open at random (II, 10, 300 A) and which give one the sense of the freshness of the conversation (II, 17, 484 A). But Montaigne loves him above all as a personality and with his own characteristic feeling for the signs of an individual, intimate life, he reads his works as a self-portrayal of their author: "Plutarch's writings, if we savor them aright, reveal him to us well enough, and I think I know him even into his soul" (II, 31, 541 A). Those who really know Plutarch know just how well Montaigne has hit the mark here. For this culture-weary, late period Greek always remained detectable in his humanity through the thin rhetorical-stylistic shell of his work, and everywhere, in the *Moralia* as well as in the *Vitae*, he intertwines his treatment of facts with the history of his own life and his family, with personal reminiscences, and with images of his hometown of Chaironea. In the *Moralia*, with only a few declamatory exceptions, he has known how to preserve the character of writing which is intended for a small circle of friends, although it is probably made up of revised lectures that he gave before the numerous pupils of his Roman period. Montaigne responded to these features. His Plutarch is not the transmitter of heroic subjects, as he is later for Corneille, Shakespeare, and Schiller. In the *Vitae* he values the adaptable portrayer of all combinations of what is human, in the *Moralia* the artist of life who is at home in the intellectual wealth of an aging antiquity and takes from it what is suited to the expression of his own taste—a Montaigne of antiquity.

The first editions of Plutarch's works (*Moralia* in 1509 from Aldus Manutius in Venice with the assistance of Erasmus; *Vitae* in 1517 in Florence) remained a matter for scholars, as did the various Latin partial translations from the *Vitae* in the fifteenth century, and from the *Moralia* by Erasmus and Budé. A few occasional French translations from 1520 on faded away without success.[36] In the sixteenth century before Montaigne, only Rabelais was influenced most predominantly by Plutarch (whom he was able to read in Greek), and he borrowed numerous anecdotes from him. However, the major effect of Plutarch in France began only when Amyot published his two translations: the *Vitae* in 1559, the *Moralia* in 1572 (in the same year as Henri Estienne's Greek-Latin edition). They are not only the most significant translation

event of the French sixteenth century (perhaps of all of French literature) and a monument of French prose which continued to be praised
into the beginning of the classical period (Vaugelas still praises them as
exemplary in the foreword to the *Remarques*), but they are also the
main source from which future French secular and cosmopolitan education draws its knowledge of ancient history, anecdotes, and wisdom.[37]
Montaigne, who knew very little Greek, read Plutarch only in Amyot's
translation. He trusts this without reservation; it never occurs to him to
look for philological confirmation.[38] He was also the first to recognize
their significance for the French language and development of a world
view. In the introduction to II, 4 he stresses the two main advantages: its
naturalness and purity of language, in which he surpasses all others,
owing to which in France one can now speak and write respectably, and
its accessibility for urbane society. Thus the translator Amyot is the one
author of contemporary French literature to whom Montaigne, in his
own words, extended the palm.

   The traces of his reading in Plutarch are evident from the earliest to
the latest Essays. Villey counted around five hundred borrowed passages. When Montaigne visited the Vatican library in 1581 he was
pleased to see a copy of the *Moralia* near Seneca. It is only in the last
years of his life that he appears to have neglected his readings in Plutarch in favor of Plato and Cicero. But his assessment never changed.
One can see from the wealth of comparisons and other figures of speech
which carried over from Plutarch into the *Essais* how deeply Montaigne
absorbed his work. His sensuousness of language connects him artistically with Plutarch, as does his inclination toward an open form. Similarly to Erasmus (foreword to the *Apophthegmata*), he experiences the
Moralia as a carpet decorated with the color of anecdote. And he is not
off the mark here. For Plutarch is accustomed to interrupting the continuity of his thoughts again and again with comparisons, quotations,
and anecdotes, and in this manner he attains a vividness that remains
with the reader better than the concept itself. He uses more a scattering
than a collecting method, which alternates between narration and meditation, and is able to skillfully conceal his unquestionably thorough
preparation in order to give the appearance of sudden inspiration; he
also uses quite varied styles. These are all characteristics of the essay as
well, and one is correct in applying this modern term to the *Moralia*.[39]
Even Montaigne's contemporaries noted that his Essay was related to
those and inspired by them. We will return to this in chapter 8.

   But there are still other ideational forces that connect Montaigne so closely with Plutarch that the similarity cannot be understood simply as an influence. As is so often the case in the history of intellectual contacts, we are concerned with the phenomenon of finding oneself through encounter with someone generically related. Thus it is imperative that we compare Montaigne and Plutarch side by side.

The Boetian, who lived in the first and second centuries after Christ, was nourished by the educational world of the late-hellenistic period which encompassed the entire Greek and Roman traditions. He had an eclectic, liberal relationship to this educational world, thus it is difficult to pin him down to one of the many philosophical movements to which he was exposed. Platonic and Neoplatonic theories, syncretisms composed of diverse parts of all possible religions and cults, belief in demons and immortality, numerology, and a kind of theodicy satisfied his broad speculative requirements. But the focus of his interests still lay in the culture of personality and the eudemonistic lifestyle. Here, too, he displayed the tolerance and generosity of the late heir. Man's knowledge of self (in the Greek sense of the feeling of a boundary in his relationship to the divine), philanthropic understanding for all ways of life, even those outside of the Greek-Roman world, moderation in the use of morally binding or even hedonistically free principles, and an inclination, completely free of melancholy, to validate man in his limitations: these are the approximate parameters of his wisdom. Stoic, Epicurean, and skeptical features are intertwined here, but no one of them gains the upper hand. It does not bother him that some contradict others. He leaves this unresolved. He shines his personal light over the acquired and the conventional; he travels the beaten paths in his own way. And though in some parts of the *Moralia* his polemic against the Stoic school or the Epicureans can take on a sharp ironic edge, one still notes that he has a liberal sense of the fact that all theories are only attempts to bring order into the matter of living, and that the theories must therefore take turns so that each has the opportunity to give of its best. And, as a sensitive spirit, he can always be influenced by the sources to which he is exposed at the moment. The difference of his age in which he came into contact with the individual literary/philosophical traditions, one after the other, does its ultimate to weave a quite contradictory cloth of his *Moralia* as a whole. They have been called "ethical feuilletons."[40] But they are excellently suited to readers who are more likely to be won over by a broad, fluctuating, personal style of thinking than by a single-minded and intolerant doctrine.

This style of thinking can be found in its purest and relatively most

uniform manifestation in the document *De tranquilitate animi*. It is the
sixth passage in Amyot's translation of the *Moralia*.[41] It contains the
noblest content of hellenistic maxims on a level that is occasionally close
to Christian ethics. Thus it was exploited early on by Greek church
fathers. There are a couple of fundamental thoughts beneath the layer of
quotations and borrowings. Man, a being composed of body and soul,
should content himself with filling out the boundaries set for him. He
should not become set on any doctrine, should not flee public life,
should reconcile himself to what is given: "to know how to adapt
oneself to the present circumstances," as Amyot translates it. He should
enjoy the favors of fate and avoid its resentments. No rigorousness
should bring tension to wise men. With the insight that human nature is
incorrigible, he should take his fellows as they are: "in making use of
them, such as they were born, you display your graciousness" (Amyot).
He should create happiness for himself using little tricks—for example,
he should imagine things with which he has become bored as if he had
lost them, and this will open his eyes to their value, which is precious
since it can be lost. Since nature has allocated to the individual man, as
to each of her creations, his inalienable way of life, the target of the ethic
of happiness is the individual; he should adapt to his own situation, but
also to the place where he is born or where he is destined to function. A
gentle joyfulness unfolds noticeably toward the end of the document.
All the shadows of the miseries of life should vanish. "For the world is
the temple that is most joyous and most worthy of the Godhead,"
despite its many inherent defects. All the vocabulary of joy is offered,
and Amyot reproduces its abundance: *gayté, sérénité, joye, liesse,
calme, espérance*. There is nothing said in the entire document about a
generally obligatory virtue. Plutarch scrutinizes all the spirit-healing
means of the various schools and "extracts honey from even the bit-
terest plant." His wisdom amounts to a gentle, somewhat weary letting
oneself be carried along, a carefully limited peace of mind in the middle
of existence, a flexibility to one's life rhythms and a distance from things
which are more a matter of temperament than of reason; there is nothing of the powerful, metaphysical glance upward, as, for example, with
the related but incomparably greater Marcus Aurelius. As we will show
in specific detail later, much of this fundamental attitude returns with
Montaigne. He always ranked Plutarch's *Moralia* higher than his *Vitae*.
In this, he follows the view of his epoch; Erasmus, Budé, and Rabelais
made the same judgment. He plundered it to a much greater degree than
the *Vitae* during all periods of his work on the *Essais*. At first, the

Moralia served him, as they did Erasmus and Rabelais, as a treasure chest of anecdotes and meaningful sayings. The *Table Talks* and *Apophthegmata* interested him as much as the pieces on morals. It goes without saying that Montaigne also behaved eclectically with Plutarch and ignored what was inappropriate for him. Thus, for example, he takes nothing, or next to nothing, of the rigorous Spartan features from the *Mottos of the Lacedaemons,* nor the doctrines of demons and the gods from the comparative religious writings. And yet the main elements of Plutarch's image of the world and man are those of his own. The un-Platonic view of the world as a temple, a view reconciled to this life, is inserted in Essay II, 12 (326 B) from *De tranquilitate* . . . with no consideration of a Christian, theological interpretation found in the first draft, or rather, with a subsequent casual harmonization of this with the pagan source. *De E apud Delphos* (chapter 18) contains remarks on the flow of all things and on man who, himself perpetually changing in the transition from his beginning to his end, is unable to comprehend anything lasting, or even the transitory nature of things; Montaigne borrows this almost literally (of course from Amyot) at the end of the same Essay, but in so doing only repeats, this time in borrowed words, something he has said himself one hundred other times in the *Essais*. Finally, he expresses one of the most impressive versions of his favorite concept of the mixed and polarized circumstances of existence with the help of the *Moralia:* the sentences of the last Essay in which the discussion concerns our life as the harmonization of high and low notes which would shatter if one did not preserve it in its mysterious contradictoriness (III, 13, 835 B)—these sentences come almost literally from Amyot's translation of *De tranquilitate.*

Compared to the *Moralia*, the influence of the *Vitae* on Montaigne is much less, both in what he borrows from it and in his regard for it. Yet the *Vitae* are also of extraordinary significance for the concrete and complex image of man in the *Essais*. Together with corresponding theories in the *Moralia* they supplied the *Essais* with their view of the mixed nature of man. And precisely through Montaigne's *Essais* this view became definitive for the future refined psychology of individuality of the French moralists.

Plutarch's biographies, which concern persons associated with important historical events and scenes, are not the writing of history. What there is of national or world-historical processes in them remains fragmentary and is not associated with any sort of comprehensive purposes or interrelationships; it is not related for its own sake, it could just as well be otherwise and is just presumed to be something that is already known in its full scope. The forces of the portrayal are concentrated on the persons themselves. Their world-historical deeds are not given more and are often given much less space than their sayings, their behavior within the smallest context, their private individuality. The great military campaigns, the battles, the interplay of interests among the political powers represent only one subject among many from which Plutarch reads the essence of a man as expressed in them. Such an essence is like a broadcasting center; everything it reaches, but only what it reaches is mentioned in the biography. For Plutarch, the only thing that is accessible is that which is human, but this is accessible in all concrete and atmospheric layers. Wonder, presentiments, and dreams belong to the latter category, but even these, no less than the physical and moral details and no less than all other occurrences that are more easily understood, are features of a particular character and a destiny that applies to that character alone. From history Plutarch makes stories, from history's long expanse of time he makes a sequence of personal moments. This so-to-speak atomizing style with its novella-like condensations brings to light material for the contemplation of individual figures, something not previously achieved in classical writing of history and biography.[42]

One certainly still finds in Plutarch many signs of the origin of classical biography in the panegyric and the intention of passing on to posterity the story of exemplary, praiseworthy persons. He himself from time to time states this as the purpose of his *Vitae* (e.g., at the beginning of "Pericles"). But this is a diminishing purpose. For he does not seek out the heroic and famous person, but rather the actual person and his characterological findings; aspects of fame only benefit him because they are well and accurately handed down objects of his curiosity about man. And although he uses the categories "good," "evil," "virtue," and "vice," he still hopes to get beyond their schematic and strives to get hold of the tangled, crossing, contradictory actualities of man in a descriptive manner. In "Alexander," the portrayal moves back and forth between the cruel inhumanity of the conqueror and the leniency and goodness or the victor of the private man without interpreting, but all the more attentively from an artistic standpoint. Plutarch's biography of Cicero portrays the vain, fame-hungry man with the same precision as the wise administrator of his office. Is his Themistocles a great or damnable man? We don't know, or better, we learn that he is both. Does this inconsistency of his characters originate in the "inability to chisel out a character

conceived according to a particular style," as has been contended?[43] Is it
only the result of his contaminating treatment of the most varied sources,
whereby he borrows contradictory material uncritically? Plutarch's attentiveness to the baffling detail and the human organism unstifled by
some preconceived notion of uniformity is too pronounced to not attest
to at least an artistic openness to the antinomies of a character. In the
period following, and at its best in Montaigne, this has become an incentive to look more deeply into man than is possible with a rhetorical or
moral philosophy scheme. And an effect of this kind is attributed to some
"inability" of Plutarch's? Interpreters of antiquity would save themselves a great number of misinterpretations if they would only pay attention to how works of antiquity are received later on!

Plutarch himself spoke several times of his intention of tracking
down "natural" individuality, the essence of which, a crossover between
good and evil, only comes to light when the observer penetrates its
public, representative behavior, but also its ideal illusion of heroics
beyond reproach, and pays attention to inconspicuous signs. The words
used in such passages in Amyot's translation become a part of Montaigne's language. For example, the following sentences could also have
appeared in the *Essais:* "And the highest and most glorious exploits are
not always those that best exhibit man's vice and virtue; often *something trivial, a word or a game,* reveals most clearly *persons' dispositions.* As such then, similar to painters who, *painting from life,* sought
purely or primarily superficial resemblances in the facial features, on
which *men's habits and characters* show like imprinted images, so must
we concede that we were primarily in search of *the signs of the soul,* by
which we formed *a portrait of every man's character and habits.*"[44] We
have given in italics the formulations that might have affected Montaigne. Of course it was known long before Plutarch that even the most
perfect man had his faults (see Plato, *Politicus,* 491c; and *Hippias Minor,* 375e). But here this obvious insight is productive in a new way
entirely for the description of the complex actuality of individual humanity. One can best see this in the comparisons with which Plutarch concludes each pair of biographies. If we pay attention not to their proclaimed intent[45] but rather to what they accomplish, we find that,
guided by a highly sensitive feeling for what is inexhaustible to individuals and what differentiates them, they are indirect means of characterization with which the view of each individual example of man can continue to be refined. As schematic as the structure of the comparisons
may be, the distribution of attributes is minimally schematic. That is,

the negative is not allocated to one, the positive to the other of the persons compared. Rather, the individual nature is revealed in the distribution of specific negatives and positives separately. It emerges that not only are qualities and reactions in the individual different under the same circumstances, but in the realm of action, the relationships of motive and effect are different. Let us state the results of Plutarch's comparisons in a formula as follows: the effect E^1 can result from the Motive M^1 in individual I^1; for another individual I^2, however, the same effect E^1 can result from motive M^2; or: motive M^1 leads to E^1 in I^1, but to E^2 in I^2. The reader can calculate further combinations for himself, and will find adequate proof of this in the text. Thus a weave of particularities arises which seen from the viewpoint of the study of man produces greater results than the inspiring or edifying effect created by the individual heroic, exemplary descriptions in the *Vitae* and taken up by the later centuries, occasionally one-sidedly, at the expense of anthropology. It is certainly also one-sided on our part, but necessary here in relation to Montaigne, that we emphasize in Plutarch the characterizing describer of men, for whom there was no uniformity, or at most an approximate similarity among individuals and their destinies. He discovered their uniqueness and the impossibility of comprehending them through any kind of general causalities and schematics. And at the same time he recognized the unique, irreplaceable gain to be made with the descriptive method, an art of portrayal which in its dedication to the phenomena observed conveys the essence of man, which is superior to any theory.

It is clear that Montaigne's moralistic interests were nourished by Plutarch's *Vitae* even though we cannot determine to what extent they first had to be awakened by that work. In Essay II, 10 he praises the writing of history as a genre for permitting us the perception of the human essence ("man in general"), specifically, "the diversity and truth of his inner qualities in the mass and in detail, the variety of the ways he is put together, and the accidents that threaten him" (303 C). This is inserted in front of the older statement referring to Plutarch's biographical work which designates it as belonging to his favorite genre of historical portrayals, that which is more concerned with what goes on inside man than what befalls him from the outside. That is, Montaigne has gotten to the heart of Plutarch's characterizational psychological method. He understands Plutarch as the teacher of an individuating observation of man which penetrates into the variety of what is particular about him (*diversité, varieté*). It is no accident that when one reads Amyot's Plutarch one often has the feeling one is reading an Essay by Montaigne. This is due only to a small extent to the similarity in the language used by the two Frenchmen, but to a much greater extent to the sensuous view of human matters that the Greek and Montaigne share, and also to the technique used in the *Vitae* of beginning with an introductory reflection, which then leads into something concrete (compare, for example, the beginning of "Demetrius"), or the interrupting of the anecdotal description with general considerations.

The most interesting factor, though, is that Montaigne valued the comparisons in the *Vitae* as the "most admirable part" (II, 32, 549 A). On the occasion of a discussion of the "folly" of ranking the Greeks above the Romans or the Romans above the Greeks, in the same passage he also again expresses his favorite thought: "But it is folly to try to judge by one feature things with so many aspects," namely, men. And he then explains how none had been able to notice differences better and with more insight than Plutarch, who ranked neither the Greeks nor the Romans higher, but rather weighed each one individually, bit by bit according to his characteristics, and then was able to comprehend them separately. Montaigne has hit precisely upon the trait that distinguishes Plutarch's comparisons. His own thinking does not simply handle the comparative method in the superficial manner of the so-called syncrisis, which assembles traditional pairs to be compared (Socrates and Cato, Lucretius and Virgil, Alexander and Caesar, Seneca and Plutarch, etc.), rather he does so heuristically in a manner that leads into the depths, a manner that recognizes that comparisons provide a better path to understanding what is incomparable than isolated observation. Since Montaigne avoids the overtones of hero worship still present in Plutarch, or at least restricts them to a few cases, he is all the more receptive to the factual subject matter concerning the study of man which is communicated in the *Vitae*. The *Essais* constitute the mediating element that establishes the connection between the newer, more modern study of morality, that is, the descriptive, nonnormative comprehension of intimate individualities, and Plutarch. Montaigne both understood the late-period Greek and at the same time expressed his own outlook when he said that it was more important to him to find out what Brutus did or said at home in his room than on the battlefield or in the Senate (II, 10, 302 A). Precisely as was the case with his reception of the Stoic school, in his assessment of Plutarch he refrains from any glorification and ethicization of antiquity. In this, Plutarch is much more accommodating than Seneca.

We can cover other sources of education for Montaigne much more quickly. None of them played a role in his educational world even close in importance to that played by Seneca and Plutarch, not even the historians whom he valued so highly.

Here, of the figures of classical literature, we will only concern ourselves with Cicero. As was true for humanism as a whole, for Montaigne, too, we can discover his relationship to antiquity as well as his own ideas on education in his relationship to Cicero, who once dominated the first two humanistic centuries as an awakening and much imitated force. Montaigne studied him at all times, increasingly in the last years of his life. He mainly studied him as a doxographic source.

Cicero, the eclectic processor of Platonic and hellenistic didactic material of all schools in an urbane form, is particularly well suited to such a study. As the mediator of "academic" skepticism he displays traits that also distinguish Montaigne: a skepticism that is again applied to the skeptical principle, a skepticism that avoids that radical doubt in favor of a probability that leaves matters open and which shields his thinking from becoming entangled in his own principles to the point of becoming unfree. It is possible that Montaigne's interest in the *Tusculanae disputationes* is based upon this common ground—which need not necessarily come from one influence. The similarity between the aging philosophy of *De senectute* and the tone of wisdom of the late Essays will be discussed later (chapter 5). Admittedly, Montaigne never speaks of Cicero without qualification. In some passages he heaps scorn upon him. He is too scholarly, too tedious, too long-winded, too likely to beat around the bush for Montaigne's taste; he dislikes Cicero's logical, definitory, "Aristotelian" treatise style, his ceremonious ponderousness (II, 10, 301 A). His frank irony against the *bien dire* often emerges (e.g., III, 7, 700 C) and he is frank in his objection that with this author, word and deed often diverge, that is, he feigns a philosophical position when it is really just an empty facility with the pen (II, 31, 641 A). Montaigne had an aversion to the constraints of form associated with treatise writing and to an artistic treatment of language, in fact to any literary devices that in their virtuosity could express what is real and what is unreal, what is believed and what is simply repeated in the same manner, creating the greatest danger that challenges man's effort to become and to know himself, and this aversion was triggered by Cicero. Montaigne treats him—as was the case with contemporary Cicero criticism (and in part, earlier as well) and would continue for some time after his death—as the original example of rhetorical insincerity. With this he clearly fits into the late phase of humanism which had come to a point of turning against its own beginnings, which included the imitation of Cicero. He is sympathetic only to the Atticus letters, that is, he takes from the mass of Cicero's writings those in which he detects the living, private man who is not stylizing himself for the sake of public display. We will return to this later.

5. CHRISTIAN SOURCES

With which Christian sources was Montaigne involved, and to what degree? We do find some traces of readings in the Bible in the *Essais*. But for him the Bible is one source of quotations among others. It only reaches from a distance into the horizon of a Montaigne who is perhaps not impious, but is non-Christian. The number of quotations is small. Including the biblical mottos on the beams of the library, one does not even find three dozen of them. Most can be found in II, 12, the Essay that proceeds from theological questions. The nearly complete absence of the Gospels is noteworthy. They are only represented in four passages, and these are somewhat unimportant ones. The Books of Wisdom of the Old Testament and the Letters of Paul take precedence. The quotations are selected such that they can be integrated into Montaigne's agnostic, fideistic thought processes without opening up the prospect of the salvation of Christ. Montaigne read the Bible with the eyes of an intellect fond of hellenistic wisdom, and thus invokes it predominantly in passages in which it shows its strongest agreement with hellenistic didactic material. This particularly applies to the Ecclesiastes, which he is so fond of quoting. Of course without knowing the least thing about a dependence of the Ecclesiastes on hellenism, which perhaps did indeed exist,[46] he felt drawn to this book, which differed so strongly from messianic and prophetic Judaism and which later also often affected men of a skeptically bitter, moody wisdom who had turned away from orthodox religiousness. It may have been less the melancholy cast of the book which moved him, more the agnostic reserve, the experience of the remoteness of God and the fragility of existence, the concept of balance, the conservatism (this classical accompaniment to all skepticism), the equality of man and animal, and then the trying out of all possible attitudes up to the joy in enjoyment, and finally the powerful theme of *vanitas vanitatum*, which, however, he adopted without the somber tone it has there. The title of one Essay (II, 28, "All Things Have Their Season") comes from the Ecclesiastes (III, 1).[47]

Montaigne's readings in theological authors are minimal. We can disregard Sebond's *Theologia naturalis;* it will be shown later what untheological results came from his occupation with this work. A mention of Thomas Aquinas (I, 30, 147 A) is as transitory as it is meaningless. The only authoritarian theological source that can be proven in the *Essais* is Augustine's *Civitas Dei*. But with few exceptions this is treated only as a source where one finds moral history, or as a means of passing on classical religious doctrines and philosophies. Montaigne does not concern himself with the apologetic intention with which Augustine presents or rejects pertinent things.

6. ESSENTIAL VERSUS FORMAL EDUCATION

What Montaigne knew of and used from the newer Latin literature and literature in the vulgar languages of France, Italy, and Spain—apart from historical and political writings (see chapter 4)—never led to a fruitful contact with an author, at least not even remotely to the degree of his involvement in Virgil, Seneca, and Plutarch. He did indeed borrow anecdotal material and ideational motifs liberally from contemporary literature, particularly from the popular moral treatises, aphorisms, and collections of excerpts to which Villey devoted his research into sources.[48] But this should not be overrated. Involvement with such writings played itself out, so to speak, in the anteroom of his intellectual dwelling. Thus a discussion of Montaigne's postantiquity sources is unnecessary here. They will be referred to when necessary in the course of our portrayal.

Nevertheless, we must go into a considerable difference between the *Essais* and early humanism in the Italian mold. It is apparent that Montaigne falls into polemical irritability whenever he is confronted with a formal, rhetorical concept of education.

The major occurrence of fourteenth- and fifteenth-century humanism was the rediscovery of classical stylized language as a creation harmoniously refined in tone and rhythm for which the ear began again to school itself. This reverence for carefully molded speech is the aesthetic equivalent of the ideistic valuation of language as the highest sign of the essence and dignity of man. The best-spoken man is the perfecter of human existence, the best speech guarantees the purest order of the intellect: these principles were revived from the Roman rhetoricians by the Italian humanists. One can find treatment in Plutarch, Leonardo Bruni, and later also in Lorenzo Valla and others of the idea that language is the cultural, legal, moral wealth that forms the basis of the state and which raises man above the animals—the "light of things" (Cicero) without which there would be barbarism and chaos. This is Cicero's fundamental thought, especially in his two works on the orator. The humanists, in this, too, following Cicero's lead, then turn this thought to the evaluation of classical literature. They conceive of it as an unsurpassable archetype of all knowledge which can ever be attained and which in this literature has achieved intellectual reality. The basis of this is Cicero's comment in the *Tusculanae* (V, 105): *Quid est enim dulcius . . . iis litteris quibus infinitatem rerum atque naturae, et in hoc ipso mundo coelum, terras, maria agnoscimus?* ["What can there be more beautiful than literary works by means of which we get to know the infinity of things and of nature and in this cosmos, the heavens, the lands, and the seas?"] This has been paraphrased countless times by humanists from Petrarch (in *De vita solitaria* II, 9, 6) on. According to humanistic doctrine, man is elevated to the level of education appropriate to his dignity by the study of classical literature—*studium litterarum*. Since the language in which the literature handed down found its archetypal form was shaped using all possible artistic rhetorical means, a longing arose for a rhetorical, formal education with which the proper understanding and also imitation of the classical work that had been handed down could be achieved. The path to the actual thing passes through the language. So factual education is first rhetorical, literary education. Eloquence, that is, the artistic mastery of language, is considered the embodiment of all the understanding as well as reproducing intellectual capacities. In the presumption that everything knowable has already been said—namely in highly stylized classical speech—the earlier humanists let all disciplines lead into the study of the *litterae*. They are accustomed to seeing every matter in the respective canonical form of language in which it is handed down, and they believe in an ideal possibility of congruence between thing and word. The consequence of this thinking is first the development of a culture of linguistic form. It is manifested in an imitative writing in Latin, in a reproductive operation that can sink as low as to produce sterile works by tacking together its own writings according to the formulae of classical texts, but at its best it is accompanied by a highly sensitive feeling for language that wants to "smell and taste" the words, as Leonardo Bruni once put it.[49] A further consequence is the exaggerated ranking of literary education above experience, that is, limiting experience to the knowledge of literary material as the only reliable source of the substance of life and of things. Just as this imitative humanism isolates language as an instrument of culture to the detriment of the substance of culture (and without yet understanding the Greek logos idea that originally supported those views), it also isolates the knowledge present in the literature handed down to the detriment of a possible spontaneous onward movement of knowledge.

A reaction against this was apparent from the middle of the fifteenth century on. It was reinforced by the empirical sciences (Leonardo da Vinci) and the awakening demands of the vulgar language (Alberti), but it could also be expressed within Latin education. The following were characteristics of the counter-movement: trust in one's personal experience of life and mistrust of mere book learning; the conviction that even the classical authorities were only fallible humans;[50] factual knowledge that pressed forward into what was undiscovered and unstated; resolute movement away from literary imitation into self-discovery, even while still making use of classical patterns. But with this the evaluation of the literary and linguistic inheritance as a whole changed. There was no longer a belief in the ideal connection between thing and word. One no longer pursued the rhetorical, formal art for its own sake, but only to develop a flexible instrument for modern authors' needs for expression, which varied according to temperament, character, and style of thinking. The stage for this was prepared in the later fifteenth century by Poliziano and the younger Pico, and attained by Erasmus in the sixteenth century. Erasmus, himself a virtuoso, even refined, master in Latin artistic prose, was able to moderate the excessive demands of the rhetorical form in favor of its ideistic content. He recognized—thus making himself the spokesman of the entire transalpine humanism of the sixteenth century— that the masking of the present with an exclusively imitated realm of speech and formula was meaningless, and he helped validate the spontaneous expressive powers of language, particularly in his *Dialogus Ciceronianus* (1528).[51] He became a champion in the fight against the artistic literarization of the natural contents of life and the soul. Despite the extent to which this arises in him from a protest for piety (namely, against all who *qui plus habent litteraturae quam pietatis,* LB, I, 1017 B; "who have more education than piety"), it has still become quite significant for the secular areas of intellectual life. With his demand for *apte dicere* instead of mere imitative *ornate dicera* (both of these being Cicero's wording), with his conception of language as a *speculum animi* and an historically changing creation, with his readiness to recognize individuals (*ingenia*) in the context of their temporal and cultural autonomy he stripped the word of its formal predominance and removed the archetypical influence from the words of classical texts. Once rhetorical humanism had been a new achievement that opposed the linguistic, aesthetic coarsening of medieval Latinism that had been expanding from the thirteenth century on. It taught one to value the beautiful statement instead of the concepts and distinctions. But in the meantime, the fate of paralysis and alienation had overtaken this humanism, and in the transalpine countries it was thus seen as a betrayal of the authenticity of objects and of souls.

Erasmus' view of language had a profound influence on French humanism, which from the beginning had not had to suffer under a puristically restrictive manner, as had Italian humanism. Montaigne, too, was affected by this influence. He was adverse to any kind of formal, rhetorical over-valuing of language. His quite highly developed feeling for the art of language, his own literary mastery was based upon a superior relationship with language. He was able to appreciate classical texts in their art form to the extent that they were literature, as we have seen. But this was a nonbinding, aesthetic appreciation that did not assign an archetypical validity to the linguistic form of the texts. He quoted them with love, but no longer with a ritualistic reverence for the coined expression with which a Petrarch used to quote them. He expressed only scorn for rhetorical terminology (I, 51, 223 B). It was typical that he had almost no works of rhetoric in his library. What he used from Quintilian were pedagogical, not rhetorical teachings. His particular sense, which responded to the inner reality of language, necessarily disapproved of the breakdown of a creation of language for the purpose of its classification into stylistic figures and grammatical categories. In himself and in others he paid less attention to what had been created than to what was in the process of being created, that is, the act of language, and like Du Bellay—the Du Bellay of *Regrets*—he strove for the naturally flowing, nonimitative expression.

His *studium humanitatis* is also a *studium litterarum*, but never with the upward striving attitude of the earlier humanists. Thus it serves as a symbol of Montaigne's distancing himself from their belief in literature when on one occasion he also repeats that frequently repeated saying of Cicero's on the joy of reading books (see the earlier discussion on readings), but he repeats it with a reversal of judgment, that is, as evidence of the arrogance of man for thinking he could possess the truth in the written word (II, 12, 360 A). Montaigne decisively relinquished the basic humanistic thought that held that language contains existence become spirit, and that the knowledge of one's literary inheritance guarantees the certainty of having knowledge. Inherited and contemporary intellectual life for him move within the same realm of the questionable. But for him, ideas that have been handed down can never replace one's new attempt to form an opinion from the standpoint of one's own individuality, which changes in phases.

Montaigne is sensitive to how literary definitions threaten to form a dividing wall between thing and man, and how they can divert the energy of their own essential education into a formalistic one in which one captures the words or the literary source of a thing, but not the thing itself (II, 17, 501 A). Simplicity, naturalness, and being oneself protest within him against rampant literarizations. His need for personal honesty encounters the other direction passed on by Erasmus, which has its origin in the *devotio moderna* of the fifteenth century and longs for a simplicity of the heart which has not been buried in a specialized theology. Montaigne carries out in the secular realm the same thing Erasmus does in the spiritual realm, namely the breakdown of a formalistic culture. Quite telling is a motif that weaves its way through the *Essais,* wherein times of the flowering of oratory are understood as times of political, social, and ethical decadence: "Eloquence flourished most at Rome when affairs were in the worst state . . . as a free and untamed field bears the lustiest weeds" (I, 51, 222 A; see II, 12, 358–359 A). He includes his own epoch in this: "Scribbling seems to be a sort of symptom of an unruly age" (III, 9, 721 B). With viewpoints such as these he can praise Sparta at the expense of Athens ("At Athens they learned to speak well, here [in Sparta], to do well" I, 25, 105 A) and, similarly to Castiglione before him, he can explain the political impotence of Renaissance Italy as a result of the overeducating of the Italians, which crippled their capacity to act (I, 25, 106 A). His mistrust of literarization also causes him to give some credit to the lack of education of the French nobility, which he otherwise ridicules. The influence of contemporary traveler's journals also played a role in these views, since they detected with satisfaction a moral purity and an absence of any cultural and literary heightening of appeal among the exotic peoples.[52]

Montaigne attained the most extreme distance from rhetorical humanism. He was suspicious of the once highly praised beauty of tone (*suavitas*) of its speech, he who himself could write so excellently, considering it dishonest seduction. And he gruffly called rhetoric the *science de gueule* (I, 51, 222 A). A man who writes in accordance with the conventional art forms is to him like a shoemaker who makes large shoes for small feet (I, 51, 221 B). His aversion to Cicero was discussed earlier; it has its place in this context. He loves to intersperse in his work anecdotes in which oratorical extravagance appears foolish. His linguistic thinking related to subject and expression also treats the splendid verbal gestures of humanistic style and the scholastic treatise-style formalism ironically, for example in the clever passage in which he tells of an Italian cook who describes to him the various degrees of appetite of his guests and the preparation and sequence of courses of a dinner using an entire offering of distinctions similar to those of school theology (I, 51, 222–223 A; perhaps also reminiscent of Horace, *Sat.* II, 4?). He never conceals his anger with authors who falsify facts for the sake of rhetorical considerations (e.g., II, 10, 304 C). Thus his disparaging judgment of the exaggerated literariness of Bembo (III, 5, 666 B) and his often repeated challenge that the books that should be read are not the best-written ones, but rather the ones containing the best thinking. It no longer occurred to him that a perfected art of language would guarantee intellectual perfection, as earlier humanism believed. One of the reasons for his sympathy with Socrates is based upon the passage in the *Symposium* (199a/b) in which the wise man announces scornfully, after Agathon's extravagant praise of eros, how his mouth grew when he only began to think about speaking. Finally, to underscore the ridiculous extent to which literary miseducation can go, he cites the example of an acquaintance who does not dare to say he has an itchy backside until he has first looked up the meanings of itchy and backside in his lexicon (I, 25, 101 C).

An awareness of the danger of an overly refined culture of language and the recommendation of a natural, simple, factual, honest way of writing is admittedly almost as old as the theory of artistic language. It is itself a rhetorical common ground that even the most skilled artists of style do not overlook. Seneca is replete with it. *Epistola* 100 is a splendid treatise on writing from the wealth of the spirit, writing that does not degenerate into empty artistry or lack of discipline. This spirit carries the art of style (*eloquentia*) with it, as it were, only like a shadow that is taken for granted, and it is convinced of what it writes.[53] Elsewhere we find: *Quae veritati operam dat oratio, incomposita debet esse et simplex* (*ep.* 40; "A speech that strives for truth must be artless and simple"), and *ep.* 59 contains the laudatory phrase (also quoted by Montaigne in III, 5) *Plus significas quam loqueris* ("You express more than you say"). Plutarch makes similar statements countless times and assures the recipients of his letters of how tired he is of speaking just for the sake of saying something well. And yet he cannot refrain from it any more than Seneca can write simply and without structure, despite his theory of honesty. The discrepancy noticeable between such fine principles and actual practice is greater in humanism than it was in antiquity. The ridiculing of literarization and rhetorization in itself is an impotent literary posture that does not bring serious improvement. Not even Erasmus is free of this. A later example from the seventeenth century in vulgar language is Guez de Balzac's *Socrate chrétien,* which pontificates in virtuoso stylistic devices on the necessity of writing from the simplicity of the heart.

Montaigne rises above these cases of literary dishonesty or semi-honesty. He has taken the old common ground seriously and, much more consistently than Seneca, Plutarch, or even Erasmus, has limited the rhetorical, formalistic culture of language to its role as servant; his principle is: do not change nature into art, rather, change art into nature (III, 5, 666 C). His resolute subjective experiences established form— that of others as well as his own—as only a transitory attempt at giving shape in the restless metamorphosis of spirit and language. We will understand this better later when looking at his language critique (see chapter 4). Because he experiences things in this way, he takes no part in the development of the neoclassical concept of art as prepared in his time by the Italian and Dutch theoreticians and then put into practice in France in poetry and prose: a concept that held to the superiority of art to nature and strove to elevate the motility, crudeness, multiplicity, and directness of nature into a controlled form, therein to calm, distance, and generalize it.

7.   ESSAY ON THE EDUCATION OF CHILDREN

All of these features of a late humanism that is making a transition into a freer conception of humanity is particularly apparent where Montaigne presents his idea of education specifically as a pedagogical principle. This takes place in the Essay "Of the Education of Children" (I, 26) and in the related Essay I, 25 "Of Pedantry." The former is a French branch of the broad pedagogical literature of the sixteenth century in Europe which extends from Erasmus, Vives, Castiglione up to the Spaniard Guevara and has an eye to feudal or royal education of nobility appropriate to their class, in which principally the educational material of antiquity from Cicero and Plutarch is used. Montaigne, too, is thinking of a noble elite, more precisely the future son of the Countess Diane de Foix ("You are too noble-spirited to begin otherwise than with a male," he gallantly tells the pregnant recipient, 109 A). Essay I, 26 was at that time considered an educational document for the nobility. But its significance also extended beyond this limitation of class to the same degree as the concept of the *honnête homme,* which arose around this same time and had influence beyond its chivalrous and courtly origins.

Since the knowledge of man was more important to Montaigne than the education of man ("Others form man; I tell of him," see above), his educational concept is not doctrinaire. It is intended to serve as recommendation, advice, suggestion, filled with the cautious knowledge that a developing person is a mystery, a creature with so many unknown forces "that it is hard to base any solid judgment on them" (109 A). No rigid process of development should be preestablished. The educator should behave as friend and helper; his role should consist in observing and listening to the individual nature of the one he is educating in order to push aside any impediments to his capacity to shape himself: "It is good that he should have his pupil trot before him, to judge the child's pace" (110 C). The guidelines to follow in educating a person lie within that person himself; the only purpose of education is to lead him to himself; there is no single standard that applies to all. This is in keeping with Montaigne's view of man which knows only individuals and builds upon the particular order inherent in each individual, an order that is life-enhancing in direct proportion to the degree to which the individual follows it. Thus an extraordinary tolerance determines the spirit of the educational process. Here, too, what is takes precedence over what should be. Montaigne is only rigid and demanding in one respect, namely in placing essential education above scientific and formal education. This is the point of the entire Essay, which is why we are discussing it here.

What we designate here as essential education is what Montaigne calls "virtue," "make him wiser and better," "know how to live well," or elsewhere, "the culture of the soul" (see chapter 1). These key words that were common at the time do not mean demureness or any such thing, rather, they refer to an excellence of any kind, an art of living and capacity for judgment of individual things from one's own powers, the right of the personality to unfold fully into what it is by nature. This can be seen beautifully in an unforgettable passage on philosophical "virtue" that was only sketched out in the first draft, but later enriched in an almost boisterous flow of language: virtue is not tribulation and subjection or well-behaved cessation of activity, it is a forceful acting, a blooming, joyousness, health of spirit, a joyful consent to every condition of life which destiny brings (119 C). The opposite of this essential education is expressed with the key words *pédant* and *pédantisme*, which is associated with, as Montaigne was well aware, the "pedants" of Italian comedy of the sixteenth century, that is, that stereotypical figure that vented the layman's irritation with scholarly affectation (compare the beginning of Essay I, 25). The pedantry at which the two Essays (I, 25 and I, 26) are aimed is the epitome of the lack of intellectual freedom and of an exercise in memory which delivers man into the hands of tradition without leading him to an awakening of the soul and to being himself. An aversion to "pedants" was the contemporary means of protection against specialization. In an epoch in which—with the rising prominence of the sciences—there also arose the risk characteristically associated with them, namely, specialists (first in the form of the humanistic scholars who specialized in literature and jurisprudence), Montaigne was the indefatigable voice warning of this danger. He passed on his concern about the decline of the intellect into specialized knowledge down to the future lifestyle of the *honnête homme,* already present in his time in its major manifestations. And he himself possesses that genuine education that consists less in being learned than in being infinitely teachable: "But the fine minds are the universal minds, open and ready for everything; if not well taught, at least teachable" (II, 17, 495 A/C).

Thus in the Essay on the education of children it is once again demonstrated how sharply Montaigne is able to distinguish between a study of one's intellectual inheritance which chokes one's reasoning ability like "too much oil chokes the lamp" and that other approach to study which broadens the spirit but also makes it secure in itself by providing it with other images of mankind. Thus his educational concept for a child being brought up is to tell him to judge critically, make choices, and frankly reject anything that he feels is unsuitable: "Let the tutor make his charge pass everything through a sieve and lodge nothing in his head on mere authority and trust: let not Aristotle's principles be principles to him any more than those of the Stoics or Epicureans. Let this variety of ideas be set before him; he will choose if he can; if not, he will remain in doubt" (111 A). Compared to the customary classification of subjects of knowledge according to the scheme of the *artes liberales,* Montaigne responds completely independently, here as elsewhere in the *Essais.* He no longer expects the child being raised to follow the rigid sequence through the trivium and the quadrivium. When he speaks of the *artes liberales,* he relegates them more decisively than his contemporaries to the ranks of preparatory disciplines. He eliminates dialectics and rhetoric entirely as being useless. And his general judgment is: "Among the liberal arts, let us begin with the art that liberates us" (117 C). This is a distant echo from the *Epistola* 88 of Seneca's, who is the major Roman source of the *artes liberales* system.[54] Perhaps for the sake of setting the aims of his Essay on the education of children, which at first was related to his specific societal rank, Montaigne reaches back to the Roman idea that the *artes liberales* are called free because they are the worthy occupation of a free man. But this only involves an isolated echo without a consideration of the whole system of the *artes* developed by Seneca. Of course there is no attempt at a theological enhancement of the *artes*. Ultimately, the Essay proves with its tentative, reluctant exploration of this century-and-a-half-old scheme just how far it has fallen into decline.

We will not pursue this further. Nor will we go into the details of Montaigne's concept of education; they are so well known that one finds reference to them in every history of educational theory. The research has determined how much of this had already been expressed by other authors, for example, the principle that learning should be made a game (Erasmus, following Plato and Quintilian)—or how far Montaigne's rebellion against the joyless, philistine compulsory schooling that he had experienced in his youth had already been surpassed in the interim by the greatly altered circumstances of the French school system.[55]

However, this does not negate the fact that Montaigne was the one who made the concept of a liberal, cosmopolitan education a part of the French nation. "It is in him that the principles derive their source and from where our secondary teaching draws again periodically each time that it revolts against the practical constraints that bring it down, in order to raise itself up again to meet its ideal mission," said Villey (*Postérité*, p. 236). Montaigne settled, not only in a pedagogical sense, that chaotic polyhistoria into which later humanism had degenerated and which Rabelais had been unable to master fifty years earlier. For despite his genial playfulness, he lacked the means to illuminate and to ease the monotony of the jumble of things and words from a calm center of personality; in the end, he intended to again make of his Pantagruel an "abyss of knowledge" (a word that could, however, be meant humorously) and to bestow a six-story, multilingual library upon the men and women of his Abbey of Thelem. Montaigne, on the other hand, valued more highly than that a free essential education with a view of the richness of the world—the happy man who is as much at home in society, at court, on the battlefield as he is in the quiet library, a sovereign partner of his intellectual forefathers and involved in a communication with them which can be discontinued, then resumed, at any time, without the restrictions of the specialist, capable of admitting ignorance, ready to engage in self-mockery, attentive to the health of soul and body, with affection for any type of humanity, well-traveled, versed in the "book of the world," respecting truth, even when his opponent possesses it, without deception about his own importance, this tiny point in the universe, and thus intolerant of only one thing, namely, arrogance, rigidity, and violence. This idea, first suspected by Rabelais, seen and lived in full clarity by Montaigne, signified the internalized return of the former Italian universally educated man (*uomo universale*), now in France, and while it was bound once again to the nobility, the idea was still such that it made that noble class the birthplace of the freest humanity the French and the Europeans had ever enjoyed.

CHAPTER III

Abased Man

It is a powerful malady . . .

[*III, 2, 620 B*]

1. ABASED MAN

One can open the *Essais* to any random passage, they are always concerned with man: ". . . the study I am making, the subject of which is man . . ." (II, 17, 481 A). Montaigne stresses his predominant theme in this and similar wording often and almost extraneously. Whether nature, being, or God is discussed, it is always for the purpose of characterizing man. These are forces to which man must submit, dark areas over which the fantasy lights of human opinion play, restlessly and incompetently. And this book, which displays all moral, physical, political, intimate characteristics of man like an inexhaustible landscape, pushes him all the way to the edge of the cosmos: an appendage without influence, uncertain in his sense of rank, unclear in his driving forces, incalculable in his reactions to destiny, much more likely to be related to the animals than to the divine, and then again capable of finding happiness and peace in the midst of his ignorance and abasement, creating the art of social intercourse, attaining the summit of friendship, poor and rich alike, a surprise with which one never fully comes to terms—"so deep a labyrinth . . ." (II, 17, 481 A).

The humanity idea in the Roman humanistic mode which rigidly and pedagogically defines the boundaries of man's essential dignity does not appear in the *Essais*. It has made way for the confused all-too-human condition. The all-too-human condition is formulated with the help of the Christian concept of the *conditio humana*, but it is brought to light with the non-Christian satisfaction of the observer in its essence. But first this essence must take form. This is accomplished when Montaigne levels all ranking: ideal type, social, even moral rank. One does not learn about man's essence by what he makes of himself, but rather by how he receives what is given him from the hands of nature. Montaigne asks, what distinguishes the soul of an emperor from that of a shoemaker? Nothing—both are cast in the same mold. A prince waging war or a neighbor negotiating privately with a neighbor, beating a servant in one's household or ravaging a province: do these not stem from one and the same root? (II, 12, 350 A). Or: "The life of Caesar has no more to show us than our own; an emperor's or an ordinary man's, it is still a life subject to all human accidents" (III, 13, 822 B). And elsewhere: "A little man is a whole man, just like a big one" (I, 20, 67 C). The guiding theme of the *Essais* is that of calling man down to earth from his pretenses. Even on the last page in a late-period, handwritten insert, he states forcefully: "Yet there is no use our mounting on stilts, for on stilts we must still walk on our own legs. And on the loftiest throne in the world we are still sitting only on our own rump"—which in the mouth of Goethe's Mephistopheles reads:

> In the end you are—what you are.
> Whether you put on wigs with a million locks,
> Whether you put your feet into endless socks,
> You still always remain simply what you are.

A certain structuring that we must keep in mind is apparent in the viewpoints under which Montaigne observes man. The first consists in abasement; he stresses every conceivable thing that forces man down into an animal helplessness. The next renounces the negative value judgments though leaving the humbled creature in his abasement, discovers this creature's life circumstances there, and describes and affirms them. Finally, the third turns back to Montaigne; this observer of man, in describing himself, seizes the closest and least falsified material to answer the question of what we really are. In the following three chapters, the study of man conducted in the *Essais* will be portrayed within the framework of these three viewpoints: abased man, affirmed man, the self. It should be pointed out first that these three viewpoints cannot be considered as an historical development, as if Montaigne had first abased, then affirmed, and finally chosen himself as subject matter. All three points of view are present from the beginning, though they are stressed differently depending on the phase of the *Essais* considered; but none of them is ever entirely absent. They represent alternating perspectives from which he attempts to gain insight into the "deep labyrinth" till the end.

The *Essais* contain countless references to man's misery, weakness, and lack of dignity. One finds formulations such as the following: "human frailty" (I, 2, 8 A); "isn't man a miserable animal?" (I, 30, 148 A); "the bane of our condition" (II, 12, 380 C); "the weakness of our condition" (II, 23, 518 A), and so forth. The conclusion of the "Apology for Raymond Sebond" is interesting (II, 12, 457 A). There, in the first draft, Montaigne repeats a comment from Seneca: "O what a vile and abject thing is man if he does not raise himself above humanity!"[56] Thus he seems to go along with the stoic ethic of surmounting one's condition. However, a later insert calls this comment absurd, and thus stresses even more strongly what Montaigne has already said in the first draft (how contradictory!), namely, that man cannot rise above his humanity (*humanité*) without the help of God. But does God help him? The *Essais* have nothing to say to this question. One of Montaigne's sharpest sentences expressing abasement can be found in II, 17: he says that of all doctrines of antiquity, his favorites are "those that despise, humiliate, and nullify us most" (480 A).

Is that Christian? It appears to be. There is great similarity between this willingness for abasement and Christian-theological trains of thought on the sinful wretchedness of man. And in fact, Montaigne makes use of such trains of thought. But he only makes use of them incompletely. He departs from them at the point where they lead into the chance of redemption and the doctrine of man being originally made in the image of God. His claiming of Christian evidence for man's animal nature is only an heuristic prelude intended to open the way to a view of human essence. To attain this goal, support from antiquity is as welcome to him as Christian support. Montaigne willingly listens to the voices that refer to man within his limits, regardless of their source, whether they come from Paul's letters, the Ecclesiastics, hellenistic skepticism, or Plato. But then he switches focus to come into agreement with the one abased. Referring to Christianity this means: he uses it in order to then reject it.

2. APOLOGY FOR RAYMOND SEBOND

This brings us to one of the trickiest questions that arise in the study of Montaigne, namely his Christianity. We will have to speak of this often. But first we must look at the text in which he provides his most

consistent threatment of the abasement of man, specifically in the context of a theological problem: the text is the "Apology for Raymond
Sebond" (II, 12), which was written in several stages between 1573 and
1580. The theological problem can be stated as follows: is a natural
theology, that is, the basing of the contents of belief upon rational
cognition, possible? Montaigne answers in the negative. Within the
framework of this negation, which spans the whole of this extensive
Essay, he brings in everything he has to say against man's claim to
dignity, power, and a higher destiny.

Montaigne's involvement with theological questions was triggered
by the French religious battles that experienced their most acute phase
between 1570 and 1590. He experienced them firsthand in his home in
southwest France. His conservative orientation rejected the Reformation as a whole without delving into individual dogmatic debates, in
fact, without even differentiating between Luther and Calvin. The impetus of the religious battles led him, by way of some personal circumstances, to an examination of a liberal movement within Catholicism,
namely, natural theology, to which he was first exposed in the form of
Raymond Sebond's *Liber creaturarum*. The fact that he simultaneously
turned against natural philosophy and against the Reformation can be
explained in that he saw in both of these a common danger: a claim to
the autonomy of human reason. This equating of the two cannot be
justified in an exact historical sense, but it was done by several of his
contemporaries. Montaigne, who was not all that particular about how
accurately he reproduced outside didactic opinions, threw together
ideas that were only vaguely similar. The fideistic evidence with which
he intended to invalidate the Reformation would to a great extent have
been unnecessary if he had recognized the strong fideistic elements in
the teachings of Luther and Calvin. Meanwhile, the skeptic Montaigne
was simply concerned with opposing the self-certainty of human reason
in any form, without considering the particular denominational camp in
which he found or suspected it. The two movements, the Reformation
and natural theology, are the occasion for him to demonstrate that
abasement of man which he required in order to establish the basis of
his anthropology and his wisdom.

Montaigne relates (II, 12, 319 A) that his father once received from
Pierre Brunel (a humanist who originally had protestant leanings, then
reaffirmed Catholicism[57]) a copy of the *Theologia naturalis sive liber
creaturarum* by Raymond Sebond with the comment that it was a useful
book opposing the *nouvelletez* (modern teachings) *de Luther*. In order

to make this book, which supposedly pointed back toward orthodox beliefs, available to the French public, Montaigne translated it in 1569, upon his father's request. And as late as the beginning of his "Apology for Raymond Sebond" (II, 12), Montaigne appears to consider it a weapon in the battle against protestantism. Over the further course of the "Apology," however, from Montaigne's fideistic standpoint, it deteriorated just as much—when less openly—into condemnation as into protestantism. Montaigne himself dimly recognized that the theses of natural theology were not orthodox. But his fideism is also unorthodox. The result was the peculiarity (not infrequent in theological disputes) of an author attempting to save traditional doctrines of faith by combating unorthodox theses with other unorthodox theses—a confusion that would not interest us here if it did not shed light on Montaigne's own thinking. To understand the processes at work, we will restrict ourselves to what is really necessary.

Sebond's *Theologia naturalis* was written in 1434–1436 and appeared in a first printing in 1484 in Lyon, went through several editions up to the middle of the seventeenth century, and had an influence on Cusanus, Bovillus, and Grotius, among others.[58] It is a part of the movement of the fourteenth and fifteenth centuries against the Latin Averroism which began with Ramón Lull. That form of Averroism (though not Averroës himself) diverted the content of its beliefs into the irrational to such a degree that no logical access seemed possible, and it derived from the contrast between mysteries and the objects of reason a doctrine of "double truth," whereby religious truth retains its validity without damage in that it can be false to one's philosophical understanding. The consequences of this division were dangerous. Irrationalized faith was no longer sufficiently safe from rationalized criticism. The method of "double truth" threatened to turn into a trick with which reason, under the protection of the assurance that it was merely speaking rationally, thus not accountably, could break down the article of faith as something nonsensical. Lack of faith settled into the gap between faith and knowledge. To drive it out, Spanish and French theologians from Ramón Lull (who died in 1315) on, by reaching back to earlier ideas, particularly those of Anselm, attempted to establish an unconditional unity of faith and knowledge, of theology and philosophy, to such an extent that they could show the accessibility of the mysteries of faith through natural thinking. Thus the extreme irrationalism of the Averroistic school which threatened faith called forth the extreme, apologetic rationalism of "natural" theology, because Thomistic doctrine proved inadequate to refute the former. While Thomas did indeed leave room for the accountability of the "natural light" of reason, he only did so in the realm of the *praeambula fidei,* while the highest articles of faith (the trinity, God becoming man, etc.) were still considered beyond the reach of natural understanding. In contrast to this, the core idea of natural theology (which we can greatly simplify for our purposes) consisted in the conviction that logical, discursive thinking was capable of producing definite grounds for even the revealed, "absurd" truths of faith which would make them compelling even to the nonbeliever. Rationalism declared itself to be the trailblazer for faith. This represents, still within the area of theology, a first emergence of the modern autonomy of thought which would later be followed in the fifteenth and sixteenth centuries by something similar in the fields of the natural sciences and secular philosophy.

Sebond develops this concept of natural theology, showing a clearly demonstrable connection with Lull. He speaks of the independent responsibility of human perception, which although it does not make revelation superfluous, still is capable of working its way toward revelation by its own means. Characteristic is the renunciation of any authority, even the Bible; this was stated in the prologue and in fact followed through in the 330 chapters of the text. Sebond speaks as a rationalized empiricist—though in the form and speech of scholastic distinctions—of the things of natural perception, of man, and of the world. Admittedly, the arrangement of these things is based upon the customary gradualistic structure that leads from inanimate to animate things, and from there to ideas and to God, like the principle of *analogia entis.* But it is significant that all of that is perceived as an immanent area of perception accessible to anyone who is able to think. Sebond borrows from Lull the motif—otherwise an old motif—of understanding nature as the visible "book" in which God has placed his "script" in a form comprehensible to man (besides the Bible, which is accessible to only a few), and in this script man again represents the "noblest letters." It is in the study of this "book" (*liber naturae, liber creaturarum, liber mundi*) as well as in man's self-analysis that the *Theologia naturalis* intends to itself arrive at the empirical, rational insight into the relationship to God of all beings and the basis of creation, the full truth of which will then be left in the hands of revelation.

What must have appealed to Montaigne in this document, and in fact did, was its character of a layman's theology. Sebond expressly recommends the ease of his nonauthoritarian method which does not depend on specialized schooling, theological or other.[59] He thus continues the vulgarization of theological thinking which began with Lull. He remains readable in terms of the demands of the sixteenth century, which had already completed the transition from the esoteric specialty type of schooling into lay education through various other figures (the greatest of these was Erasmus). But Montaigne will reject the intent of this method of natural theology, which goes beyond this moment of educational history. Indeed, Sebond himself attempted to keep within the bounds of a common human preparatory lesson, and thought of revelation as another esoteric addition to it. Nevertheless, reason takes on a power of certainty by means of which it can from within itself concoct the divine order of creation, and an essential dignity is attributed to its bearer, namely man, which comes all the more to the forefront since it is so little limited by the concept of sin. This brings forth Montaigne's objection. Similar ideas to those in Sebond's book can be found in the works of the Italian humanist theologians on the *Dignitas hominis*. The Council of Trent rejected the prologue to the *Theologia naturalis* with its extreme conceptions of lay theology, thus it has disappeared from several later editions.

It is interesting to examine how Montaigne reacted in his translation of 1569 to these two particularities of the work, lay education and the autonomy of reason.[60] Later on he confirms that the work was popular reading among educated persons of his time in the first few pages of his "Apology" (where he also effectively summarizes the meaning of Sebond's *Theologia naturalis:* ". . . he undertakes by human and natural reasons to establish and prove against the atheists all the articles of the Christian religion . . ." 320 A). He intended to intensify the elegant effect of the book and through his translation to give it an appearance that was more appropriate to society than the "wild and barbaric" original, as he put it in his dedication.[61] When later in the "Apology" he gives the impression that the translation was a quickly completed side job that he undertook at his father's request, this is not quite in accordance with the facts, but it is evidence of his intention of removing the taint of pedantry from the matter. He understood and heightened Sebond's defrocking efforts. With his translation (which was printed several times into the middle of the seventeenth century), he not only in his own time of religious battles and dogmatic controversies created access for educated man to theological questions, but he became a patron of that sophisticated vulgar theological writing that aimed at the end of all possible manifestations of the separation between esoteric theology and lay religiosity, from the products of *humanisme dévot* to Guez de Balzac's *Socrate chrétien* and Pascal's *Lettres Provinciales.*

Nevertheless, the translation displays a pronounced reticence with respect to the autonomy claim of natural theology. The sharp formulations concerning knowledge acquired through reason which are found in the prologue are greatly moderated by Montaigne in a way that leads into the future critique in the "Apology." An apodictic *Ista scientia docet omnem hominem cognoscere realiter . . . omnem veritatem* is limited in the translation with "in so far as it is possible for natural reason"; *cognoscere . . . omnem debitum* becomes "to be acquainted with almost everything." It is difficult to decide whether this is prompted by the fact that the prologue is found in the index from 1564 on. It is improbable that Montaigne toned it down simply from his own orthodox knowledge, since for example he indiscriminately repeats the completely erroneous opinion that was suggested to him that the *Theologia naturalis* is a kind of quintessence from Thomas Aquinas (II, 12, 321 A). It is quite possible that even at the time of the translation his thinking was on its way to fideistic conviction, which runs contrary to the theses of natural theology. This is suggested by a passage in chapter 208. Sebond in a few words touches upon the beauty and safety of faith. Precisely here Montaigne adds one of the expansions that are otherwise rare in his translation, and he expounds with unmistakably fideistic tones on the irrationality of faith, which constitutes an exception lying well above the human power of reason, which is capable only of incompetent opinions, indicating that this faith is not at all something neatly self-evident. It is additionally true in a general way that the speculative chapter and the portrayal of the sacraments receive the most subdued translation, apparently without intimate involvement, whereas Montaigne's writer's drive awakens in the purely anthropological chapters and brings a life to the text that goes beyond what can be found in the original—that is, in those passages that are concerned not with the results of certainty, but rather with the preludes to natural theology. Such alterations and accentuations are informative. They are a sign of the Montaigne of the *Essais*, the fideist, skeptic, and analyst of man.

Concerning the formal and linguistic characteristics of the translation, suffice it to say here that they reach a higher, or at least a more cosmopolitan level than the original. A maturing writer transforms a dry treatise that is rigid with "firstly, secondly, thirdly's" into supple prose, pulls awkward distinctions together with a summarizing expression, avoids school terminology, replaces abstract nouns with colorful images or verbs of motion, eliminates the monotonous repetition of words by using rich synonyms, reproduces impersonal, hackneyed phrases such as *Probatum est, Dictum est* with personal expressions such as "I verified, I demonstrated," uses ironic highlights or judgmental adjectives to attain a more lively shading and round out the proportionless periods into a structured fullness—in brief, he brings the product of the Catalan master's little room into the open, clear air. In this translation one can detect a spirit who is not satisfied with mere repetition, but rather who begins to recast what he touches, and one can perceive a language that, although it is still attached to the chain of the foreign model, pulls away impatiently toward an independence and sensual vividness—which is indeed attained a few years later.

And now to the "Apology for Raymond Sebond." The title of the Essay does not express what is said in it. Montaigne is not concerned with a defense of Sebond, nor with a direct rejection of him. Rather, he is concerned with retrieving theological questions from their own abstractness. What faith is, how its ideal manifestation must be constructed, these questions retreat before the observation of how faith appears in temporally, spatially, individually different humanity. Even the discussion of the religious battles of the epochs at the beginning of the "Apology" points out the fact that Montaigne is oriented toward the circle of comprehensible, current experiences. Factual man is the standard and the field of observation. He does not relativize man from an ideal model of faith, rather, he relativizes this from man. Sebond and natural theology's claims to certainty founder as unsuitable. For Montaigne, natural theology serves as an example of intellectual behavior whose lack of success can be used to demonstrate the abasement of man.

The "Apology" does not offer a set outcome toward which the author need only march forward, presenting illustrations. Rather, it contains a movement of thought which, like the many-year-long process of writing it out, changes direction several times, and is thus burdened with numerous contradictions. Despite this, a basic line of thought can be extracted from it. At first, in the first few pages, Montaigne seems to consider a natural theology possible. This is more along the lines of Thomas Aquinas than Sebond, however: a rational comprehensibility of faith is taken into account, but it is subordinate to enlightenment, which rises beyond reason (II, 12, 321–322 A). But this is followed with the comment: Do we have such an enlightenment? Have we, as the inadequate humans that we are, the capacity for pure faith? Do we have faith, other than in conceptual distortions or the disfigurements of it arising from denominational debates and political interests? And where, really, is the light and peace that would have to pervade us all if we really had faith? For it is really like this: some act as if they believed, those who believe, again, do not know what they believe, and man handles religion like wax, he makes of it the most conflicting things, draws it into any random opinion, nourishes or conceals his vices with it, believes what only habit suggests he believe . . . (322–325). The problem of natural theology initially taken up from Sebond is forced aside by these thought processes. The concreteness of what is all-too-human comes into focus. Thus we find this comment: "We are Christians by the same title that we are Perigordians or Germans" (325 B). This well-known sentence—which in all earnestness had been interpreted as a confession of Catholicism—represents nothing other than an illustration of the thought expressed shortly before this in the first draft: ". . . we receive our religion only in our own way and with our own hands . . . they are human ties." It implies that pure, blessed faith received with pure hands that are not spotted with what is all-too-human is an ideal case, it is conceivable, but it is refuted by prevailing reality. Habit and environment determine our religious behavior to a much greater extent. The revelation bestowed upon man is confined within the limits of man's powers to take it in, powers that can only process something unconditional as something conditional by burdening it with inertia, habits, egoism, emotions, and sensory needs: "It is for mortal and human religions to be accepted by human guidance" (325 A). This appears to refer only to the classical religions if one looks at the context of the passage. But the "Apology" as a whole is evidence that Montaigne is able to observe religion, regardless of which religion, only in its connection with humanity, as "mortal and human religion."

At first he makes these statements as if they were a complaint: "It should not be like this." But they represent something else, namely the determination that "this is how it is." One can see from the insertions how Montaigne reinforced this determination theoretically and anecdotally in reworking the Essay. A realistic thought has been injected in front of the theological expositions: where man is involved, there is no ideality—and we do not have access to any areas in which man would not be involved. A brave sense of the world arises in Montaigne here, and it brings a completely new point of view to the tiring controversies of the theologians (and later, the philosophers as well). It is in the literal sense a point of view, a seeing with one's own eyes: "I see this evident"

(323 C). The abasement of man is introduced with the observation that his religious perfection may be occasionally possible as "some rare nature," but it cannot generally be attained. Human reality becomes visible due to its unfortunate quality of spoiling moral and religious idealities. The possible unconditional quality of faith fades before the daily evidence of man's limitedness. Even as the "Apology" continues, and then in the later insertions—apart from consideration of the other Essays—it becomes apparent how small a step it is from this heuristic abasement of man to his complicity in his own baseness. What is real then no longer is seen as a fall from the ideal, but rather as a perpetual actuality above which an isolated, great individual occasionally rises.

But what becomes of Sebond? We see from the preceding discussion why Montaigne uses theological motifs. They provide him with the ideal form of faith, and he can use its unattainability to show the state of man. He takes them, by chance, from Sebond. But very few pages after the initial sentences of the "Apology" in which he appears to endorse natural theology he no longer treats Sebond as its representative. What attracts him to Sebond is not his rational method of providing proof, but rather his aura of being inspired. He defends Sebond as a person inspired—against rationalistic criticism. It is only when reason is divinely guided, he explains, that it has the assurance of being able to penetrate the truths of faith—and Sebond was divinely guided (II, 12, 327 A). For this reason, not because he furthered natural theology, Sebond had the right to speak. Strange reversal! Montaigne arbitrarily elevates Sebond to the ranks of the enlightened. To this extent, he is and remains his defender. And he himself walks down into the field in which the battle rages for and against Sebond, and ultimately, for and against faith. But in fact this is the same field upon which Sebond and natural theology can also be found. But Montaigne overlooks or ignores this. As representative of natural theology, he has in mind the rationalistic critics of Sebond. But since methodologically they are related to him (namely in their rationalistic handling of theological questions), in the end he still encounters Sebond; without expressly intending this or stating it, he becomes Sebond's opponent.

One can see that what happens in this confused process is simply that Montaigne permissively shifts the circumstances of the history of dogma because he is not at all concerned with a true-to-source analysis of texts. (The fact that he makes Sebond into one of the inspired ones is not necessarily a trick, although one might well expect that of him; it can be Sebond's connection with a casual remembrance of the *Illuminatio*, the

familiar identifying feature of the Franciscan-Lullian school as a whole.)
His interpretational precision is as lacking in rigor here as it was in the
treatment of classical texts. But his principle striving is all the more
determined. Under the appearance of combating Sebond's rationalistic
critics, and with the firm intention that we will see whether man can
bring forth stronger reasons than the "inspired" Sebond, Montaigne
turns against the claim of the fitness of reason as a whole.

And as soon as he gets to this point, he throws his accusation at
mankind with a vengeance: "The means I take to beat down this frenzy,
and which seems fittest to me, is to crush and trample underfoot human
arrogance and pride; to make them feel the inanity, the vanity and nothingness, of man; to wrest from their hands the puny weapons of their
reason" (327 A). Under the fury of this accusation, human reality comes
to light, and the observer finally turns to this: "Let us consider for the
moment man alone, without outside assistance, armed solely with his
own weapons, and deprived of divine grace and knowledge . . ." (328 A).
Later on, Pascal will intend to do something similar. But Montaigne does
not take Pascal's path into the problems of merciless, earthly existence
which compel one to follow the call of deliverance, a path that passes
through man into the hope of grace. Montaigne remains with man and in
man. The motif of the lack of grace (*despourvu de la grace* . . .) vanishes.
And Sebond and his theological theses vanish from the "Apology." He
has been entirely forgotten from the middle of this Essay on. Montaigne
does not even make an effort to reflect upon the extent to which the main
elements of his "Apology" precisely contradict what is written in Sebond
and what he himself once translated.

What Montaigne has to say about faith always ends up back in the
disempowerment of reason, and thus in man's abased position. He
does not intend to harm faith. To the contrary, faith remains possible;
but its content, like any sort of transcendence, is shifted into an absolute darkness. The fact that it must be said of man that he can only
believe blindly and only if he surrenders all of his natural capabilities is
noted as one of the basic signs of his powerlessness. Man comes more
in touch with his own insignificance, the more he experiences the
remoteness of God; the more willing he is to concede the incomprehensibility of God, the greater God becomes for him. This thinking leads
to fideism. This is the path Montaigne follows. But his fideism has
neither pathos nor a significant trace of mystical longing. It signifies an
intellectual awareness of human limitation. Montaigne does not strive
to go beyond this. His fideism is negative in nature: the certainty of

uncertainty. Montaigne's "theology"—if one can speak of such a thing at all—represents a detour to the anthropology of man's inner world. It requires the remoteness of God to safeguard the insignificance of man within which it is established.

Although fideistic Montaigne returns its full due to transcendence, he never concerns himself specifically with the difficult principles of faith, namely the trinity, original sin, the concept of God become man, the death of the Redeemer. He neither courts nor combats them, he leaves them alone. Renunciation of their natural knowability does not drive him to a leap into a different order of truth. There is no despair such as "I cannot reach this height with my powers"—there is no passionate longing to be pulled up by it in grace and to experience its absurdity as the overpowering glory of its truth. Expressed in Pascal's Augustinian terms: no *ordre de la charité* torments him from above and entices him to praise the deeper *ordre de l'esprit* (*Pensées*, ed. Brunschvicg, fragment 793). As greatly as he tears open the abyss between faith and knowledge, beside the discredited knowledge, faith appears only as a theoretically acknowledged chance, but not as a transforming force. Everything ends up in the factuality of man and in a consent to the limits revealed as a result of his experiencing of the darkness. One has the impression that Montaigne with his fideism is unburdening himself of the contents of faith in order to have his peace with them. What there is of piety in the "Apology" and the other Essays is to such a small extent specifically Christian, to such a great extent generally oriented to philosophy of life, that he can express it better with the words and contents of hellenistic wisdom than with Christian doctrine. This also explains his closeness to classical skepticism. Together with fideism, and even better than this, it helps him to disempower reason and determine man's abased position. This combination of interests also is a part of the basic characteristics of the sixteenth century (and the seventeenth as well), and is based upon a similarity of essence. "The combination of skepticism and fideism is classic and timeless," in Gilson's words.[62]

Modern research uses the term *fideism* in an historically more precise sense to designate the Christian doctrine of faith which rejects a reason-based treatment of the revealed truths.[63] This concerned older principles that had arisen in prescholasticism, and which were renewed at the height of scholasticism and also in late scholasticism (Duns Scotus and Ockham), and which then in the following centuries, in alliance with nominalism, Pyrrhonic skepticism, and the empirical sciences, attained considerable significance that went beyond the bounds of the theologi-

cal discipline. Fideism is the counter-movement to natural theology, but
the former is just as unorthodox as the latter. Whereas Thomas Aquinas
assigned knowledge attained by reason the task of working faith in its
own hands without rationalizing it, in natural theology, contrariety to
reason is exhausted, thus so is the transcendence of the articles of faith
as a result of their adaptation to rational understanding. Fideism, on the
other hand, avoids reproducing and safeguarding them through natural
thinking and silences the logically monitoring drive for knowledge at
the entrance of the realm of faith; rather, its logical impenetrability
serves as its most profound proof. Fideism, in a different manner than
natural theology, but with the same liberating effect, breaks down the
once existing hierarchical unity of the intellectual orders upon which
orthodox Catholicism had been building for centuries into individual
parts. Knowledge and faith separate completely. Here is one of the
origins of the doctrine of "double truth" which for free thinkers could
lead to the development of statements critical of religion. On the other
hand, in fideism, a religious inwardness is also expressed, and with
fideism's help it was also able to protect itself from the elimination of
transcendence by school theology. Thus one similarly finds fideistic motifs in Pomponazzi and the other Paduans, where they serve the hidden
purpose of dissolving the Christian structure of doctrines on the basis of
a philosophy that supposedly does not touch upon faith, as was also
true of mystics, reformers, and later the Jansenists, in other words, all
intellects who were seeking a new form for their lay piety which was
independent of the church. The latter is the reason fideism is encountered so frequently in popular and humanistic writings. After even Erasmus sympathized with it,[64] and after it received support from classical
skepticism, by the middle of the sixteenth century it had become such a
widespread movement that it can no longer be attributed to any single
author of this epoch. The Curia did not offer any resistance to it worthy
of mention before the Council of Trent; only the Papal Bull *Unigenitus*
of 1713 expressly rejected it.

Due to this general proliferation, we can no longer be sure of where
Montaigne received his fideistic impetus. It could go back to his education in the *Collège de Guyenne* where he was a pupil of Buchanan,[65]
who was influenced by Paduan fideism. However, fideism is incorporated so consistently into Montaigne's manner of thinking that here,
too, one again should speak less of one "influence"—which in any case
would be impossible to pinpoint—than of a receptivity of his intellect
that took in what his already established predisposition encountered.

The fideist Montaigne does not play a game of hide-and-seek using the "double truth" concept in the manner of the Paduans. He lacked the certainty of philosophical reason. Although he, too, at times cast critical shadows over Christian life under the guise of simply offering non-binding "opinions," the content of these "opinions" was in fact too unresolved to have a very hostile effect. It simply brushed over its object, softly raising questions. But its object, faith, does not sink. It is always there, in the distant horizon, as a transcendent foreboding and as a sign of human shipwreck. From time to time it again assumes a Christian form. The plurality of biblical aphorisms which Montaigne has inscribed in his library tower is made up of fideistically utilizable texts containing the warning against human claims to knowledge of the Godhead. One finds among them the words from the psalm *Judicia Domini abyssus multa* (Ps. 35, 7). This is found near the other phrase from the Old Testament on *Deus absconditus* (Jes. 45, 15) which is quoted so often throughout fideism both in the prescholastic period and in the sixteenth and seventeenth centuries. We then find in the "Apology" the comment that is completely Christian and in the style of mysticism and negative theology: "Our powers are so far from conceiving the sublimity of God, that of the works of our creator those bear his stamp most clearly, and are most his, that we understand least. To Christians it is an occasion for belief to encounter something incredible. It is the more according to reason as it is contrary to human reason" (368–369 A). But comments such as this are the exception, and they are only made to demonstrate the insignificance of the human capacity to know using the example of the fideistic irrationality of faith. A later insertion adds an Augustine and a Tacitus quotation, a paraphrase of Plato, and finally an additional Cicero quotation: Christian and pagan evidence together serve the same anthropological aim with no attempt to establish a hierarchy of authority. Then Montaigne takes up another motif of negative theology wherein the naming of God conceals his essence rather than reveals it (369 C). As a whole, the "Apology" frequently opposes anthropomorphic images of God, mainly with the help of classical quotations (383, 393–394, etc.). Montaigne knows that divine will is far removed from all human differentiations and levels of importance: "As if it were more or less to him to move an empire or the leaf of a tree; and as if his providence were exercised otherwise in deciding the outcome of a battle than the jump of a flea!" (394 C). But his knowledge of this does not work to the benefit of the Christian God. The agnostic conclusion is the main content and it will be combined with pieces of evidence taken from

Pyrrhonic skepticism. He even finds religions among those of antiquity which revere the incomprehensibility of God (380 B/C), but he does not find them, as was done in earlier theology, to be examples of a pre-Christian presentiment of truth. We find an example of the low energy invested in his recommendations of Christian faith in a passage in which he discusses immortality at some length (411–415). After he has established doubt, based upon the contradictions in the various philosophical and religious doctrines of immortality, not only in the possibility of deciding the question, but in the idea of immortality itself, he simply leaves everything else up to faith. But what was not a philosophical certainty will not be a certainty of faith either. Faith to him is simply a higher form of uncertainty, a nebulous view into the realm of transcendent possibilities.

Meanwhile, Montaigne was considered an ally in the conflict against the Reformation by his contemporaries. Villey provided sufficient evidence of this (see the Notes).[66] Montaigne's making this impression confirms the utility of fideism as a doctrine that safeguards faith. But with respect to Montaigne this is a misunderstanding, analogous to the other misunderstanding of reading him as a neostoic author. The real reason one counted him among the apologists for Catholicism probably lay in his strongly emphasized conservative church orientation; his practical conservatism was confused with a fundamental theoretical conviction. Otherwise, the *humanisme dévot* that developed around the turn of the century, with its simplification, adapted to the world, of Catholic doctrines of faith and with its skeptical generosity, was useful to him. François de Sales and Pierre Camus were approving readers of the *Essais*. Furthermore, the Roman Curia spoke in Montaigne's favor. The less gentle objections of their censorship of the first edition of the *Essais* consistently concerned passages of secondary significance and characteristically not the skeptical-fideistic ones.[67] But from this we can only point to the formal permissiveness of his religious comments. Their lack of absoluteness or orthodoxy first came to light when stricter intellects of the seventeenth century tested him: Pascal, Malebranche, Bossuet. Pascal in particular became his powerful opponent in that although he did include the fideistic disruption of reason in the process of faith, he considered it a first dialectical, dramatic moment; the other moment, that of possible redemption, which stemmed from the God-given essential worth of man, came into conflict with the first with the effect of intensifying faith. Seen from the standpoint of Pascal's claims, Montaigne appears as the spokesman for despairing mankind. This is a clouding of the situation which really distorts Montaigne. If Montaigne had *expressly* rejected Christianity, then Pascal's judgment would have been correct. But he is richer and wiser than Pascal perceived; he is simply operating from a different base. But in any case, one thing was revealed through Pascal's absolute requirement: that Montaigne's Christian piety was much too slight to play a role in any serious religious discussion. He cannot even represent the role of despair which Pascal reserved for him. Pascal forced him into his own dialectic as a symptom of mankind without mercy—and crushed him. Here we see an event worthy of consideration, namely that religious absoluteness can be blind to the fullness of spirits: "There are many rooms in my father's house" (*John*, 14,2).

3.   CHRISTIANITY AND CHURCH

More remains to be said about Montaigne's relationship to religion, Christianity, and the Catholic Church. He finds himself in the transition from orthodox faith to a philosophy of life version of piety in view of a transcendence that has become uncertain, to a psychologically objectifying understanding of all kinds of religious content, and also, still, to the formal conservative attachment to church institutions. This transition takes place effortlessly and without crisis, filled with awareness of what it is leaving behind, and without the sharpness engendered by enlightenment.

Montaigne, like all true skeptics, is tolerant, not destructive. He always revered great religious abilities, clear in the knowledge that he himself did not possess them. Thus in a late passage he still speaks respectfully and at length about spiritual renunciation of the world. But there is distance in his words. The last sentence of this passage begins: "And he who can really and constantly kindle his soul with the flame of that living faith and hope . . ." (I, 39, 180–181 C)—and that means: *I myself* cannot do it. As a sharp observer, though, he is able to differentiate between genuine and false piety. Thus he disapproves on one occasion of thoughtless praying and the dishonesty of men who make the sign of the cross when the bells sound and yet cannot refrain from hatred, miserliness, and injustice, as if their principle were the following: "To vices their hour, to God his hour" (I, 56, 231 B). But this interests him less because it profanes what is holy, for he sees this sort of thing in himself as well: shortly before this he confesses, even when yawning I make the sign of the cross. Rather, it interests him as a case of human inconsistency which attempts to reconcile something irreconcilable. He speaks in the same Essay I, 56 of his own praying (229–230 A/B). One finds in this passage something lacking passion or anxiety, it is not a prayer of entreaty, but rather one of resignation, related to the philosophical prayer of the Stoic school, without an intimate bond between God and the self, and infinitely removed from the mystery of the mastery of God,[68] usually just a ritualistic paternoster. One does not expect otherwise. He prefers to study religious behavior as one curiosity among all the other human curiosities. Thus he concerns himself with cases of asceticism as examples of illusionary generation of happiness, and categorizes them with the principle that the worth or lack of worth of a matter is based upon the formation of opinion or delusion (I, 14, 42 C). He treats the "spiritual death" of Paul's letters as a variation of suicide (II, 3, 260 A; presumably according to *Philipp.* I, 23). He conjectures on suggestions in instances of stigmata and ecstatic experiences, consigning them to the order of psychogenic illnesses (I, 21, 69–70 A/C). In Rome, he watches the heads of the apostles shown in San Giovanni. Afterward, he notes this matter in his journal with the calmness of someone who is not even angered by the deception he has seen through, and he acknowledges it as a curiosity of ethnology. His response to the three drops of blood on the altar plate of San Pietro in Pisa is similar (*Journal de Voyage*). He writes an Essay on odors, and does not forget the incense, the sensual stimulus to a spiritual gathering (I, 55, 228–229 B). With the late Renaissance moralist's need to track down processes of deception and delusion, he extracts religious experience from the directness of personal experience and repositions it to serve as the material for the recognition that this is how man is, to a great extent physical body, sensuality, susceptibility to seduction, even in his finest moments.

To this is added a sense of the spatial and temporal diversity of mankind. One of the major tendencies in this epoch, the comparative study of religions (Louis Le Roy, Jean Bodin), also exercises its influence in the *Essais*. Despite his practical conservatism, Montaigne preserves an extraordinary theoretical openness to all religions. He sees them as actualities that are interesting from the standpoint of cultural history and ethnography. As with all things human, he functionalizes them as creations that derive their nature from natural conditions, just as the plants and animals do, turning out one way in one climate, another in a different one. This is no different from the thinking, along Aristotelian lines, of Le Roy and Bodin.[69] ". . . the form of our being depends on the

air, the climate, and the soil where we are born—not only the complexion, the stature, the constitution and countenance, but also the faculties
of the soul," as he writes in the "Apology" (433 B). Shortly before
writing this sentence, Montaigne illustrated this by enumerating various
cults and forms of belief of various peoples (Christian peoples included): it is one of those chaotic accumulations of customs (*coutumes*)
which are so numerous in the *Essais* and which correspond to the
ethnographic empiricism of the epoch which he uses without consideration of a moral ranking to conclude that all things human are relative.
In this way he avoids any criticism of non-Christian religions. He is
more inclined to do the opposite, and on one occasion he takes the
opportunity to argue for the moral superiority of the Mohammedans,
who would put Christianity in its quite un-Christian behavior to shame
(II, 12, 322 B),[70] an argument heard rather frequently in literature of
that time and earlier.

However, where Montaigne speaks of Christian doctrines of faith, a
double restraint is apparent: restraint in the positive treatment of the
doctrines as well as in the critical approaches. We have already said that
none of the specifically Christian or even Catholic basic dogmas is
expressed. For all practical purposes, Christ is not discussed at all.
Montaigne contents himself with the formal reference to the authority
"of our beliefs." Not even this much is present in the Essay on the
education of children; there is no place in it for the religious needs of the
child being educated. Indeed, there are several passages in which without a doubt one finds a critical dig at Christian doctrines (for example,
II, 12, 385 and 411 A). But they are vague; they insinuate a critical
conclusion rather than state it openly, treat a subject in the context of
classical doctrines of the gods and the soul so that one sees these, rather
than Christianity, as the ones attacked, or they retreat so insistently to a
focus on the incompetence of mere opinion that one can find little in
their wording to accuse of insubordination. If one compares passages
such as these with French literature contemporary to them, it becomes
even more apparent how tame they are. Nowhere in Montaigne do we
find the sarcasm of a Rabelais or a Bonaventure Des Périers, who counter faith with their sensuality of life or their rationalistic enlightenment.
Nowhere do we find intrusions into faith such as those in Bodin, who in
the *Heptaplomeres* treats the paradoxes of God become man, the deliverance from sin, the mystery of the last supper and divine mercy for
those most wretched, ironically, in tones quite like those of Voltaire
(though disguised with the alibi of using a dialogue technique), as outra-

geous absurdities. Montaigne removed himself from the conflict between agreement and criticism. The reference to faith is in itself no
longer faith, but rather a methodical act for the purpose of recognizing
the limit of human essence. And conversely, the hidden criticism of
Christianity does not represent an impiety, rather it is an openness to
every kind of belief. He considers Christianity a great possibility for
human spirituality, but only one among many.[71]

But all this applies only to the theoretical realm. In actual practice it
is otherwise. This brings us to Montaigne's conservatism, behind which
a fundamental process of modern epochs emerges: the divergence of
theory and practice.

Montaigne is faithful to the Church. But he does not derive his
conservatism from agreement with the objective content of the truths of
Catholic doctrine. The Church is to him something that has been a given
and which has created order since olden times; anyone born into its
circle of influence will do well to submit to it. His approval of its
institutional power arises in the same manner as his approval—
described in the next chapter—of the positive legal axioms and inherited social systems: namely, as a act of practical conduct which cannot
be disrupted by the critical results of theoretical reflection. Montaigne's
conservatism (at the same time a classical case of French conservatism
as a whole) moves in confusing contradictions, and yet it is completely
honest. He makes absolutely no effort to evade these contradictions. He
wants them. For they represent his true self—and thus the symptom of
nonharmonizable mankind in an individual case; he broadens the latter
to learn about the former.

In II, 17 he writes: "This capacity for shifting truth . . . and this free
will not to enslave my belief easily, I owe principally to myself" (499 A).
This is one of the fullest statements of his theoretical will for freedom
which dares to attribute to itself the capacity for finding his own truth
and which remains in reserve against all outside and handed down ways
of thinking, believing, and behaving. And then there are sentences with
a quite different orientation, such as this one: ". . . always adding this
refrain, not perfunctorily but in sincere and complete submission: that I
speak as an ignorant inquirer, referring the decision purely and simply
to the common and authorized beliefs . . ." (III, 2, 612 B). Or the beginning of the Essay on prayers (tacked on after censorship by the Curia in
1582): "I put forward formless and unresolved notions, . . . And I submit them to the judgment of those whose concern it is to regulate not
only my actions and my writings, but even my thoughts" (I, 56, 229 A).

Thus we have: no submission (or at least no unexamined submission)—then again submission treated as self-evident; then reservation of his own freedom—then again relinquishment of freedom: the "contradictions" amount to a clear conflict between these opposite positions.

But this conflict is nothing other than the basic empirical knowledge that weaves its way through the *Essais,* namely that the intellect has the capacity for freedom, but not the capacity for certainty. The intellect must take on both positions: that of power, and that of impotence. In Montaigne's open writing, produced always from the particular moment, we find separate expression of ideas which when referred to one another represent a contrary interaction of the intellect's independence and need for security. The intellect when left to its own devices stumbles into disorder and lack of moderation. Thus something must be created to stop it—conversely, it must break through what stops it, it must break through authority so that it does not die. Montaigne expresses one or the other of these convictions depending on whether at the moment he has in mind the danger or the freedom of the intellect. In understanding this, we must keep in mind the fact that when he calls for authority, he means only its formal role of setting limits, not the superiority of its content: "Our mind is an erratic, dangerous, and heedless tool; it is hard to impose order and moderation upon it . . . People are right to give the tightest possible barriers to the human mind . . . They bridle and bind it with religions, [note the plural!] laws, customs . . . It is more expedient to place them in tutelage" (II, 12, 419–420 A/B). Montaigne recognizes the Christian faith in just such a manner as the chance of setting a limit to the power of the intellect which leads into impotence. The spying, curious, adventurous intellect is called to order from another sphere so that it will not perish from its adventures and its divisions: "And since I am not capable of choosing, I accept other people's choice and stay in the position where God put me. Otherwise I could not keep myself from rolling about incessantly" (II, 12, 428 A). Montaigne knows this—and yet does not cease his "rolling about incessantly." This fluctuation between freedom and submission is characteristic of him. He surrenders to it. But he is explicit that faith is an authority for him only by virtue of its function of indicating the limits of the autonomous intellect.

This formal view becomes completely clear with respect to the Church, that is, from the point at which Montaigne crosses the line from theory into practice. Abased, fluctuating man for whom all intellectual contents are shifted into possibilities among which he cannot decide requires a basis for his actions: it can be found in his historical reality. Here man acts in that he obeys and preserves what is given. There one is not seeking truth but rather a suitable order. For Montaigne, who was born Catholic, his church is the embodiment of this order. He went to confession, combatted Protestantism, sponsored a votive tablet in Loreto, and died with clergy present: "We must either submit completely to the authority of our ecclesiastical government, or do without it completely. It is not for us to decide what portion of obedience we owe it" (I, 27, 134 A). But we can also find a statement the opposite of this. One might point out that despite his subjection to Roman censorship, he did not strike out or even alter the passages for which he was reprimanded. One might further point out that he rejected any compulsion to believe (III, 11, 789 B), and that he described that visit to Loreto with unmistakable irony (cf. *Journal*), and much more. But those are theoretical matters that do not interfere with the practical, conservative attitude as a whole. Montaigne does not even from the onset place man and himself in a higher position than the strife-torn abasement of existence in the world in which, while order is possible, no order has theoretical ideality. In his thinking he may know that something absolutely right and true cannot be realized. But his practical conduct lets this insight rest. He is content with the fact that the existing order into which man is born and which bears the mark of continuance is deserving of authority. Montaigne's conservatism vis-à-vis the Church signifies the consistent fulfillment of human factuality around which all his observations revolve: being as one actually is in that which is imperfect: "We are Christians by the same title that we are Perigordians or Germans": this well-known sentence sheds light upon his conservative fundamental attitude. Each form of order is a part of general coincidence, but it is also a particular necessity. When we obey the concrete order we inherit, we obey the destiny of our essence that we can only exist within something limited. Thus the skeptical-fideistic shifting of the contents of beliefs outward into what cannot be known and their formalization into a limit to the freedom of reason can certainly be combined with the acknowledgment of their institutional authority embodied in the Church. And critical freedom can in the same manner unite with it vis-à-vis the doctrines of faith. For critical freedom falls silent in the face of the authority of handed-down historical reality. Or more accurately, it remains limited to the theoretical internal realm of individuality. The need for practical security does not obliterate this critical freedom any more than critical freedom can make changes in the order of reality as it is handed down without falling into chaos. Freedom and commitment, doubt and obedience are contrasts that arise from the split in human nature between power and impotence. Man must tolerate their contradiction to protect himself from destruction and he must reconcile the two in an alliance—not in hypocrisy, but in the honesty of being as he is: *un miserable animal.*

Expressed in this behavior are a clever sense of the world and a renunciation of the inner transformation of man by faith. Other than this, Montaigne's marriage of fideistic doctrine and institutional conservatism represents the abbreviation of a process that had been in progress from the fourteenth century on. The logical absurdity of the doctrines of salvation and the "arbitrariness of God" were then considered characteristics of religious truth, and the validity of the latter was based upon authority alone; thus authority in the sense of "curialism," that is, a ceremonial ecclesiasticism that was content with the formal subjection of Catholics,[72] was all the more strongly reinforced. To this extent, Montaigne's position vis-à-vis religion is also a reflection of circumstances in the early modern period before the Council of Trent. An additional factor for him as a Frenchman was the particular situation in his country in which as a result of centuries of connections between the Church and the office of king, an attack upon one was also necessarily experienced as an attack upon the other; the safeguarding of the Church's authority was at the same time a political requirement. However, he does not go into details here either. His conservatism is more a generally anthropological and sociological concept than a theological one. He returns in this form in the ideas of French freethinkers of the eighteenth and nineteenth centuries, always in an easily acceptable form of dogmatic casualness or even religious indifference along with an outward preservation of Church tradition and its concept of order which stemmed from the classical Roman world—reminiscent of Barrès' pointed comment: "I am an atheist, but I am Catholic."

The contemporary historical urgency of Montaigne's conservative views grew out of the Reformation battles. He saw their effect on party politics and the national, legal, and religious life in France directly.[73] He interpreted the Reformation as a break with authority, and much more with respect to the social and political consequences than consequences for the Church. This is probably connected with the fact that he knew of the Calvinists' attempt to expand theological doctrine into doctrines of political revolution. When in the *Essais* he does not make a distinction between Lutheranism and Calvinism, this is due to his indifference to dogmatic details. He only sees the anarchistic disruptions for which both were generally considered responsible. He does not attack Luther's or Calvin's doctrines of faith, rather, he attacks the reformatory politics. He considers these an overstepping of the boundaries between theory and practice, because from a doctrine that they developed themselves they derive a claim to the right to interfere in the order that was handed down to them. In the protestant principle of freedom of conscience, he, who in his own theoretical thinking exercises the greatest freedom, only perceives the negative moment without an eye for the protestants' deeper bond to authority as embodied in the disclosed word of God. Here, in the field of religious practice, Montaigne separates those who have been called from those who have not, and does so with an energy that cannot be found elsewhere in the *Essais*. Like Erasmus and Bodin, he fears that proliferation of the beliefs that one can make decisions based upon one's individual conscience will grant to those who have not been called ("the common herd" II, 12, 320 A) a personal authority that they will not know how to handle and thus can only use in a disastrous way by misusing it to apply doctrinaire force to others. This fear was not unjustified with respect to Calvinism. Additionally, it is in harmony with the generally accepted French aversion to constraints upon conscience, which probably represents one of the more profound reasons for the comparatively low level of success of the Reformation in France, and which was quite content under the formal-authoritarian Catholic ecclesiasticism.

When Montaigne occasionally does discuss protestant doctrines, he bases his criticism upon fideistic propositions. Thus when he opposes Bible reading by laymen, he responds: the Bible must not be diminished to a subject of conversation in "parlor and kitchen" or robbed of its esoteric character through translations—"Formerly they were mysteries; at present they are sports and pastimes" (I, 56, 232 C). These are the usual objections of enemies of the Reformation, but they are particularly appropriate to his fideism. If one collects everything he had to say against protestantism, one winds up with the same chain of reservations that could be found up until Bossuet: where personal decision by the individual in religious matters is permitted, man's weakness of essence will increase, the argumentative presumption of certainty will grow into an acute illness, namely verbal altercations (II, 12, 393–394, on the supper dispute); when this happens, faith is shattered, and from this, in theological matters, the danger of atheism, and in practical matters, the danger of a division into partisan sects arises—and from this the danger of a dissolution of the unity of church and state, and so forth. One could well be surprised at these reservations in Montaigne (since in fact he knows these dangers and lives with them as characteristics of really being human, even his own quality of being human) if one did not recognize that he only gives them this type of polemical meaning in practical matters. He seems in some passages in the *Essais* to proceed from the position that he would have tolerated protestantism if he had only been exposed to it from a theoretical viewpoint. But since he saw it entangled in partisan matters of the church and state politics, it was a practical problem for him.

But two passages must still be presented. They have a deeper impact, and at the same time they provide insight into how Montaigne always conducts his thinking from the viewpoint of concrete, imperfect human essence. A late insertion in the "Apology" mentions cult forms of antiquity (according to Plutarch) which are limited to a reverence for God which lacks symbols, "to a purely intellectual religion, without any predetermined object or any material admixture." But Montaigne disapproves of this: "The human spirit cannot keep on floating in this infinity of formless ideas; they must be compiled for it into a definite picture after its own pattern. The divine majesty has thus let itself be somewhat circumscribed within corporeal limits on our behalf; his supernatural and heavenly sacraments show signs of our earthy condition; his worship is expressed by perceptible rituals and words; for it is man that believes and prays" (II, 12, 381 C). Here this appears to be directed only at those classical cult forms (the Pythagorean ones), but it contains a thought that in an earlier passage was unmistakably intended to apply to protestantism: "It is still man we are dealing with, and it is a wonder how physical his nature is. As for those (The Protestants) who, in recent years, tried to construct for us a system of religious practice that is all contemplative and spiritual, they should not be astounded if there are some who think that religion would have melted away and slipped through their fingers if it did not hold fast among us as a mark, title, and instrument of division and faction rather than by itself" (III, 8, 710 B). Thus both passages make reference to man, that limited, fragile being with his mixed structure of body and soul, who is unable to comprehend the pure ideality of God if it is not transformed into symbols and words to which his senses are capable of responding. This is a criticism of the internalized service of God of protestantism, with its paucity of images and symbols. In contrast to this, Montaigne praises the appeal to the eyes and ears produced by the Catholic cult, not as a higher style, but rather as one more appropriate to man—an argument one encounters frequently in Roman Catholicism (Bossuet, Chateaubriand, Manzoni, etc.). The fundamental fideistic concept is not contradictory to this. The essence of God remains in a remote unrecognizability, but the practice of religion must guard against disappearing in an immaterial purity that no longer does justice to the human need for embodiment. Montaigne absolutely sees what is abasing about this need. But he confirms it as a fact of our essence and from it conducts his attacks on protestantism with the reproach that it overestimates limited man and encourages hubris in him.

4. RANKING OF MAN

To the question of man's rank in the totality of all existing things, Montaigne never accepts the Plotinic response whereby man is a final element in the ring of emanated beings which reestablishes the connection with the source of emanation, the original one. Nor does he accept the Christian response whereby man represents the earthly crown of creation to which all creations are allied and for the sake of which God decided upon acts of salvation. Montaigne the man is rather one point in the universe who lacks the expectation that destiny or God has an interest in him. He shares this insignificance with the environment in which he lives: home, state, continent, animals, and plants. He is decentralized, submerged in the great number of all existing things, does not know what differentiates him from them, feels small—but also protected and freed of all distress in his unknowing insignificance. This thinking is based upon Lucretian motifs.[74] Montaigne shapes them into his own awareness of life, the contours of which become clear to him in their delimitation with respect to the themes of the essential dignity of man.

The old question of man's rank has on the one hand been concerned since the patristic period (Lactantius), utilizing classical conceptions, with the establishment of the *dignitas hominis*. To this end, one used an unchanging, commonplace supply of proofs which combined Greek (in Ciceronian form) and biblical evidence. Among these, or in addition to them, or contrary to them, there was also another group of themes, those characterized as *miseria hominis* and put forth with predominantly Christian arguments into which then, during the Renaissance epochs, trains of thought from Pliny the Elder's *Historia naturalis* could be inserted. With a certain degree of simplification, the postantiquity interpretation of man could be defined from the history of these two themes, specifically by where the emphasis was placed, whether on the dignity or on the lack of dignity and misery of man. Even in Montaigne, the platitudes of the *dignitas* and *miseria* themes appear so unmistakably that we can characterize him by them.

The definitions of human essential dignity (*humanitas* in Roman usage) which affected the postantiquity Occident via Cicero and which were rooted in Platonic and Aristotelian thought state that man is a mixed configuration of animal and spiritual nature with the gift for being able to separate the latter from the former and rise up to the proximity of God. Due to the power of reason which strives upward, and especially due to the power of speech, its effective manifestation, man truly becomes man and is distinguished from the animals. The motif of the *praestare bestiis* runs throughout Cicero's writings. Then the symbolism of the body's structure is added: man is the only living being with an erect walk and an upwardly directed gaze. This anatomical symbolism came more vividly from Ovid than even, perhaps, from Cicero (*Metamorphoses* I, 85–86: . . . *coelumque tueri Jussit et erectos ad sidera tollere vultus;* ". . . he [the creator of the world] commanded man to look to heaven and to point his face to the stars"). Then biblical and theological motifs were combined with such attributes of man's dignity, taken from *Genesis* (I, 27–28), *Sapientia* (IX, 2), the *Psalms* (VIII, 7–10), and also from Lactantius and Augustine: man was created in the image of God, provided with a godlike and redeemable soul and named master over the animals. Catholic theology succeeded in inserting into this image of dignity the knowledge of the *miseria hominis*— not as a fundamental contradiction to it, but rather as a modification brought about historically in the event of sin, a modification that profoundly attacked man's empirical nature, but not his essential resemblance to God or capacity to be forgiven. The *miseria* subject can on occasion lead to a passionate, even naturalistic emotionalism of remorse (as in, for example, Innocent III's *De contemptu mundi*), but as a rule it always remains within the concept of redemption which fits into the interpretation of history which stresses God's saving grace. During the Renaissance epochs it fades before the doctrine of *dignitas,* which, revived through classical sources, also extended to secular philosophy. One even encounters it in the emerging natural sciences, which combined their rational method, their triumph of research and the awakening goal of a technical mastery of the world with Platonic, Ciceronian, biblical, and patristic statements on man's mission of dignity.

Even Sebond's *Theologia naturalis* contains the *dignitas* motif. When Montaigne translated it, he changed nothing in its formulations on the highest and noblest creation, the beautifully formed image of God, which was singled out in its capacity for speech, and which all creatures were to serve. The "Apology" devotes extensive attention to these attributes—but now with a negative response. In determining man's rank, it distances itself from Sebond to the same extent as it does in the disempowering of natural reason. The fluctuation between *dignitas* and *miseria* was in general a favorite game of contrasts in popular literature of the sixteenth century, a fashionable material for argumentation where reaching a solution was no longer necessarily the point. In Spain in the first half of the sixteenth century, for example, Pérez de Oliva worked it into a *Diálogo de la dignidad del hombre* which left the decision open, and which is interesting to us in that it presents all Ciceronian and theological commonplace elements of the double theme which are also found in Montaigne.[75] Montaigne was not acquainted with this dialogue. It is possible that the antithetical commonplace elements of man's dignity and misery were suggested to him in two treatises by the French compiler Pierre Boaistuau.[76] But he could just as easily have found them in other sources. The topic was in the air.

From the moment in which the "Apology" turns to actual man (328 A: "Let us consider for a moment man alone . . .") on, a step-by-step excising of all symbols of dignity which were customarily presented for the *dignitas* theme begins. The first reservations are aimed at the doctrine of the orientation of all created things to man, thus in opposition to his claim to mastery in the universe. The fideistic disempowerment of reason follows, and also the critique of language, the denial of a human position of preference with respect to the animal, the ethnographic relativization of the concept of beauty, and shortly thereafter, following the quotation above from Ovid's *Metamorphoses,* there is the sarcastic comment in response to the symbolism of the human body that the camel and the ostrich stretch their heads farther toward the heavens than man—so what is man's claim? "I have said all this to . . . bring us back and join us to the majority. We are neither above nor below the rest . . . in a very ordinary condition, without any real and essential prerogative or preeminence" (336 A). In offering his counter-arguments, Montaigne does not proceed in any particular order, everything is interspersed or recapitulated several times. But the result remains the same from the beginning: "The most vulnerable and frail of all creatures is man . . . He feels and sees himself lodged here, amid the mire and dung of the world, nailed and riveted to the worst, the deadest, and the most stagnant part of the universe, on the lowest story of the house . . ." (330 A). The abasement expressed in this sentence is even more drastic than the preceding quotation. There are several such passages in the "Apology." They sound like an echo of the cries of remorse of the late Middle Ages. And yet it is curious that they do not set the tone. It is as if a foreign voice intruded, a voice that stands out to anyone who has the more common, very relaxed tone of the *Essais* in mind. Those passages are instances of transitory agitation at the polemical turning points from the ideal images of essential dignity to human reality. When this has been attained, Montaigne relaxes again. The *miseria hominis* for which he decides is not wretchedness, rather, it is a gray but serviceable soberness. Thus he does not exaggerate it. His polemical agitation ebbs. He again breathes easily. In fact, he guards against painting the black-on-black pictures of a Pliny (*Hist. nat.* VII, 1) or a Lucretius (V, v. 222 ff.) of helpless man delivered up to all the elements: "those complaints are false"—and he counters them by asserting the adequate tolerability of existence, because from the abasement in which it finds itself it also receives protection and guidance (II, 12, 333–335).

The leveling comparison with animals takes up a large part of Montaigne's arguments against man's rank. And for good reason. The *praestare bestiis* is, as we say, a core of the classical *humanitas* concept. The Ciceronian ranking of man above animal because of his capacity for speech was not seriously threatened by the much-loved occupation with the problem of animal intelligence since sophistry and in the stoic school, nor by the naturalistic observation of social organisms using animal societies which came through Aristotle. Only Pyrrhonic skepticism derived doubts about the uniqueness of the human capacity from the instinctual abilities and the sharpness of the senses found in animals (Sextus Empiricus *Hypotyposes* I, 14, 62 ff.). Then in late hellenism when the Pythagorean doctrine of the presence of a spirit in all living beings was taken up again, Plutarch in his *Moralia* used animals to demonstrate their sensibleness—in the serious explanation of the work on land and water animals, and in the humorous paradoxes of the so-called "Gryllus" dialogue. Christian theology's *dignitas* concept understandably prevented the proliferation of such arguments in the centuries constituting the Middle Ages. Old Testament praise of the animals (e.g., in *Proverbia* 30, 24 ff.) had a limited effect only on the extreme *miseria* literature, for example on Innocent III's treatise *De contemptu mundi*. It was only with the revival of skepticism in the sixteenth century that the

animal comparison again became so prominent that it became commonplace when proof was offered against human superiority in reason.[77] It
stands out sharply against the background of orthodox theology, but
also against the idealistic, Neoplatonic *dignitas* system in the manner of
Giovanni Pico della Mirandola, who sets before man the choice of
degenerating to the level of the animals or regenerating himself to the
divine (*De hominis dignitate,* fol. 131v).

Montaigne's animal comparison follows that in Sextus Empiricus
and in the Plutarch documents mentioned fairly exactly. (The "Gryllus"
dialogue, by the way, had left its trace in the prologue to Erasmus' *Laus
stultitiae* and would later on also have an effect on Cervantes' *Coloquio
de los perros* and La Fontaine's fable "Ullysses' Companions.") Pliny
(*Hist. nat.* VII) and Lucretius (V, v. 223 ff.) represent further stimuli. But
Montaigne directs the point of this comparison much more sharply
against man's claim to uniqueness and certainty than was done in these
classical sources. What do we know about the animals? What do we
know at all about something that we ourselves are not, since we do not
even know this much? And then comes the unforgettable sentence:
"When I play with my cat, who knows if I am not a pastime to her more
than she is to me?" (II, 12, 331 C).[78] Animal and man are brothers
("fellows and companions") in the common cycle of nature, each a
mystery to the other, each with its own gift for preserving its life, and
the animal at times with a greater gift than man, for whom thinking
undermines obedience to the laws of nature. All proofs of the special
dignity of man are deflated in that they also apply to the animal: it has
its speech, *its* reason, *its* soul, capable of joy and suffering, *its* society, *its*
morality . . . Montaigne goes on with this for pages. We need give this
no special treatment. The meaning is clear: man is removed from his
special position and in equal rank with the animal is delivered up to a
motherly order of nature ("our mother Nature") which protects him all
the more, the more willing he is to let go of his desire to rule. Montaigne
retained this brotherhood with animals which compelled modesty even
into his last Essays. A significant portion of his thoughts on death will
be based upon this. It is connected with his unfolding skepticism, which
we will discuss later. And it was perhaps also rooted in a temperament
that was attracted to all living and existing things: "still there is a
certain respect, and a general duty of humanity, that attaches us not
only to animals, who have life and feeling, but even to trees and plants.
We owe justice to men, and mercy and kindness to other creatures that
may be capable of receiving it . . . I am not afraid to admit that my

nature is so tender, so childish, that I cannot well refuse my dog the play he offers me or asks of me outside the proper time" (II, 11, 318 A/C). The abandoned human pride gives way to a "humanity," to a good will for every sort of creature, a good will that no longer fears the command to leave the creatures for the creator's sake. This is conceivably hetero-doxical. Orthodox dogma can only understand man coming together with the animals as a sign of his fall from the original height of creation and as a reversal of the order God intended.[79] Thus later on, in his Montaigne critique, Bossuet found the animal comparison the most disturbing aspect.[80] Perhaps it is the recollection of those passages in the *Essais* which led Pascal to term man's receptivity to the seductive magic of all creatures, including the animals, terrible, and to include it among the symptoms of original sin (*Pensées,* fragment 430, ed. Brunschvicg). But another author will join in Montaigne's orientation: La Fontaine. His fables, which contain so much of the spirit of the *Essais,* recognize the animal cleverness and evil of animals and the animal cleverness and evil of man, the mutual love as well as enmity of the two, and their belonging to the nurturing realm of nature which rules in a manner so very different from what human arrogance suspects.[81]

5.   CRITIQUE OF KNOWLEDGE

Furthermore, Montaigne then contests human essential dignity on the basis of considerations of a critique of knowledge. The result is simple and in the negative: there is no certainty of knowledge. The bases given for it are neither systematic nor original, they are highly variable and vague in their terminology, axiomatic, confessional, descriptive, but not philosophically compelling, though replete with the suggestive force of a personal conviction. Their only significance lies in that they form a part of Montaigne's alternative to the idealistic image of man which was aimed at naming man the bearer of a reason that recognizes being.

Montaigne heaps deprecatory names upon reason in the earliest Es-says and to the end. He most often calls it *fantasie* and thus diminishes it to the rank of a power of the imagination, passively subject to one's impressions, playing in random combinations—that is, an unreliable instrument with which one cannot acquire knowledge.[82] It thus makes itself a party to a process of proving everything with everything: "I always call reason that semblance of intellect that each man fabricates in himself. That reason, of which, by its condition, there can be a hundred contradictory ones about one and the same subject, is an instrument of lead and of wax, stretchable, pliable, and adaptable to all biases and all measures" (II, 12, 425 A). In another passage he calls it a pot with two handles of which one can randomly grasp the right or the left one (438 B). Its contents are fantasies ("*rêveries*" 389 B), nonbinding casting about in the dark, attempts to surround a belief with the appearance of truth—and the best thinkers perhaps did not mean their speculations to be anything other than this: "I cannot easily persuade myself that Epicurus, Plato, and Pythagoras gave us their Atoms, their Ideas, and their Numbers as good coin of the realm. They were too wise to establish their articles of faith on anything so uncertain and so debatable" (379 A). No possibility of objective knowledge impedes the free flight of fantasy, which swarms through a hundred invented worlds, giving reasons for a myriad of things that do not exist (III, 11, 785 B). There is nothing so senseless that it has not been earnestly demonstrated somewhere, at least once (I, 23, 79–80 B; II, 12, 408 B—here probably from Cicero, *De divinatione*, II, 119—and even more frequently). No evidence, logical or intuitive in nature, guarantees an objective truth. Quite the contrary, the more we are filled with conviction for an idea, the more we must suspect that tomorrow the opposite idea will hit us with the same convincing impact. The truth and the lie have the same face (III, 11, 785 B). Existence does not radiate into the spirit, the spirit radiates into existence. But this radiant penetration is only the creative urge of subjectivity wanting to run free, but incapable of knowing anything. Thus all "recognitions" are only at the level of opinions, and they have merely subjective validity for the moment in which they occur.

To illustrate this fantasizing creative urge of the spirit, Montaigne uses the doxographic panorama of all didactic doctrines available to him. A major part of the "Apology" is filled with them. It was not difficult to do. His sources—Cicero, Diogenes Laërtius, Agrippa von Nettesheim, and others—provided him with examples of the compendium-like review of philosophical statements. He accumulates in no particular order whatever was thought about nature philosophy and cosmology, theories of the soul and immortality, definitions of the moral good, and so forth—a dance of fools, or a dance of death of speculations, whereby the one defeats the other, an unending throng that is destroyed by its own contradictoriness, leaving only one certainty: the powerlessness of the human intellect to attain truth. Since everything leads to this one conclusion, Montaigne does not go into a critique of any one individual doctrine within this "clatter of so many philosophical brains!" (II, 12, 383 A).

One would naturally not expect an author of the sixteenth century to see the various historical didactic opinions as the stages of a total truth, stages that are still tied to a one-sidedness requiring development in order to cultivate the antitheses of this truth's dialectical structure, which in the future are to be integrated. But one could expect that he could have performed a simple division into truths and errors and expressed a concluding preference for the truths. This is what Cicero and, in some passages, also Plutarch did, the ones from whom a portion of Montaigne's doxographical material was taken. But there is no trace of even this in Montaigne. The fact that contradictory principles are proposed does not signify a conflict between truth and error for him, rather, it is a symptom of the empty drive of the "imagination" to combine things. He concludes from the contradictions of the various intellects that there is an essential, inherent contradictoriness in the intellect. He takes the historicism of the intellect as proof of the intellect's lack of a capacity for truth. But also, admittedly, as the proof of its vividness. But Montaigne's intention in showing all these fools' dances of opinion is not merely to break down human dignity. They also provide him with a look at what we are—and can be. Speculating reason is fruitless from a philosophical standpoint, but anthropologically it is very expressive. It is the element of the intellect which runs free in the play of characters of the imagination—no more, but also no less.

We again find ourselves at a point in which Montaigne diverts the negative act of abasement into being in tune with that which is abased. At first this being in tune is psychological and anthropological in nature, determining what our makeup is, and no longer lamenting it; but it then becomes an act of being in tune in one's personal attitude, permitting oneself that which seemed contemptible: self-contradiction, impotence of knowledge, subjectivity, forming one's opinion from the moment, and endless mobility. Over the course of the "Apology," it is unmistakable how pleasure in the performance is mixed in with the critically sworn theater of didactic opinions presented. The urge to observe man and his metamorphoses becomes stronger than the initial attack upon these metamorphoses. He affirms where he initially had denied. This twist is as original as Montaigne's critique of knowledge is flat and unoriginal. Only from this point does one penetrate into the core of his thinking and his wisdom. By limiting the object of knowledge to man, knowledge again becomes possible for him, namely in the form of the descriptive observation of human essence. The same eagerness to know (*curiosité*) which he calls an illness from a fideistic theory of knowledge (II, 12, 379 B) constitutes the healthy driving force of his own anthropological direction. He cannot satisfy it, he is so eager to see how men act, think, and are. The panorama of the multiplicity of spirits of which at first there was such suspicion is transformed into a garden of enticing bright colors. Thus on one occasion he can express regret that there are no longer any books such as Diogenes Laërtius: "For I consider no less curiously the fortunes and the lives of these great teachers of the world (the philosophers) than the diversity of their doctrines and fancies" (II, 10, 303 A). In this sentence, the words "curiously, diversity, fancies" have a positive meaning. They return to the spirit its right to have dreams, as many as it wishes, and to enjoy them. This is the source of Montaigne's feeling for poetry, which we mentioned in the last chapter. And this is also the source of that curious passage from the late period (III, 13, 818) on the "spirited mind" that never rests with what it has attained, but rather hunts on, staggering, enraptured, probably filled with delusion, but also filled with power, equipped with the entire ambiguity that every living thing has, but only because of which it has life.

Montaigne then tried his hand at an analysis of the act of cognition. It essentially consisted of a repetition of the epistemological scheme from Sextus Empiricus (whose *Hypotyposes* he read in Henri Estienne's translation, which appeared in 1562) with a few changes that probably originated in his readings of Lucretius. Its basis is the acknowledgment of the mixed body/soul structure of man, that is, the fact that the body serves as both a limit and a prerequisite for the spiritual content. In contrast to Platonic, stoic, and Christian ethics, this mixed structure is not seen as a dualism that must be overcome, but rather as an interplay of two forces in the harmony of which human essence is fulfilled. That is, if one will permit such broad concepts, a "Renaissance" motif. This represents the same removal of the stigma of sinfulness from the body, the same integration of the soul into the context of nature as was done by the Italians in the fifteenth and sixteenth centuries. And like them, Montaigne also hopes to base this upon the invocation of the Christian doctrine of the resurrection of the body (II, 17, 484–485 A). Yet the focus for him is not on the resurrection, but rather on the earthly life of the body. His invocation is nothing more than a conventional argument of convenience.

The process of acquiring knowledge is described such that its capacity for modification comes to light as a result of physical circumstances, that is, as a result of material conditions in the broadest sense (II, 12, 424 A). Body and passions make our spirit corruptible. Again Montaigne explains these commonplace things more through anecdotes and everyday experiences than through strict methods. Thus we find vivid sentences such as this: "If my health smiles upon me, and the brightness of a beautiful day, I am a fine fellow; if I have a corn bothering my toe, I am surly, unpleasant, and unapproachable" (II, 12, 425 A). Further modifications of judgment then arise, he explains, as a result of climatic or other physical environmental influences, and also bonds to national, societal, class milieus, and finally as a result of the law of inertia of habit. Man has no possibility of getting beyond perspective judgments that are functionalized by his dependence upon his body and his environment. This leads into a critique of the powers of the senses. Indeed, the senses are the sole basis for knowledge, goes the Lucretian argument. They yield irreversible determinations: iron is in fact heavy, light is in fact bright, fire is in fact hot (II, 12, 444 A). And yet even the certainty of the senses is only a limited certainty, and one determined by function. For when we are concerned with evaluating perceptions, this is influenced from the outset by the mood of the one doing the perceiving: even the ugliest woman is beautiful to her lover. Thus the question arises as to whether the five senses have the capacity to capture all qualities of reality, or rather whether a reality is conceivable which has an undetermined, higher number of qualities than correspond to the five senses: a reality that is still material, yet also beyond the senses, and which man has not the capacity to perceive (II, 12, 444 A). The summarized scheme of the act of cognition which Montaigne constructs ultimately states: the imagination (*fantasie*) is bound to the material perceived by the senses; however, these provide only limited material, according to their own limited receptivity (*passion*); thus the contents of the imagination are only an appearance that says nothing about the particular object (*subject,* according to the older meaning of the word *subjectum* = *hypokeimenon*) (454 A). Therefore: "There is no knowledge" (447 B).

All this is a poor patch job and is well below the careful epistemological analyses that had been offered before by Aristotelian and scholastic philosophy. Certainly this agnosticism of Montaigne's concerns one of the modern repetitions of Pyrrhonic skepticism and a transition to the English sensualist of the sixteenth and seventeenth centuries. But this position in the history of philosophy is not the important thing. More important is the consequence for the interpretation of man. Montaigne's critique of knowledge is not a conclusion, it is an axiom. Its power lies in the determination of the value of human essence, which is brought to full expression in it. It describes, only with borrowed evi-

dence, and the philosophical content of which Montaigne is hardly a
match for, the same thing that is expressed in his critique of natural
theology and much more: the questionable position of human existence.
It is only in view of this anthropological determination of value that
there is any point in considering the "epistemologist" Montaigne at all.

6. SKEPTICISM

We have touched upon some elements of Montaigne's skepticism
earlier in this chapter. It, too, is to be seen in the context of his anthropology. It is a part of the loose flow of thoughts which move back and
forth between his awe of the hidden world principle and his study of the
limits inherent to man. One can apply to Montaigne the word of Kant
which is expressed in the preface to the first edition of his *Critique of
Pure Reason,* in which he calls the skeptic "a sort of nomad who abhors
any permanent building on the land." But it is not foolishness that
drives Montaigne away from any permanence. His skepticism is eye-
opening wisdom, not a desire for destruction. It shows that what is
unrecognizable reaches much more deeply into what is immediate to
our experience than naive intellect suspects. It tends and protects it
rather than driving it out through the inquisitiveness of our supposed
knowledge. Everything man says apodictically appears to it as a premature interruption of creation in what is eternally inexhaustible. It gives
the contradictory opinions their due and it expects to find in that which
is least probable by the standards of logic and experience a possibility
that at some time or somewhere can be realized. The fragmentation of
the spirit into the contradictions of its speculations is its triumph. For
when the spirit consumes itself, or when it runs aground, then that
which is unrecognizable remains at its height, untouched. But this is
what Montaigne's pious reverence wants to serve, the pious reverence
that constitutes the soul of his skepticism, and which one must not
overlook simply because he is no longer a Christian.

With respect to man, his skepticism signifies a further aid in the
breaking down of the *dignitas hominis.* In Aristotelian-scholastic philosophy, absolute doubt was considered timidity unworthy of human
powers of cognition. It is only allowed in that system as *hodogetic*
(direction-indicating) doubt: a weighing comparison of passages of text
from biblical, patristic, and classical sources with the aim of dialecti-
cally harmonizing what appeared irreconcilable. This type of doubting
provides the impetus to finding truth, a "little sprout at the foot of

truth," as Dante once expressed it.[83] Montaigne had nothing in common with either the preliminary doubt of Aristotelian-scholastic doctrine nor with the later methodical doubt of Descartes, who accomplishes the stripping away on a trial basis of all intellectual contents that were obtained merely authoritatively for the purpose of recovering them from his own self-certainty ("tear down in order to rebuild," *Discours de la Méthode*). For his interest is not in certainty and intellectual consciousness of dignity.

To the extent that Montaigne's skepticism uses the customary proofs, he takes them from classical Pyrrhonism. He knew Pyrrhon from Sextus Empiricus' *Hypotyposes*, which he had in Henri Estienne's Latin translation. He found further impetus in the fideistic movements of the sixteenth century already mentioned, which also made use of Pyrrhonistic motifs. The treatise *Examen vanitatis* by Francesco Pico della Mirandola (1510) provides the bases of the rational inaccessibility of the revealed mysteries in this manner. Erasmus made unambiguous claims of skepticism.[84] Agrippa von Nettesheim's *De incertitudine et vanitate scientiarum* (1530) expressly wants the resolution of all sciences understood as an argument for faith.[85] It is questionable to what extent Montaigne leans on Agrippa von Nettesheim. All that can be proven is that he borrowed a few anecdotes. The doxographic review of didactic opinions, the relativization of the natural law concept by means of historical and ethnographic variations, and other areas of agreement between the *Essais* and Agrippa von Nettesheim prove nothing, since all this can also be found in Sextus Empiricus. In addition, there is a profound difference between Montaigne's skepticism expressed in a relaxed joyousness and the hypochondriacal, gloomy anger of Agrippa's work. Newer research has recognized that Montaigne's terminology points not to contemporary language usage, but rather goes back to classical skepticism, thus Sextus Empiricus is probably his predominant source.[86] Nevertheless, he demonstrates a fundamental trait of his epoch with his close connection of Pyrrhonic skepticism and fideistic intent. He may also be encouraged in this by his own home environment; in Bordeaux and Toulouse at that time there was a noticeable accumulation of skeptical, fideistic writings.[87]

Montaigne reviewed Pyrrhonism quite accurately (II, 12, 370–371). He even accurately identified its stated ethical goal of attaining a "calm of the soul." He expands his review with a generous number of his own observations which display a remarkable desire to place himself in the fluctuating uncertainty and to rock in the "mild manner" that he praises

in Pyrrhonic disputation (372 A). Later additions to the "Apology" lead
to some changes in the nature of academic skepticism, but they still
continue this game of point and counterpoint, providing a no for every
yes, and pausing between the two without deciding between them. All
this then comes together in the formula added in 1588 which had the
misfortune of becoming a facile label for Montaigne: "What do I
know?" (393 B; see also later discussions in this chapter). It is found—
and we will come back to this later—in the midst of a passage of
linguistic criticism. In its interrogative formulation, it is intended to
bring consciousness of not knowing ("Ignorance that knows itself . . .",
372 A) even into the state of not knowing, and to avoid the still assertive
character of even a negative judgment ("I know nothing"), to avoid the
paralyzing effect of the language as a whole. Additionally, the sentence
introducing it designates the principle of doubt as *fantasie*. Thus the
extreme is attained in the self-empowerment of the skeptical method—
and in leaving the human situation, which had already become problematical from all sides, in the hands of complete uncertainty.

A glance at the wealth of thought and material in the *Essais* will
guard the reader against misunderstanding its skepticism as complacency or even nihilism which no longer considers a spiritual act to be
desirable. The book can be ironic, but it includes itself in the irony.
There is no flat sensibleness that simply shrugs its shoulders at what it
does not understand; there is no derision of those who think differently.
Quite the contrary, Montaigne has an extraordinary readiness to take
into account what all has been tried to make sense out of things, and
what still remains to be tried. His skepticism does not cripple and break
things down, rather, it develops them. In refraining from partisanship
for one of the interpretations of the world which have been handed
down, it discovers the productivity of the human spirit. And it further
discovers the fullness of what is real, that which in its concrete reality as
well as in its metaphysical roots continuously escapes interpretation. It
is in fact a peeking in (σχοπέω), a looking around for that which *is*,
before the thing perceived is impoverished in the process of being defined by language, concept, and judgment. It lies in wait for the eventful
metamorphoses of the spirits and the inexhaustibility of the factual in
order to be able to pour forth what it has seen in countless anecdotes,
reports, and confessions. It can thereby satisfy its deep need to be surprised by what is unique, what cannot be categorized, what is mysterious in material as well as human peculiarities. Thus a productive connection does exist between the concrete abundance of factual material in

the *Essais* and the skepticism in the book. The significant part of Montaigne's skepticism can be found here, in this transition from the critically examining act to the developing act, that is, from the devaluation of didactic opinions that lose themselves in something that cannot be decided to the observation of what is anthropologically and ontologically real. In fact, the ground is prepared for this in Pyrrhonism itself. In Sextus Empiricus one finds: "The skeptic pursues the observation of life without an opinion" (*Hypotyposes* III, 24, 235). But this observation has a quite different meaning in the *Essais* than it does there; here it proliferates the complex substance of life for its own sake, not simply to demonstrate an educational principle.

We see in the fideistic elements of Montaigne's skepticism the piety of which he is capable—admittedly, a philosophical, not a Christian, piety. Its object is a transcendence that he sometimes calls "God," but more often calls "nature." It has a mysteriousness that lacks contour, but which is reverently nourished. When on occasion he tries to define it more precisely, it appears to be the principle of absolute arbitrariness, which someday could make everything different than it is now. A randomness of all existing things follows from this. In the "Apology" he once explains that God's omnipotence is an omnipotence that can randomly break through what was once established (II, 12, 389–390 A). A few pages farther on it is nature that has the capacity to suddenly and at any time revoke all that till then existed (400 A/C). However, when what exists is seen as surrounded by the possibility that it can be revoked at any time, as something that can just as well be as not be, then no relationship to it is possible other than one of acceptance of its mere actuality. The skeptical nourishing of the secret, transcendent arbitrariness becomes the skeptical nourishing of the secret contingent actuality. No judgment can be permitted to generalize this actuality into a knowledge of eternal laws. The skeptical spirit lives in the expectation of limitless possibility and in the reflective viewing of reality which is inexhaustible because it is contingent. The latter, contingent reality, becomes clear in its thus designated essence in that one throws the weave of contradictory opinions over it: the confusion of pro and con has the advantage of reestablishing the many-sidedness of the phenomenon. Are these thoughts—which (though veiled and fuzzy) are the basis for the "Apology" but also for the later Essays—traces of Ockhamism with its doctrine of the arbitrariness of God, the contingency of the universe, the limitation of knowledge to observation with one's senses of unconnected facts? Let us not forget that the doctrine of Ockhamism continues to have an effect on the sixteenth century.[88] This question could only be resolved if we knew all of Montaigne's contemporary sources. But as it is, we must leave this question open. That is all the more regrettable since an answer would permit a better clarification of Montaigne's position in philosophical history. Furthermore, other elements of his thought—particularly his linguistic criticism, which will be considered in the next chapter—point to the same context.

The fundamental knowledge attained by Montaigne's skepticism is that what is known and what is best known is transformed into an unknown as soon as it becomes the object of reflective contemplation. Everything becomes a miracle. Reminiscent of Sextus Empiricus' ninth trope (*Hypotyposes* I, 14, 141 ff.) he writes: "It seems to me that among the things we see ordinarily there are wonders so incomprehensible that they surpass even miracles in obscurity" (II, 37, 578 A). The miracles do not just begin with the supernatural miracle, but rather with the ordinary, customary thing, the wonder of which is veiled only by its habitual nature (I, 27, 132–133 A). The inferential skepticism does not doubt what is, rather, it doubts the opinion that something could possibly not be. It knows that the usual criteria of probability are not adequate for deciding whether something is possible or impossible: ". . . it is foolish presumption to go around disdaining and condemning as false whatever does not seem likely to us . . . which, if we cannot be convinced of them, we should at least leave in suspense! For to condemn them as impossible is to pretend, with rash presumption, to know the limits of possibility" (132 and 133 A). Probability conclusions forget that they are based upon the temporal conditions of our thinking and experiencing, that is, they are undermined by the same endless stream of possibilities of becoming different as are all things to which they refer: ". . . neither believing rashly nor disbelieving easily" is Montaigne's rule of thumb (133 C). A thought that does not keep itself in skeptical balance and willingness to watch and see will harden into presumptuous obstinacy (the designations for this which are offered countless times are *presumption, obstination, outrecuidance*); it spoils the complex puzzle of what is real, as well as that of transcendence. Skepticism is unassumingness. It tones man down and yet in the abasement of his place in the world it opens his eye to the miracle of the world, pregnant with inexhaustibility—and the miracle of himself.

But access to these miracles leads through facts. They themselves are all the more a miracle, the more purely they are understood. Instead of looking away from them to seek reasons, judgments, prejudices, one's gaze must learn to focus upon their appearance. Montaigne has a passion for the pure facts. This is the energy released through his skepticism. He speaks of the "evidence of the facts" (II, 12, 430 A) and plays them off against the constructions of reason: "I would rather follow facts than reason" (II, 12, 430 A). Similar formulations can be found several times in the *Essais*. The principle of "things rather than reasons" is expressed most clearly, although used polemically, in the following passage: "I see ordinarily that men, when facts are put before them, are more ready to amuse themselves by inquiring into their reasons than by inquiring into their truth. They leave aside the cases and amuse themselves treating the causes" (III, 11, 785 B). This sentence contains the additional formula of the "truth of facts"; the future formula in Leibniz, "truths of fact," is reminiscent of this, but Montaigne's lacks the subordination to the "eternal truths" found in Leibniz. The "truth of facts" lies in their essence as they appear, and the perspective of the observer, limited by the moment, is a part of this essence: ". . . she [the soul] gives all her being to each matter, and concentrates all her strength on it, and never treats more than one at a time. And she treats a matter not according to itself, but according to herself" (I, 50, 220 C). From this results the demand to bring to view the appearance of isolated facts. The question of why they are and why they are as they are is silenced; they *are*—and I am constituted such that they are to me what to me they *appear to be*. But I must grasp this; if I do, then I have the only truth comprehensible to man. One must not confuse this orientation toward facts with the later positivism that believes in a limited number and in the immutability of facts, and which places them on the chain of causality. Here, on the other hand, one denies the facts none of their contingency, none of their residence in the incalculable realm of the possible, and thus none of their enslavement to what is temporary. They are a provisional state that could also be different, or at one time was different, or could at another moment be perceived differently by us.

The facts that Montaigne observes are admittedly to an overwhelming degree those of mankind, not of things: forms of life, morals, characters, all absurdities of human action and opinion, and above all the one great fundamental fact that man is so fragile and abased and yet so viable and so secure. And here is where the fruitfulness of inferential skepticism begins to unfold. Montaigne is able to listen, to project himself in, to value every reality that develops from the unlimited possibility of the human essence to be sometimes this, sometimes that, sometimes something else. Whatever men, from the cleverest to the most abstruse, say is deserving of attention, for what they say characterizes them: "Man is capable of all of this." He approaches man not with a sense of knowing it all, but rather with anthropological curiosity. Thus we find sentences such as the following, which can both refer man to the impossibility of knowing things, and thus the freedom to interpret them at will, as well as what they yield for the study of man: "We who deprive our judgment of the right to make decisions look mildly on opinions different from ours; and if we do not lend them our judgment, we easily lend them our ears" (III, 8, 704 B). And shortly before that: "There is no fancy so frivolous and so extravagant that it does not seem to me quite suitable to the production of the human mind . . . All such idle fancies which are in credit around us, deserve at least to be listened to . . ." In both passages, note the expressions "lend an ear" and "listen." Listening in, Montaigne expects everything from man. He reports ritualistic consumption of fathers among exotic peoples with the same composure as Lycurgus' recommendation that one should let thieves ply their trade, since they train the property owners to be watchful (II, 12, 437 A). It would be foolish to dismiss Montaigne's numerous fantastic anecdotes by ascribing them to a relapse into gullibility. To the eye of his inferential skepticism, their very improbability is the symbol of man's unlimited possibilities. Thus he concedes that man does achieve heroic or religious greatness—as an exception, certainly, but something of which this puzzling creature is capable; it surprises him no more and no less than "the extreme baseness of some minds, which does not astonish me and which I do not disbelieve either" (II, 32, 548 C). It is interesting to see how on one occasion he defends one of these exceptional cases (the Lacedaemonian boy who let a fox he had hidden under his robe tear him up) against Bodin's banal doubt, since to Bodin this degree of self-control appeared improbable, abnormal, and thus impossible (II, 32, 546 A). The higher level skeptic does not doubt the improbable as an individual fact but rather as a category.

There is a vast difference between this type of inferential skepticism and the later Enlightenment skepticism in the manner of a Fontenelle, a Bayle, a Voltaire. Their skepticism is namely a dogmatism of healthy human reason which is dedicated to evidence that is binding on all, and which rejects what it does not understand. It unmasks, irons out, drags down, deciphers, it smiles at metaphysical awe, and when it reviews human writing and thought, it sits in judgment of embarrassing foolishness that could have been avoided. But Montaigne considers precisely that which healthy reason cannot understand to be possible. His skepticism has a tone of metaphysical awe. It mistrusts any platitude, "that takes away their [things'] strangeness" (I, 27, 132 A). Theologians who know all about God and the Trinity and the creation of the world are as unbearable to him as the philosophers of the Enlightenment, but for different reasons: representatives of the Enlightenment know better, but he knows neither this nor that. It was skepticism that opened Montaigne's eyes to the mystery of the animals. How can man have confidence that he knows what is going on within an animal? Doubting such knowledge, he keeps watch over the reticence of the animal at a distance which is a form of closeness to the essence: "When I play with my cat . . ." (see earlier discussion).

Montaigne's doubt is something quite serious. For he first brings man on long journeys to satisfy his innate need to escape uncertainty. Montaigne first thrusts him thoroughly into it so that he loses his naive inclination to believe that one can dispense with a matter with a simple yes or no. He flings him into a sea of the undecidable. Here he drowns— or he learns to move according to the law of his individuality, which bears his weight all the more securely, the more he is in tune with himself.

7. THE MIRACLE

Finally, among the themes associated with Montaigne's skepticism is assessment of the miracle in the narrower sense of the word. This concerns one of the most widely discussed problems of his witch-burning epoch, which in its rationalist representatives attempted to explain miracles as misinterpretations of causal relationships that are simply not understood or, in the case of the witches, as hypnotic occurrences.[89]

Montaigne's judgment is not uniform. This is due less to the temporal difference of his statements on the subject than to his division between the viewpoints of theory and practice. After all we have already seen, his theoretical position appears to be as follows: he tolerates belief in miracles as a need of human speculation, and he considers the miracle possible because he considers the act of the sovereign Godhead or nature breaking through whatever presently exists to be possible at any time. He can speak reverently of miracle healings that cannot be refuted by their "improbability." "It is a dangerous and fateful presumption . . . to disdain what we do not comprehend," he writes in one such passage (I, 27, 134 A). But to the extent that belief in miracles hardens into a dogmatic claim and sits in judgment over man, namely when it burns "witches," he rejects it. However, only then.

Essay III, 11, which is concerned with the witch trials, demonstrates this. He seems quite enlightened and anticipates much that Fontenelle and Bayle will later use to argue against miracles: they are deceptive maneuvers. But Montaigne does not in the process negate the possibility of a miracle, rather, he only attacks the arrival at judgments by the witch tribunals. For these judgments are based on a presumably irrefutable certainty: that those accused *are* witches. But there is no such certainty. To show this, Montaigne presents all possible reasons for the belief that the witches' magic really only signifies lies or incorrectly interpreted symptoms of mental illness. It is much more likely, he writes, that a swindle is being perpetrated than that someone is riding through the air on a broom (789 B). He once observed a witch himself for an extended period "with the soundest attention," and the result was: "I would have prescribed them rather hellebore [the remedy used against insanity] than hemlock" (790 B). Thus here, where personal inspection led to a conclusion different from that of the authorities, he contests the miracle. Personal inspection is stronger than the terror of the authorities: "Thank God, my belief is not controlled by anyone's fists" (789 B). Montaigne bravely takes a position against a delusion of the masses and against clerical fanaticism. Here he is in fact that which he is later one-sidedly claimed to be, a herald of the Enlightenment. But only because he warns of premature certainty and because he sees how practical consequences are derived from it, and how men fall prey to them. The miracle, which is certainly possible but which is inaccessible to judgment, does not allow one to make decisions upon which to act. Precisely to demonstrate this chasm between theory and practice, Montaigne here casts doubt upon the miracle to the same degree in which elsewhere he asserted that the miracle was possible—and it does not matter at all that here he is concerned with "diabolical" miracles, and elsewhere with divine ones. For even the demonic miracle of the witches' travel is claimed by church authorities. Thus he writes this liberating sentence: "To kill men, we should have sharp and luminous evidence . . . After all, it is putting a very high price on one's conjectures to have a man roasted alive because of them" (789–790 B). Theory is the realm of conjecture, practice is the field of positive decisions; these cannot be derived from the former, rather, they must be built upon irrefutable facts; since these are not available in the case of the accusations of witchcraft, judicial authority to issue a death sentence is lacking. This is the simple, and in his time risky, meaning of his Essay on witches (the dangerous subject matter of which is hidden behind the title "Of Cripples"). Several decennia earlier, Rabelais was scorned and Dolet was burned for similar thinking.

Montaigne then appears to want to dull the critical point of his explanations. Near the end of the Essay (790–791) we find the well-known passage that one could interpret as a retreat to double truth: what I said there is of course completely meaningless, it is, like every-thing I say, a personal, confused opinion, without any intention of getting involved in the situation, and of course I subject myself to the competent authorities. Does this addition signify deception, a trick? Perhaps. But perhaps it is also only a means of raising skepticism to an irony—quite apart from the specific topic at hand of the witch trials—where it can be perceived that it is also skeptical of itself and is not a prisoner of its own principle. But it is difficult for one to gain insight into these last, floating, playful movements of his thinking. We must content ourselves with once again establishing that his Essay on witches only turns the practical consequences upside down, it does not thus affect the possibility of miracles or the belief in miracles per se. Where miracles are denied, Montaigne considers them more possible than the reasons for this denial; where they are proclaimed, he doubts them in view of the uncertainty of all knowledge. Denial of the improbable and proclaiming the existence of the improbable are both called back into the only thing allowable: a careful conjecturing about what is improba-ble. So we are left with the overall picture in which Montaigne speaks both for and against miracles. Pascal noted this: "Montaigne opposed to miracles. Montaigne in favor of miracles."[90] He is correct. Mon-taigne the skeptic pulls down the wall of the certainty delusion of both sides and opens up the broad horizon to the possible.

8. DISTANCE FROM THE NATURAL SCIENCES

Occasionally the attempt has been made to consider Montaigne a precursor of modern natural scientific thinking. From the accurate rec-ognition that his skepticism is a symptom of the exhaustion of the speculative forces in theology and philosophy, the erroneous conclusion has been drawn that it signifies the preliminary work for new methods of attaining certainty. Montaigne's love of facts is connected with experi-mental sciences. It appears that critics assumed he lacked only the deter-mination to himself take the steps that others took at his time or shortly thereafter.[91]

But the Essais lack almost all the prerequisites for the world view of the modern natural sciences. Montaigne moves along a line that originates in the hellenistic doctrine of wisdom and in anthropology, which proceeded through Christian theology, which he re-secularized, and which then proceeds into the moralistic thought processes of the seventeenth century. This line bypasses the mathematical, physical, and technical sciences. He is not ahead of them, nor does he limp along behind them, rather, he does not think in that direction at all. An association of Montaigne with the exact sciences, no matter how it positioned him, would be a distortion and would cause the best results of his thinking to appear only to be backwardness or popular philosophy.

For Montaigne, there is no knowledge in which object and thought come into complete accord. The subject of knowledge is to him a part of all existence—not an outstanding part, but rather encompassed in the character of all existing things: flowing, changing, as unreliable as these. Crudely stated, his view of the world is heraclitic. He consistently keeps all that is reminiscent of the doctrine of being of Parmenides, Plato, and Aristotle at arm's length. One of the most important and most frequently occurring memorable terms in the *Essais* is *branle, branler, branloire.* Synonyms and terms with similar meaning such as *mutation, passage, ondoyer,* and so forth, which occur just as frequently, underscore this central motif of his world view, variability. At the beginning of Essay III, 2, we read: "The world is but a perennial movement. All things in it are in constant motion—the earth, the rocks of the Caucasus, the pyramids of Egypt—both with the common motion and with their own. Stability itself is nothing but a more languid motion" (610 B). When Montaigne repeatedly describes the transitional flow into one another of contradictory things, he does not mean to show only a sequence of inadequate human illusions about things, rather he means an event taking place within the things themselves. At the end of the "Apology" he provides his most thorough presentation of his world view of changeability. It concerns a paraphrase from Plutarch's *De E apud Delphos* in Amyot's translation. Since he acknowledges agreement with the thought processes in this source, they can be considered evidence of his views. In this passage, Plutarch inserts the heraclitic doctrine of the flowing change in humans and things into the Platonic doctrine of the resting being of the divine to express the difference between what is divine and what is not divine. Montaigne also accepts this. But it is apparent that here, too, he is more concerned with determining the essence of the nondivine than the divine. He abbreviates the passages concerned with the latter in order to reproduce a broader description of the former. And the moment most important to him is the impedance of knowledge resulting from the changeability of men and things. Let us quote the pertaining sentences: "Finally, there is no existence that is constant, either of our being or of that of objects. And we, and our judgment, and all mortal things go on flowing and rolling unceasingly. Thus nothing certain can be established about one thing by another, both the judging and the judged being in continual change and motion . . . We have no communication with being, because every human nature is always midway between birth and death, offering only a dim semblance and shadow of itself, and an uncertain and feeble opinion" (II, 12, 455 A). We find this refrain often and in similar words in the *Essais*. The universal swirl dominates the "objects" as well as the "subject" and generates between the two an unceasing interplay of combinations of indeterminable movements, circling or crossing through one another. There is no prospect of escaping this confusing interplay of combinations through knowledge of regularity or even constancy. One can only surrender himself to it and describe its specific moments with the limits related to that moment. That which is real, which evades any permanent interference like quicksilver (III, 13, 816 B), and reason, which is as pliable as wax (II, 12, 425 A), cannot be brought into stable, comprehensible accord. Thus Montaigne is far removed from an epistemological intellectual inheritance—the doctrine of the possible agreement between thinking and being—which in his own century had been productive for the exact sciences and their mathematical basis. He himself did not think through his own procedure of aesthetic observation of the particular in its phase-like moments from the standpoint of its competency adequately to allow him to understand that besides it, the natural scientific method of identifying laws also was justified.

Expressed in modern terms, Montaigne does not strive for nomothetical, but rather for idiographic, knowledge. He never tires of emphasizing the variety in the (material, spiritual, character) facts: "The inference that we try to draw from the resemblance of events is uncertain, because they are always dissimilar: there is no quality so universal in this aspect of things as diversity and variety . . . Resemblance does not make things so much alike as difference makes them unlike. Nature has committed herself to make nothing separate that was not different" (III, 13, 815 B/C). And: "Their most universal quality is diversity" (II, 37, 598 A).[92] However, within the irreducible variety, the individual should be observed and exhausted to the greatest extent possible. This is the direction of Montaigne's method of experience of which he speaks so often. But no science that operates with quantitative laws and abstrac-

tions can be built upon this. Montaigne's major and magnificent movement to value what was dissimilar and thus individual led him to reach
for precisely that which could not be captured by an approach that
sought generalizing laws. Thus his concept of experience had nothing in
common with the experiments of the natural sciences. For those experiments were only a detour through the concrete world of things and
occurrences with the objective of leaving the concrete behind. In observing two falling stones, Montaigne would be interested not in what they
had in common, the law governing the two instances, but rather the
differences in the color, shape, and weight of the stones. Additionally,
for him laws lack continuity, for he allows for the possibility that nature
could turn all that was previously existing upside down. He is still
moved by the event of the late scholastic period: the nominalistic discovery of the facts that could not be anticipated through deduction and
which did not fit into any classifications and distinctions; but he does
not share the trust of his contemporaries in the natural sciences that the
collection of facts freed of the deductive system could be converted into
the generality of laws of nature.

His remoteness from contemporary sciences is most obvious when he
expresses his views on them. Only the geographic discoveries fascinated
him—for good reason, since they satisfied his relativistic hunger for
facts. But he only became mistrustful of the new discoveries in astronomy and medicine of which he learned. He was one of the first in France
who became aware of Copernicus and took him seriously.[93] But how
did he react to him? He recognized the revolutionary character of
Copernicus' teachings. But he did not conclude from this that they
contained a greater degree of truth than the earlier geocentric astronomy. Rather: "What are we to get out of that, unless that we should not
bother which of the two is so? And who knows whether a third opinion,
a thousand years from now, will not overthrow the preceding two? . . .
Thus when some new doctrine is offered to us, we have great occasion
to distrust it, and to consider that before it was produced its opposite
was in vogue; and, as it was overthrown by this one, there may arise in
the future a third invention that will likewise smash the second" (II, 12,
429 A). The new theory is thus no more than a variant among the
countless possible variants of attempts at attaining knowledge. Discoveries unhinge an old error in order to introduce a new one. The previous
changing nature of thought throws the shadow of a mere provisory
status over the new idea. Montaigne has no sense of development or
progress. He only sees replacements which, while they do eliminate

errors, do not eliminate the process of erring. Discoveries bring the old, dark horizon surrounding us into focus in a new way. In 1568, Montaigne's contemporary Louis Le Roy wrote the following, expressing pride in modern achievements: "We will fail to find that there existed in the past a century during which man's understanding and the liberal arts achieved greater perfection than now."[94] That is the fanfare of a consciousness of progress which could also be heard elsewhere, and which would later intensify to the *Querelle des Anciens et des Modernes* and which would ridicule the backwardness of the Ancients. Montaigne cannot think this way. His historical landscape of the spirit is a plane upon which men always remain at the same distance from the truth. But if the new and the old are found in *the same* abasement, then no arrogance of what is new can overwhelm the old. The old is respected in its humanity, which is not denied, even when it errs, and has the right to say that it lived and how it tried out itself and the world.

Montaigne judged the medical and mathematical discoveries in a similarly reserved manner. It is pointless to object to his decisively anti-scientific attitude by saying that he derived it broadly from untenable theories of his age and that he knew too little about astronomy, mathematics, and medicine to be equipped to renounce it. For would this refute the sense of his skepticism? Hardly. For his belief was in the borderline quality of the human essence. Even possible knowledge remains replaceable partial knowledge, thus it does not change man's destiny of being unable to attain total knowledge. No science could surpass this simple and age-old thought in the *Essais*. Nor would it want to if it had the genuine concept of knowledge, the concept that recognizes the essential boundaries of knowledge which cannot be moved by any amount of learning, no matter how greatly expanded. It is Montaigne's eternal, and thus in a more profound sense historical, mission to speak of these boundaries at which for man, because of his human essence, what is intellectually unknowable begins—and becomes a matter of intellectual indifference.

Finally, the *Essais* lack any innuendo regarding man's position of technical mastery. A few years later, Bacon will express his sentence on the noblest intellects who broaden the power of the human race over nature (*Novum Organum*, I, 129). And Descartes will want to elevate the autonomous subject who trusts in his progressive knowledge to the position of "master and proprietor of nature" (*Discours de la Méthode*). Montaigne's wisdom does not recognize any such imperialism. Along with the claims to knowledge of nature, his wisdom also withdraws the claims to will which would like to intervene in it triumphantly, planning, building, making changes. And with this, he completes his renunciation of the idea of the *dignitas hominis,* while the science of his time, making its transition to technology and rational organization, is still calling upon the biblical core of this idea: "Fill the Earth and subdue it, and have dominion . . ." (*Genesis* I, 28). Montaigne's man—who never aspires to be more than he, Montaigne, himself is—does not feel himself to be the lord of nature, but rather its protégé. To state it pointedly: he does not want the will to power, but rather the will to powerlessness.

We see a meaningful event in that just before the rational subjectivity of the modern scientific approach steps into technical mastery of the world, here in Montaigne that subjectivity of quite a different order speaks once again: indeed it is also secular, but it is closer to a subjectivity related to piety, that of human, individual well-being which, the more "subjective" it becomes, the more carefully it limits itself to listening and obeying.

CHAPTER IV

Affirmed Man

Nothing falls where everything falls. Universal sickness is
individual health.

[*III, 9, 734 B*]

1. AFFIRMED MAN

We have shown the path Montaigne took to his view of mankind. It
is a path that leads along fideistic trains of thought, and those critical of
cognition, into the depths of fragile animal nature. There, in the depths,
Montaigne encounters man as he is. He discovers that his deficiencies
define the reliable boundaries of his reality. He stops and observes man.
He immerses himself in his complicated existence and finds that the
degradation brought about through Christian theological means as well
as through those of antiquity is only a first glance, the prelude to an
affirmation that says to abased man: be what you are, be it wholly,
know yourself, and trust nature that has created you as you are. No
more despair, no longing for deliverance, no further thought that how
we are now might be the immature transitional manifestation of a
higher form of existence to which we can rise by purifying ourselves in
this world or the next.

Montaigne's descriptive study of man is only possible with the presumption of this affirmation. The critical peak of fifteen hundred years
of earlier Christian anthropology is broken off. Montaigne is a classicist
of modern moralism. From Guicciardini to Gracián and La Bruyère, the
moralists have refined our knowledge of man and have made it cautious. In their perspective, man gains in fullness and enigmatic qualities
what he loses in no longer being defined in terms of God's saving grace
or profane ethical concerns. And thus it is also with Montaigne. It is not

the extraordinary but rather the ordinary man who appears in the
Essais as the greatest of all wonders. It is only a matter of finding the
proper spotlight that allows us to be astonished at the wonder of ordinariness: ". . . from the most ordinary, commonplace, familiar things, if
we could put them in their proper light, can be formed the greatest
miracles of nature and the most wondrous examples, especially on the
subject of human actions" (III, 13, 829 B). An immeasurable task stands
before us: what appeared to be known, the ordinary man, must be
restudied without preconceptions, and without the requirement of educating him. This inquiring view has enough to do in disentangling complex facts. Perhaps it cannot disentangle them at all, but can only
quickly seize them, "the number and variety of occurrences" drives the
observer on—someone else might be able to explain what was discovered better than he: "If I do not apply them well, let another apply them
for me" (I, 21, 75 C).

The pathos of this study of man is a bright, enthusiastic joy in
surprise and discovery. Its satisfaction grows with the richness of the
material it encounters. It knows that man has at his disposal forces and
combinations of forces which cannot be summarized neatly in a single
unwavering character. For man exists in time, and the affairs of time
continuously alter the supposed character by forcing to light elements
that have been dormant, unknown even to the bearer himself: "There
are secret parts in the matters we handle which cannot be guessed,
especially in human nature—mute factors that do not show, factors
sometimes unknown to their possessor himself, which are brought
forth and aroused by unexpected occasions" (III, 2, 618 C). The observer keeps himself always open to possible new facts—whether they
are only occurring now or have already occurred. In this sense, and
only in this sense, is the historical context significant to Montaigne in a
backward as well as a forward direction: it is the field in which what
man potentially is unfolds, and is never all of what he can be, not in a
single moment, nor even in the collection of all moments. Everything is
valuable as evidence of human existence, even the most fantastic
claims. Therefore: "So in the study that I am making of our behavior
and motives, fabulous testimonies, provided they are possible, serve
like true ones. Whether they have happened or no, in Paris or Rome, to
John or Peter, they exemplify, at all events, some human potentiality,
and thus their telling imparts useful information to me" (I, 21, 75 C).
But there is actually no such thing as "man" in the singular. There is
only the plural sense of "man." In the preceding chapter we discussed

this category of difference and dissimilarity (*diversité, varieté, dissemblance*). Only in the concrete study of man differentiated by characters, times, and peoples does this fundamental category of Montaigne's attain its full validity. It compels him to see the multiplicity in others—and to live it out in himself: "Yes, I confess . . . variety alone satisfies me, and the enjoyment of diversity, at least if anything satisfies me" (III, 9, 756 B).

Much of the results of this descriptive study of man will then be found in Pascal's *Pensées*. The *Essais* have been called by some Pascal's secular Bible.[95] But Pascal reinterprets Montaigne's results. The antinomies and paradoxes of being human which Montaigne observes serenely are stretched to the breaking point by Pascal; natural reality now appears filled with symbols that evoke terror, feelings of guilt, remorse, fear about salvation: "It is appalling that man is like this." Pascal re-Christianizes what Montaigne had disentangled from Christian condemnation. As frequently as abasement motifs are heard in the *Essais*, their echo resounds again and again: men simply are this way ("This is the way men behave" III, 9, 757 B), we cannot change it ("There is no remedy" III, 13, 820 B).

2. ESSAY I, 1

Montaigne's method of pursuing his analysis of man can be seen even in the first Essay of the first book, with the title "By diverse means we arrive at the same end." Indeed, this is the first Essay only in terms of the arrangement of the text, not the first in origin; it was probably written in or after 1573. But its content justifies its preferred position. It sets up the predominant moral theme of the *Essais,* namely the question of whether one can come to an understanding of concrete, changeable man with general, rigid maxims. Montaigne would have moved it to the beginning because of the importance of this, since the last Essay of the second book, which is at the same time the last Essay of the first edition (1580), closes with the same theme, rounding the work off nicely.

Let us now look at this Essay more closely. The reader must manage a little patience for what at first are rather peripheral things that Montaigne writes there. The beginning is a banal general sentence. It reads: "The commonest way of softening the hearts of those we have offended, when, vengeance in hand, they hold us at their mercy, is by submission to move them to commiseration and pity." But is this sentence correct? "However, audacity and steadfastness—entirely contrary means—have

sometimes served to produce the same effect" (3 A)—thus is the first
sentence countered with a second sentence, precisely in the manner of
disputation in schools, where one proceeds from a *quod sic* to a *quod
non*. The second sentence is no less banal than the first. But this is not
the point, rather, the point is the insight that a general sentence is not
correct. Also, the second sentence has already moved into the qualifying
formulation: "sometimes." We certainly do not want to exaggerate this
matter—however, we must assert that hidden in the banal counter-
sentence is Montaigne's characteristic turn toward the concrete instance. That little word "sometimes" leads the trail of considerations
from the generality of a maxim into the specifics of the historical cases.
Namely, three examples follow immediately (from Froissart, Paolo
Giovio, and Bodin). In all three, events are reported in which courageous resistance moved the conquerors to magnanimity. In the second
instance (that of Commander Scanderberg) Montaigne intimates that
the response of the conqueror could have been different had the reliable
manliness of Scanderberg not prevented him from even thinking of a
show of weakness. A later insertion (4 B) provides further nuance: I,
Montaigne, would have been moved by both, the plea for mercy as well
as courageous resistance. The first version then asks what is more effective, and it decides in favor of magnanimity resulting from a high regard
for the brave opponent—but then qualifies this psychologically, in a
new point: to respond with forgiveness to the valor of the conquered is
done not only by strong and great spirits, but also by lesser ones:
"However, in less lofty souls, astonishment and admiration can engender a like effect" (4 A). Consider the formulation "however . . . have
sometimes served" which is similar to the first counter-sentence. It reveals the striving in the first Essay to show that an attitude can originate
in quite different motives and that no homogeneous causality is at work
in human affairs. But there is more. A further addition ("And directly
contrary to my first examples") reminds the reader of Alexander, who
was once so enraged by one who opposed him courageously that he had
the man tortured to death (5 B). Montaigne asks, how can this be
explained? Was boldness something taken for granted to such an extent
by Alexander that he was no longer able to respect it? This was the
conclusion in layer B of the text. But a handwritten insert poses a second
question: was Alexander envious of the other man's boldness? The
Essay breaks off without answering this question. We have only one
more sentence to add which has the final conclusion; in the first version
it is at the end, but it was displaced later by the inserts. It reads: "Truly

man is a marvelously vain, diverse, and undulating object. It is hard to found any constant and uniform judgment on him" (5 B).

But what does all this mean? A general maxim discovered to describe practical behavior is refuted in its general validity with a series of individual cases, that is, it is itself limited to individual cases. The observation recognizes that no summary, one-track judgment can do justice to the unlimited combination of what is human, nor does it permit a prediction of man's behavior. How he will act can only be found in each individual case. No causality that permits generalization can be discovered in man's changing conditions (situation, character, momentary mood). What appears identical in its outcome (magnanimous behavior by the conqueror) is not identical in its motives. What is apparently identical branches out, when considered on a case-by-case basis, according to its motives, into in each case an individual difference. An act thus has its full reality not in its formal similarity or identity with another act, but rather in its growth from its particular motive. An act of mercy can originate in sympathy or in respect for the boldness of one's opponent. If it comes from the latter motive, it could also have within it further different motives, for example, greatness or weakness of spirit. This can be continued at will. Though Montaigne does not go further in this Essay, his tendency to do so can be detected, since the later additions point in the direction of progressive particularization. He had also become aware more strongly in these of the obscurity of the connection between action and motive than he was in the first draft. While in the first draft he did point out in the case of Scanderberg that the explanation of his behavior was protected from error only due to the particular circumstances—and this means that that explanation was close to being in error—in the late draft he leaves an explanation of Alexander's behavior completely open: the reality of the act is no longer interpreted according to its motives at all, rather, it is just seen as a case that is different from all other cases. No synthesis results from the *Quod-sic-quod-non* beginning of the Essay. A school disputation would have aimed for one. Montaigne avoids rising above the contrary maxims to arrive at a third that would contain both of them or even all other cases. His "synthesis" lies in the following problematical judgment: man can sometimes act from this motive, sometimes from another.

A fundamental insight into man has been achieved: "Man is a diverse and undulating object."[96] It results in a change in the anthropological method. The tradition of performing classifications according to maxims or ethical standards, all of which presume a constancy or repeatability of situations and individuals, must be replaced with the skeptical ("spying") view of facts and their changing particularities. The observation of man changes from a schematization of archetypes into capturing views of individuals in the moment. This is the method of the discipline of morality. Thus here, in this first Essay, Montaigne applies the procedure with which he will go to work in all future efforts. And this, too, is the point in which one can pinpoint the first influence of Plutarch in the direction that we discussed earlier (see chapter 2).

Let us now compare the Essay just discussed with a text by Machiavelli. The third book of his *Discorsi sopra la prima deca di Tito Livio* contains a group of chapters that show remarkable similarity to this Essay, namely, chapters 19 to 22. We will cite some passages from these. Two great authors of the sixteenth century, the one at the beginning, the other at the end, are confronted with the same question of the make-up of that complex human reality. Both proceed by the same method of casuistic breakdown of general statements. But while the earlier work ends in a political doctrine, the later one projects so far into open factuality that only a fragmentary point of view remains. It is quite questionable whether Montaigne was acquainted with the *Discorsi*, but in any case, an influence should not be concluded from this comparison.[97]

In chapter 19 of the *Discorsi*, Machiavelli weighs two practical maxims concerning the ruling of men against one another: (1) leniency and kindness in a ruler results in obedience in the subjects; (2) harshness and cruelty have the same result. To the question of whether both cannot be considered correct, the answer is: yes, but under different preconditions; the first is appropriate in a republican state, the second in a tyrannical state. Thus this means that neither can claim absolute correctness since each is qualified by its historical position. The abstract maxims become occasional, limited, flexible recommendations due to their inclusion in the flow of changing preconditions. Chapter 21 (for which the reader is prepared in chapter 20) shows striking similarity with our Essay in its theme and formulation. Its title is: "How it happened that Hannibal achieved the same results in Italy as Scipio did in Spain through a method different from that of the latter." Montaigne uses the title: "By Diverse Means We Arrive at the Same End." Machiavelli shows how one conqueror can attain the same ends through magnanimity as another did through harshness, namely, obtain respect for himself. The relationship between conqueror and conquered is explained here from the conqueror's standpoint, in Montaigne from that of the conquered. But that is an insignificant difference in view of the agreement in the stating of the theme. Furthermore, Machiavelli reflects upon the reasons why the cruel conqueror is also successful. The result (obtaining respect), after the apparent identity is eliminated, is then further differentiated in one of its bases (cruelty). Namely: (1) men always want something new, and someone who approaches them as new, whether he treats them well or badly, will be successful, people will follow him; (2) men are ruled by love and by fear—one who wants to get people under his control can play upon the one as well as on the other, thus the cruel approach which inspires fear will also lead toward that goal. Following this Machiavelli discusses how both attitudes (kindness and force) have certain entanglements associated with them: benevolence will initially subdue those conquered, but it will also entice them to attempt an uprising to which in the end the benevolent ruler will have to respond with cruelty in order to put down the uprising. Yet the subjugating harshness destroys the love of the subjects, generates hatred, and thus new cruelty from the conqueror. "I will conclude then," Machiavelli says, that everything depends on the person who is ruler and conqueror; if only he is strong, it does not matter whether he treats his subjects in a hostile or benevolent manner. Thus we again see two opposing possibilities compared. But it follows from the empirical evidence of human nature and from historical situations that each of these can only be realized in certain cases, depending upon given premises to which the path leading to the goal of the ruler's power must be accommodated. Chapter 22 only takes this further. What is better, benevolence or strictness? The value question is asked. Authors are consulted. But they are unequal to the task, for they offer only contradictions, no resolution. So to arrive at a conclusion ("In order not to leave this part uncertain"), Machiavelli shifts the question to the character make-up of the individual rulers and the requirements of the individual forms of state. The antinomy of the abstract maxims (be kind–be harsh) dissolves in a functional plurality of possibilities which depends upon the individual persons and the particular situations. The ruler should choose the maxim that is appropriate to his nature and the form of state over which he rules.

If one then compares these texts with our Essay, one sees how both authors proceed from a *Quod-sic-quod-non* antithesis of abstract maxims to advance to a casuistry which, by observation of individual cases, supports an explanation on the ground of empirical reality. They discover that man is much too variable to be restricted to following a maxim that applies to all cases. Both Machiavelli and Montaigne set aside generality under the pressure of the diversity of history and character.

But differences do exist. The Italian is a politician or political historian. He pauses in his observation when he has discovered the relationship of human action to archetypical forms of state and has identified the rules that are organically conducive to each of these forms. However, Montaigne presses on, and though not so definitively in Essay, I, 1, all the more so in the others. He is concerned with the totality of human reality; each of its spheres is particularized, even atomized, into the countless number of individual cases. No rules are to be derived from them, least of all political ones. Man is completely at the mercy of his fluctuating indeterminability. Furthermore, Machiavelli still believes he can explain why something is in one case this way, in another different. He takes his historical and psychological need for causality into his recognition of diversity. He differentiates man, but he also seeks to decipher him in the differentiations. Montaigne dispenses with clarification, particularly in the insertions in the Essay. He does not answer the question of why Alexander tortures his bold opponent to death. Machiavelli still knows why one individual must be cruel, Montaigne no longer knows this. Finally, Machiavelli displays definite pessimism. Chapter 21, which we mentioned, contains sinister contempt for man: treat men cruelly and you will have them under your control, particularly if you intend to establish a strong state. But pessimism is a qualitative determination that makes of man something uniform. This is precisely what Montaigne avoids. As we will see, he does have some "Machiavellian" impulses, but these neither serve an amoral isolation of the energy of one who acts nor originate in a contempt for man. He leaves man undisturbed in his mixtures of good and evil, and in this he ascertains a nature that lies this side of the ethical categories. The cleverness of the Italian says excellent things about the paradoxes of human nature, that, for example, magnanimous action due to its opposite effect (rebelliousness) must turn into harshness, and so forth. But from all his insights he derives practical conclusions that are intended to serve the politician in his goal-oriented actions. Montaigne draws no conclusion. For him, it is not a matter of "in order not to leave this part uncertain," and it is no longer a matter of "I will conclude then." Both drafts of Essay I, 1 end as fragments. The puzzle of man emerges from the opposing particular cases and any judgment is denied except the following: one cannot approach man with any uniform judgment. For Montaigne, to research man means to lead man back into his mysteriousness—or in other words: free him from the predeterminations of the usual maxims and psychological hypotheses and arrive at a view that lets wave upon wave of this "flowing being" glide by. The contemplative Frenchman knows a bit more about man than the practical Florentine who, as all practical people, abbreviates what is infinite.

3.   CONTRADICTORINESS

Then, in the first Essay of the second book, "Of the Inconsistency of Our Actions," we find a classical collection of statements on the study of man. According to the results of Villey's research, the Essay probably originated around the same time as the one just discussed. But here everything is more self-contained and resolute. The perspective is broader, the anecdotes are richer in content, the reflections are more powerful. The text is filled with passages borrowed from Seneca. But in the manner of the earlier Montaigne, who as a rule did not quote prose, but only verse, literally, these passages appear in the form of French paraphrases. The Essay as a whole is based upon an ethical standard of Seneca's: the uniformity, symmetry, and internal consistency of what is morally purified, which is differentiated from the internal contradictoriness of what is average. But this had only heuristic significance in Montaigne. It helps him get a better sense of the facts of human contradictoriness. He connects an ethical purpose with this in appearance only. The separation found in Seneca of the "sick" unwise man and the "healthy" man of wisdom fades to the level of literary fiction. Earlier, we discussed how Montaigne follows the Roman moral philosophers only to the point at which the analysis of human susceptibilities moves into recommendations for healing man (see earlier discussion). This can be seen particularly clearly in this Essay. As was the case with religious absoluteness in the "Apology," here it is the ethical absoluteness of the hypothetical background against which the broken, uncontrolled contour of factual humanity stands out so sharply.

The Essay offers a description of human absurdities which is quite faithful to its subject. Anyone observing our actions, he writes at the beginning, will be at quite a loss if he tries to comprehend them from a single viewpoint "for they (human actions) commonly contradict each other so strangely that it seems impossible that they have come from the same shop" (239 A). Nero, the potentate of cruelty, is shaken when he must sign a death sentence. The Agrigentines enjoy their lives as if they were to die tomorrow, yet they build houses as if they were to live forever. The girl who in fear of being raped by an enemy soldier defends herself like a second Lucrece and attempts suicide is otherwise a "wench not so hard to come to terms with" (241 A). A soldier who is courageous but ill is cured—and he loses his courage, because he now lacks the reason he was willing to give up his life; his courage was weariness with life. Anecdotes such as these, in great numbers and all from classical sources, create the following image: man is a bundle of contradictions. This is what makes any attempt to base a constant judgment upon his factual inconstancy so questionable. If two opposing forces are fighting over us, do we have within us two souls (242 C)? This may be an allusion to the Manichaean doctrine; Pascal will refer to this passage later (*Pensées,* fragment 417). And near the end we read: "We are all patchwork, and so shapeless and diverse in composition that each bit, each moment, plays its own game. And there is as much difference between us and ourselves as between us and others" (244 A). Later additions prove this from Montaigne's personal experience and formulate it in antitheses that he poured out rapidly: bashful-impudent, chaste-sensual, talkative-taciturn, wise-dull . . . I am all this and see all these things in myself depending on which way I turn (242 B/C).

Montaigne knows how far removed he is from the literary clichés of the portrayal of man. We cannot be certain of which author he had in mind when he wrote the following sentences, but his awareness that he is taking a different path is unmistakable: ". . . in view of the natural instability of our conduct and opinions, it has often seemed to me that even good authors are wrong to insist on fashioning a consistent and solid fabric out of us. They choose one general characteristic, and go and arrange and interpret all a man's actions to fit their picture; and if they cannot twist them enough, they go and set them down to dissimulation" (239 B). A moralistic view emerges to contrast with the deductive, classifying portrayal of man in the older mode. It does not eliminate only the concept of unity of the category man, it also eliminates the concept of the unity of uniform character: ". . . judge them [men] in detail and distinctly, bit by bit," is the guiding principle of this method (239–240 B/C). No single one of our forces can become the identifying sign of our specific character; each one of these forces can be intersected by its opposing force within the same individual: ". . . one courageous deed must not be taken to prove a man valiant . . ." (242 A). The only potentially successful prospect of discovering the whole weave of contrasts in a character lies in patient observation that penetrates into individual aspects: ". . . to judge a man, we must follow his traces long and carefully . . ." (243 A). And then, with an ironic undertone, we hear this principal formula for the method: "*Distinguo* is the most universal member of my logic" (242 B). It is ironic because the words of this little sentence stem from the methodology that Montaigne is abandoning; he does not have a logical intent, nor does his "distinguishing" mean that late-scholastic tinkering with empty concepts. He means a distinguishing of uncategorizable facts, he means a differentiating view that increases the variety of what is observed through the change in viewpoint. Thus we have the following sentence from the last Essay: What I find in man "I do not attempt to arrange this infinite variety of actions, so diverse and so disconnected, into certain types and categories, and distribute my lots and divisions distinctly into recognized classes and sections . . . Not only do I find it hard to link our actions with one another, but each one separately I find hard to designate properly by some principal characteristic, so two-sided and motley do they seem in different lights" (III, 13, 824–825 B/C).

What today is self-evident to psychologists, namely the complex, contradictory layering of the character and intellectual life, was won for human knowledge by Montaigne—though not by him alone—through a strenuous stripping away of anthropological concepts of types. What did science make of man? he asks in the "Apology." A microcosm, is his response. But that favorite word of his century sounds derisive here. And what does such a microcosm look like? It is pieced together from purely artificial, that is, conceptual, elements, subelements, capacities, functions—and this "to accommodate the impulses they see in man . . ." The result is construction and falsification: "They make him an imaginary republic" which one can shift around and alter at will, ". . . and yet they still do not have him." That is, there is always something there that eludes this artificial construct (II, 12, 401 A). Montaigne recognizes that each classification is already false due to its logical ordering principle and its ranking approach because it derives the particular—the concrete man—from a generality, and because it overlooks the fact that without a leap, without a continuous new beginning of one's view, one cannot get beyond the generality and into what is particular and real: "All judgments in gross are loose and imperfect" (III, 8, 721 B). This recognition contains one of the great impulses of the *Essais*, incalculable in its uses for a study of mores, that is, for what at first is a literary art form of what later will become scientific psychology.

4. INDIVIDUALITY

Goethe's "qualitative individuality" has been discussed.[98] This apt
term can also be applied to Montaigne, just as he can be considered an
important forerunner of the concept of individuality per se from the end
of the eighteenth century. Individuals can be differentiated in his view
not by gradations of general characteristics, that is, merely quantita-
tively, but rather by each one's unique layering and combination of
them, thus this is also a shift in the values of these characteristics, in
other words, it is a qualitative approach. Individuals interest him in
view of their inimitable, vegetative growth, regardless of whether it is
great or slight. Montaigne expresses individual variation with clumsy
theoretical means, but with an adequately clear tendency, at the beginning of Essay I, 42. Even the title is programmatic: "Of the inequality
that is between us." He then writes: "Plutarch says somewhere that he
does not find so much difference between one animal and another as he
does between one man and another." The invocation of Plutarch at
precisely this point confirms what we said earlier. The comment refers
to a passage in the "Gryllus" dialogue in the *Moralia*, which in a rendering of Amyot's translation reads: "For I do not think that there is such a
great distance from one beast to the next, as compared to the distance
that separates man from man in matters of prudence, discourse, reason,
and memory." But this is not yet enough for Montaigne: "I would
willingly outdo Plutarch and say that there is more distance from a
given man to a given man than from a given man to a given animal . . .
and that there are as many degrees in minds as there are fathoms from
here to heaven, and as innumerable" (189 A). He repeated the sentence
almost literally in the "Apology" (II, 12, 342 A). This is an indication of
the importance he attaches to individual differences ("between a given
man and a given man") and the plethora (*innumerable*) of individuals.
What sets man above the animal is for him no longer logos, but rather
the capacity for greater differentiation. This concept has been expressed
several times in the period following; one encounters it again in French
literature of the nineteenth century in the works of Honoré de Balzac.[99]

On the occasion of his criticism of school medicine, Montaigne once
developed a plan of what should be considered by a good doctor in
order to begin proper treatment of a patient: his physical constitution,
temperament, moods, inclinations, manners of behaving, way of thinking . . . ; even the astrological constellation (II, 37, 586–587 A). This is
indeed tailor-made to apply to medicine. But this can only be said at all

after one has learned to see man as woven into a web of external and internal factors with particularities of character and physical body, affected by environment, these things being different for each individual. The consideration of astrological constellations can be explained in that Montaigne was seeking the individualizing conditions of man at any cost, even at the cost of a belief in astrology, which he would usually smile at. If he had known to what extent Paracelsus had anticipated him in this, he would have been more kindly disposed toward him.

Montaigne's gift of detecting what in a man is irreplaceably his own is extraordinary. It comes to its fullest development in his portrayal of himself; more on this later. The path leads through detail and intimate anecdote. For in these he senses the scent of what is alive. They serve to reveal undefinable yet describable images of each particular organism with body and soul. Man when relaxed is more likely to reveal his essence than when he is putting on his public face. This is knowledge Plutarch offered:[100] ". . . to judge a man really properly, we must chiefly examine his ordinary actions and surprise him in his everyday habit" (II, 29, 533 A). He notes that Caesar used to scratch his head, Cicero to wrinkle his nose (II, 17, 479 A). Several times he mentions Plato's report (*Phaedo* 60b) of how Socrates rubs his legs when the chains are removed from them (II, 11, 310 C). Such minor traits provide him with better insights into the natural make-up of the individual than he would find in speeches, maxims, great deeds. "Every movement reveals us" (I, 50, 219 C), if one only knows to look. The individual minor traits form the bridge across the centuries upon which he can closely approach the ancients on a human level. He once writes that he would have loved to watch while the Romans spoke, ate, walked (III, 9, 763 B). He regrets the loss of the self-portrayals of Alexander, Augustus, and Cato (II, 18, 503 A/C). He would have wished for even more familiar details than he could already find in Plutarch's writings (II, 31, 541 A). When writing of his father, he reports precisely on his stature, face, bearing, inclination to use canes filled with lead, or his trick of walking around the table on his hands (II, 2, 248 A). There are countless such passages. Is this a shortsighted restriction to minor things? Yet this care in the minor things was necessary for this reacquired act of studying the true characteristics of man. Montaigne once comments that only painters of unknown mythical landscapes can indulge in ideal images: "But when they draw from nature for us in a subject that is familiar and known to us, we demand of them a perfect and exact representation of the lineaments and colors . . ." (II, 12, 402 C). The analogy of this critique of the painter's ideal landscape to a critique of the anthropological ideal types is obvious. Montaigne demands the same true likeness in literary depiction as the art of painting had demanded of itself since the fifteenth century.

5.   LINGUISTIC CRITICISM

If this humanity is to come into full view, it has to be protected against generalizations of concept and language. As a result, Montaigne's linguistic criticism is connected with his qualitative individuality and the category of variety. We mentioned this earlier (chapter 2). It was described there in the stand it took against rhetoricized humanism and its conviction that there was an ideal correspondence between thing and word. The same criticism accompanies the examining analysis of man and here it finds its more profound necessity. Admittedly, Montaigne is no philosopher of language. He lacks the thoroughness for this. But the frequency of comments of linguistic criticism scattered through the *Essais* is striking. They support Montaigne's "heraclitic" view of the world and his individualizing view of man in that they declare that what is particular about a thing or individual about a man is linguistically inexhaustible: language and its object in each case are both intrinsically mobile; they can approach each other only in a fleeting moment, and language always brings with it the risk of transforming what is original, that is, what is different, into apparent unity with something else, and thus to destroy it. This is the fundamental concept constituting his linguistic criticism.

It is nominalistic. This is stated clearly in the sentence with which he begins Essay II, 16, "Of Glory": "There is the name and the thing. The name is a sound that designates and signifies the thing; the name is not a part of the thing or of the substance, it is an extraneous piece attached to the thing, and outside of it" (468 A). In this as in the following passages some have identified paraphrasing from chapter 191 of Sebond's *Theologia naturalis*.[101] This is correct to the extent that Montaigne in fact does follow Sebond in the theological explanation of the name of God: God cannot grow substantially in the growth of his name used by man, for the name is only an accessory of God's. But Montaigne diverges into secular considerations. He applies this thought to language per se—more precisely, to human glory, the bearer of which is language. Here he intensifies the moment of linguistic criticism. Sebond only rejects the agreement of name and thing from the standpoint of God's transcendence. Thus Sebond was able to say: "The name is what represents and signifies the thing as a whole."[102] But Montaigne only writes, in his passage cited above (II, 16), "which designates and signifies the thing"; he has dropped the word expressing "as a whole." The rest of his sentence is radically critical (the name is only an accessory, not a part of the thing, etc.). And he has also added: "the name is a sound," and this can be interpreted, especially in view of his other statements in the passage, as a distant echo of the nominalistic definition of the word as a mere *flatus vocis*. This is a profound difference from Sebond.

This concept of nominalism from the aspect of linguistic criticism means that names (words) are only standardizations of similar things that are not inherent in the things, but rather are performed after the fact (*post res*) by the subject. It is not surprising to find this thought again in the *Essais*, which stress the separation of being and thinking everywhere. This thought was also present in the Stoic school, as well as in Pyrrhonism. It could also have come to Montaigne from this source. He read in Sextus Expiricus' *Hypotyposes* (II, 8) that words are random conventions, not essential to the thing, and thus unable to state anything reliable about the thing.

Essay II, 16, as indicated, transfers the skeptical, nominalistic linguistic criticism to the problem of glory. He takes us through the train of thought whereby glory—that is, the reflection of a man in a remembering, praising, or even scorning word—and the particular man do not correspond. The man is more or different from what his contemporaries and those following say about him. We will return to this directly. What is important at the moment is the idea that man does not disappear in his glory. Since glory is seen as an exception in the function of language to recognize and preserve what is real, the idea is connected with the further thought that there is no naming and recognition which, to the extent that it remains rigid and uniform, is identical with the individual at whom it is directed. What a man sees in and expresses about another man does not exhaust his essence any more than a statement about a thing exhausts its essence (II, 16, 474–476). Montaigne's concept of language still contains elements of the classical, humanistic ennoblement of language as something promoting glory, that is, the capacity to raise the empirical deed to spiritual being and thereby preserve it. Thus he develops a part of his comments which amount to linguistic criticism on the subject of glory. But that ennobling conception only paves the way for him and is converted into its opposite. Glory is to him a chance act due to which language makes an event public. But what is known constitutes only a fragment of what is real (II, 16, 476). Furthermore, the name (understood as fame and reputation) does not affect what is unique. As he writes radically in another Essay: "Whatever variety of herbs there may be, the whole thing is included under the name of salad" (I, 46, 201 A).

Names lack essential necessity in men as well as in things. They fabricate what does not exist: absolute unity and repeatability. Language leads what is unknown and unique back to what is known and general (III, 13, 824 B). It identifies that which is nonidentical. Diderot will have the same thoughts about two centuries later.

Then other considerations also come to bear on this. For example: The word is not only inadequate to the thing, it is also ambiguous. The ancients had already recognized this. Among Chrysippus' theorems was this: *omne verbum ambiguum esse.*[103] Montaigne persistently returns to this ambiguity. The unceasing metamorphosis of intellectual life spirals in the transformation of the meaning of words. The quiescent external impression words make in sound and in written form conceals but does not eliminate this spiraling. And even when the word agrees with its meaning according to the speaker's intentions, it does not lose its fluctuating restlessness. It only expresses what is meant imperfectly and with secondary connotations that the speaker did not intend. It is an unreliable tool that projects the unsureness of the intellect outward into the world. It cannot stand up to precise examination, one can interpret it this way or that. It creates misunderstandings, the endless chain of contradictory interpretations, conflicts between sects, wars. "Our speech has its weaknesses and its defects, like all the rest. Most of the occasions for the troubles of the world are grammatical," and an allusion to the supper table dispute follows (II, 12, 392 A). Montaigne eagerly repeats what then was offered against language on the occasion of the battles over dogma:[104] ". . . there is no sense or aspect, either straight or bitter, or sweet, or crooked, that the human mind does not find in the writings it undertakes to search" (II, 12, 442 A). Dangerous distortions of the word such as these are not simply due to the interpreter, but rather are the result of the ambiguity of words. Instead of illuminating the obscurity of things, the words make them even more obscure. Thus in addition to the difficulty of understanding man and the world, man is confronted with the difficulty of understanding interpretations already made: "It is more of a job to interpret the interpretations than to interpret the things . . ." (III, 13, 818 B). Thus the word necessarily flows in the same current of inconstancy to escape from which it originally was created: "Words when reported have a different sense, as they have a different sound" (III, 12, 814 B).

But Montaigne shrewdly also perceives the positive chance in this negative determination, namely, the possibility of interpreting texts in a direction that furthers greater yields than the author knowingly put there: "The work, by its own power and fortune, may second the workman beyond his inventiveness and knowledge and outstrip him" (III, 8, 718 B). Or even more emphatically: "An able reader often discovers in other men's writings perfections beyond those that the author put in or perceived, and lends them richer meanings and aspects" (I, 24, 93 A). These are perhaps the last remnants of the Platonic doctrine of the inspired poet who does not himself know what he is saying because he is only the mouthpiece of God (Plato, *Apology* 22b, etc.). But this is used in Montaigne quite without speculation, and also justifies piecemeal his own free relationship to the works handed down to him, which he uses without hermeneutic precision. He writes during a late period: "I have read in Livy a hundred things that another man has not read in him. Plutarch has read in him a hundred besides the ones I could read, and perhaps besides what the author had put in" (I, 26, 115 A). In any case, sentences such as these are astounding suspicions coming from an intellect of the sixteenth century. They perceive how the spark of a force of meaning which rises beyond the speaker can be struck from the weakness of linguistic ambiguity. But Montaigne only touches upon this. The attitude of linguistic criticism prevails. We will not pursue this any further here. It should only become visible in its role of supporting the process of individualizing observation. For when the situation with language is such that it is more likely to conceal than reveal, then the description of concrete man can take only one path, the path that avoids fixation in words, or rather balances it with continuous new statements and by ranking images (anecdotes, stories, gestures, etc.) above conceptual interpretation. Deriving comments from observation constitutes an attempt that must be continuously regenerated from different perspectives, and which take things back as often as it establishes them. This kind of commenting only circles around its object, man, or cuts across him with pros and cons until his complex image shimmers forth from the dense web of intersecting, contradictory statements. We will come back to this later (chapter 8). However, let us note that that skeptical formula of "What do I know?" is formulated in a questioning manner from the bases of linguistic criticism described; in fact, it is included as an additional example of linguistic criticism (see earlier discussion).

The dis-covering of man in the *Essais* takes place in the quite literal sense of the removal of coverings. Among these is glory. We have indicated the reasons why, in Montaigne, the critique of glory intersects the critique of language. Under glory, besides the usual meaning of the word, he also includes honor, in fact all that men mutually consider worthy of discussion, what is reported and handed down. These meanings merge, but have in common that they all signify a falsification that man perceives via incomplete or prematurely absolute speech about something. The man who is praised is not the real man, and the real man is richer than his public reflection in his own environment or later: this is the crux of the critique of glory. The study of man in the *Essais* strives to retrieve man from the way he is redesigned by glory. It is further aware of how the consideration of glory, reputation, and honor can insinuate itself into man's behavior vis-à-vis others and, more important, himself, as a danger that threatens the authenticity of his being himself, and thus threatens the only certainty that he is granted, namely, his individual existence.

Thus in his own way Montaigne states his position on one of the major themes of the Renaissance. The theme of glory has a long history that we will not replay here.[105] Let us just review the necessary parts.

Roman ethics offered two treatments of this. In one of them, they taught that *virtus* and *gloria* were a unit, meaning that deed and virtue could only be considered complete when mirrored by glory, and there was no thought of a different means of confirming their value, for example from the deed and the virtue themselves. This was the older view, of which strong traces can still be found in Cicero. Thus Montaigne can call upon him as the representative of an ethical system that measures morality according to glory, and acts upon this, rather than upon the ideal value within what is moral itself (II, 16, 470 A, according to *De finibus* II, 15). However, due to Greek influences, the Romans became aware of the problems associated with this unity concept. Thus in Cicero himself, to an even greater extent in Seneca, and also in Pliny the Younger, we find the other concept, namely that the fruit of moral behavior is intrinsic to it, and that *gloria, fama, honos* serve only as supplements to it which can confirm it, but which are not essential.[106] Christianity intensifies this distinction into the contrast between moral inwardness for which one is answerable only before God and its reflex in the secular world, which has become meaningless. The most important elements on this can be found in Augustine's *Civitas Dei* (V, chaps. 11–19). In the Renaissance the two motifs, idealization of glory and devaluation of glory, become intertwined; this is most pronounced in Petrarch. Nevertheless, the rise of courtly cultures led to a preference for the first, all the more so because the positive concept of glory was prepared in the literary consciousness of the humanists (writing creates glory for the performers of the deeds described, the ones to whom the work is addressed, and the author himself). The Italian courts of the sixteenth century then created the bridge between the Roman *gloria* concept and the concept of the honor of one's social class. The extreme position can be found in Castiglione's *Cortegiano*. There it is explained that great deeds should intentionally be performed in view of representatives of the highest social classes in order to obtain from them the glory that is what makes performance of these deeds worthwhile (II, 8). This then applies to the consciousness as a whole of European courts and their aristocracy over the next two centuries. What man is, he is only to the extent that he is this in the view of those of his rank and in the view of princes, that is, in the eyes of the right people. A man's actions and manners are only valuable in their manifestation, that is, in the reflection of the social castes that are capable of making judgments. According to this theory, man obtains his true objective validity that includes him into the societal framework here, in the spotlight of glory and honor. What does not appear in this spotlight does not exist. It is thereby a matter of indifference whether one's reflection in one's surroundings corresponds to the real facts, that is, whether it is truly the manifestation of the facts—or whether it is only an appearance that one who is greedy for honor can create even when the moral substance is minimal or nonexistent. Thus in courtly cultures the drive for reputation took the upper hand, and this was answered by the destruction psychology of the moralists ("The world is only made up of appearances"; La Rochefoucauld, No. 256), which would later be described quite concisely and incomparably by Montesquieu.[107]

After all this, we would expect nothing other than that Montaigne would have to disapprove of the positive concept of glory in its general ethical application and in its particular societal one. From Roman antiquity, he makes the corresponding passages from Seneca's letters his own. He combines them at the conclusion of his Essay on solitude (I, 39) into a paraphrase filled with personal warmth on the independence of a philosophical state of being with oneself from the praise or criticism of the world. The most important thing he has to say about glory can be found in Essay II, 16, which—a rare occurrence—contains what the title promises. At first it appears only to be concerned with the argument that pure morality should be separated from the obsession with glory. But this is just the prelude. Montaigne is thinking less of the protection of morality (*vertu*) and its absolute value, which is confirmed in one's conscience, than of the protection of man's ability to be himself. He is seeking the level at which man is entirely himself, unadulterated individuality. The initial ethical motif gives way to the anthropological insight that there is a disparity between what man is factually and what he appears to be. Man when he enters into the view of others is already man who is exposed to misunderstanding and the attempt at leveling to bring him in line with an unreal general conception. Thus Montaigne repeats the idea that he expressed earlier in I, 46: the name is not the man. "Name" here can be understood both in the simple sense of the word and as the embodiment of all that characterizes a man from the outside. Thus we read: "I have no name that is sufficiently my own" (475 A). Thus Montaigne moves into open conflict with the courtly and societal concepts of glory and honor when he explains how deed and glory only come together by chance. Glory is not a proof of the quality of the one who receives it, nor does the quality of an act or a behavior carry with it the surety of glory: "An infinity of fine actions must be lost without a witness before one appears to advantage" (471 A). The pages we are referring to here by way of summary sound like a response to Castiglione. Montaigne stresses that also an act that is not reflected in glory—which would thus be worthless by courtly standards—retains its worth. He then, based upon such distinctions, develops a critique of the historical material which has been handed down. It is a critique of the naive belief that all that occurred was reported, and all news of what occurred is based upon truth. Montaigne is concerned with that which left no traces in glory or in reports of events: "If I had in my possession all the unknown events, I should think I could very easily supplant those that are known, in every kind of example" (476 C). What is unknown in man also extends into the past. Montaigne's doubting of the congruent meaningfulness of name, honor, reports of events, penetrates deductively into the zone of silence in what has been handed down, senses life in what is forgotten, and perceives the random nature even of the historical image that man makes of man.

But all this only adds to the basic thought that the core of concrete man can only be grasped approximately from the outside. Later on, this reprimand: "We do not care so much what we are in ourselves and in reality as what we are in the public mind" (III, 9, 729 B). This is aimed with a somewhat educational emphasis against the exclusive societal concept of the courtly-baronial culture, but it is based upon the anthropological central thought of the *Essais:* what man really is (here: "what we are in reality"), he is only with himself ("in ourselves"). When Montaigne is discussing glory and the reporting of events, as well as language as a whole, he stresses not their enlightening function, but rather their concealing function; this serves the purpose for him of honoring man who is without glory and without a name as something that is still to be discovered. This immediately leads him to the problems of his study of man to the extent that they attempt to probe others; he knows he only has solid ground under his feet when he makes himself the object. Admittedly, he then ventures into a new problem area, this time the question as to the knowability of the self. More on this later.

6. COMPLEX MAN

Montaigne's man, when freed from the sheaths of prejudices, intentional or unintentional self-falsification, public manners, and theories handed down that tend to idealize him, is the bearer of all possible contradictions. Dilthey commented once that "the concept of contradictions in an individual always arises only from the comparison of what empirically is the given with the image of a logically ordered and expediently operating spiritual context" and that the *Eidos* of an individual "connects the actual bases which are not determined by logic with a structure which organizes things expediently."[108] Something similar occurs in Montaigne. He arrives at the sharp perception of contradictions by a comparison with a possible ordered structure. But the comparison always opens up into the abandonment of such a structure (*architecture* II, 12, 401 A. The passage should be reread; we presented some of it earlier). He has no term for the "expediently ordering structure" of the individual, and he does not want one, in his fear of premature standardization. Or, in other words, he fills the structure of the individual all the way to its most intimate areas with contradictions. And at the same time he recognizes that nature, in a mysterious but empirically detectable manner, keeps the individual alive by the power of these contradictions. "Nature proceeds thus by the benefit of our inconstancy," he writes on the occasion of such an analysis of contradiction and inconstancy in Essay III, 4 (635 B). It is not a structure that encompasses the contradictions, but rather the contradictions themselves that form the particular organic configuration of a man. This is the root of the frequent formula in the *Essais,* which is not meant only empirically, but also refers to essence: "complex man, human admixture" (II, 20, 511 B, etc.). To the pressing question of where this comes from, then, Montaigne, with the usual ambiguity of his "last" responses, keeps in reserve the insinuation that this is just as much the compulsion arising from the urgency of our being as it is the rescuing action of nature. But he does not like to speak of such backgrounds. His gaze is focused on the facts in which our contradictory crossovers come to light. The following sentence shows how he drops the unknown cause ("I know not how") to get to the fact itself: "We are, I know not how, double within ourselves, with the result that we do not believe what we believe, and we cannot rid ourselves of what we condemn" (II, 16, 469 C).

His researcher's drive is completely in the sway of what Goethe once called "the wondrous complication of human nature in which the most pronounced opposites unite, the material and the intellectual, the common and the unusual, the offensive and the delightful, the limited and the limitless, one could make a long list of such things."[109] Montaigne did keep such a list, which in its wealth of material has no rival in the theoretical material of his time. Its value is not lessened by the fact that many of his observations are literary, namely of classical origin. For he is the first to pull together this fine-lined drawing of man. The fact that he retrieved the findings of classical psychology from oblivion is in itself an achievement. Measured against him, Plutarch's descriptive achievements are only a beginning (Saint-Evremond commented thoroughly on this later[110]), Seneca's analyses seem inadequate due to their ties to ethical healing, Sebond's division of men into good and evil seems much too crude. Montaigne also knew of what he was capable; he was proud of the accuracy of his description of man ("the pertinence of my description") and of its unmasking method ("to reveal by their [men's] outward manifestations their inward inclinations"), and attributed to himself a particular gift for research ("a studious bent") (III, 13, 824 B). It is interesting that he could forget his customary modesty at precisely this point.

And now a few particulars so one can see how he proceeds. The short Essay II, 20 ("We Taste Nothing Pure") concerns the interconnections among spiritual contents. He begins with the abasement motif: everything we touch is corrupted by the weakness of our human condition. But he quickly proceeds into the neutral description of how joy flows into sorrow, pleasure into pain, and none of these emotions can exist without the opposite one. It is the spirit's game of contradictions with its barely perceptible approaches to the extremes, concealed in deceptions, which is brought to view here. Much has been borrowed from Seneca. An example is the sentence "Metrodorus used to say that in sadness there is some alloy of pleasure" (510 B). But in Seneca (*ep.* 99) it is followed by a sharp rejection of the possible enjoyment of pleasure in pain because this prolongs the pain instead of eliminating it, as is appropriate behavior for the man of wisdom who overcomes emotion. We find nothing of this in Montaigne. He is interested in the complexity itself, not in overcoming it. Thus his description of it is also more precise than that in the Roman's work: "Our utmost sensual pleasure has an air of groaning and lament about it . . . when we forge a picture of it at its highest point, we deck it with sickly and painful epithets and qualities: languor, softness, weakness, faintness, *morbidezza:* a great testimony to their consanguinity and consubstantiality" (510 A). The interplay of pleasure and pain had never been stated in such a free perspective before except in the poetry of Virgil and Ovid, and then again in Petrarch and his followers up to Gaspara Stampa and Louise Labé. The descriptions of Eros in Ficino and later Neoplatonists, who are certainly acquainted with it, reinforce it didactically in their speculations. In the writings of Augustine, as in Seneca, it served as a sign of illness. Without disqualifying secular or religious ethicists, and in a strange proximity to poetry, Montaigne describes the two faces of the spirit and finds in this, as he finds in man's ambiguity as a whole, something deliberately determined by nature: "Nature reveals this confusion to us; painters hold that the movements and wrinkles of the face that serve for weeping serve also for laughing" (511 B).[111]

Then, in other Essays, he is concerned with the conflicting reaction of the spirit, which when confronted with one and the same thing sometimes reacts one way, sometimes another. In one example he comments that we can resolutely avenge an insult and rejoice in this—and then still weep: ". . . there is nothing changed; but our soul looks on the thing with a different eye . . . the turn is so quick that it escapes us" (I, 38, 174 A). And Nero again: he orders the death of his mother and weeps in taking leave of her (I, 38, 173 B). Among the spiritual forces, one tends to prevail—but in spite of this it does happen that another, a weak and hidden one, can gain the upper hand, so great is the soul's need for change (I, 38, 173 A). Or: the judge tears a scrap from the same paper upon which he has written the judgment on an adulterer to use for a love note to the wife of his colleague; another sentences men to death for crimes that he basically does not consider crimes (III, 9, 756 B). We are capable of hating unto death one who has offended us, but feeling the same toward one whom we have offended (II, 27, 525–526 A)—an observation that Tacitus had made (*Agricola,* chap. 42), and which was later repeated by La Rochefoucauld in his *Maximes* (No. 14), La Bruyère in his *Caractères* ("Du cœur," 68). The fact that one person does another harm does not prove that he hates him (III, 5, 648 C). This leads to the argument that one cannot from the ethical quality of any act draw generalizing conclusions about the attitude or the character of the one who performed the act. No single moment in a person's life which comes to light permits one to draw conclusions applying to him as a whole. For example: as Montaigne tells us, just because my *Essais* mention Theodore de Bèze (a protestant), people are not in the least justified in considering me heretical, as happened to me in Rome (III, 10, 774 C). Even if one is a thief—he has his handsome leg nevertheless (775 C). And drastically, in the same passage: if someone is a whore, must she also necessarily have bad breath? Moral equations of any type are disallowed, for example, one such as the following: the envious man always behaves enviously. Experience teaches us that men who live depraved lives are capable of dying a pure, great death (I, 19, 55 B). Montaigne also observes these types of crossover in himself: "I find that the best goodness I have has some tincture of vice" (II, 20, 511 B). He looks for this intersection of the single straight line even in the most revered characters. Thus he is fond of the thought he finds in Plato and Plutarch that heroic men have heroic vices. This will later become a leitmotif of La Rochefoucauld.[112]

The strangeness of the spirit can be seen in its restlessness, it cannot remain with the present, but longs for what is in the future, or other things, although they are not comprehensible—"the commonest of human errors" but Montaigne immediately corrects this judgment: "if they dare to call an error something to which Nature herself leads us in serving the continuation of her work" (I, 3, 8 B); thus the illusion is a trick of nature which serves to protect man. Our will cannot hold onto anything. Because the process of attaining something is finished, what he possesses is worthless to him. One should not envy man the circumstances in which he lives. Only in not having, in the tension of the desire, do goals show their splendor. One who has power suffers from a weariness of it: "Do we think that choirboys take great pleasure in music? Not so; satiety makes it boring to them . . . he who does not give himself leisure to be thirsty cannot take pleasure in drinking" (I, 42, 193 A). Love ennobles the object, possession devalues it, a lack of it overestimates its worth—erroneous perspectives that never bring us to a correct view. A restless inconsistency prevails between man and object. And the incongruence of motive and action results from man's internal inconsistency. This is a classical theme of all modern studies of mores and their unmasking psychology. Montaigne treated it at length: ". . . the strangeness of our condition makes it happen that we are often driven to do good by vice itself" (II, 1, 242 A). Common sense in life can originate in fear, heroic deeds from ambition or arrogance: ". . . no eminent and lusty virtue is without some unruly agitation" (II, 12, 427 A). Essay II, 27 ("Cowardice, Mother of Cruelty") is full of examples of the topic in its title, and it contains a subtle differentiation of all possible incongruent motives for cruelty: ". . . it is an act more of fear than of defiance, of precaution than of courage, of defense than of attack" (525 C). Montaigne notes the particularly intricate case of a czar who dreamt that one of his own soldiers was his murderer; when days later he learned that this soldier was a coward, he had him slain for that reason; the tyrant presumed in that soldier the incongruence that cowardice generates cruelty—and nevertheless missed (what scorn!) the truth, for even incongruence of motive is no law, it is only a possibility, and here it was not manifested (528 A). (The anecdote comes from Innocent Gentillet.) The Essay on fear (I, 18) concerns something similar. One is reminded of La Rochefoucauld, La Bruyère, Voltaire, and others when in II, 11 one reads that chastity, moderation, and abstinence can arise from physical deterioration—courage in the face of death and defiance in the face of danger from ignorance of the true situation: "Thus want of apprehension and stupidity sometimes counterfeit virtuous actions; as I have often seen it happen that people have praised men for something for which they deserve blame" (310 A). In such passages one should not be mislead by their ethical, qualifying vocabulary; this only plays the role of an aid to making a point clear, and Montaigne is not the last moralist who pours his new wine into old skins.

He is also interested in the illusionary effect of custom, an inertia that casts the appearance of legal or moral value over what presently exists, though objectively it is questionable. This is a real spiritual force with which the knowledge of man must come to terms to a high degree, and in a true Montaignian double perspective, it must at the same time rescue man from drowning in the flow of things. Custom is truly the major symptom of the insignificant factuality of our existence. Since, as experience teaches us, we are able to continue to exist in it, the result is that we are not forced to search for universal, ideal orders that could eliminate what is questionable in that which is presently a given. We must grasp what nature has granted to us through the signs of custom. This is the central idea of the major Essay I, 23 ("Of Custom"), in fact, of Montaigne's conservatism as a whole. We will return to this later.

Those are a few details from the description of concrete man. They have something of the narrative and random in them, yet they all point to one thing: that there is a break in man. The observer finds anything, even the most improbable, the most banal, what has already been said by others, as appropriate for demonstrating the point of the break: "Any topic is equally fertile for me" (III, 5, 668 B). Montaigne's image of man quite intentionally has the muted sound of the everyday. He does not color it, he does not darken it, he gives it nuances of gray on gray.

Otherwise, his view of man does not indulge merely in the hidden interlacing of motives and paradoxes. It also draws a bead on the obvious weaknesses and ridiculousness. This usually occurs in the form of anecdotes, whether, as in most cases, he takes them from books, or whether they are drawn from his own personal experience. The latter are the best. He is a master of anecdotal narration.[113] Just as, admittedly, he took pleasure in comedy, he himself was able to apply comedic emphasis when an arrogant fool, an eccentric, a disgraced titled nobleman occurred to him. An example would be the mocking story he relates about a smug councilman who with great effort and equal ineptitude spewed forth a "boatload of paragraphs," then disappeared into the *pissoir du Palais,* where he was heard muttering with satisfaction between his teeth: "Not unto us, O Lord, not unto us, but unto thy name give glory" (III, 10, 782 B). The image of man in the *Essais* is also made up of such stuff of laughter.

A brief look at contemporary school psychology and school ethics reveals how far ahead Montaigne has ventured. We can use the so-called *Académie du Palais* 1570/1585, established under Henry III, to which Ronsard, Baïf, Pontus de Tyard, Pibrac, and others belonged[114] as an example. Here, with royal stimulus, lectures on moral theory (according to the Aristotelian model) or on the emotions such as joy, pain, anger, envy, and so forth were given. But they were not much more than exercises in declamation. Each speaker only had the ambition of delivering his thesis in a manner that was beyond reproach from the perspective of form. There was no trace of new insights. It is an unproblematic preening with the supply of commonplace ideas that were customarily taught in the schematic characterologies of rhetoric. The characteristics of the virtues and emotions, neatly categorized, were established conventions; one simply shifted them around like markers in a game; one would indulge in the triumph of reason, and each speaker would offer his variant on this prescribed concluding topic. Tinkering with ethical universals (Anger, Envy, etc.), constructive generalizing and typing instead of viewpoints, instead of experience, and instead of consideration of the heterogeneous layering of characters is precisely the procedure with which Montaigne usually became so impatient. For example, when Ronsard in his lecture on Envy intends to "describe" the envious person, he looks like this: "The envious has a leaden expression, blighted teeth, his body skinny all over, he never sleeps: it is as if he were cross-eyed, never looking straight ahead nor lifting his eyes toward the sky, from the pain he suffers to see it so beautiful . . ."[115] This type of schematization is quite inconceivable in the *Essais*. One would counter the drastic claim quoted above as follows: "And if she is a whore, must she also necessarily have bad breath?" (III, 10, 775 C). Montaigne brings forth his proof of the labyrinthine contradictoriness of things precisely to head off the falsification of man caused by restricting him to a single characteristic. He dismissed the abstract typology that stretched all the way back to Theophrastus. Fixed types could only live on in comedy, where they had always existed by virtue of the comedy that springs from exaggeration and which makes their implausibility aesthetically tolerable. They founder in moralistic literature; one finds the last traces of them in the portraits La Bruyère inserted into the later editions of his *Caractères,* in which, however, they are surrounded by the more differentiated knowledge of man found in his other pieces. To gauge how great the distance is between the Academy and the *Essais*, which are approximately contemporary, one can compare Montaigne's Essay on anger (II, 31) with the lecture by Pibrac with the same title: in Pibrac we find a clumsy, empty conceptualizing by a moral preacher, in Montaigne the sensitivity of the moralist, relinquishing any specific definitions, attentive to phases, transitions, crossovers, attentive to externalized, internal experience. But in the process, Montaigne made use of literary material no less than did Pibrac. The scheme of the four temperaments, which was still customary in the lectures of the Academy, was of course completely abandoned in the *Essais*.

7.   OPPOSITION TO THE STOIC SCHOOL

Montaigne's observation of concrete man owes the breadth of its perspective to a considerable degree to the elimination of the "man of wisdom" in the stoic mode. In addition to what we have already said on this topic, this can be seen in his conception of the emotions. One certainly finds occasional remnants of the stoic doctrine whereby emotions are *perturbationes animi,* intrusions from lower strata which cloud one's judgment. Remnants such as this can be found in the early Essays, for example, in I, 2 ("Of Sadness"), or in I, 18 ("Of Fear"), and so forth. But the course of the explanation does not lead to the command to overcome, rather it swerves off into descriptive analysis and recommends that one tolerate and actualize the emotions for the sake of preserving one's natural humanity.

It is possible that here Montaigne adopted something of the doctrine of the Peripatetics who, in contrast to the stoic school, did not want to eradicate the emotions, but only to moderate them (II, 11, 313 C: "Moreover, the Peripatetics do not accept . . ."). Their ideas could have mainly been imparted through Cicero's *Tusculanae* and through Plutarch. The latter's treatise "De virtute morali" in the *Moralia* contains thought processes that recur in the *Essais.* They revolve around the central idea of *Eupathia,* which counters the stoic *Apathia* and permits a harmonious, moderate realization of the emotions. Plutarch considers the emotions to be necessary elements in the mixed structure of man. If they are lacking or suppressed, the soul slackens like a sail in a calm (chapter 12). Montaigne knew this treatise. But Christian tradition also accommodates his toleration of the emotions, and with reasons that were used at the time by the reawakened (since Gianozzo Manetti, Lorenzo Valla, and others) peripatetic doctrine of the emotions.[116] Augustine's polemic against the stoic *impassibilitas* is well known. He defends suffering—including suffering from the emotions—as an unavoidable part of sinful earthly existence, and as a prerequisite for the reward of salvation.[117] He invokes Peter's weeping (*Matth.* 26, 75), and Paul, who prides himself on his weakness (II *Cor.* 12, 5). But the major model is Christ himself, who, in becoming man, also took upon himself the agitation of sympathy, pain, and despondency. It concerns what Hieronymus called the *propassiones Christi.* The soteriological interest in the inclusion of the emotions in redemption allows their reality to be emphasized.[118] If God-become-man suffered, then man who follows him must also bear his suffering to demonstrate understanding of the earthly way of Christ, and as atonement (I *Peter* 4, 12–13). As long as we are men, an *Apathia* is not only impossible, it is immoral. It is hubris. But the emotions that must be suffered (and which have low value in Augustine as well) should be deflected into activity in something good (*Civitas Dei* IX, 5). Thus Christian doctrine opened up the way to seeing the humanity of the emotions. Later theology repeated the criticism of the stoic school's deadening of the emotions several times.[119] This criticism also increased in the liberal religious writings of the sixteenth century. Erasmus devoted a section to this in chapter 30 of his *Laus stultitiae*, in it reflecting a trace of the arguments of the church fathers, but the idea of natural humanity was given the deciding voice. What is the result of Seneca's demand that the emotions be conquered?, he writes. An artificial God-man who never existed and never will exist, a motionless statue of stone. In *Enchiridion*, Erasmus developed as refined a psychology of the emotions as one could imagine, only possible when one was no longer inhibited by the intent of a stoic therapy.[120] The Spanish humanist Juan Luis Vives also rejects the stoic theses and recognizes the value to life of the emotions, which are no longer ranked ethically, but only psychologically.[121] Then, shortly after the *Essais*, and again from religious considerations, François de Sales—invoking Augustine's *Civitas Dei* XIV, 9—arrived at a similar conclusion, asserting against the Stoic school: "Great folly to want to be wise with an impossible wisdom" (*Traité de l'Amour* I, 3). This is found again later in Quevedo, and, without the religious motivation, in La Rochefoucauld, Molière, La Bruyère.[122]

Montaigne has a solid place in this line. With his rejection of stoic apathy he passes on a theme that has also become one of the classical themes of the study of mores. He was supported in his application of the natural humanity idea to the doctrine of the emotions, in addition to Plutarch's influence, by that Christian train of thought; but he admittedly invokes it only rarely.

In a methodical difference from the Stoic school, his presentation of emotional life lacks any classification of the emotions, even of the more liberal type that was developed by the later Stoic school and then the neo-stoics of the sixteenth century. Furthermore, he completely disregarded the stoic claim (which was already treated ironically in Plutarch) that there was no middle ground between ἀρετή and κακία, man could rather only be wise or only foolish, only good or only evil;[123] even the moderation of this by Seneca was still too rigid: "The Stoics say that the wise man operates, when he operates, by all the virtues together . . . if from that they want to draw a like consequence, that when the sinner sins he sins by all the vices together; I do not believe them so simply or else I do not understand them, for in fact I feel the contrary . . . I ply some vices, but I fly others as much as a saint could do" (II, 11, 312–313 A/C. Note how here as well a complex fact that has been experienced—"in fact I feel"—is used to counter the simplifications of a theory.) Nor can he accept the stoic axiom of the equality of all vices. "Vices are all alike . . . But although they are equally vices, they are not equal vices," he writes at the beginning of II, 2 (perhaps from Horace, *Satirae* I, 3, v. 97 ff.). Nor do we find a trace of the distinctions of the stoic doctrine of property in his work. As we have already said, his own precise distinctions are phenomenological, not conceptual, in nature.

However, the most important aspect is that he drops the ethical invalidation of the emotions to make room for their valuation as necessary driving forces. One can see this very clearly in the "Apology." After the analysis of modifications of judgment due to the emotions (for the purpose of a critique of knowledge), he diverges and describes their indispensability for the soul's zest for life (II, 12, 424 ff.). This is another of the many passages in which he perceives the richness of man in something questionable, crosses over from abasement into affirmation. Passion, he writes there, is able to inspire us to do what is suitable more than any appeal to reason: ". . . it is perhaps tenable that she has no other propulsion and motion except by the breath of her winds, and that without agitation she would remain without action, like a ship on the open sea that the winds abandon without their aid . . . it is known that most of the finest actions of the soul proceed from, and need, that impulsion of the passions. Valor . . . cannot become perfect without the assistance of anger" (426 A/C). These sentences are based all the way down to the similes (wind, sea, ship) on the passage from Plutarch's "De virtute morali" drawn upon earlier. At the same time, it supports the ideas directly following which are concerned with the lack of congruence between motive and act: a deed that is of high ethical worth can originate in a passion that is ethically neutral. In a further incorporation of Plutarch's models (though Cicero, too, plays a part), he then comes to the point where he gives prophetic insanity its due—Plato's μανία—as the highest uplift of the spirit: "This is amusing to think about: by the dislocation that the passions bring about in our reason, we become virtuous; by the extirpation of reason that is brought about by madness or the semblance of death, we become prophets and soothsayers . . . It is a pure transport that the sacred truth inspired in the philosophical spirit, which wrests from it, against its intention, the admission that the tranquil state of our soul, the sedate state . . . is not her best state. Our waking is more asleep than sleep; our wisdom less wise than madness" (427 C). One finds no Platonism in this passage, close though it may be to Plato's *Phaedrus*. One cannot miss the fact that it uncovers an absurdity that is the greatest and most spectacular of all human absurdities, the absurdity that shows how man is most enriched by the most negative thing, that is, by madness and delusion. Montaigne here intends none other than a spiritual discovery: an eccentric stimulus can result in unexpected blessings. He does not believe in its content ("we became prophets and soothsayers"). He is no Platonist. What interests him is the paradoxical actuality of this stimulus. One can see that he loves the enthusiastic delusion, unclouded by reason, as a sign of the profound fullness of which man can be capable. He is not restricted by the fact that the fullness is illusionary and divorced from knowledge. He is comfortable with such paradoxes. His inferential skepticism in fact discovered them. He is not a convinced Platonist, but he is a wise connoisseur of man who also understands—and envies—those who are intoxicated with delusion.

This understanding wisdom no longer has anything in common with the wisdom of one whose power comes from reason. Montaigne not only turns away from stoic, even Epicurean, *ataraxia;* he even forces the peripatetic concept of moderation, at least in the doctrine of emotions, to the side. He does not remove mankind from being determined by layers of drives. Nor does he remove man from his destiny of suffering. Do not all living things suffer, and do they not live in that they suffer? "Shall we violate the general law of nature, which can be observed in all that lives under heaven, that we shall tremble under pain? The very trees seem to groan at the blows [= blows of an axe] that are given them" (I, 14, 37 A). It is human to want to avoid suffering, but it is just as human to knowingly and feelingly meet suffering's demands once it is already there. Montaigne stresses emphatically that a philosophy that suppresses the surging of the emotions does not create greatness, it creates inhumanness, encourages phoniness and lies, and it would be better to leave the realities of the living ("real substance and actions") to run their course (II, 37, 576 A). "Let it shout right out" is his advice to the ill—and to himself (II, 37, 577 A). Later we will see the significance of this willingness to suffer for Montaigne's philosophy of death (chapter 6). He challenges the stoic with: even you cannot escape human essence: "For all his wisdom, the sage is still a man: what is there more vulnerable, more wretched, and more null? Wisdom does not overcome our natural limitations . . . The sage must blink his eyes at the blow that threatens him; if you set him on the edge of a precipice, he must shudder like a child. Nature has willed to reserve to herself these slight marks of her authority, invincible to our reason and to Stoic virtue, in order to teach man his mortality and frailty . . . Let him think nothing human foreign to him" (II, 2, 249–250 A/C). Here is Montaigne's individual interpretation of that verse by Terence[124] which echoed through the whole of Renaissance literature, and which had been interpreted in so many different ways: Obey your fragile human essence, for you cannot escape it. Montaigne criticizes some of the figures he reveres most, precisely for their rigor: Epaminondas, and even Socrates. And he asks about the motive and the psychic process involved in undeniable cases of heroic self-mastery. He finds ambition and delusional obsession in the insensitivity of stoics and martyrs, not at all what they hope to project, namely, greatness of will (II, 2, 250–251 C/A). He considers the heights of pure virtue to be eccentric exceptions, and he is more interested in the subsequent relaxation when the soul again comes down to earth to its position of averageness (II, 29, 533 A). In the duel between reason and the emotions, he looks to the resistance of the latter (II, 33, 550 A and 554 ff.). He describes greatness of soul and steadfastness in such a manner that one can see these are a curiosity to him, not impossible (for nothing improbable is impossible), but of the same origin as obstinacy: "stubbornness" is called the "sister of constancy" (II, 32, 548 B). But he states all of this without dragging greatness through the mud in a true Montaignian openness to the possibility of greatness under the circumstances of abnormality.

In eliminating the stoic tension of will, Montaigne is leading French literature toward that gentle humanity in the spirit of which we find the comedies of Molière and the fables of La Fontaine. Descartes briefly interrupts this trend. A glance at his *Traité des passions de l'âme* (1649) will remind us once again of the distance between this and voluntative ethics. Descartes throws a clean net of classification (into six basic emotions and thirty-three subordinate ones) over the soul. It is woven of precise, terse definitions. He formulates the passions like a mechanic formulates the forces of matter. The passions interact with one another following laws of the proportion of their energies, and they form combinations that can be computed. No ambiguity remains. Man—always understood only as a generic being—seems transparent to the core. His spiritual structure is ranked. Only the highest of his forces can shape his model image—the force of will, this too a "passion," but a passion at one with reason and capable of making any feeling and acting profitable for an objective order. Man in the natural state is only the raw material of what he can make of himself if he brings himself to action ethically. Man is empowered to raise himself up out of his lower levels and to will himself an essential dignity wherein individuality coincides with what is general. Ethics become man's strategy against himself. They represent a method that is just as precise and clear in its rules as the method of the act of knowledge. Girded for battle, the will of reason lies in wait for body, heart, feelings. One trains them as one trains a dog (art. 50), and the reward is: "The joy of having conquered" (art. 45). However, where, such as here, the general is forced to prevail over the particular, the difficult over the easy, the compulsive over what is original, an asceticism of the inner world develops. It retains all the harshness of the Christian elements, while it suppresses the Christian establishment of meaning. But the finest virtue of Renaissance culture, easy grace, is also suppressed. This is what Castiglione once described with the word *grazia*, and what hovers over all the pages of Montaigne's *Essais*. The labyrinth of man is walled shut again by Descartes. The more profound knowledge—that in sacrificing man to his own perfection—is lost. A heavy price must now be paid, the price of inhumanity and suffering. But this suffering is then admittedly accepted again in the literature of the seventeenth century, in Racine. It does not dissipate the ethical standard, but poetically it is on the side of the spiritual forces that here sound all the more human, the more they must be submerged. It is perhaps the point of Racine's tragedy that man must express how the great forms of discipline of his existence are possible only in the realm of the tragic. Literature picks up those sacrificed where ethical law repudiates them.

But the wisdom of Montaigne is profoundly separated from both conclusions, that of the triumphant Descartes and that of the tragic Racine, because it does not share their assumptions. His wisdom does not intend to command, overcome, sacrifice, or triumph, but rather to obey, to soar feelingly and fulfillingly in humanity, which is an antimonically intersected fragment and yet is harmony. It is more blessed than the magnificent poverty of the Stoic school and of Descartes, and it is also more grateful.

8. THE STUDY OF MORES

We have called Montaigne a moralist several times, and we have discussed his classicism within the history of moral theory. Now we need to come to an agreement on the meaning of this term.

Montaigne himself never used a consistent term to designate his moralistic study of man. He simply performed it, and other than this, he was more likely to circumscribe its aim and its method than to define them. One of these circumscriptions can be found in the Essay "Of Books" (II, 10) in the form of his explaining why historians are his favorite authors. The reason, he writes, is that in their work man ("the knowledge of whom I seek") appears more alive and more complete than in other sources ("more alive and more entire . . ."), and in them, one sees "the diversity and truth of his inner qualities in the mass and in detail, the variety of the ways he is put together, and the accidents that threaten him" (303 C). This is the formulation used in the handwritten addition. Earlier, it was stated thus: ". . . the consideration of the natures and conditions of various men, the customs of the different nations, this is the true subject of moral science." The question of why he gave up the first formulation must remain open. But the two versions supplement each other. They point to that which Montaigne strives to see in man: variety, difference, internal nature. It is significant that the first version concluded its comment with the term "moral science." Although such a term is traditional, from the context it takes on a meaning that agrees with our meaning when we use the expression the study of mores.

The German loan word "Moralist," modeled on the French *moraliste,* has in common with this and with Montaigne's "moral science" the root of the Latin word *mores.* This word must be understood in its broadest meaning. It encompasses traditions of every kind, lifestyles, characters, conditions of the time, inner make-up, essence—almost everything, apart from the purely physical, associated with man.[125] *Les mœurs* in sixteenth-century French is an empirical term, free of value judgments. An author of that time writes: "As regards mores, it is only another way of saying the customs and manners of behavior governing human actions and passions."[126] One finds the same usage in Montaigne (III, 5, 656 B, etc.). The term "moral science" found in the quotation above designates the empirical, detailed knowledge of lifestyles, traditions, and natures of the various men and peoples, and also the goal of learning from these materials what man really is. Later on, the bearer and nurturer of this type of knowledge was called *moraliste.* This word had to contend more strongly and longer than *les mœurs* with a much more limited meaning also contained in the root word, that of normatively moral (*bonos mores*), and can even today be called "moral philosopher." But the broader meaning, which renounces any normative intentions, has also become quite familiar. It is used, for example, in Sainte-Beuve's sentence: "You are a moralist [*moraliste*] , and you observe the world. You have only one care, to see what is . . ." (*Port-Royal*). This corresponds to the prevailing German usage, particularly from Nietzsche on. Nietzsche Germanizes "Moralisten" on one occasion with "*Menschenprüfer*," examiners of men (*Menschliches* II, Section 5). On another occasion, he speaks of "La Rochefoucauld and those other masters of the examination of souls"; they "resemble marksmen with precise aim who hit the bullseye repeatedly—but it is the bullseye of human nature" (*Menschliches* II, Section 36).[127] In an historical sense, when one speaks of the moralists, one is referring to a group of French authors of the seventeenth and eighteenth centuries (which is not a valid limitation). In a conceptual sense, one means intellects who answer the question of what man is by observing and describing all means of manifestation of man with respect to matters of the spirit, customs, the history of customs, society, and politics, always considering the differences in place and time—they do not actually answer the question, rather, in view of previously undiscovered layers, depths, interrelationships, they continuously pose the same question again as the ultimate in unanswerable questions. Since man, the moralistic object, is a contradictory, fragmented thing, the moralistic portrayal tends to use the open literary forms, which do not require a system but rather allow for repetitions, variations, nuances, every pro and contra. But above all, the study of mores, which has outgrown its original site, namely, satire, refrains from ethical judgments and refrains from making ethical decisions for others, or at least pushes these practices to the background. It is not moral teachings. Nor is it a moral philosophy, that is, a philosophy that discovers moral standards in something general or metaphysical. The fact that it is not this represents its most significant negative definition.

When Montaigne speaks of the *science morale,* one does hear something of the older concept of the *philosophia moralis.* In the classical view, this represented the first element of the three-part philosophy, and it was concerned with recognition of the highest good and the moral way to live one's life.[128] In the theological view (analogous to natural theology), this was the realm of natural ethics and preparation for the dignity of grace. But these conceptions have disappeared in Montaigne. Yet he is not alone in this. In 1530, Agrippa von Nettesheim defines *moral philosophia,* in contrast to general ethical reasoning (*ratiunculae*) as being concerned with *vario usu, consuetudine, observatione, ac communis vitae conversatione,* and he comments that they must be *mutabilis* because the *singulae nationes* have their own specific ways of life which preclude a universal concept of good and evil (*De incerti-*

tudine . . . chap. 54). Thus it has become an empirical, relativistic study of human diversity which changes according to times and peoples. Later on, then, Cardano classifies under moral philosophy—not exclusively, but preferably—that which is concerned with the knowledge of human habits, particular national traditions, the balancing forces inherent to an individual life.[129] These are randomly chosen examples of a change in the concept, indicating a profound change (beginning as early as the fifteenth century) in the view of man.

The study of mores as we understand it here was not confined to France. However, the term usually brings to mind names such as Montaigne, la Rochefoucauld, Saint-Evremond, La Bruyère, and so forth. But they owe their position of honor not to the uniqueness of their ideas, but rather to their psychological intelligence and their literary artistry which perfected the open form of expression, which is suited to thinking about *mores,* in the essay and the aphorism. In this respect, they represent the highest level of the European study of mores, and Montaigne is the first classical writer of this level. The Italian and Spanish preliminary forms of the Essay cannot compare with him or Saint-Evremond, nor can Guicciardini's *Ricordi* or Quevedo's *Sentencias* compare with the aphoristic virtuosity of La Rochefoucauld and those coming later. Yet one must consider the French moralists in a category with the moralists of Italy and Spain from the standpoint of the history of ideas. In doing so, the extent to which this unit is expressed through mutual influences of the authors upon one another is of lesser importance. For the drives encouraging moralistic thinking derive less from literary interchanges among the moralists than from the events in the European intellectual realm, mainly from the end of the fifteenth century on, which necessitated this type of thinking and paved the way for it. Among these events was the fading of the theological power of the system and the separation of individual areas of life from a ranked order and into individual areas of worth (state, class, etc.). Instead of an ethical, metaphysical type of idea which applies to all parts and rules over all of the ranked areas, several isolating ideas of an empirical, practical nature appear. The best-known example of this is the concept of reasons of state which, while it does not expressly endorse the inapplicability of general ethics for political practice, at least acknowledges it for cases of conflict. A new technique of political intercourse emerges in this context, represented by the position of the diplomat. The *Relationen* of the Italian diplomats reveal how observation of men and situations developed in the soil of the preservation of political interests, an observation that is all the more acute because it is limited to the finding of pure facts and it examines the facts as symptoms of the self-centered interests of others against which one must weigh one's own. The prevailing "idea" in such specialized areas is tactical cleverness—in fact, it is not an idea, but rather a method that strives to be able to handle any man, any situation by seeing through it and protecting oneself. The totality of life is broken down into countless, changeable conditions that one must approach with changeable responses. This is also reflected in the societal life of the courts. The style of disguise in an aristocratic culture based upon rank (one wants to appear to be something) produces the psychology of unmasking and destruction. Initially it serves as a defense for its bearer. But then, as in the political realm, it becomes fundamental knowledge that man acts in accordance with hidden motives that do not match the effect and which must be brought out under a guise. The complete dissolution of a general norm of living among the leading classes of Europe due to their particular interests is also expressed in theology. It now attempts to make moral precepts useful for particular cases—whereby Spanish moral theology of the sixteenth century takes the lead. This led to the casuistry of the Jesuits—perhaps the most striking event of moralistic thinking, since here, changeable human reality is made independent in all its details, and despite opposite intentions, the destruction of the moral idea becomes dramatically evident.

Thus quite diverse historical-societal, political, and theological processes lead to the development of the empirical, moralistic concept of man. We were only able to touch upon it. They all have the erosion of a universal standard in common. Readings in the classical historians and moral philosophers and the influx of modern travel and discovery literature encourage this image of man, filled with facts and relativities. Even when it is hidden in other literary genre (novellas, novels, satires, historical writing, etc.) it shows the characteristics that will then come together in the individual literary form of the study of mores: antinomical contradictoriness, reality free of norms, changeability, differences in individuals, classes, peoples, countries, continents, emergence from the customary categories of the doctrine of the affects, incongruence of motive and action, movement of life in a destiny that is understood as a randomness of endless combinations, incalculable, and usually running counter to probability. This image of man can be expressed in a practical, tactical cleverness of interests, or it can be elevated to a philosophical anthropology, or even further to a true wisdom. These are differences in level, but

they remain within the same common ground. There is no doubt that
any moral absoluteness has collapsed in the moralistic attitude. But this
destruction is offset by the wealth of knowledge about human reality
which is gained. For this reality can only be revealed completely and
profoundly to a perspective that is oriented toward individuals and
changing situations. Thus the method used in the study of mores as a
rule is more likely to describe than to theorize. Even the literature of
aphorisms and maxims, as much as it may appear to work in formulae
at times, separates "men" into individual cases and unlimited combinations, and it pushes aside what has already been said beneath the unceasing change in the perspective of the observer. It can often be felt how
closely the writings of the moralists approached poetry. Jacob Burckhardt and Dilthey both discussed this from different standpoints, but
with the same results. Burckhardt writes: "One could also rank among
the philosophers those to whom life has become objective to such a
degree that they appear to stand above it and bring it to light in many-
faceted sketches: a Montaigne, a La Bruyère. They represent the transition to the poets." And Dilthey says of the moralists (whom he calls the
"Lebensphilosophen," the "philosophers of life"): "Their eyes remain
focused on the puzzle of life, but they despair of ever solving it by means
of a generally applicable metaphysics or a theory of world coherence;
life should be interpreted from within itself—this is the major idea
which connects these philosophers of life with experience of the world
and with poetry."[130]

If one wanted to portray the origin, character, and achievement of
the moralists in its full extent, one would have to begin with the societal,
national historic, theological, and humanistic assumptions outlined
above, expand into an analysis of Guicciardini (especially *Ricordi*),
Quevedo, Gracián, supplement their complex picture of man with poetic figures in, for example, Bandello, Cervantes, Shakespeare, and into
the broad field of the European study of man in the courtly period
obtained in this fashion, introduce the French moralists. Such an undertaking would demand its own book. But only in this way would Montaigne's position in the history of moral thinking really become clear.
Here we must return to a monographical description of our author.

The most general characteristic his *science morale* shares with the
European study of mores is the disregarding of morals. While moral
standards do appear frequently in the *Essais,* they are relativized, sometimes also treated ironically, or interpreted as a burst of personal inclination, but never presented as a "should." Montaigne, too, eliminates the

concept of a greatest good, upon which a morality binding to all would
depend, in the multiplicity of relative maxims, particularly since he sees
how this concept is defined now this way, now that, and finally disappears again and again in the clashes of opinions (II, 12, 435 A/C; also cf.
I, 53, 224–225 A). He is also convinced that a man's individual aptitude
cannot be changed by any kind of upbringing ("a pattern all his own, a
ruling pattern, which struggles against education" III, 2, 615 B). Moral
unification is thwarted by the differences of men: "Men are diverse . . .
they must be led to their own good according to their nature and by
diverse routes" (III, 12, 805 B). Of course none of this means that
Montaigne intended to be immoral. One finds enough passages in the
Essais on loyalty, decency, honesty, a sense of honor, and there are even
quite passionate passages, especially against lying (II, 19, 505 A). But he
issues these principles more as custom and personal taste than as a
doctrine. Only freedom ennobles them: "I am lax in following duties to
which I should be dragged if I did not go to them . . . If the action does
not have something of the splendor of freedom, it has neither grace nor
honor" (III, 9, 738–739 B). As Friedrich Gundolf put it, "Montaigne is
no disciplinarian, rather, he is more of a connoisseur of virtue, just as he
is a connoisseur of greatness and grace, but virtue tastes best to him of
all the values."[131] He even goes so far as to evaluate his own behavior in
the context of the persons at whom it is directed; if they are indecent, his
own decency irritates him, nor is his conscience bothered if he acts
illegally toward those who accept illegality (III, 12, 814 B). Hidden
behind such admissions is his consciousness of how our existence is an
interlacing of good and evil. This makes him cautious and allows him to
choose what is right only as the most favorable temporary arrangement
in the face of uncertainty: "That is why, when the various details and
circumstances of a matter have so perplexed us that we are powerless to
see and choose what is most advantageous, I find the surest thing to
do . . . is this: to cast ourselves into the course in which there is the most
decency and justice, and since we are in doubt about the shortest path,
to hold always to the straight path" (I, 24, 93 A). The right thing does
not have an absolutely justifiable priority.

9.   SEPARATION OF THEORY AND PRACTICE

Like all moralistic thinking, the *Essais* are also based upon the separation of theory and practice. We spoke of this earlier when discussing
Montaigne's position on denominational questions (see chapter 3). We

will add to this here: "The virtue assigned to the affairs of the world is a virtue with many bends . . . so as to join and adapt itself to human weakness; mixed and artificial, not straight, clean, constant, or purely innocent" (III, 9, 758 B). This is one of his many comments in which morals take a back seat to worldly wisdom. Moral purity is perhaps conceivable and it can be taught ("a scholastic and novice virtue" he calls it in the same passage). But practical action has its own case-by-case orientation. The sixteenth century worked through this separation in the relationship between morals and politics, and in the debates about the idea of reasons of state. One should not be surprised that Montaigne decides in the direction of political realism. To him, its necessity is one more sign of the divisions in our human essence.

In fact, he never offered a coherent position on the current theoretical problems of the state, and he never gave special treatment to the idea of reasons of state. He only touches upon these topics. But he touches upon them proceeding from the same question that was a contributing factor to the origin of modern political realism (particularly of a Machiavelli or Guicciardini). It is the question about the conflict between the possible balancing of usefulness and morality, practical needs and duty—expressed in classical terms, *utile* and *honestum*. This was treated in antiquity by Cicero in the third book of his *De officiis*, chapters 19 to 33.[132] Sixteenth-century discussions often invoked Cicero. The pairing of the concepts of *utile-honestum* appears in the whole of contemporary theoretical literature concerned with morals and the state. One finds it in Machiavelli's *Discorsi*, Guicciardini's *Ricordi*, and also in the works of the later French historians. Bodin places it under the *loci communes*, according to which one can categorize historical material (*Methodus . . .* , chap. 2). It is the title of one of Montaigne's Essays: "Of the Useful and the Honorable" (III, 1), which we will discuss in detail later.

But there is a considerable difference between Cicero's manner of solving this conflict and that of later political realism. Cicero does not treat the conflict as an antinomy of irreconcilable realms. He understands it as a dialectical process on the various levels of morality. It is wrong to kill a relative; but if the relative is a tyrant, then killing him is an act of justice in favor of the state. The killing is indecent (*turpis*) from the viewpoint of private ethics, but from the viewpoint of the ethics of state, expediency (*utilitas*) is transformed into a moral value (*honestas*). Thus what at first appeared here to be subordination of ethical absoluteness to the practical requirements of the particular case is in reality a subdivision of morality according to ranked areas of application. Morality itself is not destroyed, it is merely made functional. Cicero makes an effort to evade an antimony between *utile* and *honestum*: "Utility did not conquer duty . . . , rather, duty joined forces with utility. Thus we see that no conflict between utility and duty can arise at all."[133] However, he only allows a break in the straight moral line in actions of the state as an exception. Nevertheless, for later political realism, the opposition of practical necessity and morality does become an antinomy that can lead to the sacrificing of morality, and indeed may do so. Expressed with the classical terms: *utile* and *honestum* are heterogeneous realms of value. Political necessity is given its own, independent legality with which it is possible for moral principles to coexist, but coexist without a right to object or appeal.

This is Machiavelli's well-known solution. In his model of a powerful state he decides upon a concept of reality which is required by the rapidly changing positions of an earthly configuration of purposes. And it also includes the concept of a human essence which would be destroyed if it opposed this reality with inflexible norms. Reality can be mastered in no other way than by tactical adaptation from case to case. (*Discorsi* III, chap. 9: "As it is proper to change with the times . . .".) Utopian thinking is replaced with a method that states (*Principe*, chap. 15): "It seemed to me more correct to stick directly with the factual reality of a matter and not to rely on an opinion about it. For there is such a great difference between life as it is and life as it should be that someone who abandons what one does for what one should do is more likely to cause his ruin than his preservation." Guicciardini goes several steps farther in particularizing what is real to individual moments that are free of norms and which are to be handled on a case-by-case basis. He even drops something Machiavelli still attempted, namely, an association of political situations to archetypes which can be found in Roman history, and thus can be considered as guides. Rather, in his work, everything real is included under the category of dissimilarity. He writes: "The smallest petty thing when it changes can result in a conclusion—derived from it—also changing. One must not assess occurrences of the world from a distance, rather, one must judge them day by day and draw one's conclusions in this way. The essence of things is such that one finds none in which some sort of disorder does not prevail; thus one must take them as they are."[134] It is well known how in France the attempt was made to moderate the consequences of this type of thinking. Thus Bodin in particular, despite all realistic insights, strove for the idea of a state under the rules of law; he strove to once again couple the political world of facts, which the Italians had separated out as an independent realm, to a higher principle.[135] We need not explain this here. It suffices to establish to what extent the separation of theory and practice, morals and politics, norms and actuality had been taken at the time Montaigne wrote his *Essais.*

Montaigne only mentioned the name of Machiavelli twice in passing (II, 17, 497 A and II, 34, 556 A). When in another passage he touches upon the advocates of an amoral power politics ("Those who, in our time . . .," II, 17, 492 C), this need not necessarily refer precisely to Machiavelli. Some have taken the further progression of this passage as a response to Machiavelli. If we assume it is, then the response is not strong enough to turn the Machiavellian spirit around. What is Montaigne's objection to allowing a prince to break his word? Moral indignation? A recommendation of truthfulness? The latter, yes, but for very unidealistic reasons: if one breaks one's word, one will probably be successful the first time, but will thereby make one's partners mistrustful, and the next time they will not negotiate with the one who broke his word. One who is dishonest destroys his own advantage; in actual practice, therefore, honoring one's given word is more advantageous than uncomfortable and entangling lying (II, 17, 492 C). One can see that Montaigne is quite far removed from moral indignation. Honesty simply strikes him as the more advantageous tactic. His answer belongs within the same pragmatic realm as the "Machiavellian" principle. Thus there can be no claim of a "refutation" of Machiavelli. Thus, elsewhere, he can also allow for the suitability of perfidy: "As for us who . . . hold that the man who has the profit of war has the honor of it, and who say, after Lysander, that where the lion's skin will not suffice we must sew on a bit of the fox's . . ." (I, 5, 17 A). Montaigne thinks no differently than one thought in France even before Machiavelli; in this sentence one hears words that one can find in Commynes.[136] The unavoidability of amoral decisions in practical matters for Montaigne results less from political orientation than from his fundamental insight into the fragility of humanity, which is not capable of ideality: "The weakness of our condition often pushes us to the necessity of using evil means to a good end" (II, 23, 518 A). Montaigne is no "Machiavellian"; he does not preach power politics or immorality. But he is clever enough to know that man when he moves into the sphere of political worldliness will have to leave many of his noble scruples at home. He acknowledges the immutability of the weak "human condition" and its paradoxes in every area. He is open to the facts, even the fact that in certain cases, man must act amorally. He concurs in the distinction Machiavelli makes between "life as it is and life as it should be." Thus it is not an accident that his formulation "truth of facts" (III, 11, 785 B) agrees with Machiavelli's formulation "stick directly with the factual reality." But he does not simplify man in a mere evilness, rather, he shows him in a polarity: man *can* act justly and well, but it can also happen that he *must* act unjustly and evilly. His unprejudiced eye perceives the remaining light where others only see darkness. Thus he protests expressly against Guicciardini's pessimism, which traces every action to a base motive. "No corruption can have seized men so universally that someone would not escape the contagion," he says, in an assessment of Guicciardini's historical writing (II, 10, 305 A). He does not see merely power, amorality, and lack of conscience even in political matters. His thinking is more highly differentiated than that of the Machiavellians. And he has no taste at all for acting exclusively to serve a purpose in favor of war and state. On two occasions (II, 36, 573–574 A and III, 1, 609 B) he stresses a humanitarian act by the Theban general Apaminondas, namely that he paused in the midst of a battle to spare a guest who was fighting in the enemy ranks: "It is a miracle to be able to mingle some semblance of justice with such actions" (609 B). We should keep in mind how Corneille later resolved the same conflict: Horace broke the human tie between himself and his sister's lover because he had become his political enemy. ("Alba has named you, I no longer know you . . .," *Horace,* II, 3.) For Montaigne, warlike and state purposes are not great enough to supercede humanitarian feelings in every case.

Nevertheless, with his orientation toward facts he is at the level of the Florentine realists. His handling of the classical problem of the conflict between *utile* and *honestum* is informative in this respect. He dedicates the Essay III, 1, which was mentioned above, to this issue. After the introductory sentences, one reads the following: "Our structure, both public and private, is full of imperfection. But there is nothing useless in nature, not even uselessness itself. Nothing has made its way into this universe that does not hold a proper place in it. Our being is cemented with sickly qualities . . . Whoever should remove the seeds of these qualities from man would destroy the fundamental conditions of our life" (599–600 B). From the beginning, the ethical question that the title contains is subordinated to an analytical observation of existence, an observation that detects the indispensable nature of what is "imperfect," of "sick characteristics," for the preservation of life. The mystery of why it is thus is not aired. There is only a vague comment that nature permits nothing that is useless, and everything has its place in the universe. But the mystery is a fact that can be learned and can be described in concrete terms. Montaigne stresses the following as such a concrete manifestation of the polar association between "illness" and "life": "In every government there are necessary offices that are not only abject but also vicious. Vices find their place in it and are employed for sewing our society together, as are poisons for the preservation of our health . . . The public welfare requires that a man betray and lie and massacre . . ." (600 B/C). This is a Machiavellian atmosphere. Montaigne dissociates himself personally from these evil actions necessary to the state ("Let us resign this commission to more obedient and suppler people," 600 C). But he still displays an astonishing openness to take what is morally of lesser worth into consideration. He neither praises nor scorns it: he simply sees it. He sees the incompatibility of the practical realm of usefulness (*utile*) and the morally ideal realm (*honneste*). Here is one among many of his comments on this subject: "I do not want to deprive deceit of its proper place; that would be misunderstanding the world . . . There are lawful vices, as there are many either good or excusable actions that are unlawful" (604 B). The factuality of the world runs alongside, not above, and not below, the normative ideality. Montaigne clarifies the collision of the two anecdotally. For example: a commander orders someone to commit treason, and afterward punishes the treasonous underling who has obeyed the order because he has committed treason—though ordered to do so (605–606, from Plutarch). The number of these kinds of anecdotes proves how animated Montaigne's interest in such entanglements is. One can also see this in that he elucidates and evaluates the classical anecdotes, which quietly contain this casuistry, but do not explain it, in light of the problem it contains. And then he writes: "Those are dangerous examples, rare and sickly exceptions to our natural rules. We must yield to them, but with great moderation and circumspection" (607 B). These are indeed exceptions, but one must yield to them . . . And despite his advice of caution and moderation in purposeful amoral action, the awareness that a pure morality would have a destructive effect on life remains.

Yet Montaigne seems to vacillate. Shortly after this we read: "The example that is proposed to us for making private utility prevail over our pledged word does not receive enough weight from the circumstance that they introduce into it . . . for the rights of virtue must prevail over the rights of our obligation" (608 C). This is a late insertion. Does morality, then, have the last word? But the vacillation can be found even in the first pages of the Essay. For it is part of the problem itself as Montaigne sees it. The contradictoriness of which this Essay is a particularly informative example consists in the change in perspective with which he illuminates the matter first from the advocate's viewpoint, then from that of the opponent. The alternation of perspectives is an attempt to capture the complexity of the matter. The relationship of standard and reality, morality and practical necessity, is so entangled that no generally applicable solution is possible, not even one in which the realm of utility is given absolute priority. Concrete man can only decide on a case-by-case basis. A sentence near the end of the Essay reveals the occasionalistic solutions: "Let us not fear . . . to consider . . . that the common interest must not require all things of all men against the private interest . . ." (609 B). Political purposes may thus demand not everything but some things from our personal purity as a sacrifice. The Essay concludes by simply placing the possibility of two different ways of acting (morally or practically) side by side, leaving everything open to the field of countless different cases in which sometimes one way, sometimes the other, is advisable. In the course of these considerations, which can so easily be interpreted as absence of conscience, we must always remember that Montaigne does not intend to teach free discretion without obligation, rather, he wants to identify what our existence is really about.[137]

Otherwise, he returns often to the intersecting weave of our nature which is visible in the political and social spheres. In III, 9 he discusses the moral breakdown in public life of his time and asks how a state can exist under such conditions. And yet it does exist: "In fine, I see from our example that human society holds and is knit together at any cost whatever." Because, he continues, with men, the situation is similar to that of a pile of things that one just throws anywhere; somehow, by shaking and jolting about it arrives at an order, entirely by itself, and better than a design could accomplish. King Philip founded his city entirely with villains: "I judge that from their very vices they set up a political system among themselves and a workable and regular society" (730 B). That is, the social order is independent of any moral order. What is mysterious about this ("It is a marvel . . .," 730 B) is that a matter is capable of life although all signs point to decay. An order can develop even from what is depraved ("their very vices")—"a regular society." Montaigne shows the paradox in sharp contrast: *vices—juste*. Here the word *juste* no longer means "just," but rather means suitable. In society and state he sees structures free of values. The order they

achieve by stringing together individual "disorder" is puzzling but factual, confirmation of the absurdity in everything human. It is in such
findings concerning the structure of man's essence that we discover the
basis of Montaigne's "Machiavellian" trains of thought. In view of this,
it is of subordinate significance when from time to time practical,
shrewd maxims in the nature of the *prudentia* that were so extensively
interpreted in the Renaissance literature are found in the *Essais*.

10.   CRITIQUE OF LAW

When one withdraws the ethical basis from human society and renounces the idea of a universal morality, one consequently also renounces
the idea of a universal law. Montaigne commented on the law in various
ways. He did not do it as the jurist that he was. What he said was so
lacking in specialization that it could also have come from one not versed
in the law. For nowhere more than in the field of legal scholarship was the
specter of pedantry so threatening to this century. The image of the
anemic Doctor of Jurisprudence, stuffed full of quotations from commentary and devoid of any healthy human understanding, was a favorite
object of scorn in the literature of the Renaissance. Thus Montaigne
carefully avoided disrupting the man-of-the-world tone of his *Essais* with
specialized legal learning, although he had it at his disposal because of his
occupation. There is even next to nothing to be found about the reform of
legal thinking, which had been on the rise from Valla and Budé on. This
reform consisted in the urbanization of legal language, a return to Roman
sources of law (which had been buried in commentary), and in the nurturing of the natural understanding of law. One only finds traces in the
Essais of the latter, and only now and then. But Montaigne did not want
to advance legal reform. He simply wanted to exemplify, using the special
case of the life of the law, what he always wanted to exemplify, namely the
impossibility of understanding the fluid, contradictory essence of man
using normative general precepts, and he wanted to free man from the
web of legal statutes in order to restore to him his own reality, individual
and different from case to case.

Only a few decades before Hugo Grotius created the modern rationalistic basis of natural law and recognized the existence of reason per se in
the law,[138] Montaigne once again summarized the entire course of proof
against the idea of natural law, proof that was widespread from classical
skepticism on, and which was repeated frequently during his century.
This once again illuminates, from a different angle, his distance from

rationalism. He writes the following in the "Apology": "But they are
funny when, to give some certainty to the laws, they say that there are
some that are firm, perpetual, and immutable, which they call natural,
which are imprinted on the human race by the condition of their very
being" (II, 12, 437 A). This passage contains a simple formulation of the
natural law idea (perhaps from Cicero), but also the aspects that Montaigne had to reject, namely the certainty and immutability of some
fundamental rules of law, as well as their general applicability, which
was supposed to proceed naturally from human essence, which was
assumed to be identical in all. And he then continues that the actual
difference in the forms law takes in various peoples at different times
refutes the presence of a uniform idea of law. So even here we find that
empirical relativism with which we have become familiar. This is what
causes him to write the sentence that Pascal would later sharpen to a
famous formula: "What am I to make of a virtue that I saw in credit
yesterday, that will be discredited tomorrow, and that becomes a crime
on the other side of the river? What of a truth that is bounded by these
mountains and is falsehood to the world that lives beyond?" (437
A/C).[139] In addition to this, there is the further objection that the supposedly natural norms of law are embroiled in eternal dispute; thus they
lack the most fundamental proof, that of the *consensus omnium*. The
natural law idea is to Montaigne a hypothesis that identifies what has
many variations and thus profanes the make-up of man's essence. An
element of the argument that it is an animal defect of man that he is
unsuitable for natural law can probably also be detected here (438 B).
But as we will now see, here, too, this echo of the theological abasement
motif is ultimately silenced.[140]

Without exception, the law of Montaigne consists of positive rules of
law which he understands historically, not as the unfolding of an idea of
law which has no history behind it. He is a pure legal positivist in the
sense of a sentence written later by Hobbes: *Auctoritas, non veritas fecit
legem* (*Leviathan*, chap. 26). Thus one reads the following in the "Apology": "The laws take their authority from possession and usage; it is
dangerous to trace them back to their birth. They swell and are ennobled as they roll, like our rivers" (440 A). He indicates how the rational-
ists ("these people who weigh everything and refer it to reason") fail to
recognize precisely this empirical origin of law in the lawlessness of a
former power situation or in mere custom. Since law did not originate
from reason, reason cannot establish law. Necessity brought man to
society: "This accidental link afterward takes the form of laws; for there

have been some as savage as any human opinion can produce, which have nevertheless maintained their bodily health and long life as well as those of Plato and Aristotle could do" (III, 9, 730 B). This thought of an empirical, illegal origin of the system of laws is not new. It comes from sophistry and was imparted to the *Essais* via Plutarch. But it is significant that Montaigne turns this once again to his favorite paradox, namely, that something that runs counter to values (here counter to law) can be the prerequisite for the "health" of a structure (here society). Or even that injustice must occur for justice to arise: ". . . a man is forced to do wrong in detail if he wants to do right in gross" (III, 13, 820 B).[141] This type of statement is made in the later Essays without any condemnation, in contrast to Bodin, for example, who in *Les Six Livres de la République* also provides legally positivistic explanations, but then combats them. Rather: ". . . there is nothing just in itself . . ." (III, 13, 820 C, following a sentence from the elder Aristippus taken from Diogenes Laërtius). One would not find a statement like this uncontested in the work of any ranking theoretician of the law in the sixteenth century. Montaigne can in fact call justice a "noble virtue," but he then turns his attention to real situations in which justice is no more than ". . . the hodgepodge of the first laws that fall into our hands, and their application and practice, often very inept and very iniquitous . . ." (II, 37, 580 C). This is the same shift in perspective which we find in his assessment of Christianity: he can acknowledge it as a great idea, but in reality, he sees it as a habit determined by milieu and spoiled by human discontent. Rules of law are normative not by force of their legality but rather by force of their authoritarian presence: "Now laws remain in credit not because they are just, but because they are laws" (III, 13, 821 B). There is no more lamenting the animal fragility that is the cause of this. Montaigne declares quite openly that the plan of an ideal state under the rule of law is ludicrous ("ridiculous and unfit to put into practice," III, 9, 730 B). While he has Plato's utopia and the Aristotelian types of the best forms of government in mind, the target he hits is, in general, the fundamental concept of natural law when he writes: "Such a description of a government would be applicable in a new world, but we take men already bound and formed to certain customs" (III, 9, 730 B). Man as he is now cannot be corrected; thus we must take him as he is in the old world, which is now our world . . . Once again, his orientation toward factuality has turned an initial abasement into consent.

But to what extent can human action even be classified under laws? To what extent can a legal case be resolved by a textbook finding of the law? Questions such as these are posed several times in the last Essays. The response is negative. It leads to an even further undermining of legal structures than the positivistic interpretation accomplished. The following sentences serve as evidence of this: "What have our legislators gained by selecting a hundred thousand particular cases and actions, and applying a hundred thousand laws to them? This number bears no proportion to the infinite diversity of human actions. Multiplication of our imaginary cases will never equal the variety of the real examples. Add to them a hundred times as many more: and still no future event will be found to correspond so exactly to any one of all the many, many thousands of selected and recorded events that there will not remain some circumstance, some difference, that will require separate consideration in forming a judgment. There is little relation between our actions, which are in perpetual mutation, and fixed and immutable laws" (III, 13, 815–816 B). This passage is vintage Montaigne, and classical for moral thinking as a whole. It shows in stark contrast the discrepancy between what is the given on the one hand (the endless variety of human behavior) and what is selected out and rigidly defined on the other (a hundred thousand cases anticipated in laws). Even the most broadly differentiated branching of legislation cannot equal the endless branching of actual cases. There is always something left over, an act that is in some way different than the precedents and the cases already legally registered. And it is precisely this, what is left over, what is different, which ignites critical consciousness and denies that what is fluid can be captured in what is fixed. The special case that cannot be anticipated thus is shown once again to be superior to the generalized case to which it was supposed to be subordinated. The problematical discoveries of a life of law reveal that man cannot master his own concrete actuality even in legal respects. The conclusion Montaigne draws from this is that decisions as to what is right and the administration of justice are best left to the specific moment and to common sense, "according to the circumstances and at sight, without being bound to precedents, past or future" (III, 13, 816 B). For each case has its own set of problems and its own solution. To put it concretely: "For every foot its own shoe." The fundamental thought of the *Essais* as a whole is behind this comment: since the spirit that projects its attempts to produce order into the flowing mass of what is real is repeatedly forced to capitulate to what is new and surprising, it is wise to accept that flowing reality.

Admittedly, this is no longer a legal conclusion, but rather a philosophical one. Montaigne guards against introducing it into the legal life. He is too well aware of the difference between theory and practice to do so. Actual practice with a few improvements and a certain simplification of the legal process can stay as it is. Theoretical knowledge is satisfied when it knows man's make-up, when it knows that as a result of the "sickness of his essence," jurisprudence must also be "sick," but it is a "sickness" from which order and "good health" are possible. So what must be emphasized is that when Montaigne gets involved in individual items of evidence involving the problem area of law, the intentions in question are always only intentions that are meant theoretically, and which are directed at a knowledge of man's essence. An example of such an item of evidence would be the story from his own experience about the *paysants* who find a severely wounded man in the forest who has been attacked by robbers. The man begs their help, but they do not dare fulfill his request because the law suspects those found at the scene to be the guilty parties, and they have neither the money nor the skill to prove their innocence (819 B). This story shows how the law, together with the corruption of justice (only someone with money can obtain justice), absurdly, but in fact, inhibits humane behavior; law and reality do not work together, but rather in opposition to each other; the law does not provide for the presence of innocent persons at the scene of the crime, thus it does not bring order to reality as it should, but rather it confuses reality. Thus Montaigne is simply attacking the same thing from a different angle when he uses the infinite possibilities for interpretation of laws and commentaries as proof of the unsuitability of reason which formulates laws to express itself in ways that cannot be misunderstood (II, 12, 439 A; III, 13, 818 B; etc.). We need not review this. It ends in the same results as his linguistic criticism. Incidentally, here he goes considerably further than the contemporary humanistic criticism of the commentaries and the interpretations of them used to resolve questions of the substance of the law.[142] For this criticism hopes to expose amidst the undergrowth of the commentators and post-commentators those Roman sources of law which represent the pure, unfalsified law, and which should at least be granted historical honor.[143] But for the *Essais,* even the law taken in unadulterated form from the source is a thing of uncertainty; the interpretation of it, as is true of the interpretation of any human statement, is entangled in ambiguity.

11. CONSERVATISM

In the context of all of these thought processes presented which serve to dissolve established norms and law, we once again encounter Montaigne's fundamental conservative attitude. We mentioned it earlier when discussing his formal fidelity to his faith and the Church (chapter 3). Even in his understanding of the life of the state and society, it appears as security against the dangers of theoretical consciousness which arise when guidelines for practical actions are to be derived from it. Theoretical consciousness withdraws the claim of being able to decide what is just and what is unjust; but combined with this skeptical relinquishment there is relinquishment of the will to revolt against what exists presently. Skepticism breaks down the ideality of the currently applicable norms, yet it strengthens their actual validity. It deduces the possibility of existing even under absurd conditions. It advises man not to interfere with the conventional circumstances into which he is born— to observe forms without taking into account that their contents could be absurd. "Doubt leads to form," in the words of Paul Valéry;[144] that sentence could also appear in spirit in the *Essais*. In view of the questionability of finding meaning in what is given, the skeptic could be lost in chaos if it weren't for the fact that he, like the simplest of men, simply makes up his mind to comply practically with what is given. He shrewdly obeys the darkness of pure factuality which he himself has recognized as the side of all things which face us. Montaigne has looked deeply into the fragility of state, society, and law. Nevertheless, he does not oppose it, not with the idealism of a revolutionary or the nihilism of one who has despaired. His feel for reality guards him against such excesses. He is calm in knowing that the all-powerful gliding of all things will pass over present conditions; one cannot anticipate what the future will bring; and it will not bring something better, only something different, and that different thing will come of its own accord when it is time. He does not dream of the world's capacity for attaining perfection. He avoids the helplessness of theoretical skepticism by making the leap into practical reason, which is indeed an inconsistency, but signifies acknowledgment of a rift running through human nature. This at least permits him to selectively act and live in a meaningful way within the conventional realm. What presently exists is good to the extent that it has only scantily proven its worth and has become a habit. The terms for differentiating what is suitable in matters of state, society, family, morals are not just—unjust, but rather order—disorder. And order here has no other role than to be a rule of the game, a stopgap measure in an existence in which everything proves to be a stopgap measure—an organized randomness. It is indifferent to value judgments, but it serves to sustain life.

Montaigne said often that in the political world, every maxim is possible and also false. For here, "the diversity of human events" operates particularly intensely, and no maxim can eliminate the fact that every state is defective due to the defectiveness of everything mortal (II, 17, 497 A). Therefore: ". . . in public affairs there is no course so bad, provided it is old and stable, that it is not better than change and commotion" (II, 17, 497 A). A little later we find the following sentence, which is repeated with various changes elsewhere in the *Essais:* "I readily let myself be led by the general way of the world" (II, 17, 498 C). On another occasion we find it stated quite obviously: "We may wish for different magistrates, but we must nevertheless obey those that are here. And perhaps there is more merit in obeying the bad than the good" (III, 9, 760 B). Even the established orders have arisen from human will—and this means from inadequate arbitrariness, but they have the advantage of the beaten path upon which one can walk a little way through the wilderness: "The most plausible advice that our reason gives us in the matter is generally for each man to obey the laws of his country . . . And what does reason mean by that, unless that our duty has no rule but an accidental one?" (II, 12, 436 A). The intelligent man will in practice—though only here—become an Everyman. What differentiates him from one who is not intelligent is not his actions, but rather the thought that guides his obedient actions as Everyman. And he would conceal this thought: "You must stoop to the level of the people you are with, and sometimes affect ignorance . . . in common usage it is enough to retain order" (III, 3, 624 B). The hidden thought knows this: nothing is so meaningless that it could not be actualized somewhere and some time as a social order; thus, also secretly, he does not take the present order any more seriously than any other (I, 23, 79 B). Who would dare attribute so much sense to himself that he would consider himself capable of doing away with the nonsense, either subtle or glaring, which prevails in all human matters?

Essay I, 23 represents good evidence of this skeptical-conservative attitude. Its title is its leitmotif: "Of Custom, and Not Easily Changing an Accepted Law." After Montaigne pours out a wealth of historical curiosities of various peoples and customs over several pages, thereby putting the norms of the countries and times in perspective as "customs," he turns and connects each time and each country to the custom arising from it. In the first version, indeed, he still speaks critically of the "prejudice of custom" which lays itself over the true nature of circumstances (84 A). But the term becomes a positive one, even in the first version, but even more so in the inserts, and it seems as if one could already hear the echo of Hippolyte Taine's equally affirmative formula "hereditary prejudice" (*Les Origines de la France contemporaine*, Livre III, chap. 3). For this actual, namely lawless origin that covers the nature of conditions is at the same time the force that shapes order, and it is thus the condition necessary to a country's viability. Human society must protect its particular continued existence, not an inherent sensibleness—for this does not exist. In the theoretical look at the multiplicity of different "customs" the arrogance is taken out of what is native custom and is called law, and one is made conscious of the limitlessness of what is human. However, the prerequisite for one's social and personal existence is found in a practical loyalty to one's own customs. We cannot know whether a form of state and society which transcends time and nation is possible, but we can know that there is an organic and historical closeness of peoples with their particular forms of state, determined by their particular conditions of nature, which have the relative, that is, human value of suitability.[145]

Someone who, like Montaigne, does not think in terms of natural law, is even less able to think in revolutionary terms. Revolutionary thinking presumes the conviction of an ideality of law which is based in natural law, and belief in the concept of an historical corruption of law; it is the belief that it is possible to legitimately reverse that corruption. Montaigne, as we have seen, does not share this conviction; rather, he sees each idea of justice as intertwined with that of injustice. Thus he does not recognize any revolutionary program, not even in the modest form of proposals for reform. This agrees with the purely descriptive character of his and all studies of mores. Even the structure of the state, like the structure of nature, is constructed such that no human intervention is possible without disrupting it. Therefore: "Nothing presses a state hard except innovation; change alone lends shape to injustice and tyranny . . . But to undertake to recast so great a mass, to change the foundations of so great a structure, that is a job for those who wipe out a picture in order to clean it, who want to reform defects of detail by universal confusion and cure illnesses by death . . . The world is ill fitted to cure itself . . . Whoever proposes merely to remove what is biting him falls short, for good does not necessarily succeed evil . . . the oldest and best-known evil is always more bearable than an evil that is new and untried" (III, 9, 731–732 B/C).[146] In the state as well the fundamental paradox is repeated, namely that the "health" of a structure is possible not in spite of, but because of the "illness" of all living things: "All that totters does not fall . . . nothing falls where everything falls. Universal sickness is individual health" (III, 9, 733–734 B). Revolutions would only represent change with a very high price tag in the midst of the same, unchanging inadequacies.

Montaigne is, typically enough, far removed from repeating his friend La Boétie's *in tyrannos* cry. He quite correctly sees in his *Servitude volontaire* (1548) rhetoric[147] consisting of literary commonplace arguments, and he reports that La Boétie lived according to a quite different principle, namely "to obey and submit most religiously to the laws under which he was born" (I, 28, 144 A). This is simultaneously a defense against the misuse of his friend's writings by the Huguenots and an expression of Montaigne's own conservatism. He is equally far removed from the movements of the Monarchomachs of his age[148]—and not only because they came from the protestants. In his years of public service as a parliamentary councillor and then as mayor of Bordeaux, and then later in the course of his diplomatic missions, he made a conservatism consisting of unwavering loyalty to the king the basis of his actions. (Read, for example, the long letter he wrote to Henry III in 1583.[149]) The conservatism expressed in the *Essais* agrees to a great extent with what at the time was taught by Le Roy, Michel de l'Hospital, Bodin, and so forth.[150] But one must not overlook the fact that in Montaigne's case it has a significance that transcends politics to the same extent that his critique of life under law transcends juridical matters. He establishes as the other side of the coin the fundamental thought that man is enmeshed in a web of antinomical conditions the mystery of which must not be disturbed. Injustice is still better than disorder. The free man is the one who binds himself to finite reality in recognition of the universal failure of ideality, in order to avoid chaos. He has the freedom of one who knows. And since Montaigne can in this manner tolerate the tension between theory and practice, he can also combine his cosmopolitan breadth, which opens up the horizon of all things human for him, with his limited, practical conservatism.[151]

12.   SOURCES OF THE OBSERVATION OF MAN

Here we must consider the sources from which, to even a greater extent than from the classical works on moral philosophy, the *Essais* received material for their illustrative needs in pursuing the study of man. We refer here to the historians. They satisfy Montaigne's inclination to speak of men more by narration than argumentation, to speak of them anecdotally, colorfully, stressing individuality. Earlier, we quoted a passage from Essay II, 10, in which he explains why these are his favorite reading materials: man appears in them as more complete, multifaceted, vital, changeable, and in greater detail, with his inner make-up more apparent than elsewhere. Even on the first pages of his Essay on the education of children he admits on the one hand how little desire he has to work through Aristotle or any rigorous discipline and on the other hand what "special inclination" draws him to the historians, for which—and what a revealing comparison!—he hunts no less than he hunts for the poets (I, 26, 107 A).

Montaigne's historiographic erudition is quite extensive. He prepared the groundwork for this several years before his work on the *Essais*. As the end of his life approached, he read historians far more frequently than other authors. The writing of history is the only genre in which he does not make a distinction in the quality between classical and more modern sources: "In this kind of study of history we must leaf without distinction through all sorts of authors, both old and new, both gibberish and French, in order to learn in them the things of which they variously treat" (II, 10, 303 A). Here his thirst for facts disregards any canon. Bodin possibly facilitated this for him. His *Methodus ad facilem historiarum cognitionem* (1566), with which Montaigne was thoroughly acquainted, treated classical and more recent historians side-by-side as of equal worth in chapter 4.

Montaigne knows everything of importance from these historical writings of antiquity, from Herodotus to the authors of the late Caesar period. The only noticeable gap, which we addressed earlier, was Thucydides. Of course Plutarch forms the centerpoint and dominates him to such a degree that he also reads the annals and universal historians with the eyes of Plutarch: he is not interested in the great political threads, but rather in the intimate personalities. His sympathy with Herodotus must be emphasized. Montaigne became acquainted with his work rather late (in the second edition of the French translation of Saliat, 1575), and he took a particularly large number of legendary and moral history details from him. What attracted him to Herodotus was probably that he found in him that prescientific manner, so appropriate for Montaigne, of portraying history as a loose series of novella-like, vivid individual stories, without forging causal links between them or clarifying motives—and thus produced the prerequisite for the relaxed reading session "in detached pieces" which Montaigne valued so highly. And he spoke of Tacitus with special warmth. Along with Muret, Bodin, and Du Vair, Montaigne was one of the first prominent French readers of

Tacitus. He discovered in him—as did Guicciardini before him, and
later La Rochefoucauld, Amelot de la Houssaye, Gracián, and so
forth—the author of enigmatic political and moralistic cleverness.[152]
This admiration for Tacitus is characteristic for him as well as for those
involved in the study of mores as a whole in the sixteenth and seventeenth centuries. For this bitter intellect offers a unique nourishment for
the examination of the soul, as refined as it is destructive, which is
practiced in the modern study of man which was schooled in the courtly
and societal world of reputation. Montaigne claims to have received the
impetus to read Tacitus from a friend who was a member of the nobility
(III, 8, 718 B). But it is just as probable that he received impetus from
Bodin, who in the fourth chapter of his *Methodus* makes a few excellent
comments on the realistic astuteness of the *Annals*. It is clear from Essay
II, 20 (511 A) that Montaigne knew this passage. But it is also possible
that the comparison of the present with the Roman period of the tyranny of the Caesars, which was so prevalent in French pamphlet literature of the sixteenth century, and the resulting inclination to read their
historians, also had an influence on him. What he says about Tacitus is,
except for the Plutarch passages, the most extensive assessment he ever
made on an historian of antiquity. It can be found in Essay III, 8. Among
other things, it says: "I know of no author who introduces into a
register of public events so much consideration of private behavior and
inclinations . . . This form of history is by far the most useful" (718–
719 B). It is not surprising that he places him close to Plutarch because
of this capability. This is followed by the determination that Tacitus'
judgments do not always agree with the series of events portrayed;
namely, he allowed the latter an ambiguity that exceeded his own at
times biased judgment (". . . the matter he is presenting to us, which he
has not deigned to slant one little bit," 719 B). This determination
corresponds to Montaigne's own method of skeptically leaving things
their own ambiguity. He is all the more receptive to the curious, quiet
characteristic of the *Annals* when they surround men and events with an
impenetrability that precludes any conclusive judgment, in order to
leave the door open to one or another, or a third, conjecture. This could
only be noticed by someone who had read Tacitus himself, not Bodin on
Tacitus. He must have also found it appealing that Tacitus, by his own
admission, vacillates as to whether necessity or chance rules an occurrence (*Ann.* VI, 28). Of the numerous material borrowed from the
Annals and the *Histories*, let us mention the longest, the report on the
death of Seneca (II, 35, 566–567). His only complaint is about Tacitus'

style. It is too trenchant, just like Seneca's style—though "more meaty" than the latter (719 B). This is along the same lines as his aversion to postclassical Latinism, which was described earlier.

Of modern historians, he knew the French chroniclers of the kings from Joinville to Commynes, and a greater part of the memoire writers, especially the Guillaume brothers and Martin Du Bellay.[153] In a passage in which he speaks of them (II, 10, 303–304 A), he makes a distinction between "quite simple" and "exceptional" historians. The simple ones are the narrators who intend to do nothing more than report completely what was, without personal involvement, and who thus leave any judgment up to the reader. The exceptional ones, on the other hand, select, test, draw conclusions, place suitable speeches in the mouths of the historical figures (*paroles convenables*) (that old artistic device of history), and impose their judgment upon us. One cannot mistake which type has Montaigne's sympathies. Of course it is the "simple" type of historian who produces reports in the manner of chronicles and refrains from any arranging or judging, not the "exceptional" one who interjects his judgment and his art between the material and the reader. Could he be thinking of Livy as one of the latter? The qualification of "exceptional" in any case takes on an ironic tinge. Since Montaigne is seeking pure factualness free of prejudgments, he chooses the French chronicles. He mentions Joinville, Froissart, Commynes, and praises their "frank simplicity, natural simplicity, frankness, and freedom of writing" (304–306). Perhaps in this there is an element of his delight expressed elsewhere in the freshness of the language found in the older, indigenous literature, of which he is quite fond without any humanistic contempt. But even more significant is the delight he takes in the work of these chroniclers who showed him what men did and were, pure from the source and unadulterated. He appears for a moment to prefer Commynes, perhaps because of his tendency to prefer to analyze the individual case rather than to provide general constructs and not to leave any reflection without an opinion. Yet he then finds that there is too much bias involved, and thus questions Commynes' reliability. Nevertheless, it is worthwhile reading him for the "private words and actions of certain princes of their time" (306 A)— whereby Montaigne then moves back into his "Plutarchian" mode.

He also knew the Italians from Giovanni Villani to Paolo Giovio. But his preferred subject was Guicciardini (II, 10, 305). Bodin's careful assessment of him was already available (*Methodus*, chap. 4), and it attributed to him superiority over all modern, and possibly even classical, historians, as well as an unbiased mind. Montaigne says this also:

he is precise, true and free, and he is an expert in the subjects he discusses from his own experience. His only reservations concern the literary form, he finds it has too many speeches and digressions, and a bit of "scholastic prattle." He also protests against Guicciardini's simplification of man as a thoroughly immoral creature, as we have already noted. Nevertheless, it is noteworthy that of the two great Florentines he chose not Machiavelli, but Guicciardini, who much more decisively than the former, and without his doctrinaire state objectives, furthered the consciousness of man's unfathomable nature and the precision of presenting facts.

In the passage from II, 10 mentioned above, Montaigne inserts a third category between the "simple" and the "exceptional" historian. This category is for those who spoil everything by bending and cutting material to match their own inclinations, who leave out what they do not understand or cannot express in "good Latin or French" (304 B). This strikes a blow at the biased and the rhetorical historians, and thus against the most common form of humanistic writing of history. The same aversion to placing form before facts which dominated Montaigne's literary judgments emerges here in his historiographic judgment. It is significant that he does not mention Pietro Bembo, whose Venetian history (1531) was a classic example of a puristically tortured imitation of Latin historiography.[154] Protests had already been raised by Lukian, and later from Leonardo Bruni on, against the manipulations of rhetoric in history writing. Nevertheless, this remained only a rhetorical commonplace practice. The idea of expecting the truth unrestricted by any considerations of style in the writing of history only began to prevail effectively over the course of the sixteenth century, following the Latin interpretation of Aristotle's *Poetics* with their instruction of *verosimile* to poetry, but *verum* to history. It is not surprising that Montaigne joins the polemics against rhetoric in the writing of history. For him, history means what is "realistic," that is, the absolutely true-to-facts genre, a view that will finally come to prevail in the seventeenth century.[155] He wants from the historian a knowledge of the facts in the form of his own experience; this, and not his rhetorical elegance, establishes his worth. Thus the *Essais* support a main concern of Bodin's *Methodus*. Montaigne praises Guicciardini, the Du Bellay brothers, but also Caesar and others precisely because they have the distinction of being both eyewitnesses and political practicians.

Montaigne refrains from evaluating the material handed down in written histories pragmatically. There are really only traces left in him of

Cicero's formula *historia vitae magistra*.[156] He uses historical knowledge
not to develop a prognosis for the future, but rather to diagnose the
essence of man, and the diagnosis achieved with the help of historical
material is: no prognosis is possible. In the education Essay he can
recommend history to the child being educated as a gallery of great men.
But a later insertion turns the meaning of readings in history in a completely different direction: they are to become the "the skeleton of philosophy, in which the most abstruse parts of our nature are penetrated"
(I, 26, 115 C). It is also understandable that in his work the classifying
method is breaking down, that is the method of arranging historical
material by life situations, moral concepts, and so forth, this method
that was also taught once again by one of Montaigne's great contemporaries, Bodin. Bodin showed in chapter 3 of his *Methodus* how the
historical facts should be separated by the *loci communes* (virtue, vice,
occupations, law, commerce, family . . .) in order to be able to remember them by means of this cataloging, but also to obtain an exemplary
treasurehouse of knowledge of human life.[157] The underlying concept
here, the exhaustibility of facts by means of concepts used for classification, was no longer workable for the *Essais*. Thus there are very few
passages in which one finds that Montaigne read an historical source
according to Bodin's formula.[158] Perhaps he had this formula of Bodin's
and his predecessors' in mind when he expressed his objection to the
classification of material for the study of man which we reported above.
The countless individual stories he borrows from the historians are
considerably more than mere memorizable examples for a schematic,
moral framework. In the *Essais* they achieve their own life and do not
strive simply to illuminate an abstract higher principle. It often seems as
if in recounting them, Montaigne for the first time comes upon their
surprising meaning, and he forgets his reason for quoting them, instead
pursuing this newly discovered meaning. Thus, for example, in II, 29,
"Of Virtue," at first, the theme is to be proven anecdotally in the usual
manner; but the observer is surprised to discover that the virtues reported in the historical anecdotes aren't really virtues at all, but are
instead the consequences of various emotions. Thus the materials lead
the Essay in a different direction altogether than was originally intended. Montaigne undulates in the stream of what is always new, or
newly interpretable, which he obtains from historical sources. This also
explains the countless instances in which an anecdote runs directly counter to the context of an Essay or even of the sentence immediately
preceding it. It is only an exception for the historical anecdotes in an

Essay to be grouped uniformly around the theme expressed in the title. As a rule, they diverge in all possible directions. Other than this, Montaigne has the endless possibilities for evaluation afforded by the anecdotal historical material that he intersperses with his own emphasis, as well as the provisional nature of what he said about them: "And how many stories have I spread around which say nothing of themselves, but from which anyone who troubles to pluck them with a little ingenuity will produce numberless essays. Neither these stories nor my quotations serve always simply for example, authority, or ornament. I do not esteem them solely for the use I derive from them. They often bear, outside of my subject, the seeds of a richer and bolder material, and sound obliquely a subtler note, both for myself, who do not wish to express anything more, and for those who get my drift" (I, 40, 185 C). In contrast to the intent of the humanistic collections of examples, and Bodin's intent, his anecdotes and examples are far more likely to be problematical than demonstrative. They melt back into the ambiguity of living beings. This explains why he relates his historical proofs so frequently without drawing a conclusion from them.

The *Essais* do not contain a constructive concept of history. Here it is really not much more than the whirling fair of what is human. Broader contexts, subjects of a higher unity (nations, peoples, institutions) do not appear. There is no discussion of the Roman, Greek, or French state, but only of individual Romans, Greeks, Frenchmen. (The passage in III, 9, 733 B on "the state of Rome" is only an apparent exception, for this is concerned with an essential law of being human with Rome used as proof.) Montaigne feels no need to observe dramatic movements with broad horizons. His individualizing orientation resists any comprehensive syntheses in the field of history, as in all other fields. Although he reads Sallust, Livy, Augustine (*Civitas Dei*), their approach of dividing history into periods has not left the slightest trace in his work. He cannot even think in the simple directions of the Annals and Chronicles. Characteristically, he did not even take on from that broad panorama of cultural and societal history from Lucretius' fifth book (v. 1011 ff.). Nor does one encounter in his work patterns of human development such as can be found at the time, for example, in Le Roy (*De la Vicissitude . . . ,* 1575). To Montaigne, history is a jumble of actions, gestures, brief conversations, moral or social circumstances, traditions, character traits. All of this is presented in an attractive manifestation, but it remains unconnected, nonbinding, and without chronological graduation by proximity and remoteness. Just as Montaigne does not recognize development in himself, but only sees a directionless occurrence of different things, this is also his response to the historical appearance of man. He need not first inform himself through historical data that our essence is changeability, for he already knows this. The more unhistorically he observes history, the more likely he is to find in it what his moralistic interest is seeking.

The *Essais* receive a further influx of facts related to the study of man from the traveler's journals of the sixteenth century. These were reports that were highly important for broadening the Europeans' geographical and ethnographical horizons. They appeared in Latin, Italian, Spanish, and French, and covered discovery, colonization, and missionary journeys to western and eastern continents.[159] Apart from its empirical material, this literature also stimulated or furthered ideas that are a part of the fundamental intellectual content of the sixteenth century: religious tolerance arising from contact with other religions—the relativization of political and ethical norms due to knowledge of orders of life pursued by foreign peoples—disruption of the authority of the ancients due to discovery of their geographical errors, or their lack of knowledge, and so forth. Montaigne is well read in this literature of travel, which, when it was not originally written in French, was available in French translations. It is obvious that he would have welcomed their empirical and ideational content to satisfy his fundamental relativistic attitude toward facts. However, the emergence of his interest in travelers' journals only took place after 1580. Until that time, his readings hardly took him beyond the cultural circle of the Mediterranean Sea and Western Europe. However, from 1588 on his *Essais* are filled with examples from peoples of South America and the Near and Far East. We can see how fully he immersed himself in the stream of facts from the ethnographical writings in Essay I, 23 ("Of Custom"), for example, which we have already used as one of the most important proofs of his theoretical relativism and his practical conservatism. The first version was still quite moderate with its examples (taken from classical texts) of the "customs" of foreign peoples. Later supplementation (from 1588 on) adds what he has found in the meantime in Lopez de Gomara and Simon Goulard:[160] ritualistic customs, the nature of priesthood, greeting ceremonies, customs of love and marriage, prostitution, foods, manner of combat among primitive peoples. He moves into a remarkably agitated style which, with its elliptical sentences and pages-long, anaphorical "where . . . where . . ." (which abbreviates a preceding "there are places where . . .") has a somewhat benumbing effect, almost as if the intention were to let the reader feel that he cannot master the mass of factual material (80–82 B/C). A similar addition is inserted into the "Apology." This is also taken to a large extent from Gomara, and he squeezes it into overly long sentences that can scarcely be followed to the end, and the syntactic structures of which threaten to break under the weight of the examples, and wherein the writer in some passages, in increasing haste, only piles key word upon key word (II, 12, 431–433 B/C). The language whirls along in the whirling of the facts breaking in. One does not find such chaotic pages often in Montaigne. For brief moments they move the *Essais* along the same thread as the jumble of things found in an Agrippa von Nettesheim, a Rabelais, a Henri Estienne (*Apologie pour Hérodote*). But these are only the excessive clarification of his fundamental thought concerning the great variety of what is human, and this thought is so close to his heart that it can enrapture the *Essais* to the point of abandoning its otherwise so measured tone.

The *Essais* thus have a special connection with the theme of the "noble savage" dealt with so often in the travelers' journals, the primitive man of North and South American lands, the Pacific Islands and Africa, who is untouched by European cultures. The travelers' literature describes how he lives a modest and content existence of innocence—a reminder that man can live in peace if he only allows nature to guide him.[161] Hovering over this discovery, which is more ideological than realistic, is the memory of classical literature, the knowledge of the humanists, which joyously discovers that here, among the exotic peoples, we find the golden age of the poets, here is Plato's Atlantis, here are the Elysian Fields . . . Or, in Christian ideology, in the "noble savage" one welcomes the safeguarding of free will and natural morality which were left to man even after the Fall from Grace. Literary though the framework was in which this new knowledge of primitive peoples was displayed, it proved to be strong enough to activate one of the major tendencies of that age: the critique of culture and of Europe.[162] It was indeed a curious moment in the sixteenth century when, based upon the experiences of world travelers, people felt they could say that an age-old dream of mankind, the paradise of innocence, was not a dream at all, it was reality.

Montaigne offered an opinion on this theme of the "noble savage" in his Essay "Of Cannibals" (I, 31). The fundamental attitude upon which it was based is clear from the following sentence: "I think there is nothing barbarous and savage in that nation . . . except that each man calls barbarism whatever is not his own practice; for indeed it seems we have no other test of truth and reason than the example and pattern of the opinions and customs of the country we live in" (152 A). Added to this skeptical solution of the concept of barbarism there is a second idea, cultural criticism. Montaigne assembles everything that can be said in favor of these "cannibals": their honorable way of waging war, their moral instinct, their modest needs, their patriarchal order, their poetry (here we find the well-known passage on folk songs of the savages: 158 A). He handles their eating of the dead without indignation, for he sees that it has ritualistic motives. He also finds it horrible and barbaric. But he adds immediately that it is even more barbaric to kill living men—a blow struck against the European death penalty and human torture (155 A). But what is "barbarism" anyway? It is to be free of the worries caused by the human intellect and human tricks, a life lived in the happiness of undistorted closeness to nature. And this brings Montaigne to his favorite theme: "It is not reasonable that art should win the place of honor over our great and powerful mother Nature. We have so overloaded the beauty and richness of her works by our inventions that we have quite smothered her" (152 A). He illustrates this once again later, using the same object, when he criticizes the Spanish colonization of the New World as poisoning the primitive peoples with European barbarism (III, 6, 693 B). Montaigne is not the only one who thought this, and who reevaluated the concepts of "culture" and "barbarism."[163] But he merged what was a contemporary commonplace thought into his own vivid consciousness of the problems of European arrogance about their education and culture, which he contrasted with the breadth of all non-European possibilities of being human, which are called "barbaric" only because of prejudice. But just how much he is otherwise concerned with getting beyond the literary coloration of this picture of nature is revealed in these words: ". . . it seems to me that what we actually see in these nations surpasses . . . all the pictures in which poets have idealized the golden age . . . They could not imagine a naturalness so pure and simple as we see by experience" (153 A). His image of natural life (although the classical myths and utopias play a role just as much as the reports of discoveries) prefers to remain in what is factual, what can be experienced, and it resists any sort of infatuation. And then he relates the story about three savages whom he had the opportunity to see a few years before in Rouen: how they were no less amazed at European ways than the Europeans were amazed at them, the savages.

The Essay, "Of Cannibals," is a fine product of inferential skepticism. It looks outward into a cosmopolitanly broad horizon and smiles at the opinion that everyone should think as we do, or as if everything that others represent were contemptible barbarism. The ethnographical dis-coveries of the Renaissance encouraged this skepticism. Montaigne used these discoveries in forming his own particular wisdom: whatever and however and wherever man may be, he is in the right, a creature of this earth who is defective, but worthy of affirmation.

CHAPTER V

The Self

I do not make it my business to tell the world what it
should do . . . but what I do in it. That is my practice: do as
you see fit.

[I, 28, 142 C]

There is no description equal in difficulty . . . to the description of oneself.

[II, 6, 273 C]

1. THE PATH TO THE SELF

Montaigne replaces the question of what man is with the more precise
question: what are men? But he does not stop there. He gets even more
precise: what am I? The most dependable path to human reality, which
emerges all the more naturally the more individual it is, leads through
one's own essence. Observation of self provides the most immediate
information on what makes up being human. Certainly this is limited
information, since it applies only to the self. But in its very limitation it
provides a penetrating look into the direct workings of being human in
that particular, thus real, instance. This look discovers more than what
philosophers, ethicists, and metaphysicists believe they know about man.
Montaigne's conviction that the particular is richer than the general, and
that one can never come to the end of the labyrinth that is human existence, becomes definite in his observation of himself. He himself is to
himself the most surprising labyrinth, but also the most attainable one,
and the one most valuable for attaining knowledge.

Several detours were necessary before he had the security he needed
to write the *Essais* as an account of his own individuality. But even the
foreword of the first edition in 1580 designated this to be the guiding
thought behind his work: "I want to be seen here in my simple, natural,
ordinary fashion, without straining or artifice; for it is myself that I
portray. My defects will here be read to the life, and also my natural

form . . ." The emergence of his investigation and presentation of himself is usually set approximately in the years 1578/1579.[164] In any case, the corresponding programmatical statements are prevalent around this period. For example: "The world always looks straight ahead; as for me, I turn my gaze inward, I fix it there and keep it busy. Everyone looks in front of him; as for me, I look inside of me; I have no business but with myself; I continually observe myself, I take stock of myself, I taste myself. Others always go elsewhere . . . as for me, I roll about in myself" (II, 17, 499 A). Then, later, in the third book and in the simultaneous supplements to the first two, and finally in his late handwritten insertions, he continues to find new ways of formulating this striving: "I am hungry to make myself known . . . I, who see myself and search myself to my very entrails . . ." (III, 5, 643–644 B). Or: "I study myself more than any other subject. That is my metaphysics, that is my physics" (III, 13, 821 B). He claimed that he was so skilled in making himself his own object that he was able to observe himself like a neighbor, like a tree (III, 8, 720 C). In such statements, expressions such as the following are repeated several times: *se taster, se gouster, se sonder.* They also appear in the Sebond translation, where they enliven the bland expressions used in the original, for example, in chapter 224: ". . . that everyman might examine and prove himself." This not only shows that Montaigne's self-analysis was stimulated by theological ideas, but also that this, his particular passion, was stirred up even before the *Essais.*

In this way the *Essais* became the most personal book that had appeared to date in world literature, despite all its precursors in the various categories of autobiography, confessions, memoirs, and letters. This is one of its many differences from the works of the next great French moralist, La Rochefoucauld. The author disappears in his terse maxims just as surely as a mathematician disappears behind his formulae. Montaigne, on the other hand, distributes his most human intimacies with methodical honesty. "This is a sincere book," he writes in the foreword. He proceeds according to the principle that what is faulty represents the most reliable contours of what is real, even with respect to himself. His honesty, which causes him to withhold as little as possible, is free of any tendency toward pathological self-revelation (Rousseau), any literary self-stylization (Petrarch), any torturous wallowing in conflict and misery (Cardano). He becomes entangled in his all-too-human qualities neither with misery nor with vanity. He has at his disposal that compelling power that flows from people who have the courage to be themselves completely. He only gets better the better one knows him. On one occasion, Sainte-Beuve said: "Montaigne is a neighbor for all of us; one can never know too much about his neighbor," and earlier he repeated that fine comment by Madame de La Fayette, who, in contrast to some earlier guardians of aristocratic etiquette, was not at all offended by Montaigne's sometimes quite uninhibited confessions: "It would be enjoyable to have a neighbor like him."[165] These must indeed have been generous spirits upon whom this generous spirit had to depend in order to be understood in the freedom of his being himself.

In a philosophical and anthropological sense, Montaigne exercises the principle that every person is most closely related to himself: "We are nearer to ourselves than the whiteness of snow or the weight of stone are to us" (II, 12, 421 A). Self-knowledge is of greater urgency than knowledge of things. In determining such priorities of insight into the self, he is following both classical and Christian strivings. We will discuss this further later. He continues along the path once pointed out in the Delphic oracle "Know thyself." He fulfills in the secular realm what Augustine posed in the beginning of a religious knowledge of salvation: *Quid autem propinquius me ipsi mihi,* and *Nihil sibi ipsi praesentius quam anima.*[166] ("But what is closer to me than I am to myself? . . . Nothing is more present to itself than the soul.") But in his case, this leads not to an ethical result, but rather to one concerned with the study of man. Insight into one's own individuality brings the essential features of being human into focus to an elevated degree. Among these are above all diversity, existence in what is absurdly contradictory, what scorns any characterological scheme and is intensified even more because the observer of self is forced to change his standpoint and evaluation of himself just as he would of any object: "If I speak of myself in different ways, that is because I look at myself in different ways. All contradictions may be found in me . . . Bashful, insolent; chaste, lascivious; talkative, taciturn; tough, delicate; clever, stupid; surly, affable; lying, truthful; learned, ignorant; . . . and whoever studies himself really attentively finds in himself, yes, even in his judgment, this gyration and discord" (II, 1, 242 B/C). Man who comes into the greatest proximity to himself must differentiate still further that image of man which has already been liberally differentiated through objective observation, that is, he must release any apparent unity into contradiction. In the process, Montaigne is fond of using moral terminology, for example, in the sentence that can represent many others: "When I confess myself religiously to myself, I find that the best goodness I have has some tincture of vice" (II, 20, 511 B). But the moral beginning ("goodness—tincture of vice") is only an apparent one. Montaigne means something in accord with his nature. This becomes clear in the continuation of the passage just quoted: it says, anyone who listens carefully to himself will always hear "some false note of human admixture, but an obscure note, perceptible only to himself. Man . . . is but patchwork and motley." Thus the analysis of the self can best listen to the hidden mixed nature of man; and this is the whole point of it, not moral improvement.[167] Thus the formula for the image of man based on pure factuality—"This is the way men behave" (III, 9, 757 B)—corresponds to the formula for one's own factual essence, which receives itself and leaves itself as found: "I am made that way" (II, 17, 492 B).

Montaigne obtains the freedom to be himself in that he frees himself, as he frees all others, from the validity of any model. He expresses this eloquently and clearly as follows: "Because I feel myself tied down to one form, I do not oblige everybody to espouse it, as all others do. I believe in and conceive a thousand contrary ways of life . . . I am as ready as you please to acquit another man from sharing my conditions and principles. I consider him simply in himself, without relation to others; I mold him to his own model" (I, 37, 169 C). This leads to the attainment of a liberating height of understanding of oneself, because the more one perceives one's own uniqueness, the more one is open to an understanding of the uniqueness of others. Montaigne agrees to the random multiplicity of men with the unbroken tone of his individuality without feeling shamed by others or shaming them. Thus here, in the *Essais,* self-knowledge becomes the source of a noble tolerance for any form of being oneself. What is surprising in this is that the legitimacy of the self as Montaigne practices it as well as the self-observation of limited individuality again attain a general applicability, though admittedly a different one than the one based upon an identity that can be evaluated ethically: it addresses men in their different individualities and exhorts them to actualize human existence in that they develop it in their particular, irreplaceable uniqueness. "He who pushes, finds, and accepts his own limits is more universal than those who never feel theirs," as Paul Valéry once put it.[168] This unintentionally applies precisely to the spirit of the *Essais.*

2.   THE DIFFICULTY OF SELF-ANALYSIS

Montaigne had a quite well thought-out critical awareness of the effort required for self-analysis. This alone would suffice to elevate the

Essais above the level of mere memoirs. He, who called himself the "king of the matter I treat" (namely his own individuality, III, 8, 720 B), he, who can say that he is "the most learned man" there is in the knowledge of himself (III, 2, 611 B), and who frankly admits that his book is unique in the world due to the determination with which he has made himself his own object (II, 8, 278 C)—he also knows that the observation and reproduction of the self is exposed to no lesser risk of deception and premature fixation than the observation of objective humanity. For the falsifying image that others have of us threatens from the outside. And self-distortion threatens from within. The individual generally deviates no less from his real essence in what he believes he knows about himself than an outside observer might deviate from it. Self-analysis not only uncovers, it also unintentionally covers. It shapes the self according to the schemes of terms and evaluations; by putting it into language, it brings it into the essential danger inherent in language of only being able to express what is true with addition of the lie, and of burying what is unique under its apparent identity with something else. In order to be able to communicate, it deteriorates into attempts to arrange by embellishment: "Now, I am constantly adorning myself, for I am constantly describing myself" (II, 6, 273 C). Thus we find such critical sentences as the following: "It is a thorny undertaking, and more so than it seems, to follow a movement so wandering as that of our mind, to penetrate the opaque depths of its innermost folds . . . There is no description equal in difficulty . . . to the description of oneself" (II, 6, 273 C). The observer of self finds he must make a continuous effort to avoid a premature conclusion to his efforts. For even in self-analysis, that supposed result limits what by its very nature is limitless, and one who believes he has come to the end can be assured that he has not yet even reached the beginning: "Thus in this matter of knowing oneself, the fact that everyone is seen to be so cocksure and self-satisfied, that everyone thinks he understands enough about himself, signifies that everyone understands nothing about it" (III, 13, 823 B). In the recognition that the self is a continuous process the visible aspects of which tell only part of the tale while the whole retreats or can be traced only by lining up its randomly comprehensible movements—in this recognition Montaigne is superior to all studies of man from antiquity and post-antiquity. He has made the discovery that man understands himself all the less, the more he is occupied with himself: "The more I frequent myself and know myself . . . the less I understand myself" (III, 11, 787 B). He confesses that his insights into himself have borne no fruit other than a sense of how many more insights he must still achieve (III, 13, 823 B). The man who in his own company has the only true proximity to human reality will here immediately encounter the surprise of all that is real, namely that it is incomprehensible. In proximity to himself, man becomes to himself the most alien being and the greatest of all wonders. But the observation of the self takes priority over all other studies of man precisely for the sake of this discovery of simultaneous proximity and remoteness, which cannot be made this vividly in any other way. Where am I really, where does the self reside, where are the boundaries beyond which I am no longer a self, but rather an imitation of someone else, or a product of anonymous forces? Where is the unity of my characteristics and the place that guides all the reactions of my inward self, which seem so familiar and yet foreign, so thoroughly under control and yet so self-willed, so good and yet so evil? Questions such as these hover over the *Essais*. Montaigne knows that the striving to find the familiar and yet so foreign form of the self has the greatest prospect of success when he, as it were, furtively, waiting under cover, and without making any prejudgments, takes a wait-and-see approach to its movements, in order to then capture them in their diversity, which deviates from all expectations: "I do not find myself in the place where I look; and I find myself more by chance encounter than by searching my judgment" (I, 10, 26–27 C).

One can see that such a search for self is anything but complacency and idle, vain small-talk. It is a high degree of methodically thought-out resistance to the concealing layers of ethical and societal structure and to literary clichés. It is resistance to those complacencies with which man escapes into an Everyman existence, rather than being an individual. It is so easy for a man to be like everyone else rather than to be himself. Montaigne's search for self is an attempt to convert these centrifugal tendencies into centripetal ones. Knowledge of man means listening in on the individuality in oneself; listening in on the individuality in oneself is an attentive listening away from imposed or barely perceptible tones of "education": "There is no one who, if he listens to himself, does not discover in himself a pattern all his own, a ruling pattern, which struggles against education" (III, 2, 615 B). What ranking this "basic form" of individual essence has is unimportant: if it is safeguarded and listened to with fidelity to the self, the goal is attained. Montaigne disapproves of man shaped by public education and attitude as a creature corrupted by the loss of himself. One's task in knowledge as well as in conducting one's life is to eliminate this corruption. But this is extraordinarily difficult and out of the ordinary, even if one's own nature is a quite ordinary one. Only people with highly developed powers of reflection, such as Montaigne, are able to tolerate in themselves the counterpoints of peaks and valleys, light and dimness, power and triviality and to take upon themselves this quite puzzling discontinuity as the real empirical knowledge of the self of a living being. But people such as these also hesitate to come to the end of themselves and to believe sometime they will know, once and for all, what they are. "Only common souls readily achieve the sincere expression of their personality," as Gide once put it.[169]

An element is repeated in Montaigne's perception of himself which we described earlier when discussing his general determination of man's situation, namely, abasement. This seeker of self who is awkwardly avoiding the loss of self is not afraid to be the least significant one. This self-abasement is based upon the thought that one can very well be a self who is conscious of his uniqueness, a person, and yet at the same time, depending on his station, can be a person like thousands of others, temperamental, vacillating, moody, unexemplary. "The meanness of my subject," he says on one occasion, meaning himself (II, 17, 495 B). He finds the courage to speak of himself because this object is so "barren and meager" that there is no danger of vanity (II, 18, 503 A). "I, who am only a little gosling," find it easy to live in mediocrity (III, 7, 699 B). "Anyone who wants to verbally abuse me is always right" (III, 9, 749 B). One could continue reproducing comments such as these indefinitely. All this takes a direction that is analogous to toning down the objective concept of man. Reality should be found and entered; according to the essential order of what is human it can be found in that which is deficient. Even in the search for self, moral or characterological or intellectual devaluation ushers in the affirmation of devaluation as that which is factual. In fact, the reversal of devaluation into affirmation takes place most frequently when Montaigne speaks of himself. Man who has rejected all illusionary levels of rank secures the ground upon which he can feel at home because nature has placed him there. No matter how inadequate one's own essence may be, self-discovery will uncover what is supportive as well as tolerable in one's own inadequacy. The characteristic persistence with which Montaigne emphasizes his average humanity serves a moralistic drive for knowledge that describes without making value judgments, and his joy, which seems like passion, in tracking his own weaknesses is the joy of getting hold of reality.[170] Admittedly, irony is liberally mixed in with the seriousness of his self-diminishment, as is a certain arrogant pleasure in pulling the wool over the eyes of superficial readers who take it too literally. He avoids any remorseful emotionalism. For there are no feelings of guilt associated with his deprecating discovery of himself. Nor does he want to only say negative things about himself at any price: "If I seemed to myself good and wise or nearly so, I would shout it out at the top of my voice. To say less of yourself than is true is stupidity, not modesty" (II, 6, 274 C). Montaigne has the wonderful ability to sidestep both dangers, the delusion of vanity, but also the delusion of worthlessness. Taking both into account he learns to look closely at what he is. He knows that he is small, but also great; perhaps not great by virtue of his own morality, but by virtue of his capacity to elevate for reflection that which is ordinary and confused in the self: "I consider myself one of the common sort, except in that I consider myself so; guilty of the commoner and humbler faults, but not of faults disavowed or excused; and I value myself only for knowing my value" (II, 17, 481 C; III, 9, 766 B).[171] If I know that I am average, then I am no longer average. On one occasion, he cleverly expresses this as follows: I need not worry about avoiding stupid statements as long as I recognize them as such (II, 17, 496 C).

Montaigne was fond of appealing to classical examples with his study of himself. He quoted the Delphic oracle "Know thyself" several times (III, 9, 766 B; III, 13, 823 B; etc.). His source here is Plutarch's *Moralia* document "De E apud Delphos," in which the oracle is interpreted at the end as an admonishment to mortals to heed their own weaknesses. "Recognize the limits that you cannot exceed and be guided by this" was a modern humanist's interpretation of the saying.[172] Amyot in his translation of Plutarch reproduced this passage in the *Moralia* as follows: "Know thyself is a warning and reminder to mortal man of the imbecility [weakness] and debility of his character." This sounds much like what we find it in the *Essais*. In fact, Montaigne understands self-knowledge as insight into one's own inadequacy. He can also invoke Socrates for this (see chapter 2). What is admittedly lacking in his approach is the moment of subjection to the divine which is so important in the Greek work.

3. COMPARISON WITH AUGUSTINE

At the same time, this is where its difference from Christian reflection on the self becomes apparent. For that always has the characteristic of a striving for salvation. The pious man who looks upon himself perceives his poverty before God. He can only speak of himself under the presumption that he is "advertising his weaknesses" (II *Cor.* 11, 30). The beginning of a Christian knowledge of oneself is an ashamed abandonment of the arrogance with which man forgot his origin in creation and his later remoteness from God. *Qui bene se ipsum cognoscit, sibi ipsi vilescit,* one reads in the *Imitatio Christi* (I, 2; "Whoever really knows himself well will be insignificant to himself"). But this is only the first, negative phase of the process. It is followed by a second, positive one. And this is described unforgettably by Augustine. Even in the *Soliloquia,* the goal of all knowledge is defined as follows: *Deum et animam scire cupio* (I, 11, 7). Self-knowledge is the path to a knowledge of God. Thus it takes priority over all knowledge of things. The *Confessiones* contain the following well-known sentences: *Et eunt homines admirari alta montium . . . et relinquunt se ipsos* (X, 8: "Men enter and admire the high mountains, but they do not see themselves"); this is the original expression of the occidental introversion as a whole, which repeatedly—and from Petrarch on, even under a renewal of classical stimuli—emerges beside objective studies of the world and calls men back to contemplation of themselves.[173] Those sentences can still be detected in the occidental analysis of the soul when spiritual stimulus diminishes and worldly psychology remains. Christian self-examination recognizes man's place in the order of created beings. If in the initial, negative stage it has perceived the condition of sin of *miseria,* in the continuing, positive stage it perceives the soul's capacity to be redeemed, its capacity for God, and thus *the dignitas hominis.* But what it first encounters is the soul's unfathomability, the *ingens sinus animi, penetrale amplum et infinitum,* which cannot exhaust itself; *quis ad fundum eius pervenit? (Conf.* X, 8: "the vast depth of the soul; the endlessly broad inner self; who can penetrate to its foundation?"). Precisely this that is unfathomable is superior to external things because it encompasses their individual being through remembrance (*vi memoriae*). And, to a much greater degree than external things, the unfathomable soul demands explanation from a perspective of divine origin. It identifies itself in its caverns and caves (*in antris et cavernis, Conf.* X, 17) as the place closest to God and most intimately permeated by him: *Tu autem eras interior intimo meo . . . (Conf.* III, 6). It strives to make this proximity even closer. Penetrating into itself, it transcends itself. *Transibo et hanc vim meam . . . ut pertendam ad te, dulce lumen (Conf.* X, 17: "I want to transcend even this, my power, to come to you, sweet light"). The soul concerned with itself awakens from its contrite fear of being lost to a pious fear in the face of the wonder of its being created by God and to an ascent leading inward into love for its source. *Descendite, ut adscendatis* (*Conf.* IV, 12). These two stages of self-knowledge will remain a common element to the entire Augustinian, mystical direction of theology in the Middle Ages and later.[174] They can also be seen in Petrarch, though in somewhat diluted form. Traces of them can even be found in Cardano.

This is also true of Montaigne's study of the self initially. It is possible that he was inspired to do this early on by Sebond. For precisely in his translation of related passages of the *Theologia naturalis* is where we find a few of the most striking elaborations. Sebond's first chapter explains (with unmistakable Augustinian expressions[175]) that man is most closely related to himself, and that self-knowledge is the truest and only path to a knowledge of human nature. Man only knows with certainty what he knows in his own inner experience. But Sebond only uses this customary thought to safeguard the *dignitas hominis*. Montaigne does not share this conclusion. The *Essais* persist in an equating of self-knowledge and self-abasement. But one need not even see this as Christian. Christian introversion in general and Sebond's trains of thought in particular indeed paved the way for the turning to the self in the *Essais*, but nowhere do they penetrate further than a vivid command. When Montaigne undertakes "to penetrate the opaque depths of its innermost folds" (II, 6, 273 C), one is struck by the parallels in this and similar formulations to the expressions from Augustine quoted above (*Conf.* X, 8 and X, 17). However, similar words by the two authors point in different directions. Montaigne only retains *animam scire cupio* from the Augustinian *Deum et animam scire cupio*. And he does so without any striving for salvation, any need to experience an inspiring event in his own inwardness. His restlessness is no longer that *inquietum est cor meum donec requiescat in te* (*Conf.* I, 1). Rather, it is a philosophical restlessness that comes to rest in the assurance of individual actuality. The Socratic art of self-analysis, which was spiritualized by Christianity, had in fact already become secularly psychological again before Montaigne. But in his thinking it first took the form of an ethically indifferent observation of one's own essence. From the initial ranking of one's own nothingness—as the reality of what he is—he leads into a living out of the laws of his own self, without regret, the same thing that once led Goethe to say of man's resolve, "to explain that what is right is that which is appropriate to him" (*Dichtung und Wahrheit* III, 11).

Thus one should only take it in the loose sense of the word when on occasion Montaigne calls the *Essais* a "confession" (II, 17, 495 B), his portrayal of himself as "when I confess myself" (II, 20, 511 B; III, 5, 643 B). In the Cardano section of his *Geschichte der Farbenlehre*, Goethe places Montaigne beside Cellini and Cardano. He sees the autobiographies of the latter two and the *Essais* as a kind of confession in which the writers "rather comfortably speak of their faults," whereby "that which before this would only have been nervously told to the priest as a secret in the confessional is now presented to the entire world with a bold sort of implicit trust . . . Thus the confessions we mentioned seem to us to point to a certain degree to Protestantism." Montaigne reinforces the latter part of this comment to the extent that he himself writes on one occasion: "In honor of the Huguenots, who condemn our private and auricular confession, I confess myself in public, religiously and purely" (III, 5, 643 B). As justified as the comparison of the *Essais* with Cellini and Cardano may be (we will return to this in a moment), they have very little to do with confession in the sense of a religious confession, even in its protestant form. Montaigne drops the limits to confession precisely because there is no longer religious timidity sanctifying it. If one can use this anywhere, here one can call him a "Renaissance nature" which is not ashamed of its own growth before anyone. The partisanship for the "Huguenots" expressed in the quotation above is a little joke. The expression "to confess oneself religiously" is a play on the double meaning, still common then, of *religieux* (pious, but also conscientious) and means the thoroughness of his self-analysis. Even the invocation of Augustine found directly following the quotation is inconsequential; it does not even prove that he was even acquainted with the *Confessiones*.[176]

Rather, the character of the self-contemplation practiced in the *Essais* can be defined precisely in its remoteness from the *Confessiones*. Augustine's book portrays the stages in the ascending path to salvation: *lo quale fu di non buono in buono, e di buono in migliore, e di migliore in ottimo*, as Dante so simply expressed it (*Convivio* I, 2). This path is layed out between fixed starting and end points. Only those events in one's own life which are related to the dynamic of grace are brought to mind. Autobiographical recounting has a teleological, final character that interprets what has occurred as the soul's progressive movement into the proper relationship with God. It occurs when one is at the peak of fulfillment: it is a retrospective discussion of oneself with God concerning previous aberrations and enlightenment, it is a single, long prayer of thanksgiving. The book's fervor comes from a fully flowered knowledge of the intellectual plan and the hints that controlled the course of one's own life and lead one to that culmination in which the soul sacrifices itself to the will of God: *Et hoc erat totum: nolle quod volebam, et velle quod volebas* (IX, 1: "But it was thus: not to want what I wanted, and to want what you wanted"). And this knowledge knows that its power of self-illumination is the last and crowning stage of grace received.

The self is undoubtedly a puzzle for Montaigne as well. But its astonishing agitations do not have a transcendent plan. He escapes from its inability to be interpreted into the vague and uninterpreted concept of "nature." He only knows its boundless, contradictory change in form, "a perennial movement," as in the things of the external world (III, 2, 610 B); but he knows it thoroughly, for he experiences it. Since the agitations of the self remain unplanned, Montaigne cannot select a main event by means of which his self or his life would have come to an ideal completion, and from which everything else could be classified into either inhibiting or preparatory phases. He carefully avoids the concept of a development even with respect to himself. He only differentiates greater or lesser degrees of honesty with which he feels able to pursue and learn about the undulating movements of his own, antinomical disorder. He never makes distinctions between the individual realms of his life or between various intellectual conditions that are based upon their rank. Every trivial detail from every realm or condition is in his eyes worthy of being a symptom for—stated paradoxically, as it must be—the amorphous form of his individuality. When he speaks of his faults, appearing to moralize and falling back on customary terms, he is speaking of characteristics, but not of something that must be overcome. The moments of life and self which he relates have something strangely random about them, and they remain surrounded by the half-light of possible future random events from which an entirely different self could emerge. Nowhere in the *Essais* does one find the description of a crisis with a prelude of "not yet" and a postlude of the solution. This separates it as profoundly from Augustine as from Descartes, behind whose purportedly autobiographical *Discours de la Méthode* is hidden the universally applicable case of seeking truth, introduced through crisis, via extra-personal human reason. Finally, even the progression of Montaigne's self-portrayal is adapted to all this: it is not a look back from a height already attained, but is rather a synchronous accompanying of urgent instances: "I take it in this condition, just as it is at the moment I give my attention to it" (III, 2, 610–611 B).[177] The *Essais* are a monologue in a form similar to a diary in which one is never quite sure of the intended audience, other than the writer himself; it is not God, in any case.

What Montaigne achieves with this is an extraordinary, clear, many-sided illumination of his self and he can linger undisturbed in the realm of honest, empirical observation that leaves nothing out. For the sake of achieving this, he surrenders any unambiguousness of his self, any preju-dicial image, any entelechy-based structure, and any connection with extra-personal orders. His self is an open synthesis the contents of which are boundless and chaotic; the more contradictory, the more welcome. But even when this empirical observation of self threatens to disintegrate into mere details, it still contains, and this is what matters, its specific way of understanding the self. The fact that it avoids creating a centralized structure and deriving the individual moments of the self from this as something evident is both its principle and its outcome. To understand oneself here means to understand that the self is an interplay of surprising factualities that can never be expressed as a totality, which are interlocked in mysterious ways and yet, again mysteriously, together are capable of life. No salvation-oriented self-analysis, no self-analysis proceeding according to the idea of an entelechy, could have advanced as far into this astounding problem area as did this empirical observa-tion of self. In this observation of self, as in the observation of others described earlier, Montaigne had to clear the path of claims for creating structure ethically and religiously in order to follow it to the point where man emerges as he is.

4.   COMPARISON WITH AUTOBIOGRAPHY

How do the *Essais* relate to other genre of self-portrayal, particularly autobiography? Nowhere does Montaigne speak of the great autobiog-raphies of antiquity or the Renaissance, at least not in connection with his self-portrayal. Only in one passage does one find: "We have heard of only two or three ancients who opened up this road, and even of them we cannot say whether their manner in the least resembled mine, since we know only their names. No one since has followed their lead" (II, 6, 273 C). But who are the "two or three ancients" whom he could con-ceive of as his precursors, but from whom he hesitantly turns away since only their names are known? The conjecture of two commentators,[178] which goes back in part to an observation made by Pierre Coste, that Montaigne was thinking of Archilochus, Alcaeus, and Lucilius, cannot be proven. That he suspected in the verse of these three authors (spoken of in the Renaissance as well, although their fragments were not known then) something related to his own unceremonious openness is conceivable. But we do not know whether he was thinking of them precisely here. All that can clearly be concluded from the passage is that he was conscious of the originality of his undertaking as the first one to risk making himself the object of a book.

We need not get into the complex history of autobiography.[179] But we must briefly mention what connects the *Essais* with it in individual cases, but separates it from autobiography in a vastly greater number of cases.

As far as antiquity is concerned, what connects them is what is most general, and it also concerns not fully developed autobiography, but rather philosophical contemplation of the self, such as that practiced by Seneca. We have already discussed this. Additionally, there are stimuli in Horace's *Satirae* (in which it is legitimate for the author to speak of himself according to the rules of the genre), and in letters. Of the latter, this comment applies primarily to Cicero's letters. But their influence was essentially only as a model for the use of an intimate tone and the open form of the *Essais;* thus we will discuss this elsewhere (chapter 8).

Petrarch deserves first mention among modern writers. However, Montaigne never invoked him regarding the topic of self-analysis which we are considering here. Nevertheless, with his interest in his own secular self-ruled individuality, Petrarch represents the beginning of a line at a later point in which one finds Montaigne, who is indeed a much stronger personality around whom the air is much fresher and Petrarch's vain ambiguousness has disappeared. Petrarch discovered the dangerous, and at that time new, claim of subjective humanity to make the world and images of the world a game of its own perspectives. Knowledge of intellectual figures which had been handed down from the past replaced a binding subordination to an authority and the knowledge of the objective coherence of things. He randomly chose from what was handed down what was useful to him, because his only rule was: care and satisfaction of his own taste. As often as he described historical figures, essentially, he only understood himself and only knew how to use himself as reliable material for interpreting man. In his case it is already true that he no longer reveals his own periods of suffering and happiness as examples, as Seneca did, from which others were to learn the methods of salvation like pupils from a teacher. When Petrarch describes himself as a pitifully weak creature, one can detect how the

aesthetic enticement of this "being sick" which interests him is stronger
than his public assurance that he remorsefully wishes to improve himself. This internal avoidance of an ethos corresponds externally to an
aversion to any sort of obligation in one's occupation and how one
conducts one's life. He only apparently places his individuality under
the concepts of guilt and remorse. But he persists in a lyrical enjoyment
of his fragility, which he adorns with melancholy tones of Christian
conscience. Human inadequacy is still theoretically derived from the fall
from grace. But since the ethical force leading to remorse and transformation has become weak, an art of describing spiritual confusion and
disquiet previously unattained to this degree of refinement arises—
primarily in the letters and the *Secretum*. To this is added the gift of
being able to relate the most concrete things about the self graphically.
Details of his personal life are infused into all his writings, even the
historiographic ones. It seems as if he were unable to stop their flow, so
powerful was the urge to reveal the self.

What Montaigne and Petrarch have in common is patently clear. But
for the Frenchman, the regulatory ideas Petrarch sought to use to find
access to the self, other than a few remainders, had vanished, particularly the idea of an existence in original sin. The Christian shadow of
conscience in man's consciousness, which even in Petrarch only remained as a stimulus, had evaporated. The self-affirmation of a joyful,
even conscience-less character that was fulfilling an organic, natural law
when it confirmed its own animal narrowness and settled in to live
within it had broken through completely in Montaigne. Plutarch's complacency in his own impotence, the vacillation between the spiritual
pathology of Augustine and that of Cicero or Seneca, all of which he
acquired by reading, has given way to an honest drive for knowledge
which is able to rise above the given literary lines. Petrarch has every
intention of looking at himself, but he never escapes from the masks and
imitations. Montaigne has the will and does escape them—it is precisely
for this reason that he understands the danger of self-stylization to quite
a different degree than Plutarch ("I am constantly adorning myself, for I
am constantly describing myself" II, 6, 273 C). Man of the fourteenth
century who was interpreted in Petrarch adhered with half his force to
the memory of being a creation of God which was thrust out of paradise, a freak.

Although the *Essais* were written closer in time, in subject matter
they are further removed than the much older Petrarch from the autobiography of Benvenuto Cellini (1558/1562). Montaigne did not know it.

It represents the most vehement creation of Italian Cinquecento prose. The eagerly egocentric Cellini wrote it in the full conviction of his artistic greatness. It is stuffed full of adventures and events to which the language is barely equal, it is completely unhumanistic, sometimes titanic, sometimes burlesque, but always naive and lacking in reflection of the deeper meaning of a self-analysis. Precisely this defect separates it from Montaigne, despite the existing general correspondence of his and Cellini's unlimited legitimacy of the self. It is best apparent, from the contrast between the *Essais* and Cellini, how with the empirical matter that the Frenchman exhibits, far more is involved than simply the raw concern with the subject matter.

On the other hand, Girolamo Cardano's *De vita propria* is much more closely related to Montaigne's work. It was written around 1575 when the author was advanced in years, and was published for the first time in 1643 in France by Gabriel Naudé. Thus Montaigne did not know it. All the more astounding, considering all the differences in temperament and world view, is what they have in common, what arose simultaneously on French and Italian soil. Cardano's autobiography, written in a chaotic Latin, does not proceed chronologically, but rather analytically. It proceeds through the author's opinions on individual philosophical, religious, moral, and medical topics, and describes his behavior in the various spheres of his life (marriage, career, travels, etc.). Its unity consists in its expression of subjectivity removed from context. The book continuously reaches forward or backward again, and surrenders in a confusing and digressing manner to chance inspirations of memory or associations arising from the topics just considered. Cardano declines any ideal claim to himself. "Good" and "evil" are only auxiliary terms, they are not measures of one's own essence. He does call his self-portrayal a confession (chapter 13); but this is not a confession before God, although the final chapter is an attempt to give that appearance. The meaning of the undertaking lies in its knowledge of being human (*conditio humana*) based upon what lies closest at hand, one's own individuality. Cardano establishes without remorse that he, like all others, is a mixture of filth and gold. There is nothing cheerful or apollonian in the image of himself he presents. He casts even himself among the rest of the rabble filled with a misanthropic attitude. But passionate honesty guides him. He speaks of his disfigured, sickly body, of his soul that has sunken into wretchedness, and then of mysterious beckonings he has received from a higher realm, one does not know whether divine or demonic. He denounces classical autobiography because it tends to revise life into a process of ideal self-fulfillment (chapter 13; he does not actually mean autobiography, but rather Marcus Aurelius). He himself wants nothing but brutal factuality. He views himself as a strange organism, sees his natural functions and his contradictions with the eye of the diagnostician, discovers in the events of his life what is inconsistent between cause and effect, and from all this draws the conclusion that man is confusion. But he has a very highly developed consciousness of the uniqueness of what he, and precisely he, is. He seeks with hundreds of banal or even pathetic details to bring himself to light as a person: carbuncle on his face, preferred writing implement, longing for fame, love for his son . . . And all this despite the fact, or because, he knows that his own essence lacks any comprehensible form and is a mere plaything of what is unpredictable. This man sees clearly how defective he is, and yet he remains what he is. Instead of striving for remorse or improvement or discovering meaning, he uses his energy to strive for an investigative observation of the self. It pleases him, for it opens up to him new territory: humanity of a natural, unstandardized, individual reality.

This is the same new territory that was discovered in the same time period in the *Essais,* and using the same method. Independent of each other, Cardano and Montaigne created a view of the self that is far removed from the characteristics of a so-called "typical" autobiography, that is, far from the interpretation of one's own life as a structure that unfolds logically from phase to phase, which can be presented in a factual completeness including the external circumstances of contemporary history. In each of them, everything is fragment and conglomerate, but it also has at every point a density of symptoms at which the puzzle of one's own nature is illuminated all the more surprisingly, the more one dispenses with external order and rounding. Cardano's *De vita propria* is in this respect the only work of all autobiographical literature which can seriously be placed beside the *Essais,* as thoroughly different as Montaigne's situation is, as little as his life can be compared with the adventurous turmoil of the Italian's, and as little as his cheerful solitude can be compared with the feelings of terror of the latter, who was shrouded in his belief in demons, magic, and astrology.

Montaigne very seldom speaks of the events in the history of his time which affect his life. His individuality extends into itself, not into the external realm of its epoch. He does not feel driven to look for prerequisites or reflections of his self in contemporary events. He is unable to penetrate to that magnificent contrapuntal interaction of person and epoch which Goethe later experienced and described in *Dichtung und*

Wahrheit. For what he wants to know about himself, the conditions of his century are just as much a matter of indifference as is the chronological progression of the course of his own life. He understands the effect he has in the public world much more as a matter of Fortuna than as a result of his personal powers: "My actions would tell more about fortune than about me" (II, 6, 274 C). Thus it is also again just a matter of a lax use of the word when on one occasion he calls the *Essais* "memoirs" (III, 9, 751 B). Occasional reports on the conducting of his public office (namely in III, 10) are indeed reminiscent of the conventions of *mémoires,* but their aim reaches beyond the brief intention apparent at first and into observation of the self, which is developed here using the random material provided by his own practical actions. As he puts it expressly, "It is not my deeds that I write down; it is myself, it is my essence" (II, 6, 274 C). Or, with the customary decorative modesty: "I cannot keep a record of my life by my actions; fortune places them too low. I keep it by my thoughts" (III, 9, 721 B).

Thus there is nothing remaining in the usual literary genre of subjective statements which could be called a direct model for the *Essais.* Confessions, soliloquies, autobiographies, memoirs: they did indeed make the *Essais* possible in a very general way, just as they made the occidental contemplation of the self of postantiquity possible everywhere, but also no more. Montaigne was correct in his conviction that it was something new and unheard of to make the self-portrait of "a completely ordinary person" the object of a literary undertaking: "It is the only book in the world of its kind" (II, 8, 278 C)—or, in a passage that was later crossed out: "I have spurred myself to break the ice and show our . . . [the rest of this is torn off]" (III, 5, 678).

5.   PERMISSION TO SPEAK OF ONESELF

This consciousness of originality still had one tension to overcome, something that we today are not easily able to feel, but which is a part of the circumstances surrounding the *Essais.* One notices that Montaigne apologizes several times for speaking of himself because this is only appropriate for great and famous men, but for others it is an affront to decorum. The beginning of Essay II, 18, for example, addresses this. Elsewhere, he writes: "Custom has made speaking of oneself a vice, and obstinately forbids it out of hatred for the boasting that seems always to accompany it" (II, 6, 273 C). And: "We must pass over these common rules of civility in favor of truth and liberty" (III, 8, 720 B). Any reserva-

tions against speaking of himself which he considers, but also decisively
counters, were an integral part of critical judgment at his time and later.
His friend Etienne Pasquier, who otherwise had great respect for Montaigne, tried to dismiss his speaking of himself in the *Essais* as the
infirmity of old age. Scaliger and other scholars vent their annoyance
with it. Mlle. de Gournay had to expressly come to her foster father's
defense against attacks on his personal confessions. People appeared
disconcerted by the fact that this "stoic wise man" chose this manner of
expression, and they disapproved of the third book of the *Essais*, considering it a decline. Precisely that which was most characteristic of Montaigne had an alienating effect. Pascal's cry is well known: "What a
stupid idea his self-portrait was!" (*Pensées*, fragment 62). The logic of
Port-Royal and Malebranche is a variation of these reproaches. Even
Coste finds it necessary in the foreword to his ten-volume edition of the
Essais (1724) to defend Montaigne's practice of speaking of himself,
and even Montaigne's English friends in the nineteenth century felt they
had to do something similar.[180]

Discussion of the question of whether an author is permitted to speak
of himself is quite old. In antiquity, it belonged in the discipline of
rhetoric.[181] As a rule it was answered in the negative. For to speak of
oneself attracted the suspicion of vanity, a vice that was to be avoided by
sophisticated rhetoricians and authors. The question was even considered in the discipline of ethics. Aristotle considered it a merit of high-
minded persons that they did not speak of themselves (*Nic. Ethics*,
1125a). Yet exceptions were permitted. For example, in old age, presum-
ing the speaker were a famous, exemplary person; Cicero, for example,
once speaks of this exception (*De senectute*, 9–10). Or there is the
illustrious man per se, who may preserve his *virtus* in writing to the
benefit of those who follow: Tacitus in the introduction to *Agricola*.
Plutarch took a position on this question in the *Moralia*. In the small
treatise "How One Can Praise Oneself without Causing Harm" he
turns strongly against speaking of oneself because, as with the earlier
rhetoric, he can only see it from the viewpoint of "vainglory." However,
it seems permissible to him in cases of "emergency," if one must defend
oneself against slander, or if, when one has fallen into misfortune, one
wishes to protect oneself against humiliating pity from others: thus
defensive and heroic praise of oneself is permitted. These things were
then explained again in the literature of postantiquity. Best known is
Dante's apology, derived for epic reasons, which is found in the *Divina
Commedia* for mentioning his own name *di necessità* (*Purg.* XXX, 62–

63), or the omission at the beginning of the *Convivio,* where he repeats the opinion of the "rhetoricians" that speaking of oneself should be condemned, and where he then (invoking Boëthius and Augustine) allows for two exceptions: defensive and virtuous (that is, to serve others) praise of oneself. Christian theology justified these principles in its own way early on by invoking the Pauline "boasting of one's own weakness" (II *Cor.* II, 31). In general, it only permits speaking of oneself before God and priests unless what one says is valuable for one's fellow man as testimony of one's own path to salvation. On the other hand, in autobiographic writings of the Renaissance one again finds mention of those sentences from Cicero's *De senectute,* Tacitus' *Agricola,* and Plutarch's treatise used for the purpose of justifying portrayal of oneself to spread one's own glory. Finally, courtly society of the sixteenth and seventeenth centuries was also concerned with the question, but it advised against speaking of oneself, considering this unseemly. Every document on education, from Castiglione and Della Casa to Chevalier de Méré, discusses this. The decency of the courtly gentleman, Christian attitudes, and rhetorical schooling were unified in their rejection of speaking of oneself. Even Voltaire advised authors: "Speak of yourself as little as you can." Goethe sees it quite differently: "The question of whether one may write one's own biography is quite awkward. I consider one who does so the most courteous of men. When one opens one's heart, it is quite unimportant what one's motives may be in doing so."[182]

These things, which to today's reader probably seem inconsequential and antiquated, had to be touched upon to show the conventions with which Montaigne had to contend. The courage required for him to speak of himself was much greater than we might be inclined to concede at first glance today. It was opposed by prohibitions of several centuries' standing. All of the reasons just mentioned for this prohibition, as well as the provisions under which speaking of oneself was permitted, are heard in the *Essais,* only to be rejected. We will not quote each of these.[183] The force and the philosophical content of the study of the self were too strong in Montaigne to be held back by inhibitions of rhetoric, religion, or societal concepts of propriety. In fact, they grew during the process of eliminating these inhibitions. He only occasionally concedes to a common motive when he calls his talk of himself the privilege of his "old age." But he abolishes the two alternatives to which speaking of oneself has been restricted, namely, self-praise or self-reproach. He treats self-reproach, which he appears to practice, as an heuristic method, as we have seen. Thus he also removes himself from a judgment from the perspective of a situation often discussed in moral theology, namely that ostentatious confession of one's sins is disguised vanity or an evasion of genuine remorse. His confession of unworthiness is the recognition of his own reality, free of value judgments. Here, to express the "vices" is done not to save one from the "vices" themselves, but rather from ignorance of the self. He dares to speak of himself only "in favor of truth and liberty," as he states it in the important passage quoted above (III, 8, 720 B). It required a special awakening of modern consciousness to be able to see in self-analysis not vanity or remorse for sin, but rather the most valuable source available for knowledge of man. Montaigne accomplished this awakening. From a philosophical viewpoint "the most courteous of men" and the most courageous and cheerful, he reaches his hand across two centuries to Goethe, whose comment quoted above breaks through the conventions of concealing the self with the same free-thinking spirit found in the *Essais*.

6.   LACK OF REMORSE

Montaigne's relationship with himself, the source of his understanding of himself, is defined through and through by a lack of remorse. Just as he removes guilt from his objective image of man, he removes it from himself. He is very well aware of his shortcomings, his weaknesses, his failure to attain an ideality, whatever its bases. But to him these are facts, inexplicably there, prevailing unavoidably, in fact, equipped with the mysterious sense of being constituents of the organic order of individuality which would fall apart without them. Thus he also lacks the ethical stimulus inherent to the feeling of guilt: despair, remorse, the desire no longer to be like this, regret, the drive for redemption. Indeed, he was not an evil or even criminal man, as Cardano was at times. He possessed, as did thousands of others, the degree of decency necessary for men to live together. This in itself eliminated the opportunity for a personal, moral feeling of guilt (which he definitely would have taken upon himself in the event of evil deeds). But also absent is that deeper sense of responsibility which seizes a man when he believes in the moral, spiritual, and religious perfectibility of human essence as a whole. Thus he can write sentences such as the following: "I have something still worse than inadequacy: that I hardly mind it, and hardly try to cure it" (III, 10, 784 B). "I let myself go as I am" (II, 10, 297 A). "I have not . . . corrected my natural disposition by force of reason, and have not troubled my inclination at all by art. I let myself go as I have come" (III, 12, 811 B).

This obedience to his own factuality which prevailed against remorse was so important to him that it was his concern in one entire Essay: III, 2 ("Of Repentance"). Not that he rejects remorse. His psychology comes to terms with it just as one comes to terms with a known mental phenomenon. But it considers it ineffective, delusional. It cannot combat a person's basic make-up. Man is truer and more genuine when he accepts himself than when he makes himself into something; for his essence is not his own work. Therefore: "I can do no better. And repentance does not properly apply to the things that are not in our power" (617 B). It is wise to leave that which I was as it was, and not to fear that which I will become: "If I had to live over again, I would live as I have lived. I have neither tears for the past nor fears for the future" (620 C). A different, passive will takes the place of active remorse: the will to be obediently true to oneself. In looking back over the totality of his life, Montaigne notices that he has fulfilled the make-up of his own individuality, and thus has enjoyed the blessing of an order which is, though inscrutable, rich with metamorphosis: "When I consider the behavior of my youth in comparison with that of my old age, I find that I have generally conducted myself in orderly fashion, according to my lights" (617 B). This brings a peace into which remorse cannot penetrate. This is reminiscent of Goethe's statement: "I can say this straight out, for what concern is it of mine, I did not make myself" (to Eckermann, March 30, 1824). Apart from all individual differences, Montaigne shares with Goethe this experience of the pressure of individuality which must be satisfied despite any injuries it may do to men and mores, and which knows it is secure within a deep trust in the intricate weave of the self. Thus: "My professed principle, which is to be wholly contained and established within myself" (618 B). This by no means casual, in fact, quite bold, tolerance of oneself has the prudence not to judge prior behavior after the fact, for it knows that this behavior arose in its own time from the irrepeatable interplay of opportunity and the nature of the self at that time: "I find that in my past deliberations, according to my rule, I have proceeded wisely, considering the state of the matter proposed to me . . . I am not considering what it is at this moment, but what it was when I was deliberating about it" (617–618 B). This represents, when applied to a relationship to himself, the same respect for his own rights and for the uniqueness of the moment which he grants to other men, peoples, and times—for indeed all of human essence consists of mere moments that have their own laws. Thus his assessment of his own youth is also one of tolerance; it does not come from the perspective of old age, for old age is no longer in its youth, and thus would only distort it; rather, it comes from the reproductive empathy with one's former youth: "Now that I am no longer in that state, I judge it as though I were in it" (619 B). He allows himself to be vain or idle or moderately disloyal; it is simply inherent in man to be vain or idle or disloyal. Even our unsuitable and suitable characteristics are elements of life without which we strange beings would die out. All the way into his last Essays Montaigne remained fond of the thought that self-knowledge and self-transformation are two different things, and remorse can be a betrayal that man perpetrates against his own nature, which has been placed in his hands: "I would indeed correct an accidental error, and I am full of them . . . But the imperfections that are ordinary and constant in me it would be treachery to remove" (III, 5, 667 B). Montaigne is a surprising example of how a man can relinquish active ethics and yet pursue involvement with himself as a very serious matter. He offsets the loss of ethical absoluteness in the absoluteness of knowledge which goes along with self-discovery. In fact, the loss of the former is necessary to make the latter possible. That fine sense for listening within himself perceives the hidden harmony of the forces that guide the self only when the admonitions of conscience are silent. *Propriam naturam sequamur,* Montaigne quotes from Cicero (III, 9, 756 C, from *De officiis* I, 31). What he means is admittedly different from the stoically conceived nature that guarantees the correspondence of man and a world structure that is understandably rational. It is the realm of what is irrational and contradictory. It makes no response to speculative questioning—and yet, in the manner of an individual order of the self, living is possible because it is imposed upon us. When a man becomes and knows what he is, he is already sound.

7. HIS OWN INDIVIDUALITY

Montaigne wove the description of his own, concrete individuality into all of the characteristics of his relationship to and understanding of himself described up till now. In the process, he delves so often into small and very small details that it appears as if he had lost sight of the philosophical meaning of his discussion of himself and simply wanted to chat about himself. And that is the case in many individual instances. But even then, the description has a further meaning, namely to assure the unmistakableness of his person. His drive for individuality is afraid of nothing so much as it is afraid of distortion: "I would willingly come back from the other world to give the lie to any man who portrayed me other than I was, even if it were to honor me" (III, 9, 751 B). His awareness of originality is also supported by this precision of portraiture: "Authors communicate with the people by some special extrinsic mark; I am the first to do so by my entire being, as Michel de Montaigne, not as a grammarian or a poet or a jurist" (III, 2, 611 C). Instead of his professional characteristics ("extrinsic mark . . ."), which are somewhat foreign to individuality, as something one shares with others, his interest is in the extra-professional but clearly individual elements of his human essence ("entire being . . . Michel de Montaigne"). He presented himself so precisely that no Montaigne legend could develop, for example, like the legends that arose around a Rabelais or a Shakespeare. He presented a portrait of himself, not a myth. His contemporaries confirmed that he was indeed as he portrayed himself in the *Essais*.[184] The occasional assurances that he feels inhibited due to considerations of decency from revealing everything, unadorned, about himself are the last traces of the convention of propriety against which he expressly allows his self-description to prevail. But in view of the intimate, erotic, and physiological confessions in III, 5 and III, 13, they turn out to be ironic embellishments.

Montaigne finally left his one-time stimulus Sebond behind with this concreteness. In the *Theologia naturalis* one reads that man is only prized because he is the image of God (that is, due to his general rank), not *quia talis vel talis est,* which at the time Montaigne translated as: *ny pour quelque consideration qu'on ait eu de ce qu'il est Pierre ou Guillaume*[185] ("nor for any consideration that one might have had of his being Peter or William"). Now Montaigne is only interested in what is not general, "our own affairs and Michel, who concerns us even more closely than man in general" (III, 9, 726 C). Unlike Seneca in his self-analysis, Montaigne does not simply take daily details for granted. He grasps these as the reality that contains life. He discovers, even with respect to himself, that what is insignificant, inconspicuous, imperceptibly transitory, tells more about a man than things that are publicly and didactically memorable. He is the Plutarch of himself. Under the magical glance of his sense of individuality, his lines and wrinkles, ugliness, faults, the intimacies of his body and his spirit become the definitive contours of a self-portrait.

Thus we learn everything we might wish to know about his person. He has a somewhat stocky, plump build. This irritates him a little, for it detracts from his other features: his broad forehead, his gentle eyes, his moderately large nose and small mouth and ears, his white, even teeth, his full, dark brown beard, the fresh complexion, his lack of body odor, and the proper proportions of his extremities. He mentions his bald head several times. He is pleased with his dense moustache; scents, to which he is quite sensitive, cling to it for a long time—once, in his youth, the scents of a woman's sensual kisses. His gait is rapid and steady, but his legs are so fidgety and restless ("like Chrysippus") that he cannot sit quietly at any ceremony. His good eyesight saves him from needing to wear glasses. When reading, he places glass over the paper to cut the glare. His voice is loud and forceful. He loves to use forceful language in conversation, and easily gets excited. He likes to scratch his ears, eats rapidly, and sometimes bites his tongue in the process. He dislikes long mealtimes, thus ("like Augustus") he generally only comes to the table after the others have already begun. He isn't picky and makes do with what is placed before him, but he does pay attention to the digestibility of the foods. He avoids overloading his stomach, prefers salty foods, likes to drink ("more than Augustus"), and sometimes prefers white wine, sometimes red (this passage irritated Scaliger[186]). He worries about a well-functioning digestive system; he considers speaking of this, and extensively at that, to be permissible for one who is a "soldier and native of Gascogne." This and similar revelations as a whole, as he admits, are affectations of old men, who have the liberty of being concerned extensively with their physical well-being. (This will quite apparently characterize the style of his old age.) His temperament is moderately sanguine, midway between joviality and thoughtfulness. Conflict and hatred are contrary to his nature; he is more inclined toward compassion, yet displays great coolness toward his wife and child. He loves animals so much that he frees them immediately when he has captured some. He is jumpy and anxious. But as a whole, he is ruled by "the vice of indolence," but this, in his opinion, also has the advantage of protecting him against a restless ambition. He had the fault of laziness even in his youth. The job of managing his household bores or irritates him; he performs the duties associated with it as quickly as possible. He places no restraints upon himself in dealing with those in his service. If someone angers him, he scolds him thoroughly—and the anger is gone. He does not harbor long resentments and grudges. He sees through the incongruent motives of his moral qualities with a sharp eye: he knows he is brave, but from weakness, modest and obedient, but for convenience. He suspects the deception of the passions in his desires— but he says this so charmingly: "I am somewhat tenderly distrustful of the things I wish for" (III, 10, 775 C). He only feels he can praise one trait in himself, and that is a love of truth. To him it is the sign of a free man's essence; only slaves have the need to lie. He puts it well as follows: "I admit the truth when it hurts me, just as when it serves me" (III, 5, 675 B). He happily tolerates contradiction for the sake of truth. He finds himself free of obstinacy. Nevertheless, on one occasion he also mistrusts this sense of truth as a possible consequence of his indolence.

He is thoroughly ready to experience and live out the entire entanglement of human existence. For no objective knowledge, no anthropological definitions can compare with natural firsthand experience; only this has the power to perceive the human essence in its internal clarity: "I know better what is man than I know what is animal, or mortal, or rational" (III, 13, 819 B).[187] In one instance Montaigne spoke of "a person" whom he described as follows: "no middle position, always being carried away from one extreme to the other by causes impossible to guess; no kind of course without tacking and changing direction amazingly; no quality unmixed; so that the most likely portrait of him that men will be able to make some day, will be that he affected and studied to make himself known by being unknowable" (III, 13, 825 C). This passage has always been understood correctly: he means himself.[188]

The most productive act of finding the self is observation of one's spontaneous reactions of taste and intellect. To solve the problem of a matter to him means to listen as passively as possible for the natural answer that his own nature gives to it. He knows from his skeptical schooling that things only emerge in a changeable, subjective appearance, and that although the possibility of objective truth is lost in this, the nature of the individual spirit unfolds in it. Every soul is the queen in its own realm in that it dresses everything it encounters in its own garments, he writes (I, 50, 220 C). His is as well. Saturating everything with its own colors it acquires everything with a deeper intimacy than factual knowledge can accomplish, and in the process it acquires itself. Even if clarity regarding a matter is not possible, clarity of its observer regarding himself is possible. Since any knowledge can only amount to "it seems to me," Montaigne collects all such instances of "it seems to me" in order to discover himself in them with precisely the same unmistakability as he discovers himself in his physical or character traits. Giving up claims to objective truth, he retreats into subjective truthfulness, which consists in the individual relating to a matter in a manner that is true to himself. He is in fact a "lyrical philosopher,"[189] to whom, similar to the lyrical poet, things can become his soul's medium.

No Occidental author before him dared with such resoluteness to keep his thinking within the realm of merely private opinion, and yet to publish it for the sake of self-description. According to Hegel, opinions are: "random thoughts," "imaginings which I can have this way or that, and someone else can have differently." "An opinion is mine; it is not per se a general thought." "Truth stands facing opinion, and opinion blanches before it."[190] These are precisely the definitions that apply to Montaigne, but with different value placed upon them. Does this make him unphilosophical? His opining, modest as Cinderella, stays away from the great seekers of systematic, objective truth, and has no intention of competing with them. And yet he does not see himself "blanch" before them—or if so, only ironically. He sees himself flash in the colors of his own nature. While the *Essais* apparently do nothing other than to break everything down into inconsequential subjectivisms, a process of powerful crystallization of self-awareness is taking place in a person who is ready to accept his uniqueness, and who gains solid ground beneath his feet when he "only" forms an opinion. All ideas presented in the *Essais* are meant ultimately to be understood as the self-portraiture of their author. At the same time, they are permeated by the suspicion (generally only allowed poets) that what is close to the essence of a thing becomes apparent in what is most illusionary, the subjective coloring (*teinture* I, 50, 220 C), that is, the transformation due to the inwardness that differs from person to person, and from phase to phase. The perspective of the individual, thoroughly conscious of its relativity (but no longer as an inferiority), discovers itself as an example of the truth of "appearance." There is also another significance to such a reduction of thoughts to mere "opinions." It is the recognition of the high degree of uselessness of philosophical thinking which need not praise itself, strive for acknowledgment or defend itself, but is rather concerned fully with continually questioning things and itself and its bearers. By intending only to be opinion, it retains the mobility necessary for such an occupation. It knows that it need not blanch before one who follows its train of thought—even if he does it in his own way and has a different opinion.[191]

8.   REFLECTIONS ON OLD AGE

The motif of old age plays a dominant role in Montaigne's self-portrayal. We spoke earlier about the fact that, and why, he wanted his *Essais* understood as meditations of a man on the threshold of old age, or actually living his old age (see chapter 1). Here we must say a few more things about this.

The old age motif is a welcome means of self-deprecation for Montaigne: you are listening to an aged spirit here, so listen to him without the expectation of learning much from him. "Here you have . . . some excrements of an aged mind," he writes bluntly at the beginning of III, 9. Classical and humanistic typologies of aging are intertwined with the need to particularize his own individuality still further, namely by limiting it to his current stage of life. From the fundamental discovery that a life can only understand itself fragmentarily, he withdraws to his condition of being old and exhausts it, existing in it and learning about it. In his customary manner, he intends the exhibition of his "old age" to be as ironic as it is serious. It is ironic in the excess pressure of such an exhibition. This degrades what is so close to his heart, the earnest will to find the self in what is real, which for him is always what is momentary. The more he abandons himself to his being old, the more he feels himself to be immediate in his humanity. Other than this, he is in fact a classical author of old age. He has quite purely actualized the advantages—and also a few defects—of this stage of life: skepticism, tolerance, gentleness, irony, calm wisdom, remoteness from all business, the maturity of closeness to death, but also a certain gossipy quality and the tendency to speak at length about what is comfortable or beneficial to him. Yet he confesses to the deficiencies no less lovingly than to the advantages. In fact, in nurturing the inclinations of his old age, his spirit grows and truly becomes what he was intended to be to the extent that one might say he became younger with old age. Perhaps he was in such a hurry to become old, or to be seen as old, because he perceived this.

It is striking how early he lets his "old age" begin. When he withdraws to his tower at the age of thirty-nine, he is already speaking of "what little life remains to me." As a forty-year-old, he feels he is at the threshold of old age. And to live past forty seems to him an unusual favor. The forty-six-year-old speaks bluntly of *ma vieillesse*. Looking back, he determines that he was fully a man at twenty-five. On another occasion, he writes that the highpoint of life lies around thirty-five; this is when great deeds are accomplished. This can be seen in the example of Alexander, who at thirty-three had already subjugated the inhabited world. And he evaluated the stages of life according to their biological vigor, and thus saw old age as a weakening of vitality and cooling of the blood. The decay of the body parallels the decay of the soul; it, too, begins to develop wrinkles, "to smell sour and moldy." In 1588 he inserts a comedy-like stereotyped picture of an old man into an Essay (perhaps his fellow countryman and neighbor Gaston de Foix): a petulant, spiteful, hypochondriacal man, meddling mistrustfully in everything, stingy, and drolly made fun of behind his back by all.[192]

But he is also prepared to acknowledge the advantages of old age and to find them in himself, though without praising them more than they deserve. He considers among these to be above all the permission to enter into contemplative seclusion and to take leave of all that keeps others at a distance from ourselves: "We have lived enough for others; let us live at least this remaining bit of life for ourselves . . . We must untie these bonds that are so powerful, and henceforth love this and that, but be wedded only to ourselves" (I, 39, 178 A). He sees his favorite occupation, observing himself, as the most appropriate means of obeying the law of old age. Admittedly, he describes this observation as if for want of something better he simply has no alternative but to look into himself. He does not pride himself in his *vita contemplativa* as an ethical achievement, for he sees in it, as everywhere, a mixture of decay and favor. Thus he knows without illusions that the virtue of the old man comes about entirely of itself and without credit to him simply because his passions have faded away (II, 11, 310 A and III, 2, 619 B—a theme much beloved in future moral theory[193]). Finally, he is far removed from expecting a guarantee in his position as an old man that he has become wiser, namely, wiser in the sense of some moral example. Thus in a late period he writes: "Since then I have grown older by a long stretch of time; but certainly I have not grown an inch wiser. Myself now and myself a while ago are indeed two; but when better, I simply cannot say. It would be fine to be old if we traveled only toward improvement. It is a drunkard's motion, staggering, dizzy, wobbling, or that of reeds that the wind stirs haphazardly as it pleases" (III, 9, 736 C). This is one of the most informative passages for Montaigne's understanding of himself. He sees his life breaking up into disconnected phases, none of which, not even the last, brings an increase in value, but only a change, always a new form of his unending tumbling about in the winds of chance. A comment of Goethe's is appropriate here, even if it does not break down the unified direction of life as profoundly as does Montaigne: "A man does indeed become someone different in the various stages of his life, but he cannot say that he becomes someone better."[194]

Montaigne's wisdom, which is an outgrowth of his sense of age, avoids the air of the noble, dignified old man who has knowledge of all

secrets. It obediently consents to the flow of the tides and to the deficiencies as well as the favors that each of them brings. This is expressed
beautifully in three sentences from his late period which refer to his body,
but which can be extended to his feeling for life as a whole: "I have seen
the grass, the flower and the fruit; now I see the dryness—happily, since it
is naturally. I bear the ills I have much more easily because they are
properly timed" (III, 2, 620 C). In another passage he writes: "If health
itself, sweet as it is, happens to revisit me by fits and starts, it is rather in
order to make me regret it than to return into my possession; I no longer
have anywhere to harbor it" (III, 10, 773 C). An entire Essay lingers in
this mood of old age: III, 5 ("On Some Verses of Virgil"). We know that
Gide wept when reading it (*Journal*, 3-17-1904). The aged man here casts
a somewhat melancholy glance back at the joys of love of the period of his
youth. But he does not get lost in the melancholy. It is now too late for
love, he is mature, too mature—it is an infirmity, he believes, and he is
happy to let himself be seduced into foolishness in small portions, for
what is the point of an all-too-great sedateness, the overcast skys of old
age? But he knows that such a youthful thing as love only develops its
proper hue in a youthful heart. He does not deceive himself about how
much forgery goes into the late ardor that age, which is taking its leave,
spreads over life: "In farewells we exaggerate the warmth of our affection
toward the things we are leaving. I am taking my last leave of the world's
pastimes; here are our last embraces" (644 B). When he yields in this
Essay to the memories of love, the tenderest and the crudest, he does so to
make his spirit younger. But he also knows how much foolishness attends
doing so. Montaigne yields to both: homesickness filled with delusion,
and awareness of the delusion. He mourns his lost youth with the naive
sorrow of the old man, and yet accepts that the past can never be brought
back again. He hauls in what joy there is to haul in, then lets it out again,
because the time of joy is past. Old age hurts him, and then he is amused
that it hurts him. He flees his miserable condition and yet returns to it. He
feels driven to the bluff and complains about it, but does not become
sullen. And then comes the core sentence: "My judgment keeps me indeed from kicking and grumbling against the discomforts that nature
orders me to suffer" (640 B). Reason does indeed see the order of the
tides, the distress of crippling old age, and the senselessness of revolting
against it—but it also sees the human right to suffer from it. It is good as it
is, even when it hurts; but one may say that it hurts, for the pain is a sign
of the order itself. Like any phase of life, old age has the double nature of
being a providence and a burden. What remains to one who has aged is

his spirit: this must bloom and turn green like mistletoe on a dead tree (641 B). Montaigne has the rare wisdom to step aside at the proper time and leave the field to youth: "I am ashamed to find myself amid this green and ardent youth . . . Why should we go offering our wretchedness amid this sprightliness . . . They have strength and right on their side; let us make way for them, we have no hold left" (682 B).[195] He does not expect of old age what belongs only to youth, and does not expect from youth what is only seemly for old age. He knows that everything has its own time. This wisdom of old age is not a didactic ringing from the lofty heights. It is cheerful obedience and all conceivable caution to evade at least the worst error of old men: being at odds with life, which is slipping away from them. This is payment enough for the loss of the "roaring, vigorous, free good health" of earlier years. Finally, what applies to the entire essence of man applies also to old age: in knowing its fragility, it rises above it: "An avowed ugliness and old age is less old and less ugly to my taste than another that is painted and glossed over" (683 C). Montaigne's reflections on old age, which he kept very personal, in many passages have literary models; they combine old and general educational material with an individual view of himself. This is perhaps at least the case for the fact that he considers the beginning of his "old age" to come so early. Perhaps he is thinking of the teachings in the Bible whereby, using the example of Christ, life becomes complete in the thirty-third year. It is also possible that he has in mind Aristotle's determination that the middle of the curve of life—the ἀκμή extends from the thirtieth to the forty-ninth year. The Roman division, on the other hand, as a rule defines *senectus* as beginning only with one's sixtieth year; in Roman terms, Montaigne's age at the time of his work on the *Essais* would fall within his *juventus*. Then again, the periods of the High Middle Ages and the Renaissance lean toward an earlier onset of old age. Thomas Aquinas believes it begins at fifty, Dante and others at forty-five. Petrarch, following the customary equating of *senectus* and a turning inward, writes his look back over his life at the age of forty-six. The poet Alain Chartier (deceased 1449) declares that his life is moving toward its end at forty years. At thirty-seven, Erasmus wrote his *Carmen heroicum de senectutis incommodis*. Cellini begins his autobiography by designating the fortieth year of life as the period when a man should record his life. Ronsard declares himself an old man at fifty, and so forth. Thus it is difficult to decide whether Montaigne in calling his fortieth year his entrance into old age was simply following a literary model or custom, rather than following his inclination to ascribe to himself the prerequisite for an attitude that he finds appropriate to him—contemplativeness, freedom, occupation with himself—which he can justify with the customary typology of old age.[196]

He adheres to this customary typology in the double sense that old age to him is both the time of wilting and the time of self-observation. The history of the doctrine of the ages in life shows that sometimes the one, sometimes the other perspective prevails. The Bible recognizes both the motif of the evil burden of old age and the motif of the wisdom of old age. Solomon is the Old Testament prototype of the venerable, mature old man. In hellenism, the view represented by Aristotle was canonical. It can be found in his *Rhetoric* (II, 12–14), wherein knowledge of the ages in life had its appropriate place in the knowledge necessary for the orator's schooling. In this passage, he describes old age negatively: It is the period of "too little," the sullen, petty, egoistic, miserly, and weak cast of mind.[197] In support of this, we have the physiological description, stemming from Hippocrates, which is repeated in other Aristotelian works: with aging, the body becomes dry, cold, moldy.[198] These deprecating judgments were opposed by others, usually older ones, which speak of the dignity of the wise old man who is knowledgeable about life, and who, freed of passions, enjoys clear joyfulness of the spirit and is an example for youth. One finds such comments in, for example, the first book of Plato's *Politicus,* in which Socrates and Cephalos converse about it (328e ff.). As the Bible does with Solomon, the Greek world offers Nestor, Sophocles, and Plato as prototypes of wise old men who were still productive at very advanced ages. Even Plutarch is aware of this positive assessment.[199] Roman literature with few exceptions (Horace, *Ars poetica* v. 156 ff., or Ovid, *Metam.* XV, 199 ff.) spoke out for respect of old age. Here we will only mention the most important memorial that became so extraordinarily influential in postantiquity, namely Cicero's *De senectute.*[200] It is positioned as the rescuer of *senectus* from the customary disapproval placed upon it. It describes how biological decay is balanced out by the harmony, security, and maturity, characterized by moderation, of one's intellectual powers, which only becomes possible when the tumults of passion are silenced. Thus old age, instead of being seen as decline, is considered the pinnacle of the moral person. At that height, man holds the autumn harvest of the only products that are worthwhile in gentle contemplation devoted to the muses and to philosophy. In full possession of experience, he grants the young his help and radiates dignity. Only now can he understand, thankful in his blessings, the law of nature, even that which leads to his corporal end. Appreciating death, the great peace to come, in advance, he is completely fulfilled and ready to take his leave. He neither scorns the things of life nor overvalues them. He knows that they are only given us to remain with us a short time, not for us to own. So much for Cicero.

Traces of these typologies are unmistakable in the *Essais*. Montaigne had both Aristotle's negatives and Cicero's positives in mind. His reflections on growing old seem from a historical standpoint to be a continued examination of the two opposing assessments. And he unites the two. As everywhere, here, too, he is able to bridge what is contradictory. The body's wilting constitution provides the fundamental dimensions of his approach. Like Aristotle, he, too, speaks of a drying and molding of the body and spirit without glossing over this outrage. But at the same time he perceives what is good in this: a contemplative turning inward, permission to speak of oneself; these are motifs from Cicero's *De senectute*. We know that he read this work over and over. Much in it was used in the *Essais*, especially consent to the flow of the tides and trust in nature, which arranges everything so well.[201] But unlike Cicero, he does not ennoble the image of the contemplative old man. He leaves it immersed in the deep shadows of biological decline. He practices his *vita contemplativa* ("melancholy humor" with the old meaning of the word *melancholy* = state of observation, II, 8, 278 A) as something questionable, something not happily, but rather fatally, intended for the old. One can look at his art of living as an attempt to live and think appropriately to his age, yet without satisfaction at being old. He strives to soften the damages of old age of which his experience and a literary psychology of types make him aware: timidity, sullenness, fear (Aristotle), and strives to exploit the advantages that another psychology of types grants to old age: leisure, observation of self, distance from life (Cicero)—and in all this, obedience to the diminishment as well as the enrichment of this stage of life. From this insight into the double essence of the twilight of his life, an insight that is neither despairing nor vain, but down-to-earth and clear, arose his powerful work, the *Essais*.

9.   THE SELF AND OTHERS

Among the objects that are a part of Montaigne's observation of himself is also his relationship to other people. The *Essais* are extensively concerned with the different situations in which others step into the circle of the self: friendship, love, marriage, company, office, travels.

Montaigne's care of the self does not degenerate into eccentricity. It is thoroughly open to human interaction, and it acknowledges being together as a necessary way of life. But just as his study of man as a whole sees social existence only as a tactical task and as formal, conservative security in what is insecure, his own relationship to others is independent of any extra-personal, ethical definition. It remains within a zone of freedom, terminability, and detachment which permit him the preservation of his individuality along with tolerance of the individuality of others. Interaction with others interests Montaigne almost exclusively as an opportunity to let his own possibilities unfold (in travel, or in the societal culture). Or perhaps he kept this interaction (for example, in conducting the affairs of his office) in the foreground of a mere role-playing, an external accommodation, which did not in any way engage his personal substance.

There is only one exception to this, namely, in friendship. Montaigne experiences in this a loving devotion to the other. He appreciated friendship in its full depth as the unending, rare harmony in which the self becomes itself through the other, and the other becomes himself through oneself, a perfect union of commitment and freedom. One perceives that here, and only here, Montaigne, who was so concerned with being true to the self, was able to get outside of himself. He sacrificed his self to the friend because he received his self back from the friend in an elevated form.

There are numerous passages in the *Essais* (and not simply in the long Essay on friendship I, 28) which are among the most beautiful to be found in world literature on this subject. They have their own worth, even though many of the classical formulae of friendship are included in them. Montaigne makes the old thought that friendship is "the sweetest and most perfect fruit of human life" his own, the good fortune of one's very personal sphere of life, of which kings and potentates are cheated because all those around them tremble, and no one dares to approach their humanity in free equality and in love (I, 42, 195 A, from Xenophon's *Hiero*). He himself experienced this ideal case of a friendship, the good fortune of humanity in solidarity which must fend for itself, as the greatest and most original event of his life in his relationship with La Boétie. In it he was granted, to use words from Goethe's *Winckelmann*, "that delight that springs forth from the joining of similar natures," and there were years (the letters following La Boétie's death bear witness to this) in which he, too, "felt his own self only in the form of the friendship." Indeed, he occasionally indicates that he found the return of classical human nature in his friend (II, 17, 500–501 A, etc.). But those are echoes of a humanistic romanticism with which, as the letters reveal, the friends at that time surrounded themselves. With the maturity of his feeling of friendship, he no longer needed to first be convinced of such qualities in order to love. What drew him to La Boétie was not the air of the ancients which he once believed he could breathe in his presence. Rather, as he recognized later, it was the incomparable essence of his friend. He loved him for a reason that is as obscure as the reason for any love: "because it was he"(I, 28, 139 C; see also the later discussion on this topic in this chapter). He mourned this friendship all his life. The rare periods of melancholy to which he admits are connected with the remembrance of it. He is tortured with it in the midst of his trip to the baths (*Journal*). A handwritten late insertion into the *Essais* confesses that he made a comforting shrine of this sadness: "O my friend! My regret for him consoles and honors me. Is it not a pious and pleasant duty of my life to be forever performing his obsequies? Is there an enjoyment that is worth this privation?" (II, 8, 286–287 C). The content of his life becomes the remembrance of the one lost. He never again experienced a similar friendship. Shortly after La Boétie's death he wrote to Michel de l'Hospital that his friend had freed him from the misery of the mediocrity of the century as the only one who compensated for all that was deplorable and crass in that period.[202] About ten years later he repeats that he has only known one truly great man, meaning of course the greatness of natural humanity, and this was La Boétie (II, 17, 500 A). In his thoughts of his friend, he betrays his hidden need to honor uncommon humanity, and his need for a corrective to his down-to-earth, ironic knowledge of a general mediocrity. This need was not satisfied by his experience with the other people who were part of his sphere of life. Not even his knowledge of the ancients sufficed; here, as there, his psychologist's eye sees the entanglement of greatness and weakness all too clearly. But he was able to pay homage to his friend without reservation. Occasionally he hints that the *Essais* are exhausted continuation, now lacking the addressee, of the intellectual intimacy once nurtured with his friend, and that he would come out of himself even more if his friend were still alive (I, 40, 186 C; III, 9, 752 B). And when he turns to the subject of friendship, he always elevates his speech to a characteristic loftiness and soft rapture which stands out dramatically in the midst of the usual tone of the *Essais*. This cannot be explained from the popular effusion that emerged from the Eros apotheoses of Neoplatonic writings and the lofty style of classical texts on friendship alone. His feeling for friendship is much more than a merely literary practice. The classical archetypes, which cannot be overlooked, only gather in their vessels what flows from a deeply moved heart.

This is shown very clearly in Essay I, 28 ("Of Friendship"). It is concerned with La Boétie through and through, and it completely keeps the subject within the realm of personal experience. Written around 1576, thus thirteen years after his friend's death, he moves within an elevation of feeling and language which does not drop off even in the later insertions; if anything, it intensifies. Montaigne speaks with the melancholy of one who loves and whose loved one has died, and with him, his own soul's period of genius. He begins by differentiating friendship from other relationships (love of women, marriage, children, siblings). Friendship is unique, not guided by particular aims, an association of common interests in which a person seeks out another for his own sake, an intellectual desire that does not grow weary when it is satisfied, but rather grows, a blending in which the line separating I from you disappears: "In the friendship I speak of, our souls mingle and blend with each other so completely that they efface the seam that joined them, and cannot find it again. If you press me to tell why I loved him, I feel that this cannot be expressed, except by answering: Because it was he, because it was I" (139 A). This ironic observer of average mankind is seized with such trust in the unusual quality of that bond between souls that he plays with the thought that a directive from heaven designated him and his friend for each other long before they met; "We sought each other before we met . . . I think it was by some ordinance from heaven" (139 A). The two befriended souls see each other lovingly all the way to their innermost foundation. Each finds himself through being mirrored in and seeming to lose himself in the other. A give and take prevails between them, whereby the taker is the benefactor, for he permits the other the happiness of giving. What they are and have in common is indivisible. No secret need be kept from the other. I do not break an oath when I disclose to him something I have sworn to keep to myself, "to the one who is not another man: he is myself" (142 C). But something so unique is not repeated; one has only one friend or none: "Nothing is extreme that can be matched" (142 C). Anything else is common camaraderie or a pact made for a particular purpose. And to make what is extraordinary in this friendship even more extraordinary, Montaigne refrains from expecting understanding of it. He finally returns from this enraptured remembrance to his current present: If I compare the rest of life remaining to me with the four years of that union, it is only smoke and dark, mournful night. "Since the day I lost him . . . I only drag on a weary life" (143 A). Such gloom reveals a wound that was never to heal. It is part of the spiritual picture of his individuality, none of which he is inclined to suppress, not even the longing for the good fortune he once had of being able to merge completely into another person and believe in uncommonness.

There is no doubt that Montaigne's personal experience of the heart was the life source of this, his noblest, most human, and warmest Essay. He himself says that the literature lags behind his experience: "For the very discourses that antiquity has left us on this subject seem to me weak compared with the feeling I have" (143 A). Nevertheless, it cannot be denied that classical paradigms and formulae join in on all sides, in fact, so extensively that someone who reads this Essay only from a curiosity for historical parallels could discover nothing but a repetition of such formulae in it—even in Montaigne's assurance that was just quoted that he had experienced things that had never been spoken before. The insertion of his own material into previous literary formulations, which he certainly did not conceal, and in fact revealed in quotations, also bears witness to that characteristic of humanistic education which influenced Montaigne. For him it is a means, though a secondary one, of experiencing friendship, of becoming comprehensible to himself, which must be taken seriously. Additionally, the use of these preexisting formulations was even closer at hand, since the topic of friendship took up considerable space in the writings of antiquity which he read, not to mention contemporary literature.[203] Thus a quick comparison of the Essay on friendship with the literary tradition is indicated here.

Any trace of the otherwise so influential *Lysis* by Plato is notably absent. We can only suspect the reasons for this. Perhaps they lie in the fact that this dialogue does not treat the subject in the precise manner Montaigne sought due to the ambiguity of the Greek term φιλία, that this work keeps it floating between thesis and antithesis and ends with Socrates' confession that he and his partner are unable to discover what a friend really is. It is possible that here, in his most human sphere, Montaigne was unable to use Socrates' ironic dialectic. But other influences can be identified. The elevated tone could in part be modeled on the elevation of style of the two books on friendship (VIII and IX) in Aristotle's *Nicomachean Ethics*. Several details also point to this (whereby we are bypassing the question of whether Montaigne read them there or in the works of later compilers). For example, the comment found at the beginning of the Essay that friendship is the high point of human society originates in the *Nicomachean Ethics* (VIII, 1). The idea of an ideal bond that is elevated above all practical interests, in which the friend loves his friend only for his own sake, is also modeled there (VIII, 3). In fact, the famous sentence that was added later in handwriting, "Because it was he, because it was I" (139 C) could be a variation of Aristotle's sentence when he said that in a nongenuine friendship, the person loved is only loved because he brings practical advantage or happiness, and not because he is who he is, which is as it should be (VIII, 3, 1156a). When Montaigne states that in friendship—in contrast to marriage—interaction does not use love up, but rather increases it, we hear echoes of the final sentences of Aristotle's ninth book. He invokes Aristotle directly when he repeats the formula that even then has long been proverbial: "Friends are one soul in two bodies" (144 C). Then a fair amount of material was brought in from Epicurean writings. A universal thought of this school held that friendship was an esoteric protection of those who were rare and wise in the midst of the generalized mediocrity of the world, a lovingly understanding and giving interaction between men who were not enticed by what pleased the majority.[204] Montaigne's conception of friendship as a whole is attuned to this thought. The expression "the one who is not another man: he is myself" (142 C) contains in a slightly altered form the definition of a friend, now also proverbial, as an alter ego.[205] Montaigne could also have been exposed to all these definitions through Cicero's *Laelius* (*De amicitia*), which he read and frequently quoted or paraphrased. It is common knowledge that Italian humanists and Neoplatonists then renewed the classical idea and cult of friendship with all the usual characteristics of being uncommon, of friendship nurturing the enjoyment of ideas among like-minded people, and with a somewhat romantic notion of saving the last trace of classical spirit and genuine humanity from a world in decline by means of friendship.[206] Much in Montaigne's Essay is in harmony even with these innovations, particularly the Neoplatonic idea (to be found, among other sources, in Castiglione's *Cortegiano* II, 30) of a harmony of souls preordained in the stars, an idea with which Montaigne plays.

We will have to be content here with that brief discussion. But we still must point out the difference that Montaigne's image of friendship no longer has much room for that ethical prerequisite of friendship of Aristotle, the Stoic school, Cicero, Seneca, and the Renaissance Platonists that genuine friendship was only possible among virtuous persons. For him, it is an association of free humanity, the phenomenon of a person becoming one with the unrestricted rich nature of the other, a fullness of emotion which originates in deeper layers, does not need objective, ideal qualities, and thus does not have the intention of bringing about an objective increase in worth of the universal human essence, nor of being a showpiece for those seeking paragons. Montaigne understood his friendship as an event of concern solely to him and his friend. He withdrew its brightness into the private, hidden realm. In so doing, he deviated from tradition (with the possible exception of epicurean tradition). But even the areas of harmony with that tradition cannot conceal the fact that his impulse did not at all come from literary models, but rather was so original and strong that despite all humanistic accommodation to prior literary formulations, he was able to find memorable new words with their own sound. He would not have sought out those earlier formulations at all if the matter itself had not been of such direct significance in his life. As can be said for all great authors, for Montaigne, particularly in this special case of the apotheosis of friendship, it is nearly impossible to untangle earlier literary formulations from his original effort. Just as love poetry need not lose any of its life simply because what it says has already been formulated before, here the preshaping of the idea of friendship by tradition does not dispossess his inner experience. This experience was genuine, the flowering of his spiritual history. He does not harm it by willingly directing it back into formulations of earlier times.

Montaigne also had something to say about his relationship with women. But for him this ranks well below friendship and does not extend into the innermost spheres of his spiritual life. A sober reasonableness in marriage, which he respects as one respects any useful institution—uninhibited physicality in lovemaking, which he sees all in all only as a gallantry with a vigorous, but transitory, sensual glow: these are the basic characteristics. Of his own marriage, he reports coolly that he entered into it not because of a decision of his own, but because of outside advice. He would not have joined in this union of his own free will, as he had such a powerful need for independence: "Of my own choice, I would have avoided marrying Wisdom herself, if she had wanted me" (III, 5, 648 B). But he settled in, a process that permits one to tolerate any imperfect situation, and he then fulfilled, with his conservative orientation, the duties of convenience required for an orderly household.

His comments on physical love (found mainly in Essay III, 5) show the lack of inhibition typical of his century. They are witty in the manner of humanistic humorous writings, with a wealth of aphoristically collected comments on jealousy, betrayal, cuckoldry, coquetry, and all in all have that penetrating intelligence that is so easily awakened in France in the observation of sex play. They are completely lacking in Platonic ennoblement, which passed from Italy through Renaissance literature. One finds not the slightest trace of the lyrical inwardness of a Louise Labé, or the spiritual Eros of some of the novellas and writings in verse by Marguerite de Navarre in them. Yet Montaigne never becomes crude, sordid, or misogynous. He is revealed to be a master of the worldly, erotic culture of play. He understands the artful introduction of difficulties which intensify attraction, and he has the patience born of experience which allows him to wait for the proper moment for conquest. But basically this is all a triviality to him, and one is advised to enjoy even the deception, the trinkets, and the woman's vain craving for admiration as one enjoys a spice, rather than to fret about them: "This is a passion that with very little solid essence mixes in much more vanity and feverish dreams: it should be satisfied and served accordingly. Let us teach the ladies to make the most of themselves, to respect themselves, to beguile and fool us" (671 B). Eros, which is concealed behind courtly, polite masks, is an animal drive, "the pleasure of discharging our vessels" (668 C). Montaigne, who found such lofty words for friendship, sees love for a woman as little more than a physical business, and erotic desire as a "ridiculous titillation" that betrays us when the gods are having fun with us (668 C). For a moment he touches upon the thought that the double essence of sexuality, drive and shame, reflects the split in our humanity into the burden of original sin and the conscience of our higher destiny (669 B). This is one of the last passages in the *Essais* in which we encounter remnants of Christian anthropology. But it fades quickly. A handwritten addition sharply emphasizes: "Are we not brutes to call brutish the operation that makes us?" (669 C).[207] Man, who is a mix of body and spirit, cannot deny any part its due; no part is lower or higher than the other. Why not obey desire, since we must also obey pain? (681 B). Moderate erotic satisfaction is recommended as beneficial to one's health. Sexual abstinence, like any rigorousness, appears to be an absurdity that is an affront to the harmony of our given corporal-spiritual human essence. He writes this witty comment: "I find it much easier to bear a suit of armor all one's life than a virginity" (655 B). Thus he refrains from reticence in this Essay as well, calling upon lascivious quotations from the Roman eroticists (Catullus and Martial) to relate his earlier sexual experiences, triumphs, and disgraces. But all

of this, in personal as well as universal matters, is considered homage to
the elementary forces of nature offered by a natural, innocent man who
through the crudeness does not forget the decency of the heart. He knew
no great passionate love that reached to the depth of his being, nor did
he wish to. It would have robbed him of his freedom and his moderate
center.

For here, in this center surrounded by a field of distance, he has his
security, his "lair" (*taniere*), as he puts it several times, reflecting a
popular classical and Christian image of self-contemplation. He only
surrenders to his strong inclination to interact with others to the extent
that he feels he is secure within it. The many contradictory comments in
the *Essais,* sometimes about withdrawal from the world, other times
about the need for social interaction, can be quite simply organized by
saying that Montaigne wanted to guide interaction with others from the
inner chamber of his self-possession and self-regulation. The clear alert
eye with which he looks at the world is the eye of a scout dwelling in the
well-protected fortress of his individuality who lets in only the colored
pictures, but not the passions and limited aims of the world's hustle and
bustle. This is an orientation that he shares with Seneca. Thus the Essay
that he dedicated to solitude (I, 39) is a personally tinged paraphrase of
corresponding core passages from Seneca's letters. Solitude here means:
the soul being with itself, a meeting on the self, assuring oneself of one's
own inclinations and forces—in Seneca's words: *secum morari, sibi
amicus esse, recedere in se ipsum (ep.* 2, *ep.* 6, *ep.* 7). And in the words
of the Essay: "We must reserve a back shop all our own, entirely free, in
which to establish our real liberty and our principal retreat and solitude.
Here our ordinary conversation must be between us and ourselves, and
so private that no outside association or communication can find a
place . . ." (177 A). This is no anachronous seclusion from the world,
rather, it is an inner refuge that is always at his disposal, a refuge that
does not prevent the spirit from giving the world what it expects, and
taking from it what pleases the spirit. The more secure his self-
possession, the more agile is his art of relaxing, disregarding himself,
following along with the diversity of others: "We must not nail ourselves down so firmly to our humors and dispositions. Our principal
talent is the ability to apply ourselves to various practices . . . We are
not friends to ourselves, and still less masters, we are slaves, if we follow
ourselves incessantly" (III, 3, 621 B), Montaigne can thus comment, and
he says it even more clearly a few pages later: "I would admire a soul
with different levels, which could both be tense and relax, which would

be well off wherever fortune might take it, which could chat with a neighbor about his building, his hunting, and his lawsuit, and keep up an enjoyable conversation with a carpenter and a gardener" (623 B). Thus a natural rhythm between humane openness to the world and philosophical retreat into one's own realm arises.

The most appropriate milieu for Montaigne's need for people is the aristocratic culture of society ("outward behavior," I, 26, 122 A) which was offered to him by the times and his station in life, and which his *Essais* helped to reshape. Its most artistic creation is the discussion. He devoted an entire Essay to it: III, 8, ("Of the Art of Discussion"). It is one of his most capricious, lighthearted pieces, a *bréviaire* of *honnête-homme* education, and it was still read as such even in the seventeenth century. It concerns the game of disputation in a social setting, when the various intellects battle one another as in a tournament, without obstinacy or sensitivity, with the ability to listen, to grow through contradiction, to incite new contradiction by defending one's position vigorously so the discussion does not flag, and at the end one arrives at the same choreographed order in which the victor is not the one who knows better, but rather the one who has kept most closely to the rules of the game. The entire Essay exudes freedom and cheerful forcefulness. And as closely connected as it may be to the aristocratic educational literature in the manner of Castiglione, and even farther back with Cicero's *urbanitas* idea, one cannot mistake the fact that here Montaigne brings in his own experience, or, rather, his ideal of intellectual intercourse with others, thus portrays himself in the situation of sociability. The culture of discussion he describes arises from the skeptical principle of the possibility and the right of any forming of opinion, one's own or that of others. Sociability becomes graceful communication among the witty who meet one another in a condition of common human ignorance. Their opinions romp along behind truth, which always evades them. But they comprehend what remains to man: the happy, refreshing restlessness of the hunt which keeps the spirit alive and during which it is magnanimous to grant others the same freedom in which one feels so good oneself.

However, where interaction with men leads into the social and political structure and thus into public office and duty, Montaigne withdraws even more resolutely into the lair of the self, and from there oversees the required tasks as a person does when he takes over a role without identifying with it. His culture of individuality becomes quite clear when it collides with the demands of the social order. He certainly

recognizes the necessity of public action, and he did so in the performance of the duties of his various offices and missions. But as we
discussed earlier (chapter 4), in the public order he only sees a creation
bound to its milieu which has no higher quality of being right than any
other. In his adaptation to it, which he does in accordance with his
conservative orientation, he becomes conscious of his own nature to an
intensified degree. To Montaigne, the best thing about man is the part
that strives against seizure by society. Thus he only wants to go far
enough in his concern for the well-being of the world that the world and
his human essence are served equally.

He speaks of this extensively in the Essay III, 10, presumably written
in the years 1586/1587, which has the programmatical title "Of Hus-
banding Your Will." The Essay carefully marks off the boundaries of
office and freedom with respect to each other. The emphasis lies where
Montaigne renders an account of how he conducted his office as mayor
of Bordeaux. The first sentences establish his main subject: "In comparison with most men, few things touch me, or, to put it better, hold me;
for it is right that things should touch us, provided they do not possess
us" (766 B). Two types are compared: on the one hand, individuality,
which is based in itself and which keeps its distance, and on the other
hand, all those who are pompously lost in external aims and are tortured by the "impossibility of closing the shop, even only for the eve-
ning," as Jacob Burckhardt, whose views were so close to those of
Montaigne in this and many other respects, once put it.[208] Of the first
type—and this is Montaigne himself—we find statements such as this:
"My opinion is that we must lend ourselves to others and give ourselves
only to ourselves" (767 B). Or: "We must husband the freedom of our
soul and mortgage it only on the right occasions; which are in very small
number" (767 B). In these formulations, there is once again much that
originated in Seneca, but his personal experience is fused with it, and of
course it lacks Seneca's pull toward morality. The Roman only backs the
Frenchman up in what is in his nature to begin with, the nobility of
distance. Quite secure within himself, he determines the degree to which
the outside world may approach him. Classically the antitype he scornfully rejects: the mass of duty fanatics and business-mongers, lacking
substance, humorless, undignified, and zealous; completely lacking the
art of relaxation; what they are, they are not for their own sake; raised
to servitude; involved in everything, whether it concerns them or not;
fellow travelers in the large and small dealings of the world due to an
inability to stick with themselves; seeking business for the sake of

busyness, and seeking rest in restlessness; in bondage to others and a burden to themselves (767 B/C).[209] "It is for little souls, buried under the weight of business, to be unable to detach themselves cleanly from it or to leave it and pick it up again," as he puts it in another Essay (III, 13, 851 B). In setting the boundaries of being oneself with respect to one's ties to the world, we are not concerned here with destruction of the latter or with a recommendation of anarchistic absence of duty. What Montaigne seeks is a preservation of priorities in which ties to the world and duties to the social order are on a lower rung. But the problem lies in how one can unite the social order's claim on the individual which cannot be ignored with his free possession of himself. This is the central problem of Essay III, 10, and it was an effort Montaigne made on a practical level during his service as mayor. The solution consists in a tactical reconciliation in which one does what is required with decency, consideration of the circumstances, and moderate zeal without thereby selling one's soul: "I do not want a man to refuse, to the charges he takes on, attention, steps, words, and sweat and blood if need be . . . But this is by way of loan and accidentally . . . I have been able to take part in public office without departing one nail's breadth from myself, and to give myself to others without taking myself from myself" (770 B/C). Happy is the one who, like Montaigne, can say this of himself! For the details of social and political action, the rule of occasional accommodation to rapidly changing situations and to the course of the world, which cannot be guided by an ideal standard, applies. Compensation for this is a cheerful position of standing above the fray. But as a whole, the general rule that applies is to make oneself available to the world only on a "loan" basis, and to cleanly separate the man from the function ("skin and shirt"), preserving what is actual in the man, and in performing the function, playing a role that does not consume any of what is actual in the player. Thus in the following sentences we read the heart of Montaigne's manner of conducting his life: "We must play our part duly, but as the part of a borrowed character. Of the mask and appearance we must not make a real essence, nor of what is foreign what is our very own. We cannot distinguish the skin from the shirt. It is enough to make up our face, without making up our heart" (773 B/C). The addition of "but as the part of a borrowed character" inserted into these metaphorical formulations shows that Montaigne emphatically means what is externally imitative, exchangeable, terminable in official actions.[210] Thus even when one is carrying out a public office the relationship of the self to the other is that of a game—though admittedly one that must be played with greater care because of the greater danger of a loss of substance than is the case in the game of conversation. And then comes the most succinct formulation: "The mayor and Montaigne have always been two, with a very clear separation" (774 B). He even advises princes to practice the same separation of man from function: "But the judgment of an emperor should be above his imperial power, and see and consider it as an extraneous accident; and he should know how to find pleasure in himself apart, and to reveal himself like any Jack or Peter, at least to himself" (774 B).

Montaigne was able to think this way because he is neither impressed by power in others nor sees it as desirable for himself. In a fine, short Essay, "Disadvantage of Greatness" (III, 7), he turns a well-known dictum of Caesar's around, saying: I would rather be third in Périgord than first in Paris; "I have a distaste for mastery, both active and passive" (700 B). It is the misfortune of kings that they have to change men into servants, that they are forced to have subjects rather than equals around them. How dull must be a dignity to which all defer! "It is a pity to have so much power that everything gives way to you . . . Imagine man accompanied by omnipotence: he is sunk . . . his being and his welfare are in indigence" (701–702 B). These are notable, superior words. And they do not lose their significance because the ancients said something similar.[211] Proceeding from spirits of free humanity such as these who want to indulge themselves in the simplest of circumstances, not in power, Montaigne relates the following Diocletian anecdote: when he was begged after his voluntary abdication to take up the crown again, he responded, "You would not ask this of me if you had seen the beautiful rows of trees that I myself have planted at home, and the fine melons I have sown" (I, 42, 196 B).[212]

Just as Montaigne does not guide his own actions with consideration of any particular faction, but rather by its feasibility in the given moment and by the principle of decency, he keeps his judgment of others free of any partisan viewpoints. He evaluates opponents and friends by their personal quality. For what are the positions of friend and foe other than temporary groupings on the surface which rest upon the natural human essence incongruously, narrowing it? He thinks with approval of Caesar and Pompeius who did not extend their political differences into personal invective, but rather continued to show each other respect (III, 10, 775 B). What are wars and world affairs anyway, when we lose our human dignity in them? Swollen out of proportion, consequences of laughable futility which have outgrown the original cause. Says Montaigne: "Our greatest agitations have ridiculous springs and causes. What a disaster our last duke of Burgundy incurred because of a quarrel about a cartload of sheepskins!" (779 B). Homer understood this correctly: Greece immersed itself in fire and blood for the sake of an apple. This is among the popular ideas of that epoch; one finds it in Erasmus (*Laus stultitiae,* chap. 23) and Bodin (*Les Six Livres de la République* IV, 1, and IV, 7); Rabelais made of it his satire of the *guerre picrocholine.* This is also a part of Montaigne's intellectual property, understandable from his concept of life in which the joy in what is rich in colorful variety is peculiarly interlaced with a usually ironic, and sometimes bitter, disgust at the senselessness of altercations, large and small. One's actions should be attuned not to partisanship, but rather to the summary unworthiness of the course of the world.

This is the source of that reserve in social and political action, protective of the self's essence, which Montaigne heeded and expressed as being appropriate to his nature, both from objective motivation and as the right thing to do, that is, as relief from the doubtful course of the world where it is better to do too little than too much: "Abstention from doing is often as noble as doing, but it is less open to the light; and the little that I am worth is almost all on that side" (783 C). In looking back on his period of public service in which he performed in accordance with these principles, he finds: "all went well, I did not neglect any task, even though I operated without arrogance, great exertion, commotion or passion, just following my inadequate nature, remaining true to myself" (783–784 B). Is it not best, then, that a person obediently go along with the essence given him? A kind of secret convergence between this and happiness then assures, with less likelihood of being disturbed, that nothing will happen which is more questionable than the universal questionable condition. Essay III, 10 ends with this element of wisdom.

In Montaigne's manner of conducting his life, service in public positions is the most external concession individuality makes to the claims of the world. But he opens himself to the contents of the world much more willingly when they brush over him without a danger of inhibiting the self, when they are pictures of diverse human essence satisfying his thirst for facts with authentic experience. This happens when he travels. Travel permits him contact with others, observing and rambling on, without losing himself to them, and at the same time causing the best-hidden strings of his personal self to resonate with the broadened horizon of his study of man, allowing him to dip outwardly and inwardly into the flow of the living. We spoke earlier (chapter 4) of Montaigne's preference for travel literature. The experience of men in time and space which this facilitates is the specific way in which the sixteenth century experiments moralistically, that is, discovers human reality under the viewpoint of its unclassifiable and unending variety, and compares this to the rigid, abstract generic concept of "man." And Montaigne takes part in this moral experimentation in his personal behavior by traveling himself. He is fulfilling the principle of his Essay on education, namely, that everything becomes a book for us, not just printed matter, but also and especially the living world of men.[213] "This great world . . . is the mirror in which we must look at ourselves to recognize ourselves from the proper angle. In short, I want it to be the book of my student," he wrote then (I, 26, 116 A).[214] Just as the body becomes supple through exercise in all manners of living, the mind becomes supple through an openness to all customs and through practical adaptation to them. In the assurance of all that is possible among men, he becomes sure of himself.

Montaigne loved travel. Beyond any particular material aims, he enjoyed the lovely oportunity to look around in the world. The longest of his travels took place in 1580/1581. Shortly after the first two books of the *Essais* appeared, he departed to move to Italy via Southern Germany where he hoped to find a cure for his kidney stones in the baths. He kept a journal about this, and it was first published about two hundred years later (1774) with the title *Journal de voyage de Michel de Montaigne.*[215]

The contents of this journal show that it concerns more than just a trip to the baths. He does note in agonizing detail the precise passage of the stones, their composition and size, his constipation and flatulence, the effect of the baths on the functioning of his kidneys—for which he has the necessary sense of humor: *C'est une sotte coustume de noter ce qu'on pisse.* But he records much more than this, in fact, everything that strikes him about people, customs, cultural creations, things. The *Journal* is a notebook of his wide-open, thoroughly observational feeling for facts: *j'y considerai toutes choses fort particulierement.* One can hardly detect that it is written by someone who is ill, its curiosity is so healthy and lively. Everywhere he goes, he adapts to local customs, *pour essayer tout à faict la diversité des moeurs et façons.* Thus he orders local dishes of the particular area even when they do not appeal to him, takes part in local customs, refuses any attempt by his host to be considerate of his French habits, avoids his fellow countrymen as much as possible because they inhibit his process *d'acquerir des connoissances estangieres*, learns Italian and writes a part of the journal in that language.[216] He enjoys sliding into what is foreign by imitation; this is how he makes personal experience (*essayer*) his own, this experience that is the only thing that can guarantee him authentic knowledge about things and people. The text of the journal is quite dry. It is possible that this can be attributed in part to the fact that the first half was dictated to a secretary. But this does not let up much even in the second half. It is the dryness of factual observation, which for the time being suspends judgment and concentrates on recording what is seen as precisely as possible and collecting material for later evaluation. And in fact there is much from it which is taken up again and processed with careful reflection later in the *Essais*. But in any case, here, too, the magic of his personality shines through the dryness of the writing. Montaigne has the gift of communicating his shading to even the most unsophisticated notes, even notes that due to dictation are sometimes quite crude. One closes this book with the feeling one is taking leave of an old friend.

What stands out most about the journal of his travels is the wealth of everyday details. Thus he records the culinary customs of the different cities, the condition of the beds, the dishware, the kitchens and ovens in the inns. He makes note of the technology of a draw-well, the curiosity of public clocks in Basel which are all set ahead one hour, the layout of the mill canals in Constance. He notes how Italians bear their swords in contrast to the Germans, or how in one place, people of the French party wear a flower behind their right ear, those of the Spanish party behind the left. When Montaigne enters a city, like any travel writer of the time, he first establishes the geographical situation, waterways, boundaries, coat of arms. He always checks whether what earlier travelers have said can be confirmed. Artistic constructions mainly interest him as technical achievements. He notes the quality of the marble and measures the circumference of the dome when visiting the Florentine cathedral; in Sienna he behaves similarly. He has no eye for artistic value. One does find several mentions of sculptures (among these, Michelangelo's Moses), but he limits his comments to simply saying he finds it "beautiful." His orientation is more toward man's activity in handicrafts, in making things and building things, and then toward anything related to the history of customs. He includes in this category various faiths, cults, and sects; they serve as a sort of local color for specific regions. In Basel, he attended religious discussions between Zwinglians, Calvinists, and Lutherans and noted the differences between them without stating a position of his own. He showed the same neutrality in conversing with the Jews in the synagogue of Verona about their religious service. In Loretto he listened to the story of the Turk who dedicated an expensive wax candle when he was in dire need and was willing to try "any kind of rope," even a Christian one, and he listened *fort particulierement et curieusement* to the report of a miracle healing.

The description of his stay in Rome is central. Yet it is hardly Rome of antiquity which captures his interest. He looks around in this center of the classical, Latin universe not with the eye of the humanistic enthusiast, but rather the eye of the realist. He pays attention to the past, but he does not let it gain the upper hand. As was true of the northerner Erasmus, he is insensitive to the national, political symbolism of awakening which had been spun around the ruins of this old city of the Romans by Italian humanists. The possibility of archaeological digs did not occur to him. Our knowledge of ancient Rome, he writes, is abstract and theoretical (*une science abstraicte et contemplative*); what meets the eye is only Rome of the present, which rises above the grave of Rome past with its new and different life; of ancient Rome there remains only the warning of how destiny can conspire against fame and power. And then he describes what he sees before him: the mix of peoples at the Corso, the inns, the folk festivals, the cult forms in the churches, the Vatican and its library, the execution of the leader of a band of bandits, a daring public display of horsemanship, and a circumcision ceremony. He visits the Pope (Gregory XIII) as one visits any of the sights, pays close attention to his physical appearance and his Bologna dialect, takes his gracious words of blessing as Italian phrases of courtesy. He does not lose his composure in standing before the head of Catholic Christianity. One has the feeling that Montaigne, the man ill with kidney stones, sees this healthy old man who has been spared gout and colic with a secret envy.

All of these things are placed side by side with no differentiation of rank. He tells with equanimity of foolishness, delusion, injustice, but also intelligence, beauty, and decency. This is intentional leveling: the world is made up of mere facts that we should not dwell upon; judgment of these must remain open because the judgment, too, depends always on the accident of one's own manner of thinking, the limitations of which should be transcended precisely by means of travel. *J'escris icy en liberté de conscience,* Montaigne confesses, and this freedom from conscience is expressed in tolerance for all that is possible among men. Later on, remembering his trip, he will say: "The diversity in fashions from one nation to another affects me only with the pleasure of variety. Each custom has its reason" (III, 9, 753 B). The empirical character of this traveler's journal can certainly be derived from its purpose, which is to be a notebook in which everything he sees is simply to be recorded in the order of its appearance. But the leveling treatment of placing everything side by side, the great and the small, the foolish and the reasonable, is also characteristic of the *Essais*. In fact, the unranked mass of facts found in the *Journal* corresponds to Montaigne's overall manner of looking at things, and travel is the manner of acquiring experience that is appropriate to his outlook, wherein he would rather lose himself skeptically in the inexhaustibility of what is real than to dogmatically close his eyes to it.[217]

However, fundamental reflections upon his travels appear only in the *Essais,* specifically, in the sections written after his return from Italy, thus in the third book (especially in III, 9), and in the preceding books, in the insertions of the B and C layers. Here Montaigne attains clarity about the methodical fruitfulness of his travels. In contrast to his Essay on education, what he has to say about this he says from his own experience. In the art of travel, he discovers a natural gift of his individuality. There again, one of the most notable contrasts between him and the moral philosophy of the ancients emerges. A frequently repeated commonplace belief of antiquity is that man cannot escape his internal ills by a change of location, thus he is better off turning inward. One finds the following in Seneca: *Mutare te loca, et aliunde de alio transire, nolo . . . Tam frequens migratio instabilis animi est. Coalescere otio non potest, nisi desiit circumspicere et errare* (*ep.* 69: "I do not want you to change your residence and to move from place to place. For such frequent wandering betrays an unsteady nature. It is not compatible with leisure if it does not stop looking around and running around everywhere;" cf. *ep.* 28 and Horace, *Carm.* II, 16 and III, 1, etc.). Christian literature is also familiar with this idea (*Imitatio Christi* I, 20). Montaigne also agrees with it briefly in an earlier stage of the *Essais* (I, 39, 175–176 A). But he abandons that warning to the degree that he no longer sees merely a defect in the "malady," namely the inconstancy of our essence, but also sees man's viable manner of being, which is secretly both protected and protective. The *animus instabilis* of the Seneca quotation above recurs in the *Essais* under the key words *branle* and *branloire.* But we know the tone they have in Montaigne. He, who experiences himself in the unceasing metamorphosis of his essence, adapts to it. Thus, for him, travel becomes a purpose in itself which is adequate for his agitated, internal boundlessness: "I undertake it [a journey] neither to return from it nor to complete it; I undertake only to move about while I like moving. And I walk for the sake of walking" (III, 9, 747 B/C). This is the source of his lack of concern about reaching a destination: "Have I left something unseen behind me? I go back; it is still on my road. I trace no fixed line, either straight or crooked" (753 B). What he is seeking, that which is randomly diverse, can be found everywhere; it approaches the wanderer on its own, it need not be purposefully sought. The destination is nothing, the travels everything: "Yes, I confess, I see nothing . . . that I could hold myself to; variety alone satisfies me, and the enjoyment of diversity . . ." (756 B). He does not travel to have things better, but merely to have them different.

Montaigne is not embarrassed to be unwise, in a school sense, in having these inclinations. He is very well aware of the futility of eternal roving. And he is also aware of the futility of the "wisdom" that forbids it. What is the point of such wisdom, then? Better to unwisely give oneself to one's natural futility—that is his wisdom. Life will not be robbed of its agitated images and its many colors; it wants to enjoy them (746 B). Freed by the cosmopolitan openness of intellectual and physical travel, and without damaging its loyalty to itself, the self participates along with other elements in the determination of humanity as filled with restlessness. The aimless wandering of travel, like one's own life, is at its destination every day, namely, in experiencing endless agitation: "My plan is everywhere divisible; it is not based on great hopes; each day's journey forms an end. And the journey of my life is conducted in the same way" (747 B). And thus for Montaigne this is true: to be able to be and to know what he himself is, he needs that look into the world, and the tribute to its futility, which is also its wealth.

CHAPTER VI

Montaigne and Death

A death all my own . . .

[III, 9, 748 B]

An artless boldness . . .

[III, 12, 807 C]

1. THE GENERAL ROLE OF THE THOUGHTS ON DEATH

Montaigne completes his discovery and portrayal of himself in his reflection upon death. He, a man who is so intent upon making the content of his essence clear, must also become comfortable with the reality of a future in which he will no longer exist, and with how he will cope with the transition without becoming untrue to himself. He proves an observation that can be made freely, namely that the thought of death increases in importance, the greater a person's sense of individuality.

Human thought has always recognized that the future hour of death with the uncertainty of when it will come only deceptively disguises the finality of death, while death itself, as a certainty that it will come, is timelessly inherent in living beings as an essential mortality that casts the shadows of what is most alien into what is alive, and yet belongs to what is alive as clearly as breathing and growing.[218] Montaigne knew this also. Thus he collects his preliminary insight into the future death of his own individuality into a profound observation of the permeation of death into all of its content. Individuality only really becomes aware of its fullness when it includes mortality in its conception, something that is qualitatively different from an event that touches it from the outside, and when one's individuality has perceived how it feels in the thorough sensing of this mortality. This discovery of death from the perspective of personal, inner experience does not occur from the beginning in the

Essais, but it occurs to a rapidly increasing degree, and finally, with great purity. This makes the work one of the greatest texts on death of the postantiquity Western world, the greatest since the *Ackermann aus Böhmen* by Johannes von Saaz and before Quevedo's *Sueños,* Pascal's *Pensées,* or Bossuet's *Sermon sur la mort;* admittedly, it is quite different from these. Montaigne's reflections upon death in their autonomy seem veiled in the motifs of hellenistic wisdom on death which he included. But he does not parrot these without rejuvenating them through his own honesty. The question guiding his selection of classical quotations and borrowed concepts is not that of how man should behave with respect to death, but rather how I, Michel de Montaigne, conduct myself vis-à-vis death.

There is nothing somber or grisly about the discussions of death in the *Essais,* as there is, for example, in French dance of death literature of the Late Middle Ages or some Spanish prose texts of Montaigne's time. When he speaks of death, his tone does not change: it remains calmly observational, there is no despondency, nor is there festiveness, he simply occupies himself with this as he does with any ordinary matter. Occasionally, to express concepts such as "dying" or "preparing for death" he uses familiar expressions such as "give up the ghost" (III, 9, 743 B), "pack up my odds and ends and strap my bags" (III, 9, 753 C), and so forth.[219] Goethe's comment on Montaigne's "unschätzbar heiteren Wendung" (see earlier discussion) also applies here. "We should spread joy, but cut down sadness as much as we can," as he puts it at the conclusion of his reflections on death (III, 9, 748 B). Montaigne is a friend of death, but without the exuberance about death in the manner of the mystics or the later romantics. His thinking about death breathes clean air, and avoids euphemism and gloomy consolation. It shows great, quiet courage, yet is very different from the stoic mastery of death which several contemporaries erroneously saw in him.

But when one hears him speaking of death with such measure, cheerfully, breaking off again and again from his subject, this does not mean that he treated death as innocuous. Quite the contrary, he recognized it in its full dignity of being the most serious event a person experiences. He calls death "ordinary" only because it is the destiny of all living beings and death is inherent in them along with life itself; its monstrousness does not represent an exception, it is no catastrophe of the existing order, but is the order itself: an ordinary monstrousness. Man dies of the "common fate" (III, 13, 837 C). Montaigne expresses this ordinariness of death against the naive forgetfulness about death, but also against the arrogance of the person who believes that destiny or heaven has designed an individual death particularly for him (compare II, 13, 458 A ff.). Yet in this ordinariness he does not exculpate the essential power of death, this "impossibility which suddenly becomes reality," as Goethe once expressed it (to Eckermann, 2-15-1830).

If it is a sign of barbarism—specifically, that spiritual barbarism that comes at the end of cultures, not at the beginning—that man flattens death to a simple biological expiration, then Montaigne represents the bearer of the highest form of spiritual culture: its sign is to allow oneself to be deeply penetrated by mortality as an essential characteristic of being human, and to find a response to it. His cheerful response comes with full knowledge of the character of death, which both destroys life and is a part of it. It consists in an obedient consent to the "mixtures," that is, to the interlacing of contrasts, the interplay of which sounds dissonant and yet is the condition of our existence. Montaigne lifts death to a rank at which its power, its paradoxical oneness with life, becomes visible, but so do its accessibility and one's ability to bear it. He disposes over a culture of death in which he encounters antiquity and yet remains himself.

The weight he gives to the problem of death is not fully expressed in the fact that the words "death" or "dying" appear in the titles of three Essays, namely, I, 19; I, 20; and II, 13. For these three sections, including the later insertions in them, contain only parts of his thinking on this. One can only really understand its full scope through about twenty further Essays and his countless other approaches to this subject in passing. The most content-rich of these are found in the third book, particularly in III, 9; III, 12; and III, 13, under titles that do not refer to death. So even in thinking about death, he shows his usual manner of speaking of things he had not planned to discuss. He need not expressly make death his topic. For it is everywhere, it appears beneath his finger, whatever he touches. In describing his travels or his eating habits he stumbles upon it, or when reflecting upon the deceptions of the intellect, or the customs of various peoples, also when he is concerned with the correct, meaning natural, behavior of men, or in observations on solitude, age, illness: that is, in contexts that probably suggest thoughts of death, without requiring them, in certain instances, while in other instances this would be quite unexpected. And he also leaves the subject repeatedly to move into completely different realms. But even this uncalculated, fragmentary discussion underscores how death, like a magnet, draws one's mental powers to itself even through apparently indifferent matters.

Otherwise, we do not encounter the emergence of a final, uniform, easily reported certainty of the meaning of death in the *Essais*. Here, too, as everywhere in the *Essais*, the late, handwritten insertions run counter to what was said earlier, or they adapt to and even broaden it, even though Montaigne had left the older viewpoint behind long before this.[220] It is not easy to be clear about his thinking on death, for he himself was not clear about it. He tries out ideas, makes no final interpretation, does not admit finally to one; in fact, he relates to death in the manner of the *essai*, the attempt, which always approaches the matter from the context of the moment, and without correcting the contradictions, admits inexpressly that he has not finished with it. This is his method, here as with all topics in the *Essais*. This method is particularly appropriate here, with the most difficult thing with which one must come to terms. Feeling its way, taking it back, approaching it from another angle, the experimental method truly realizes the uneasiness death causes man—certainly to an even greater extent than Montaigne himself intended. In the absence of a final word on death, he himself remains under the control of its essence, which moves within the living, changeable, frightening or healing, sometimes seeming like the most ordinary thing, sometimes terrifying as the most absurd of all things and stronger than anything else, or similar only to love, driving objective thinking and inner experience apart as if they were two completely different manners of comprehension, yet one as necessary as the other. The fact that Montaigne did not conclude his statements on it makes him richer than his predecessors and richer than his later opponents in the realm of thoughts on death.

Nevertheless, several tendencies can be extracted from what he says. The most persistent—and yet the quietest—is his evasion of the Christian interpretation of death. The other is the gradual stripping away of stoic doctrines of death. This essentially involved an exemplary ethical system for behavior toward and in death; while it did recognize in death an essence that is inherent in life, it detects in the mastery of one's natural fear of death man's greatest chance of preserving his freedom, which goes so far that it determines the coming of the hour of death, that is, in suicide. Montaigne does share the stoic, in fact, classical wisdom on death, namely the striving to come to terms with death and leave metaphysical speculations about it open. Furthermore, he shares with it the thought, arising from a simple analysis of life, that death is born into every living thing. But his own, individual particularity rests in how he develops all this further. He individualizes death to a much greater degree than any classical philosopher. It becomes increasingly important to him as his own, future dying. He orients on this—not as some earlier ethic might recommend, but rather as his own individuality, one might even say his own spiritual taste, makes it appeal to him: not at all heroic and exemplary, but rather such that his individuality as it is extinguished gives its last, most individual response, which no one need imitate, but which is true, because once again it allows him to be entirely by himself. He wants to be individual, not in an immortality, but rather in the manner of his dying, and in the anticipation of it. He has drawn death so deeply inside himself that he can no longer comprehend his own individuality other than as a transitory figure. Thus he wants no fame coupled with his death. He does not consider growing beyond himself in his hour of death. Remaining at home in the realm of what is human and average, he lets go of the attempt to argue fear away. If death is a fact, then so, too, is its shadow, the fear of death, and it is a fact to which he has a spiritual right. He places himself at death's disposal and yet does not deny that he suffers from its annihilating power.

The most original aspect of Montaigne's relationship with death lies in his trust in predeterminative nature. He suspects that nature can master death better than any ethical discipline. In obedience to this nature—which he always terms wiser than man—he attains the most extreme distance from the stoic triumph of death. It is a fearlessness without a claim to be master over one's vassal death, a cooperative humility that takes on all that is the lot of imperfect human existence, the *condition humaine*, and it fears death as an enemy just as it cherishes it as a possession.

The tendencies just mentioned, which, to repeat this, remain in flux to the end, will be described in the following. We will disregard the fluctuations themselves in order to note the levels and stages more definitively for the purpose of clarity.

2. THE DEATH OF OTHERS

Montaigne like anyone has his external knowledge of death first from the experience of others dying. The most meaningful experience of death in his world appears to have been the death of his friend La Boétie

(1563). We have the long letter he wrote to his father shortly thereafter, which represents his most significant prose before his translation of Sebond and before the *Essais:* a work of art that inserts a precise description of the spiritual and physical phases of dying into the unmistakenly literature-dependent idealization of stoic, Christian, heroic dying.[221] Later on he returns often to the subject of his friend, but never again to his dying. He speaks only in passing, when at all, of the death of his father and his five children. He had a deeper involvement with the view of those dying of the plague during the great epidemic (in 1585). In his report of it (III, 12, 801 ff.) we find poetry that is a characteristic mix of melancholy and consolation; one can see how moved he is by this animalistic, mute readiness of those ill, in fact, even of those who are well, who let the vineyards die, who dig their own graves and lie down in them while still alive. One of the most important turns in Montaigne's attitude toward death is connected with this observational experience. We will return to this point.

One hears nothing in the *Essais* about further deaths in his external circle of acquaintances. It seems that he wants to push the possible death of those closest to him away: "Our own death does not frighten us enough? Let us burden ourselves also with that of our wives, our children, and our servants . . ." (I, 39, 178 A). A sentence that exudes coldness; one can perhaps excuse it only with the urgency Montaigne felt to identify and process death with as little disturbance as possible in its highest reality, which only comes into being in one's own inwardness, and in the face of one's own destiny of death.

All other knowledge of dying has literary encouragement. Admittedly, this does not remain mere literature. Death passed on through literary means—from the mass of classical as well as modern history and anecdotes—is no less of an event to him than that which he has seen with his own eyes in others, or that which awaits him himself. Montaigne has a penetrating curiosity about death. It even dominates that letter about La Boétie. It drives him to extract instances of death handed down orally or in literature from the cool, mere report of them and to reproduce them with his own characteristic urgency and sometimes also his characteristic breadth. It was customary in biographical and anecdotal humanistic literature when dividing up material to devote a special category to death, just as there are other categories for youth, one's office, marriage, and so forth. For example, Erasmus in his *Apophthegmata*—classical aphorisms grouped by authors and historical figures—always concluded one of these groups with the comments of the particular figure on death or when dying: these were end points in the portrait of the figure and the highest confirmation of his moral essence. Montaigne, too, hardly ever forgets when speaking of a great man to report of his death. But in his case, this is more than the fulfilling of a biographical and literary scheme. It is his receptivity (and usually it relates back to himself) to the urgency of the reflection on death: ". . . so I have formed the habit of having death continually present, not merely in my imagination, but in my mouth. And there is nothing that I investigate so eagerly as the death of men . . . nor is there a place in the histories that I note so attentively . . . I have indeed a particular fondness for this subject" (I, 20, 62 A/C). He is also attracted by behavior of any kind which dying men exhibit. It opens to him the diversity of men and the inconclusive nature of the relationship to death, with which each person copes as he can.

But he is not only interested—as the humanists generally were—in the deaths of exemplary men of antiquity. Beside the great examples of Socrates or stoic Roman men and women we find—with equal weight—the deaths of anonymous persons, simple people with their composure, even criminals who joke upon the scaffold (I, 14, 33–34 A). And when, in a late passage, he chides Tacitus for sliding so quickly over "these noble deaths as if he were afraid to bore us with their number and length" (III, 8, 719 C), this comes—and one should not be misled by the use of the expression *belles morts*—less from admiration of an heroic triumph of death than from curiosity for all that is stirred up in one who is dying, what is going on with and around him, and what he said last.

3.   PRELUDE: ESSAY I, 20

In the Essays of the first book, the concern initially is the acquiring of a definitive consciousness of death of a general nature, and also the conquering of the fear of death—and all of this in a classical manner. Montaigne is still speaking with impersonal neutrality. He is not yet alone with himself. His self is a representative for the genre of man. He tests out, using classical texts, how a man can prepare for death. He begins where all reflections upon death begin: divorcing death from its mere negativity. This takes place through the insight that it is something universally necessary, thus it represents an order. This insight does not remain within an impartial objectivity like any factual knowledge. Rather, it becomes an aid to man's behavior vis-à-vis death. For man perceives death as an evil, the greatest among the evils of pain and poverty (I, 14, 65 A). Rising to the knowledge that death is an act "in the universal order of things,"

Montaigne also attempts to disperse the fear of death. His intention is to make it understandable as a false view of a law which, since it exists, cannot be evaded, and is thus unable to evoke fear in the manner of an out-of-the-ordinary catastrophe. An intellectual process also strives to disburden death, remove it from the emotional realm of suffering inwardness, and declare this to be an "error." The person who reflects upon the ordering character of death will change his behavior into an attitude, his fear into freedom which wills that which must unavoidably be. We hardly need stress that all of this is classical. Lucretius and Seneca are behind it. The death ethic shared by the Stoic school and Epicureanism, wherein a sovereign, self-experiencing state of being natural is a subordinate personality that forces one astray, forms the lead Montaigne follows when he enters the problem of death.

The long Essay I, 20 (presumably written in stages between 1572 and 1580) paces out the classical extent of the problem to all sides—and steps beyond it.[222] Many have wanted to restrict Montaigne's thoughts on death to this Essay—presumably because the repetition of familiar, commonplace maxims from Lucretius and Seneca make this into a relatively comfortable reading session. What is already known always has a tendency (unfortunately, in research as well) to be accepted more easily than what is new, particularly when, as is true for Montaigne, the new material is expressed equivocally, disconnectedly, unnotably. There is no question but that this Essay shows most clearly how Montaigne came by means of hellenistic moral philosophy to his first major understanding and to the categories of the death problem. He was reinforced by that moral philosophy in the tendency he already had to define the question of death as the question of one's behavior vis-à-vis death, specifically, excluding Christian motifs. There is not a single Christian quotation in this Essay. There is only an echo of a passage from *Ecclesiastes* (56 A: *Eccl.* III, 12), and this passage is possibly eudemonistic. The best wisdom on death from antiquity (Horace, in addition to Lucretius and Seneca) went into the Essay, harmonized in many voices, and was passed on to posterity through it. Montaigne extends it, permeates it with his own calm passion. The classical verses and statements he quotes or paraphrases are not simply lined up, one after the other, as in a compilation of maxims. A single thread passes through all of them, a single voice repeats them. They have already climbed beyond the level of educated reception, and they ring out as surely and strongly as if they came from a timeless, unauthored fundamental knowledge of mankind. They are genuine, an acquired yet also cultivated element of Montaigne's spirit, and, although they are repetitions, they are neither weakened nor empty: they are humanistic in the best sense of the word.

The title ("That To Philosophize Is To Learn To Die") is a reproduction of a sentence by Cicero (*Tusc.* I, 75), which for its part goes back to Plato's *Phaedo* (64a). In late antiquity and in the Middle Ages it served as one of the definitions of philosophy per se. Initially, Montaigne worked within the Platonic meaning of the sentence in that he, too, proceeds from the superiority of the soul to the body, philosophical thinking being the soul escaping the body, metaphorically understood as death, with the expectation that physical death is the final freeing and return home of the soul. But Montaigne, who is completely non-Platonic, abandons this quickly to understand that sentence in its simple meaning: to philosophize is to consider death in advance and to rehearse for it. To do this requires that first we assure ourselves of its nature by a look at its preeminent position: death is of all emergencies the only unavoidable one. It is so much a part of us that our continued living is already a favor that has slipped away from death. It is always there, it comes through the most improbable incidents, a wound received while combing one's hair, a stumble on the threshold of the door, an accident while one is playing ball. Its monstrous nature makes use of the most laughable means. In repeating these things which have been said so often in all literatures—even of his time, his intention, like that of others who said these same things, is to dissolve the common forgetfulness about death. For: "The remedy of the common herd is not to think about it. But from what brutish stupidity can come so gross a blindness!" (57–58 A). Let us make note of this sentence, for later on, Montaigne will value "brutish stupidity" quite differently. But he uses this common polemical motif against those who are frivolous to achieve the certainty of death. The man who does not consider death from the beginning commits an act of negligence for which he must pay in the hour of his death. One can still detect from afar the language of the dance of death poetry of the Late Middle Ages when one reads in some of the best known comments: "They go, they come, they trot, they dance—of death no news. All that is fine. But when it comes, either to them or to their wives, children, or friends . . . what torments, what cries, what frenzy, what despair overwhelms them!" (59 A). Death, once it has become a certain necessity, must be mastered by accustoming oneself through practice—the usual conclusion: "Let us learn to meet it steadfastly and to combat it . . . let us take an entirely different way from the usual one. Let us rid it of its strangeness, come to know it, get used to it. Let us have nothing on our minds as often as death . . . Amid feasting and gaiety let us ever keep in mind this refrain, the memory of our condition" (60 A). There are also Christian traces in such sentences, but they are pale and fading, detectable perhaps in the last expression, but without a conclusion that carries beyond antiquity. It is taken literally from Seneca that reflection upon death in advance is a reflection in advance upon freedom; one who has learned to die has unlearned how to be a slave (60 A). The master is the soul that has prepared to follow necessity.

But now Montaigne relaxes the heroic motif. He begins to look at himself and to be alone with the death he has thought over beforehand. A more intimate rumination replaces the general ethic of death. He relates how in his youth, when he was in the midst of conversations with women, he would be able to withdraw into silence: others saw this as lovesickness, "whereas I was thinking about I don't remember whom, who had been overtaken days before by a hot fever and by death, on leaving a similar feast . . ." (60–61 A). A cleaving together of death and life, both aware and felt, arises, but not at the expense of the one or the other. Death retains its destructive force, understood in its nature of being a part of life. One does not have a "more dangerous" life at sea or in battle than one does at home and in external safety: the constitution of life itself (which is what makes it truly our condition) is a surrendering of death. Thus there is no lesser or greater proximity to death in space and time, there is only always the same essential proximity.[223] Conversely, death does not devalue life. It continues to function, though admittedly moderated in its zeal. It no longer takes itself quite so seriously, it flows into what is fragmentary, not without courage, but softly renouncing, ready for itself as it is ready for its extinguishing. Here, in this passage, Montaigne finds one of the most beautiful sentences expressing his composure: "I want a man to act, and to prolong the functions of life as long as he can; and I want death to find me planting my cabbages, but careless of death, and still more of my unfinished garden" (62 A/C). This behavior is one expressed often in hellenistic antiquity, in Plutarch's *Moralia* or Epictetus' *Enchiridion:* composure arising from being admitted into the connectedness of death and life where the shadow does not suppress the light, the light does not overpower the shadow. This is no longer asceticism, no radical reversal in how one conducts one's life, no heightened defiance of death.

The familiarity with death which Montaigne approaches has nothing voluntary about it. Quite the contrary, it arises through a withdrawal of the will which gives room to the control that man carries within him: nature. This characteristic, which is so important to Montaigne's attitude toward death later, can be detected as early as Essay I, 20. Individual certainty of death looks through the self into a depth from which, without its help, it is led into reconciliation with death—a reconciliation that then need only be elevated from imperceptibility to reflection. One sign of this reconciliation is illness, another is aging. The consideration of illness and aging as symptoms of death's inherence in life is again classical. But in antiquity, they were one means of proof among many which served to make death tolerable. Montaigne, on the other hand, sets these above the others: "Nature herself lends us her hand and gives us courage . . . I notice that in proportion as I sink into sickness, I naturally enter into a certain disdain for life. I find that I have much more trouble digesting this resolution to die when I am in health than when I have a fever" (63 A). Man detects what will happen or has already happened without his exercise of will. He receives that which is most difficult. It is not he, but rather nature, which has the courage for death. The flow of time in its creations—stages of life—already represents a gentle dying from stage to stage: "But, when we are led by Nature's hand down a gentle and virtually imperceptible slope, bit by bit, one step at a time, she rolls us into this wretched state and makes us familiar with it; so that we feel no shock when youth dies within us" (63 B). Man is continuously in the process of change, the child "dies" in the youth, the youth in the man, the man in the old man, and all this is the gentle prelude to what in one's final dying intensifies only in degree, thus dying essentially signifies no more than that change in life itself: this is one of the most widespread thought processes of classical wisdom on death,[224] frequently repeated in later literatures as well. It is particularly well suited to Montaigne's profoundly passive attitude. The words *douce, insensible, apprivoiser* are already the key words for his own relationship with death. Another subject replaces the human subject consisting of will and reason, namely, nature, which has invited death into itself from the beginning.

Thus it is reasonable that Montaigne lets nature itself speak in the last part of the Essay. This is a greatly expanded imitation of the little speech which Lucretius (III, 933–963) lets nature make to man. (The numerous insertions of B and C come from the same source, combined with paraphrases from Seneca.) The fact that Montaigne imitates precisely this artistic device of a speaking nature is based in that "naturalization," namely the shifting of the subject of the willingness for death into a being that precedes man. This is also the passage in which the supply of classical information on death appears with the greatest density, showing how it is common to both stoic and Epicurean teachings. Montaigne effortlessly plucks the ripest words of wisdom from the tree of the ancients. But the resonating, gentle lyrics of this speech belong to him alone. He puts these words in nature's mouth: "Your death is a part of the order of the universe; it is a part of the life of the world" (65 A). To flee death means not to want to be man. With birth, your life, and your death as well, begin. You lessen life in the process of living, and the work of your life is building death. While you are living, you are already in death, and death is already behind you when you are no longer alive. Death does not concern the dead or the living: the latter because he still exists, the former, because he no longer exists.[225] Nothingness after death is no different than the nothingness before your birth. So where is death to be feared: Only in the fear itself—in error. If you have lived one day, then you have lived through all of them. Surely you see that I have my tides, you have yours as well. Does not everything age along with you? Does it not comfort you that your lot is that which all endure? A never-ending life would be less tolerable to you than that which I have given you: you would curse me if I had not invented death. I have deliberately mixed a little bitterness into it, just so that you will not live too immoderately. Why are you anxious about your last day? It does not create your end, it only completes it. "All days travel toward death, the last one reaches it" (67 C; almost literally taken from Seneca, *ep.* 120, 18): the final dying is only the last actualization of death, which is always present.[226]

Essay I, 20, which closes with a brief epilogue to this speech "of our Mother Nature," in emulating classical thought, has achieved several things. It has stated an objective consciousness of death in the form of a simple observation of death's inherence in life. He hopes in this way to overcome the common forgetfulness about death. Because what is living strives to suppress its antagonist, death, by forgetting, it must be reminded of the banality of its essential mortality, and thus be elevated above its banal behavior. For to have death inwardly present at all times is no longer banal, rather, it is "philosophical": "to philosophize is to learn to die." But this inward presence must also be disburdened of fear. As was the case with the classical reflections, here, too, at this stage of the *Essais*, the intellectual character of the objective knowledge of death is accompanied by the phenomenon that the fear of death by the living appears to be an "error." The fearless attitude toward death is to come about by means

of a logical operation: death is a universal part of the order, "therefore" it
cannot be frightening. But even here Montaigne moderates the energy of
this battle against fear and thus emerges in his own, personal nature. This
was not recognized by his contemporaries. A certain Claude Expilly in a
"cleaned up" edition of the *Essais* in 1595 in Lyon preceded it with a
sonnet, in which we read the following: "Montaigne, . . . in what ancient
school did you learn so well about frightful death and glorious scorn? . . .
Magnanimous Stoic . . ."[227] One can find numerous similar heroizations
by readers of that time.[228] But they miss the spirit of his relationship with
death. The few passages in I, 20 which appear to justify them must not be
taken in isolation. For despite some literary accommodations, from the
very beginning, this relationship had nothing glorious about it. Rather, it
sought a kind of comfort, a harmony, which one cannot actually will for
oneself, rather, it tends only to come as a gift.

Later, right at the beginning of the Essay, Montaigne inserted a rather
long passage which, with provocative enjoyment, calls sensual pleasure
(*volupté*) the highest content of perfection (*vertu*): "I like to beat their
ears with that word, which so goes against their grain" (56 C). He
expressly separates its "divine and perfect pleasure" from the "more
lusty voluptuousness." Differentiating spiritual pleasure (which does
justice to all man's requirements, including the corporal ones) from
primitive sensual pleasure, he wants to elevate the relationship with
death into the realm of spiritual pleasure which does not diminish any
part of man at the expense of another. When he writes, still in this
insertion, the following traditional sentence: "Now among the principal
benefits of virtue is disdain of death," this "contempt" of death still
attains its composure in what directly follows: "a means that furnishes
our life with a soft tranquillity" (57 C). It is also conceived as an
overcoming of what is adversative, thus does not require heroic tension.
Admittedly, this passage is a later insertion. But the ground is laid for it
in the earlier draft, and it reveals even more clearly what was already
stirring there: a readiness for the contradictory and yet interlaced powers of death and life—a gentle conciliatory quality that is much more
likely the source of Montaigne's objective knowledge of death than the
product of it which he acquired by thinking.

There is little accomplished in seeing an "Epicurean" influence in all
this, as is usually done. For what is really involved is a relaxation that
characterizes Montaigne's nature everywhere, and which, by the way,
was also adequately expressed even in the early stage with his often-
noted practice of smiling at "excessive virtue" (I, 39, 178–179). This

relaxation will to an increasing degree define his relationship with death. In this sense, Essay I, 20 is a prelude to his future attitude, but it is only a prelude. He will retain the knowledge of death's inherence in life all the way to the last Essay (compare III, 13, 837 C; 846 B; etc.). But he will go much more deeply beneath the voluntary surface than was the case here, and he will much more decisively replace the objectifying concept with his inner experience.

4.   REJECTION OF SUICIDE

How far removed Montaigne is from the voluntary mastery of death can be seen in the fact that he does not share the classical consistency of which he was well aware: suicide, which according to stoic theory is a morally valid possibility of being in charge of death, retrieving death from its random occurrence in time and bringing it under the control of man when this life seems intolerable.

Essay II, 3 ("A Custom of the Island of Cea"), written around 1573, is concerned with this. "The most voluntary death is the fairest," we read in the beginning, borrowed from a statement by Seneca. But as becomes immediately apparent, this is simply a report, not his own conviction: "This does not pass without contradiction" (253 A). Another report follows: Christian reasons in opposition to suicide. They do not appear for the purpose of teaching Christian doctrine. Rather, like the classical statements, they are only material underscoring the impossibility of deciding the matter according to any generally applicable standards, an impossibility hidden behind the pro and contra of judgments. The entire Essay swings back and forth between pro and contra. Montaigne can just as well unmask individual instances of suicide by revealing their pathological motives as he can make others understandable from the situation that occasioned them. But no case is held up as an example of a rule that can be universalized. He subdivides "the" suicide into diverse processes that he then observes not ethically, but psychologically, as he does with any other object of his interest in the study of man. The leading thought of this Essay is not: this is how death is—or: this is how I behave vis-à-vis death—rather, it is: this is how varied people are, some seek death for this reason, some for that reason.

While the transformation of a core element of the classical death ethic into a psychological curiosity is in itself highly revealing, Montaigne's own quite unstoic attitude toward death emerges clearly in several sentences. With the impetus of certain Augustinian admonitions (that only God may call one home, and that it is more courageous to wear the chain than to break it), but forgetting their Christian meaning, he writes: "As for the opinion that disdains our life, it is ridiculous. For after all, life is our being, it is our all . . . it is against nature that we despise ourselves . . . It is by a similar vanity that we wish to be something other than we are" (254 A). The insult to life implied in suicide runs counter to Montaigne's obedience to life, which is essentially identical to his obedience to death. It is appropriate to preserve life not because it has a high value (quite the contrary, even its evils are so trivial that it is not worth calling upon death for their sake, 255 A), but simply because it is an actuality. It is absolutely a fundamental characteristic of the *Essais* that they do not derive any disallowance of the rights of life from their acknowledgment of death. Montaigne lets nothing dissuade him from the urgency of thinking about death (not even when later he deliberately transforms this thinking into forgetting), and he lets nothing convince him that death, which annihilates life, therefore makes life worthless. He profoundly comprehended the contradictory, chance nature of existence which is only possible through the antagonism of life and death, and he accepted it in obedience to both antagonists. He loves that which is mortal, and, lovingly, does not shut himself off from his own mortality. He never becomes sick to death. On the contrary: "The most barbarous of our maladies is to despise our being" (III, 13, 852 B). He notes as absurd the fact that there are peoples who curse birth and bless death, who condemn the sun and sanctify the darkness (III, 5, 670 B). He never had the inclination to summon death in order to escape death's shadow over life. To think this way is indeed a frequent motif, just as much of the Old Testament as of Greece and Rome, in fact, it is a universally human one, and it contains a noteworthy paradox: the possibility of death in all the content of life is what produces suffering (illness, misfortune, old age), and life that becomes anxious at these messengers of death flees into death itself to find peace from its messengers; it finds its happiness in that it leaps into the cause of its worry, in that it actualizes fully what has become intolerable when only partially actualized (cf. Lucretius III, v. 79 ff.). But one will find none of this in the *Essais*. And when Montaigne does discuss the *taedium vitae*, or disgust at the barrenness of biological functions that always remain the same, and because of which a man seeks death, he does this using an event reported by Seneca (*ep.* 87) which he uses as an example of a manner of death, but not to teach weariness with life (II, 13, 461–462 A).

Then, in Essay II, 3, we find the further objection to death freely chosen: it makes the error made by all summary judgments, namely, it simplifies what is complex, it fixes in place what really moves within the wealth of endless possibilities. What do we know that would allow us to believe all hope is gone? What happened to Joseph? Under the most extreme distress he rejected the advice to end his life, and he was correct in doing so: for fortune, "beyond all human reason," deflected the danger (255 A). This is quite a mundane thought, simply stated without profundity. But it has its substance, which can easily be drawn out when one remembers many other passages in the *Essais*. Namely, despair that becomes a judgment and an action that ends life does not take into account the powers unrelated to reason in the push and pull of circumstances (fortune); suicide destroys the concealed possibilities for the sake of what is real at the moment, it sacrifices the whole to be rid of a single element that in its despair it sees as absolute. Montaigne's obedience to life forms a close bond with his deductive skepticism—a skepticism that not only doubts what we consider real, but also considers possible what we doubt. He objects to suicide as the premature leap of an inadequate judgment. Actuality, which is always laden with what is different, and which cannot be hauled in or anticipated by any judgment, takes away life's right to throw itself away. Thus Montaigne's reflection upon suicide, with all its apparent casualness in the development of its train of thought, is a step farther in the disempowerment of the will and the return to obedience: with respect to death when it comes, and with respect to life as long as it lives.

He remained faithful to this view and never thought differently about suicide. This interests him, as does any heroic kind of death, as always from the perspective of the diversity of what is human. But personally he wants nothing to do with it. How well it fits his obedient wisdom that he thrusts aside precisely what is the "most Roman" of behaviors vis-à-vis death! Yorck von Wartenburg writes Dilthey once on the occasion of a reflection upon the imperial feeling for power of the Romans, something that permeates all realms of life: "Rome is the seat of metaphysics, in contrast to transcendence. Not Rome nor any Roman understands death."[229] Montaigne appears to have sensed what is expressed here: having death at one's disposal is forwardness and rebellion, power's betrayal of "transcendence," that is, of an essence of obedience which defies interpretation. This is permeated more profoundly by an obedient will than by a will that cannot conceive of its own demise and which then hopes to wring a last, despairing triumph from that unavoidable demise.

The better Montaigne comprehends death, the more his relationship to suicide becomes a psychological and aesthetic one. This can be seen nowhere more clearly than in Essay II, 35 ("Of Three Good Women"), in which he relates Roman suicides, lastly that of Seneca. He does it with a writer's care, which transforms the sources into a new work of art, and in part expands them considerably—especially the report from Tacitus' *Annals,* into which he incorporates beautiful contrasts of color and speech (the blood-red water, for example). Precisely this makes clear that he is more concerned with the observation than with the emulation of powerful, exceptional persons of antiquity. He allows the ancients suicide only as a magnificence of the period, which, however, has nothing to do with him. On these pages, there is a tellingly large amount of energy available for lovely narration. When Montaigne's innermost attitude is engaged, he is accustomed to express himself more concisely.

Other passages can also be mentioned. He frequently speaks of the prototype of the Roman position vis-à-vis death, the younger Cato. An example can be found in II, 11 ("Of Cruelty"). He is somewhat skeptical about the assumed coolness of emotion and moral motivation of Cato's suicide: "I believe without any doubt that he felt pleasure and bliss in so noble an action, and that he enjoyed himself more in it than in any other action of his life . . . I go so far in that belief that I begin to doubt whether he would have wanted to be deprived of the occasion for so fine an exploit" (309 A). Was Cato's suicide thus Cato's manner of personal pleasure, a confirmation of the power of his "virtue," which was quite grateful for this opportunity that offered itself? Montaigne does not force his doubt upon the reader, and he makes an effort to resume speaking more respectfully. But the mood of an unclouded veneration is now lost. Doubt—as the ironic Montaigne knows very well— has left behind it the thorns of mistrust that with Cato there could have been something quite different going on than simply a noble act of protest against the dishonoring of his country's freedom. In any case, for Montaigne this suicide remains a single occurrence that can be explained from the circumstances of that particular individuality. Thus, again, everything is treated psychologically. A half page later the comparison with Socrates' death emerges, quite to the Roman's disfavor, whom he finds too tense, too lacking in cheerfulness (309 A). It is the same distinction the *Essais* make between the "tense" Seneca and the relaxed Plutarch. So even in making an historical assessment, Montaigne's sympathies lie with the obedient, passive relationship to death.

What is most important, however, is inserted before this in an addition. There we read that only Cato could have died thus. The same thing would have been inappropriate for others. For: "Every death should correspond with its life. We do not become different for dying. I always interpret the death by the life" (309 C). This means, the authenticity of one's dying can be seen in the extent to which it is in harmony with one's individual life, not in the extent to which it obeys an obligatory norm. There is no universal, teachable conduct in death. Each must die as he can in remaining true to himself. Anything else is a lie: "We do not become different for dying." Montaigne's doubt as to whether man can be changed by moral norms—and his doubt in the benefit of such a transformation—is expressed here. When he inserted the sentence just quoted, he himself had long been at the point of leaving his own future death at the discretion of his own, particular humanity. He prepares for this in that he takes away from the forms of death handed down in literature any claim they may make to being exemplary. (Even in the case of Socrates, he can become critical: see III, 2, 620 C.) As he stresses repeatedly, there is no universally compulsory qualification of death: "Death is frightful to Cicero, desirable to Cato, a matter of indifference to Socrates" (I, 50, 220 C). Or: "Death has some shapes that are easier than others, and assumes different qualities according to each man's fancy" (III, 9, 752 B). The truth of death in each case is to be found only where it becomes concrete, namely, when it encounters the inner experience of the particular man, and in his hour of death. It is authentic only as an individual event. It is as varied as individuals. With this variety, Montaigne does not concern himself with one exemplary death when he is on the lookout for others' dying.

5.   INNER EXPERIENCE

Montaigne's real interest, however, is in one's inner experience before death. He knows of this both from testimony by others and—this exclusively later on—from his own incidents and meditations. If death is the most intensive event in a life (be it in the dying itself, or in the conceptual anticipation of it, or in some sort of threat to one's person), then here the qualitative superiority of inner experience over objective knowledge is all the more valid. And how one feels when death encounters what is living says more than this, to be permeated with death's approximations says more than the concept of death: "It is the approaches that we have to fear; and these may fall within our experience" (II, 6, 268 A). In fact, the highest reality of death consists not in the isolated act of dying, but rather in the shadow its threat casts over what is living. Only one's feelings of the inwardness of being close to death allows the perception of death's full nature, as, for example, one can only perceive the full nature of an illness through first having it and through one's feelings while having it and—because this comes from within—it means considerably more than the pathological diagnosis.

Montaigne's important change in direction and the magnitude of his thoughts on death are indicated by the fact that he aims for this highest reality. It is quite characteristic of this that Epicurus' sophism, which he reported in a late insertion in I, 20 (66 C), remained simply a report and did not play a role in his final view of death, that sophism whereby death does not concern the living because they are in fact living, and does not concern the dead, because they are in fact no longer living. A sentence such as this, in the eyes of inner experience, is an idle one, a game that does not extend to the reality of death.

As a marker of the expression just described, one finds numerous formulations such as the following in the *Essais: savourer, goûter, tâter, essayer la mort.* It is connected with the literary stimuli, never completely shed, of Montaigne's reflections on death when, in the process of his penetration into the inward reality of death, some things are reminiscent of the classical ethic and its practicing of strength of spirit in dying. Thus even the Essay that revolves the longest around the anticipatory experiencing of death, II, 6, has a classical starting point. Even the title bears a key term of Stoic ethics: "Of Practice." Montaigne first presents the report from Seneca (*De tranquillitate animi* XIV) of Canius Julius, who is sentenced to death. Before his execution he makes known his decision to remain clearly conscious up to the last moment, in order to perhaps perceive what happens with the escaping soul. Montaigne, like Seneca, praises the double value of this decision: an insight that furthers truth, and moral courage. And yet we can assume that despite the wealth of ethical vocabulary offered ("singular virtue and firmness . . . with all my powers intent," 267 A), the ethical act of self-mastery and overcoming fear fascinates him less than this process of an insight that pushes into the extreme, making even one's demise into an experience to be observed. Everything that we have shown to this point about his attitude toward death is evidence of this, and the further progression of the Essay does also, and then there is the following sentence that he writes elsewhere, and probably at the same time: "It is very far beyond not fearing death, to want to taste it and relish it" (II, 13, 461 A). The point is not moral example, nor is it simply fearlessness (this is a kind of byproduct), rather the point is to capture death in one's own inwardness, which will "taste" its quality. Ethically, this is more indifferent than in Seneca—only by a nuance at first, but this slight deviation leads, in the continuation of further reflections upon death (which will proceed up to the affirmation of fear), to the later major distance of Montaigne from the Roman ethic concerned with one's "bearing."

Essay II, 6 has as its core the portrayal of an accident which Montaigne suffered presumably prior to 1570. He exploits this in a manner that goes considerably beyond what he said in 1, 20. He must have also had that accident in mind when he was writing I, 20. But only here, in this text that was presumably composed between the further work on I, 20 (1574?), his theme becomes the concrete, personal experience of the proximity of death connected with this accident. This is remarkable. He shows how he is seeking several means of access to a matter simultaneously. Essay II, 6 does not "contradict" Essay I, 20. But it shifts everything into the aspect of inner experience to such a degree that something vastly different emerges from that Essay.

With great precision and over several pages Montaigne relates the following: When riding on horseback, he was run down by another horse, thrown, and in the process so severely injured that he lay unconscious, his companions taking him for dead. As he was carried home he regained consciousness, but so slowly that he felt himself to be closer to death than to life. With an alertness to the intermediate stages of consciousness which can also be detected elsewhere in the *Essais,* the text describes that awareness of wavering between death and life: "It seemed to me that my life was hanging only by the tip of my lips; I closed my eyes in order, it seemed to me, to help push it out, and took pleasure in growing languid and letting myself go. It was an idea that was only floating on the surface of my soul, as delicate and feeble as all the rest, but in truth not only free from distress but mingled with that sweet feeling that people have who let themselves slide into sleep" (269–270 A). Then he reports the first utterances and physical movements, involuntary reflex movements that his environment, not his memory, preserve, and which are told to him afterward. Then he returns again to the contentment he felt in his condition: "Meanwhile my condition was, in truth, very pleasant and peaceful; I felt no affliction either for others or for myself; it was a languor and an extreme weakness, without any pain . . . It would, in truth, have been a very happy death; for the weakness of my understanding kept me from having any judgment of it, and that of my body from having any feeling of it. I was letting myself slip away so gently, so gradually and easily, that I hardly ever did anything with less of a feeling of effort" (272 A). The fear of death only begins with the return of clear feeling, that is, as the proximity to death again recedes. And it is only at the end that he becomes aware of the accident itself, the shock effect of which initially wipes out his memory of it. In conclusion, he writes: "This account of so trivial an event would be rather pointless, were it not for the instruction that I have derived from it for myself; for in truth, in order to get used to the idea of death, I find there is nothing like coming close to it . . . What I write here is not my teaching, but my study; it is not a lesson for others, but for me" (272 A).

The pages contain a classical description of the progression of spiritual and physical phases following an accident.[229a] But the actual theme is the experiencing of the proximity of death: "now that I have tried this out by experience" (271 A). The experience has the knowledge value of an experiment that lacks all intention and planning of a designed experiment in the sense of the natural sciences, which, in Montaigne's opinion, increases the guarantee of genuineness. The state of mind during the transition between life and death is recognized. Thereby—naturally—not only is the process a passive event, but the one affected himself, Montaigne, intensifies his own passivity. Pay attention to the expressions used in the quotations, such as: "to let myself go, to let himself slide, to let himself slip away," and so forth. The one who feels he is close to death surrenders. As long as he is in a state of semiconsciousness, he observes this occurrence, which deep within him is not an act of will, but rather an obedience that precedes will, which the weak remnant of will supports. The several divergences of the text to other "reflex movements" (particularly 271) show how very interested Montaigne is in such symptoms that precede will. He seeks an "it" within the "I"—an "it" that is not of an individual nature, but rather forms the deep layer of individuality which precedes will, where individuality is embedded in guiding, healing forces that might work differently in others. The whole process is euphorically transfigured. In a remarkable accumulation, the words for this closely follow one another: "took pleasure; free from distress; sweet feeling; very pleasant and peaceful; without any pain; so gently, so gradually and easily . . ." The proximity to death seems to be enclosed in a happy, almost tender harmony. The subsequent description cannot get enough of saying this again and again. This was apparently the most astounding thing about the entire experience to him.

Montaigne does make brief mention several times of the physiological bases of this euphoria. But it would be erroneous to see this as explaining the reconciliation with death in terms of physiological conditions. Rather, for him these conditions actualize an order which nurtures the person. They are means and symptom, but not basis. He calls this order "nature." His view does not stop with its physiological materialness, rather it passes through this to the helping, healing relationship of "nature" to the person. He occasionally personifies it in a classical manner, as we have seen (I, 20, 64–65). But this is more a metaphorical substitute than a metaphysical category. In the *Essais* he carefully guards skeptically against stating precisely what he means by "nature." His thinking is indeed based in a belief in nature, but it is neither naturalistic nor materialistic. The only thing that is unmistakable is that he experiences nature as operating universally, as the motherly element, as a transcendent, yet unknowable, though perceptible, blessing: "I shall know it well enough when I feel it" (III, 13, 821 C). What we generally mean today with the word "nature" would for Montaigne be only a fragmentary, functional front side of the prevailing order that he "felt," an order that in its lap holds all contradictions, and which will "one day" be able to throw out all of our knowledge of the laws of nature (cf. II, 12, 400). Dying is a part of this rule of nature. It is seen all the more favorably, the less it is deflected by thinking, intending, and any lower physical feeling. Precisely the fact that Montaigne stresses how his experience of reconciliation with death took place while physical pains were silenced shows that he means a disposition that cannot be encompassed with terms such as "body" or "soul." One could more appropriately apply to its profoundly internal seat in the center of the person the concept of the heart as Augustinian theology and later Pascal understood it, if it is not to point in a theological or mystical direction, something Montaigne scrupulously avoided. In any case, the familiarity that he feels coming to him along with death is not "naturalistic" any more than he seeks its basis in the physical circumstances that merely trigger it.

The major significance of the entire passage consists in the fact that Montaigne intends to make the experience of a factual closeness to death his own in his reflection as a possession that he can no longer lose at some future time. He perceived the qualitative superiority of such experience over the objective knowledge of death: "What I write here is not my teaching, but my study." He does not put aside what objective knowledge of death he has acquired, namely, the insight into death's inherence in life, and into its ordering character. But this insight only attains its inner fullness in a reconciliation resulting through one's living through death's essential proximity: "In order to get used to the idea of death, I find there is nothing like coming close to it" (II, 6, 272 A). Here, in the case of his accident, this is a physical proximity: Montaigne physically touched the edge of death. In other cases, it can be a matter of thinking ahead which creates a certainty of one's own future death, and is thus also an essential proximity. In both cases, the definitive act is a listening in to one's inner mood. This is where he finds happiness: man is also equipped to cope with frightening death. Montaigne does not speak of strength of spirit, virtue, force, and such. Rather, he speaks of that happiness and of the readiness to consent to the rule that precedes will. The irrevocable contradiction between death and life opens up into a paradoxical unity that can be tolerated from a deep layer of the self for which one who has been reconciled no longer asks. A familiarity with death has developed, almost a tenderness, which encompasses the threat-ener of life as well as life itself—an ethically neutral double love that need no longer "overcome" death with great effort and consider life worthless because it can be annihilated. What is negative about death is not argued away in the process: it remains the destroyer, the enemy. But one can offer a hand to this enemy, an enemy with which one is friends. He is not nearly as bad as we commonly believe. For death is a posses-sion of the self, just as old and with just the same nature as this self.[230]

6. THE DIVERSIONS

The attempt emerges ever more strongly to bring death into inner experience in as pure a form as possible. In this context, we can consider a passage in Essay III, 4 ("Of Diversion"). The Essay concerns the eudemonistic technique of mastering something with which it is difficult to come to terms by turning one's mind to other thoughts: it is a simple process that supports the natural tendency we have toward diversion and forgetting. In the process, the conversation turns to death, and more specifically, to the question of whether a man can tolerate focusing with full consciousness upon his own death right before his own eyes. The answer is, only Socrates was capable of that. Montaigne goes through a series of cases in which the person was unable to tolerate this: the layer of an individual which operates with will and reason is not equal to dealing with death.[231] Man who stands face-to-face with death creates "diversions" for himself, for example, by thoughts of immortality, or by prayer. With great boldness, Montaigne dares to write that the dying who occupy themselves with prayer and the afterlife can certainly be praised for their piety, but not for their courage in the face of death: "They avoid the struggle; they turn their consideration away from death, as we amuse children while they are being lanced" (632 B; compare Lucretius IV, 11 ff.; Horace, *Sat.* I, 1, 26 ff.). And one page later: "Our thoughts are always elsewhere; the hope of a better life stays and supports us, or the hope of our children's worth, or the future glory of our name . . ." (633 B).

For a religious mind, words such as these are outrageous. They psychologize pious behavior and declare it to be an escape and a weakness. Montaigne is seldom as frankly free-spirited as he is here. But to get to the foundation of man—specifically, the foundation of his greatest experience, death—Montaigne risks everything. But this in itself shows the weight the thought of death has for him: this is what drives the best hidden element of his fundamental convictions to light. Montaigne does not criticize the faith of dying persons. Nor does he recommend it. And he writes in a revealing addition by hand: "Indeed the arguments of philosophy are all the time running alongside the matter and sidestepping it, and barely brushing the crust of it" (634 C), and this is followed by an ironic, brief abstract of classical syllogisms on death. This means that even objectifying thinking about death is a diversion from death, a missing of its reality. Paul Valéry once expressed this as follows: "The object reputed as being of the greatest importance can only allow the most 'superficial' description. Death, for example, can only be thought of or reflected upon illusorily . . . That is why, when I muse on it or read some author who lingers over it and studies it thoroughly, I soon have the impression that we are thinking about something else" (*Autres Rhumbs*).

The fact that Montaigne only once, and never again, reviews the other classical sophism that states that the non-being after death is like the non-being before birth (I, 20, 65 C)[232] is presumably connected with this search for the full, that is, internal, reality of death. Perhaps he detected what an intellectual deception was perpetrated in this against the consciousness of self, for which the former state of "not yet being" is a matter of vast indifference, and for which the future state of "no longer being" is vastly difficult to interpret, and to which, therefore, these two artificially identified "nots" seem fundamentally different from each other.

Since Montaigne wants to keep inner experience as pure as possible,

he asks, in III, 4, about the "diversions." Since the forces of will and
reason are unable to stand up to death (for "still they are men, and most
heavily so," quite ponderously average men, 634 C), are diversions
recommended? Montaigne answers: yes, but better natural than "artificial" ones. Nature already provides for the withstanding of death, and
this fact of being taken care of is preferable to faith and theory for
Montaigne. All of this will only really become understandable later
when we have brought in other Essays. Here we need only emphasize
that he suppresses the objective knowledge of death even more strongly
than before (now also including the religious *ars moriendi*) as something
casual and unreal, something that only reaches the "outer crust" of
death, even in the best cases. The full reality of death only opens up
when one is freely alone with it, and when one listens to one's own
individuality, through which nature provides a quite different "diversion" from that which knowledge and pious faith can provide.

7. "MY" DEATH

Being alone with death, knowing "my" death, dying "my" death:
these leitmotifs are heard more and more clearly in the *Essais*. His
aversion to deathbed-itus is characteristic. Even the epilogue of I, 20
speaks with disquiet of the weeping women, friends, children, servants,
standing around the dying person with the doctors and priests, the
curtained room and lit candles. For all these things are veils for and
disruptions of something that must be withstood in its full, painful
harshness. Montaigne returns to this. It happens in Essay III, 9, in the
passage in which he grumbles about the objection someone makes to his
travels because he could die in a foreign land. Montaigne loves travel.
But he knows that when he travels, death always travels with him; any
day of travel, just like any day of life, can bring the end. There is no
greater provisional aspect to travel than to any other form of living, and
no less of a chance of being I, myself, whether in living on or in dying: "I
feel death continually clutching me by the throat or the loins . . . death
is the same to me anywhere" (III, 9, 747 B). He would in fact prefer to
die this omnipresent death in a foreign land, "rather on horseback than
in a bed, and out of my house, away from my people." This takes up
again something which was said earlier ("I want death to find me planting my cabbages . . ." I, 20, 62 A), but it extends it by including the
longing to be alone with himself. He doesn't want any of the wailing of
those left behind around him. If the person dying can be in need of

anything in this time of great need, it is only a gentle hand to ease his condition "to scratch him just where he itches—or one should simply leave him alone entirely" (748 B). But where is there such a friend? Montaigne feels himself to be alone since the death of La Boétie. Thus he also prefers to die his own, solitary death. He also knows himself to be too human to be able to provide his environment with an exemplary death: "It is not my idea to prove or display my fortitude in this act of dying. For whom? Then will end all my right to reputation . . ." And then the crowning sentence follows: "I am content with a collected, calm, and solitary death, all my own, in keeping with my retired and private life" (748 B).

If one considers the human and religious care associated with pious dying—farewells to those close to one, presence of the priests, confession, the last rites—then what Montaigne says there looks like inhuman, impious coldness. It is again the meditation upon death which leads him to one of his greatest instances of boldness. (Perhaps he is also thinking of the passage in *Phaedo*—117c—in which Socrates sends the women away, in order to die "in blessed silence.") When he imagines himself dying, he imagines himself looking not at God or his wife or child, but rather at himself, or within himself, and again, not to examine his conscience, to repent, to transform himself in a last effort—but rather to be alone with himself undisturbed, and to be with death, remaining true to his own nature, which, however it may be, should not falsify itself.[233] For the sake of the truth of his own death—*une mort toute mienne*—he takes this "egotism" upon himself: "Dying is not a role for society; it is an act for one single character" (748 B).[234] He fears nothing as much as alienation from himself. Even in his ceasing to be, he does not want to let his self slip away, nor the reality of death, which only becomes apparent to direct inner experience and animal weakness. He wants his dying, like his living, to be completely anonymous—and like the innermost center of the person, which cannot enter into any proclamation of fame (*réputation*) without being spoiled by it. Thus even in his style of death he displays the aversion to fame as the great falsifier, just as he expressed this so vividly elsewhere. Metaphysical and ethical interests are silent. The only thing to be endured is the pure occurrence of an animal suffering of death. He is so serious about this that even God, faith, and the love of men would disturb him.

This "entirely self-contained" death also allows for suffering, for fear. For the one dying is after all a human person who is like everyone—and who only knows this a bit better than others ("I con-

sider myself one of the common sort, except in that I consider myself
so," II, 17, 481 C). One may suffer the animal fear of death. For it
belongs to the truth of dying. Only the other fear must be banished, the
fear of a death distorted into a catastrophic event. Thus the honest
intention of suffering the fear of death is a further reason to be alone
when dying. No one need hear my groaning, he writes—or if there is no
other way, then let it only be strangers who are present. "Let us live and
laugh among our friends, let us go die and look sour among strangers";
if I need help, then I will pay someone for it, he will not become a
burden to me, "letting you reflect and lament as you like" (748 B). Only
here, in suffering, is death completely "mine," *une mort toute mienne.*
The passivity of suffering is a part of the receiving of death, and Montaigne prepares himself for this, leaving it up to his nature as to how it
deals with the new arrival.

The expression *ma mort* ("my death") which is used several times
(also compare III, 13, 845–846), which has replaced the earlier *la mort*
("death"), expresses the major step he has taken from the objective
knowledge of death to a closeness to death in his individual inwardness.
The "my" is a possessive: the death in me which has grown with me—
and it is an affective word, such as when one says "my darling"; it is
death, just as I most wish it to be. Here, the *Essais,* guided by thoughts
of death, have entered into a realm in which man discovers at the most
fundamental level that he really is only, as he always has been, a lone
individual. Montaigne sees death as the last chance to preserve the self
against disappearance into universality and against the degradation of
simply being an example of a genre. And in fact it is thus: if death is
taken as the universal transitoriness, then it levels man from the outside,
making him a mere number among the countless ones to whom the
same thing happens. But in the actualization of his dying—*une mort
toute mienne*—the lone individual saves himself from within from the
gray leveling process, and he makes the banal, universal death something new, nontransferable, true—like when the banal, overused love
becomes true and new in "my" love.

8. THE AFFIRMED FEAR OF DEATH

Here we cannot avoid the frequently misused, trendy word "existential," and can probably speak of Montaigne's existential honesty in
view of the differentiation he undertakes between the knowledge of
death and the inner experience of death. Knowledge can calm one's fear

of the catastrophe of death, for it knows this: death is a part of the order, it is born along with every living being when he is born; but experience, be it in dying itself or in becoming aware of the physical and spiritual messengers of death, cannot deny that it hurts, and that it is an adversary. The following sentence expresses this differentiation clearly: "I saw death nonchalantly when I saw it universally, as the end of life. I dominate it in the mass; in detail it harasses me" (III, 4, 636 C). Montaigne's obedience, with all its knowledge of the ordering character of death "in the universal arena," accepts animal fears "in the small arena." His honesty admits to the shadows of sadness which the proximity of death casts upon one's feelings for life. In the same passage, when discussing his attack of kidney stones, he writes: "Finding myself in this plight, I considered by what slight causes and objects my imagination fostered in me the regret for life; out of what atoms the gravity and difficulty of this dislodgment from life built itself up in my soul; for what frivolous thoughts we made room in so great an affair: a dog, a horse, a book, a glass, and what not counted for something in my loss" (636 C). He knew to what great extent life consists in adhering to the small things; when they founder, it is already the great death. Even before death, he consents to that small, easily confused, temperamental humanity. This is why we repeatedly find those side-swipes at the stoic coldness of emotion: "It is a sign of a hard and obstinate nature to feel no emotion about them" (636 C). And then, interpreting a thing through thinking about it will fail when the thing itself is there: "And no matter how great a man's wisdom, he can never grasp, through his judgment alone, the cause of another's grief in all its intensity; his understanding is always enhanced by actual presence, when the eyes and ears have a share in it" (636 B). Since suffering is one of the realities of death which extends into the living, in familiarity with suffering, one's familiarity with death grows. Pain may be suffered quite unhindered ("let it shout right out," II, 37, 577 A) so that a man can become entirely that which he is destined to be: a temperamental creature. It is as if Montaigne wrapped himself in his suffering. In and through it he finds his right and his help, not in some flight into a particular "bearing." This would be a lie. "No dialectic can convince the eye not to close to keep out a speck of dust—or the head not to avoid a threatened blow," as Quevedo later writes.[235] We find no more of Seneca's *athleta,* or of *dura vincere, bonam clausulam imponere,* and however else the formulae of voluntary mastery of death may read (Seneca, *ep.* 13, *ep.* 77).

Perhaps it is now clear that these "unstoic" characteristics do not
indicate cowardice or a lower form of Epicureanism. For these characteristics also involve effort. It is, if one may say so, the effort of passivity.
Just as Montaigne receives, rather than "shapes," all the contents of the
self, he also receives his own mortality. He takes even his destination of
death into the wealth of his essence. With the fullness of his content, he
even calls its annihilation good. The effort he must make is that of
clearing away the strains of the ethical, metaphysical, and religious
interpretations of death, and to grasp the reality of death precisely
where philosophy (in the classical sense) and religion want to "overcome" it: in the shadow of fear, the natural sign of existence's association with death. He tolerates what is contrary about death, and at the
same time tolerates the sense that fears it: if he were to abandon it, then
he would lose his humanity. The ground that threatens to slip from
beneath his feet in his fear is at the same time the element that supports
him. This is why he makes the effort of passivity, why he has the "courage to be afraid in the face of death."[236]

These views should admittedly be brightened up as much as possible,
should be as free as possible of tragic tones. Since Montaigne allows
himself so completely to be the average creature, his affirmation of
suffering goes along with the hope of having a death in which suffering
is reduced as much as possible. Thus on one occasion he meditates upon
the place where he would like to die: a place free of noise, dirt, smoke:
"I try to humor death by these frivolous circumstances, or rather to
relieve myself of any other encumbrance, so that I can give my attention
exclusively to it, which will easily weigh me down enough without any
other load. I want death to have a share in the ease and comfort of my
life. It is a great and important part of it, and I hope that from this day
forth it will not belie the past . . . It is only an instant; but it is of such
gravity that I would willingly give several days of my life to go through
it in my own way" (III, 9, 752 B). This page contains almost all of the
basic characteristics of his views of death: the idea of death lying in wait
at all times, the acknowledgment of its seriousness, the need to protect
oneself from any disturbance when one is dying (here again the lack of a
desire for anyone in attendance, for he wants to concentrate completely
on death and to think only of it: *m'attendre à elle*)—and all this is
grouped around the primary motif of *mourir à mon aise, le [l'instant]*
passer à ma mode. The expression *à mon aise* (comfortably, contentedly,
in accordance with my own taste) was found once before, in Essay I, 20
(59 A), but more timidly then, and there it was also called into question

by what followed. Now it is decisive. He spends more time imagining this death "in accordance with my own taste": He would prefer a gentle death (*une mort molle et douce*), or, if it has to be a sudden death, he would rather be slain by a falling wall than fall off a precipice, rather die of a bullet wound than a sword thrust, he would prefer Socrates' cup of hemlock to Cato's act of violence, he would prefer to die "in the channel of a shallow river" than in a fiery furnace (752 B)—that is, to the extent possible, he would prefer not to intensify what is terrible in the essence of death by terrible circumstances. For fear enough is present when the time of dying comes.

Montaigne does not fool himself about the fearful foolishness of his taste for a gentle death: "So foolishly does our fear consider the means more than the result!" (752 C). He is not embarrassed about this foolishness, or if so, only to the degree that he would be embarrassed to be a temperamental human being. But his entire relationship to life and to himself fits into this middle position. What matters is that one not overlook the fact that with these easily misinterpreted "Epicurean" ideals he still remains quite close to death: "so that I can give my attention exclusively to it," he writes expressly. He does not cover it up, he does not downplay it, nor does he evade it, rather, he individualizes and naturalizes it—the latter in the sense in which we interpreted his concept of nature above. If his need to be true to himself were not so great, then he would not have written the sentence that places the true weight of dying precisely in the preservation of trueness to the self: "It is of such gravity that I would willingly give several days of my life to go through it in my own way" (752 B).

He alternates between the ideals of a euphoric and a sudden death. In one instance, he praises Caesar's response to the question of which death would be most acceptable to him: "The least premeditated and the quickest." And he adds in an insertion: "If Caesar dared say it, it is no longer cowardice for me to believe it" (II, 13, 460 A/B). Or, on another occasion: "I plunge head down, stupidly, into death, without looking at it and recognizing it, as into a silent and dark abyss that swallows me up at one leap and overwhelms me in an instant with a heavy sleep free from feeling and pain . . . I wrap myself up and nestle in this story, so that it must blind me and sweep me away furiously with a sudden and numbing attack" (III, 9, 742 B). This is the passage that aroused the horror of the Jansenists: "dreadful words that indicate the complete extinction of all religious sentiment."[237] Of course, this passage and similar ones are statements of a particular occasion that are contradicted by others in which Montaigne wants to die a fully conscious death. But these other statements are no more Christian than the first ones. Although one does hear stoic and Christian echoes on some pages of the *Essais,* what Montaigne is not becomes quite unambiguous in his reflections upon death: he is neither stoic nor Christian. This once again confirms for us in another manner how that which is most worthy of thought and most threatening to man leads Montaigne, more than did anything else, to the perception of his innermost essence. He found himself in every respect through death.

9.   DIFFERENCE FROM THE CHRISTIAN INTERPRETATION OF DEATH

A look at the essential features of the Christian interpretation of death will make clear how far removed Montaigne is from it. The only point of contact which one would expect between the ideas of death in the *Essais* and in biblical sources would be in the Old Testament, and there again only in those parts that included hellenistic material, that is, the Books of Wisdom and Proverbs. There is also a passage from *Ecclesiastes* in Essay I, 20, quoted once. But neither in quotations nor in ideas do the *Essais* make use to the slightest degree of those biblical texts upon which the Christian concept of death is based, namely, *Genesis* II, 17 and III, 19 (mortality of man as the curse of the Fall of Man) and the Letters of Paul, particularly *Ad Rom.* V, 12 (*per peccatum mors*) and VI, 23 (*stipendia enim peccati mors*).[238]

In contrast to Greek and Roman antiquity, these texts, and with them all of later theology, define death as an abnormality that was brought into humanity, which was originally free of death, by the first man's sin of will—thus it is defined as a disorder that arose historically, and which in the case of man uses the order of death which is natural for other creatures as a means, thus its meaning is not intrinsic.[239] The significance of death for Christian consciousness is as little exhausted by the metaphysical necessity of death, which as always can be justified, than it is by the biological, physiological process of dying. It is defamed ethically through original sin.

But it is again also glorified. For man who consists of body and soul is freed by death from empirical physicality and returns home "to the dwelling which is of heaven" (II *Cor.* V, 1 ff.). This fundamental idea, which is Platonic, and was also common in antiquity, now takes the following burdensome turn: the afterworld that receives the immortal soul is the court of God. Death only begins the process of the soul's final fate. There it must first be decided whether it can remain before God or whether it will be cast out by him—whether man must suffer only the *prima mors* and not also the *secunda mors*, as Augustine's formulae put it.[240] This adds an eschatological fear to the physical, animal fear of death: in dying, man worries whether hell or salvation awaits him.

Hellenistic philosophy always played with the alternative that death either extinguished the soul along with the body, or brought it into immortality, and then added that neither one was to be feared—for one would bring the peace of no longer being, the other the good fortune of happiness. *Quid igitur timeam si aut non miser post mortem aut beatus etiam futurus sum?* ("What should I fear, then, if after death I am either no longer unhappy, or in the future happy?") Cicero writes.[241] This alternative of *aut non miser—aut beatus sum,* which comes from the skeptical practice of leaving the question of immortality open, gives way to the Christian one: *aut miser—aut beatus sum.* Immortality is certainty and no longer a skeptical game. But this new alternative places a monstrous weight upon death. Whereas for hellenistic antiquity the possibility of no longer being as well as the possibility of immortality fill the dying person with *alta securitas* (Seneca, *ep.* 24), from the Christian viewpoint, the impossibility of no longer being, that is, an unavoidable immortality, is the cause of great fear and great hope in the dying person.

Thus Christianity has stressed, more powerfully than has ever been done before, the dual nature of death, a terror and a salvation. It has given death an urgency that can transform the individual's entire earthly life, and in fact should do so. If death by its historical origins is sin, and its completion is the gateway to the decision of whether a man will be cast out or saved, then it necessarily produces an anxiety that goes deeper than that of the classical interpretation. For in Christian terms, there is no such thing as death in the strict sense of the word (as no longer being), and even in the *secunda mors,* in being completely cast out in the afterworld, man's soul lives on.

It is precisely this inability to be annihilated by death which compels man to decide for or against his only chance, namely, in his earthly existence to wipe away the guilt that is part of this life, burdened with original sin. Physical death limits earthly life and thus "working as long as the daylight lasts" (from *John* IX, 4), that is, man's freedom to purify himself, to weave eternity into what is temporal, create "splendor" from "sorrow" (from II *Cor.* IV, 17), and it thus increases the moral potency of life. Death, disorder in terms of its historical origin, is incorporated into the order of the history of God's saving grace, it becomes a means of penance.

Due to this interpretation, the negativity of death becomes a blessing in Christian ethics—the *poena nascentis* becomes a *gloria renascentis* (*Civ. Dei* XIII, 6), and this is all the more true, since the man who is prepared to die has been preceded by the grace-bringing death, the divine, blessed, physical death of Christ.[242] The terror of animal death should remain, however, for this is precisely the source from which salvation arises: the devaluation of earthly life, the force of the soul pushing away and into God, and in the hour of death the eschatological fear of whether the man can prevail before his judge, since he himself can only assess the inadequacy of the life he has lived, but not how the penance he has done will be acknowledged. Precisely this moment of eschatological fear of death which must be fully endured (developed by the Church fathers[243] and prevailing in vulgar literature of the High Middle Ages) appeared to an intensified degree around Montaigne's time, namely in the movements of the Reformation and Counter-Reformation.[244] The calmer, the more composed, the more stoic one's dying, the more suspiciously it appears to represent a lack of soul and grace. On the other hand, the more difficult the battle of death, the more effective one's penance, the more genuine one's acceptance of responsibility, the greater one's faith, the more probable that one will receive grace. The agony of death becomes service. Thus, for the Christian, death should retain the full tension of its double nature to the end: it should simultaneously be the curse of guilt and the chance for purification, both fear and hope, disorder and the order of salvation.

We are not pursuing these matters in their full depth, not even in the theological variations that are quite different in their details. Yet it is probably sufficiently clear that no bridge leads from them to Montaigne. When he gives the fear of death its due, this is connected with the permission to show emotion, certainly furthered by Christianity, which is a part of modern psychology and philosophy of life, in fact, with the Christian presumptions of the concept *condition humaine*. But he himself no longer knows this. He thinks of the fear not as a sign of repentance and conscience, not as penance or service, but rather as obedience to his factual human essence in the face of the factual essence of death. So even this single moment of his basic beliefs about death which could possibly be interpreted in Christian terms in fact is not Christian. His non-Christian thinking even about the problem of death does not really create conflict with the remaining Christian elements that are a part of him for historical reasons. He need not express himself polemically against them at all. His avoidance of anti-Christian polemics is not merely fear of the censor. He develops his own basic convictions simply, guided by antiquity, as if those quite different observations did not even exist.[245]

One does not find the slightest trace in the *Essais* to indicate that Montaigne saw death as a consequence of guilt. For him, its monstrousness has its own weight. Death and the life that strives against it are seen as the fundamental antinomy of existence and as an order that can be derived neither metaphysically nor historically. Montaigne knows nothing of the powerful spiritual tension between defamation and glorification, between abnormality and death's function in the history of God's saving grace. He does not see mortality as a warning of man's divided essence, namely, that he is infinitely contemptible as long as he is temporal, infinitely valuable if he is part of what is eternal.[246] For him, too, the *memento mori* is of extreme urgency. But not to weave something eternal into what is temporal, rather, to bring the factuality of what is human to view, namely his association with death, so that he can endure this in a true state of being with himself. The proportions taken on in the course of an individual's life should not be violently shifted in death. For the proportions in life are secretly shaped by the death that is inherent in life, and thus they are more valid than a transformation one attempts in the hour of death.

Furthermore, he has no idea of immortality, either in the Platonic or the Christian sense. The passages in which he speaks of such an idea are the same few in which one can detect an anti-Christian sharpness. Even the classical myths of immortality are a matter of such indifference to him that he only treats them doxographically, as elements in his panorama of speculative delusions of man who is not conscious of knowledge (II, 12, 386–387 and 411). The anti-Christian barb concealed in this is directed against the ideas of reward and punishment. Montaigne has a strong aversion to balancing the accounts of life, short as it is, in terms of profit and loss, heaven and hell. Here is but one quotation from the many passages in the *Essais* in which the idea of immortality is evaded: death is "a quarter hour of suffering, without consequence, without harm, [thus] does not deserve any particular precepts" (III, 12, 804 C). Any eschatological fear of death is lacking, even to the extent of brooding uncertainty, which about a century later Hamlet with combined doubt and fear takes into account as the dread of something after death (*Hamlet* III, 1, v. 78). Montaigne's inferential skepticism is silent here: it does not keep open the possibility that man could be immortal, although it otherwise keeps so many possibilities open, even the miracle.

The basis of this is probably deep within his experience of himself. He does not separate his self from its randomness and transitoriness, but rather it is precisely in these that he experiences its reality. He knows himself to be all the more human, the more aware he is of his transitory nature. He does not experience transitoriness as a defect, but rather as a value, not as danger, but as security. Like his view of the world as a whole, his conception of himself is marked by his taking the risk of discovering the suitability of what is mortal. Thus in him one does not even find that kind of personal instinct for immortality which is possible outside of a religious unambiguity. The "gushing out of spiritual acts over life which is always ready to die" which is felt by every highly organized man in his case does not lead to an "intuitive idea of a continuation of life."[247] He captures it in the honesty of his recognition that everything about him is so transitory, so random, and in the enjoyment of the novelty of this courage to recognize as well as fulfill his own mortality. Goethe's well-known sentence on nature's obligation "to indicate another form of existence to me when the present one can no longer tolerate my spirit" (to Eckermann, 2-4-1829) is completely inconceivable in the *Essais*. And for the same reason Montaigne excludes the idea of immortality in an afterlife, he completely lacks the classical idea of an afterlife in this world through fame, which was also widespread during the Renaissance.

All statements on the subject in the *Essais* lead to the same result: death means to no longer be: "Once out of being, we have no communication with what is" (I, 3, 10 C). In dying, "the leap is not so cruel from a painful life to no life" (I, 20, 63 B), "passing into exemption from all torment" (I, 20, 64 C[248]). The classical comparison with sleep which Montaigne also used freely signifies with its analogy of unconsciousness the extinguishing of the self. The passage quoted above from III, 9 (742 B) is even stronger in its expression of no longer being. In antiquity, only Lucretius was this decisive. Montaigne shifts death (in accordance with its factual quality) absolutely into nothingness—but only in order to become all the more familiar with man's view of his future nothingness. Paul Valéry's sentence "Death speaks to us in a deep voice only to say nothing" (*Mauvaises Pensées*) would also be possible in the *Essais*, along with the honesty required to say it. In the Romance literatures, perhaps only Leopardi's poetry and *Operette morali* define death as no

longer being with similar decisiveness. The harsher, the more remote
Montaigne makes the factual character of death, the more he discovers
in himself nature's reconciliation with it, which precedes will and ratio-
nality. To completely expose and look clearly at both of them, the harsh,
alien matter of no longer being and the state of being equipped for it
which comes from the protection of nature, he must avoid Christian
interpretations. For these would have denied him his experience of the
full reality of death and his readiness, as bold as it is gentle, to find
shelter within annihilating death, just as the living person finds shelter
in the home of sleep.

If one wants to weigh all this from the viewpoint of the Christian
world, one could say this: Montaigne intends to interpret and withstand
death from a pre-Christian, that is, classical, understanding of death as
an order—but at the same time from the Christian definition of man as
a temperamental being—but without the devices of grace and faith
which are part of the Christian religion. He takes death as seriously as a
Christian, though for different reasons, but he denies himself Christian
comfort. He, the average and random man who shares in the "the bane
of our condition" (II, 12, 380 C) wants to remain alone and subject
himself, alone, to his own nature and his own death, finding the latter in
the former, the former in the latter, and in both the harmony they have
with one another—and to have his own distance from Christianity. He
remains silent about this last element. But it is the most informative one,
at least from an historical standpoint.

10.   THE REFLECTED FORGETTING OF DEATH

The description of the plague deaths in III, 12, which was mentioned
in the beginning, illuminates the conclusions to which Montaigne comes
in the "naturalization" of death. How gripped he is by the deaths of
these simple people, this obedience in the face of an emergency which,
to them, as something universal, has also become a matter of indifference! When he sees them parting with life without tears and without
astonishment, digging their own graves, when he sees some who are
even afraid death may overlook them and leave them in terrible loneliness, and how they arrive at a place where one would otherwise arrive
only with a calculated ethic (*resolution estudiée et consultée*), but do so
without any "philosophical" effort and with an animalistic obedience,
when he sees all this, the whole, constructed *commentatio mortis* becomes questionable, for it accomplishes no more than *cette sotte*

simplicité of the uneducated, even the animals (802 B). One can see in creatures such as these what we have come to with all our knowledge: "We have abandoned Nature and we want to teach her her lesson, she who used to guide us so happily and so surely" (803 B). Is it not better, then, to do as those creatures do, to go back to nature and forget death, to entrust our endurance of it to the hour of death itself, in which nature will point the way? When philosophy advises us to practice any ills that could befall us in advance, it is better to say: "On the contrary, the easiest and most natural thing would be to unburden even our thoughts of them" (803 B). To withstand death's gaze (that is, in the full clarity of consciousness), one needs a stability that can be acquired only through long and hard effort, in Seneca's words—but Seneca added *nisi a sapiente* (*ep*. 30). And this is not in our text. Montaigne does not weigh things according to "wise men" of the exceptional sort. The man of the middle position, he himself, is his concern. And that man should not build an ethical structure. Rather, and this sentence is the key: "If you don't know how to die, don't worry; Nature will tell you what to do on the spot, fully and adequately. She will do this job perfectly for you; don't bother your head about it" (804 B). Cicero's sentence *Tota philosophorum vita commentatio mortis est* (*Tusc*. I, 30), the source of the title of I, 20, is quoted again here, but with ironic intent (804 C). Only the "scholars" (*docteurs*) find a meal tastes worse when they think of death. And then, again with an eye to the simplicity of animals and the common people, he writes: "For Heaven's sake, if that is so, let us henceforth hold a school of stupidity" (805 B).

This was presumably written around 1588 and it sounds quite different from Essay I, 20, which is about ten years older. Then there were the *memento mori*, sharp words against the "brutish stupidity, brutish nonchalance" (58–59 A), but now there is an invoking of common and animalistic forgetfulness about death, a praise of, and desire to imitate, the "stupidity" and "profound nonchalance" (805 B), and then the key term expressing the simple patience with death: "school of stupidity." One finds reference often in classical literature, particularly in those Montaigne used, such as Cicero (*De senectute* 75) and Seneca (*ep*. 24, 36, etc.), to the intellectually weak, to children, farm girls, and their death. It is possible that here he owes something to literary stimuli, particularly in the early stage, for example, when on one occasion he uses the cheerfulness of the "poor beggar at my door" as a model (I, 39, 179 A). But at the later stages, this motif fits in so well with the parts of his attitude on death which were developed in the intervening period that here, too, as is often the case in the *Essais*, the possible literary influence is at best a symptom of his attitude (which repeats compatible things found in books as confirmation of its own position), rather than this literature being a cause of his attitude. Anyway, this reference to simple people in classical literature is meant as follows: if even these people can do what you can, philosopher, then you should be ashamed of your imperfection and strive to be more of a philosopher.

With this step into forgetfulness about death, Montaigne completes his "naturalization" of death. Nature itself informs its miseducated creatures that they can tolerate death when it comes, even without having practiced it in an artificial anticipation. After all, it is within nature itself, nature gives birth to it along with every living thing. Nature's a priori understanding with death is so complete that she herself teaches one to forget death until it arrives. But then, too, it does not destroy her structure. Death's arrival is no less in the order of things than is its being forgotten before it arrives. The meditations on death in Essay III, 12 continue what Montaigne discussed in II, 6: his personal experience of the factual proximity of death in the accident in which he perceived that death, if only we withhold our own will, will be died with reconciliation. He confirms this experience with his observation of the victims of the plague. He expands it by adding the motif of forgetting, and relinquishes "philosophical" *commentatio mortis*. And now he also confirms and expands his readiness to surrender to a level in which the antagonists of life and death are friends and come to terms with one another without the intervention of his will and his reason.

The philosophical quality of this relationship with death is not lessened by the fact that Montaigne speaks of ignorance, forgetting, nature. For this is a highly reflective forgetting, a highly reflected naturalness. That is different from primitive dullness. And there is some preliminary consideration of death even in this last stage of the *Essais*. But it is a consideration that considers and follows along with the way of nature, which has an understanding with death from the beginning, namely, a forgetfulness of the future act of death. This forgetting is the result of a knowledge of death's ordering character, and it is a result of that inwardness which is on familiar terms with death. Reasonable knowledge and internalized familiarity are so solid that death can be trusted in forgetting it.

In these reflections, Montaigne again takes up something he did once before (namely in the major section on animals in II, 12, 336 ff.): leveling man and animal. Here, too, in his view, the animal is something quite different from a creature artificially defined simply by subtracting all

human elements. Man and animal are born together and sheltered together in the lap of nature. Montaigne allies that which distinguishes man
according to the classical terms *humanitas* and *dignitas,* namely his reason, and particularly, the capacity to anticipate death, with the peace of
the animal who does not "know" death and yet is capable of it because it
has death before it only in the sense of the event when it occurs, but it
already has death behind it in the sense that the structure of life as
determined by nature is tied to death, thus it can "forget" it. Man and
death are thus also understood not as two alien elements that collide, but
rather as a part of each other, wedded from the beginning before any
factual, external encounter occurs. Yet the forgetting of death does not
decrease its importance or the fears that it engenders in the one dying
when it approaches, or the fears that are associated intrinsically with its
essence. Forgetting silently keeps the "courage of fear before death"
ready, but does not call upon the fear prematurely. The one who forgets is
at peace in his confidence that nature, which has an understanding with
death, will help him withstand the fear when he is dying. He can wait for
death as he waits for a fruit to ripen on its own; while waiting, the hands
that will pick the fruit will also ripen on their own.

Montaigne concludes his meditations on death in III, 12 with a paraphrase of the speeches of defense of Socrates from Plato's *Apology.* The
paraphrase is quite loose, assembled from randomly arranged and abbreviated or expanded sections of the original (805–807 B/C). If one compares it with the paraphrase from Tacitus' *Annals* on Seneca's death (II,
36) the difference is strikingly obvious. There we find heroic, pathetic
action and gesture, here contemplative speech, calm bearing of the one
destined to die; there, aesthetic distance, here, personal involvement by
the narrator. Montaigne sees Socrates as "interpreter of natural simplicity" and his speech as a guarantee of the possibility of that natural,
obedient death. It is characteristic in this that he considerably intensified
the agnosticism of Socrates which was found in Plato's text (whether
death was total annihilation or a transition into an afterlife of the soul).
In Plato, that is (see *Apology* 40b/e), one reads: it could after all be the
case that the soul does not die. One does not find this in Montaigne. He
does not want to know what becomes of us after death. It is a matter of
such indifference to him that farther down (807 B) he briefly touches
upon the uninspired thought (probably from Lucretius, I, vv. 262–264,
and repeated frequently in the Renaissance) that death is a placemaker
for new life, and then immediately drops it again. He is not concerned
with speculation, but rather with one's behavior vis-à-vis death—here,

the consideration of the *si nonchallante et molle consideration de la mort* displayed by Socrates (807 B). This rivets him all the more because it is modeled by his favorite, Socrates, this wise man who is like all of us, and who has the courage for death "not because his soul is immortal but because he is mortal" (811 C). And then we find the central sentence that contains the comment that we find as a motto: "In an unstudied and artless boldness and a childlike assurance, it represents the pure and primary impression and ignorance of Nature" (807 B/C). Montaigne knows "unartificial boldness" and the difficulty of behaving thus. It is "unartificial" because it dispenses with the tricks of the customary philosophy of death. But this is also why it is difficult. For as the *Essais* have stated repeatedly, "art" is always closer at hand than nature, which requires the effort of passivity to allow nature to follow its course: "art cannot reach it" (808 B). And a boldness is the "unartificial" behavior because it dares to be as nature is, and because it makes all of man's great pride, will, and reason superfluous. The paraphrase and analysis of Socrates' speech reflects Montaigne's own basic attitude toward death and his own "artless boldness."

11.   DEATH AND WISDOM

The last Essay of the third book also speaks of death here and there. But nothing thematically new is discussed. Obedience, however, has become several degrees calmer and more cheerful. The author speaks of illness and old age, messengers of death with which he converses as he does with death. He drafts a speech of his spirit to himself. One is reminded of Nature's speech in I, 20, in which the objective knowledge of death is spoken in its words. Now, Montaigne's completion of his turn inward into himself is expressed in the changed roles. The theme of the inherence of death in life, again detectable here (837), remains embedded in the inwardness, and in an almost lyrical atmosphere. The earlier words of comfort spoken by an outside, personified nature have become an internal dialogue of the self. Montaigne is now in nature. He avoids the speculative problem of its essence even more than he did earlier. He feels this essence ("I shall know it well enough when I feel it," 821 C) and need no longer personify it, to make it a simile for a concept. The artistic device of the internal dialogue with the self symbolizes the fact that he, immersed in nature as he is, himself possesses the comfort he needs. He has at his disposal the forces and counterforces of existence and obediently lingers within them.

The most beautiful passage can be found where he is thanking his illness: "Consider how artfully and gently the stone weans you from life and detaches you from the world; not forcing you with tyrannical subjections . . . but by warnings and instructions repeated at intervals, intermingled with long pauses for rest, as if to give you a chance to meditate and repeat its lesson at your leisure. To give you a chance to form a sound judgment and make up your mind to it like a brave man, it sets before you the lot that is your condition, the good and also the bad . . . If you do not embrace death, at least you shake hands with it once a month" (837 B). The illness at the same time forms the bridge between life and death. Standing on this bridge, man sees both and blesses both. It is good when the pains of the illness disappear, but it is also good when they are there. Because—and one cannot miss this knowledge of Montaigne's—in the pain, perfect joy is born: to be initiated into the totality of the human essence.

He is also grateful to old age, and again, it is his form of old age: "God is merciful to those whose life he takes away bit by bit; that is the only benefit of old age. The last death will be all the less complete and painful . . . Here is a tooth that has just fallen out, without pain, without effort . . . Both that part of my being and several others are already dead, others half dead . . . Thus do I melt and slip away from myself. How stupid it would be of my mind if it were to feel the last leap of this decline, which is already so far advanced, as acutely as if it were the whole fall" (845 B). What appeared threatening, illness and old age, is really, if one only allows them control, the healing force against that which is the fundamental threat: death. The gentle inclination toward death of old age which Montaigne expresses here has an extraordinary similarity to the last pages of Cicero's De senectute, though, again, admittedly, without its speculative Platonizing tendencies. He also supports this similarity subsequently with literature, through several quotations from it. We will not go any further into this. For these quotations do not express any sort of dependent imitation, nor do they externalize in something merely literary something that has long been in the process of inner growth. For all of Montaigne's courage in awaiting death as the absolute state of no longer being, he does not make it into something meaningless. Death's coming is for him the last of the tides in the organic cycle of his life, from which, "having had enough of his days" (plenus dierum: Genesis XXV, 8), he is ready to part, blessed and not beaten by death.

The last words spoken in the Essais on death complete the consent in life and death, without the one being scorned by the other. For, indeed, both are one. The more authentically a life is lived (and this means: the more prepared for what is endurable as well as what is transitory), the more capable it is of dying: "I am reconciling myself to the thought of losing it [life] without regret, but as something that by its nature must be lost; not as something annoying and troublesome.[249] Then too, not to dislike dying is properly becoming only to those who like living" (853 B/C). Love of life and love of death are joined. In such a dual love for the antagonists, which cannot be denied in their opposition, Montaigne brings his human essence into balance. Furthermore, the closer a life knows it is to death, the more intense it becomes. It gains in depth and fullness what it loses in time: "Especially at this moment, when I perceive that mine is so brief in time, I try to increase it in weight; I try to arrest the speed of its flight by the speed with which I grasp it . . . The shorter my possession of life, the deeper and fuller I must make it" (853 B/C).

Directly following this we then find the happiest sentences of wisdom in the *Essais,* filled with transfigured peace—also arising directly from the last thoughts on death, thoughts that encompass all the earlier ones: ". . . wherever she [my soul] casts her eyes, the sky is calm around her: no desire, no fear or doubt to disturb the air for her, no difficulty, past, present, or future, over which her imagination may not pass without hurt" (854 B/C). Thus it was death—we must state this one more time—which permeated this man, Montaigne, most intimately, and brought him to himself.

12.   MONTAIGNE'S DEATH

The question of how Montaigne died, and whether he had the death he wished for himself, remains. Most of what we know of his death comes from the letters of two friends: Estienne Pasquier and Pierre de Brach.[250] Neither was present in his hour of death. The sources of their reports are unknown. Thus the question of what in these was legend or adjustment and what was truth must remain open.

Pasquier relates that three days before his death, Montaigne suffered a paralysis of his speech organs, but remained fully conscious. He expressed in writing his wish to take leave of neighboring nobility. After they had arrived, he had a mass said in his room. As the priest was celebrating the consecration, he folded his hands, attempted to raise himself, and expired.

Pierre de Brach expresses himself more generally: Montaigne died cheerfully. He only adds one, but a valuable, element, namely, that the dying man complained that no one remained with him to whom he could communicate the last thoughts of his soul (*les dernières conceptions de son âme*). The letter then diverges into relating an earlier crisis of illness (probably 1588) in which Montaigne, given up for dead by the doctors, and himself convinced of his imminent death, had then already demonstrated strength of spirit and peace.

It is noteworthy that only Pasquier speaks of Montaigne's Christian death. Was this so obvious that the other friend could simply skip it in his report, or was it merely a legend, or did it not fit into the classical stylization that de Brach gave to Montaigne's death, as did Lipsius?[251] We don't know. Yet it is conceivable that he had a Christian death. It would have been a last act of his conservative, religious orientation, something never denied, which, for example, allowed him to state on one occasion: "At the very beginning of my fevers and the maladies that lay me low, while still whole and in the neighborhood of health, I reconcile myself with God by the last Christian offices" (III, 9, 751 B). This Christian death would only "contradict" the non-Christian views of death in the *Essais* to the same degree as his conservatism as a whole "contradicts" his frank thinking—namely, they are only contradictory in a very well thought out and intentional and tolerable sense which he derives from his adaptation to human inadequacy and its necessary separation of theory and practice. Thus his Christian death really does not contradict his fundamental attitude toward death. Unless one goes beyond what can be known and sees in this a sign that death, about which he thought in so un-Christian a manner, called him in that holiest moment of the Communion, when the bread became the body of Christ? But who can decide this?

De Brach's story is just as possible. It is curiously like a confirmation of the wish expressed often in the *Essais*—conceived not without remembrance of antiquity—to have a friend present when he is dying, someone to whom the one departing can leave his last insights. The wish was unfulfilled. We know nothing of what was going on within Montaigne at the end.

Both reports agree in one respect, however. Montaigne died in an orderly, manly, obedient manner. His own process of dying did not reverse anything that he wrote about death in the *Essais*.

CHAPTER VII

Montaigne's Wisdom

Laetus in praesens animus . . .

Horace [Carm. *II, 16*]

1. WISDOM AND KNOWLEDGE

Most of what one may call Montaigne's wisdom has already been touched upon in our discussion so far, however, only from an approach that made it seem to be only a byproduct of his study of man and his understanding of himself. But now his wisdom will be summarized and described for its own sake. To do this, we need do no more than to follow to the end those threads with which we began earlier, then interrupted, and to group them insofar as this is possible in view of the casualness with which Montaigne expresses his wisdom.

Montaigne's wisdom is fragmentary and gets by with little. It repeats what has been said before with the necessity of a natural drawing of breath. It does not merely think, but rather fills what is thought with its inward involvement. In fact, it only thinks about that which is capable of evoking its inward involvement. Montaigne is concerned with intellectual self-preservation rather than a theoretical clarification of "problems." To make this increasingly secure, it requires constant new penetration of intellectual and moral situations which are always the same, but which for it are quite acute. The completion of this act which brings the world and the self into harmony is called wisdom. It is something quite different from progressive investigative thinking. What it considers worthy of thought takes on a substance that is not lessened by the incompleteness of the factual treatment of the particular topic. This substance is often nearly impossible to comprehend, particularly when it is present only as a fluctuation in tone of a thought that may be quite banal, as an excess that originates in levels other than the intellectual one.

For Montaigne, too, wisdom is more than the sum of all objective knowledge. He does not make it dependent upon the possession of doctrines of being originating in natural philosophy or theology, or the possession of individual factual bits of knowledge. That sentence of Cicero's, so often repeated, in which he defines wisdom (*sapientia*) as *divinarum humanarumque scientia,* does not apply to Montaigne.[252] He sees in wisdom an order of inwardness, a healing, which is superior to factual knowledge and the knowledge of being, as was true also of some late hellenistic thinkers, such as Petrarch or Erasmus, and some individual Christian mystics. Montaigne separates *scientia* and *sapientia.* Despite the unmistakably fideistic and theological origin of his critique of knowledge, he presents the general category of the wisdom of salvation in secular form. Wisdom to him is the path to the health of his natural essence. And with respect to the totality of being, wisdom mistrusts knowledge as a premature closing off of the transcendent content of things, and as an intervention that interrupts the trusting contact between self and "nature," a contact that can be perceived, but that is difficult to interpret. Skepticism and ignorance are the elementary conditions of his wisdom. They open up areas that are more evident to intuition than to reason, and which one thus cannot teach, but can only attempt to communicate in their subjective accessibility, or which one can sometimes only circle around in a monologue.

Thus in the later Essays, the last traces of impersonal types of theories of cosmology and nature philosophy disappear and make way for a few very simple concepts such as "nature," "world order," and "fortuna." For this is where Montaigne's manner of conducting his life finds adequate support. He withdraws completely into his process of becoming aware of himself, and the sense of coming to terms with world, nature, life, and destiny which comes to him along with this awareness. He is as a whole continuously face-to-face with the whole and within the whole. Thus his wisdom is also more than a tactical prudence about life, despite the degree to which he can be concerned with this, as we have seen. A comment by Jacob Burckhardt (from the beginning of the *Weltgeschichtlichen Betrachtungen*) applies to him: "We hope through experience not so much to become clever (for another time) as to become wise (forever)." As one of the living, he serves all sides of the living. But from individual experiences, he rises to an encompassing familiarity that knows, as if it always had, all joys and pains, all dissonance and harmony, events that fail and those that succeed, because this familiarity has been initiated into a structure of existence in which the contradictory parts require one another to preserve the whole. This wisdom renounces any activist will that believes in the capacity of the whole as well as the individual element to be improved. It loves to receive, not to command—whether the command is an action or a claim of speculative reason which overpowers the flow of things. It indeed has a feeling for the rare, brilliant moments of life. But it knows that these are exceptions, and it does not expect lasting satisfaction from the major events arising from these, but rather expects this from the small painless moments when the shoe does not pinch, and when sleep was satisfying. It settles in with what is closest at hand, because this is what endures, and it gains a foothold in the lowlands where no storms rage and no lightning strikes. This is like a return of the spirit of Horace.

2. MONTAIGNE'S WISDOM

Montaigne admittedly did not like to call himself wise. For the term *wisdom* was for him too strongly encumbered with the idea of a voluntary, ascetic ethic. We have seen that he wants nothing more to do with this. The "philosophical scorn for transitory and mundane things" arouses his contempt (III, 9, 728 B) and displeases him as a lack of obedience to the contradictory human essence. He is unable to treat mere effort as proof of greatness. "The world . . . thinks nothing beneficial that is not painful; it is suspicious of ease," he writes critically (III, 13, 832 B). To avoid being confused with this type of glorious and dramatic wisdom, he calls himself foolish, small, unwise. When he does, very rarely, speak of his *sagesse*, it is with an ironic use of the word, or with a reevaluation of the old meaning. For example: "I might be considered wise with the kind of wisdom I consider folly" (III, 5, 644 C). His own essence of wisdom prefers to express itself from case to case, rather than to claim an idea that would bring it into the unpleasant company of the demanding ethicists dedicated to overcoming situations. From his perspective, relaxation, not tension, leads man to maturity. The unforgettable passage that he inserted into his education Essay later, and in which he speaks of cheerful philosophy, is completely guided by this conviction (I, 26, 119–120 C; see also earlier discussion). It objects to the common idea, going back to Hesiod (*Works and Days*, v. 289 ff.), that virtue is a mountain before which the gods have placed the sweat of effort. Quite the contrary, it is a blooming plain from the beginning on, and it broadens into a gentle, easily walked elevation. The image of the mountain (an original symbol of Christian ethics as well) emerges repeatedly in the *Essais,* only to be rejected: "Greatness of soul is not so much pressing upward and forward as knowing how to set oneself in order and circumscribe oneself. It . . . shows its elevation by liking moderate things better than eminent ones" we find at a late period (III, 13, 852 C).

We find a nice witness to the liberating effect of this "finer moral" of relaxation which "does not float in the ether of lofty maxims" in Herder, who on one occasion, writing with an eye to Montaigne and his kindred spirits in later periods (Sterne, Swift, etc.), wrote: "For our northern, pressured, gloomy life, all writings are beneficial in which our soul is relaxed, widened, and made gentler. It is the condition of a day-laborer to constantly spur himself, to drive others, and to feel pressured by them . . . Human nature is a victim of restless effort; during rest, during the acting out of informal exercises, it acquires merriness and strength. Unrelenting zealousness seldom leads anywhere else but to fanaticism and exaggeration, which cannot be corrected by anything but by a depiction of what it is, by a light, joyous imitation of its own character" (*Briefe zur Beförderung der Humanität,* fourth collection, 51). These sentences, even though they do not refer to Montaigne alone, but rather refer generally to the reawakening of the classical art of the *otium* at the beginning of German Classicism, contain the heart of Montaigne's culture of life.[253]

3.   THE CLASSICAL MODEL

The concept of moderation is a part of this. This concept is the moment in his wisdom which connects him most strongly with classical moral philosophy, where the rule of μεσότης (*moderatio*) represents the unifying bond between the most varied instructional trends. He could find it in all the eclectics whom he preferred. He had several sayings concerning this put on the beams of his library, even some of biblical origin. Even in a late period, he wrote: "Shall I, who in all matters have so worshipped the golden mean ἄριστον μέτρον of the past, and have taken the moderate measure as the most perfect . . ." (III, 13, 845 C). He dedicated an entire Essay to *modération* (I, 30) and in it, he admitted to his distaste for excessive morality. The concept of moderation destines his wisdom to spiritualize what is close at hand, rather than to strive for the steep heights. It constitutes the gentle monitor of a will to live which is open to all contrasts, but can only safely abandon itself to them when a balance between the contrasts has been achieved. Even sensual desire can be enjoyed under this prerequisite: "Philosophy does not strive against natural pleasures, provided that measure goes with them; she preaches moderation in them, not flight" (III, 5, 681 B/C). Practicing moderation protects one against dehumanization in an ideal unconditionalness as well as in common vice, brings body and soul back into the innocence of nature, which itself exercises moderation in everything, and within its broad boundaries, free, many-sided humanity flourishes. Thus through the marriage of fullness and moderation, once again in the *Essais* we find what Cicero once called the *magnitudo animi multa humanitate temperata* (*Ad. Att.* IV, 6: "the humanly relaxed height of the spirit"), which meanwhile had again blossomed in the Italian courts, arising from the same source of the Roman culture of life. Montaigne's wisdom has become classical for France, a preshaping of all later forms of wisdom to be found there. Even today, this wisdom is so strongly connected with the concept of moderation that in the term *sagesse* the French understand exercising moderation. Valéry defines it thus: "Wisdom is knowledge in so far as it moderates all things, itself in particular" (*Mauvaises Pensées*).

4. AFFIRMED DELUSION OF LIFE

Despite Montaigne's strong awareness of the fragility of being human, his concept of life is not gloomy. Pessimistic authors displease him, as we have seen. He appropriates Seneca's idea (*ep.* 99) that life is neither a good nor an evil, but only becomes the one or the other depending upon what we make of it (I, 20, 65 C). When something undeniably torturous occurs, he does not gloss over it. He takes it on and gets through it, trusting that it has its logic, simply because it exists. Escape, anger, and vituperation would only be another kind of dependence upon an evil; the path to freedom leads through obedience, which sees how healing comes from something threatening, and how an evil can make room for a good that would otherwise be unable to unfold. Montaigne never generalizes an individual evil to see it as an embodiment of the totality of life, but rather, he limits it to the cases in which it arises. In the instances in which the *Essais* rise to a value judgment about life (which seldom occurs), they are more likely to see it as worthy of a smile because of its triviality than deserving of lamentation because of its misery. In his Essay from the middle period (I, 50) Montaigne takes up the usual contrast of the laughing Democritus and the weeping Heraclitus[254] to declare his sympathy for the former. There he writes, for example: "The things we laugh at we consider worthless. I do not think there is as much unhappiness in us as vanity, nor as much malice as stupidity" (221 A). Man is not worth being mourned. This is stated here with a degree of sharpness which will be moderated later. The evaluation of human essence as a triviality (*vanité, inanité*) remains; but it no longer derives a conclusion of worthlessness from this triviality. Since good fortune and misfortune are not perceived as divisive opposites, but rather as complementary elements of a hidden harmony, no tragic tone emerges in the *Essais*. Nor, admittedly, does an enthusiastic one. Instead of these extremes, what prevails is the conciliatory idea, though it also casts a shadow, of how delusional everything is.

The long Essay III, 9 has the title "Of Vanity." It treats all of its subjects (household management, state, travel, etc.) expressly or secretly under this key word, a word which like delusion means both the objective insignificance of the matters themselves as well as the overvaluing of them, and furthermore means illusion. All terms that Montaigne uses liberally precisely in this Essay to characterize the course of life and humanity (*diversité, varieté, branler*) seem to converge in the generic term *vanité*. But the significant aspect in this Essay is the decision to understand what is delusional as what is possible in life. Even if everything is trivial, that is, fickle, there is still within this triviality the chance of pleasure: "I apply myself to make use of vanity itself, and asininity, if it brings me any pleasure" (762 B). Should we become obstinate because what tickles us is delusion? Rather, "Our humors are not too vain if they are pleasant; whatever they may be, if they give constant contentment to a man capable of common sense, I would not have the heart to pity him" (763 B). The world is constructed such that even the most terrible delusion copes with it. Also: delusion that knows itself and its delusional objects has understood itself as a condition of existing. The others are, so the reasoning goes, like I myself, "full of inanity and nonsense. Get rid of it I cannot without getting rid of myself. We are all steeped in it . . . but those who are aware of it are a little better off" (766 B). Montaigne pushes out with the highest degree of reflection into the totality of the human essence, which is so indefinable and astonishing that it equals senselessness. But the same reflection works its way back to the point where it can again lead into naivety. It completes the circle and itself heals the break it caused in the life drive through knowledge of what is delusional. The wise man rouses himself to carry out what he has seen through in his delusional state. He suspects in the pleasure of subjective delusion the compensatory gift for the objective triviality of which the stuff of life consists. There is an echo of the proverbs of *Ecclesiastes* in trains of thought such as these. *Per omnia vanitas* was inscribed on one of the ceiling beams of Montaigne's library. The title of Essay III, 9 and his first sentences are modeled on *Ecclesiastes*. The change from the knowledge of delusion to hedonistic decision is completely in the spirit of that Old Testament author (cf. *Eccl.* II, 24; III, 12 ff.; etc.), about whom Renan said: "Like all gifted pessimists, he loves life."[255] Stimuli from Epicurus and Horace may have also played a part in encouraging in Montaigne an attitude that spanned possible reasonableness and possible foolishness like two games, one of which counts for as little as the other. The knowledge of delusion teaches one to tolerate life even at the expense of bending one's intelligence before the intelligence of the wind: "But what of it? We are all wind. And even the wind, more wisely than we, loves to make a noise and move about, and is content with its own functions, without wishing for stability and solidity, qualities that do not belong to it" (III, 13, 849 C).

The wisdom of delusion was addressed before in the sixteenth century, by Erasmus. Montaigne knew him. Research has established traces in the *Essais* from the *Adagia, Apophthegmata, Colloquia,* and *Laus stultitiae.*[256] There is a fair amount of affinity in attitude between these two spirits. Like Montaigne, Erasmus also nurtured a relaxed philosophy of life which was moving away from activist bustle and turning to inwardness, a philosophy that clung to the simplest needs of the *homo humanus,* unheroic, unhistrionic, tolerant of the infirmities of humanness, open to the colorful variety of individuals and opinions, concerned about closing the gap between the scholarly and the unscholarly which had been torn open by humanism, and convinced that the right to grasp was close at hand in our own nature, of which he had a semi-Pelagian idea that already deviated considerably from the dogma of original sin. The fact that these general features of Erasmus' (we are leaving out the philological and theological ones) recur in Montaigne is connected in part with the fact that he, too, as all of the French sixteenth century, felt the aftereffects of the processes that originally made an Erasmus possible. Namely, in the fifteenth century there was the disintegration of the distinctions in concept of late scholasticism in favor of an education that first, even for Erasmus, is called *pietas,* and in Montaigne is given the secular, humanistic term *culture de l'âme.* Thus we need not be dealing here with an influence by Erasmus on Montaigne. What we have is the similarity in a similar intellectual situation from which both men turned to the same classical sources, namely, hellenistic-Roman moral philosophy. However, the similarity becomes astoundingly great in the theme dealt with here. It builds a bridge from the *vanitas* idea of the *Essais* to Erasmus' boldest work, *Laus stultitiae*.

In this mischievous, insightful, cryptic little work, fired by the spirit of Lucian, there emerged in Erasmus an understanding of the absurdities, the two-sided qualities and entanglements of the structure of life, an understanding that before this was only a muted association. It pulls all content, even its author's own, into a turmoil of derision, irony, and also humor, like the "spring after a long winter" (chapter 1).[257] Folly, which here makes its greatest speech, is an ambiguous creature. It sometimes appears as a dangerous, life-destroying madness. Under this symbol, the writing becomes a satire against the corruption of the Church, monastic life, and the princes. But folly also appears, and this predominates, as a delusion that serves to preserve life. And this brings us to the theme that is the reason for our discussion of Erasmus here. With a sharp eye for life's trivial capability (chapter 18) he looks over the turmoil of the world. Man, we read in one example, has his physical origin in the most comical thing, the frenzy of breeding, and he is destined to be objectively unfortunate: *calamitatibus humana vita obnoxia* (chapter 31). But the same nature placed the means of salvation at his disposal, namely, the illusionary transfiguration. What devalues man, namely delusion, at the same time heals him. *At quanto felicius, sic errare . . .* (chapter 20), and: *Non falli, miserrimum est* (chapter 45). Thus the work indulges in ridicule of the ideal construction of the wise man in the stoic mode, for the only man who is real is the one who rides the waves of his natural transitoriness. A flexible wisdom oriented toward what is two-sided and farcical in the turmoil of life looks after this man. This wisdom knows that man can be great from time to time, but it also knows that even the most noble deed, the purest feeling, does not come into being without the cunning of nature which blinds him with illusion. Even religious "folly," the *stultitia crucis*, appears to it to be of the same cloth as the usual delusion of euphoria, dream, and forgetfulness (chapters 65–66). Reinterpreting Plato's cave allegory, Erasmus no longer makes a distinction between those who climb to the light and those who remain in the cave, for all that matters for both is that, regardless of whether they are blind or dazzled, they feel fortunate (chapters 45 and 67). These are bold paradoxes. They are only apparently softened by the assurance in his title and foreword that the author intends to write nothing more than a joke, an exercise in style (*declamatio*) for his entertainment and that of his friends. In the twilight lying over the *Laus stultitiae,* one can never quite discover how seriously Erasmus took his paradoxes himself. It is enough, though, that they have been stated, and that they have indicated the confused nature of humanity with a boldness that is unique up till then in the literature of postantiquity.

When Montaigne treats the *vanitas* idea in the manner we have seen, it seems like the resolute development of what Erasmus casually called notion and idea. (Similar developments appear in Rabelais and Cervantes.) The two men, Erasmus and Montaigne, have in common the fact that they compensate for the concept of the objective triviality of the totality of life with the escape of subjective delusion. They both have in common the fact that they replace ethical unconditionalness with a humanity of modest averageness, and they shelter man in a wisdom that lies beyond the inconsequential contrast of reason and irrationality. Both also have in common the fact that they praise illusion as the mover of the human soul which brings happiness, regardless of whether the illusion manifests itself in the simplicity of fools or in the vision of believers, or in the poets' process of getting outside of themselves. Both authors have in common a discontinuation of arrogance toward animals and the desire to become as they are: *ad brutorum ingenium stultitiamque quam proxime accedere* (*Laus,* chapter 35: "to approach the foolishness of the animals as closely as possible")—"that our sapience learns from the very animals" (III, 12, 803 B). Both have in common their legacy from *Ecclesiastes,* and from Horace, whose much-cited verse *misce stultitiam consiliis brevem* (*Carm.* IV, 12, 27: "Mingle a dash of folly with your wisdom") appears both in the *Laus stultitiae* (chapter 62) and in the *Essais* (III, 5, 640).[258] Finally, both have in common the fact that they do not come to tragic or nihilistic conclusions as a result of their knowledge of what is trivial. They are able to preserve a free, undamaged cheerfulness that tends more toward humor than satire, as if it were a pleasure to be surrounded by triviality. This is perhaps the most commanding wisdom of these spirits of the late Renaissance.

5.   THE ANTINOMICAL STRUCTURE

We have already had frequent opportunity to speak of the fact that Montaigne leaves the striving for correction out of his concept of man and life, as well as his conception of himself. For: "The world is ill fitted to cure itself" (III, 9, 731 B). Inadequacies in which constructive and idealistic minds saw interruptions of a preestablished, restorable order he understands as unalterable consequences of an order in which good and bad are necessarily interlaced. Thus instead of concern for salvation or improvement, he sees a contemplative, obedient awareness of the antinomical structure. A core passage about this can be found in the sentences that he takes almost literally from Plutarch (*De tranquilitate animi,* chapter 15 in Amyot's translation), and which harmonize so organically with the leitmotifs of his thinking that they have become his own: "We must learn to endure what we cannot avoid. Our life is composed, like the harmony of the world, of contrary things, also of different tones, sweet and harsh, sharp and flat, soft and loud. If a musician liked only one kind, what would he have to say? He must know how to use them together and blend them. And so must we do with good and evil, which are consubstantial with our life. Our existence is impossible without this mixture, and one element is no less necessary for it than the other" (III, 13, 835 B). This topic of antinomies recurs in his work in numerous (usually anthropological) variations. Mainly coming to him through Plutarch (including the *Vitae*), it represents a continuation of the classical formula of the *concordia discors* which originated with Heraclitus.[259] But in Montaigne it no longer has the earlier cosmological breadth. He is not concerned with the creation of a clear metaphysical scheme. He is satisfied with the rapid reassurance of a dissonant harmony which comes by means of the concepts he found in material handed down to him which had already been derived and diluted. His glance is too shy (or too "skeptical," too "fideistic," one might say) to ask about their ontological or theological bases. What he seeks is the contact with that dissonant harmony through experiencing and viewing its everyday symptoms, and he seeks the security of a wise fundamental attitude that calmly vibrates along with the restlessness of polar tension.

Montaigne has a curious gratefulness and a pleasure in discovery in becoming aware of the antinomical law of life. In a passage in which he is speaking of the destructive civil wars of his epoch, this pleasure emerges in the following words: "So my curiosity makes me feel some satisfaction at seeing with my own eyes this notable spectacle of our public death, its symptoms and its form. And since I cannot retard it, I am glad to be destined to watch it and learn from it" (III, 12, 800 C). This pleasure of observational insight ("curiosity, seeing with my own eyes, learn from it") sound likes this in the words of another wise man:

"The disorder in question will be changed for us from confusion to an intellectual treasure. We do not want to find a subject of affliction in it, but rather a source of wealth." And: "Our contemplation is not only a right and a duty, but also a noble need, it is our freedom in the consciousness that we have of our boundless universal interdependence and the flow of necessities." And: "Instead of happiness, the goal of any good mind is knowledge. Not by indifference to a misery that can just as well fall upon us, but rather because we realize the blindess of our desires" (Jacob Burckhardt).[260]

Someone who, like Montaigne, has insight resonating in the antinomical law of life, and thus no longer attributes any particular importance to differentiating between good fortune or misfortune will expect the negative from the beginning, and will give it the opportunity to express itself and to fade away, all with moderation. The *Essais* contain a sentence that is like the decision to also pay tribute to the dark side and what is evil in existence: "In truth, and I am not afraid to confess it, I would easily carry, in case of need, one candle to Saint Michael and one to the dragon . . ." (III, 1, 601 B). This is then preserved in actual practice in life when one prepares oneself to the smallest detail to cope with the passage of evil, a kind of *non resistere malo* (*Matthew* V, 39) in everyday affairs. Has a servant betrayed me? "You have to leave a little room for the dishonesty or improvidence of your servant . . . let that surplus of fortune's liberality run a little more at her mercy: the gleaner's share" (III, 9, 727 B/C). Am I uneasy about a court case concerning my vineyard? "And often it is not as bad to lose your vineyard as to go to court for it" (II, 17, 489 B). Am I irritated by household trouble? I let it rest, "There is always something that goes wrong" (III, 9, 725 B). Why be afraid of thieves? They wish me no harm, nor I them (III, 9, 742 C). Hundreds of such little words of wisdom on daily living, scattered through the *Essais,* are the small change of the gold of wisdom: a yielding approach to evil serves an order that would collapse without that evil. How many are able to hear the secret music within the dissonance of reality?

6. DOCTORAL IGNORANCE

Man's agreement with himself and with the whole is all the more likely to come about, the more his effort for objective discovery of the whole relaxes. Montaigne speaks several times of "the way of the world" and "the law of the world."[261] But these concepts remain ambiguous. They mean the social order, or the cosmic order, or both together. The only thing that is unambiguous is that they are intended to designate a whole that is replete with its own laws (in the manner of the *concordia discors*), into which the self, also a disharmonious whole that has its own laws, is inserted. And this insertion takes place in the form of a feeling contact that connects the inside of one's own being with the "order" that prevails within himself as well as external to him, in factual matters. Thus we find a sentence such as the following, which supplements what was said in the preceding chapter in discussing thoughts of death: "In this universe of things I ignorantly and negligently let myself be guided by the general law of the world. I shall know it well enough when I feel it" (III, 13, 821 C). To the degree to which skeptical restraint calls the intellectual comprehensibility of the "order" into question, it taps the inner evidence of that feeling contact that is experienced in one's own, natural and direct essence of what it is to be alive: "The knowledge of causes belongs only to Him who has the guidance of things, not to us who have only the enduring of them, and who have the perfectly full use of them according to our nature, without penetrating to their origin and essence" (III, 11, 785 C). I don't know where I am standing, but I sense that I am looked after by the place in which I have been put: this is the fundamental mood of this wisdom. Where reason can no longer find its way, obedient existence will find its way. It no longer fears ignorance, but rather uses it to completely attain its inner fullness.

Montaigne's agnosticism, as we have seen, came about through theological-fideistic and Pyrrhonic stimuli. Later on, it became a personal constituent of his wisdom, and it grew beyond the last remnants of an epistemological doctrine to which earlier he still clung. Thus it can now be expressed with great emotion, as if moved by a feeling of happiness: "Oh, what a sweet and soft and healthy pillow is ignorance and incuriosity, to rest a well-made head!" (III, 13, 822 C). But even this ignorance, which is enjoyed as a blessing, is not primary, but rather of a higher rank. It has taken the detour over the attempt at knowledge, and in the failure of the attempt, has discovered the path to wisdom. Only one who is experienced in the desire to know can achieve knowing ignorance: "The difficulties and obscurity in any science are perceived only by those who have access to it. For a man needs at least some degree of intelligence to be able to notice that he does not know; and we must push against a door to know that it is closed to us" (III, 13, 823 B). First the unsuccessful effort to find knowledge is needed before man is granted the leap down into his initial state of being natural. But this leap continues to tremble within him, and in this way it makes the contact with the "order of the world," which the animal also has, the content of reflected inwardness. Only after elevation above animal essence in the failed attempt at knowledge can the following sentence be spoken: "We must become like the animals in order to become wise, and be blinded in order to be guided" (II, 12, 363 C). Thus the wise man approaches the animals and those who are simpleminded as one who behaves as they do, and yet is more than they, because he has acquired that which they are only through dullness. He has *l'ignorance doctorale* (I, 54, 227 C), the doctoral ignorance.

We also find in Montaigne an echo of the *docta ignorantia* formula that originated with Augustine and Pseudo-Dionysius and was revived by Cusanus, Pico della Mirandola, and Bovillus (Charles de Bovelles), and which combined what the anti-Aristotelian, fideistic, philosophy-of-life tendencies, associated with the *Devotio moderna,* of the post-Middle Ages centuries strove for: a higher order of wisdom arising from the crisis in knowledge. Montaigne applies the basic principle of blessed ignorance to the concrete process of living one's life. He, too, knows the reliability of acting by instinct is threatened by the pallor of thought. Guicciardini had said pointedly, *Io ho visto molte volte, che chi non ha il giudizio molto buono giudica meglio (Ricordi* II, 155: "I have often observed that one who does not have a particularly good faculty of judgment judges best"). In the *Essais* we read: "It is likewise true that for the uses of life and for the service of public business there may be excess in the purity and perspicacity of our minds . . . These must be weighted and blunted to make them more obedient to example and practice, and thickened and obscured to relate them to this shadowy and earthy life" (II, 20, 511 B; also, III, 9, 725 C). The life order is obscure; only the fading of the theoretical intellect in an appropriate manner can respond to its mystery and its absurdity. Only in yielding to the moment can the harmony that has always existed between the prerational, internal forces and the careful, outside forces be effective.

7. OBEDIENCE

All elements of Montaigne's wisdom go back to the fundamental attitude of obedience. *Obéir, obéissance, suivre,* and similar terms are frequent in the *Essais.* Montaigne is no longer a naysayer to what is around him for the sake of "something higher." He says no to that higher thing because it disrupts the tranquility of what is around him and it disrupts the natural movement of man within himself and within the dissonant harmony of the whole. He feels happier being a creature who is guided than one who does the guiding: "I am strongly of this opinion, that it is much easier and pleasanter to follow than to guide" (I, 42, 193 A). His thinking and his manner of conducting his life are oriented toward obedience, consent, resignation. We were able to show this earlier with the example of his conservative accommodation to church, state, societal order, and customs. But this practical conservatism is only a particular application of his universal affirmation of what is randomly given, be it bad, cruel, frightening, illegal, ridiculous, or the opposite of these. Once a man has gotten through the randomness of such differences and has achieved the neutral essence, he will obtain the more profound well-being of an existence that knows itself to be secure in its openness to everything that is its lot.

Several quotations will illustrate this. They add to what was cited in the previous chapter in the discussion of a willingness for death. They combine self-confidence with a confidence in the obscure, yet helpful, "order." "Let us let things take their course: the scheme of things that takes care of fleas and moles also takes care of men who have the same patience to let themselves be governed as fleas and moles. There is no use in our shouting 'Giddap'; that will indeed make us hoarse, but not get us ahead. It is a proud and pitiless scheme. Our fear and our despair disgust it and delay it from coming to our aid, instead of inviting it to; it is obliged to let disease run its course, as well as health . . . Let us follow along, in God's name, let us follow!" (II, 37, 583 B). Or: "I readily let myself be led by the general way of the world. Happy the people . . . who let themselves roll relaxedly with the rolling of the heavens" (II, 17, 498 C). What do we know about the stars, other than suspicions, "we who have no dealings with them except obedience?" (II, 12, 330 A). And then the particularly vivid, easily remembered statement: "In short, we must live among the living, and let the river flow under the bridge, without caring, or, at the very least, without being upset by it" (III, 8, 709 C). It is one of Montaigne's fundamental perceptions that the deliberate will is more likely to drive away than attract what it wants, and conversely, that it is more likely to attract what it fears than to drive it away. As castle lord, he relates on one occasion, he does not protect his house against the passing hordes of the civil war. All his doors remains open, because: "Defense attracts enterprise; and mistrust, offense . . . I have no guard or sentinal but that which the stars provide for me" (II, 15, 467 C). Passivity disempowers the enemy and lets it fall flat in a void. It if still strikes me, what does it matter! "When in danger, I do not think so much how I shall escape, as how little it matters that I escape . . . Not being able to rule events, I rule myself, and adapt myself to them if they do not adapt themselves to me" (II, 17, 488 B).

This type of attitude goes all the way to the complacency of letting everything proceed as it will. Is this a decent but cowardly philistine approach? Sometimes it appears to be.[262] But Montaigne gazed long enough at the pitiless face of the world order, perceived all too often, even in major things, the mysterious capacity those who are fragile have to bear things and the silent encouragement of all things that would rather be received than mastered for him not to adjust his actions in the small matters of daily life to this as well. Amusement at himself is liberally added to this. Behind this obedience there is a piety without dogma. It is serious but not oppressive, reverent but not frightened. It later neutralized its partially Christian origin, which was still perceptible in the earlier Essays. One might almost speak of a trust in God which could also get by without God. However, it is in agreement with classical as well as Christian texts of wisdom in which man declares that he is not master, but is rather the protégé and servant of the one who rules. One could gloss the *Essais* with sentences from the golden book of the Late Middle Ages, the *Imitatio Christi*—for example, with this: *Per solam fugam non possumus vincere, sed per patientiam . . .* (I, 13: "We cannot conquer by mere flight, but rather by endurance"), or with another: *Sicut res eveniunt, sic se homo internus illis accommodat* (II, 1: "Man must inwardly accommodate things as they occur"), but one would have to eliminate their spiritual meaning. One could (and Montaigne himself did) add words from Seneca—for example the ones quoted earlier: *Nihil invitus facit sapiens. Necessitatem effugit: quia vult quod ipsa coactura est (ep. 54)*—or the comment, now proverbial, which originated with Cleanthes: *Ducunt volentem fata, nolentem trahunt (ep. 107)*, only here, one must eliminate their heroic intent of "rising to the ranks of the gods." One could remember the verses from Juvenal's tenth satire (v. 347 ff.), which "are among the most agreeable of all of Roman poetry":[263]

> *Si consilium vis*
> *Permittes ipsis expendere numinibus, quid*
> *Conveniat nobis . . .*
> *Carior est illis homo quam sibi . . .*

> If you ask me for advice,
> Leave it to the discretion of the gods themselves to examine
> What is good for us . . .
> Man is more precious to them than he is to himself.

And there are countless others such as these from *Ecclesiastes,* Epicurus, Epictetus, Marcus Aurelius. Montaigne agrees with such wisdom resounding from all camps. And as in these, in his work the piety of obedience is also expressed in the continuing, varying repetition of the same; since it is a spiritual situation, like the lyrical situation of a poem, it needs this repetition that per se constitutes a formal characteristic of all wisdom.

8. NATURE

Montaigne's piety, free of myths and dogma and skeptical of knowledge, is thankful to have again acquired what hubris destroyed—an ear for the language of nature: "I accept with all my heart and with gratitude what nature has done for me, and I am pleased with myself and proud of myself that I do" (III, 13, 855 B/C). The key word "nature" brings us to another of his simple as well as universal fundamental concepts. We spoke of it somewhat in the preceding chapter. But what does he have in mind with the term "nature"? One would search in vain for a precise statement on this. But in any case, we can completely eliminate some definitions of the natural sciences. That which is materially vivid is indeed reflected in the countless metaphors found in the *Essais,* but not for its own sake. Montaigne's relationship with nature is not directly related to the senses. The *Essais* contain no landscapes, as are found liberally in French lyric poetry of his time. The "landscapes" of his travel journal are plain geographical descriptions of the position of cities. From the mass of classical texts which influenced his conception of nature, he avoided precisely those passages that contain poetic descriptions of stars, seas, mountains. On one occasion he admits that he does not even notice when there is a full or half moon, or when it is spring or autumn (III, 13, 846 B). Nature is present for him only when he looks within himself. To him it means the whole that covers all individual elements, the home of all dissonance, transformation, and disorder. But as vague as this concept of the whole remains, its quality is just as emotionally full. The *Essais* speak of nature as if they were speaking of a personal being: it commands or recommends, instructs, leads, comforts, offers its hand, gives, speaks.[264] All of these terms are aids to expressing the affective relationship of trust and care between man and nature. Montaigne's conception of nature is unambiguous only in this respect. He honors nature in its majesty, in its eternal variety, in its giant expanse, in view of which man notices how insignificant he is, that is, he is a dot in the universe (I, 26, 116 A; reminiscent of Cicero, *Somnium Scipionis,* III–VI). But more important to him is the consciousness that man is not lost, nature does not forget him, that miniscule dot is under her protection. Thus we find that oft-repeated classical phrase: "our mother Nature" (compare Seneca, *ep.* 90). And this is also the source of the relationship of obedience to nature: "We wrong that great and all-powerful Giver by refusing his gift, nullifying it, and disfiguring it. Himself all good, he has made all things good" (III, 13, 855 B/C). It is not only outside man, but also within him. Here its unknowable essence is accessible in inner experience. It is the real power of organization of individuality: "Let us also call the habits and conditions of each of us nature; let us rate and treat ourselves according to this measure, let us stretch our appurtenances and our accounts that far. For in going thus far we certainly seem to me to have some justification" (III, 10, 772 B). The self-fulfilling, individual process of being oneself is the right way to come into contact with nature. One need do nothing other than to grasp what nature has given one, each individual in his own way: "As she has furnished us with feet to walk with, so she has given us wisdom to guide us in life" (III, 13, 822 C).

It is obvious how un-Christian this affective relationship with nature is. In Christian terms, nature signifies an *ens creatum,* strictly separate from God, its creator. Montaigne no longer preserves this separation. Characteristic of this is a passage that is found even in the first draft of the "Apology" wherein it first goes back and forth between the concepts of "God" and "nature" and then ends in the equivalence "God and nature" (II, 12, 337 A). All the way to the last pages of the *Essais,* one can replace the word "God," which becomes less and less frequent, with the word "nature" at will without altering the meaning of the pertaining sentences. In Christian terms, it is not considered good to follow nature, although nature itself, as something that has been created, is good: *vivere secundum creatum bonum, non est bonum,* thus not *vivere secundum totum hominem,* Augustine teaches (*Civ. Dei,* XIV, 5). *Homo per se satisfacere non potest pro peccato totius humanae naturae,* Thomas Aquinas teaches (*Summa theol.* III, 46, art. 1). But Montaigne praises Socrates: "He did a great favor to human nature by showing how much it can do by itself" (III, 12, 794 B). If one wanted to search for theological conditions in Montaigne's conception of the trustworthy, autonomous healing power of nature at all, one might consider the Pelagian and semi-Pelagian ideas passed on by Lactantius and taken up again in the fifteenth and sixteenth centuries: the doctrines of salvation and grace lost power here due to the view that nature was damaged not fundamentally, but only in passing, by the Fall of Man, and as a result of this, man's freedom of will from its nature suffices to attain the good as long as it follows the principle of moderation. Erasmus' sympathy for these ideas is well known.[265] But it is questionable whether Montaigne knew anything about this easing of doctrine. Additionally, the Pelagian ideas themselves point to classical origins, in fact, their first appearance in the fifth century was nothing other than the resistance of the hellenistic intellectual inheritance to Augustine's absolutely supernatural doctrine of grace. And in those classical origins one also finds the demonstrable sources of Montaigne's concept of nature. Externally, this can be seen in the fact that he quotes liberally from corresponding passages in Lucretius, Cicero, Horace, Seneca, and so forth.

Lucretius sees in nature the universal mother, impregnated by "Father Ether." She bears all living things, nurtures them, and takes them back inside herself (II, 991 ff.; V, 259–260). The Stoic school from its beginnings to Seneca and Marcus Aurelius defines it as the creation of divinely ordering reason which binds all existing things in the endless chain of causality and fills them with usefulness. In most hellenistic schools the following ethical application is added to such metaphysical interpretations: general objective nature is at the same time the nature that rules within man, therefore the principle of "life in accordance with nature" brings man into harmony with the highest level of world reason. But since nature understood in this way always remains superior to corporal drives, "non-nature," *vivere secundum naturam* takes on the character of acquired morality, it becomes the triumph of the divine over the animal. *Dedit tibi illa* (sc. *natura), quae si non deserueris, par deo surges,* Seneca writes (*ep.* 31: "nature gave you what makes you like God, if you do not squander it"; compare Cicero, *De legibus* I, 24–27). In Italian and French Renaissance literature, all of these views are resurrected. Objectively, there, too, nature appears as a practical causality of the whole, or as a fruitful, motherly giver; in both versions, it is sometimes subordinate to divine providence, sometimes its equal. (Remember Vallas' sentence: *Natura idem est quod Deus.*) Applied to man, it appears as the instinct to do right, whereby we might quote the maxim of the Abbey of Thelem by Rabelais: *fay ce que vouldras*—a maxim that in no way means lack of restraint, but rather refers to the uncovering of an originally good predisposition in which a man must once again immerse himself in order to be a creature of "honor and virtue" with pleasure and grace.[266]

Most of what Montaigne says about nature resembles these conventions, though one cannot pin him down to the one source or the other. One can easily see what he suppressed in what was handed down to him here as well. He does not speak of a calculable usefulness, causality, and reason in nature. Without speculative support, he believes in its hidden economy because he "feels" it. He is only preoccupied with its giving, motherly relationship to man ("that great and all-powerful Giver," III, 13, 855 B). One can interpret this historically from the perspective that he was more likely to follow Lucretius than the Stoic school. And while the nature idea handed down from hellenism and the Renaissance places man in a clear ethical order, he does not separate nature from non-nature, but rather from human artificiality (art). He broadens nature into a much more encompassing totality, to the embodiment of all factual things that we are before we deliberately educate ourselves. Under nature's guidance—praised as lightly and gently as by Seneca and Rabelais—he sees himself drawn further than would be conceivable according to the conceptions of Cicero, Seneca, Valla, Rabelais, and so forth: not merely drawn to "honor and virtue," but under some circumstances not in that direction at all, but rather to foolishness, delusion, minor sins—and yet toward what is right. He feels he is sheltered in this indifferent, obscure totality that rises above human evaluations and intentions, and encompasses all from the outside and from within. His agnosticism, which deepens the transcendence of nature, also deepens his emotional relationship to it, his obedient, "existing" contact.

9. REACTION TO ILLNESS

Montaigne's reaction to illness is also connected with this obedience to nature. He speaks of it often using the subject of his kidney stones. But he does not speak like the pathologist who is studying its objective symptoms. Rather, he speaks from its subjective configuration of pain. It interests him as a shade of his spiritual well-being, as an individualizing feature of his person and his destiny, and also as a task for his wisdom, namely to reconcile with a threat. There is no serious effort to systematically eliminate it. He does not defy it, does not dress it up, he simply lets it take its course. Obedience grants physical suffering, whether it can be cured or not, its own place in the dissonant order. He knows all too well that to evade a pain would have the consequence that the suffering due him would become a burden elsewhere instead so that its predestined weight would be preserved. Thus we find comments in which he applies the instruction of the Sermon on the Mount, *non resistere malo,* to the particular case of illness: "We should give free passage to diseases; and I find that they do not stay so long with me, who let them go ahead . . . Let us give Nature a chance; she knows her business better than we do . . . They [the diseases] are conjured better by courtesy than by defiance. We must meekly suffer the laws of our condition" (III, 13, 834–835 B). Illnesses are the signs of the essential mortality of all that is alive. Similar to Paracelsus—but presumably without having borrowed it from him[267]—he understands it as a kind of living being that has its own independent processes of growth and death: "Troubles have their life and their limits, their illnesses and their health. The constitution of diseases is patterned after the constitution of animals . . . He who tries to cut them short imperiously by force, in the midst of their course, prolongs and multiplies them, and stimulates them instead of appeasing them" (III, 13, 834 B/C). Here one has the true Montaigne: Don't intercede, just let things take their course. In contrast to school medicine, he turns over the act of healing to nature itself. In this obedience, which is far more than a medical maxim, we find the deeper basis of his satire on physicians, which otherwise uses the same arguments found commonly during that epoch.[268] Always on the lookout for the good within the bad, he discovers that one illness frees one of another. Or, he discovers the appropriateness of precisely this illness, renal colic, to his intense temperament: it does not sneak in, it comes violently—this seems a benefit to him, for he has "his" illness, just as he intends to have "his" death (III, 13, 839 B). And then again he is amused by the fact that observers of his tortures consider him more heroic than he is—good, then my illness also has the advantage that it is good for my moral reputation (III, 13, 836 B). But he is joking; he does not want the moral reputation or the heroic intention. As with his death, with his illness he knows there is the blessing of the moment in reserve: when its attacks come, the gift of enduring it, a gift from nature itself, will come also. He sees through any other comfort at which he catches himself as possible self-deception, as delusion. But why should it be otherwise? Delusion also heals pains. But what if the pains are worse tomorrow? Well: "Tomorrow we shall provide other ways of escape" (III, 13, 839 B). One can see how during illness he has his full wisdom at his disposal: a readiness to suffer, a knowledge of the delusion of comfort, and yet the feeling of good fortune in being alive, which is behind that suffering and delusion and comfort.

10. FORTUNA—EPICUREANISM

Finally, besides the *ordre du monde, nature,* and so forth, another concept appears in the *Essais* to designate the whole into which man is introduced: *fortune.* It means, as in ordinary usage, sometimes good fortune, sometimes misfortune, but in both cases, it has the character of randomness. It lacks any sort of classification into a providence or a causality. *Fortuna* here is a collective name for what is factual in the course of the world and of life, for its contradictory and incalculable nature, for its ethical, judicial, logical incomprehensibility and its absolute power over men. This indeed corresponds to some classical opinions, particularly with Plutarch's concept of *tyche,* but it need not be derived exclusively from sources such as these in the *Essais*. It fits in organically with all the other elements of Montaigne's thinking. Montaigne illustrates what it means to act with the help of the idea of Fortuna: it is to blindly reach into the sea of chances, whereby success and lack of success are equally independent of will, and are equally dependent upon the favor or disfavor of the hour. Fortuna facilitates or foils it; but when it helps, it is not the captive of the will, and in foiling it, it is not the enemy of the will. It is absolute, indifferent and, as it were, subjective arbitrariness, the original image of the distance between human will and the course of the world. Thus when man succeeds, this should not be considered a contribution, when he fails, it should not be considered incompetence. Just as man is not adequately expressed in his language, his name, his reflection in his fellow man, he is not adequately expressed by the results of his will. To stress a favorite discovery that the effect of one's will can be the opposite of what one intended, Montaigne twice cites the example of Caesar's murder by Brutus and Cassius: they killed for the sake of freedom, and yet helped the lack of freedom to prevail (because the murdered Caesar was followed by principality and empire). This is an example used often in contemporary literature and analyzed in the same way, and here Montaigne is speaking clearly from the heart of his century.[269]

But the twist in this idea of Fortuna which is specifically Montaigne's is this: Fortuna can also fulfill one's desire, by "chance." The occasional congruence of will and effect is merely one variation on the universal incongruence, the lack of a connection between man and situation which can be mastered. Montaigne paid attention precisely to such variations that deceive the will into thinking it has done something correctly. He relates in his travel journal how a great man, the French ambassador, had been trying for a long time without success to be allowed to see the Seneca manuscript in the Vatican; but he, the low-level nobleman Montaigne, did not make an effort to gain access to it— and he was allowed to see it. *La fortune m'y porta, comme je tenois . . . la chose desesperée (Journal)*. Thus it is Fortuna's particular absurdity that it is fond of slapping all hope in the face, and she is just as fond of surprising someone who is mistrustful beyond his expectations with her favor. And what conclusion can be drawn from all this? The conclusion that for Montaigne results from every experience: give up a planning will. To intend and to plan are no guarantee that one will attain one's goal; renunciation and hopelessness do not represent a certainty that one will fall short of one's goal; when a door is open, chance will slam it closed, when it is closed, chance will open it. There is no comprehensible connection between wish and fulfillment, between renunciation and loss, rather, absurdity prevails. But this does not frighten the wise man. He experiences the blessing of the whole even through this discontinuity, a whole which, as absurd as it may act in individual matters, forms a shelter for obedient man even by means of the absurdities.[270]

11.   MONTAIGNE'S EPICUREANISM

The "Epicurean" element of Montaigne's manner of conducting his life is based in obedience and piety toward nature: one must make the greatest possible use of all the content of the human essence: "The most barbarous of our maladies is to despise our being" (III, 13, 852 C). In the early stage, Montaigne was still able to express this using Christian motifs, that is, that mild one which—from Erasmus to François de Sales later on—promises man a gentle grace: God takes us as we are, "she [divine law] stretches out her arms to us and takes us to her bosom, no matter how vile, filthy, and besmirched we are now and are to be in the future" (I, 56, 236 A). The physical body is among the gifts of "God" (or, nature, as it is put later) and the things "in common" which we have. Because it has been given, it is a good. Let us cease separating what a ruling order has brought together, body and soul. The body must also be obeyed. Furthermore, body and soul mutually balance out their deficiencies, and this is how it should be: "Let the mind arouse and quicken the heaviness of the body, and the body check and make fast the lightness of the mind" (III, 13, 855 B). The triviality of what is corporal appears of its own accord, no differently than does the triviality of the spirit. Nature has already assured that its goods, body and soul, not only supplement one another, but also limit one another and horrify one another. Thus there is no need at all for our ascetic efforts; if we simply are what we are, then we will automatically weary of that which disrupts our equilibrium (III, 13, 849 C).

When joys are given in body or soul, they should be received along with their shadow of triviality. Why should one who renounces joys not also renounce breathing? Why not renounce light, since he is already foolish enough to renounce all that is given (*gratuit*) and which does not even require effort? (III, 13, 850 B/C): "I consider it equal injustice to set our heart against natural pleasures and to set our heart too much on them . . . We should neither pursue them nor flee them, we should accept them" (849 B). The reflected obedience in the face of one's lot gives enjoyment its rank of wisdom. For under this assumption, enjoyment is free. And Montaigne can with his full temperament express the hearty joy and happiness, this *gaillardise*, which is the inheritance of his southern home. "We should take part up to the utmost limits of pleasure," which is admittedly followed directly with: "but beware of engaging ourselves further, where it begins to be mingled with pain." And: "We must hold on, tooth and nail, to our enjoyment of the pleasures of life, which our years tear, one after the other, from our hands" (I, 39, 181–182 A). Elsewhere: I would run through the whole world to find joy, and if somewhere there is a man to whom my cheerful essence appeals, and who appeals to me with his cheerful essence, he would only have to whistle, and I would come and give him an example of joy in flesh and blood, "I, who have no other aim but to live and be merry" (III, 5, 640 B). Then again, in a more muted tone, and with an eye to what is uncertain in what we do, there is a sentence that unites skepticism and the expectation of happiness, one of the loveliest sentences Montaigne ever wrote: "Since there is a risk of making a mistake, let us risk it rather in pursuit of pleasure" (III, 13, 832 B).

One could call all of this Epicurean, assuming one meant by this the genuine, spiritual Epicureanism. It is no accident that the theologians of *humanisme dévot*, such as Pierre Camus and François de Sales, wished the Epicurean in Montaigne so well.[271] Pleasure (*volupté*) in the *Essais* means: indulging in the gift of the fullness of existence ennobled by moderation and contemplation. Thus in late passages we find a large number of comments such as: "As for me, then, I love life and cultivate it just as God has been pleased to grant it to us" (III, 13, 854 B). Or: "My trade and my art is living" (II, 6, 274 C). Or: "We are great fools. 'He has spent his life in idleness,' we say. 'I have done nothing today.' What, have you not lived? That is not only the fundamental but the most illustrious of your occupations . . . Our great and glorious master-piece is to live appropriately" (III, 13, 850–851 C). This is the spirit of Horace in its outlook and almost in its wording as well:

> . . . *ille potens sui*
> *Laetusque deget, cui licet in diem*
> *Dixise "vixi"* . . .
>
> . . . a man is master of himself
> And happy, if daily
> He can tell himself: "I have lived"

These verses (which come from Ode III, 29, which Montaigne apparently liked especially, since he quotes from it several times) are cited in another Essay, I, 11 (28 A). Finally, in one of the last sentences of the *Essais,* we read: "It is an absolute perfection and virtually divine to know how to enjoy our being rightfully" (857 B). Montaigne does not shy away from being an Epicurean in this sense: a free, happy achiever of the *condition humaine* under the banner of the trivial.

12.   PEACE IN THE MIDST OF RESTLESSNESS

Then on the final pages of the *Essais* Montaigne has come to the pure form of his wisdom. Although the terms he uses to express it are simple, almost meager, although nothing is finally fixed and for many themes, even to the end he leaves open the possibility of a different "opinion," still everything is mature, satisfied, and clear in the essential features. Montaigne came into the clarity of what found his center. There is a mild festiveness on these pages which accompanies the work to its conclusion. Each sentence has its own weight. New expressions constantly flow toward him, for he himself is in the stream of harmonious sounds. He is in eudemonia, in "geglückten Dasein" (a successful existence).[272] He knows all of its content and lives it to the full, from solid comfort to content release and on to patience with pain, all moods of a person who has both feet on the ground, looking out over its breadth, accustomed to the horizon of what is uninterpretable, prepared for the delusional elements of the whole. That man seems most mortal to him who dreams of his immortality. Montaigne's humanity is contentment. Within it he has made himself comfortable, as he did within the decline of his aging. He promotes the art of uniting the divine with the earthly, the reasonable with the unreasonable, the strict with the mild, the appropriate with the inappropriate (855 C). He doesn't need metaphysics or dogma to make this reconciliation, he only needs to listen to himself. He wants to very clearly know the enjoyment of his own human essence, which vibrates along with the dissonant, harmonious whole in order to be grateful: "Others feel the sweetness of some satisfaction . . . I feel it as they do, but it is not in passing and slipping by. Instead we must study it, savor it, and ruminate it, to give proper thanks for it to him who grants it to us" (854 B). Peace develops within him from this thankful self-awareness. This man who suffered so much and who knew so much about the restlessness in others and in his own self and in everything which exists—was in the core of his being acquiring a peace that he preserved in the midst of the changes and fears in that he gave himself to them. It is the peace of a strong, lithe swimmer faced with a flood the depth of which is unfathomable, the eddies incalculable.

On one occasion, Montaigne comments that there is a grace of simple naturalness which is like a secret light (*secrette lumiere*) inaccessible to the normal eye. He said this in thinking of Socrates (III, 12, 793 B). But one can also say it in thinking of Montaigne. The Socrates figure of the *Essais* is essentially himself. And that secret light falls across the best pages of his *Essais*. It is the reflection of his wisdom. And just as this was not acquired by means of any knowledge, it cannot be overtaken by any advance in knowledge. For nothing in which men expressed, under whatever didactic shell, that which is human, can become outmoded: for this is obedience in the face of the fullness and heaviness of existence, and the astounded observation of its limitless, contradictory manifestations that are superior to any interpretation.

CHAPTER VIII

Montaigne's Literary Consciousness and the Form of the *Essais*

1. THE WRITER

Montaigne the writer, to whom we will now turn, had two original accomplishments: the creation of the essay and the shaping of a highly developed writer's consciousness with which he accounts for his essay-istic writing. Both serve to round out the image of a thoroughly organic intellect who obeys his own nature, not only in what he says, but also in how he says it, and in how he justifies the "how" of the saying.

We will begin with an analysis of his consciousness as a writer. This presents him with several questions: why am I writing, for whom am I writing, how am I writing, and why in this particular way? Thus it concerns the questions of meaning, audience, and form.

Montaigne certainly does not raise these questions simply because it was a rhetorical requirement that an author express himself on the *causae scribendi* of his work. In his work, there is very little of the usual pragmatic self-justification of prose writing (to preserve memorable events, to establish fame, the charitable duty to permit others to share in one's accumulated knowledge, etc.) to be found. The reasons he gives for his writing form an imperative part of his overall reflection upon the self, for the writing itself is an aid to this reflection. Thus one can observe how repeatedly in the midst of his examination of himself he moves into an examination of his activity as a writer. Reflecting upon his own nature, reflecting upon his own thinking, reflecting upon the literary expression of both of these: they are the different phases of one and the same act. Here, to a degree found nowhere else before, the consciousness of the writer is a part of the self-observation of his own individuality. One could say that the *Essais* provide a running commentary on themselves. There have been many authors who wrote commentaries on themselves, the last in the early and high Renaissance periods, from Dante's *Convivio* to Lorenzo Magnifico's *Commento sopra alcuni de' suoi sonetti,* and the treatise by Juan de la Cruz on his religious poem *En una noche oscura.* But these involve subsequent clarifications of the instructional content that the writer had already set forth in his literary work. For Montaigne, on the other hand, it is an intensified self-discovery. In writing, as everywhere else, he turns himself over to his own nature. Reflection upon his writing serves the purpose of collecting more symptoms that will enlighten him as to this nature. Furthermore, this reflection watches over and encourages the uninhibitedness of the writing which flows into the pen; thus, analogously to everything else, it safeguards the internal laws of his being.

In Montaigne, the writer's consciousness has different aims than it did in the following centuries when the prevailing question was, how could the writer acquire rank and social standing after he left the institutions of the Church and the universities? In the first chapter, we traced the somewhat intricate process whereby Montaigne invoked his nobility in order to assure the *Essais* of a space in which to be heard, and yet at the same time elevated himself beyond the bonds of the nobility to avoid negatively influencing the higher, universally human rank of essential education (*culture de l'âme*) he wished to nurture. But he had no intention of founding a separate, independent class of writers. He did count himself among the *écrivains,*[273] but without any sociological flavor. He was certainly the first writing layman in France who resolutely did not want to appear as a theologian, jurist, or philologist, and in this, he certainly introduced the nonspecialized, urbane literature of the *honnête homme.* But this has nothing to do with the societal tendencies of later phenomena of this nature. And to the extent that others did want to invoke him in this respect (predominantly in the eighteenth century), at most this applied to the effect of his work, not to his intentions.

2.   THE QUESTION OF MEANING

The writer's question of meaning (why am I writing?) in the *Essais* receives the same answer as the question of the meaning of self-observation. For Montaigne, writing only signifies communicating with others as a second or third aspect. It is precisely this communicating that is problematic for him: "But is it reasonable that I, so fond of privacy in actual life, should aspire to publicity in the knowledge of me?" (III, 2, 611 B). Here, writing is a self-directed recordkeeping of one's own individuality, a registration of its content and the content of the world in its subjective reflection, moment by moment, as it passes by. The effect of putting it down in writing makes it possible to objectify it, and through this, one's own essence can be understood. The terms common at the time for the process of writing which he preferred to use are informative: *mettre en registre, enregistrer, mettre en rolle, enroller, contreroller.* Early on, he commented that in order to be able to study the strangeness (*estrangeté*) of the "chimeras of his spirit" in full precision and at leisure, he had begun to record them ("to put them in writing," I, 8, 21 A). This type of writing supports the crystallization of the content of one's consciousness; only with the help of their "registration" or "recordkeeping" can they come to the full expression that is necessary so the observer of the self can know how things stand with him. A silent or merely oral monologue is not enough: "For those who go over themselves only in their minds and . . . in speech do not penetrate to essentials in their examination as does a man . . . who binds himself to keep an enduring account, with all his faith, with all his strength" (II, 18, 504 C). And a few sentences later: "In order to train my fancy even to dream with some order and purpose, and in order to keep it from losing its way and roving with the wind, there is nothing like embodying and registering all the little thoughts that come to it. I listen to my reveries because I have to record them."

We find statements such as this very frequently. This shows with what originality-conscious attentiveness Montaigne reflected upon the meaning of his writing. It represents a written exercise in the overall process of trying himself out, it is not a subsequent addition to a finished result, rather, it is an accompanying process of capturing his own process of change, the graphic curve of fluid subjectivity. As we have already described, Montaigne is permeated by the conviction that the self is not completely present at any one point, and that it only achieves an approximate insight into itself from a viewing of all the stages in which it experienced all of its metamorphoses. He feels himself all the more drawn to writing things down true to the moment, for it is the only means he has to keep himself in view over the expanse of time and thus in the wealth of his own labyrinthine twists and turns. In a late passage, he expresses this as follows: "It [my book] may know a good many things that I no longer know and hold from me what I have not retained . . . If I am wiser than it, it is richer than I" (II, 8, 293 C). I am wiser than my book: for in the images of what I have been, I learn how everything came to me only to founder. My book is richer than I am: for it preserves all that has foundered, and which was no less I than all which is now present, and it contains the totality of my essence. Writing safeguards against the danger that Montaigne feared most, that is, falsification of himself; in this case, it safeguards against falsification due to forgetfulness, or due to a memory that is not fixed. Montaigne educates himself by making himself into a picture. His writing enables him to look at what he has been later on, and it makes it easier for him to come into reflected harmony with his changeable factuality. It is an instrument of truthfulness and it guarantees trueness to his own nature. Therefore: "I have no more made my book than my book has made me—a book consubstantial with its author, concerned with my own self, an integral part of my life; not concerned with some thirdhand, extraneous purpose, like all other books" (II, 18, 504 C).

From time to time, other motivations are put forth for his writing. For example, he wrote to relieve boredom, or because he had nothing better to do. Reassurances such as these can characteristically be found in Essays addressed to ladies of the nobility (II, 8, 279 A and II, 37, 574 A)—and with good reason, for it is a tone appropriate for giving the air of a nonpedantic leisure. These are societal considerations, and also literary conventions that go back to antiquity, conventions of which humanism made extensive use.[274] An affectation such as this, which no reader tended to take any more seriously than was intended, cannot conceal the fact that Montaigne's *Essais* had become very close to his heart. He loves them as the child of himself and his muse (II, 8, 293 B/C). It is another convention, in fact, to call one's own books "children."[275] But this expression regains an original warmth when he uses it. When one sees how thoroughly he reflects upon his *Essais*, how he takes them up again and again, improves them, expands them, one can no longer believe his claim that he is simply passing the time. He himself is the first and most thorough reader of his book—similar to Petrarch (*mea scripta revolvere, Famil.* I, 9). He carries it along with him on his trip to Italy. The writing was a process of making his spirit, which was always in motion, visible; thus when the author rereads what he has written, he is again set in motion toward the never-ending act of self-observation. This is combined with astonishment that from time to time he no longer understands himself, and with the conclusion: I am continuously someone else (II, 12, 426 B and I, 10, 26–27 C). Intentionally written from the moment, what is written carries within it the unique-ness and thus the volatility of the moment. Precisely because it can be incomprehensible later, it becomes a means of obtaining information for perceiving complex individuality. In practice, the result of his involve-ment with his own book is that Montaigne in supplementing and cor-recting it only changes the first version stylistically, but not in content, or only minimally in content, something that he not only expressly admitted (II, 37, 574 A/C), but which was confirmed by critical studies of the corrections.[276] Something that has been said once, even if it contains embarrassing material, is valuable evidence; it would be a betrayal to eliminate it. He comments on his insertions nicely and with a self-satisfaction that is softened by irony: "These are only overweights, which do not condemn the original form, but give some special value to each of the subsequent ones, by a bit of ambitious subtlety" (III, 9, 736 C). These insertions are in fact unconcerned that they might be contra-dictory in the context into which they are inserted. For they, too, are born of the moment. But all this only underscores the preeminence of orientation to the self in this writing, which we have described, and the specific meaning that he attributes to his writing.

One can furnish various classical and Christian analogies to this determination of the meaning of his writing. Roman literature of moral philosophy was from time to time passed off as *secum loqui* or *sermo intimus*.[277] But as a rule this remained subordinate to the motive of instructing others, whereby we refer to the beginning of Seneca's *ep.* 27 (*De communi malo tecum colloquor, remedia communico. Sic itaque me audi, tamquam mecum loquar. In secretum te meum admitto et te adhibito mecum exigo:* "I am speaking with you about our common suffering and calling you my remedy. So listen to me as if I were speak-ing with myself. I am introducing you to my innermost self, and in your presence I am examining myself"). Only in Christian writing did the internal dialogue rise above the intention to communicate and instruct. This occurs most powerfully in Augustine's *Soliloquia* and *Confes-siones,* that is, where the pious man seeks "God and the soul." In the former (I, 1) it is explained how writing is the indispensable means of keeping a firm hold on the phases of the investigation of the self and the dialogue with God; on a basis thus secured, the fluctuating process of seeking becomes more certain in its aim and more courageous toward itself. This type of writing assumes the character of a religious journal intended for the writer himself. Augustine calls his *Soliloquia (Retract.*

I, v, 1) a *commonitorium* (written reminder). This is then repeated in the *Confessiones*. The writing of this work is an accompanying (not subsequently reported) realization of a self-examination before God which is completed at the highest level, namely, in the reflected vision of the spiritual path of life; the external communication of this is not the primary concern (the readers are only considered witnesses and listeners), rather, the primary concern is the writer reassuring himself by means of his writing. Later, we find something similar in Petrarch, in his soliloquy-like writings (especially in the *Secretum* and in the letters), though, admittedly, here it is toned down to an autopsychology that is only half religious, half secular, but which still displays a rather purely emerging awareness that the writing process is an accompanying act in internal dialogue which serves to relieve (*levamen animi, Fam.* XII, 5) as well as to objectify the inwardness. Montaigne is related to these classical, Christian, and Petrarchian motives to the same extent that he is related to the corresponding attempts and developments in the investigation of the self. The fact that, in this respect, one can bring both Augustine and Petrarch so close to him only confirms for us from another perspective that he is their secular heir. The differences are self-evident here as well (cf. chapter 5). The orientation to himself is so strong in his writing that the other classical and also humanisitc motive, namely, writing for the purpose of establishing fame, has no point of entry in the *Essais*.[278]

3.   THE QUESTION OF AUDIENCE

And now to the question of audience. Montaigne posed this question expressly: "And then, for whom do you write?" (II, 17, 498 C). If one looks through his responses, a confusing impression emerges. He is not clear about whom he is actually speaking. The uncertainty of his idea of his audience confirms his writing's orientation to himself. He can easily imagine, as he once confesses, that no one at all will read him. But he does not lose faith in the usefulness of his writing because of this, and the experimental turning outward results in a stimulating drive for a process of turning inward and for intensification of self-analytical clarity: "Painting myself for others, I have painted my inward self with colors clearer than my original ones" (II, 18, 504 C). All the same, he also knows that thinking, to the extent that it cannot avoid becoming language, becomes subject to the communicative function of language. With the transition from silent to written meditation, one necessarily enters the public realm. The fact that Montaigne recognizes this is what really prompts his question about audience. The fact that, due to the communicative function of language, he is operating under a constraint that interferes with the directness of his being alone with himself intensifies his uncertainty in answering that question. The foiling of his desire for solitude by his sociable temperament, which was described earlier (chapter 5), recurs here: wherever he touches upon the question of audience, it happens in such a manner that one can see how greatly it remains subordinated to his internal dialogue.

Sometimes he appears to consider his readership to be quite a small circle, for example, in his foreword "To the Reader" of 1580. There, indeed, he addresses the reader directly. But we then read that he intended the book for his relatives and friends so that when he is no longer with them, they will have a faithful picture of his person. This is first of all the style of the memoir: one hopes to preserve himself for the remembrance of those of his lineage—of course with the difference that Montaigne is not thinking of having an exemplary effect on his children and grandchildren, but simply wants to pass on a precise portrait of his person to those close to him. He repeats this in another passage: "This is for a nook in a library, and to amuse a neighbor, a relative, a friend, who may take pleasure in associating and conversing with me again in this image" (II, 18, 503 A). A few sentences further this again becomes questionable—is it then not all that important to him to be unforgotten by those close to him? Apparently, for this motive of limiting his readership to an intimate circle arises from another source. It comes from the need of a convincing pretext for portraying his private individuality. The drive to discover his essence which has become so strong in Montaigne is still far too closely connected with the feeling that he is doing something risky for him to get by without the help this motive provides.[279] Over the years, he drops it. On one occasion later, after the sentence "I am hungry to make myself known," the following comment slips out: "and I care not to how many, provided it be truly" (III, 5, 643 B). In addition, the fictitious limitation of his audience to family and friends has the advantage that it comes in handy for his heuristic self-abasement: I am so insignificant that if anyone is interested at all, at most those closest to me might be interested in my confessions. Moreover, the limitation promotes a genuine longing. Montaigne's spirit, which is averse to any sort of abstraction, requires in every venture something that can be closely imagined. Thus for his writing also, if he is thinking of it in relationship to readers, he needs the certainty that familiar people will listen to him. This also explains his comments, to which we referred earlier, in which he indicates he would prefer to have La Boétie as a reader. When this work, which has become known world-wide, gives the impression in certain passages that it is nothing more than conversation among family and friends, it puts the reader, whoever that may be, into that state of relaxed humanity in which Montaigne himself lived, and in which he wanted to be understood.

Then again he seems to have been thinking of broader or very broad circles. Alongside statements such as "I write my book for few men" (III, 9, 751 B), we find others such as "when a man has mortgaged his work to the world" (III, 9, 736 B) and many similar to this in which he speaks of *le public*. But what is his conception of audience and world? It is certainly not obvious that he meant the educated nobility. The occasional dedication of individual Essays to noble ladies proves nothing, as this is the usual style in dedications, and does not exclude the possibility that it is also aimed at a larger readership. He sometimes addresses the *honnête homme*, other times man in general. And then again he will attempt to divide his readership by educational levels and seek out what fits among them, as in the passage in which he poses the question of audience. There he makes a distinction between the scholars: they only have knowledge of subject matter, and the vulgar spirits: but they have no feeling for the grace and content of a document, and the strong, self-assured spirits: these are the ones to whom he wishes to speak, but they are rare, they have neither name nor rank, and it is an effort half lost when he hopes to please them (II, 17, 498 B).[280] In any case, this affirms that he is not thinking of a bland public, nor of a class of nobility, but rather the bearers of genuine essential education. And when, as here, he counts on these, it is still with doubt as to whether he can reach them at all. The hope of a public which is beginning to acquire a more precise definition thus immediately collapses again. Earlier, in another Essay, he posed the following educational schema: farmers at the lowest level, philosophers at the highest, and in the middle, those who are a "mix" (*les mestis*); he counts himself among these last; the *Essais* might be able to speak to them (I, 54, 227 A/C). Thus here he is again lowering his audience. On other occasions, he refers vaguely to *le peuple*, a term that in literary language of the time simply meant the public. In one of these passages we read: "Amusing notion: many things that I would not want to tell anyone, I tell the public; and for my most secret knowledge and thoughts I send my most faithful friends to a bookseller's shop" (III, 9,

750 C). This is the exact opposite of the intimacy of friend and family:
he defines the recipient of his writing as a neutral public, the anonymity
of which spares him shame about what he confesses.

There is no more to be said. In the question of audience, which is
answered sometimes one way, sometimes another in the *Essais*, only one
thing is constant: Montaigne expects them to have an effect, and he
expects the reader to be interested. In the third book, he notes with
satisfaction the success that the first two books have had (III, 9, 736–
737 B). On one occasion he confesses that he deliberately keeps his
writing loose so that the reader is obliged to pay close attention (III, 9,
761–762 B). But he is unable to say who this reader might be. Montaigne does not speak to a particular societal or occupational group, nor
does he speak to the nation (as Du Bellay and Pasquier emphatically did
at that time), he speaks even less to Christianity, and least of all is there
an appeal to posterity. He has no publicist tendencies. Unlike the writer
type of the eighteenth and nineteenth centuries, he does not want to
educate a public for himself, step in for an ignored righteousness, formulate interests that are in the air, bring enlightening ideas into circulation.
Cautiously, he hopes for those of like mind in whom he can awaken the
desire for freedom: "God grant that this excessive license of mine may
encourage our men to attain freedom, rising above these cowardly and
hypocritical virtues born of our imperfections" (III, 5, 642 C). The
publication of his book is a risk in uncertainty. He sends out what he has
written, may it have an effect where and how it will. The main aim has
been accomplished: he has found himself in the process of writing. The
fact that a public did indeed emerge, from the aristocratic citizen of the
world in the seventeenth century to the best intellects of the nineteenth
and twentieth centuries, belongs on another page, it belongs to the
history of its influence, which is no longer directly connected with his
attitude of uncertainty with respect to his audience.

4. THE QUESTION OF FORM

Montaigne poses and answers the question of form—How am I
writing, and why am I writing in this way?—in a much more uniform
manner. He is aware that he is the opposite of the disputational artistic
prose of the humanists. He is clear about how unusual an effect the
open form of his essayistic prose must have. And thus he feels compelled
to justify it and to demonstrate its connection in growth to his own
spiritual nature. Here is the point at which his self-awareness and his

awareness as a writer are most directly merged. Open-form prose has a long history before him. But only with Montaigne did this prose become independent in the Essay, also, its particular capability as art was discovered, and its aesthetics were developed. Thus he is simultaneously the creator and the first theoretician of the Essay.

The open form of the *Essais* resembles a stroll, and this is how Montaigne wants it. For the thinking itself is taking a stroll (*promener mon jugement*, I, 50, 219 C). He compares it with wandering around in a gallery (I, 26, 122 A). Thus we find the agreement expressed in this well-known sentence: "My style and my mind alike go roaming" (III, 9, 761 C). This vagabondage of style is sometimes connected with the casualness of dress of the urbane man, the coat tossed on at an angle, comfortable and somewhat baggy stockings are considered elegant (I, 26, 127 B). But it is more, namely, the literary repetition of the yielding to the moment which he practiced in his living and thinking, and its unpredictable productivity. The same words that Montaigne used to characterize his thinking—"an unpremeditated and accidental philosopher!" (II, 12, 409 C)—return in the characterization of his speaking and writing: "My plan in speaking is to display extreme carelessness and unstudied and unpremeditated gestures, as if they arose from the immediate occasion" (III, 9, 735 B). In writing as well, he depends upon freedom leading farther than planning. Thus he sets out without knowing where the journey will take him. The greater interrelationships can be reached beginning from any random point, "for all subjects are linked with one another" (III, 5, 668 B). He knows that the inward connection of the most varied topics of an Essay which are created by their relationship to the author would be expressed even without a controlled structuring: "My ideas follow one another, but sometimes it is from a distance, and look at each other, but with a sidelong glance" (III, 9, 761 B). In this type of improvisational method he perceives things that would not otherwise emerge within the limited beam of a single topic. Deviations from the path lead to new riches. "But there is profit in change," he writes after one digression (II, 25, 522 A). But are these really digressions at all? They are the reality of which an Essay is made, the fluid line of expression of his flowing subjectivity.

In one passage, Montaigne relates that he watched a painter as he filled in the remaining empty areas around a fresco "with grotesques, which are fantastic paintings whose only charm lies in their variety and strangeness," and he applies that to his *Essais*: "And what are these things of mine . . . but grotesques and monstrous bodies, pieced together of diverse members, without definite shape, having no order, sequence, or proportion other than accidental?" (I, 28, 135 A). The word "grotesques" that Montaigne used here expressed a fixed concept in artistic technique. In the language of painters of that time, it designated the adventurous heterogeneity of randomly mixed ornaments and scrolls of plant and fable motifs in which the mood of fantasy could be expressed, in contrast to the closed, composed depictions of dignified subjects.[281] Montaigne chose this word deliberately; he could count on the fact that it would imply the disqualifying determination of style which that term contained. Later he uses another image: "It is only an ill-fitted patchwork" (III, 9, 736 C), a poorly executed job of inlay, a mosaic—and, remaining within the image, he calls the additions of the various layers *quelque embleme supernumeraire,* some extra ornaments.[282]

These are the usual disqualifications with which he typically adorns his entire self-description. They mask with irony what is closest to his heart: the determined abandonment of composition, that is, as it was called in classical rhetoric, the *dispositio (taxis, oikonomia),* or as the moderns called it, the *ordo tractandi.* The composition of an Essay by Montaigne, which is only associative, is in fact the most extreme antitype to Latin humanist prose, even to works in the vulgar languages, such as Calvin's *Institution de la Religion chrestienne.* Montaigne has an aversion to the treatise structure which is arranged by who, what, why, by first, second, third, by the syllogistic sequence of steps (whereby it is amusing to observe that he himself once says "second" without having said "first": I, 26, 129 A). He does use an occasional *Item* taken from school language to make a joke (I, 46, 201–202 A), as Rabelais frequently did with this formula and other similar ones. He pokes fun at Cicero's ceremonious marking of parts of speech and comments: "For me . . . these logical and Aristotelian arrangements are not to the point" (II, 10, 301 A). Just as he praises Seneca and Plutarch for the fact that they have written *à pieces descousues* (disconnectedly) and can thus also be read this way, he claims this quality for himself: "I speak my meaning in disjointed parts, as something that cannot be said all at once and in a lump" (III, 13, 824 C). His specialty is content and spontaneity, not compositional preparations. "I, who have more concern for the weight and utility of the arguments than for their order and sequence," he comments on one occasion at the beginning of a "diversion" (II, 27, 528–529 C).

Casualness in form and gesture—the *ordo neglectus*—was indeed the taste of the times in the fine arts, poetry, and societal appearance.

Men had learned since the fourteenth century to value the charm of effortlessness. A letter of Petrarch's outlines the aesthetics of the *habitus neglector,* in contrast to the *magnus cultus (Famil.* XVIII, 7). Castiglione counts it among the qualities characterizing the perfected man of the world that he must be capable of *sprezzatura* (casualness) (*Cortegiano* I, 26). A feeling for the beneficial effect of the *negligenze artifici* (*La Gerusalemme liberata* II, 18) extends all the way to Tasso. Thoughts of Horace and Ovid, who recommended something similar, may be behind all this. Furthermore, it is a long-time convention for an author to introduce himself with "affected modesty" and assure the reader that he would be incapable of writing artistically.[283] But one does not get far if one attempts to derive Montaigne's self-characterization as a writer solely from this popular practice and rhetorical affectation. He only imitates these things because they satisfy the needs of his nature, and he can also justify them from the basis of his nature. He abases himself as a writer using the customary modesty formula to serve precisely the same purpose as when he abases himself as man and philosopher using the formula of *miseria hominis.* He used the modesty formula as a well thought-out sign of his own reality and its unlimited development. He makes use of the open form of the *ordo neglectus* which he appears to disqualify, although he recognizes its charm (I, 28, 135 A), because it is the natural outflow of his conception of the world and his absolute subjectivity. The world with its universal changeability, the antinomical character of life, and complex, inconstant man preclude a regulated depiction, that is, a depiction that closes what is open, makes of what is many-sided something one-sided, and dresses up what is imperfect: "Whoever writes about it only . . . according to the rules leaves out more than half of it" (III, 5, 678 C). The unrecognizability of the whole—"I do not see the whole of anything" (I, 50, 219 C)—and the inconstancy and changing perspective of the observer—"I may presently change" (III, 2, 611 B)—forced a fragmentary approach to the depiction. The two poles (object and observer), each both internally mobile and moving constantly into new constellations due to the changing relationship to the other, can only arrive with the help of an equally mobile form at the only appropriate reproduction, namely, an approximate one. In this, the fluid modality of world and existence (*branloire perenne*) is repeated in written form; writing that obediently conforms to this modality discloses it by accompanying it to its fulfillment in language. The contents of a self-portrait are also not suited for a rhetorically and logically disputed artificial structure: "What I chiefly portray is my cogitations, a shapeless subject that does not lend itself to expression in actions" (II, 6, 274 C). And last, the personal urge for freedom is added to the object-based rejection of controlled form. Montaigne is comfortable in a manner of writing which does not have a "memory" as a prerequisite. His frequent assurance that his memory is deficient is not merely a side-swipe at the pedants with their knowledge of subject matter. It is also a refusal of rhetoric. The doctrine of memory (*memoria*) is a part of rhetoric, and it encompasses the "literal memorization of a completed written composition" for the purpose of recitation.[284] Memory reproduces the carefully subdivided speech, thus it is at the mercy of constraints. It is thus understandable that the freedom-loving Montaigne finds another reason for an open form when he rejects the premeditated aspect that requires memory; it would rob him of the productivity of the moment, the core impulse of his writing: "I shall have to avoid any preparation, for fear of binding myself to some obligation on which I should be dependent" (III, 9, 735 B). But where everything is so attuned to everything else, thinking and behavior on one side with writing on the other, casualness of form in writing can no longer be simple imitation of what is fashionable, and the assurance of "lacking art" can no longer be mere repetition of a commonplace convention. Fashion and convention are transformed into the necessity of that which is organic.

In the midst of reflections upon his style of writing, Montaigne suddenly invokes Plato and the *furor poeticus*. As a postscript to a "digression" he writes: "I have run my eyes over a certain dialogue of Plato, a fantastic motley in two parts, the beginning part about love, all the rest about rhetoric. The ancients do not fear these changes, and with wonderful grace they let themselves thus be tossed in the wind, or seem to" (III, 9, 761 C). Presumably he means the *Phaedrus*. What interests him in it is the motley of colors (*bigarrure*) of its themes and its improvisational pace. "Let themselves be tossed in the wind":[285] this key word is reminiscent of the definition of the essence of man formulated elsewhere: "But what of it? We are all wind" (III, 13, 849 B). But that other key word, motley (*bigarrure*), had appeared before: "Man . . . is but patchwork and motley" (II, 20, 511 B).[286] This re-emergence of two fundamental anthropological concepts in a description of style is no accident. In the sweeping, fragmentary method of the Platonic dialogue Montaigne detects an agreement with that which he considers essential in men and in himself. He writes: "I love the poetic gait, by leaps and gambols. It is an art, as Plato says [*Ion* 534b],

light, flighty, daemonic." And farther down: "The poet, says Plato
[*Laws* 719b], seated on the tripod of the Muses, pours out in a frenzy
whatever comes into his mouth, like the spout of a fountain, without
ruminating and weighing it; and from him escape things of different
colors and contradictory substance in an intermittent flow. He himself
is utterly poetic." Between these sentences, Plutarch's "Demon of Socrates" is discussed, "in which he [Plutarch] forgets his theme, in which
the treatment of his subject is found only incidentally, quite smothered
in foreign matter"—a quite correct description, for this dialogue in the
Moralia does in fact speak of all possible things: political relationships,
dreams and visions, the story of a scuffle is slipped in, and the theme
of the title emerges almost at random, purely in association with the
language, and is dropped again in the same manner. Montaigne responds enthusiastically: "Lord, what beauty there is in these lusty
sallies and this variation, and more so the more casual and accidental
they seem" (761 C). Montaigne makes sure one cannot overlook the
extent to which all this is a self-characterization of the *Essais* using the
mirror image of Plato and Plutarch. Montaigne shifts both Plato and
Plutarch, and also himself, into proximity of poetic enthusiasm—not
for the sake of the inspirational history, but rather in view of the
leaping pace ("gait by leaps and gambols"), the quality of being
driven, the quality of being carried away by ideas and temperament. In
this passage as one reads further the double meaning of *furor* is also
expressed: in negative terms it is a pathological symptom of mental
chaos resulting from the essential human inclinations—and in positive
terms it is the happy satisfaction of precisely these human inclinations.
As in his thinking as a whole, in his consciousness as a writer Montaigne takes up the motif of the *furor poeticus,* with the same turn-
about from self-deprecation to self-fulfillment. All thinking is only the
projection of the rays of subjective fantasy into the darkness of what is
unrecognizable, the generation of colorful, delusional images from the
pleasure of mental alertness—thus I "think" in the form of dreaming
which resembles poetry; all speaking and writing is only the attempt to
hurry after the volatile fading multiplicity of things and of myself—
thus I write in an independence that resembles poetry. If one examines
the paraphrase from Plato's *Laws* ("The poet, seated on the tripod of
the Muses . . .") in the source, one finds that Plato was speaking re-
proachfully: he sends the confused, lying poet out of the state. Montaigne included this reproach without comment and surrendered to
what was so blameworthy—he too was "only" a poet and spoke

whatever came to his lips. Montaigne himself aspires to this closeness of the Essay to poetry, in the form of a disqualification. His writer's consciousness is clear about what his Essay is: it is a meditative occasional poem in open-form prose which makes no claims in comparison to dignified art, and yet, or perhaps because of this, which has a "wonderful grace" and is beautiful in its vigorous, free play with diversity. This introduces the aesthetics of the Essay, and the pioneering disqualification disappears again. In view of the trains of thought which Plato developed, these can hardly be considered Platonic any more. But they have the advantage of being Montaignian.

5. THE TITLE OF THE *ESSAIS*

But why did Montaigne select the title *Essais* for his book, and what does this title mean? It will be valuable to pursue this question since it can shed light upon the genesis of this literary genre.

The title fits in with the titles popular at that time for miscellany-type documents, such as *Disputations, Sentences, Mots dorés, Entretiens, Mélanges, Variétés, Diversités,* and so forth. Montaigne was the first author to call his book *Essais*. In contrast to the later imitators of this title, he does not associate any literary concept with this, but only a methodical one. It is uncertain when he decided upon it. There are very few passages in the book in which he refers to it with this name. And these are found late, for the first time in the fourth edition, and then in the handwritten insertions. Otherwise, when he is talking about his book as a literary product, he speaks of *mon livre, mes escrits, mes pieces, ces memoires,* or deprecatingly of *ce fagotage, cette fricassée, cette rapsodie, mes brisées,* and so forth.[287] But he prefers to reserve the term *essai* (and *essaier*) for designating the method of thinking, manner of living, and self-discovery. This is revealing about the reason he titled the book the way he did.

The root of the word *essai* is in the postclassical *exagium:* to weigh, weight, mass. Its derivatives in the Romance languages go back semantically to the expanded meaning of "attempt," evidence of which can be found in the fourth century, while the concrete meaning of "mass" only persists in Latin; the Romance languages have also generated a series of new concrete meanings, of which here we will only mention "taste sample" and "foretaste or sample foods and beverages." In France in the sixteenth century, there are various meanings for *essai:* practice, prelude, sample, attempt, temptation, taste sample—and for *essaier:* to feel, test, taste, experience, lead into temptation, undertake, expose oneself to danger, take a risk, weigh, weigh up, make an attempt. Clément Marot writes in the foreword to his *Adolescence Clémentine* (1532): "These are works of youth, these are trial strokes; nothing more indeed than a little garden . . . wherein you will never see a single shoot of worry." His opponent Sagon would head a pamphlet with *coup d'essay*. In Marot's use of *coup d'essay* (first work, *primitiae*, experimental piece) the ground is prepared for using *essai* as a modesty title for a literary work.[288]

In Montaigne we find: "Reader, let this essay of myself run on" (*Laisse, lecteur, courir encore ce coup d'essay* . . .), as an apology for a digression (III, 9, 736 B); here, as the context reveals, *coup d'essay* approximately means improvisation. Thus we have transcended the meaning of the beginner's trying things out to arrive at *essai* and *essaier*. This becomes apparent in a passage that is at the same time a fundamental statement: "If my mind could gain a firm footing, I would not make essays, I would make decisions; but it is always in apprenticeship and on trial" (III, 2, 440 B). The skeptic shys away from final conclusions and is content with learner's attempts. The word used for this, *essaier*, clearly shows its connection with Montaigne's method of seeing things as provisional, leaving everything open, of an experimenting sort of involvement with the self, and the renunciation of the practice of instructing others. We find the same in other passages, for example: "I set forth notions that are human and my own . . . as children set forth their essays to be instructed, not to instruct" (I, 56, 234 C). When he uses the word *essai* as the title of his book, in his epoch one heard very clearly the reference to the "beginner status" which it expresses. Thus La Croix du Maine writes in 1584: "This title is terribly modest, for if one wants to take the word *Essays* as meaning trial or apprenticeship, these are extremely humble and lowly . . ."[289]

The passage most important for the methodological meaning of the word is found at the beginning of I, 50. There the object of discussion is the *essais de jugement*, and Montaigne writes: "Therefore in the tests that I make of it [my judgment] here, I use every sort of occasion. If it is a subject I do not understand at all, even on that I essay my judgment . . . I stick to the bank . . . Sometimes in a vain and nonexistent subject I try to see if it [my judgment] will find the wherewithal to give it body . . . Sometimes I lead it to a noble and well-worn subject . . . There it plays its part by choosing the way that seems best to it." Here, grouped around the words *essai* and *essaier*, we have everything that characterizes Montaigne's thinking all together: the occasional impetus, the promenading pace, the consciousness of inadequacy, the readiness to "stick to the bank" without regret if he cannot proceed farther, but also the expectation that a deeper penetration could succeed—and as a whole, the inclination to feel good during all of this experimental passivity. And that is also the prevailing meaning of *essai:* testing oneself for the purpose of discovering one's own power or powerlessness, one's own nature per se: "As for the natural faculties that are in me, of which this book is the essay . . ." (I, 26, 107 A). Since his resolve to penetrate into his own nature through all which was alienating and clichéd continued to grow stronger over the years, he wrote critically in the third book: "We neither essay them [our faculties] nor know them. We invest ourselves with those of others, and let our own lie idle" (III, 12, 808 B). Because for him this always concerned an experiment upon himself, the term related in meaning, or even identical in meaning, namely, "exercise," could be used instead of *essai* (II, 17, 498 A).[290] The word *experience,* too, in the sense of passive self-discovery elevated to reflection, is used (II, 37, 579 A: "this essay—this experience"). This is how, for example, he "experiences" death; in the passively received event he "tastes," "feels" it, tries it out: "There is a certain way of familiarizing ourselves with death and trying it out" (II, 6, 268 A). His book is the expression of the sum of these experiences of himself: "All this fricassee . . . is nothing but a record of the essays of my life" (III, 13, 826 B). La Croix du Maine, who was mentioned earlier, thus explains this second meaning of the title using the same passage: "This book contains nothing other than a full declaration of the life of the aforementioned Monsieur de Montaigne." One further finds the meaning of "risk" for *essaier,* confirmed in Nicot with *periclitari,* and finally, its illustration using the graphic *sonder,*[291] which means *critical testing.*

One can see from all this that Montaigne intended the title of his book to be understood in view of the methodological meaning of *essai.* He did not intend the title to be the designation of a literary genre, as when a poet would title his poem "Poem of . . ." One must expand the title with something such as this: *Les Essais de ma vie, Les Essais de mon jugement, Les Essais de mes facultés naturelles,* and so forth. All meanings that fall within the conceptual field of essai for language awareness of that time should be included: *coup d'essay, apprentissage, épreuve, exercitation, expérience, jeu, sonder, goûter, tâter.* It is indeed a modest title, but it expresses what is real (and not a popular affectedness): the desire to exist in one's own temporary state. The title of this book is his best motto—even to the extent that it has the feature of so many of Montaigne's terms, a fluctuating breadth of meaning.

Translations of the title in his time and later show how correctly it was understood. Justus Lipsius writes in a letter in 1583: *Montani librum Gallicum Gustuum titulo* . . . With this, he has simply translated back into classical Latin what was part of the meaning in late and middle Latin of the word *exagium,* as well as its Romance language derivatives, that is, the meaning of "foretaste," "taste," "taste sample." Montaigne himself sometimes makes use of this meaning. For example, when he says speaking of his medical self-discoveries: "For anyone who wants to try it I have tasted it like his cupbearer" (III, 13, 927 B). Or: "I continually observe myself, I take stock of myself, I taste myself" (II, 17, 499 A), where the synonymous expression *et je m'essaye* could have been added automatically. A seventeenth-century reader, A. de Laval, protested Lipsius' rendering of the term with *gustus* and, citing a verse by Ovid, proposed *conatus,* which he explained with this addition: "that is, to essay, to try to see if he would succeed in writing . . . as apprentices do." De Thou and Sainte-Marthe also translate it with *conatus*—and correctly, since this word, which has the same meaning as *adumbratio* (sketch), was used in classical Latin to differentiate what was unfinished from what was complete. The same Sainte-Marthe also calls the *Essais* a *Miscellaneorum libri.* However, Sainte-Beuve did not agree with *conatus,* since he felt it had too much of a connotation of effort and strain: *lusus* (game) would be better. This, too, can be justified, both from Montaigne's overall attitude and from the evidence of several passages. "The play of my judgment," he writes, along with "I essay my judgment" (I, 50, 219 C). Then *tentamen* emerges again, for example, by the German Buddäus in the eighteenth century; the fact that Leibniz called his Latin essays *Tentamina* fits in with this. The translation of the *Essais* into other living languages reveals a similar understanding of the meaning of the title. The first Italian translation, by Naselli (1590), is titled *Discorsi morali, politici e militari*—the second, by Canini (1633), was *Saggi* . . . *ovvero Discorsi naturali, politici e morali.* This agrees with the concept then common of *Discorso, Discours* for presentations in loose, essayistic form; Machiavelli's *Discorsi* are the best example of this. By the way, the second posthumous (and garbled) edition of the *Essais* in 1595 had the subtitle: . . . *Thresor de plusieurs beaux et notables discours.* In Spain, Montaigne's admirer Quevedo speaks of his *Essais o Discursos.* Supposedly, an unpublished Spanish translation existed in the seventeenth century and it had already received the Church's Imprimatur: *Experiencias y varios discursos.* Florio's English translation (1603) carries the title: *The Essayes, or morall, politike and Millitaric Discourses* . . . And finally, there is J. J. Bode's masterful rendering into German, despite its numerous errors in language and adaptation of style: *Montaignes Gedanken und Meinungen über allerley Gegenstände* (1797)—a title that in language usage of that time expressed the contrast to the closed system of knowledge even more sharply than we can perceive today. Lichtenberg, for example, customarily used the words *Gesinnungen* (views), *Meinungen* (opinions), *Gedanken* (thoughts) to distinguish freely reflecting subjectivity which is saturated with experience from the ordered but unincorporated knowledge of the schools.[292]

In these translations of the title *Les Essais* we find a reflection of the wealth of meaning which Montaigne himself placed in it. A literal rendering—with *Saggi, Ensayos, Versuche*—did not become established at all, or if so, only hesitantly, in living languages before the nineteenth century. But all of those alternative titles were available, and each of them captured at least *one* essential element of that wealth of meaning and the methodological orientation of the title. But meanwhile, the word "essay" had already come into circulation as a generic designation. Thus the title had become a literary term. Montaigne himself had not intended this, but it became a consequence of the work's form characteristics. In France, it began with Coëffeteau; in 1607 he published his *Essay des questions théologiques.* Pierre Camus (*Essay sceptique,* 1610) and others followed. Quite important, even the most important, authors issued scientific, philosophical, and theological treatises under this title, in part with an eye to the cosmopolitan propriety which recommended an unpedantic appearance, and in part from a deliberate fragmentarism, for example, Descartes, Pascal, Nicole. But this title only became a general trend as a result of the English influence. Bacon used it for the first time as the designation of a genre in 1597, probably outwardly borrowing from Montaigne, but with the correct idea that the essay as a prose form had classical roots. "The word [essay] is late, but the thing is ancient: for Seneca's Epistles to Lucilius . . . are Essaies, that is dispersed Meditacions," he writes in the foreword to the second edition of his *Essayes.* Bacon's *Essayes* are in any case quite different from Montaigne's work; their didactic, maxim-like, dry and cool style and their limitation to an audience of persons of the court and politicians has nothing to do with the colorful, lovable, capricious, and generally human Frenchman. This also applies to Robert Johnson's *Essaies* (1607). On the other hand, the *Essayes* of William Cornwallis (1600, final version in 1637) live in the spirit of Montaigne and have the same writer's consciousness he had. Starting with England, the essay as an artistically cultivated, urbane genre permeated by autobiographical elements and a strong subjectivity made the transition in both the title and the thing itself—and even in the English orthography—into world literature. France profited from this English configuration and proliferation of the structure which arose in their countryman Montaigne. We will not take this topic any further. The task of writing the history of the essay on the basis of world literature still remains incomplete.[293]

6. SOME SPECIFICS ON THE ESSAY FORM

We do not need to analyze the form of a Montaignian Essay in all its detail here. We will merely content ourselves with a few of its elements. The picture will be rounded out by all that we have described so far. We can apply to Montaigne's Essay what Herder once said at the beginning of his *Briefe über das Lesen des Horaz* about the poetry of the Roman: "Elegant charm and grace were his muse. One feels, one enjoys the elegant charm; the grace speaks to us in shapes and features, in movements, words, gestures, soulfully, warm-heartedly; who would want, intend to fix in place the dance of these movements, cut apart the play of these features?"

Only in the period before the *Essais* did Montaigne cultivate a strict disposition. An example of this was presented earlier (chapter 1), the letter on the death of La Boétie. In the translation of Sebond, his resistance to the treatise style had already emerged; the translator sought to rid the text of the ponderous apparatus of divisions in the original (compare chapter 3). The first Essays begin with a completely different method. Montaigne placed himself in the depths of contemporary miscellany and anthology literature, that is, the *Leçons,* the centos, and the collections of platitudes and examples. Villey described them and their classical models (Valerius Maximus, Aulus Gellius, Stobaeus, etc.) and showed how one could identify in individual early Essays the particular cento used by the sequence of quotations in it.[294] In the initial imitation of the compilatory method, Montaigne suspected he was on the path that would lead him to his own form. But he quickly distanced himself from the pure cento-type form. He transformed the practice, common in those writings, of assembling the various opposing opinions on a particular matter into the inner compulsion of his skeptical thinking. The anthology-like accumulation, the diversity of material loses its pedantic instructive quality in his work. He has fun with it, but with a philosophical artery from which he pours new blood into the suffocating lot of real facts of written-out compendia. What in the *Leçons* and the centos was fad and confusion in his work becomes style that makes use of the disorder because it can be the vessel of an organic order.

Montaigne's essayistic writing begins several degrees farther back, so to speak, than treatise writing, namely, in the process of thinking and association which was still in motion. Let us look at the beginning of II, 4: "Let Business Wait till Tomorrow." The title theme comes from Plutarch. The treatise style, after an appropriate preamble, would head straight for the subject. But instead of this, Montaigne begins with praise of Amyot, the translator of Plutarch, that is, with a secondary source of a secondary source. But for him the topic of the title is bound up with the most personal moments, namely, his readings of Plutarch in Amyot's translation, his own relationship to that which is Greek, and his opinion on Amyot's role in French artistic prose. All these "incidental matters" are just as important to him as the title theme, and they must thus come out on paper, and not to satisfy a *prooimion* required according to a rule of rhetoric. The later Essays display such beginnings in "secondary sources" so widely that one can identify a deliberate style in the abandonment of proper school divisions of text. Montaigne makes as little formal distinction between *prooimion* and *narratio* as he does between primary and secondary sources. It is one of the fundamental features of the Essay that it does not separate the subject about which it is speaking from the personal conditions that led the author to that subject, nor does it separate it from the associative links it has to other subjects. The occasions for reflection, regardless of how or where they originate, are also preserved in that reflection. The maxim of classical writing, "creating is choosing" (Taine), does not apply here. A created order that came into being by singling things out would represent for the living spirit, which is in a principal sense always like a beginner, that is, always "essayistic," a falsification of the order that is related to growth, the order that appears automatically in the relationship between object and thinking.

The relationship of the Essays to their particular titles is informative. In the first book, the contents most frequently agree with the titles, but this is much less the case in the second and third books. But even when they do agree, the relationship is quite a loose one. Montaigne says as much. He opens Essay I, 46 ("Of Names"), which is relatively faithful in its subject matter, with the words: "Whatever variety of herbs there may be, the whole thing is included under the name of salad. Likewise, under the consideration of names, I am here going to whip up a hodgepodge of various items." The weak association between the title and the content of an Essay increases with the years. The title in the end is only a hook upon which the bundle of different types of material is hung. Montaigne knows this, and intends it to be thus (III, 9, 761 B/C: "The titles of my chapters do not always embrace their matter . . ."). His orientation toward linguistic criticism is behind this: no name can capture the wealth of a thing; the incongruence of thing and language leads the writer to neglect consistency with the title, and the incongruence of title and content of an Essay is thus a symbol of the core theme of the *Essais* per se. This is why we find numerous titles that do not "fit"—the ironic one of II, 12, or, to skip over a few, the titles of the third book: III, 5; III, 6; III, 9; III, 11. Then again, he can be in the mood to provide an adequate title even there: III, 1 ("Of the Useful and the Honorable"); III, 2 ("Of Repentance"); and so forth. This is admittedly no assurance that there will be no long "digressions." Pasquier laughed bad-temperedly at these inconsistencies: "Montaigne took pleasure in pleasantly displeasing." Thackeray joked with better intentions that Montaigne could just as well have given every one of his Essays the title of another one, or he could just as well have called one "Of the Moon," another "Of Fresh Cheese." In III, 5, the pages-long "Introduction" concludes with "But let us come to my theme" (644 B); the name of the Essay is "On Some Verses of Virgil," but these are not the "theme" (or only very peripherally), rather, love is the theme. Sometimes the titles are a means of hiding dangerous contents, like the key words in Bayles' *Dictionnaire*: for example, III, 11 carries the title "Of Cripples," but first he discusses witch trials, and at length. Sometimes the titles are simply jokes, such as Rabelais loved (he speaks of this in the prologue to *Gargantua*), or Stendhal (*La Chartreuse de Parme*), or Sterne in England, Jean Paul in Germany.[295]

Within an Essay, then, everything is wavy line, outgrowth, and outgrowth of the outgrowth. For example, if Montaigne is reasoning about marriage and love and the comparison occurs to him that marriage and love have as little to do with each other as nobility of one's station in life and virtue, he quickly loses himself in an observation on nobility and virtue (III, 5, 646–647). He lets the flow carry him until it takes him to a place where he decides to stay a while: "I am prone to begin without a plan; the first remark brings on the second" (I, 40, 186 B). Thus III, 9 begins with pages of musing on everything imaginable, incomplete, without depth, until suddenly, as if from nowhere, clear concentrated realizations about the paradoxical law of life which is so central to him emerge: "Universal sickness is individual health." But these passages are also merely a meditation of the occasion, far removed from the dimly suspected destination for which he had set out. Each point touched upon in the manner of taking a stroll can (but need not) become the spark that lights the flame. From the standpoint of composition, this requires linking digression to digression, because they are all mere possibilities that can lead into the inner order, namely, into the relationship the author has with the structure of life and of the self.[296] The inner form of the *Essais* resembles a journey on which one leaves the wide throughway that ignores the surrounding landscape for the sake of leading directly to the destination in order to move into the forest. The traveler walks on, discovers unknown or forgotten trees, plants, animals, and suddenly finds himself at the throughway again, but richer and more knowledgeable than before.

Probably only the "Apology" was planned according to a division by subject and was intended to be a kind of treatise. There are signs of this. But in the execution, the system of divisions becomes so weakened that variously attempted efforts of Montaigne's critics to reconstruct them lead in each case to different results.[297] Here, as in other cases in which there is an original intention for the layout of the piece, the act of writing does not fill out that intended layout, but rather diverges from it or grows beyond it. The distribution of the contents lacks proportion. One could even reverse the order of some sections of the "Apology"; its compositional arrangement is not in any case compelling.

Montaigne himself states that the length or brevity of individual pieces is determined by external motives and not by the final exhaustion of the topic (III, 9, 762 C). The extent of a piece has its own life, the content has its own, different one; the two are not composed within each other's constraints. In any case, the long Essay, as we find predominantly in the third book, is the more appropriate form for the unending lines of continuing reflection. Some Essays—not merely the two directly following II, 16—have no well-defined beginning, rather, they seem to continue others, or to begin in the midst of an interplay of thoughts the first parts of which were not written down. As we learn from occasional comments (III, 12, 796 B: "I was writing this . . ."), Montaigne did not write individual Essays continuously, even in the first draft, but rather worked on them at various times. One could detect this easily in the *Essais* even if he had not related how he wandered around in his library, leafing through first this book, then that one, sometimes "musing," sometimes "setting down" or "dictating" (III, 3, 629 B).[298]

The *Essais* have a more sharply defined form, at least at times, only in one aspect, namely, the conclusion. Here, even in Montaigne, the old Romanic sense of art which was preserved in the epigram, the sonnet, and in prose stirs again, it is a sense that is a virtuoso master of the ambiguous, maxim-like, concise point that both closes off what went before and brings in further reverberations. He himself admits his inclinations in this direction (II, 10, 303 B; against Cicero's long *clausulae*). The conclusions of I, 31; II, 25; III, 2; and III, 9 shows that he is a master of the suggestive brief punchline. But these, too, are only an elegant ceasing to speak, not an end to the thinking.

One can thus summarize the characteristics of the Essay as it was created by Montaigne and recognized and developed further in later works as an independent genre as follows. The Essay is the organ of a way of writing which does not intend to be a result, but rather a process, just like the thinking that comes to an unfolding of the self in the process of writing. In the Essay the particular character of this thinking, skepticism, has found its means of becoming modern artistic prose in everyday language. This prose does not at first dare to call itself art due to external considerations, but it is art. Since skepticism avoids judgments and classifications, the Essay even in form avoids wholeness, divisions, and didacticism. It is deliberately fragmentary. Since the skepticism replaces constructed contexts with observation of individual things, the expandable Essay also opens itself to sensual and inner observation; it describes, relates, expresses, and in this manner it attests that the depiction of what is observed captures its truth, something that cannot be comprehended in a concept, more purely and protectively than discursive analysis. Its open form actualizes in writing what cannot be concluded about the substance of the world and of life, as well as of the author's self-discovery. It is like a slightly clinging garment that repeats the lively or soft breaths the spirit takes. It lives from the generative force of the moments, each of which appears singly, as if there were no others. It makes it possible in writing to shift even the perspectives and to move everything under changing exposure, whereby no one becomes the ultimate one. It is able to play along with the entire combinatory game of things in themselves, the self in itself, and their interplay with one another. In the process of leveling external and internal facts into a factuality that is no longer separated into main issues and peripheral ones, it reveals the secret that rules over the totality of the world and life, and it no doubt arranges the details of this secret quite differently than we, who are caught up in goal-oriented and customary thinking, are in a position to know. It has the broadest space for contradictions, and it takes away from them the character of a logical offense. It is the means of expression of an intellect which faces the world as a continuous beginner, and always faces itself anew. This is the source of its magic, a magic that belongs to everything that is just beginning, the broad horizon still before it and the courage for adventure within it. Unlike a classical work, it is not a creation that can be separated from the author, for its purpose lies in its subject which becomes real by looking at itself and things in reference to itself. It is "nature," not in the sense of an untouched rawness, but rather a naturalness that is rediscovered because it has been lost, and it is smoothed out only with urbane irony and moderation. It is nature at the reflected level which strives to reach beyond art and culture because it has wearied of them as antinature. It is the product of a high and late epoch of education which has become critical of itself: a primitive could not have written or understood the Essay. But the educated spirit that has passed through much knowledge and many cultural experiences understands it, heaves a sigh of relief in it, as Montaigne himself heaved a sigh of relief when he cut a path out of the cultural masses into the open spaces of natural subjectivity and learned to play with those masses. It is significant that Montaigne's alleged pupil Charron felt he had to "order" the *Essais* in order to bring their ideas, in the form of his book *De la sagesse,* to the scholars. But that was death to the spirit of the *Essais.* Charron fell back into the form of knowledge and thinking which Montaigne had left behind.

The opinion has been advanced from time to time that Montaigne's Essay, because it is an experiment, can be looked at as a parallel in philosophy and history of form to the experiments in the natural sciences of those epochs. This is quite tempting, but it is erroneous. Because here we must once again make a distinction. The experiment in the natural sciences is a systematic intervention that attempts to test or confirm preliminary assumptions; it operates according to a rigorous method, avoids random perceptions, separates the laws of what occurs from the occurrence itself, and aims for what is universal, transferable, what permits the prediction of the same effects when the causes are the same. But the Essay "experiments" with passive, "nonrigorous" methods (which is really a rigorousness of another order), it permits inner and outer occurrences to approach one another as they will, it undertakes a journey at random and is prepared to wind up somewhere completely different than it could foresee. As a structure somewhere between prose and poetry, it is open to reflection as well as observation, to factual interests as well as mere moods, it can formulate, but it can also narrate, and in all this, it grants what is individual prerogative over what is universal, whether its approach to it is through reflection or observation. It isolates it to the disadvantage of what is universal, not conversely. Thus it does not represent a parallel to the scientific method of that time, but is instead its opposite in content and form. It is the literary creation of the other great movement of the modern intellect which is separate from the natural sciences: moralistic phenomenology.

Finally, Montaigne's Essay is the writer's way of pursuing the wisdom of obedience. Its casualness of form has the same beauty as the vegetative-like growth that distinguishes the spirit of its author. It is not even merely an "expression" of his obedient freedom. Rather, it is this freedom itself as directly as a person's speech is this freedom itself, and is not merely an "expression" that one could picture oneself without in the belief that even without it, one would still be present in one's full essence.

7. THE OPEN FORM

Seen historically, the *Essais,* as has already been noted, are a special case in that extensive mass of open-form prose literature which had long been manifested in complications, miscellany, free treatises, letters, dialogues, diatribes, and so forth, and had become generally popular again from about the fifteenth century on. It is found here in Latin and vulgar language texts, elegant or crude, and in theoretical as well as narrative genres. Some clear lines lead back to models, usually of late antiquity, among which one might mention the widely read *Noctes Atticae* by Aulus Gellius with its principle of *ordo fortuitus* (cf. Montaigne's favorite word for techniques in thinking and prose, *fortuite*). In products such as these one can note a tendency toward wildness, but one also sees the natural vessel for the empiricism that relishes fact and occurrence, something that tends to break through repeatedly in late and transitional epochs. While Boccaccio was still ordering his novellas by themes, persons, days, and numbers and subordinating them to the unity of a concrete societal situation (noble social circle in a country seat in Tuscany), about two hundred years later, Bandello issued his only as a collection without an overall order as to subject, time, or composition. They are: *Una mistura d'accidenti diversi, diversamente e in diversi luoghi e tempi a diverse persone avvenute e sanza ordine veruno recitati,* he writes in the foreword to the third part of the *Novelle* ("A variety of different events which happened in a different manner in different places and times to different persons, and related without any particular order"). In this richly configured formulation we can see how he relishes the worldwide random variety. The lack of order in itself becomes a feature of modern novelistic literature, particularly in France. "What order must be kept when it is a laughing matter?" Guillaume Bouchet asks in the foreword to his *Sérées* (1548). Rabelais' novel is the monumental outgrowth of this independence. The situation is similar in theoretical prose. Dante's *Convivio* was still a strict treatise, divided by distinctions, layed out with an eye to completeness (though it was never completed); it is a vulgar-language reflection of the Latin school style of the High Middle Ages. On the other hand, the later Italian lay writings—for example, those of Alberti—are rich in anecdotes and digressions, mixing conversation on factual matters with the personal. They make extensive use of the dialogue in order to picture the societal realm from which they come or upon which they hope to have an effect. The Latin prose of the humanists presents the same image of a loosening up. Valla's *Elegantiae and* Poliziano's *Miscellanea* can be mentioned in this context. In France, Budé uses his studies of pandects, the *Annotationes* (1508), filling them with associatively sprinkled-in material from all areas of classical culture, but also with personal observations on the political situations of the epoch. It is no different in his work on coinage (*De Asse,* 1515), of which he himself said that what was most important could be found in the digressions, also characteristically invoking Cicero's letters. The body of commentary and interpretation in the fifteenth and sixteenth centuries also moved into a peculiar deviating expansion and frequently made use of the text being commented upon only as an opportunity to get into essay-like variety. Thus, for example, Vives' explanations of Suetonius, Isocrates, and so forth consist of *bons mots* of personal taste and eclectically collected masses of material; Vives is not the main combatant against the scholastic treatise technique for nothing. Erasmus' *Colloquia,* and also some sections of his *Apophthegmata* lie within the same realm. In the writing of history, in Latin, but even more so in the vulgar languages, an unbridled development of the individual at the expense of the whole proliferated; it was a continuing process of wandering off into the secondary circumstances of the event under discussion. Even Machiavelli can be cited under this point of view. In his Livius interpretations (the *Discorsi*) he includes all of his observations on politics, leading an army, questions on administration, and so forth. Etienne Pasquier, who is particularly interesting here because he was close to Montaigne in time as well as personally, is the main representative of free-form historiography in the vulgar languages. His *Recherches de la France* (first appearing in 1562) show an almost complete disruption of form in favor of the study of facts, anecdotes, and curiosities. Some sections of this book are extraordinarily closely related to Montaigne in both title and content. One chapter on dreams contains a sentence that proves the great extent to which his writer's consciousness was clear about the aesthetic charm, but also the usefulness, of the open form for a manner of thinking which plays off "nature" against "art": "Here is a miscellany. It is not said that a prairie variegated with an infinite variety of flowers, Nature's disordered products, be not just as pleasing to the eye as the Gardeners' artistically tilled flowerbeds." Montaigne could also have written this.[299]

There are endless numbers of examples. But it is more important to remember the reasons which led to this triumph of the open form and joy in variety. They can be found in the various antischolastic tendencies of a religious, philosophical, scientific, and urbane nature. From the fourteenth and fifteenth centuries on, a layman's piety had been emerging stronger than before, and it offered resistance to the school-based theological speculations and subtleties and withdrew into the simple, artless word.[300] Of the writings of popular theology which came into circulation from the Frenchman Gerson on, there is a tangled line that can nevertheless be followed leading via the authors of the *devotio moderna* to Erasmus and his rejection of the treatise style that is chopped up into distinctions and divisions, and which to him appeared to threaten the *pietas*, evangelical purity. Compare what he says about this in the *Ratio seu Methodus perveniendi ad veram theologiam*.[301] Fideism, which had meanwhile been renewed, accommodated this free orientation toward form, as did the skepticism that went along with the fideism. It is no accident that fideists and skeptics—Francesco Pico della Mirandola, Agrippa von Nettesheim, and later Francisco Sanchez— were among those furthering the natural style that was freed of divisions. And from another side, secular humanism was exercising influence in the same direction. Those renewing hellenistic moral philosophy are nurturing a humane essential education, and they react no less strongly to the late-scholastic intellectualism than do those trying to renew piety. Whether the "authentic thing" one is seeking is Christian simplicity or the secular personality of the caliber of antiquity—what unites these is the turning to a relaxed form of expression. In the secular case, one can see this as early as Petrarch. Instead of the syllogistic structure of periods, he loves the free sequence of suggestive sentences and, with Cicero's letters as his model, he strives to make a connection to colloquial language, or at least what he takes to be colloquial language. In addition, we see the beginnings of the academies and courtly cultures with their conversations held among urbane people of both genders and the nurturing of a code of propriety applied to the arts of conversation and writing. The requirements of good breeding also call for the writer's instrument of an open form, in fact, real elegance comes into the matter from this urbane side. What Erasmus says in Latin in the letter of dedication of his *Apophthegmata*—that the *ordo neglectus*, the *non molestum esse,* is appropriate for the nonpedantic educational path of princes and their educators—had already been compulsory for vulgar-language writings at the end of the Quattrocento of Upper Italy, and it would remain so into the flowering of courtly culture in Spain and France. This open form that could be used so variously was also suitable for the new scientific attitude of unspoiled healthy human reason which sought facts instead of concepts, views of life rather than interpretation by authorities, and it was also well suited to the reception of the massive flood of material arising from the broadening of ethnographic and geographic horizons.[302]

There are certainly considerable differences within these various processes which we have quickly sketched. Yet all of them work together to further that particular writer's orientation of which Montaigne would become a master. They are a part of the prehistory of the *Essais* with respect to both its spirit and its form.

8.   LETTER AND ESSAY

In classical times as well as in the Renaissance there were two genre which predominantly used the open-style form, namely, the letter and the dialogue. Montaigne not only reproduced a moral-philosophy type of thinking which rejected the constraints of system, changing it to the study of mores, he also reproduced their free-form language and changed it into the Essay. Letter and dialogue, along with the generically related diatribe, were the major means of expression used for the moral philosophy of hellenism. Montaigne does not use these genres, but he sympathizes with them, from the correct feeling that they are the earlier stages of his Essay in world literature, mainly in their classical manifestation. Thus we find the most effective impetus for his own language of form not in the *Leçons,* anthologies, and miscellany of his epoch, but rather in the classical letter and dialogue, apart from Plutarch's *Moralia,* which for its part is also drafted in a dialogue-like or essayistic form. Thus an overview of the letter and the dialogue and their characteristics which could be developed into the Essay is indicated here. In providing this, we will restrict ourselves to the authors that Montaigne read.

The letter as it was adopted and transformed from the Greek didactic letter by the Romans is an agile product in which a consciousness of individuality, which is restricted in other genres, can unfold more freely because it is written under the assumption that the writing of it serves to allow a personal exchange of opinion among friends and relatives.[303] The letter adheres to this presumption even when it is intended for publication. It offers the possibility of introducing private, intimate speech and casual subjectivity into prose literature. Its Roman master is Cicero. Less in the *Familiares,* which were edited and stylized for the public, than in the *Epistulae ad Atticum* (published posthumously in 60 A.D.) did he treat the genre as a means of expression for a richly shaded chat. He was able to express himself so personally in these letters that one could use them to reconstruct his life and his spiritual make-up. It has been said of them: "The faculty of the reflective interior life to fully manifest itself in the instantaneous expression appears here to be displayed in the natural flow of discourse" (Misch, as cited earlier) and they have thus been considered a major origin of autobiographical writing per se. Cicero's letter can discuss all possible questions, whether political, scientific, or concerned with moral philosophy in an informal alternation that is held together only by the unity of the one writing it. The writing process enjoys the freedom of saying everything, *quidquid in buccam venit* (*Ad Att.* I, 12) and surrendering to the productivity of the moment.[304] The flexibility of the Ciceronian letter consists, in accordance with universal classical practice, first in its adaptation to the particular intended recipients and the variations in style and tone resulting from this. But after this, it consists in the communication of the *privata cotidianaque vita* (*Ad Quintum fratrem* I, 1, 36) in which the author, freed of his official and dignified existence, finds the time and leisure for self-contemplation. Many of the letters directed to Atticus are like diaries filled with the moods a person can only reveal to those close to him, weariness, self-reproach, feelings of remorse, genuine suffering, but also a holiday mood or self-irony: *Ex epistolarum mearum incon-stantia puto te mentis meae motum videre,* he writes on one occasion (*Ad Att.* III, 8, 4: "You will probably detect my inner restlessness in the changeable behavior in my letters"). The letters remain rooted in quite concrete situations, not only of the writer himself, but also of the recipi-ent, particularly when Cicero is recommending political maxims, like in his correspondence with his brother Quintus: the letters refer to his brother's particular situation at the moment, for which help is indi-cated. He carefully avoids a doctrinaire tone, everything is to have a human warmth to it. The agility and mobility of his own spirit is also revealed in the fact that Cicero loves the unrestricted swinging between pro and contra when he is expressing his opinion on a particular matter.

Cicero created a literary category of immeasurable effectiveness with his letters. While Seneca's didactic letter later on has a different purpose, it still contains the elements we are interested in here. There has been mention of the "essayist" Seneca with good reason.[305] Even the letters of Pliny the Younger are essay-like. But here the still relatively great directness of Cicero's Atticus letters has retreated from a calculating stylistic aim. The concrete situation from and for which they claim to have been written is artificial, their casualness is an arrangement calcu-lated for its effect on the connoisseur; the particular addressee only represents an invented motive (or an after-the-fact recipient of a dedica-tion) for the writer to allow him to express random thoughts in personal reflections and in an elegant dilettantism that feigns leisure. They intend to function as a whole, a picture book of all kinds of things with a variable style. They are usually set up such that from insignificant start-ing points they broaden into digressions. They deal with demanding topics, but also banal everyday matters, they describe a landscape, a villa, a banquet, a day in the life of an old man, and they do all this with coquettish self-contradictions. But what is most important is the fact that here, despite all of the rhetoricizing, the essential features of the letter are acknowledged as laws of the genre. Additionally, these fea-tures had already been introduced before this in the poetic epistle, as Horace proves.

When Petrarch took up the letter again in a more personal form after the epistolographical tradition of the Early and High Middle Ages, which was never destroyed, but which receded in the treatise style, this took place in direct imitation of Cicero's Atticus letters that he had discovered. (He was not yet acquainted with the *Familiares*). He is also the one who exploited the Ciceronian letter as a source for the knowledge of the intimate humanity of the Roman. His own letters pass on to his century and those following the Ciceronian elements of the genre as forms of written expression which can be learned, forms that alternate between artistic (even artificial) and familiar types of style. Petrarch writes them both for the sake of their public effect and to discharge subjectivity. To explain to his friends *animi mei status, animi mei effigies*, as an element for obtaining the *fragiliora et humiliora* which were not permitted in high art is his admitted intention in the latter case (*Fam.* I, 1). They are intended to be intellectual intercourse with the like-minded rather than didactic anonymity. A broad, even boundless range of subjects can be touched upon in them, but the letter always remains oriented to the feeling, opinion-forming author who is more concerned with self-expression than subject matter knowledge, the author who says of himself: no one should forbid me to go wherever I wish, to flee from whatever frightens me, to attempt what has not been attempted, to walk upon friendly and short paths, to hurry or to rest, to deviate from the path or to reverse my direction (*Fam.* XXII, 2). If he is speaking about a subject, he does not refrain from relating how he came to this subject. An example of this can be found in the *Seniles* (XVI, 1): there he explains, beginning with the topic of Cicero, the development of his relationship to Cicero; the well-known panegyric to the Roman is completely embedded in Petrarch's own course of education. The intentionally personal perspectives are not balanced out in their contradictions. The organization of the letters does not depend on the order of the facts or on a logical sequence. It simply results from the mood of the moment and a taste for change, whether this taste is satisfied in a change in style related to the addressee (in accordance with a classical rule of the genre) or whether it consists in the joy in the variety of what is worthy of discussion. Petrarch brought the germ of the Essay placed in the letter by Cicero (and Seneca) a little further.

We can skip over the other humanistic products. From the sixteenth century on, the letter nurtured as a genre of art also appears in the vulgar languages. In Italy it begins with Bembo and Aretino. In Spain, we find the *Epistolas familiares* by Antonio de Guevara (1539 and frequently): these are reflections which are kept familiar in tone, filled with anecdotes, short stories, and examples, reflections of a nature that tends in part toward publicity, and reflections that lighten their eclectic masses of material (taken in part from Plutarch's *Moralia*) with a studied lack of composition—they are a kind of treasure chest of the average man's education, and they had enormous influence, including in France, where in Guterry's translation, entitled *Epîtres dorées,* they circulated and were also known to Montaigne. In France, Estienne Pasquier then boasted of having brought the vulgar-language art letter to his country-men. His collection of letters is admittedly dependent upon Cicero and Pliny the Younger. As he himself states, it includes "all kinds of wares," this admittedly in an extremely chaotic form. Pasquier even developed a little work on the aesthetics of this genre, and in the last letter he comments that he intended to offer nothing more than "a history of my inclinations."[306]

"A history of my inclinations": this also applies to Montaigne's work. The points of agreement between the Essay and the letter are obvious. Montaigne himself admits at a late time that he came close to using the letter form for his writings: "And I would have preferred to adopt this form to publish my sallies, if I had had someone to talk to" (I, 40, 185–186 C). Only what appears to be a secondary reason prevented him from doing so. But to him it was a good reason: he lacked someone to address them to, thus he lacked an honest prerequisite; it was inimi-cal to his sense of honesty to write fictitious letters. The passage quoted is an indication that he himself felt how suitable the letter was for his own spiritual nature and, as the preceding sentences, which we have not quoted here, make clear, that he sensed the kinship between letter and Essay. He owned and knew the most important literature in letters from Cicero and Pliny the Younger to Guevara. He also knew that the Italians were in the forefront of this. From them he had "a hundred different volumes of them; those of Annibal Caro seem to be the best" (I, 40, 186 B). His judgment on Caro was appropriate. For his *Lettere familiari* (1581) were indeed the best that the epistolography of Tuscany had to offer; they were valued very highly both at that time and later on in the writing of the history of literature.[307]

The letter, because it contained hidden essays itself, paved the way for and furthered Montaigne's Essay. In letter and Essay we find the same: free drifting from one subject to another, the intertwining of discussion of the factual and the personal, the expression of a contempla-tive or even only capricious mood, the explanation of the *mentis meae motus,* as Cicero put it, and Petrarch similarly, the self-contradiction, the perspective use of pro and contra, and the permission to improvise (Cicero's formula of *quidquid in buccam venit* returns in Montaigne, though in a different context, but indirectly related to the *Essais:* "what-ever comes into his mouth" III, 9, 761 C). In both cases we find instead of the firm marble of great art the malleability of a language which finds its way back to its natural function; in both cases, a genre in which man reverses the depersonalization that occurred in the great work of art, yet he does so in a manner that itself becomes a work of art; in both cases, we find a product in which the intellect can devote itself to its deepest tendencies, in which he can tear down what he builds, and where he is free to participate in the productivity of the moment which requires no other justification than that it is there. But it was not antiquity, but rather the modern epochs of antiformalist thinking in the tug-of-war with late scholasticism which were able to allow these freedoms to flourish to such an extent that they freed themselves of the letter form that still encased them and were able to become the self-aware essay form. The point of crossover occurred with Montaigne.

And this is also why he went beyond the letter to a considerable degree. He freed himself completely from the treatise style that was still an option in the letters of Petrarch, Erasmus, and Budé, and he also completely eliminated the last remains of a reluctance to speak uninhibitedly of oneself which they still dragged along with them. We know from Petrarch that before his letters were published he weeded out anything that was too concrete or random in the first draft, which was intended merely as correspondence.[308] Montaigne, on the other hand, reinforced precisely what was most personal. In the Essay, he perfected the process and the literary language of modern subjectivity, while Petrarch, operating from a classical bias, anxiously wanted to tone this process down. In this way, and in an entirely different, superior manner, Montaigne coped with the variety of material and digressions which weighed upon the letters of Guevara or Pasquier like a wild chaos; he played where these dragged. But above all, in the transition to the Essay he eliminated the affected quality of the humanistic and vulgar-language letter, and also the set-up situation in which one pretended to have an addressee. His judgments on the literature of letters turn out accordingly. Although, like for Petrarch earlier, he finds Cicero's Atticus letters valuable "because in them I discover his personal humors" (II, 10, 302 A), in him as well as in Pliny the Younger he disapproves of the fame-hungry publication of letters that never really served as actual correspondence (I, 40, 183 A). He even directs a sharp comment at Guevara (I, 48, 213 A). He recognizes with aversion the fashionable illness of the contemporary art letter which had become the playground of empty exercises in style, and which had made of what was once the genre of directness a genre of vain coyness. He distanced himself from the letter for all these reasons. And he fulfilled the possibilities for the expression of free subjectivity which the letter contained with more beauty and power than the authors of letters, who were inhibited by rhetorical considerations. In any case, he had to create something different, the Essay, which could carry itself and had no further need for fictions.

9. DIALOGUE AND ESSAY

Now to the dialogue. Together with the letter, it is part of the prehistory of Montaigne's open-form language. And it is so all the more since the letter, as has been repeated like a formula from antiquity on, is "half of a dialogue." What the two have in common with one another they also have in common with the essay: "They allow an informal manner of presentation, and they offer a form for explaining objects that do not lend themselves to a systematic treatment."[309]

Montaigne expressed his sympathy for the dialogue several times, specifically the Platonic dialogue. We have already quoted a core passage from III, 9. Another pasage can be found in the "Apology" following an explanation of the Socratic method and Greek and academic Roman skepticism. First he notes of various philosophers with satisfaction that they have more a seeking and doubting than instructing writing style, then this is expanded to include Seneca and Plutarch, and finally we read: "Plato seems to me to have favored this form of philosophizing in dialogues deliberately, to put more fittingly into diverse mouths the diversity and variation of his own ideas. To treat matters diversely is as good as to treat them uniformly, and better, to wit, more copiously and usefully" (II, 12, 377 C). We recognize Montaigne's favorite words, which are emphasized here, and we also know that he saw a skeptic in Plato. In his view, the dialogue is the writer's actualization of the withholding of judgment, the impossibility of fixing in place either the spirit or the subjects, and the linguistic means of improvisational subjectivity, which can depict its wealth and changing perspectives by distributing material among several persons. Thus in this declaration of sympathy he expresses some of his own consciousness as a writer. Montaigne is, by the way, not the last person to interpret Platonic dialogue in this way. Something similar was done in more modern research; compare what Hirzel says on this (*Dialog* I, 245). Shortly before this, Walter Pater (*Plato and the Platonism*, 1893) emphasized in the Greeks' dialogue technique the skeptically essayistic method, a "literary form which is particularly suited to a versatile but hesitant consciousness of truth" which "never comes to an end, so to speak," "paves the way, clears the atmosphere or wipes the slate of the spirit clean," "does not make any assertions, but rather structures a temperament," and "experiences the remnants of what is questionable as the salt of the truth."[310] It is obvious that these assessments apply only to some of the Platonic dialogues (the *Apology, Lysis, Protagoras*, etc.) and one of the methods, but not the entire content of Plato's philosophy, which even when it shifts and hesitates clears away what is confused and leaves behind it an unforgettable luminescent trail of knowledge. All that is important to us here is the influence that can emanate from these characteristics of Plato which are treated as one-sided. In Montaigne, like three hundred years later in Pater, we find repetition only of the manner in which some of the classical imitators of the Platonic dialogue understood and adopted it, like the representatives of academic Roman skepticism and Plutarch. Like the letter, the dialogue has become a permanent genre. It is not necessary to speak of the mass of medieval and humanistic products. What the Renaissance centuries offer in this respect in Latin and the vulgar languages is analogous to the history of the letter. Almost all branches of knowledge can be presented in dialogue form. Among them is the methodically rigorous dialogue worked out according to the Aristotelian model, in the manner of Galileo, for example, and also the more relaxed didactic dialogue such as that written by Tasso,[311] in number and prestige far behind the essay-like type that was particularly preferred by eclectics of moral philosophy (for example, Alberti). The latter represents a structure quite rich in digressions in which everything that interests the author or any commonplace idea that must be considered can be mixed in under the guise of something coming up randomly in conversation. It adapts itself to the back and forth of semi-joking, semi-critical opinions that are played off against one another, and it is equipped to provide a hearing for the doxographical and empirical masses of material by distributing them among various roles, leaving the author his flexible freedom. Additionally, this dialogue shows to what great an extent the courtly, societal culture in which the layman's education blossomed was a culture of conversation.[312] The greatest philosophical event in Italy, the work of Giordano Bruno, which arose almost simultaneously with Montaigne's *Essais*, consists of dialogues. In France, the doxographs and skeptics that Montaigne used were dialogue writers: Pontus de Tyard, Pierre de La Ramée, Guy de Bruès, and Jacques Tahureau, who was filled with Lucianic-Erasmian wickedness, and whose *Dialogues* (1565) were in Villey's view among the precursors of the *Essais*.

Thus we can say this: Montaigne's Essay, in direct contact with classical sources, but invigorated by the taste of his time, combined the genres of the letter and the dialogue, which were related in both their origin and their development, into a newly created form. Montaigne made use of their common atectonic, unstable organism admittedly to outdistance those who provided his impetus. This is the significance of the essay in the history of form of modern prose. (Let us only mention peripherally the fact that the essay arose in a time in which the plastic arts of the transalpine countries also made the transition to an open form.[313]) While the letter prepared a means of expression for the subjectivity of the author and for proliferation of a variety of subjects, the dialogue provided the basic skeptical orientation with a means of representation which could do justice to the many faces of the facts by changes in perspective. A fact that applies to the dialogue analogously to the transformation of the letter is that Montaigne relinquishes the literary ponderousness, the conversation between persons which was after all only feigned, in order to present directly something that till then was hidden in fiction: the intellect speaking with itself.

10.   LINGUISTIC AND STYLISTIC DEVICES

Now we must say a few things about the linguistic and stylistic devices of Montaigne's prose. Here, too, we see a uniting of practice and the accompanying theory. Montaigne practices his linguistic art while at the same time reflecting upon it. His reflections on the theory of style only seldom employ rhetorical school terms. Rather, they move within summary expressions of taste on the types of style he prefers in other authors as well as on his own style. These expressions are found in the broad horizon of his nominalistic and skeptical linguistic criticism. As was just explained, this is also manifest in practice. Specifically, Montaigne's aversion to fixing words by means of definition is striking. His terminology fluctuates and is filled with equivocations. Favorite words such as *branler, curiosité, raison, âme, fantaisie, humeur, sagesse, folie,* and many others sometimes mean one thing, sometimes another. They take on the particular meaning intended in each instance not from customary or perhaps his own, consistent usage, but rather from the context in which they appear. This lack of sharpness in terminology certainly has its historical basis in the general conditions of language in his time, when there was a lack of semantic precision to the theoretical vocabulary. (The only exceptions to this are Calvin and Bodin.) But Montaigne does not fight against this deficiency. He makes use of the uncertainty of meaning of contemporary vocabulary. If one may put it pointedly, he is the philosopher of ambiguity. And it is possible that the *Essais* and their fluid speech would only have been possible in this preclassical fluctuation of the French language.[314]

As we said earlier, Montaigne is the first French author of note who wrote in French. But he uses this language in the full awareness of what a rapidly changing vehicle he is entrusting himself to. He asks himself whether his *Essais* will still be understood in fifty years in view of the fact that the French language "slips out of our hands every day, and has halfway changed since I have been alive" (III, 9, 751 B/C). The feeling of disquiet that the French language changes "every fifty years" was shared by many in the century. Geoffroy Tory complained about this in 1529 in the foreword to his *Champfleury*.[315] This disquiet became the impetus for attempts of grammaticians to codify the language. But Montaigne did not experience it as disquieting at all to presume he might no longer be understood in fifty years.[316] Rather, he experienced this as confirmation of general as well as his own particular transitoriness, which he wants in order to be real. Writing in French thus provides him with another chance to preserve obedience to what is finite. None of his contemporaries came upon an idea such as this; they work against the inconstancy of their mother tongue; he, on the contrary, immerses himself in it. This also applies in another respect. Several times he speaks of the lesser powers of the French language in comparison to Latin or Greek. This, too, is a statement often heard in his time. With humanism, an intensified feeling of inferiority came into the vulgar languages. But it also awakened the courage to build these languages up to the level of the ancient languages; the Cinderella mother tongue was to become queen. But the fact that Montaigne writes in French has nothing to do with this sort of ambition. He has no interest in the national and cultural-political goals in a language program of a Du Bellay, a Pasquier, and many others. He never expresses the need to secure for French, which he so loves and has mastered, a triumph over Latin. The admitted inferiority of this language does not limit him. Quite the contrary, it drives him even more strongly to make use of this language, as one who is imperfect obeying what is imperfect. We know this element of his wisdom: in what is imperfect it respects the pauper's nobility of what is real.

One must understand his love for the French language from this basic orientation and less so from the influence of the language program of the Pléiade (which was slight anyway). He gave this love beautiful if not uncritical expression. Thus we find in III, 5: our language is bountiful, we read here, it is only a bit lacking in finesse; but one should elevate and foster what one does have, particularly what comes from the jargon of hunting and war (665 B).[317] He also rejoices in the earthy element of the language of farmers and tradesmen. He knows that what was once its colorfulness can be worn away by use, but it can also be regenerated so that it can glow again with its old force. Because he is so deeply convinced of these treasures, he finds intolerable those "many French writers of the time" who, instead of taking what is there, destroy themselves and their subject with "miserable affectations and contrivances," with cold and absurd frills. This probably goes against the mannerism of the post-Ronsard poets, and perhaps even against Ronsard himself. In this context, one then also finds one of his most important confessions on the art of style of the vulgar languages. Good authors, he writes, do not bring in new words, "but they enrich their own, give more weight and depth to their meaning and use; they teach the language unaccustomed movements, but prudently and shrewdly" (665 B). Use what is given, enrich it with new charm and depth, but do so carefully and without neologistic degeneration: principles such as these (perhaps encouraged through Quintilian) in fact guide Montaigne's own style, which is nicely balanced between long-established faithfulness to the language and a moderate yet clear and quite personal motor ability of the language. Its force comes from below, from words into which the French meanings of all levels of the people have been deposited, what they see, hear, taste—but its harnessing comes from above, from a taste that has been ennobled by its contact with the ancients.

Any subject matter of language is proper to him, without limitations of societal standing or landscape. His comments on this are well known. If French is not adequate, then the language of Gascogne can fill the gap; he wants to use words from the halls of Paris, sentences as one can hear them in the street; he will orient himself to usage, not the rules of grammar, and he would rather his "son" learn to speak in the pubs than in the schools for orators. As a whole, this is an orientation to language which is similar to what Henri Estienne once expressed thus: the French language is like a rich man who not only owns a lovely house in the city, but also has many others in many country locations in which he can enjoy himself when the urge for a change in climate comes over him. In practice, however, Montaigne is hesitant, as is most of his epoch, to use provincialisms. He even uses archaic language only with great care. We do not find in the *Essais* that chaos of words found earlier in Rabelais, who accumulated lexical lists. Montaigne's range of language is large, but an overview is possible. Neologisms only appear in larger numbers in the later years, most of them in the handwritten additions. They serve to provide greater precision and vividness, and they serve his personal style which evolves continuously toward freer writing, though without contradicting the principles outlined above.[318]

Montaigne has said of his style: "I have naturally a humorous and familiar style . . ." (I, 40, 186 B). With this, he uses a traditional term to indicate the ranking of his writing. It involves the *humile atque cotidianum sermonis genus* (*Quintilian* XI, 1, 6) which, because of its use in comedy later also took on the auxiliary designation of *stilus comicus* and represented the lowermost of the three style categories, of which the other two were called *genus mediocre* and *genus sublime*.[319] Since these terms for style categories simultaneously cover content, expression, and composition, the generic position of the *Essais* is expressed entirely with the designation *stile comique:* a product of an everyday way of thinking, familiar way of speaking, and relaxed composition. Thus again we find self-abasement—and again its reversal into the affirmation: "but of a form all my own," he continues. Montaigne, the moralist of averageness, who for the reasons described places himself and mankind quite low in the universal order of rank, reaches consistently, when he wants to characterize his undertaking in terms of style typology, for the category of style which is available for the raw material of life. But this assignment of the *Essais* to a style type such as this is only a whim that makes use of convention and behind which what is real flourishes, namely, the joy in the discovery of the individual form of self-presentation. Moreover, Montaigne freed the "lower" category of style from its limitation to "lower" subjects and also used the familiar linguistic material for "middle" and "high" subjects.[320] Thus traditional rhetoric's demand for agreement between content and level of style, in fact, the hierarchy of styles per se, was penetrated. The agreement becomes a different one. The style of the familiar expression and relaxed composition, instead of expressing the rank of the subjects, now expresses the subjectivity of free observation and thus the individuality of the observer; the style is "a form all my own."

This also forms the basis for a comment full of self-irony: "If I were of the trade [namely, the writer], I would naturalize art as much as they artify nature" (III, 5, 666 B/C). "To naturalize art," this means: to make it permeable to the natural make-up of the author and to write in an unrhetoricized individual style of expression. Montaigne has a sensitive feeling for the antinature of a merely decorative style of embellishments and frills. He found Italian and Spanish Petrarchism intolerable (II, 10, 299 A; he is referring to what we call baroque literature today). Also intolerable to him are any authors who "mount on horseback because they are not strong enough on their legs," who leap and twist instead of walking with their natural gait (299 A/B). As we said earlier (chapter 2), he does not stand alone in his aversion to the declamatory super-culture. In France, he was preceded particularly by Du Bellay with his *Regrets*, this most personal lyricism of the century, and it, too, admittedly written in the *style bas,* as "diaries" and "secretaires of my heart."[321] We need not go into the classical origins of such an aesthetic of a style of expression and honesty. They can be found in Horace and Quintilian, also in Seneca.[322] It is enough that this aesthetic reappears in Montaigne as a part fitting in with all other parts of his organism as intellect and writer.

Here it is appropriate to quote the sentences reviewed earlier (chapter 2) in the wording Montaigne used in III, 5 (664–665 B) to describe the style of Lucretius and Virgil. For these sentences do not refer only to the Roman poets, rather, they contain an evaluation of style that can be applied very well to the *Essais* as well. Whether intentionally or not, Montaigne describes at the same time his own content-rich spontaneous style, which is guided by idea and fantasy, and is dense and sinewy, filled with the power to have an effect, nourishment for powerful intellects, and thus something different from the pleasing facility with form of the mere virtuoso: "This is not a soft and merely inoffensive eloquence; it is sinewy and solid, and does not so much please as fill and ravish; and it ravishes the strongest minds most. When I see these brave forms of expression, so alive, so profound, I do not say 'This is well said,' I say 'This is well thought.' It is the sprightliness of the imagination that elevates and swells the words . . . This painting is the result not so much of manual dexterity as of having the object more vividly imprinted in the soul." And these sentences are also simultaneously the fulfillment of their aesthetics. Just as in the thoughts, in the linguistic expression we are confronted with an antithesis. But it is not overextended, rather, it is varied into several types. Type 1: "This is not a soft eloquence . . . ; it is . . ." Type 2, similar, but stronger: "I do not say 'This is well said,' I say 'This is well thought.'" Type 3, inserted between them: "and does not so much please as fill . . ." and later repeated: "This painting is the result not so much of manual dexterity as for having . . ." A sentence with no antithesis is inserted: "It is the sprightliness . . ." In this antithetical but liberally diverse overall structure there are a number of figures of speech. There are two highly accentuated adjectives with parallel rhythm: *Elle est nerveuse et solide* ("it is sinewy and solid"); the fact that there are two occurs as a counterbalance to the attribute in the first clause. Its accents established by the force of expression repeat: . . . *qui esleve et enfle les parolles . . .* (". . . that elevates and swells the words . . ."). Then comes a part of the sentence completely dominated by alliteration: *qui ne plaist pas tant comme elle remplit et ravit le plus les plus forts espris* ("and does not so much please as fill and ravish; and it ravishes the strongest minds most")—as if strung together with hammer blows, yet with a slight relaxation in the beautifully falling end of the sentence. And then we have the rapidly following metaphor: first the work "fills" the reader and "carries him away," whereby the image of the wind which fills the sails appears in somewhat concealed form— later it is there (even though not completely expressed in words, it is indeed there in the force of imagination): the boisterous fantasy "elevates and swells" the words. The entire passage is designed to be spoken, heard, and seen with the inner eye.

Another passage, this one a confession: "The speech I love is a simple, natural speech, the same on paper as in the mouth; a speech succulent and sinewy, brief and compressed, not so much dainty and well-combed as vehement and brusque . . . rather difficult than boring, remote from affectation, irregular, disconnected and bold; each bit making a body in itself; not pedantic, not monkish, not lawyer-like, but rather soldierly, as Suetonius calls Julius Caesar's speech" (I, 26, 127 A/C). The idea is the same as before, but it is emphasized with even more passion and the reference to the freedom of composition is expanded. Again, what he strives for in the idea of style is already there in the language. The relatively long sentence forms a thoroughly articulated structure. Montaigne's individual sentences are often like this, whereas the groups of sentences move into the unstructured open form again. Thus we have an example here of the claim "each part making a body in itself." The sentence too is aimed above all at sounding and being heard: in the sinewy, masculine ("soldierly") rhythmics of the affective accents, in the audible figures of speech of alliterations and rhymed endings (*-esque*), in the proportions of elements in two parts provided in his outline, but not monotonous, rather, extremely variable, and in the course to the end of the period, which thanks to the brief rest inserted ("each bit . . .") lets one catch one's breath and brings the expressive urge toward relaxation in a falling conclusion to the sentence ("as Suetonius . . ."). The liberally used adjectives and attributes serve in no way as a mere *amplificatio*, rather they are

necessary in their meaning, just as the numerous figures of speech serve
the thought that is close to Montaigne's heart and are not affected varnish
spread over a passage that says nothing.[323]

We have moved from Montaigne's reflections on style to inspection
of his style in practice. Montaigne is one of the great prose writers of his
nation. The *Essais* also represent a monument of the history of style in
French literature. Its prose is not merely an "example" of artistic prose
of the sixteenth century, rather, it is its own word that has arisen from
the possibilities of that century, as were only the prose of Calvin, Rabelais, and, at some distance, Amyot. The other prose authors of that
period, the satirists, historians, novelists, are only variants of a type, and
one cannot identify them straightaway from their texts as one can with
those just mentioned, and with Montaigne. A German with a refined ear
once made the judgment that Montaigne "was granted the most individual tongue with which ever a Frenchman had spoken."[324] One must
guard against the repeatedly heard opinion that the taste for the open
form and the "humorous and familiar style" exclude artistic work and
control. Anyone who has such a highly developed awareness of style
also writes with a monitored style. Lack of structuring and lightness,
letting oneself be carried along by concrete linguistic material and the
forces of motion inherent in oral language are not a writer's negligence.
They are characteristics of an art which lets down the dividers between
thinking, seeing, feeling, and saying in favor of a unified organism. No
one succeeded in doing this again in France until the Marquise de Sévi-
gné in her letters. That artistic intent is at work is apparent, if one has
not already recognized it in the prose of the *Essais,* in the detailed work
Montaigne put into the corrections; the majority of them are stylistic in
nature.[325] His art consists in elevating "what is unsophisticated" to the
level of intelligent grace. In doing this, he succeeded completely in avoiding that affectedness that so often set in in the history of prose when one
attempted to be "natural." Because he himself was nature, his writing
also became nature intensified to become art. Certainly his natural style,
like any writing that is style at all, required preestablished rhetorical
means. But they do not go beyond the bounds that must be reached to
allow the thought to attain its linguistic maturity. They are rhetorical
without, due to rhetoricizing, taking what is said away from the subject
matter and point of view that it contains. They represent adornments,
not embellishments. A Romance sense of form was expressed even in
Montaigne's natural style, however—and at that time this was not at all
something self-evident—it was expressed by means of a special func-

tionalization of expression of the usual rhetorical figures of speech that revealed the author's individuality no less than did his presentation of life and himself. Thus a look at style is necessary for a complete understanding of the *Essais*.

In the following, what we say about this is admittedly only a sketch that hopes to point out only a couple of elementary elements. Thus we will limit ourselves to passages that demonstrate concentrated stylistic intent. Since they correspond without exception to concentrated content in thought and viewpoint, they are suitable to make clear the unity of thinking, seeing, and style which is not as clearly revealed in other passages in which Montaigne speaks with less intensity.

Visual figures of speech (tropes) take absolute priority, and among these, the metaphors. Montaigne's aversion to abstraction, his skepticism that lets the eye that is blinded by the universe recover by viewing what is individual and close at hand, his feeling for the uniqueness of an event as well as for the interwoven quality of events among one another, his comfortable dwelling in milieu and everyday situations: all this encourages the wealth of images in his language even further. Tropes are his stylistic passion. His productivity in the use of these is quite unusual in France of the sixteenth century. The only writer at about that time who can be compared with him is Shakespeare. One can hardly even think of the Spanish and Italians in this regard; their use of metaphor is too conceptual. In France, the wealth of tropes does not recur until the work of Victor Hugo, Balzac, and Proust. Montaigne's wealth of images is one of the reasons he is repeatedly considered alongside the poets. Montesquieu notes boldly: "The four great poets: Plato, Malebranche the father, Milord Shaftesbury, Montaigne." De Sanctis writes: *Mondi nuovi poetici ci erano allora, ed erano i mondi che creavano Camoes, Cervantes, Montaigne, Shakespeare e Milton.* Sainte-Beuve, who calls Montaigne "the true poet," expresses it more precisely: "His style is a perpetual figure of speech, renewed with every step; one only receives ideas from him in the form of images; and at each moment they appear under different, ready and yet transparent images . . . Montaigne is like the Ovid and the Ariosto of style."[326]

In the earlier Essays, the metaphor (and the simile) is short as a rule. Later on it gains in breadth, tending toward the expanding metaphor wherein a second and new image is generated out of the first one. The handwritten additions after 1588 are filled with tropic figures of speech, as they are with proverbial and folksy sayings. Conceptual material seldom remains in a conceptual form. Sometimes the language carries it

over into visualization. An example of this follows, where the thought
is: "Since it is the privilege of the mind to rescue itself from old age,"
and the image illustrates this as follows: "Let it grow green, let it flourish meanwhile, if it can, like mistletoe on a dead tree" (III, 5, 641 B)—it
is an expanding metaphor that extends what is first the isolated process
of turning green and blossoming to the image of mistletoe on the dead
tree. Or the language can bring the thought directly into the sensual
event, skipping over its theoretical stage: "to rub and polish our brains
by contact with those of others," we read, and we understand what is
meant: we form our spirit on the spirit of others (I, 26, 112 A). Here is
another example of the same kind: "I would rather fashion my mind
than furnish it" (III, 3, 622 C). This means I prefer essential education
to the dead matter of knowledge. But to translate it back in this manner
is already false. One thereby forgets that for thinking, which works by
watching, the metaphor represents what is real, and the "direct" expression represents what has been derived. Montaigne is quite impatient to
get from what is merely thought to what can be seen. He has a finely
tuned sensitivity for the metaphorical content inherent in the language
which comes from its origin. Long before Vico and Herder he suspected
that the majority of words and expressions were tropes that had died
out. The simplest word that comes to his pen suffices to ignite that
impatience. He follows the signals of the language, acts quickly, recalls
what is half extinguished back to life, and generates new life with it. A
fine example of this is the following passage from III, 11 (790 B). There
he says: the questions arising through experience are endless, thus I do
not answer them, *je ne les desnoue point;* this word *desnouer* (It.
snodare, today it has been replaced with *résoudre*), which has long since
been functionalized, "to release the knots," becomes an image genera-
tor, and he thus continues: *aussi n'ont elles point de bout; je les tranche
souvent, comme Alexandre son nœud.* The "knot" has no "end," I
"hack through" it, as Alexander did to the Gordian knot: using the
image that he develops from a trope (*dénouer*) which had declined, he
visually represents the complete thought that is also so revealing of his
thinking.

With this regenerative use of the vivid inheritance of his language,
everything blossoms from his pen, becomes familiar, close, and friendly.
He scoops from the fullness of an active linguistic memory. Certainly
many of his most beautiful images are of literary origin, coming from
Plato, Cicero, Seneca, and also several contemporary texts, but predominantly Plutarch's *Moralia.* By the way, Erasmus had also discovered the

fertility in tropes of the latter. His collection *De parabolis sive similibus* is carried in the main by that work. Montaigne's love of Plutarch was intensified by this stylistic characteristic of the Greek (and his translator Amyot). Yet Montaigne's productivity in images cannot be explained simply from the influences upon him. Simply because he carries this within himself, Montaigne reacts sympathetically to this and other models in their metaphorical passages and reproduces them. But the number of such reproductions remains modest when compared to the number of images he creates himself.

Montaigne displays extraordinary mobility in his use of tropes. There are very few metaphors that appear consistently with a particular idea or concept in the *Essais* (like *estamine*—sieve—for "capacity for critical judgment," I, 26, 111 A and II, 12, 393 A). He avoids the danger of allowing a metaphor to solidify into allegory, whereby one also notes that he avoids using the customary allegories at all (for example, in the passages on Fortuna, or on death). Just as his conceptual terminology fluctuates, his transformation of facts into images fluctuates, in fact he is able to say the things he says often always using new images. He converts practically all of his ideational material into a visual form with the help of material for tropes which he finds in the realm of the farmer, soldier, sailor, merchant, craftsman, and from hunting, medicine, the kitchen.[327] The preferred images are those of bodily movement of any kind, such as walking, wandering, dancing, riding, jumping, staggering, creeping, mountain climbing, falling . . . Here is one example representing countless others: "My conceptions and my judgment move only by groping, staggering, stumbling, and blundering; and when I have gone ahead as far as I can, still I am not at all satisfied" (I, 26, 107 A). With a certain amount of caution—since corporal tropes are old and obvious—in these instances where one represents what is inside in a corporal image one can see a reflection of his favorite idea of the unity of body-soul, the "structure made up of such close and brotherly correspondence" (III, 13, 855 B). "Let us bind it together again by mutual services," he continues in this passage, and he also actualized this intention stylistically. Abstract beings are transformed rapidly into living beings. "Vices . . . : once they prick me, they stick to me and will not go away without shaking" (III, 5, 667 B). He sees the vices and feels them in his body, little demons or monsters which dig their claws in and which he has to shake off. A sentence is seldom satisfied with a verb that cannot be visualized. Thus, for example, a "study" will be quickly followed by the forceful "savor and ruminate," a crescendo of sensuousness (III, 13, 854 B). Anything that was not concrete enough in the first version is remedied by a later addition: (B) "Prayer wins me, threats repel me"; (C) "favor makes me bend, fear makes me stiffen" (III, 9, 723). As a rule, an alert faithfulness to the image prevails. When the text is loosened up with an amassing of images, no images that are incompatible with one another are used. This can be seen in the following sentence on Amor, which works with metaphor and synecdoche: "See how he goes reeling, tripping, and wantonly playing; you put him in the stocks when you guide him by art and wisdom, and you constrain his divine freedom when you subject him to those hairy and callous hands" (III, 5, 684 B). With the image of Amor who has fallen into the "hairy, callused hands" (of the old men), even the first of the divine swaying and romping gains in force; even the image, not quite consistent in itself, that he is "put in the stocks" when one "guides" him with artistic wisdom, does not spoil it. Let us briefly refer to a particularly lovely example of faithfulness to the image. It is the magnificent passage added in the late period to the Essay on the education of children about joyful virtue (I, 26, 119 C: "She has virtue as her goal . . ."[328]). The idea is divided into the picture of a lovely landscape with shaded, softly rising paths, and the complementary picture of a rugged, steep, inaccessible, rocky cliff overgrown with thorns. The verbs originated in the common metaphorical area of landscape, all speaking of processes that one can picture in a landscape. Montaigne's ability to make something visual is so great that he really sees the content of his metaphors. Once he has entered into the sensuous realm, he no longer leaves it; it becomes total and absorbs all that does not relate to the senses into itself. And it is thanks to this gift for metaphor that a reading of the *Essais* is so refreshing and still brings joy even when one does not want to struggle with the thoughts it contains. One walks upon healthy soil in the open air, and guided by a man who is happy in his body and in things.

But this sensuousness is satisfied not only in the play of images of the imagination, but also in the sound effects of the words. This is not the case throughout, but applies to many core passages, and particularly in the late period Montaigne's prose is aimed at the ear, language monitored by the ear. Its simple means include the various figures of speech related to sound, a kind of "pictographic writing for the ear."[329] It appears in various forms, as alliteration, assonance, prose rhyme, sound symbolism, grouping of emphatic accents, as word-based figures of speech, which are hardly distinguishable from those based on sound, such as *annominatio*, *anaphora*, and so forth. We will be content with just a few examples. On one occasion, Montaigne tells of his moustache, which aids his sense of smell; the aroma of gloves, of a handkerchief, adhere to it for an entire day; and then: "The close kisses of youth, savory, greedy, and sticky, once used to adhere to it and stay there for several hours after" (I, 55, 228 B). The full voluptuousness is expressed in the two epithets *gloutons et gluans* ("greedy and sticky") together, and these make the eager, slippery, sticky quality of a sensual kiss positively audible by means of alliteration, parallel rhythm, and the liquid consonant *l* sliding after these in the following verb. In another passage, the endless possibilities for the discussion of political opinions are expressed by the following climax of words with the same ending: *Il s'y trouveroit tousjours, à un tel argument, dequoy y fournir responses, dupliques, repliques, tripliques, quadrupliques* ("In such an argument there would always be matter for answers, rejoinders, replications, triplications, quadruplications") (II, 17, 497 A; note how the inserted *repliques* is there more for the series of sounds than for the sequence of meanings). A sentence that Montaigne found modeled in Plutarch-Amyot, which there still hesitantly made use of the *figura etymologica* (. . . *le feit carder à coups de carde et de peignes de cardeur* ["had him so carded with the cards and combs of this carder"]) he intensifies using a chiastic sound-based figure of speech: *le fit grater et carder à coups de cardes* ("had him so scratched and carded with the cards") (II, 27, 530 C). Or we find: . . . *subjects graves et qui grevent* ("are grave subjects and grieve us") (III, 5, 638 B); *L'ardeur querelleuse gourmande tous-jours l'amoureuse ardeur* ("the quarrelsome ardor always dominates the amorous ardor") (II, 33, 552 C). These are means that were not scorned in Seneca or religious Latin prose either. They are admittedly more reminiscent of the linguistic craftsmanship of the Rhétoriqueurs and the Gascognian Du Bartas. But Montaigne never uses them or any other figures of speech to the point of obtrusiveness. These figures of speech are enjoyable to him, just as riding, dancing, making love, or a good meal are enjoyable. They may at times border upon refinement, but as a rule they remain comprehensible from the expressive force of the passage.

One also finds a number of word-based figures of speech. Some, as we have just seen, can also be seen as sound-based figures of speech, that is, the *figura etymologica,* which is the repetition of the root of a word in a different inflection or derivation. Essay III, 9 begins this way. Its title, "Of Vanity," kinetically generates the first sentences, for which it represents the upstroke (which might be added to the variants of Montaigne's moods in creating titles). The title is intended to be read with them, thus the beginning reads as follows: "Of vanity. There is perhaps no more obvious vanity than to write of it so vainly. What the Divinity has so divinely told us about it . . ." Sometimes we find word accumulations. We mentioned one of these, separated with the help of the anaphoric "where . . . where . . . where . . ." (I, 23, 80–81), and tried to make it understandable as an intended build-up of facts for the sake of an insight into the relativity of human customs. One finds a quite unusual example in the "Apology." Here, an army of verbs is offered to describe the capacity of expression of the hands and the head: forty-seven verbs for the hands, twenty-one for the head (II, 12, 332 C). This is probably based upon a passage in Quintilian (*Inst. orat.* XI, 86), but how it has grown! It is a jumble of words in the manner of Rabelais, and there is no other comparable example in the *Essais,* nevertheless, it serves its purpose, because it is intended to create an extreme counterpressure to the doc-trine of the *dignitas hominis,* according to which it is language guided by reason that distinguishes man; but the gift for gesticulation which the hands and the head possess (later also the eyebrows and the shoulders) refutes this, and Montaigne lets that army of verbs storm in to overrun the opposing opinion. Among the word-based figures of speech that also have an audible effect is the chiasma of this type: *Qui se faict mort vivant est subject d'estre tenu pour vif mourant* ("He who acts dead when still alive is subject to be thought alive when dying") (III, 9, 748 C).

Then there are meaning-based figures of speech. As with all rhetori-cal devices, Montaigne only uses the simplest ones here. Typically, pleonasm and hyperbole are almost completely absent. But there is extensive use of antithesis, this original form of all artistic prose. He writes of begetting and killing: *Chacun fuit à le [l'homme] voir naistre, chacun suit à le voir mourir* ("Everyone shuns to see a man born, everyone runs to see him die") and a handwritten addition continues the dance: *Pour le destruire, on cherche un champ spacieux en pleine lumiere; pour le construire, on se musse dans un creux tenebreux et contraint* ("For his destruction we seek a spacious field in broad day-light; for his construction we hide in a dark little corner") (III, 5, 669 B/ C). The other figures of speech used along with this are obvious. And there are also occasional instances of playing with meaning: *Il [le lecteur] se repentira de s'y (aux Essais) estre amusé. C'est mon* [= certain], *mais il s'y sera toujours amusé* ("But he [the reader] will after-ward repent of having wasted his time over it. That may be, but still he will have wasted his time over it") (III, 9, 762 B); first *s'amuser* in the meaning of "to occupy oneself," which was common at that time (Nicot: *occupare*), then in the other meaning of "to amuse oneself."

Finally, there is the complex sentence. Montaigne loves the pointed short sentence, but he also likes the extended rhetorical period. The legacy of the two types is combined in the *Essais:* the laconic style of Seneca and the discursive, or narrative, broad style of Cicero and Livy. Both types had been widely imitated in vulgar-language artistic prose of the Romance Renaissance literatures. But Montaigne lets neither of these types predominate. The rich, epigrammatic, terse formulations remain a variant of style in the overall form of the *Essais;* the narrative or reasoning periods represent the counterbalance to those without for their part disrupting the labile Essay structure. The relationship of these two types to each other changes over the years. In general, the long rhetorical periods decrease in favor of the maxim style, though they appear freely in the latest insertions when anecdotal or historical material, or a personal experience, is related.

Short sentences are preferred when a reading of Seneca has preceded them. Montaigne is indeed master of his language, but he is also sensitive enough to impression to be influenced by models with a strong style. Thus in the Essay on solitude one comes across a few pages in which he combines and paraphrases several passages from the Lucilius letters, and does so in such a manner that the result is a series of unconnected, self-contained maxims, quite in the manner of Seneca (I, 39, 182–183). This is an early example. But we find this later on as well. Read the passage in III, 10 which begins: "He who does not arrest the start has no chance to arrest the course" (778 C)—a Seneca imitation. Montaigne knew the effectiveness of a sententious concentration: "Before or after, a useful maxim or a fine touch is always in season. If it does not suit what precedes or what follows, it is good in itself" (I, 26, 126 A/C). We see that he experiences a maxim—and this in a late addition to the passage—as the appropriate form for an inspiration with no context which can have an effect on its own. These are the first stirrings of the French taste for aphorisms which will repeatedly reemerge later in conjunction with a nonsyllogistic style of thinking. Montaigne is capable of writing complete maxims. Thus we find the following one on jealousy: "Of all the diseases of the mind it is the one that the most things serve to feed and the fewest things to remedy" (III, 5, 658 C). Or: "For 'a good wife' and 'a good marriage' are said not about those that are so, but about those that are not talked about" (III, 5, 662 B; probably from Plutarch). He can spread terse sentences such as these over half pages. For example, the beginning of III, 2 contains a select piece of laconic prose. Because of this art, Pasquier said of him: "He's another Seneca in our tongue." What has Montaigne not been called: *notre Socrate, notre Horace, notre Sénèque, notre Plutarque . . .* , and yet each of these names captures only one of his many faces.

However, the laconic aspects are submerged again and again in the narrative or epic flow of thought of the *Essais*. This flow can swell to an undulating breadth and accumulation of rhetorical periods. Then Montaigne's comfortable urge to tell a story comes into force. And he can tell a story marvelously. One sees this best when he is reproducing something from an earlier model. For example, there is the Pacuvius story from Livy in III, 9 (732 B): the retelling is longer then the original, but along with the length it gains in vividness, becomes more dramatic, has more artistic delaying elements, and achieves better preparation of the concluding point. When occasionally he moves into overly long periods, he often does not have a firm syntactic grasp of them. They are defective, the mass of material gets jammed up, and it creates emergency exits for itself in anacoluthon, synesis, ellipsis, and other such constructions. This can be attributed to the circumstances of language at that time. Montaigne had no reason to change much about these deficient circumstances. They, like the semantic deficiencies, represent for him a chance for freedom of movement, not resistance, but rather a path. And it is astounding how despite this, his periods succeed in being clear, rhythmic, to the point, and his narration or reasoning does not become chaotic despite all the syntactic problems.

Let us leave it at these indications. It has certainly been made clear that the rhetorical means used in the *Essais* are not merely there artistically, rather, they are there for something, for an idea, for a manner of thinking, or even only for a stirring of the temperament and for the joy of play. Their use, which as a whole can in no way be considered excessive, but rather is closely reined in, confirms that they are subject to the control of a desire for expression. The organism of Montaigne's spirit which circulates as the life blood through everything he writes is perceptible in his prose. It is worked out to the last detail, but not rhetoricized, it consists of personal acts of selection, not empty imitations—in short, it is style in the sense of the modern individual style, *une forme mienne,* "a form all my own."

Notes

CHAPTER I

1. *Unzeitgemäße Betrachtungen* (Schopenhauer als Erzieher, section 2). The passage on Plutarch cited is in Montaigne III, 5, 666 C, and it reads: "I cannot be with him even a little without taking out a drumstick or a wing"; Nietzsche drastically softened this. Villey discovered that the passage imitates a sentence from Boaistuau, whom Montaigne read widely (*Théâtre du monde*, 1558). This is a good example of how quotes can expand in meaning as they travel from hand to hand. On another occasion Nietzsche speaks of the fact that Montaigne signifies a "coming to rest in oneself, a peaceful being for oneself and exhaling" (*Unzeitgem. Betr.*, Richard Wagner, section 3).

2. Confirmed by Chapelain (*Opuscules critiques*, ed. Hunter, 1936, p. 479).

3. There is extensive evidence of this presented at the end of the ten-volume edition of the *Essais* obtained by Pierre Coste in 1724, summarized under the heading *Jugements et critiques sur les Essais de M.* Also Villey, *Postérité*, p. 308 ff.

4. The expression *cultura animi* is only found once in classical works, namely in Cicero, *Tusculanes* II, 13 (*cultura animi philosophia est . . .*). More frequently found is the term with the same meaning, *cultus animi* (Cicero, *De finibus*, V, 54, etc.). Whether Montaigne uses the expression (not to be found anywhere else in the *Essais*) *culture de l'âme* from the cited Cicero passage or from one of the humanists cannot be determined. J. Niedermann in *Kultur. Werden und Wandlungen des Begriffs von Cicero bis Herder* (Bibl. dell'Archiv. Roman., series I, vol. 28, 1941) only provides one piece of evidence from humanism before Montaigne (p. 64: Fil. Beroaldo). Petrarch (whom Niedermann does not name, as he does not name Montaigne) uses the customary *cultus animi* (*De remediis . . .* II, cap. 117, ed. 1649, p. 655). Only from Bacon on do we find *cultura animi* in general use (Niedermann p. 104; p. 128 ff.). The

meaning that Montaigne apparently intends is that of Cicero, and it is similar to the meaning of *humanitas:* ethical-urbane refinement, in contrast to raw power.

5. The inscription and the mottos on the beams have been reproduced in, among others, Armaingaud, *Œuvres complètes de Montaigne,* 12 vols., Bordeaux, 1924–1941; vol. XII, p. 423 ff.

6. Best publication in Armaingaud, vol. XI; also in *Œuvres complètes,* ed. M. Rat, p. 1347 ff.

7. The etymology is contested; *resver* already means "to rave" or "speak nonsense" in Old French. Montaigne uses *resveries* almost synonymously with *songes, fantasies, imaginations, opinions,* and so forth, words all of which are meant to express the undoctrinary, noncompulsory, and private nature of his thinking. Core passage: ". . . reveries, which are the dreams of the waking, and worse than dreams" (II, 12, 451 C). Jean Nicot, *Dictionnaire françois-latin,* 1583, gives the following for *resverie: deliratio, ineptia.* More in J. Jud, "Rêver" (in *Romania,* 1936) and finally in Fr. Schalk, "Somnium . . ." (in: *Exempla romanischer Wortgeschichte,* 1966).

8. The sentence is the more pointed reproduction of a statement by Pherekydes passed on in Diogenes Laertius (*Omnia quippe indico potius quam aperio,* Villey, *Les Essais, publiés d'après l'exemplaire de Bordeaux . . . ,* 5 vols., 1906–1933, [*EM*], IV, p. 239 A), but Montaigne clearly applies it to himself.

9. In the preface to her edition of the *Essais,* 1625, p. III recto. About the editor: M. H. Isley, *Marie le Jars de Gournay: Her Life and Works.* The Hague, 1963.

10. *Französische Geschichte . . . ,* book V (ed. 1924, vol. I, p. 320).

11. *Journal 1889–1939,* Bibliothèque de la Pléiade, 1940, p. 183; also, Sainte-Beuve: *Causeries du Lundi* IV, p. 94.

12. Letter to Justus Lipsius of April 1593; quoted from Villey, *Postérité,* p. 352.

13. Since the following pages only concern a quick orientation in what is already known, specific evidence from the sources is not included here.

CHAPTER II

14. The prospect of going into Montaigne's standards for and technique of quotation is appealing. But this would only be meaningful if one compared them to the techniques of quotation used in antiquity, in humanism, and in contemporary vulgar literature. Only then would Montaigne's specific ratio between convention and original work come to light in this respect. Additionally, one would have to go into a general aesthetic theory of quotation and its role in the communication among the various intellects. We will only indulge in a few brief remarks. Montaigne reflected extensively on his use of quotations; *emprunts, allégations* are the terms he uses. The most important passages can be found in: I, 25, 100 C; I, 26, 111 A; I, 26, 126–127 C (Je tors . . .); II, 10, 296 C; III, 12, 808–809 C. A quotation in the *Essais* does not mean that the author quoted is considered an absolute authority. Nor does it mean, as it did in antiquity, that he should be honored (occasionally the Romans called the act of quoting *laudare*). Montaigne commented on only one occasion that quotations

from great authors were intended to conceal his own weaknesses (II, 10, 297 C). In quoting, Montaigne is allowing authors whom he seeks out where they please him to have their say. Thus the direction of his quotations—as has always been true of literary, nonscientific quotation—usually proceeds away from the source toward his own context, with the moment of surprise in which the expression quoted takes on a breadth of meaning it did not have in the passage in the source. (Plutarch had already collected examples of this sort of handling of quotations: *Table Talks* IX, 1.) One can frequently find quotations that run contrary to the intent and spirit of their source. But one only finds quotations at the beginning of an interpretation of them in III, 5 (645 B, from Virgil). As a rule, the quotation is found in the midst of a train of thought which continues through the borrowed comment. The expression is newly and ingeniously focused by the thought, the thought is brightened up or varied or clarified by the expression. One can see how much knowledge Montaigne presumed in his readers by the fact that one can only understand a number of his quotations if one knows the context in the original—or looks it up. A wealth of the most beautiful passages in Latin poetry and prose is expressed in the *Essais*. But they are always found in a vital connection with the author quoting them. Montaigne avoids vain decoration by quotation almost completely. In his middle and late periods, he avoids—even if not completely—quoting from simple school learning, which along with the commonplace themes also promptly provided the phrases of the authors of antiquity (which were available in the centos, anthologies, etc., and thus expected) (compare his comments in III, 12, 808 C: "These concoctions of commonplaces . . ."). He usually quoted the wording literally, thus not from memory. Until 1580, he only used quotations in verse, whereas he paraphrased prose borrowings in French. But from 1588 on, even the latter are almost always quoted in the original. For discussion of quotation in antiquity, see M. Bernays, "Zur Lehre vom Zitieren" (in: *Schriften zur Kritik,* 1903), E. Norden, *Die antike Kunstprosa,* 1909, p. 89 ff., and W. Kroll, *Studien zum Verständnis der römischen Literatur,* 1924 (unrevised reprint in 1964), p. 289 ff. Seneca's several reflections on quoting come under consideration as a classical impetus to Montaigne's standards for quoting (especially *ep.* 16 and *ep.* 33). One can read what the humanists thought about quoting in: Petrarch, *Famil.* XXII, 2; Leonardo Bruni, *De studiis et litteris liber* (in: *Human.-Philosoph. Schriften,* ed. H. Baron, 1928, pp. 12–13); Erasmus (in addition to the prefaces to the *Adagia* and the *Apophthegmata;* also *Laus stultitiae,* cap. 64 of the Kan edition). Later on, there were important comments by Gracián, *Agudeza,* discurso 34 (*Obras,* ed. 1669, vol. II, p. 211 ff.); humorous ones by La Bruyère in the *Caractères* ("Des jugements," no. 64). Excellent pages were written a few years ago by Valéry Larbaud, *Sous l'invocation de Saint-Jérome,* 1946, p. 215 ff.; one will find comments there, too, on Montaigne's use of quotations. More recently, see M. Metschies, *Zitat und Zitierkunst in Montaignes Essais,* 1966 (an appendix contains an extensive bibliography on the history and theory of quoting).

15. For the history of the bee allegory, see H. Gmelin, "Das Prinzip der imitatio . . ." (in: *Romanische Forschungen,* 1932), and J. von Stackelberg, "Das Bienengleichnis" (ibid., 1956).

16. *Bildung und Wissen,* new ed. 1947, p. 18.

17. Quoted from the selected edition of aphorisms by E. Vincent (Sammlung Dieterich, no. 75, 1942), p. 347.

18. In his content-rich and still quite worthwhile article "Montaigne und die Alten" (in: *Vorträge und Aufsätze,* 1905, p. 378). Another work that is much weaker and lacks Bruns' expertise, and is also unreliable in many passages, is that of P. Hensel, "Montaigne und die Antike" (in: *Vorträge der Bibliothek Warburg,* 1928); regarding subject matter, there are only excerpts from Villey's *Sources.*

19. The expression "I do not gnaw my nails over them" recurs several times and probably goes back to Horace, *Sat.* I, 10, v. 71.

20. He makes a comment about Terence which at the same time is an example of his own feeling for art, which pays attention not to what is done, but how it is done: ". . . the perfections and beauties of his style of expression make us lose our appetite for his subject. His distinction and elegance hold us throughout; he . . . so fills our soul with his charms, that we forget those of his plot" (II, 10, 299 A).

21. More on this in C.-A. Fusil, "La Renaissance de Lucrèce au XVIᵉ siècle en France" (*Revue du XVIᵉ siècle,* 1928). Also, G. D. Hadzsits, *Lucretius and His Influence,* 1935.

22. The history of the Horace reception in Montaigne's century is described by R. Lebègue, "Horace en France pendant la Renaissance" (*Humanisme et Renaissance* III, 1936).

23. U. von Wilamowitz, *Hellenistische Dichtung in der Zeit des Kallimachos,* 1924, I, p. 91.

24. "Portrait français de Montaigne" (*NRF* 1933, p. 650).

25. The most important passages: II, 12, 368 C; 375–376 C; 376–377 C; 399–400 C; 408 C.

26. The source for this passage is in *Tusc.* V, 10 (*Socrates primus philosophiam devocavit e caelo et in urbibus conlocavit et in domus etiam introduxit*), and not, as Villey indicates (*EM* IV, p. 440 A) in *Acad.* I, 4. The basis is probably Xenophon, *Memorabilia* I, 1, 11–16. The formula was a familiar quotation, as in Erasmus, *Colloquia* ("Ad lectorem"): *Socrates philosophiam e coelo deduxit in terras* . . . (*LB* I, 905 B; *LB* is the designation of the ten-volume Erasmus edition by Leclerc, 1708 ff., which appeared in Leyden, *Lugdunum Batavorum*).

27. From antiquity: Xenophon, *Symposium,* 2; Seneca, *De tranqu.,* 15; Valerius Maximus, *Dict. et fact. libri,* VIII, 8 externa. Contemporary influences are: Erasmus, *Apophthegmata* (passim); Rabelais, prologue to *Gargantua* (*Œuvres,* ed. Lefranc, 1913, I, pp. 5–6); Castiglione, *Cortegiano* II, chap. 42 ff. Even L. B. Alberti in *Della Famiglia* speaks with illusion to Socrates of *quelli comici filosofi* (meaning philosophers who behave and express themselves simply) . . . *pieni di giuoco e riso, e non vacui di prudenzia e sapienzia, con molta grazia e dignata* (Libro quattro, p. 271 of the edition by Capasso, s.d.). The invocation of the laughing and playing Socrates served as an example from an authority for the urbane motif of Renaissance education *risu relaxare animum*

(like Erasmus in the preface to the *Apophthegmata*). Montaigne himself confesses that in his old age he would prefer to play "at cobnut or with a top" (III, 5, 640 B), in a definite imitation of Socrates.

28. In a letter in which he inveighs against the commentators of the *Nicomachean Ethics* because they were always thinking only about *casuum monstra* rather than what was more common for men. (Quoted in A. Renaudet, *Préréforme et Humanisme*, 1916, pp. 281–282).

29. On hellenism, we refer to: J. Kaerst, *Geschichte des Hellenismus*, especially vol. II, 1926; U. von Wilamowitz, *Hellenistische Dichtung*, 1924, especially vol. I, chap. 1: "Die Umwelt"; P. Wendland, *Die hellenistisch-römische Kultur in ihren Beziehungen zu Judentum und Christentum*, 1912; W. Tarn, *Hellenistic Civilisation*, 1952 (German: *Die Kultur der hellenistischen Welt*, trans. G. Bayer, 1966); M. Rostovtzeff, *Die hellenistische Welt, Gesellschaft und Wirtschaft* I–III, 1955–1956. Here I can of course only speak summarily without consideration of the periods of hellenism, as Wilamowitz did, as cited above (and also in his summary of Greek literature in Hinneberg's *Kultur der Gegenwart*).

30. Compare, for example, Petrarch, *Fam.* XXIV, 5, where he expresses criticism that Seneca's life and what he taught were contradictory. The beginnings of such criticism can be found in Dio Cassius. Still later in the seventeenth century it became commonplace to call Seneca a hypocrite. Compare the frontispiece of the first edition of La Rochefoucauld's *Sentences et maximes*, which shows a Seneca bust in which Amor (as *amour de la vérité*) has removed the philosopher's mask. (La Rochefoucauld, *Œuvres*, ed. Gilbert-Gourdault, "Album.") Similarly to Montaigne, later Diderot was to defend Seneca (*Œuvres complètes*, ed. Assézat et Tourneux, vol. III, p. 160).

31. On neostoicism: L. Zanta, *La Renaissance du stoicisme au XVIe siècle*, 1914, and J. Eymard d'Angers, "Le renouveau de stoicisme en France au XVIe siècle" (in: *Bulletin de l'Association G. Budé*, 1964).

32. *Griechische Kulturgeschichte*, new ed. 1956–1957, vol. III, p. 364.

33. See G. R. Hocke, *Lucrez in Frankreich*, diss. at Bonn, Cologne 1935, p. 16 f., and S. Fraisse, *L'Influence de Lucrèce en France*, 1963.

34. C.-A. Fusil, as cited in note 21, p. 265.

35. When Montaigne says in the sentence summarized here that Plutarch has "a liberal hand, inexhaustible in riches and embellishments," this is a reflection, very rare in his work, of humanistic use of a text in the sense of the *copia dicendi*, in which one reads the author for the passages that one can use as decoration (*ornatus*) in the form of quotations woven into one's own speech.

36. More in M. Treu, *Zur Geschichte der Überlieferung von Plutarchs Moralia*, 1877; J. Platard, *L'Œuvre de Rabelais*, 1910, p. 229 ff.; R. Hirzel, *Plutarch*, 1912, p. 109; G. de Stefano, "La découverte de Plutarque en France" (in: *Romania*, 1965); also, R. Aulotte, *Amyot et Plutarque. La tradition des Moralia au XVIe siècle*, 1965.

37. The fact that the French read Plutarch in Amyot's translation even today is due to the two-volume edition of the *Vitae* which G. Walter prepared for the *Bibliothèque de la Pléiade* in 1940. The orthography has been updated, Amyot's

preface removed (it can be found in an incomplete edition of Amyot's translation of the *Vitae* in: *Société des textes français modernes*, vol. I, 1906; also in B. Weinberg, *Critical Prefaces of the French Renaissance*, 1950, p. 101 ff.).

38. There is one exception, however. In the *Journal de Voyage* (p. 276 ff., ed. D'Ancona) he relates how he got into a dispute in Rome over individual passages, admittedly with the help of scholarly friends who first had to clarify the original meaning of the Greek for him.

39. U. von Wilamowitz, *Die griechische Literatur des Altertums* (in: Hinneberg's *Kultur der Gegenwart* I, 8, 1905), p. 166. Hirzel, *Plutarch*, passim. Here also on p. 44 the note that eighteenth-century classicism was again accustomed to criticizing Plutarch's medley of styles.

40. M. Pohlenz, in *Hermes* XL (1905), p. 292.

41. *Les Œuvres morales de Plutarque, translatées de grec en françois . . .* in the Geneva edition of 1621, vol. I, p. 209 ff., to which I had access. In the following, I am quoting the *Moralia* in Amyot's translation, since this is the one through which Plutarch affected Montaigne. About the work *De tranquilitate . . .* : Pohlenz in *Hermes* XL (1905).

42. Plutarch's anecdotal style of presentation was noted several times even in the fifteenth century; for example, see A. Rinuccini, *Lettere ed Orazioni*, ed. V. R. Giustiniani, 1953, p. 163.

43. Namely, W. Graf Uxkull-Gyllenband, *Plutarch und die griechische Biographie*, 1927, p. 115.

44. *Alexandre* I (ed. Walter, Pléiade, vol. II, p. 323). Also see *Nicias* II, (vol. II, pp. 8–9), in which, besides the key words found in the quote above (*mœurs, naturel,* etc.), the others are also found: *humeurs,* and *Cimon* V (vol. I, p. 1079). For the reason already stated, I am also providing the quotes from the *Vitae* in Amyot's translation.

45. See *Demetrius-Antonius* X (vol. II, p. 953) and *Dion-Brutus* V (vol. II, p. 1099).

46. See *Das Buch des Predigers . . .* trans. and explained by A. Allgeier, 1925, p. 3 ff.

47. In view of the many similarities between Montaigne's thinking and the Ecclesiastes, at one time a Montaigne admirer attempted to portray the themes in the *Essais* as a development of verses from the Ecclesiastes: W. Vischer, "Der Prediger Salomo im Spiegel Montaignes" (*Jahrbuch der Theologischen Schule Bethel,* IV, 1933). This goes well beyond what is justified, apart from the fact that the similarities are based mostly upon a common third element, the hellenistic philosophy of life.

48. Among contemporaries who possibly served as inspiration for Montaigne, one could suspect Etienne Pasquier, with whom Montaigne was personally acquainted. A treatise-style letter of Pasquier's to the humanist Turnebus, presumably from the year 1564, contains the most extensive anticipation of the themes in Essay II, 12 which could be imagined. This letter is the first item in the tenth book of Pasquier's letters, which were first published as a collection only in 1586, but which had been in circulation as individual letters before this time. See notes 77, 104, 139, and 306 below.

49. *Ep.* VII, 4, quoted in Ph. Monnier, *Le Quattrocento . . .* , 1908, I, p.

230. On Ciceronianism: R. Sabbadini, *Storia del Ciceronianismo*, 1885. On anti-Ciceronianism: M. W. Croll, "Juste Lipse et le mouvement anticicéronien" (in: *Revue du XVIᵉ siècle*, 1914).

50. This thought, which recurs in Montaigne (II, 12, 409 B: *Quoy qu'on nous presche . . . c'est l'homme que donne*) can be found in Petrarch (*De sui ipsius et multorum ignorantia*, ed. Capelli, 1906, p. 40 and p. 72), then in L. B. Alberti (*Della Famiglia*, p. 180), and in Agrippa von Nettesheim (*De incertitudine et vanite scientiarum . . .*, chap. I), and so forth.

51. For example, *De oratore* III, 10, 37. Erasmus uses this Ciceronian formula against "those who ape Cicero" but who merely practice *ornate dicere* instead of *apte dicere*. The *Dialogus Ciceronianus* by Erasmus is available in a Latin-Italian edition (by A. Gambaro, 1963). Erasmus' concept of the *speculum animi* can be found, for example, in *Laus stultitiae*, chap. 5, ed. Kan.

52. See G. Atkinson, *Les Nouveaux horizons de la Renaissance française*, 1935, p. 346 ff. Also Montaigne II, 12, 351 A.

53. The image of the *eloquentia* as shadow can also be found, though used differently, in Plutarch's work on the education of children, with invocation of Democritus.

54. See the more recent *Senecas 88. Brief. Text, Übersetzung, Kommentar* by A. Stückelberger, 1965.

55. More on this in P. Porteau, *Montaigne et la vie pédagogique de son temps*, 1935, p. 61 ff. For limitations with respect to the older humanistic principles of education, see E. Garin, *L'educazione umanistica in Italia*, 1949. Also see the older work by W. H. Woodward, *Studies in Education during the Age of the Renaissance*, 1906.

CHAPTER III

56. From Seneca, *Natur. quaest.*, praefatio: *O quam contempta res est homo nisi supra humana se erexerit!* Montaigne uses the word *humanité* mainly to designate humanity and a natural quality of being human, never in the sense of the higher ethos and dignity of essence (of the Ciceronian *humanitas*). His avoidance of the latter meaning of the word, with which he must have been acquainted, is precisely a tendency of his "humanity," which experiences an ideal model as a falsification of a natural being human. However, the meaning of *humanité* = *grace, benignité*, which is not necessarily connected with the normative dignity of essence, does appear on occasion (II, 11, 318 A). The gossipy, presumptuous, and trivial book by Ms. Tavera, *L'Idée d'humanité dans Montaigne*, 1932, is also worthless for Montaigne's concept of humanity.

57. More specifics on this in Busson, *Sources et développement . . .*, p. 104 ff.

58. Raymundus Sebundus is the Latinized name of the Catalan Ramon de Sibiude (according to the 1436 manuscript of the *Theologia naturalis;* there is also evidence for Sebeyde, Sabieude, Sabauda; Montaigne Frenchified the Latin form in his translation to Sebon, and in the "Apologie" to Sebond). Sebond was a theologian, physician, and humanist, and in the last years of his life he lived and taught in Toulouse. The full and original title of his work (reminiscent of

Bonaventura and Guillaume d'Auvergne) was: *Liber creaturarum seu Naturae seu liber de homine propter quem sunt creaturae alia*. The title *Th. nat.* (which we are retaining for the sake of simplicity) did not originate with Sebond at all, but rather appears later, but is suggested by the methodical explanations of the prologue. For more on the author and the work: M. Menéndez y Pelayo, *Historia de los Heterodoxos españoles*, 1880, I, book 3, chap. 5; J.-H. Probst, *Le Lullisme de R. de Sebonde*, 1912; Coppin, *Montaigne traducteur . . .* These documents contain critical references to the remaining literature available. Also see Busson, *Sources . . .* passim, and E. Gilson, *La Philosophie au moyen âge*, 1947, p. 465 ff.; and finally J. S. Révah, *Une source péninsulaire au XVIᵉ siècle: La Théologie Naturelle de Raymon Sebond*, 1953.

59. Compare the following expressions (even stronger in Montaigne's translation): "This doctrine opens before every man the path to an understanding of the saintly Doctors: . . . This doctrine is common to the laymen, the clerics, and men of every sort" (Armaingaud, vol. IX, p. VI and p. VIII). In the edition of the original which I have before me (Venice 1581): *Prologus*, unpaginated.

60. Specifics in Coppin, *Montaigne traducteur . . .* especially p. 67 ff. I only want to comment regarding this valuable work that it attempts to derive too many ideas in the *Essais* from Sebond. Also, the Latin models are omitted in the presentation of Montaigne's translation vocabulary. The second edition of the Sebond translation (1581) has been corrected. In 1957, Montaigne's pocket edition of his translation was found among rare books. It contains numerous entries in his own hand (see *Bibliothèque d'Humanisme et Renaissance*, 1958, p. 372).

61. Armaingaud, vol. IX, p. III.

62. *Philosophie au moyen âge*, p. 655.

63. Fideism is treated by: H. Haldimann, *Le Fidéisme*, 1907 (inaccessible to me); Busson, *Sources et développement . . .* passim; H. J. J. Janssen, *Montaigne fidéiste*, diss. at Amsterdam, Nijmegen-Utrecht, 1930. Presentation of medieval fideism (from Petrus Damianus to Ockham) in Geyer and Gilson, as cited above, and in the protestant histories of dogma by Loofs and Harnack. Effect of fideism in poetry: H. Weber, *La Création poétique au XVIᵉ siècle en France*, 1956, vol. 1, p. 49 ff.

64. A. Renaudet, *Etudes érasmiennes*, 1939, pp. 126–127.

65. Janssen, as cited above, p. 21, and Montaigne I, 26, 128 ff.

66. *Postérité*, p. 112 ff; p. 210 ff. Also Busson, *Sources et développement . . .*, and Janssen, as cited above, each passim, as well as Busson, *La Pensée religieuse de Charron à Pascal*, 1933, p. 203 ff.

67. *Journal*, ed. D'Ancona, pp. 294–295 and 329; there too, in the commentary, the incriminated passages.

68. See *Matthew* XI, 12 and Dante, *Paradiso* XX, verses 94–96.

69. Aristotle, *Politics*, VII, 7. Bodin, *Les Six Livres de la Republique*, V, 1 and *Methodus* V.

70. Compare Henri Estienne, *Apologie pour Hérodote*, 1566 (ed. Le Duchat, 1735, p. 42). The argument for the frequent superiority of the heathens goes back to Gregory the Great's *Moralia* (Migne, *Patr. lat.* LXXV, col. 518). Also compare Dante, *Paradiso* XIX, verse 104 ff.

71. H. Busson arrives at the same results in "La pratique religieuse de Montaigne" (in: *Bibliothèque d'Humanisme et Renaissance,* 1954).

72. Brief summary of "Curialism" in A. von Harnack, *Lehrbuch der Dogmengeschichte,* 1931, p. 424 ff. F. S. Brown's *Religious and Political Conservatism in the Essais of Montaigne,* 1963, is rather flat and lacking in new insights.

73. Details in M. Dréano, *La Pensée religieuse de Montaigne,* 1936, p. 133 ff., in which a number of unpublished sources is evaluated.

74. Montaigne's source was presumably the Lucretius passage VI, verses 678–679, which he used as one of the mottos on the beams in his library and also quoted in II, 12, 389. Also see Petrarch, *De remediis . . . ,* and later Pascal, *Pensées,* fragment 72 (Brunschvicg ed.), though used differently.

75. Accessible in the edition *Biblioteca de Autores Españoles,* 65 (*Filósofos*), 1929. Extensive material on the earlier history of the double theme of *dignitas* and *miseria hominis* in Burdach-Bernt, commentary on the *Ackermann aus Böhmen,* 1917, p. 314 ff.; also: H. Baker, *The Dignity of Man,* 1947; W. Dürig, s.v. (in: *Reallexikon für Antike und Christentum* III, 1957); J. Kamerbeek, Jr., "La dignité humaine. Esquisse d'une terminographie" (in: *Neophilologus,* 1957); A. Buck, "Die Rangstellung des Menschen in der Renaissance" (in: *Archiv für Kulturgeschichte,* 1960).

76. On this, see Villey, *Sources,* passim. Villey can prove that various passages borrowed by Montaigne come from Boaistuau, but he overestimates this author's influence.

77. Evidence in Villey in *EM* IV, 219 A. Also, Francesco P. della Mirandola in his *Examen vanitatis . . .* 1510. (More specifics in Strowski, *Bulletin italien* V, 1905, p. 311 ff.). N. Machiavelli in his poem in tercets, *Dell'asino d'oro,* and Estienne Pasquier, *Lettres* (1586) X, 1. See M.-L. Henry for the Old Testament view of animals in *Das Tier im Bewußtsein des alttestamentlichen Menschen,* 1958.

78. Stendhal paraphrases the sentence in *Lucien Leuwen* (ed. H. Martineau, 1927, III, p. 383: "Your cat is not caressing you; he is caressing himself on you").

79. Augustine, *Civ. Dei* XIII, 3; Thomas Aquinas, *Summa theologica* I, IIae, qu. 13, art. 2. The orthodox Catholic didactic opinion is summarized in Laurent. Janssens' *Summa theologica ad modum commentarii in Aquinatis summam,* 1918, vol. VII, p. 32 ff., there with express rejection of Montaigne. Also see Sebond, *Th. nat.,* chap. 89: *Quod bonum hominis non consistit in aliquo quod sit commune hominibus et bestiis.*

80. *Traité de la concupiscence,* ed. Urbain Levesque, 1930, pp. 58–59. Also *De la connaissance de Dieu et de soi-meme,* chap. 5, section 7, and *Sermon pour la fête de Tous les Saints,* troisième point.

81. For another side of the animal observation, see P. Schunck, "Die Funktion der Tiergeschichten in der Apologie de R. Sebond" (in: *Z. für franz. Sprache und Literatur,* 1964).

82. This meaning of *fantasie* corresponds to stoic word usage, particularly the stoic equating of *phantasia* and *pathos.* See G. Kilb, *Ethische Grundbegriffe der alten Stoa . . .* Diss. at Freiburg, 1939, pp. 6–7. Through this connection, of

which Montaigne was aware, his use of the word became even more distinctly pejorative.

83. *Paradiso* IV, verses 130–132. Also compare *Convivio* IV, 1514 and the proofs from Aristotle and Thomas provided with respect to this passage by Busnelli-Vandelli in their edition (*Opere di Dante*, vol. V, 1937, pp. 190–191). I am bringing Dante into this here only because Montaigne quotes him himself. In I, 26, 111 A we find the following verse (of course obtained secondhand): *Che non men che saper dubbiar m'aggrada (Inf.* XI, 93). Precisely this quotation demonstrates the difference. Dante stresses the benefit of doubting (which to him is equivalent to questioning) because it results in the benefit of precise instruction.

84. In addition to the proofs supplied in Renaudet (see note 64 above), there is also *De libero arbitrio* (LB, IX 1215 D).

85. Preface (p. 7 of the 1537 edition) and chap. 97 passim. It must be emphasized that the complete title of Agrippa's work was: . . . *et de excellentia verbi Dei.* These last words were later omitted, which contributed to distorting the fideistic meaning of the treatise. Agrippa is a skeptic in favor of the truth of faith; knowledge is devalued because it lies under the curse of the fall of man from grace. Thus one does not capture Agrippa's intent when, as often happens, one only sees the Pyrrhonic skeptic in him. The exact title of Francesco Pico della Mirandola is: *Examen vanitatis doctrinae gentium et veritatis Christianae disciplinae.*

86. F. Strowski, *Montaigne. Sa vie publique et privée*, 1938, p. 163, in which the author reports on a work in progress (never published, to my knowledge), a lexicon of Montaigne's philosophical language, and summarizes the findings: "We had found that Montaigne exactly modeled his technical terms after Greek and Latin words employed by the Ancients. He retained in the copy the precise meaning belonging to the original in the passage from which he drew his inspiration."

87. Villey, *Sources* II, p. 157 ff.

88. Cf. E. Gilson, *Philosophie au moyen âge*, chap. 9, sections 3–4, particularly p. 654 ff., and also by the same author, *Philosophie médiévale* II, p. 170.

89. More detail in H. Busson, *Sources et développement . . .* , passim, especially p. 43 ff. and p. 181 ff., and also Villey, *Sources* II, p. 344, and A. M. Boase, *Montaigne et la sorcellerie* (Bibliothèque d'Humanisme et de Renaissance, 1935, p. 402 ff.).

90. Fragment 814 (ed. Brunschvicg). Diderot makes a quite similar comment: *Œuvres,* ed. Assézat, XVI, p. 486.

91. G. Lanson, *Les Essais de Montaigne*, 1930, p. 276 ff., and L. Brunschvicg, *Le Progrès de la conscience dans la philosophie occidentale*, 1927, vol. I, p. 121.

92. In addition: "If our faces were not similar, we could not distinguish man from beast; if they were not dissimilar, we could not distinguish man from man" (*Essais,* III, 13, 819 C). This is a thought that is important for Montaigne's concept of individuality, which will be described in the following chapter. Villey found the sources for the sentences on dissimilarity. "Resemblance does not make things so much alike . . ." comes from Amyot's translation of Plutarch;

"Nature has committed herself . . ." is from Seneca; "If our faces were not similar . . ." comes from Augustine. But when one reads the context in these sources, one finds the following: In Seneca (*ep.* 113, 16) the concept of dissimilarity serves to refute the stoic doctrine according to which the virtues were living beings; Seneca countered this by saying one cannot compare different things, and everything is different. In Augustine (*Civ. Dei* XXI, 8), the concept is an element of proof for the claim that God, who had already visibly created all things different from one another, in a miracle can even make them dissimilar to themselves, for example, when he transforms the dead into eternal inhabitants of hell. In neither source does the concept have the weight that Montaigne gives it; it probably represents a commonplace device of Heraclitic origin which is used for demonstration purposes. The Plutarch passage is a bit different (*Moralia,* in the discourse on hatred and envy, from the cited edition of the Amyot translation, p. 337): in it, the differences in the emotions are demonstrated using the concept of dissimilarity. So as literally as Montaigne may have taken passages from Seneca and Augustine, he accentuates them quite differently; what in the sources is only touched upon, in Montaigne becomes the central issue. Of his classical sources, only Plutarch did advance work in this, and Montaigne's concept of dissimilarity could only develop freely in the ground of human analysis prepared by Plutarch. Before Montaigne, the dissimilarity concept appeared in a broader application in the works of Cusanus and Paracelsus (regarding the latter, compare the quotations, which agree with Montaigne to a remarkable degree, provided by E. Metzke in "Erfahrung und Natur in der Gedankenwelt des Paracelsus," *Blätter für Deutsche Philosophie* XIII, 1/2, 1939, pp. 89–90); the concept is then known to be continued in Leibniz.

93. On this, see Plattard, *Etat présent . . .*, pp. 42–43.

94. *Considérations sur l'histoire . . . universelle,* quoted in Atkinson, as cited above, p. 404.

CHAPTER IV

95. The expression stems from Stapfer (quoted in Pascal, *Œuvres,* ed. Brunschvicg, vol. XII, 1925, p. 70).

96. How successful this formula was is shown in Villey, *Postérité,* p. 200. Classical preliminary stage in, among others, Horace, *Sat.* II, 7, v. 7: ". . . *pars multa (sc. hominum) natat . . .*"

97. As far as I can see, no one has observed what is explained here. Villey only established a formal similarity of the *Essais* with the loose style of the *Discorsi* (*Sources* I, pp. 28–29). G. Atkinson attempts in a short article with the ambitious title "La forme de l'Essai avant Montaigne" (*Bibliothèque d'Humanisme et Renaissance* VIII, 1946, p. 129 ff.) to make a case for a chapter of the *Discorsi* (I, 28) as a unique case of the use of the essay form before Montaigne, but provides rather inadequate reasons.

98. G. Simmel, *Goethe,* 1921, p. 151. In a discussion of the first edition of my book (in: *Romanistisches Jahrbuch* III, 1950, p. 590) the comment was made that one could not use terms such as "individuality," "personality," and so forth for Montaigne's trains of thought because he did not use these terms himself. Cer-

tainly, he did not use them. But what is meant with these designations—from the eighteenth century on—is in his work, as the evidence we provide in our section shows. One could just as well contest calling Montaigne a moralist because he never called himself this. It is not sound methodologically in interpreting texts to use only designations that the texts themselves contain. The history of an idea quite often precedes the appearance of a word that fits it, and interpretation also consists in finding the appropriate word, even if it arises later, for an idea that arose earlier.

99. Compare Gracián, *El Criticón,* Ia parte, crisi 11, at the beginning, and also (in a softer form) La Rochefoucauld, *Réflexions diverses,* no. xi (in *Œuvres,* ed. Gilbert, 1868, p. 307). Balzac in "Avant-Propos" of the *Comédie Humaine* (ed. Conard, vol. I, p. XXVI ff.).

100. However, also see Terence, *Heauton.* II, 3, v. 282 ff.: the insight into the *vita cotidiana* also permits an insight into the nature of a man.

101. Coppin, *Montaigne traducteur,* p. 113 f.

102. In Montaigne's translation, Armaingaud IX, p. 343.

103. The sentence is found in Aulus Gellius (*Noctos Attic.* XI, 12). In the later Roman theory of *interpretatio iuris* also, which is incorporated into the rhetoric, the knowledge of the ambiguity of the word plays a major role; more on this in J. Stroux, *Summam ius summa iniuria,* 1926, passim, and also in his *Römische Rechtswissenschaft und Rhetorik,* 1949, and in K. Büchner, *Humanitas Romana,* 1957.

104. For example, Pasquier, *Lettres* X, 1 and Agrippa von Nettesheim, *De incertitudine . . . ,* chap. 3.

105. The following can serve as an orientation: U. Knoche, "Der römische Ruhmesgedanke" (*Philologus* LXXXIX, 1934); E. Zilsel, *Die Entstehung des Geniebegriffs,* 1926, p. 111 ff.; H. Friedrich, "Odysseus in der Hölle" (*Geistige Überlieferung, Zweites Jahrbuch,* 1942, p. 180 ff.); U. Leo, "Petrarca, Ariost und die Unsterblichkeit" (in: *Romanische Forschungen,* 1951).

106. Besides the passages in Knoche as cited above, the following come under consideration: Cicero, *Somnium Scipionis,* passim; Seneca, *ep.* 7, 19, 21, 22, etc.; and Pliny *ep.* I, 8.

107. *Esprit des lois* IV, 2. For example: *On n'y [monarchies] juge pas les actions comme bonnes, mais comme belles; comme justes, mais comme grandes; comme raisonnables, mais comme extraordinaires:* aesthetic, not ethical, values are the mode. Compare this in Montaigne: "In proportion as a good deed is more brilliant, I deduct from its goodness the suspicion I have that it was performed more to be brilliant than to be good: put on display, it is half sold" (III, 10, 783 B). Here, Montesquieu's comparison "good actions—beautiful actions" is anticipated in the antithesis "good—brilliant." There is even an echo of the sentence from La Rochefoucauld cited above in the *Essais:* "Our world is formed only for ostentation" (III, 12, 793 B).

108. *Ges. Schriften* V, p. 232.

109. *Italienische Reise* (WW., Weimarer Ausgabe, I, 32, pp. 201–202).

110. *Jugement sur Sénèque, Plutarque et Pétrone,* 1664 (in: *Œuvres choisies,* ed. A.-Ch. Gidel, s.d., pp. 267–268).

111. We find the same thought processes in Giordano Bruno, *Della causa . . .*

(1584), fifth dialogue (in: *Opere italiane*, ed. G. Gentile, 1907, I, p. 255 f.f.). Perhaps originating in Cusanus?

112. Plato, *Polit.* 491e; *Gorgias* 525e; *Hippias Minor* 375e; Plutarch, *Demetrius* 1/2. La Rochefoucauld, *Sentences et maximes*, nos. 182 and 190. Related to this, Corneille, *Trois Discours . . .* , I, and on Cleopatra, his *Rodogune*.

113. Anything necessary on this in C. H. Eickert, *Die Anekdote bei Montaigne*, diss. at Cologne, Erlangen, 1937.

114. E. Frémy, *L'Académie des derniers Valois*, 1887 (on p. 221 ff. reprints the lectures held there); see also F. Neubert, "Die Académie du Palais unter Hch. III . . ." (*GRM* XXI, 1933, 11/12). Neubert's attempt at classifying the lectures of the academy into a morality in the manner of Montaigne is not tenable. One cannot justifiably speak of "personal experience" which Neubert hopes to discover in these lectures (p. 468). More in F. A. Yates, *The French Academies of the 16th Century*, London, 1947.

115. Also accessible in Ronsard, *Œuvres complètes*, ed. G. Cohen (Bibliothèque de la Pléiade), II, p. 1042.

116. More on the antistoic tendencies in Manetti and Valla in E. Garin, *Der italienische Humanismus*, 1947, p. 50 ff. and p. 57 ff.

117. This and the following according to *Civ. Dei* XIV, 9; and IX, 4–5. Also compare Lactantius, *Divinae Institutiones*, VI, 17.

118. See the article "Affekt" by A. Vögtle in the *Reallexikon für Antike und Christentum*, ed. by Th. Klauser, 1941 ff., cols. 171–172.

119. For example, Thomas Aquinas, *Summa theol.* I, IIae, qu. 24, arts. 2–3.

120. Erasmus, *Ausgewählte Werke*, ed. by H. Holborn, 1933, pp. 44–46. The passage is interesting in our context in that it is based upon the insight that man is not a unit that can be comfortably interpreted. Much of the preparatory work is done here for what Montaigne will say about the complex spiritual "labyrinth."

121. Vives, *De anima*, book III, introduction (in the modern Spanish translation of the "Collección Austral," 1945, p. 188). It also contains the equating of affects with the enlivening wind of the soul.

122. Quevedo, *Obras en prosa*, ed. L. Astrana Marin, 1941, pp. 1849–1850; Molière, prologue to *Tartuffe;* La Bruyère, *Caractères* (*De l'homme*, no. 3). Also compare Calderón, *El sitio de Breda* (*Comedias*, ed. Keil, 1827, vol. I, p. 238).

123. In the *Moralia* fragment on the inconsistencies of the stoics.

124. From *Heauton.* I, 1. Erasmus uses it similarly to Montaigne, *Laus stultitiae*, ed. Kan, chap. 30. For more on the wealth of available literature on the statement "Homo sum . . ." see K. Büchner and J. B. Hofmann, *Lateinische Literatur und Sprache*, 1951, and J. Marouzeau in his Latin-French edition of Terence.

125. Compare Seneca, *ep.* 121, beginning.

126. Desportes (quoted in Frémy, *L'Académie des derniers Valois*, p. 232).

127. Further passages in Nietzsche: *Menschliches* I, section 36; II, section 33 and section 72; *Wanderer und sein Schatten*, sections 19–20, and so forth; see also "moralist" in the sense of "tactician" in German usage: Kant, *Zum ewigen Frieden*, appendix I: ". . . a political moralist who forges morals that are condu-

cive to the advantage of the statesman." The history of meaning of *moraliste* or "Moralistik" is quite complicated and cannot be presented here. One would have to show how the much older concept, mainly expressed from Nietzsche on using this word, of an analytical, psychological, nonnormative observation of man was expressed earlier using other terms (usually circumscriptions).

128. Seneca, *ep.* 89, 14: *Ergo cum tripertita sit philosophia, moralem eius partem primum incipiamus disponere . . .* ; then nature philosophy follows as the second part, and logic as the third part. *Science morale* in the seventeenth century could still be interpreted as: *la doctrine qui règle la vie et les mœurs,* according to the editor of Amyot's translation of Plutarch's *Moralia,* 1621, in the preface.

129. Cardano, *De Vita propria* (written in 1575), chap. 44. In it, but only at the end, jurisprudence is classified under the *scientia moralis.*

130. Burckhardt, *Weltgeschichtliche Betrachtungen* (ed. R. Marx, Kröners Taschenausgabe, 1935), p. 217; Dilthey, *Ges. Schriften* V, p. 370.

131. Fr. Gundolf, *Caesar,* 1925, p. 169.

132. R. Hirzel, *Untersuchungen zu Ciceros philosophischen Schriften,* 1882, II, p. 727 ff.

133. Hirzel, as cited in note 132, p. 729.

134. *Ricordi* (in: *Scritti politici e Ricordi,* a cura di Palmarocchi, Scrittori d'Italia, 1933), II, nos. 114 and 126. The *Ricordi* (see this edition, p. 369, note 1 concerning the title) were only published in their entirety in the nineteenth century; however, we can quote them as the most concentrated version of thoughts which also form the basis of Guicciardini's *Storia d'Italia.* Also compare the introduction by E. Grassi to the translation of the *Ricordi* which he edited (Fr. Guicciardini, *Das politische Erbe der Renaissance*).

135. More in Fr. Meinecke, *Die Idee der Staatsraison,* 1929, and P. Mesnard, *L'Essor de la philosophie politique au XVIᵉ siècle,* 1952.

136. "All things considered, whoever gains the advantage will receive the honor." And: "Those who win always have the honor of it." Commynes, *Mémoires,* ed. Dupont, 1840 ff., vol. I, p. 266. Montaigne's comment on the lion's and fox's skin concerns an adage of antiquity presumably handed down by Plutarch; Villey, *EM* IV, 13 A.

137. This distinguishes him from Bodin, who also permits amoral means to promote "good" purposes, but thereby restricts himself entirely to the realm of teaching practical political wisdom. Compare G. Cardascia, "Machiavel et Jean Bodin" (in: *Bibliothèque d'Humanisme et Renaissance* III, 1943, pp. 158–159).

138. E. Wolf, *Große Rechtsdenker,* 1963, p. 253 ff.

139. In Pascal: "A comic sort of justice that has a river for its boundary! Truth on this side of the Pyrenees, error on the other" (fragment 294). Villey, (*EM* IV, 268 B) found impetus for Montaigne's sentence in Erasmus' *Querela pacis* and named the other forerunners (Sextus Empiricus, Agrippa von Nettesheim). One can also add that E. Pasquier said something similar in his letter to Turnebus (*Lettres* X, 1) which has been mentioned several times already; also, Le Roy: "What is good one day is bad another . . . , here holy, there profane . . ." (quoted in Atkinson, as cited above, p. 411).

140. Not until Montesquieu would anyone dare again to base a doctrine of

society and state, when not one of natural law, at least one of a law of types, on the following sentence: . . . *j'ai cru que, dans cette infinie diversité de lois et de moeurs, les hommes n'étoient pas uniquement conduits par leurs fantaisies* (*Esprit des lois,* préface). Did this great admirer of Montaigne have his fellow Gascognian in mind when he formulated this?

141. Villey, (*EM* IV, 499 A/B) suspects the source of this sentence to be a passage from Plutarch's *Moralia.* But it could just as well have been a paraphrase of a classical adage, *Summum ius summa iniuria,* then familiar from Erasmus' *Adagia,* which came in this form from Cicero (*De officiis* 133). See note 103 above. The classical meaning of the adage, which tended to be quoted to recommend caution against too literal or improper interpretation of law, is different than the one in Montaigne, and it does not have the fundamental meaning of being critical of law as it does here. Also compare Terence, *Heauton.* IV, 5, v. 796: "ius summum saepe summa est malitia."

142. Compare, in addition to the passages in Budé (L. Delaruelle, *G. Budé,* 1907, p. 96 ff.), also Erasmus, *Laus stultitiae,* chap. 51 (ed. Kan), and in Thomas More's *Utopia,* the version of a legal system limited to the simplest basic laws (ed. Delcourt, 1936, p. 166).

143. On this, see P. Koschaker, *Europa und das römische Recht,* 1947, pp. 106–109.

144. *Variété* IV, 1938, p. 45.

145. This corresponds to the theories also developed by Bodin (*Les Six Livres . . .* V, chaps. 1 and 6) in which he advises the statesman to heed the *locorum ac regionum ratio.* But Bodin then restricts this consideration of the historical individualism of states with the concept of the absolute law.

146. The last sentence is the more strongly emphasized paraphrase of a passage in Livy (XXIII, 3). Also compare the following passage in Essay III, 12: "Plato likewise does not consent to have the repose of his country violated in order to cure it" (797 C); this refers to Plato's seventh letter. Montaigne's conservatism can also invoke Plato elsewhere, in III, 9, 732–733 C, also *Polit.* VIII, 546a, and so forth.

147. Research into sources has confirmed this. See L. Delaruelle, "L'inspiration antique dans le Discours de la servitude volontaire" (*Revue d'Hist. litt. de la France* XVII, 1910).

148. Concerning this, see P. Mesnard, *L'Essor de la philosophie politique,* p. 473 ff.

149. Armaingaud XI, p. 215 ff.

150. The quotations from Le Roy provided by Atkinson as cited above, p. 411 ff., are particularly informative. Also Guy de Pibrac, quoted by Montaigne himself (III, 9, 731 B), expresses the same ideas in his *Quatrains,* 1584.

151. P. Hazard on the occasion of discussing Molière addressed the question of how greatly the French considered conservatism of this kind, surrounded by the free-thinker movement and skepticism, a conservatism that was found through all the more modern centuries, to be a fundamental characteristic of their nation. The comments also apply to Montaigne and can thus be presented here: "He did like everyone else. An innovator in thinking matters, he remained a traditionalist in political and governmental ones. The man who would take

note of this contradiction would not be wrong; and he would be entirely correct
if, in addition, he recognized one of the eternal traits of our mind . . . We are the
first to accept classical ideas. We are at the same time revolutionaries and
traditionalists." ("Ce que Molière représente pour la France," in: *Molière, articles . . . recueillis et publiés par M. Mignon*, 1931.)

152. Amelot de la Houssaye in the *Discours critique,* which preceded his
translation of the *Annals* (*Tacite, avec des notes . . .* , 1690), in which Tacitus'
analyses of the sixteenth and seventeenth centuries are collected, mentions neither Montaigne nor Bodin. Compare also to what follows: J. von Stackelberg,
Tacitus in der Romania, 1960.

153. More in Villey, *Les Livres d'histoire utilisés par Montaigne,* 1907, and
A. Masson, "Notes sur la bibliothèque de Montaigne" (*Bibliothèque d'Humanisme et Renaissance,* 1939, p. 475 ff.).

154. Bembo is only mentioned by name in III, 5, 666 B, and is treated
ironically as a man of letters, here presumably directed against the *Asolani* or
against his lyric poetry.

155. Compare Chapelain's statements in a letter to G. de Balzac in 1638
(*Opuscules crit.,* ed. Hunter, 1936, pp. 393–394).

156. *De oratore* II, 36. In Montaigne's age, quoted in Amyot's foreword to
the translation of the *Vitae* or in Bodin's *Methodus* (foreword).

157. A wealth of material on the proliferation of this method in the sixteenth
century can be found in P. Porteau as cited earlier, p. 178 ff.

158. Villey gives an example, *EM* IV, 343 B below. Racine will still read
Homer.

159. Illustrated in the work by G. Atkinson, which has been mentioned
several times already and which is invaluable for enriching our knowledge of the
sixteenth century in France.

160. More on these authors in Atkinson. Exact specification of sources can
be found in Villey, *EM* IV, 54 ff.

161. This view is, however, contradicted by other authors, for there was also
an image of the backward, barbaric savage, especially by the Jesuits who hoped
to civilize the conquered lands. Atkinson, cited above, pp. 146 ff. and 164 ff. In
addition: Pasquier, *Lettres* III, 3, and Bodin, *Methodus,* chap. 7.

162. More on this in A. Castro, *El pensamiento de Cervantes,* 1925, p. 181
ff., which contains an excellent overview of European cultural weariness in the
sixteenth century and its battle with the idea of progress. We also find here some
proofs from Erasmus.

163. Atkinson, as cited above, pp. 167–168. Also J. Höffner, *Christentum
und Menschenwürde,* 1947, and G. Cocchiara, *Il mito del buon selvaggio,*
1950.

CHAPTER V

164. Villey, *Sources* II, p. 216.
165. *Nouveaux Lundis* II (1864), p. 155.
166. *Confessiones* X, 16; the second sentence (source not cited) in Gilson,

Philosophie au moyen âge, p. 467. On the Christian theme of self-knowledge, also see E. Gilson, *L'Esprit de la philosophie médiévale*, 1932, II, p. 1 ff.

167. These passages refute the superficial and vain criticism that Rousseau directed at Montaigne on one occasion when he said: "I had always laughed at the false naiveté of Montaigne who, while pretending to confess his faults, is quite careful to offer only the likeable ones; whereas I felt that there is no human interior, pure as it may be, that does not harbor some odious vice" (*Confessions* II, 10, *Œuvres*, ed. Musset Pathay, vol. II, p. 33). Compare the sentence quoted above from Montaigne, II, 20, 511 B, which says precisely the same thing that Rousseau here claims as his own discovery.

168. *Mauvaises Pensées*, 1942, p. 148.

169. *Morceaux choisis*, 1930, p. 86.

170. Compare to this the sentence Lichtenberg once wrote regarding his self-analysis: "Persons who are well versed in the observation of themselves and who thus secretly know themselves to be great often rejoice in the discovery of their own weakness" (*Schriften*, 1844, vol. I, p. 126, quoted according to P. Requadt, *Lichtenberg*, 1948, p. 28).

171. This concept of ignorance and abasement which knows itself and is thereby rescued goes back to Socrates (Plato, *Apology*, 22a–f). It becomes theological in Augustine's principle of *sui conscium esse*. It then returns again in Pascal with the theological meaning that Montaigne removed from it, which understands one's becoming conscious of one's own abasement as the impetus for purification: *Pensées*, fragment 397 and fragment 416.

172. Fr. Klingner, "Humanität und Humanitas" (in: *Beiträge zur geistigen Überlieferung*, ed. H. Küpper, 1947, p. 27).

173. Petrarch, *Famil.* IV, 1 and *De . . . ignorantia*, ed. L. M. Capelli, 1906, p. 25.

174. For example, Bonaventura, *Soliloquia* (ed. Quaracchi, VIII, p. 30a); later, *Imitatio Christi* III, 42, 1.

175. For example, *Nulla res magis vicina, magis propinqua . . . est quam ipsemet sibi . . .* The first chapter of the *Theologia naturalis* is easily accessible in the original in Armaingaud X, p. 464 ff., in which it is reproduced as a comparison with Montaigne's translation.

176. The passage is somewhat unclear and could also have the *Retractationes* in mind. But this changes nothing in our conclusion.

177. The introductory passage in this Essay from which the sentences quoted here were taken is thoroughly interpreted in Erich Auerbach's book, *Mimesis*.

178. Namely, Villey, *EM* IV, 195 A, and Armaingaud III, p. 103. If Montaigne had knowledge of Lucilius, it presumably would go back to Horace, *Sat.* II, 1, v. 32 ff.; compare the beginning of Essay II, 17.

179. I direct you to the well-known work by G. Misch, *Geschichte der Autobiographie* I, 1949. Also, B. Groethuysen, *Philosophische Anthropologie*, as cited above, passim.

180. Pasquier: *Lettres* XVIII, 1; Mlle. de Gournay: Villey, *Postérité*, pp. 72–73; Port-Royal: *La logique ou l'art de penser* III, 20, section 6 (ed. 1775, pp.

308–310); Malebranche: *La Recherche de la vérité* III, 3, chap. 5 (in: *Œuvres,* ed. Roustan-Schrecker, vol. I, 1938, pp. 367–368); English friends of Montaigne: cf. the paper on Bayle St. John, *Montaigne: The Essayist* (1858) in Dédéyan, *Montaigne chez ses amis anglo-saxons,* I, p. 311 ff., particularly p. 326. Bayle St. John's book is the best written in the English language on our author, alongside Emerson's Montaigne essay in *The Representative Men.*

181. More on this association can be found in E. R. Curtius' "Dichtung und Rhetorik im Mittelalter, *Deutsche Vierteljahresschrift für Literaturwissenschaft und Geistesgeschichte* XVI, 1938, vol. 4, p. 456. One can add to the passage from Cicero's *De invent.* quoted there his *De officiis,* I, 137. Also compare Servius on *Aeneis* I, 378. For discussion of the background of classical resistance to speaking of oneself, see: W. Kroll, *Studien zum Verständnis der römischen Literatur,* 1924 (reprinted 1964), p. 25 ff.

182. On Christian theology: Augustine, *Confess.* X, 3 and *Retract.* II, 6. Also compare Pascal, *Pensées,* fragment 100 (p. 377 of the small Brunschvicg edition) and the Logic by Port-Royal (as cited above, p. 311). On the Renaissance: see also Rabelais, in *Pantagruel* VIII (*Œuvres,* ed. Lefranc III, p. 102). De Thou took the motto for the *Commentarius de vita sua* from the introduction to Tacitus' *Agricola,* which Alfieri would also do for his *Vita scritta da esso.* On the Christian attitude of the seventeenth century: it is interesting how these various motifs come together in Port-Royal's Logic (as cited above, pp. 307–311); it is said of Pascal, for example, that he had sufficiently mastered *véritable rhétorique* to know that an *honnête homme* should not speak of himself (p. 307). On Voltaire: see the article "Auteurs" in *Questions sur l'Encyclopédie* (*Œuvres,* Geneva 1775, vol. XXI, p. 536). On Goethe: *Bedeutung des Individuellen* (W.W., Weimarer Ausgabe, I, 36, p. 276, and the Hamburger Ausgabe, X, p. 536).

183. These passages are in: II, 6, 273, C; II, 18, 503 A; III, 5, 641–642 B; III, 8, 720–721 B.

184. Villey, *Postérité,* p. 190.

185. Armaingaud IX, p. 215; *Theologia naturalis,* chap. 125.

186. Villey, *Postérité,* p. 73. Similar criticism was also found in 1771 from the pen of President Bouhier, reprinted in Dédéyan, as cited above, vol. II, p. 14 ff., especially pp. 22–23.

187. This means: in that man is and experiences himself, he knows better what human essence is than if he were to determine it definitely/objectively, for example, as in the well-known comments from antiquity to which the quotation refers (*animal rationale et mortale*). Several times, Montaigne makes comments from which it is clear how highly he values the evidence of inner experience. We will return to this in the next chapter. Here we will only present one passage in which he explains that when speaking of an illness, the only one who knows what he is talking about is one who himself has had it; and then he continues that whoever speaks of it without having experienced it himself will have happen to him what happened to the town crier who was to proclaim a lost horse and precisely described its appearance, its coat, its height, its ears—but when the horse was brought before him, he did not recognize it (III, 13, 827 B). What Montaigne is getting at with these considerations is similar to what Pascal will

later call the *esprit de finesse*. It concerns the insight that even the most precise, objective knowledge and discursive analysis of a matter is not sufficient to identify the matter in its reality if it has not been experienced, that is, perceived in its axiomatic totality by means of internal evidence.

188. Passages with his portrayal of his own person: II, 17, 485–486 A; I, 26, 108 A; I, 55, 228–229 B; III, 13, 848–849 B/C; III, 11, 786 B; III, 13, 830–831 B/C; III, 13, 843; III, 12, 814 B; II, 8, 291 A; II, 4, 263 A; II, 17, 490 A; I, 38, 173 B; II, 17, 492 B; III, 13, 823–824 B.

189. K. Voßler, *Frankreichs Kultur und Sprache*, 1929, p. 236.

190. Hegel, *Vorlesungen über die Geschichte der Philosophie*, ed. J. Hoffmeister, 1944, pp. 24, 27, and 88.

191. The key terms Montaigne uses to designate his mere opinions are: *mes fantasies, mes resveries, mes ravasseries, mes humeurs*. See note 7. The most frequent of these is *mes humeurs;* the most important passages can be found in Villey, *EM* V, but these could be expanded considerably. In Montaigne, the word *humeur* contains both the original concrete meaning of "juice," "liquid" (II, 12, 453 A), as well as that usage stemming from Galen's humoral physiology applied to the doctrine of the four humors (II, 12, 425 A: "melancholic humor, choleric humor"), but also, and this meaning is prevalent, the carry-over of the term, which was commonly done in the sixteenth century, to the character and the life of the soul. *Les humeurs* are the inclinations, attitudes, random thoughts which go along with one's personal nature. In keeping with his view of man as *subject ondoyant*, Montaigne appears to feel the original meaning of "liquid" in this word more strongly than was commonly the case. The inclination of his language, which pushes toward sensuousness and freshness of image, probably found in the word *humeurs* a very useful aid that fit in with the other images of fluctuation and flow, a word that at the same time expressed both the subjectivity and the mode of inconstancy. In Seneca we find: . . . *quanto facilius animus accipit formam, flexibilis et omni umore obsequentior (ep.* 50, 6). Here the closeness of *umor* and soul ("the pliant soul, more yielding than any liquid") is so remarkable that one would have to suspect that Montaigne was thinking of this passage.

192. Passages with comments on age: II, 17, 486 A; I, 20, 58 A; I, 57, 237 A; II, 32, 545 A; I, 28, 139 C; I, 57, 238 A; II, 36, 571 A; II, 2, 248 A; III, 2, 620–621 B; II, 8, 285 B.

193. Le Rochefoucauld, *Sentences et maximes*, no. 93, no. 192; La Bruyère, *Caractères* ("Des esprits forts," no. 6). Also from antiquity: Seneca, *ep.* 26, 3.

194. Quoted from Simmel, *Goethe*, p. 260. Unfortunately, as is the case throughout this excellent book, he does not reference the source.

195. Compare the clever sentences of a similar tone, filled with renunciation, by Saint-Evremond ("A. M. le Maréchal de Créqui . . .," in *Œuvres choisies*, ed. Gidel, pp. 401–402).

196. Bible: Psalm 90, 10; *Eph.* IV, 13; Aristotle: *Rhet.* II, 12–14; Dante: *Convivio* IV, 25, ed. Busnelli-Vandelli, vol. II, p. 304 (here, too, quotations from Thomas); Petrarch: *Fam.* I, 1; Alain Chartier: from P. Champion, *Histoire poétique du XVe siècle*, 1923, p. 40; Erasmus: *Opera, LB* IV, p. 755 ff. The *Carmen heroicum* is a collection of all aging formulae. Even though its inten-

tions are more rhetorical than autobiographical, the thirty-seven-year-old's des-
ignation of himself as an old man remains a fact, and this is also confirmed in a
passage in a letter which came shortly thereafter. See Ronsard: *Œuvres*, ed.
Cohen, I, p. 784. On the typology of ages in one's life, compare J. G. Herder,
Seereise nach Nantes (offset edition of 1911, p. 103 ff.); J. Grimm, *Rede über
das Alter*, 1860 (in: *Kleinere Schriften*, 1867 ff.); Fr. Boll, "Die Lebensalter" (*N.
Jahrbücher f. d. klass. Altertum* XVI, 1913, p. 89 ff.); A. Dyroff, *Der Peripatos
Über das Greisenalter*, 1939; E. R. Curtius, "Zur Literarästhetik des Mittel-
alters II.", *ZRPH* LVIII, p. 143 ff. Finally, we refer to the fine description of
stages in life in Dilthey (*Ges. Schriften* V, p. 217 ff.).

197. Dyroff, as cited above, p. 34, shows that he also thought otherwise.

198. Material in Dyroff, as cited above, pp. 30–33. Compare Br. Nardi,
Saggi di filosofia dantesca, 1930, p. 123 ff.

199. *Moralia*, in the short treatise on the question of "whether an old man
might still be permitted to take over affairs of state."

200. Dyroff, as cited above, p. 35 ff., reveals the Greek sources. In the
sixteenth century, Erasmus devoted a long, respectful passage in his *Convivium
religiosum, Colloquia* to it. In Germany, we have the somewhat archaic translation by R. A. Schröder, 1924.

201. Compare the following side by side: "I have seen the grass, the flower,
and the fruit . . . happily, since it is naturally . . ." (III, 2, 620 C) and Cicero,
Cato maior II, 5: *Sed tamen necesse fuit esse aliquid extremum et, tamquam in
arborum bacis terraeque fructibus, maturitate tempestiva quasi vietum et
caducum . . .*

202. Armaingaud XI, p. 196.

203. Villey (*Sources* I, pp. 16–17) refers to the fact that in 1579 in Paris, Bl.
de Vigenère's translation of three classical texts on friendship appeared. These
were Plato's *Lysis*, Cicero's *Laelius*, and Lucian's *Toxaris*. For more on classical
ideas on friendship, see E. Curtius, "Die Freundschaft im Altertum" (in: *Altertum und Gegenwart*, 1892), and P. Lain Entralgo, "La amistad en la antiqua
Grecia: Platon y Aristoteles" (in: *Eco. Revista de la cultura de occidente*, 1963).
Also: E. Klein, *Studien zum Problem der römischen und griechischen Freundschaft.*, diss. in Freiburg i. Br., 1957 (typewritten).

204. J. Mewaldt, *Die geistige Einheit Epikurs*, 1927, p. 10.

205. The classical sources are easy to find in Büchmann's *Geflügelten
Worten* s.v. *alter ego*.

206. See Bembo, *Fli Asolani*, ed. Milan 1808, pp. 151–152: even in our
broken-down world, there is still friendship, thus *il vero odore antico* has not
died completely.

207. One will find a response to this statement in Kierkegaard's private
papers when he says that "the mind is precisely modesty" and where Kierkegaard again takes up the spiritual-religious standpoint that Montaigne himself
had eliminated from the passage in the B layer preceding this sentence.

208. J. Burckhardt, *Briefe*, critical edition by M. Burckhardt, 1963, vol. V,
p. 98.

209. Pascal was probably inspired by this passage in his fragment on *Di-*

vertissement (*Pensées*, fragment 139). Montaigne's phrase "their mind seeks its repose in movement" can be compared to Pascal's "seeking rest through so much labor" (Turnell, p. 177), which could be added to Brunschvicg's commentary.

210. These words may have been written with certain passages in Cicero's *De officiis* in mind. In it, the two concepts contained in *officium*, office and role, have a common ethical, rigid reference and are understood as of equal weight as "binding duties." See G. Kilb, as cited above, p. 55 ff. Concerning emphasis of the old themes of life = playing roles, which was common in Roman moral philosophy, though sharply differentiated by Montaigne, the passages in Epictetus' *Enchiridion* 19, and Marcus Aurelius XII, 36 are informative. The sentence *Mundus universus exercet histrionem*, reproduced before the quotation from Montaigne above, stems from E. R. Curtius' *Europäische Literatur und lateinisches Mittelalter*, 1948, p. 146 ff.; it is indicated that it originated with Johannes von Salisbury.

211. Namely in Xenophon, *Hiero*, a document Montaigne used several times. The theme of the inhuman isolation of powerful persons recurs later in Racine: *Bérénice* III, 1 (Titus) and *Iphigénie* I, 5 (Agamemnon).

212. Did this anecdote have an effect on Moltke's comment in response to the question of what there was left to him of joy in living after the great successes that lay behind him, when he said "seeing a tree grow"? Moltke was fond of the *Essais*. It has been reported that he carried the book in his saddle bags when he rode his horse (van Seeckt, *Moltke*, 1931, pp. 62 and 183).

213. The recommendation that one travel was commonplace in all of the educational literature from the fifteenth century on, and it is possible that in I, 26 Montaigne at first was only recommending travel because he was following this common practice, which was connected with a general reversal of the educational concept of book learning to one of real personal experience. Montaigne's principle that the traveler should adapt to all customs and peoples is also found in Castiglione (*Cortegiano* II, 22:". . . *che sappia accommodarsi ai costumi delle nazioni ove si trove* . . ."); still, here this is more a rule of politeness.

214. The metaphor of the "book of the world" suggested here is probably something Montaigne took from Sebond, the foreword to the *Theologia naturalis* (in Montaigne's translation: Armaingaud IX, p. XI: "*A cette cause bastit elle* [*l'intelligence divine*] *ce monde visible et nous le donna comme un livre propre*"). Sebond, in turn, took it from Lull, who may have found it in Bonaventura (compare Probst, *Le Lullisme* . . . , p. 30, and Gilson, *Philosophie au moyen âge*, p. 464). For more on the age and the broad proliferation of this metaphor, see E. R. Curtius, "Schrift- und Buchmetaphorik in der Weltliteratur" (*Deutsche Vierteljahresschrift für Literaturwissenschaft und Geistesgeschichte* XX, 1942, p. 359 ff.), the Sebond passage could well be added to the rich material it contains. Cusanus (whom Sebond knew) also called nature a *libri Dei* (Cassirer, *Individuum und Kosmos* . . . , p. 57).

215. See the *Notice bibliographique* in M. Rat's edition of the *Journal* (1942; this addition has limited value, since it only reproduces the Italian part in French translation). A later edition by Ch. Dédéyan (1947) is filled with printing errors. In the following, quotations will be taken from the edition by D'Ancona.

Let us also note that Goethe valued the *Journal* very highly; proof of this can be found in V. Bouillier, "Montaigne et Goethe" (*Revue de litt. comparée*, 1925, p. 572 ff.).

216. The part begins: "*Assaggiamo di parlar un poco questa altra lingua . . .*, " p. 419. D'Ancona made the following assessment of Montaigne's Italian: "*un poco ricorrendo alle forme auliche, e un poco porgendo orrecchio al parlar vivo . . . Troveremo parecchie reminiscenze francesi . . .*" (p. 419). Montaigne did not write out of arrogance about his education, but rather as an adaptation, as an Italian "attempt" (*assaggiamo . . .*). It is the only foreign language in which he expressed himself, and he only did so here. Also, in sixteenth-century France, due to the elevation in the rank of Italian writing to the status of the third "classical" literature, the use of Italian was fairly widespread (E. Walser, *Studien zur Geistesgeschichte der Renaissance*, 1932, p. 86, and H. Chamard, *Histoire de la Pléiade*, 1939, vol. I, p. 116 ff.).

217. I will refrain from listing the many passages that form the basis of my review. One can find them quickly using the Register in D'Ancona's edition.

CHAPTER VI

218. Compare, for example, *De senectute*, 74: "*Moriendum enim certe est, et incertum an hoc ipso die.*" What later became a dictum: "*mors certa, hora incerta.*" Also, *Lucas* XII, 19–20, etc. For a modern source, see: G. Simmel, "Tod und Unsterblichkeit" (in: *Lebensanschauung*, 1918), p. 104; and M. Heidegger, *Sein und Zeit*, 1941, p. 258.

219. On further familiar death metaphors that were particularly numerous in the sixteenth century, see E. Huguet, *Le Langage figuré au XVIe siècle*, 1933, chap. 13, p. 241 ff.

220. One example: I, 14, 46 C (stoicizing, though from the late period).

221. Compare what was said in chapter 1.

222. It is very difficult to review this Essay for its final form contains all imaginable attenuation and different additions. I am essentially working here with the earliest and the middle draft (A and B).

223. Very similar is the conversation about the tightrope walker in Gracián, *El Criticón*, 3a parte, crisi 11: "*Dime, ¿no caminas cada hora y cada instante sobre elhilo de tu vida, no tan grueso ni tan firme como una maroma, sino tan delgado como el de una araña y aun más y andas saltando y bailando sobre él?*" (Ed. Cejador, 1914, II, p. 312).

224. Such as Seneca, *ep.* 24: *Quotidie morimur; cum crescimus, vita descrescit;* Plutarch, *Moralia* (several times, e.g., in the *Trostschrift an Apollonius*); Quevedo, *La Cuna y la sepultura*, chap. III (*Obras en prosa*, 1941, p. 1097). On classical, particularly stoic, teachings on death: E. Hoffman, "Leben und Tod in der stoischen Philosophie" (in: *Platonismus und christliche Philosophie*, 1961).

225. For a critique of this "clever dialectical expression," which is most common in Epicurus (Diog. Laërtius X, section 125; also see Lucretius, III, v. 866, and Cicero, *Tusc.* I, 38), see M. Scheler, "Tod und Fortleben" (in: *Schriften aus dem Nachlaß* I, 1933), p. 18.

226. The countless texts of antiquity and late antiquity which model these reflections that result in the understanding of death by means of a knowledge of its inherence in life cannot be listed here. The oldest is probably Heraclitus, B 20. Regarding Montaigne's sources, anything necessary can be found in Villey (*EM* IV). We must add that these reflections were quite tenacious, enduring uninterrupted even by Christianity. One finds them in Augustine (*Civ. Dei* XIII, 10), in the *Ackermann aus Böhmen*, in Quevedo (in the lovely *Carta a D. Manuel Serrano*, 1635, *Obras en prosa*, 1849 ff.), in Gracián, and so forth, and in more modern times, again in Simmel, *Rembrandt*, 1917, p. 89 ff., and in Scheler as cited above passim—in the latter, though, without any apparent literary dependency. They even reach into the analyses of the "Sein zum Tode" in Heidegger's *Sein und Zeit* (p. 236 ff.), or into Rilke's poetry, or Valéry's volumes of aphorisms.

227. Villey, *Postérité*, p. 34.

228. Namely Lipsius, Pierre de Brach, Florimon de Raemond. Evidence in Villey, *Postérité*, p. 30 ff. and p. 350 ff.

229. *Briefwechsel W. Dilthey und Graf Yorck v. Wartenburg*, 1923, p. 120 (letter of March 4, 1891 from Rome). The judgment does not apply to Roman philosophy on death as a whole. Quite apart from a few softening passages in Seneca, a few aphorisms from Marcus Aurelius (IV, 48; IX, 3; XII, 36) are enough to make it clear that at least the Romans of the late Caesar period "understood" [*begriffen*] death in the sense in which Von Wartenburg uses the term "Begreifen."

229a. See K. Jaspers, *Allgemeine Psychopathologie*, 1946, p. 306 ff.

230. The idea that for men there is no "single" death, but rather, in each person's case, there is his "particular death," is also expressed later by Quevedo when, in his *Sueño de la muerte*, he has Death speak the following words: *La muerte no la conocéis, y sois vosotros mismos vuestra muerte: tiene la cara de cada uno de vosotros . . .* (*Obras en prosa*, p. 211).

231. Compare to this La Rochefoucauld, *Sentences et maximes*, no. 26 and no. 504.

232. Classical: Lucretius III, v. 972 ff.; Seneca, *ep.* 54; Cicero, *Tusc.* I, 12.

233. The opposite of this would be "to become normal" in dying by fulfilling the ritual duties. An example of this is Don Quixote's death (ed. *Clásicos Castellanos*, vol. VIII, 1923, pp. 324–325). Don Quixote begins, as death approaches, to make pious speeches, to make his testament, and so forth. Those present thereupon consider him cured of his madness, seeing his earlier madness as a common kind that is fortunately now leaving him: death makes him "normal" (at least apparently).

234. The theater metaphors in this sentence could well be an echo of antiquity's common comparison of "death equals the last act in the drama of life." Compare Cicero, *De senectute*, last sentences; Seneca, *ep.* 77; Marcus Aurelius XII, 36; and so forth.

235. *No puede alguna dialéctica persuadir al ojo que no se cierre al polvo que le ciega, ni a la cabeza que no se aparte del golpe que la busca,* as cited above, p. 1850. See our chapter 4, and the sentence quoted there from the *Essais* II, 2, 250 A/C.

236. To use a sentence from Heidegger: "Das Man läßt den Mut zur Angst vor dem Tode nicht aufkommen" (*Sein und Zeit,* p. 254).

237. *La Logique ou l'art de penser,* ed. cited above (note 180), p. 310 (IIIe partie, chap. 20, section 6). The protest applies at the same time to a passage in Essay III, 2 (617 B) on remorselessness.

238. A combined quotation from *Phil.* I, 23 and *Romans* VII, 24 (deliverance from the body and return to Christ) appears once in II, 3, 260 A as evidence of a lesser form of suicide motive. Also compare K. Rahner, in: *Lexikon für Theologie und Kirche* X, 1965, s.v. *Tod.*

239. On this subject, see H. Thielicke, *Tod und Leben,* 1946, p. 13 ff.

240. *Civ. Dei* XIII, chap. 3, and the following chapter.

241. *De senectute,* 67. Also compare *Tusc.* I, 25 and Seneca, *ep.* 24. The alternative probably goes back to Plato, *Apology,* 40b/c.

242. *Matthew* XXVI, 37–38. Augustine, *Civ. Dei* XIII, chap. 6: *Sic per ineffabilem Dei misericordiam et ipsa poena vitiorum transit in arma virtutis . . . Tunc enim mors est acquisita peccando, nunc impletur iusitia moriendo.*

243. Augustine as cited above, chap. 7; Gregory, *Moralia,* 16–18. Later, the Spanish equivalent of this by Luis de Granada, *La Gula de pecadores (BAE VI),* p. 34, and in Calderón, *El gran teatro del mundo,* v. 1211; see the French version in Pascal, *Pensées,* fragments 194–195.

244. On Luther: see Thielicke as cited above, p. 129. On Catholics: H. Bremond, *Histoire du sentiment religieux,* vol. IX, chap. 5, "L'art de mourir," particularly p. 335 ff.

245. Quite untenable is M. Dréano's attempt (in his well-informed yet superficial book cited above, *La Pensée religieuse de Montaigne,* p. 361 ff.) to win Montaigne back for Christianity based precisely upon his thoughts on death. The fulfillment of the obligations of the Church which Dréano uses as evidence belongs within the realm of his formal conservatism. It says nothing at all—or, rather: it says all the more about his lack of Christianity in that it does not prevent him from thinking in an un-Christian manner. To distinguish Montaigne's attitude toward death from that of authors of the late Middle Ages and of his own time would be useful: see E. Dubruck, *The Theme of Death in French Poetry of the Middle Ages and the Renaissance,* London, 1964.

246. "O death . . . , you teach him [man] these two truths, opening his eyes to a better knowledge of himself: he is infinitely contemptible in that he is temporally finite; and infinitely estimable in that he enters eternity," Bossuet writes in the preamble of his *Sermon sur la mort.*

247. Quotations according to M. Scheler, as cited above, p. 46, where he is seeking the "psychological" prerequisites of the idea of immortality. Also compare Simmel, "Tod und Unsterblichkeit," as cited above, p. 112.

248. The sentence found on the same page, "Death is the origin of another life," sounds Christian, but it comes from Lucretius: death is a placemaker for new life (*De natura rerum* I, v. 262 ff.). This comes out more clearly in III, 12: "The failing of one life is the passage to a thousand other lives" (807 B). See A. Tenenti on the dissemination of this thought at the time in *Il senso della morte e l'amore della vita nel Rinascimento,* 1957.

249. Cf. Seneca: *Hoc ipsum solatium est, aequo animo perdere quod periturum est* (*ep.* 98), something that eluded Villey.

250. Pasquier, *Lettres* I, 18 (also available in the edition of the *Essais* prepared by Coste, 1724, vol. IX, p. 312 ff.). Pierre de Brach, letter of February 4, 1593 to Lipsius, reprinted in Villey, *Postérité*, pp. 350–351. There is also an earlier letter by de Brach on the death of Montaigne, a letter of October 10, 1592. I was unable to gain access to it. The portions of it passed on by Strowski (*Montaigne* . . . , 1938, pp. 265–266) say nothing new when compared with the later letter. A few more details that we can skip are reported by a source cited by Armaingaud (I, p. 45).

251. Compare his letter to Mlle de Gournay of May 22, 1593, reproduced in Villey, *Postérité*, p. 352.

CHAPTER VII

252. *De officiis*, II, 5. Literally in the foreword of Charron's *De la sagesse*, in the foreword of Descartes' *Principia phil.*, section 2, and so forth. A valuable collection of doctrines of wisdom in European writings of the sixteenth century can be found in E. F. Rice, Jr.'s *The Renaissance Idea of Wisdom*, London, 1958. On the classical differentiation of wisdom/science: Br. Snell, *Meinungen der Sieben Weisen*, 1952; W. Burkert, *Weisheit und Wissenschaft, Studien zu Pythagoras, Philolaos und Platon*, 1962.

253. And also all that the literatures of the Renaissance included under the key word of grace (*grazia, grâce*, etc.), the loveliest example in the first book of Castiglione's *Cortegiano* (chaps. 26–28). A sovereign sense of the perfection of man in the cheerful purposelessness of leisure is expressed here, encouraged by the spirit of Cicero. There is a direct line from *De oratore*, the basic text of urbane, Roman humanity, to the *Cortegiano*.

254. On the proliferation of this commonplace image, see Villey, *EM* IV, 155 A.

255. Renan, *L'Ecclésiaste*, 1890, p. 40.

256. Villey, *Sources*, especially II, p. 214 ff.

257. As earlier, I am quoting from the following edition: Μωρίας εγχώμιον, *Stultitiae laus Des. Erasmi Rot. Declamatio*, ed. J. B. Kan, The Hague, 1898, and the chapter divisions used in this. On the subject of "Wahn," among others: B. Könneker, *Wesen und Wandlung der Narrenidee im Zeitalter des Humanismus*, 1966 (in this work, p. 248 ff. on Erasmus).

258. Numerous other classical stimuli come under consideration for the theme of "happy foolishness" in Erasmus and Montaigne. Erasmus himself used this in the *Adagia*, where one finds it using the index *iuxta locos* under the heading *Fortunata stultitia* (*LB* II, 83 of the appendix). The *Adagia* (*LB* II, 702–703) also contains—as does the *Laus stultitiae*, chap. 38—the anecdote about Argiver Lykas, who was obsessed with sitting in the theater and enjoying comedies; after he was cured of his madness by the doctors, he became unhappy. This anecdote (which comes from Horace, *ep.* II, 2, v. 128 ff.) recurs in Montaigne under the sentence: "I think they will not deny me this, that if they could add

order and constancy to a man's state of life and maintain it in pleasure and tranquillity by some weakness or infirmity of judgment, they would accept" (II, 12, 365 A; with quotations from the Horace passage).

259. *Concordia discors:* for example, in Horace, *ep.* I, 12, 19 (cited by Montaigne himself in II, 12, 402—though, just as in Horace, he uses it as an ironic allusion to world mysteries that cannot be solved); in Ovid, *Metam.* I, v. 433; in Lucan, *Pharsalia* I, 98; and so forth. Also compare Plotinus, *Enneads* II, 3, 16, Boëthius, *De consol. philosoph.* IV, metrum 6, v. 16 ff., and Augustine, *Civ. Dei* XI, 18. The Plutarch passage forming the basis of the quotation from III, 13 just offered contains, almost literally, Heraclitus' fragment 51 (cf. *Moralia,* ed. Pohlenz-Sieveking, vol. III, 1929, p. 210), to which, from the standpoint of meaning, one could add the further Heraclitus fragments A 22, B 8, and B 10, at least in the manner in which they have been understood in post-Socratic philosophy. Other passages on the subject of antinomies in Montaigne: III, 1, 599–600 B; III, 5, 677–688 C; III, 9, 756 B; and so forth. Also cf. Castiglione, *Cortegiano* II, chap. 2, and T. Tasso, *Prose,* ed. Guasti, 1875, I, p. 155. In antiquity and postantiquity, the formula also applied to the doctrine of world harmony and to music. On the concept of world harmony including *concordia discors:* L. Spitzer, *Classical and Christian Ideas of World Harmony,* ed. A.-G. Hatchey, Baltimore, 1963.

260. J. Burckhardt, *Historische Fragmente,* ed. W. Kaegi, 1942, p. 207. *Weltgeschichtliche Betrachtungen,* ed. R. Marx, 1935, pp. 11 and 270.

261. Passages: II, 12, 375 C; II, 17, 498 C; III, 13, 821 C; and so forth.

262. A. Thibaudet declared, half jokingly, half seriously, that Montaigne was the greatest archetype of the small *Français moyen: NRF,* 1933, p. 648.

263. J. Burckhardt, *Erinnerungen aus Rubens,* ed. H. Kauffmann (Kröners Taschenausgabe), s.d. p. 18.

264. Montaigne had undertaken this personification even in his translation of the *Theologia naturalis.* Cf. *homo tenetur de jure naturae = nature mesme le luy commande* (even nature commands him to do it); *Credit quod melius est pro humana natura = Il est guydé à ceste creance par la main mesme de la nature* (He is guided in this belief by nature's very hand). Quoted from Coppin, *Montaigne traducteur . . . ,* p. 180. Also see N. Dow, *Montaigne's Conception of Nature,* 1940 (inaccessible to me). An overview of the personification of nature in antiquity and in the Middle Ages can be found in E. R. Curtius, *ZRPH* LVIII, 1938, p. 180 ff.; also, further literature can be found there. Furthermore, K. Deichgräber, *Natura varie ludens. Ein Nachtrag zum griechischen Naturbegriff,* 1954.

265. Cf. *De libero arb.* (*LB* IX, cols. 1221–1223) and *De conscribendis epistolis* (*LB* I, col. 416a). Additional material in Renaudet, *Etudes érasmiennes,* pp. 335–336.

266. Valla: see Garin, as cited above pp. 50 ff. French Renaissance: Busson, *Sources et développement . . . ,* p. 254 ff., and Atkinson as cited above passim. Rabelais: ed. Lefranc, vol. II, pp. 430–431.

267. The two mentions of Paracelsus in the *Essais* are vague and do not prove that Montaigne read his works (II, 12, 429–430 A and II, 37, 586 A). The idea discussed here is also Platonic: *Timaeus,* 89c/d. Cf. W. Leibbrand, "Gesundheit und Krankheit im abendländischen Denken" (in: *Studium Generale,* 1953).

268. This is mainly found in Essay II, 37. Just as in Agrippa von Nettesheim and Erasmus (for example, the "Funus" conversation in the *Colloquia*) there is ridiculing of the demanding ignorance, the bickering over opinions, the money hunger, the fraudulent behavior of physicians. The belief that one is better off leaving healing to the discretion of nature is a commonplace view in literature of that time (Quevedo, *Obras en prosa*, pp. 1879–1880), which is known to still play a major role in Molière (*Malade imaginaire* III, 3).

269. The fortuna idea in Guicciardini agrees almost literally (*Ricordi*, IIa series, nos. 30, 31, 85, 126, etc.). Montaigne is farthest removed from the *fortuna* idea of Machiavelli; he has no interest in the resistance of *virtù* to *fortuna*.

270. Fortuna passages in the *Essais:* II, 4, 263 A; II, 20, 511 B; III, 5, 674 B/ C; III, 9, 733 B; III, 2, 618 C; III, 8, 714 B; III, 8, 713 B; I, 24, 175 A; III, 12, 812 B/C; III, 9, 764 B. Caesar's murder: II, 3, 255–256 A and III, 9, 731 C (similarly to Erasmus, *Laus stult.*, chap. 24).

271. Villey, *Postérité*, p. 192 ff. One can count the frequent mentions of Montaigne in the letters of François de Sales among these as well. Some sections of his *Introduction à la vie dévote* also read like spiritual paraphrases of the *Essais*. Compare the following side by side: *Introduction* III, 31 (*Œuvres complètes*, ed. Ch. Florisoone, vol. II, pp. 89–90) and Montaigne III, 13, 851–852.

272. This lovely rendering of the Greek word from W. Szilasi, *Macht und Ohnmacht des Geistes*, 1946, p. 21.

CHAPTER VIII

273. For example, I, 21, 75 C; I, 40, 185 C; and so forth. He uses the word only in the meaning of "author"; we do not find in his work the meaning of *scriptor*, writer or scribe, which was still associated with the word at his time (and to some extent in modern French as well).

274. In antiquity: Cicero, *De senectute*, 2; Pliny the Younger, *ep.* I, 9. In the vulgar literatures of the fifteenth and sixteenth centuries, there was similar material, parallel to the Latin writings, in Leonardo Bruni, Machiavelli, Bandello (all three contain the following several times: *scrivere per mio spasso*), in Rabelais, Marguerite de Navarre, Ronsard (type: *écrire pour passetemps*), etc.

275. In the passage from II, 8 mentioned, and before this also, one finds the popular classical anecdotes about men who took upon themselves poverty, persecution, and death for the sake of their books. On the definition "my books = my children," E. R. Curtius, ZRPH LXII, 1942, pp. 490–491. One can add to this: Ficino (Ph. Monnier, *Le Quattrocento . . .* , vol. II, p. 84) and Erasmus (Huizinga, *Erasmus*, German by W. Kaegi, 1936, p. 147).

276. Coppin, *Etude sur la grammaire . . .* , especially pp. 13 and 34.

277. Examples from Cicero, and so forth in R. Hirzel, *Der Dialog*, 1895, vol. I, p. 520. This designation is also known in poetry: Hirzel, vol. II, 14 (Horace). The basis for the expression *sermo intimus* is probably Plato, *Theaetetus* 189e (thinking is the soul speaking with itself).

278. One can see which definitions for the meaning of writing were commonplace in Montaigne's time in, for example, Cardano's *De vita propria*. There, in

chapter 45, the author justifies his writing, and derives their development from the following motives: obeying the instruction of a dream; giving in to pressure from friends; creating fame for himself; passing the time during idle hours; instructing men; furthering scientific knowledge; providing himself with comfort and clarity; to thank God and Mary; and so forth. This is an enumeration of the traditional motives, just as the relating of justifications for his own writings in itself is a traditional practice.

279. One can also think of a literary convention. It was a commonplace motive in Roman literature that a work would first claim only to be a manuscript written for friends (on this, see W. Kroll, *Studien zum Verständnis der römischen Literatur,* p. 117 ff.). Petrarch offers something similar; in his letter "Ad Socratem suum" (*Fam.* I, 1) of 1350, for example, he assures the reader several times that, at least with respect to his letters, he only hoped for a very small audience of connoisseurs within his circle of friends—assurances that are clearly repeated from classical models. Later, we find this sort of thing again in Goethe; compare the evidence assembled in Gräf's *Goethe über seine Dichtungen,* 1901 (vol. I, nos. 720, 729, 863: his own works are actually only intended for friends).

280. A three-part schema of levels of education such as this can be found frequently in literature of that time, although the schema is filled in variously in the details. Examples are Machiavelli, *Principe,* chap. 22; G. Bruno, *Cena delle ceneri,* Dialogo I; also compare E. Zilsel, *Entstehung des Geniebegriffs,* p. 191.

281. The word goes back to *grotta,* from *krypta,* because such paintings were found in the ruins of Roman palaces. The grotesque style was employed by Raffael, Giovanni da Udine, and others. On this subject, see Vasari, *Vite degli Artefici* in the chapter on Giovanni da Udine. Some information on the history of the grotesque style can be found in K. Borinski, *Die Antike in Poetik und Kunsttheorie,* 1914, I, p. 188 ff. Also compare W. Kayser, *Das Groteske,* 1957.

282. *Emblème* in Montaigne, as often in others in the sixteenth century in France, did not have the derivative meaning, present at that time, of "symbol" or "epigram," rather it was used with the original meaning of "mosaic" or "part of a mosaic." Compare Rabelais, *Pantagruel,* book V, chap. 38 (ed. Plattard, 1929, pp. 145–146, *emblemature*). The word *marqueterie* used a little before this is still in use in modern French to designate a literary potpourri; see Littré.

283. Some information on this can be found in E. Norden, *Kunstprosa,* p. 595 ("Such affected modesty was known to be a topos of the prooimion"), and in E. Curtius' *Deutsche Vierteljahresschrift für Literaturwissenschaft und Geistesgeschichte* XVI, 1938, pp. 457–458. On *ordo neglectus:* see Horace, *ep.* II, 2, v. 124; Ovid, *ars amatoria* III, v. 153; and so forth.

284. R. Volkmann-C. Hammer, *Rhetorik und Metrik der Griechen und Römer,* 1901, p. 60.

285. Probably an imitation of a statement of Socrates (Plato, *Polit.* 394d): "I don't yet know; but we must go in whatever direction the wind of speech drives us, as it were." Also compare the passage of the *Essais:* "... breath of her winds ..." II, 12, 426 A, which we quoted above in chap. IV.

286. *Bigarrure* at Montaigne's time was also a title for books of hodgepodge and miscellany: Villey, *Postérité*, p. 348 (Des Accords, 1586), and H. Morf, *Geschichte der französischen Literatur im Zeitalter der Renaissance*, 1914, p. 225 (Tabourot, 1582). The title can still be found in the eighteenth century (Tiphaigne de la Roche, *Bigarrures philosophiques*, 1759). Additionally, *rapiessement, rappiecer* in the verb form are also recurring terms in Montaigne's definition of style: I, 28, 135 A.

287. Some examples: *Essais:* III, 5, 666 B; III, 8, 718 B; I, 26, 128 C; I, 40, 185 C; III, 9, 758 C; *Mon livre*, etc.: "To the Reader," II, 12, 425–426 B; II, 10, 297 A; III, 9, 751 B. Devaluing characterizations can be found quite frequently and easily according to the examples noted above in Villey, *EM* V.

288. Etymological and history of meaning material in Wartburg, *FEW;* Du Cange, Forcellini, Nicot, Godefroy, Littré. The Latin equivalents of *essai, essaier* in Nicot are: *proludium, praeludium, tentamentum, praelusio; tentare, attentare, experiri, facere periculum, periclitari, probare, praeludere*. On Clément Marot: *Œuvres*, ed. P. Jannet, s. d., IV, p. 189. On Sagon: Ph. A. Becker, *Clément Marot*, 1926, p. 95 and pp. 307–308. Rabelais calls his Gargantua prologue *ce prelude et coup d'essay* (ed. Lefranc, I, p. 7), two synonyms that confirm Nicot's translation back using *essay = praeludium*. More on the history of the meaning of *essai:* A. Henry (in: *Romance Philology*, 1949–1950) and A. Blinkenberg (in: *Mélanges offerts à M. Roques* I, 1951). In his notes on the *Ephemeriden*, Montaigne uses *essai* once in the sense of "sampling a food" (*Œuvres complètes*, ed. M. Rat, p. 1409).

289. Villey, *Postérité*, p. 347.

290. *Exercitation* can, like *essai*, also mean exercise in stylistic composition. In I, 28, Montaigne says of La Boétie's *Contr'un:* "He wrote it by way of essay" (135 A), and a few pages later: ". . . was treated by him . . . only by way of an exercise . . ." (144 A).

291. On "risk": III, 9, 735 B; III, 13, 830 B. On *sonder:* I, 50, 219 C; II, 12, 427 A.

292. On Lipsius: Villey, *Postérité*, p. 344. On Laval: ibid., p. 108. The Ovid verse, which Villey does not footnote, is reproduced in an inexact version and comes from *Tristia* IV, 10, v. 26. On De Thou and Sainte-Marthe: in Coste's edition of the *Essais* of 1724 (available to me in the 1779 edition, vol. IX, pp. 309–310). Ménage also speaks of *Montani conatus* (Dréano, *Pensée religieuse*, p. 470). See Sainte-Beuve: *Port-Royal*, 10th ed. vol. II, p. 446 note. See Buddäus: Bouillier, *Montaigne en Allemagne*, p. 12. On Italian translations: the same, *Montaigne en Italie et en Espagne*, pp. 13 and 15. (The erroneous statement in Thibaudet's *Essais* edition, p. 22, can be corrected according to this.) On posthumous edition of the *Essais:* Villey, *Postérité*, p. 356. See Quevedo: *Obras en prosa*, p. 912. On unpublished Spanish translation, see Bouillier, *Montaigne en italie . . .*, p. 59. (I was unable to gain access to R. Sáenz Hayes's "La posteridad de Montaigne en España" in: *Nosotros* I, 1936.) Florio: this is the translation (1603) that Shakespeare used. Unfortunately, I cannot go into the much-discussed and complex question of Montaigne's influence on Shakespeare. Contrary to prevailing opinion among the English, German, and French scholars of English, I am not convinced that this influence amounted to much. The only thing solidly

established is the proof that Shakespeare read the Florio translation. But the parallels of the ideal kind cited in the research in the main concern cases of commonplace things for which Montaigne only played the role of vehicle, or things that could also have come to Shakespeare from other sources. This was often the case in the sixteenth and seventeenth centuries: one read Montaigne as a compiler of what was in general circulation, and noticed what one already knew. What was specific to Montaigne was noticed by very few; I don't believe Shakespeare was among these few. Pascal was among them; from the unconditionality of his Christian consciousness and the passion of his resistance he recognized quite clearly what was unique to Montaigne. On the question of Shakespeare and Montaigne: I. M. Robertson, *Montaigne and Shakespeare*, 1897; G. C. Taylor, *Shakespeare's Debt to Montaigne*, 1925 (p. 3 here contains further literature references); S. Türck, *Shakespeare und Montaigne*, 1939; M. Deutschbein, "Shakespeares Hamlet und Montaigne" (*Shakespeare-Jahrbuch*, vols. 80–81, 1946, p. 70 ff.). Lichtenberg: Evidence in P. Requadt, *Lichtenberg*, p. 128. It should also be added regarding Bode's translation that the publisher, C. A. Böttiger, in vol. 6, p. 106, reports a few changes about Bode's manner of working, from which one can see—apart from Bode's understandably inadequate schooling in the history of language—how the many errors arose. The translation is a monument, but cannot be quoted from with respect to Montaigne.

293. See Descartes: *Discours de la Méthode*, ed. Gilson, 1939, note pp. 79–80. Pascal: *Essai sur les coniques*, 1640. Nicole (*Essais de morale*, 1671) states in vol. I, Avertissement, p. II an interesting reason for his choice of title, which is far removed from Montaigne. Nicole is also among the spokesmen for the Jansenist criticism of Montaigne (vol. VI, p. 211 ff.). It is similar to Pascal's criticism and is probably dependent upon it as well; for example, Montaigne becomes the despairing, merciless nature. See Bacon: foreword to the 2d edition, reprinted in *A harmony of the Essays of Bacon*, ed. E. Arber, 1871, pp. 158–159. Cornwallis: cf. sentence quoted above from Montaigne II, 18, 504 C "And if no one reads me . . ." with the following passage from Cornwallis: "I write to my selfe, and my selfe profits by my writing. If a strange eye carries it to a strangers judgement, and hee profits not by it, I am not sorry nor displeased, for I meant it only to my selfe." Quoted from W. L. MacDonald, "The Earliest English Essayists" (*Englische Studien* LXIV, 1929, p. 37). Further literature on the English essay is noted in this article. On the essay in general: Herm. Grimm, *Fünfzehn Essais. Neue Folge*, 1890, foreword; G. Simmel, *Philosophische Kultur*, 1923 (introduction); M. Bense, "Über den Essay" (in: *Merkur*, 1947, no. 3, p. 414 ff.); L. Rohner, *Der deutsche Essay*, 1966.

294. *Sources*, II, p. 1 ff., and, with valuable new material, Porteau, as cited above, p. 198 ff. Porteau admittedly considerably exaggerates the "influence" of the anthologies and centos.

295. On Pasquier: Villey, *Postérité*, p. 79. On Thackeray: Dédéyan, as cited above, vol. I, p. 288. One could note a minor point on the subject of Montaigne's characteristic fluctuation, namely that even the types of title are nonuniform. Sometimes they are maxims (I, 1 and I, 20), sometimes a designation of the content, either in the form derived from Latin titles, *De* . . . (I, 2), or with *Sur* . . . (III, 5), or without any preposition (II, 3). Only the third book has

greater uniformity, as it also does in form of speech and orthography. We find similar fluctuations in types of titles of Amyot's translation of the *Moralia*.

296. The fact that the digressions contain the real and most important subject matter was recognized in 1607 by Dominicus Baudius, who also distinguished himself with other intelligent judgments about Montaigne; Coste in his *Essais* edition as cited above, vol. IX, p. 345 ff., reproduces a rather long utterance from this: *noster tum mirabilia effundit, quum aberrat a proposito . . .* Montaigne would certainly have agreed with the sentence from Pliny the Younger (which L. Sterne would invoke later): *non enim excursus hic eius sed opus ipsum est* (Pliny, *ep.* V, 6; Sterne, *Tristam Shandy*, books VI, VII, IX).

297. Reconstructions of the plan can be found in Villey, *Sources* II, p. 74, and in Porteau in his separate edition of the *Apologie* of 1937 (which is valuable because it includes all variants), p. XX ff.

298. The comment that comes in here, *et dicte . . .* , indicates that at times Montaigne interchanges writing and dictating. He also says this elsewhere (II, 37, 574 A; III, 9, 737 B). Two additions in the Bordeaux copy are in the hand of Mlle de Gournay (Villey, *Postérité*, p. 38). The expression *dicter* in Montaigne can also be understood literally, and does not mean "to write," as did *dictare* in late Latin writing (cf. Norden, *Kunstprosa*, p. 954 ff.) and *dicter* frequently in France of the sixteenth century. Semantic information on *dicter, diter* in the sixteenth century can be found in Huguet, *Dictionnaire de la langue française du XVIᵉ siècle*, s.v. *diter*. On the contested question, which will probably never be put to rest, of whether or not a systematic train of thought can be derived from individual Essays: M. Parslow, *Montaigne's Composition: A Study of the Structure of the Essais of the Third Book*, Ann Arbor, 1956; R. Sayce, "L'ordre des *Essais* de Montaigne" (in: *Bibliothèque d'Humanisme et Renaissance*, 1956); M. Baraz, "Sur la structure d'un essai de Montaigne" (in: *Bibliothèque d'Humanisme et Renaissance*, 1961); R. Etiemble, "Sens et structure dans un essai de Montaigne" (in: *Cahiers de l'Association internationale des Etudes Françaises*, 1962). The dissertation by W. E. Traeger, *Aufbau und Gedankenführung in Montaignes Essays*, 1961, treats the determination that the *Essais* are loosely composed as a fault. Traeger's efforts to prove in the *Essais* "a chain structure greatly complicated by the intersections of and reversions to themes" (p. 230) proceed, only in different words, to the same conclusion: a loose layout of the *Essais* in the nature of proliferative growth. Incidentally: is it permissible to so obstinately ignore Montaigne's self-characterizations of his approach to style, as is done here?

299. Aulus Gellius: *Noct. Attic.*, praefatio 2. This contains a few titles of such works of miscellany from the postclassical period (6–10). Bandello: *Opere*, ed. Fr. Flora, 1934, vol. II, p. 247. Also cf. vol. I, p. 6. Bouchet: *Sérées*, ed. 1873, vol. I, p. XIV. Budé: L. Delaruelle, *G. Budé*, 1907, p. 159 ff. Pasquier: *Recherches . . .* V, 41, in the edition of 1611 to which I obtained access, p. 703.

300. On these questions, also compare: P. M. Schon, *Vorformen des Essays in Antike und Humanismus*, 1954.

301. *Ausgew. Werke*, ed. by Holborn, particularly pp. 190–192.

302. See the extensive description by L. Olschki, *Geschichte der neusprachlichen wissenschaftlichen Literatur*, vol. II, 1922, p. 1 ff.

303. H. Peter, *Der Brief in der römischen Literatur*, 1901. G. Misch, *Autobiographie passim*, and W. Kroll, *Studien* . . . , p. 216 ff. M. Roustan, *La Lettre (Evolution d'un genre)* 1902 is not accessible to me. Additionally: F. Neubert, "Einführung in die französische und italienische Epistolarliteratur der Renaissance" (in: *Romanistisches Jahrbuch*, 1961). An historical sketch of the art letter and its acknowledgment as a literary genre was written by F. Cascales, *Cartas filológicas* (1634), ed. J. García Soriano, I, 1951, p. 9 ff.

304. The formula *quidquid in buccam venit* is traditional with occasional slight variations; Peter, as cited above p. 102 (Pliny the Younger), p. 239 (Hieronymus), p. 425 (Poggio).

305. R. Hirzel, *Der Dialog*, 1895, vol. II, p. 33. Similarly, Misch, as cited above pp. 249 and 251. Even Bacon traced the essay back to Seneca's *dispersed meditacions*.

306. Guevara: available in *BAE* XIII, ed. E. de Ochoa, 1934. Pasquier: *Lettres*, in the edition I have of 1597, folios 30, 420, and 435.

307. See G. Toffanin, *Il Cinquecento*, 1929, p. 531 ff. and *Il Cinquecento* (compilation ed. by E. Cecchi and N. Sapegno), 1966, p. 551 ff. Compare Chapelain's assessment in a letter of 1635 (in *Opuscules*, ed. Hunter, 1936, p. 473) in which he ranks Caro alongside Cicero as models of the genre. See also A. Caro, *lettere familiari*, ed. A. Greco, I, II, 1957.

308. G. Pasquali, *Storia della tradizione e critica del testo*, 1934, p. 457.

309. Hirzel, *Dialog*, vol. I, p. 305; G. Wyss-Morigi, *Contributo allo studio del dialogo all'epoca del Rinascimento*, 1947; A. Hermann and G. Bardy, *Dialog* (in: *Realenzyk. für Antike und Christentum*, 1957). Let us note concerning the designation of "halved dialogue" that even Tasso, turning the formula around, says in his *Discorso sull'arte del Dialogo*: "*bisogna scrivere col medesimo stile il dialogo e l'epistola, perchè il dialogo è quasi una sua parte*" (*Dialoghi*, in *Prose*, ed. C. Guasti, II, 1875, p. 247).

310. Since I was unable to check in the English original, my quote is from the translation: W. Pater, *Plato und der Platonismus*, German by H. Hecht, 1904. The passages quoted: pp. 205–206; p. 218; p. 228. In this book, as in his novel *Gaston de Latour*, 1889, Pater provides excellent descriptions of Montaigne.

311. Indeed, Tasso says of the dialogue writer that he stands "*quasi mezzo fra'il poeta e'l dialettico*" (as cited above, p. 226), but his own dialogues tend more toward the didactic tone than toward a poetic prose.

312. Details in Olschki, as cited above, vol. II, p. 316 ff.

313. Compare to this the chapter on "Geschlossene und offene Form" ["Closed and Open Form"] in H. Wölfflin, *Kunstgeschichtliche Grundbegriffe*, 1915 (and subsequently).

314. The terminological lack of sharpness in the *Essais* is one of the most dangerous obstacles to the interpreter. This has become apparent as early as with his first readers, for example, Lipsius, who interpreted several words and expressions, particularly in the death Essay, back to a traditional meaning, when the terms had already been transformed in Montaigne's usage, causing Lipsius to understand them as key terms of a position from which Montaigne had already completely turned away.

315. Accessible in the photocopy edition issued by G. Cohen in 1931; in it, *Aux lecteurs*, recto.

316. He assumed correctly, by the way. In 1635, Mlle de Gournay has to apologize for the "outmoded" language of the *Essais* in order to attract readers who now were indeed repelled by the *Essais* for reasons of language (Villey, *Postérité*, p. 64). But after a further half-century his prose was again treasured for its patina and seen as a kind of archetype for the expression of personal independence: La Bruyère in the fifth edition of his *Caractères* (1692) inserts an imitation of the style of the *Essais* ("De la société," no. 30). Then in the eighteenth century, Coste (as cited above, vol. I, p. XXX) asserts that one can no longer translate Montaigne's "outmoded" words into modern French without sacrificing *la naïveté, la vivacité, les grâces de l'auteur.*

317. Ronsard expresses it quite similarly: ed. Cohen, vol. II, pp. 999–1000.

318. Comments on the material of language: I, 26, 127 A; I, 26, 128 A; III, 5, 667 B; III, 8, 707 B. See also Henri Estienne: *Precellence du langage françois,* quoted according to F. Brunot, *Histoire de la langue française,* vol. II, 1922, p. 176. On the question of provincialism, compare chapter 2 of the third book in the same volume of Brunot, also the work of E. Voizard, still useful in some aspects, *Etude sur la langue de Montaigne,* 1885, especially p. 242 ff., and M. Lanusse, *De l'influence du dialecte gascon sur la langue française,* 1893 (in this, p. 175 ff. on Montaigne's Gascognisms). The *Lexique de la langue des Essais* by Villey and Norton (*EM,* vol. V) is an indispensable aid, but it is incomplete and unreliable in a few instances. More on Montaigne's language and style: M. Rat, *Montaigne écrivain,* 1957; P. Bonnet, *Jeux phoniques et jeux de mots dans les Essais,* 1960; A. Lorian, "Montaigne. De l'impératif" (in: *Zeitschrift für Romanische Philologie,* 1964); M. Recksick, *Montaignes Verhältnis zu Klassik und Manierismus,* diss. at Bonn, 1966 (in this, see chap. 7: Montaignes Satzbau . . .).

319. The designations fluctuate; the Quintillian ones given here are the most frequent. The three-part schema remains about the same. More in Volkmann, as cited above, p. 53 ff., and W. Kroll, *Rhetorik* (Pauly-Wissowa, 1937), 35 ff. Montaigne's formula of *comique et privé* may go back to Horace (*ars poetica,* verses 90–91): *privatis carminibus dignis socco* ("nonfestive verse suitable for comedy").

320. *Verbis e trivio quaesitis dignitatem ac splendorem conciliat,* comments D. Baudius, who has already been quoted (Coste, as cited above, vol. IX, p. 345). These formulations show that at that time one was very well aware of what was unusual about the prose of the *Essais* with respect to rhetorical school meaning. Today these things would be a matter of indifference; we no longer think in the schema of rhetorical typology, and thus, at least in the average man's education, we have lost the feeling for the fact that intellects into the eighteenth, even the nineteenth centuries, were very concerned with it. E. Auerbach, *Mimesis,* 1947, browses through classical and postantiquity literature using the typology of the three categories of style or, respectively, where they reveal themselves, and he derives the "Aufhebung der Stiltrennung" [abolition of the separation of styles] from the Christian need to represent the paradox that the eminence of the Messiah was manifest at the lowest social level (p. 76 ff. and p. 148 ff.) Auerbach

implies in passing that this abolition in Montaigne's case can also be traced back to a Christian origin. Montaigne himself is fond of invoking the simplicity of the poor in spirit (especially in II, 12). But much more frequently he invokes Socrates who spoke "like the women, coachmen, and carpenters" (III, 12, 793 ff. from *Symposium* 221–222), and Montaigne's own *stile comique* appears to have been encouraged by this rather than Christian influences. This is analogous to the whole self-discovery from self-diminishment: Christian tradition triggered it (compare our chapters III and IV), but his classical education preferred to confirm it using the Socratic model.

321. Sonnet I, vs. 11–14. Also, sonnets III, v. 11; IV, vs. 7–11; but especially XXI, vs. 5–8, etc. The fact that the lyric poets of the *Pléiade* experienced the *style bas* as an appropriate type of style for love poetry which turned away from Petrarchism and strove toward naivete is indicated in various comments by Ronsard: H. Chamard, *Histoire de la Pléiade*, vol. II, 1939, p. 240.

322. Seneca: *ep.* 100, 114, 115. The latter contain the phrase *oratio cultus animi*, which at that time one read as: *oratio vultus animi*, according to the Lipsius edition from Leiden (in the edition of 1639 which I have, p. 455). Montaigne himself quotes from Quintilian: "It is the heart that makes a man eloquent" (III, 5, 665 C; cf. *Inst. orat.*, X, 7, 15). See Norden, *Kunstprosa*, p. 307 ff. on this question as a whole.

323. By chance I came across a comment on style in Erasmus which has a striking similarity to Montaigne. It can be found in one of his letters aimed at those who "ape Cicero," October 13, 1527: . . . *malim aliquod dicendi genus solidius, adstrictius, nervosius, minus comptum magisque masculum* (ed. Allen, VII, no. 1885, p. 194). Each of these qualifications can be found again in Montaigne: *solidus = solide; adstrictius = court et serré; nervosius = nerveux; minus comptum = desreglé, descousu, non peigné; magisque masculum = soldatesque*. But Montaigne is even more resolute, as one can see by comparing how the text goes on in Erasmus. What is the source of this similarity? Perhaps it is from a source the two authors had in common, Quintilian and his comments aimed against the Asian, effeminate style? Or could Montaigne have been acquainted with this letter, which according to Allen was published for the first time in 1529 and then frequently included in collections of Erasmus' letters?

324. C. Justi, *Winckelmann*, 1943, vol. I, p. 260. The rather long characterization of Montaigne given there is excellent. Winckelmann made for himself numerous though disconnected excerpts from Montaigne (in the edition by P. Coste, 1724), presumably with the intent to collect important passages from Montaigne, but also important quotations from antiquity. Photocopies of these excerpts were in the possession of W. Rehm, who turned them over to me to look through a few years before his death.

325. This was determined from Coppin's analyses, *Etude sur la grammaire* . . . Main elements: the corrections (particularly the approximately three thousand of them in the Bordeaux copy) achieve greater variation in vocabulary, avoid repetition of words, eliminate superfluous epithets, are aware of considerations of sound. In lexical, syntactic, and orthographic respects there is no uniformity to them and they frequently conflict; Montaigne does not submit to any rule here, in fact, he does not even turn a decision he has made himself into

a rule; the handwritten additions again contain forms that were crossed out in the last version. He only casually follows the changes in the French language which had come into usage since the first version.

326. See Montesquieu: *Pensées et fragments inédits,* ed. G. de Montesquieu, vol. II, 1901, p. 490. See Fr. De Sanctis: *Storia della letteratura italiana* II (in: *Scrittori d'Italia,* vol. 32), p. 192. On Sainte-Beuve: "Qu'est-ce qu'un classique" (in: *Causeries du lundi* III, 1850, p. 52), and *Port-Royal,* 10th ed. vol. II, pp. 443–445, in which there is a nice summary description of the style of the *Essais.* On Montaigne's style, see F. Gray, 1958; G. Lanson, *L'Art de la prose,* 1908 and frequently thereafter, chap. 3.

327. A useful survey can be found in W. Schnabel, *Montaignes Stilkunst, eine Untersuchung vornehmlich auf Grund seiner Metaphern,* 1930. Nevertheless, this work, like most of this kind, is arranged according to the subject matter of the metaphors, but not according to the ideas expressed with the metaphors, thus it shows the means but not the act of productivity, and thus it also does not show the degree of mobility with which Montaigne put his often-repeated ideas sometimes in one visual image, sometimes in another. On Montaigne's tropes: see M. Hamel, "Les images dans l'essai III, 10" (in: G. Palassie, *Mémorial du Ier Congrès des études montaignistes,* 1964), and M. Baraz, "Les images dans les Essais de Montaigne" (in: *Bibliothèque d'Humanisme et Renaissance,* 1965).

328. An extensive analysis of this passage can be found in M. Roustan, *Précis d'explication française,* 1923, p. 201 ff.

329. The expression comes from Lichtenberg, quoted according to G. Gerber, *Die Sprache als Kunst,* 1871, II, p. 127.

Index

Designer: UC Press
Compositor: Huron Valley Graphics
Text: Sabon
Display: Sabon
Printer: Edwards Bros., Inc.
Binder: Edwards Bros., Inc.